PRODUCT LIABILITY DESK REFERENCE

1998/99 Edition

PRODUCT LIABILITY DESK REFERENCE

A Fifty-State Compendium

1998/99 Edition

MORTON F. DALLER

Editor-in-Chief

ASPEN LAW & BUSINESS
A Division of Aspen Publishers, Inc.

This publication is designed to provide accurate and authoritative information in regard to the subject matter covered. It is sold with the understanding that the publisher is not engaged in rendering legal, accounting, or other professional services. If legal advice or other professional assistance is required, the services of a competent professional person should be sought.

— From a *Declaration of Principles* jointly adopted by
a Committee of the American Bar Association and
Committee of Publishers and Associations.

ISBN: 1-56706-903-7

Printed in the United States of America

About Aspen Law & Business

Aspen Law & Business — comprising the former Prentice Hall Law & Business, Little, Brown and Company's Professional Division, and Wiley Law Publications — is a leading publisher of authoritative treatises, practice manuals, services, and journals for attorneys, financial and tax advisors, corporate and bank directors, and other business professionals. Our mission is to provide practical solution-based how-to-information keyed to the latest legislative, judicial and regulatory developments.

We offer publications in the areas of banking and finance; bankruptcy; business and commercial law; corporate law; pensions, benefits, and labor; insurance law; securities; taxation; intellectual property; government and administrative law; matrimonial and family law; environmental and health law; international law; tort law; legal practice and litigation; and criminal law.

Other Aspen Law & Business products treating product liability law and litigation issues include:

> **1998 Wiley Expert Witness Update**
> **Product Liability Case Digest**
> **Preparation of a Product Liability Case**
> **Psychological Experts in Personal Injury Actions**

ASPEN LAW & BUSINESS
A Division of Aspen Publishers, Inc.
A Wolters Kluwer Company

SUBSCRIPTION NOTICE

This Aspen Law & Business product is updated on a periodic basis with supplements to reflect important changes in the subject matter. If you purchased this product directly from Aspen Law & Business, we have already recorded your subscription for the update service.

If, however, you purchased this product from a bookstore and wish to receive future updates and revised or related volumes billed separately with a 30-day examination review, please contact our Customer Service Department at 1-800-234-1660 or send your name, company name (if applicable), address, and the title of the product to:

Aspen Law & Business
A Division of Aspen Publishers, Inc.
7201 McKinney Circle
Frederick, MD 21701

CONTENTS

INTRODUCTION

This is the sixth commercially published edition of what has become a popular resource for product liability lawyers across the United States. The *Product Liability Desk Reference: 1998 Edition* is designed to serve as a handy first-stop practice tool for several types of readers:

- the attorney handling product liability litigation in more than one state;
- the corporate in-house counsel or the litigation management professional who is handling product liability in more than one state;
- in-house counsel at the liability, casualty, or property insurance company concerned with claims and litigation management.

For each of the 50 states, and the District of Columbia, the book provides a succinct summary of state product liability doctrine, rules, and procedures. Information for each state is in the same format, allowing easy comparison across state lines.

Each summary is designed to provide an overview. In order to be useful each summary must therefore be brief, which is, of course, very difficult. The summaries are not designed as full-scale research tools, but rather as starting points for assessing the merits or pitfalls of litigation in a particular jurisdiction.

The *Desk Reference* was created because of the many significant differences among state product liability laws. For example, four states do not recognize strict liability as a separate cause of action. Those that have adopted strict liability have a wide range of statutes of limitation: most have a two-year limitation, eighteen have a three-year statute, four have a one-year statute, and five have other provisions. Similarly, many states provide statutes of repose, whose provisions vary widely. In the rapidly developing area involving "spoliation of evidence" there are many significant differences in state law. Codification of product liability law is also increasingly popular, with 19 states having done so for at least a portion of their laws.

Product liability law is quite volatile in many states, with rather frequent decisional changes and less frequent statutory changes and amendments. In 1997 the Illinois 1995 Tort Reform Act was struck down in its entirety by the Illinois Supreme Court. Connecticut now applies a modified consumer expectation standard and Georgia now applies a risk-utility standard in design defect cases. Many other changes have taken place. Accordingly, the contributing editors and I will provide an annual revision of this book.

We have for the 1998 edition new contributing editors for California, Colorado, and Maryland.

On behalf of all the contributing editors, I hope that the reader and user of *Product Liability Desk Reference: 1998 Edition* will find the book a useful and practical tool.

Morton F. Daller
Editor-in-Chief
Daller Greenberg & Dietrich, LLP
Valley Green Corporate Center
7111 Valley Green Road
Fort Washington, PA 19034
(215) 836-1100 / (215) 836-2845 (Fax)
Email: mdaller@dallergreenberg.com

March 1998

CONTRIBUTING EDITORS

ALABAMA

Brittin T. Coleman, Esquire
John E. Goodman, Esquire
Bradley Arant Rose & White LLP
2001 Park Place Tower, Suite 1400
Birmingham, Alabama 35203
(205) 521-8000 / (205) 521-8800 (Fax)

ALASKA

John B. Thorsness, Esquire
Ronald H. Bussey, Esquire
Sean P. Edwards, Esquire
Hughes, Thorsness, Powell, Huddleston
    & Bauman, L.L.C.
550 West Seventh Avenue, Suite 1100
Anchorage, Alaska 99501-3563
(907) 274-7522 / (907) 263-8320 (Fax)

ARIZONA

Warren E. Platt, Esquire
Bruce P. White, Esquire
Snell & Wilmer
One Arizona Center
Phoenix, Arizona 85004-0001
(602) 382-6000 / (602) 382-6070 (Fax)

ARKANSAS

Katherine Bennett Perkins, Esquire
Rose Law Firm
120 East Fourth Street
Little Rock, Arkansas 72201-2893
(501) 375-9131 / (501) 375-1309 (Fax)

CALIFORNIA

Arnold D. Larson, Esquire
Mary P. Lightfoot, Esquire
Iverson, Yoakum, Papiano & Hatch
One Wilshire Building
624 South Grand Avenue, 27th Floor
Los Angeles, California 90017-3328
(213) 624-7444 / (213) 629-4563 (Fax)

COLORADO

R. Eric Peterson, Esquire
A. W. Victoria Jacobs, Esquire
White and Steele, P.C.
1225 Seventeenth Street
Suite 2800
Denver, Colorado 80202
(303) 296-2828 / (303) 296-3131 (Fax)

CONNECTICUT	Francis H. Morrison III, Esquire
	James H. Rotondo, Esquire
	Jessica J. Mitchell, Esquire
	Day, Berry & Howard
	Cityplace
	Hartford, Connecticut 06103-3499
	(860) 275-0100 / (860) 275-0343 (Fax)
DELAWARE	Allen M. Terrell, Jr., Esquire
	Frederick L. Cottrell, III, Esquire
	Richards, Layton & Finger
	One Rodney Square
	P.O. Box 551
	Wilmington, Delaware 19899
	(302) 658-6541 / (302) 658-6548 (Fax)
DISTRICT OF COLUMBIA	Patrick W. Lee, Esquire
	Mark A. Behrens, Esquire
	Michael R. Greco, Esquire
	Crowell & Moring
	1001 Pennsylvania Avenue, N.W.
	Washington, D.C. 20004-2595
	(202) 624-2500 / (202) 628-5116 (Fax)
FLORIDA	Lawrence P. Bemis, P.A.
	Lance A. Harke, Esquire
	Sarah B. Clasby, Esquire
	Steel Hector & Davis
	200 South Biscayne Blvd.
	Miami, Florida 33131-2398
	(305) 577-7000 / (305) 577-7001 (Fax)
GEORGIA	James R. Johnson, Esquire
	Jones, Day, Reavis & Pogue
	3500 One Peachtree Center
	303 Peachtree Street, NE
	Atlanta, Georgia 30383-3242
	(404) 521-3939 / (404) 581-8330 (Fax)
HAWAII	David J. Dezzani, Esquire
	Mark B. Desmarais, Esquire
	Roy J. Tjioe, Esquire
	Gregory F. Geary, Esquire
	Goodsill Anderson Quinn & Stifel
	1800 Alii Place
	1099 Alakea Street
	Honolulu, Hawaii 96813
	(808) 547-5600 / (808) 547-5880 (Fax)

IDAHO

Rex Blackburn, Esquire
Bruce C. Jones, Esquire
David W. Gratton, Esquire
Evans, Keane LLP
1101 West River Street, Suite 200
P.O. Box 959
Boise, Idaho 83701-0959
(208) 384-1800 / (208) 345-3514 (Fax)

ILLINOIS

Frances E. Prell, Esquire
Colin Smith, Esquire
Burke, Weaver & Prell
55 West Monroe Street, Suite 800
Chicago, Illinois 60603
(312) 263-3600 / (312) 578-6666 (Fax)

INDIANA

Richard D. Wagner, Esquire
Mark J.R. Merkle, Esquire
Krieg DeVault Alexander & Capehart
One Indiana Square, Suite 2800
Indianapolis, Indiana 46204-2017
(317) 636-4341 / (317) 636-1507 (Fax)

IOWA

S. P. DeVolder, Esquire
Lewis, Webster, Johnson, Van Winkle & DeVolder
620 Liberty Building
418 6th Avenue
Des Moines, Iowa 50309-2407
(515) 243-1000 / (515) 288-7000 (Fax)

KANSAS

Heather S. Woodson, Esquire
Stinson, Mag & Fizzell, P.C.
7500 West 110th Street
Overland Park, Kansas 66210-2329
(913) 451-8600 / (913) 344-6777 (Fax)

Thomas P. Schult, Esquire
Stinson, Mag & Fizzell, P.C.
1201 Walnut Street
P.O. Box 419251
Kansas City, Missouri 64141-6251
(816) 842-8600

KENTUCKY	John L. Tate, Esquire W. Kennedy Simpson, Esquire Catharine C. Young, Esquire Stites & Harbison 400 West Market St., Suite 1800 Louisville, Kentucky 40202 (502) 587-3400 / (502) 587-6391 (Fax)
LOUISIANA	William J. Hamlin, Esquire William C. Ellison, Esquire Bordelon, Hamlin & Theriot 701 South Peters Street, Suite 100 New Orleans, Louisiana 70130 (504) 524-5328 / (504) 523-1071 (Fax)
MAINE	Bernard J. Kubetz, Esquire Thad B. Zmistowski, Esquire Eaton, Peabody, Bradford & Veague Fleet Center, Exchange Street P.O. Box 1210 Bangor, Maine 04401 (207) 947-0111 / (207) 942-3040 (Fax)
MARYLAND	Daniel R. Lanier Miles & Stockbridge 10 Light Street Baltimore, Maryland 21202-1487 (410) 385-3651 / (410) 385-3700 (Fax)
MASSACHUSETTS	John C. Bartenstein, Esquire Ropes & Gray One International Place Boston, Massachusetts 02110-2624 (617) 951-7000 / (617) 951-7050 (Fax)
MICHIGAN	Xhafer Orhan, Esquire Edward M. Kronk, Esquire Daniel P. Malone, Esquire Lynn A. Sheehy, Esquire Phillip C. Korovesis, Esquire Butzel Long 150 West Jefferson, Suite 900 Detroit, Michigan 48226-4430 (313) 225-7000 / (313) 225-7080 (Fax)

MINNESOTA	George W. Soule, Esquire Bowman and Brooke 150 South Fifth Street, Suite 2600 Minneapolis, Minnesota 55402 (612) 339-8682 / (612) 672-3200 (Fax)
MISSISSIPPI	William H. Cox, Jr., Esquire Lewis W. Bell, Esquire Watkins & Eager PLLC The Emporium Building, Suite 300 400 East Capitol Street P.O. Box 650 Jackson, Mississippi 39201 (601) 948-6470 / (601) 354-3623 (Fax)
MISSOURI	Robert A. Horn, Esquire Blackwell Sanders Matheny Weary & Lombardi Two Pershing Square 2300 Main Street, Suite 1100 P.O. Box 419777 Kansas City, Missouri 64141-6777 (816) 983-8000 / (816) 983-8080 (Fax)
MONTANA	James A. Poore III, Esquire Poore & Hopkins, PLLP Suite 303 The Florence 111 North Higgins Avenue Missoula, Montana 59802 (406) 543-3487 / (406) 721-4346 (Fax)
NEBRASKA	William M. Lamson, Jr., Esquire Raymond E. Walden, Esquire Kennedy, Holland, DeLacy & Svoboda Kennedy Holland Building 10306 Regency Parkway Drive Omaha, Nebraska 68114-3743 (402) 397-0203 / (402) 397-7824 (Fax)
NEVADA	Stacey A. Upson, Esquire Vargas & Bartlett 201 West Liberty Street P.O. Box 281 Reno, Nevada 89504-0281 (702) 786-5000 / (702) 786-1177 (Fax)

NEW HAMPSHIRE	Fred J. Desmarais, Jr., Esquire
	Jeffrey B. Osburn, Esquire
	Wiggin & Nourie
	The Parish House
	20 Market Street
	P.O. Box 808
	Manchester, New Hampshire 03105
	(603) 669-2211 / (603) 623-8442 (Fax)
NEW JERSEY	Gerhard P. Dietrich, Esquire
	Tracy Canuso Nugent, Esquire
	Daller Greenberg & Dietrich
	2 White Horse Pike
	Haddon Heights, New Jersey 08035
	(609) 547-9068 / (609) 547-2391 (Fax)
NEW MEXICO	Kenneth L. Harrigan, Esquire
	Modrall, Sperling, Roehl, Harris & Sisk
	Sunwest Building
	500 Fourth Street, N.W., Suite 1000
	P.O. Box 2168
	Albuquerque, New Mexico 87103-2168
	(505) 848-1800 / (505) 848-1889 (Fax)
NEW YORK	Thomas E. Reidy, Esquire
	Andrew M. Burns, Esquire
	Nixon, Hargrave, Devans & Doyle
	Clinton Square
	P.O. Box 1051
	Rochester, New York 14603
	(716) 263-1000 / (716) 263-1600 (Fax)
NORTH CAROLINA	H. Grady Barnhill, Jr., Esquire
	William F. Womble, Jr., Esquire
	Womble Carlyle Sandridge & Rice, PLLC
	P. O. Drawer 84
	Winston-Salem, North Carolina 27102
	(910) 721-3600 / (910) 721-3660 (Fax)
NORTH DAKOTA	Patrick W. Durick, Esquire
	Larry L. Boschee, Esquire
	Pearce & Durick
	314 East Thayer Avenue
	P.O. Box 400
	Bismarck, North Dakota 58502
	(701) 223-2890 / (701) 223-7865 (Fax)

OHIO	Robert C. Weber, Esquire Jones, Day, Reavis & Pogue North Point 901 Lakeside Avenue Cleveland, Ohio 44114 (216) 586-3939 / (216) 579-0212 (Fax)
OKLAHOMA	John C. Niemeyer, Esquire Linda G. Alexander, Esquire Niemeyer, Alexander, Austin & Phillips P.C. Three Hundred North Walker Oklahoma City, Oklahoma 73102-1822 (405) 232-2725 / (405) 239-7185 (Fax)
OREGON	Elizabeth A. Schleuning, Esquire Roland F. Banks, Jr., Esquire Schwabe Williamson & Wyatt Pacwest Center 1211 S.W. Fifth Avenue, Suites 1600-1950 Portland, Oregon 97204-3795 (503) 222-9981 / (503) 796-2900 (Fax)
PENNSYLVANIA	Morton F. Daller, Esquire Eileen M. Johnson, Esquire Mark S. Kirby, Esquire Daller Greenberg & Dietrich Valley Green Corporate Center 7111 Valley Green Road Fort Washington, Pennsylvania 19034 (215) 836-1100 / (215) 836-2845 (Fax) Email: mdaller@dallergreenberg.com
RHODE ISLAND	George Vetter, Esquire Gordon P. Cleary, Esquire Vetter & White 20 Washington Place Providence, Rhode Island 02903 (401) 421-3060 / (401) 272-6803 (Fax)
SOUTH CAROLINA	Edward W. Mullins, Jr., Esquire William H. Latham, Esquire Nelson Mullins Riley & Scarborough, L.L.P. Keenan Building, 3d Floor 1330 Lady Street P.O. Box 11070 Columbia, South Carolina 29201 (803) 799-2000 / (803) 256-7500 (Fax)

SOUTH DAKOTA	Arlo D. Sommervold, Esquire Woods, Fuller, Shultz & Smith 300 South Phillips Avenue, Suite 300 Sioux Falls, South Dakota 57102 (605) 336-3890 / (605) 339-3357 (Fax)
TENNESSEE	W. Kyle Carpenter, Esquire J. Ford Little, Esquire Woolf, McClane, Bright, Allen & Carpenter, PLLC Suite 900, Riverview Tower P.O. Box 900 Knoxville, Tennessee 37901-0900 (423) 215-1000 / (423) 215-1001 (Fax)
TEXAS	James Edward Maloney, Esquire Maria Wyckoff Boyce, Esquire Stephanie Kay Copp, Esquire Baker & Botts, L.L.P. One Shell Plaza 910 Louisiana Houston, Texas 77002-4995 (713) 229-1234 / (713) 229-1522 (Fax)
UTAH	Stephen B. Nebeker, Esquire Rick L. Rose, Esquire Eric D. Barton, Esquire Ray, Quinney & Nebeker 400 Deseret Building 79 South Main Street P.O. Box 45385 Salt Lake City, Utah 84145-0385 (801) 532-1500 / (801) 532-7543 (Fax)
VERMONT	Karen McAndrew, Esquire Cathy Nelligan Norman, Esquire Dinse, Knapp & McAndrew, P.C. 209 Battery Street P.O. Box 988 Burlington, Vermont 05402-0988 (802) 864-5751 / (802) 864-1967 (Fax)
VIRGINIA	Michael W. Smith, Esquire Mary Metil Grove, Esquire Christian, Barton, Epps, Brent & Chappell 909 East Main Street, Suite 1200 Richmond, Virginia 23219-3095 (804) 697-4100 / (804) 697-4112 (Fax)

WASHINGTON	John D. Dillow, Esquire Perkins Coie, LLP 1201 Third Avenue, 40th Floor Seattle, Washington 98101-3099 (206) 583-8888 / (206) 583-8500 (Fax)
WEST VIRGINIA	R. Kemp Morton, Esquire Krista L. Duncan, Esquire Huddleston, Bolen, Beatty, Porter & Copen 611 Third Avenue P. O. Box 2185 Huntington, West Virginia 25722-2185 (304) 529-6181 / (304) 522-4312 (Fax)
WISCONSIN	Frank J. Daily, Esquire Michael J. Gonring, Esquire Quarles & Brady 411 East Wisconsin Avenue Milwaukee, Wisconsin 53202-4497 (414) 277-5000 / (414) 271-3552 (Fax)
WYOMING	G. G. Greenlee, Esquire Murane & Bostwick 2020 Carey Avenue Suite 750 Cheyenne, Wyoming 82001 (307) 634-7500 / (307) 638-7882 (Fax) Thomas R. Smith, Esquire Murane & Bostwick 201 North Wolcott Casper, Wyoming 82601 (307) 234-9345 / (307) 237-5110 (Fax)

PRODUCT LIABILITY DESK REFERENCE

1998/99 Edition

ALABAMA

A. NEGLIGENCE

Product liability theories grounded in negligence (i.e., negligent manufacture, design, failure to warn, and negligent instruction) are available to plaintiffs under Alabama law, notwithstanding the advent of Alabama's version of strict liability (see section B, *infra*). Contributory negligence in the use of the product, misuse of the product, and assumption of the risk are complete defenses to negligence claims.[1] The statute of limitations for negligence actions is two years.[2]

B. STRICT LIABILITY

Alabama's version of strict liability, known as the Alabama Extended Manufacturer's Liability Doctrine (AEMLD), was judicially created in 1976.[3] While incorporating much of the lexicon of and rationale underlying section 402A of the Restatement (Second) of Torts, AEMLD purports to retain the "fault" concept of a negligence action.[4]

1. Plaintiff's Prima Facie Case

An AEMLD plaintiff must prove he suffered injury or damages to himself or his property by one who sold a product in a defective condition unreasonably dangerous to the plaintiff as the ultimate user or consumer if (a) the seller was engaged in the business of selling such a product and (b) the product was expected to, and did, reach the user or consumer without substantial change in the condition in which it was sold. If such showing is made, the seller is negligent as a matter of law, even though he may have exercised all possible care in the preparation and sale of the product.[5] In cases alleging a design defect, plaintiff must prove that a safer, practical, alternative design was available to the manufacturer at the time the product was manufactured, the utility of which outweighed the utility of the design actually used, in light of a variety of factors.[6] The fact that the product failed in furthering or performing its intended use, or the fact of an injury, is not itself sufficient to prove liability.[7] Ordinarily, expert testimony is required to prove defectiveness and causation.[8] The fact that a product has been modified by the buyer does not necessarily relieve the manufacturer or seller of liability, but the plaintiff in such an instance must show that the injury was not caused by the change, or that the alteration or modification was reasonably forseeable to the defendant.[9]

2. "Defect"

The jury in an AEMLD case is instructed that a product is defective if it is "unreasonably dangerous," or is not fit for the ordinary purposes for which it was intended, or does not meet the reasonable expectations of an ordinary consumer as to its safety. Plaintiff does not have to prove the specific negligent conduct that caused the defective condition, but he must prove a defective condition in the product and that the defect proximately caused his injury.[10]

3.   Defenses Under AEMLD

   a.   No Causal Relation

   The defendant may show that there is no causal relation in fact between her activities in connection with handling the product and its defective condition. This defense is not available to a manufacturer where the defect is in a component made by a third party or to a defendant who distributes a product under its own trade name.[11]

   b.   Assumption of the Risk

   The defendant may show that any danger associated with its product was either apparent to the consumer or was adequately warned against by the defendant. If the user or consumer discovered the defect and was aware of the danger, and nevertheless proceeded unreasonably to make use of the product and was injured, he is barred from recovery.[12]

   c.   Contributory Negligence and Product Misuse

   Contributory negligence is a defense in AEMLD actions, and is defined as the plaintiff's failure to use reasonable care with regard to the product.[13] Product misuse is a related but distinct defense, defined as the plaintiff's use of the product not intended or foreseen by the manufacturer or seller.[14]

4.   Crashworthiness

A plaintiff can recover on a claim that a defect in a product (usually an automobile) was not the proximate cause of a collision but nonetheless enhanced the injury sustained in the collision. To do so, the plaintiff must show the existence of a safer, practical alternative design that would have reduced or eliminated the plaintiff's injuries, the utility of which design outweighed the utility of the design actually used in light of a variety of factors.[15] All AEMLD defenses are available to the defendant.

5.   Successor Liability

A successor corporation that purchases the assets of its predecessor is liable for the defects in the predecessor's products if (1) there was an express agreement to assume such obligations, (2) the transaction amounts to a de facto merger or consolidation, (3) the transaction is a fraudulent attempt to evade liability, or (4) the asset transferee's business is a "mere continuation" of the transferor's business.[16]

6. **Failure to Warn**

A manufacturer owes a duty to warn if he knows, or reasonably should know, that his product is unreasonably dangerous when put to its reasonably intended use.[17] Products that are "unavoidably unsafe" are nonetheless not defective or unreasonably dangerous if they are accompanied by adequate warnings and instructions.[18] A plaintiff who fails to read an allegedly inadequate warning cannot maintain a failure-to-warn claim unless the alleged inadequacy is such that it prevents her from reading it.[19] A manufacturer cannot be held liable for failure to warn the ultimate consumer where the manufacturer did relay an adequate warning to an intermediate party and the intermediate party failed to pass on the warning.[20] A product is not defective under AEMLD if the manufacturer fails to warn of open and obvious dangers associated with it.[21]

7. **State of the Art and Industry Standards**

That a product was or was not "state of the art" is neither a part of the plaintiff's prima facie AEMLD case nor an affirmative defense, but rather goes to whether the product is unreasonably dangerous and thus defective.[22] Evidence that a product complied with, or did not comply with, regulatory or industry standards is admissible.[23]

8. **Nonsale Transactions**

AEMLD applies to any transaction whereby a product is placed in the stream of commerce, including by sale, lease, free sample, or demonstration.[24] However, the supplier must be in the business of supplying the product and not merely involved in isolated or occasional sales or leases of it.[25]

9. **Statute of Limitations**

The Alabama statute of limitations for personal injuries not arising out of contract, which includes AEMLD and negligence actions, is two years.[26]

10. **Spoliation of Evidence**

Failure by a party to preserve material evidence in a product liability case can warrant sanctions, up to and including dismissal or default.[27] The Alabama Supreme Court has refused to recognize a "spoliation of evidence" cause of action.[28]

C. BREACH OF WARRANTY

1. **Nature of the Cause of Action**

Breach of warranty is a viable product liability theory in Alabama. Although there is no warranty cause of action for wrongful death (see section D, *infra*), a breach of warranty action can be maintained for compensatory damages, including pain and suffering, between the time of the accident and death.[29] In such an action, no compensatory damages are recoverable for the loss or worth of the life of the decedent. In a warranty action, a seller's warranty, whether express or implied, extends to any natural person if it is reasonable to expect that such person may use, consume, or be affected by the goods and who is injured in person by breach of the warranty.[30] Thus, lack of privity is not a defense in personal injury cases.[31] The proof required in a nondeath warranty product claim is essentially the same as that required in an AEMLD claim. Punitive damages are not recoverable in a breach of warranty action.[32]

2. Statute of Limitations and Miscellaneous

The statute of limitations for a breach of warranty action is four years.[33] In cases of personal injury caused by consumer goods, the statute begins to run when the plaintiff's cause of action accrues, that is, when the plaintiff first suffers injury.[34] In the case of nonconsumer goods, the statute of limitations begins to run from the date of sale, unless the warranty sued upon expressly extends to future performance of the goods.[35] Notice of any breach by the buyer to the seller is a condition precedent to recovery under a warranty theory, even in personal injury actions.[36] However, a warranty beneficiary (as opposed to the buyer) need not give such notice.[37]

D. WRONGFUL DEATH

1. Nature of the Claim and Nature of Damages

Under Alabama's wrongful death statute,[38] as interpreted, the *only* damages recoverable by the plaintiff are punitive damages, their amount depending on the nature of the defendant's act, his degree of culpability, and the need for deterring the defendant and others from committing similar wrongful conduct.[39] The product liability wrongful death plaintiff need not show wanton, reckless, or intentional conduct, but merely the same proof required to make out a standard negligence or AEMLD claim. Evidence of loss of earnings, loss of enjoyment of life, and contributions to family are inadmissible because they are irrelevant. As noted in section C, *supra*, a wrongful death plaintiff can also bring a claim (or a separate action) in warranty for compensatory damages incurred during the period of time between accident and death.[40] In addition, an action by a personal injury plaintiff survives his or her death, meaning that representatives of such a plaintiff may pursue the existing personal injury action (for recovery of exclusively compensatory damages) *and also* pursue a wrongful death claim (for recovery of exclusively punitive damages).[41]

2. Proper Capacity of Plaintiff

The decedent's "personal representative" is the proper party plaintiff in a wrongful death action.[42] In the usual case this is the administrator or executor of the decedent's estate.[43] However, if the dependents of a decedent, as defined in Alabama's worker's compensation act, have a statutory right to bring suit for workers' compensation benefits against the decedent's employer, such dependents (rather than the "personal representative") also have the right to bring a wrongful death action against a third party potentially liable for the decedent's death.[44]

3. Foreign Application of the Wrongful Death Statute

The statute requires that all actions arising under it be brought in Alabama courts; courts in other states have, however, applied the statute to actions brought in those states.[45] The Alabama statute cannot be used to support an action brought in Alabama where the wrongful act was committed in another state.[46]

4. Statute of Limitations

All actions for wrongful death must be commenced within two years of the death of the decedent.[47] This limitations period is contained within the wrongful death statute itself, and is thus considered a part of the plaintiff's prima facie case rather than an affirmative defense.[48]

E. CONTRIBUTION AND INDEMNITY

If the separate acts of more than one defendant proximately result in one indivisible injury to the plaintiff, all defendants are jointly and severally liable for the entire damage, although the plaintiff is entitled to only one recovery.[49] Contribution or indemnity among joint tortfeasors is not allowed, except when an agreement exists between the liable parties clearly indicating indemnity of the type of conduct in question.[50] A further, very limited exception to the no-contribution rule exists (though its applicability is not entirely clear) when the party seeking indemnity is totally without fault but is held liable solely because of an absolute nondelegable duty to the injured plaintiff.[51] In general, proof of facts sufficient to establish a right to indemnity will also establish a no-causal relation defense to liability under AEMLD.

F. FICTITIOUS PARTY PRACTICE

A product liability plaintiff may designate a fictitious defendant in her complaint if the defendant's true name is not known.[52] When the true name is discovered it may be substituted, and the substitution will relate back to the time of original filing for statute of limitations purposes, so long as the fictitious party's true identity was not known to the plaintiff at the time of filing and the plaintiff has exercised reasonable diligence in discovering the fictitious defendant's true identity.[53] The presence of fictitious defendants is disregarded for purposes of removal to federal court.[54]

G. MISCELLANEOUS

1. Collateral Source Rule

In cases in which the plaintiff claims medical expenses that have been or will be reimbursed as an element of damages, it is questionable whether the product manufacturing defendant can introduce evidence that these expenses have been or will be paid.[55]

2. **Substantial Evidence Rule**

Motions for summary judgment and directed verdict are governed by the "substantial evidence" standard, meaning evidence of such quality and weight that reasonable persons exercising impartial judgment could reach different conclusions about the existence of a fact to be proved.[56]

3. **Punitive Damages**

Except in wrongful death actions, punitive damages are by statute not recoverable unless the plaintiff proves by "clear and convincing evidence" that the defendant consciously or deliberately engaged in oppression, fraud, wantonness, or malice with regard to the plaintiff.[57]

Brittin T. Coleman
John E. Goodman
BRADLEY ARANT ROSE & WHITE LLP
2001 Park Place, Suite 1400
Birmingham, Alabama 35203
(205) 521-8000

The following language is included pursuant to Rule 7.2 of the Alabama State Bar Rules of Professional Conduct:

No representation is made that the quality of the legal services to be performed is greater than the quality of legal services performed by other lawyers.

ENDNOTES - ALABAMA

1. E.g., *General Motors Corp. v. Saint*, 646 So. 2d 564 (Ala. 1994); *Campbell v. Cutler Hammer, Inc.*, 646 So. 2d 573 (Ala. 1994); *Williams v. Delta Intl. Mach. Corp.*, 619 So. 2d 1330 (Ala. 1993); *Brown v. Piggly-Wiggly Stores*, 454 So. 2d 1370, 1372 (Ala. 1984); *Rivers v. Stihl, Inc.*, 434 So. 2d 766, 773 (Ala. 1983).

2. Ala. Code §6-2-38(l) (1993 Repl. Vol.).

3. *Casrell v. Altec Indus.*, 335 So. 2d 128 (Ala. 1976); *Atkins v. American Motors Corp.*, 335 So. 2d 134 (Ala. 1976).

4. *Casrell*, 335 So. 2d at 132; *Atkins*, 335 So. 2d at 137.

5. *Atkins*, 355 So. 2d at 141; Alabama Pattern Jury Instructions (Civil) §32.08 (2d ed. 1993) (hereinafter APJI).

6. *Beech v. Outboard Marine Corp.*, 584 So. 2d 447 (Ala 1991); *Elliott v. Brunswick Corp.*, 903 F.2d 1505 (11th Cir. 1990), *cert. denied*, 498 U.S. 1048 (1991); APJI §32.25.

7. *Sears, Roebuck & Co., Inc. v. Haven Hills Farm, Inc.*, 395 So. 2d 991, 995 (Ala. 1981); *Townsend v. General Motors Corp.*, 642 So. 2d 411 (Ala. 1994).

8. Id.

9. *Sears, Roebuck and Co. v. Harris*, 630 So. 2d 1018 (Ala. 1993); *McDaniel v. French Oil Mach. Co.*, 623 So. 2d 1146 (Ala. 1993).

10. *Taylor v. General Motors Corp.*, — So. 2d —, 1997; WL 677042 (Ala. 1997); *Atkins*, 335 So. 2d at 142; APJI §32.12.

11. *Atkins*, 335 So. 2d at 143; APJI §32.16; *Foremost Ins. Co. v. Indies House Inc.*, 602 So. 2d 380, 381-382 (Ala. 1992).

12. *Atkins*, 335 So. 2d at 143; APJI, §§32.17, 32.18.

13. *General Motors Corp. v. Saint*, 646 So. 2d 564 (Ala. 1994).

14. *Saint*, 646 So. 2d 564; *Kelly v. M. Trigg Enterprises, Inc.*, 605 So. 2d 1185 (Ala. 1992).

15. *General Motors Corp. v. Edwards*, 482 So. 2d 1176, 1191-1192 (Ala. 1985); APJI §32.22.

16. *Colonial Bank of Ala. v. Coker*, 482 So. 2d 286, 292 (Ala. 1985); *Rivers*, 434 So. 2d at 771.

17. *Gurley v. American Honda Motor Co., Inc.*, 505 So. 2d 358, 361 (Ala. 1987); *Rivers*, 434 So. 2d at 773.

18. *Purvis v. PPG Indus., Inc.*, 502 So. 2d 714, 718 (Ala. 1987); *Stone v. Smith, Kline & French Labs.*, 447 So. 2d 1301 (Ala. 1984).

19. *E. R. Squibb & Sons, Inc. v. Cox*, 477 So. 2d 963, 971 (Ala. 1985).

20. *Purvis*, 502 So. 2d at 719.

21. *Entrekin v. Atlantic Richfield Co.*, 519 So. 2d 447, 450 (Ala. 1987); *Ford Motor Co. v. Rodgers*, 337 So. 2d 736 (Ala. 1976).

22. E.g., *General Motors v. Edwards*, 482 So. 2d 1176. See also *Elliott v. Brunswick Corp.*, 903 F.2d 1505 (11th Cir. 1990), *cert. denied*, 498 U.S. 1028 (1991) (applying Alabama law).

23. E.g., *General Motors v. Edwards*, 482 So. 2d at 1198; *Dunn v. Wixom Bros.*, 493 So. 2d 1356 (Ala. 1986).

24. *First Natl. Bank of Mobile v. Cessna Aircraft Co.*, 365 So. 2d 966, 968 (Ala. 1978).

25. *Baugh v. Bradford*, 529 So. 2d 996, 999 (Ala. 1988).

26. Ala. Code §6-2-38(l) (1993 Repl. Vol.).

27. *Capitol Chevrolet, Inc. v. Smedley*, 614 So. 2d 439 (Ala. 1993). See also *Campbell v. Williams*, 638 So. 2d 804, 817 n.9 (Ala.), *cert. denied*, 115 S. Ct. 188 (1994) (jury can be instructed that spoliation is sufficient to support an inference of negligence).

28. *Christian v. Kenneth Chandler Construction Co.*, 658 So. 2d 408 (Ala. 1995).

29. *Benefield v. Aquaslide 'N' Dive Corp.*, 406 So. 2d 873, 875-876 (Ala. 1981).

30. Ala. Code §7-2-318 (1993 Repl. Vol.).

31. *Bishop v. Sales*, 336 So. 2d 1340, 1345 (Ala. 1976).

32. E.g., *Geohagen v. General Motors Corp.*, 291 Ala. 167, 279 So. 2d 436, 438 (1973).

33. Ala. Code §7-2-725(1) (1993 Repl. Vol.).

34. Id. §7-2-725(2) (1993 Repl. Vol.); *Moon v. Harco Drugs, Inc.*, 435 So. 2d 218, 220 (Ala. 1983).

35. E.g., *Simmons v. Clemco Indus.*, 368 So. 2d 509, 510 (Ala. 1979); *Stephens v. Creel*, 429 So. 2d 278, 282 (Ala. 1983).

36. Ala. Code §7-2-607 (1993 Repl. Vol.); *Simmons*, 368 So. 2d at 513.

37. Ala. Code §7-2-318 (1993 Repl. Vol.); *Simmons*, 368 So. 2d at 513.

38. Ala. Code §6-5-410 (1993 Repl. Vol.); see also id. §6-5-391 (1993 Repl. Vol.) (wrongful death of minor).

39. E.g., *Deaton, Inc. v. Burroughs*, 456 So. 2d 771, 776 (Ala. 1984).

40. *Benefield*, 406 So. 2d at 875-876.

41. *King v. National Spa and Pool Inst.*, 607 So. 2d 1241 (Ala. 1992).

42. Ala. Code §6-5-410 (1993 Repl. Vol.).

43. *Downtown Nursing Home v. Pool*, 375 So. 2d 465, 466 (Ala. 1979), *cert. denied*, 445 U.S. 930 (1980).

44. Ala. Code §25-5-11 (1993 Repl. Vol.); *Baggett v. Webb*, 46 Ala. App. 666, 248 So. 2d 275, 282, *cert. denied*, 287 Ala. 725, 248 So. 2d 284 (1971).

45. E.g., *Stevens v. Pullman, Inc.*, 388 So. 2d 580 (Fla. App. 1980); *Spriggs v. Dredge*, 140 N.E.2d 45 (Ohio App. 1955).

46. E.g., *Spencer v. Malone Freight Lines, Inc.*, 292 Ala. 582, 584, 298 So. 2d 20, 22 (1974).

47. Ala. Code §6-5-410 (1993 Repl. Vol.).

48. *Downtown Nursing Home*, 375 So. 2d at 466.

49. E.g., *General Motors*, 482 So. 2d at 1195.

50. *Crigler v. Salac*, 438 So. 2d 1375, 1385-1386 (Ala. 1983).

51. *Consolidated Pipe & Supply Co., Inc. v. Stockham Valves & Fittings, Inc.*, 365 So. 2d 968, 970 (Ala. 1978).

52.   Ala. R. Civ. P. 9(h).

53.   Ala R. Civ. P. 15(c); *Kinard v. C. A. Kelly & Co.*, 468 So. 2d 133, 135 (Ala. 1985); *Ex parte Klemawesch*, 549 So. 2d 62, 64 (Ala. 1989).

54.   28 U.S.C. §1441(a) (1988).

55.   See *American Legion Post No. 57 v. Leahey*, 681 So. 2d 183 (Ala. 1996), declaring unconstitutional Ala. Code §12-21-45, which is similar to the product liability statute §6-5-522 on the same subject.

56.   Ala. Code §12-21-12 (1995 Supp.); *West v. Founders Life Assurance Co. of Fla.*, 547 So. 2d 870, 871 (Ala. 1989).

57.   Ala. Code §6-11-20(a) (1993 Repl. Vol.).

ALASKA

A. CAUSES OF ACTION

Product liability actions may include causes of action for (1) strict liability, (2) negligence, (3) breach of an implied or express warranty, (4) design and/or manufacturing defect, or (5) failure to warn or inadequate warning.

B. STATUTES OF LIMITATION

Causes of action for personal injury[1] and wrongful death[2] are subject to a two-year statute of limitation. The time period does not begin to run until plaintiff "discovers, or reasonably should discover, the existence of all elements of his cause of action."[3] This has also been defined as the time at which the plaintiff should have begun an inquiry to protect his rights, whether or not he knew of the technical cause of the defect.[4] It is not necessary that the plaintiff suffer all of his damages or even know the full extent of his damages before the cause of action accrues and the statute begins to run.[5] Strict liability or negligence claims asserting only damage to personal property are governed by the six-year limitation period for causes of action accruing prior to August 7, 1997 and by the three-year limitation period for causes of action accruing on or after August 7, 1997.[6] Claims based on breach of an express warranty must be brought within four years of the breach, or, in the case of a warranty that explicitly extends to future performance of goods, within four years of the date the defect is or should have been discovered, provided however that that day is still within the warranty period.[7] Claims based on a breach of an implied warranty, such as merchantability or fitness for a particular purpose, must be brought within four years from date of purchase, since implied warranties never extend to future performance.[8]

C. STRICT LIABILITY

1. The Standard

Alaska's theory of strict product liability is as follows: "A manufacturer is strictly liable in tort if an article he places on the market, knowing that it is to be used without inspection for defects, proves to have a defect that causes injury to a human being."[9] Strict liability in tort can also be imposed in cases where a product defect "creates a situation dangerous to persons or other property" and in fact causes personal injury or property damage, but in an action based on strict liability where no personal injury is involved, plaintiff must show actual property damage as opposed to mere economic loss.[10]

2. "Defect"

The focus in a strict products liability action is on the product itself, not on the conduct of the manufacturer.[11] A product may be defective because of a manufacturing defect, a design defect, or a failure to contain adequate warnings.[12] A product is defective in design if (1) the plaintiff proves that the product failed to perform as safely as an ordinary consumer would expect when used in an intended or reasonably foreseeable manner, or (2) the plaintiff proves that the product's design proximately caused injury and the defendant fails to prove, in light of the relevant factors, that on balance the benefits of the challenged design outweigh the risk of danger inherent in such design.[13] The ordinary expectation of the consumer is an objective test.[14] A design defect will be the legal or proximate cause of a plaintiff's injury if the product's defect was more likely than not a substantial factor in bringing about the plaintiff's injury.[15]

A product may also be defective if its reasonably foreseeable use involves a substantial danger that would not be readily recognized by the ordinary user of the product, and the manufacturer fails to give adequate warning of such danger.[16]

3. Contributory Negligence/Assumption of Risk

Alaska is a "pure" comparative negligence state,[17] and the comparative fault of a plaintiff in a product liability suit is considered by the jury.[18] Assumption of risk is not a complete defense to a product liability action, but will only be admissible to prove a plaintiff's comparative fault. A defendant must show that plaintiff had actual knowledge of the defect and voluntarily and unreasonably encountered that known risk.[19] For cases accruing after June 11, 1986, the law on comparative negligence has changed and requires a purely objective assessment. Alaska statutory law requires that the jury allocate fault among all named parties to the lawsuit, and in so doing, consider the nature of the conduct of each party at fault and the causal relation between the conduct and the damages claimed.[20] The statute defines fault in product liability terms as including breach of warranty, unreasonable assumption of the risk, misuse of a product, and the unreasonable failure to avoid an injury or to mitigate damages.[21] A jury may not allocate fault to nonparties and may only allocate fault to parties to the action, including third-party defendants and settling or released parties.[22] For causes of action accruing after August 7, 1997, the jury may also allocate fault to a non-party who was responsible for damages whom the other parties did not have a reasonable opportunity to join as a party to the action.[23] Mixed results have been obtained at the trial court level on the right of a plaintiff to obtain an affirmative recovery when a defendant, for purposes of allocating fault, after the statute of limitations in the underlying action has run.[24]

4. Sale or Lease

Strict liability in tort is not confined to sales transactions, but extends equally to commercial leases and bailments.[25] No sale exists, and strict liability does not attach, where a product is merely serviced or repaired.[26]

5. Inherently Dangerous Products

A product may be defective despite warnings of obvious dangers if the product is so dangerous that such warnings would not protect the "inadvertent plaintiff."[27]

6. Successor Liability

There are no Alaska decisions in this area.

7. Privity

Alaska does not require vertical privity of contract between a consumer and a manufacturer where the injuries claimed consist of more than pure economic loss,[28] either in cases based on strict liability in tort[29] or in cases based on breach of warranty.[30] It remains unclear whether lack of horizontal privity is a defense.[31]

8. Failure to Warn

A faultlessly manufactured and designed product may nonetheless be defective if it lacks an adequate warning of how to safely use the product.[32] Manufacturers must warn of dangers not readily recognized by the ordinary consumer, and there is no duty to warn of open and obvious dangers.[33] In most cases, for a warning to be adequate, it should (1) clearly indicate the scope of the risk or danger posed by the product; (2) reasonably communicate the extent or seriousness of harm that could result from the risk or danger; and (3) be conveyed in such a manner as to alert the reasonably prudent person.[34]

Plaintiff carries a "more likely than not" burden of proving a causal relationship between the alleged failure-to-warn and the injury; the failure must be a substantial factor in bringing about the injury.[35] A factor is considered substantial only when it can be shown that (1) the accident would not have happened "but for" the failure-to-warn, and (2) that such failure-to-warn was so important in bringing about the injury that a reasonable person would regard it as a cause and attach responsibility.[36]

9. Post-Sale Duty to Warn

There are no Alaska decisions in this area.

10. Substantial Change/Abnormal Use

For liability to attach, a plaintiff has the burden of demonstrating that the product was (1) defective as marketed and (2) the defect existed at the time it left the manufacturer's possession or control.[37] A substantial alteration or change in a product after it leaves the manufacturer, that is shown to have proximately caused plaintiff's injury, will ordinarily defeat a claim based on strict tort liability.[38] The plaintiff must first demonstrate, however, that a defect existed at the time the product left the manufacturer, and then the burden shifts to the manufacturer to demonstrate that the injury resulted from the alteration and not from the defect in the product.[39]

11. **State of the Art**

State of the art, or conformity with industry-wide practices, will not insulate a manufacturer from liability,[40] but the jury may consider such evidence to determine the existence of a defect,[41] the feasibility of other designs,[42] or to consider whether the defect was scientifically knowable to the manufacturer.[43]

12. **Standards**

Compliance with industry standards is not a defense and is considered to have little probative value, but it may be considered by a jury to determine the existence of a defect[44] or the feasibility of alternative designs.[45]

13. **Other Accidents**

Evidence of prior or subsequent accidents may be introduced to demonstrate the existence of a product defect, provided that the incidents took place under substantially similar circumstances and conditions.[46]

14. **Misrepresentation**

Alaska has not judicially adopted the Restatement (Second) of Torts section 402B and has not decided any misrepresentation cases outside of those cited in the breach of warranty context, discussed in section E, *infra*.

D. NEGLIGENCE

The unique significant feature in Alaska's law of products liability is that liability for claims accruing after March 5, 1989, is determined on the basis of several liability only. In such cases, each defendant's liability, including settling or released parties, is limited to that percentage of fault allocated to it by the jury.[47] This system of fault allocation applies to strict liability as well as to negligence claims.[48] As discussed above in section C3, a jury may not allocate fault to nonparties, but can only allocate fault to parties to the action, including third-party defendants and settling or released parties.[49]

E. BREACH OF WARRANTY

Breach of warranty as a basis for a product liability claim is, in most cases, merely an alternative form of relief.[50] However, in cases involving solely economic harm, the warranty remedies of the Uniform Commercial Code provide the only basis for a product claim.[51]

F. DAMAGES

Punitive damages are appropriate in product cases only where the defendant is shown to have acted with reckless indifference toward the safety of its customers or acts wantonly or maliciously, such as to shock the conscience.[52] Punitive damages may not be awarded unless proven by clear and convincing evidence.[53] For causes of action accruing after August 7, 1997, punitive damages are capped at the greater of three times compensatory damages or $500,000 unless there is proof that the conduct was motivated by financial gain, in which case the cap is the higher of four times compensatory damages, four times the amount of the financial gain or $7 million.[54]

1. Contribution

The Uniform Contribution Among Joint Tortfeasors Act was repealed in Alaska. Consequently, there is no right of contribution against a co-tortfeasor for claims accruing after March 5, 1989. However, since Alaska is a pure comparative negligence state, a jury should allocate liability to each party to the action only in relation to its comparative fault.[55] In the absence of contribution, equitable apportionment is available as a means of bringing in other tortfeasors to the lawsuit.[56]

2. Pain and Suffering

Damages for pain and suffering are limited to $500,000 for each claim based upon a separate injury or incident; this limitation does not apply to damages for disfigurement or severe physical impairment.[57] Pain and suffering must be consciously experienced.[58] Pain and suffering contemporaneously with death is not compensable.[59]

3. Minor's Right to Sue for Loss of Consortium

A minor child is entitled to loss of consortium damages when his or her parent is tortiously injured.[60] Similarly, a parent is entitled to recover for the loss of a child's society when the child is tortiously injured by a third party.[61]

4. Emotional Distress

Sensory or contemporaneous observance of an accident is not required for one to recover for emotional distress.[62] Instead, the test for recovery is reasonable foreseeability that the claimant would suffer emotional harm.[63] Damages for emotional distress where there has been no physical injury are ordinarily restricted to instances involving intentional or reckless conduct of an extreme or outrageous nature.[64] Plaintiff may recover for negligent infliction of emotional distress without physical injury only where there is a pre-existing relationship that establishes a duty to refrain from activity that presents a foreseeable and unreasonable risk of causing emotional harm, and in the case of a bystander claim.[65] Only damages for severe or serious emotional distress may be recovered.

5. Implied Indemnity

An innocent supplier of a defective product found liable on a theory of strict liability is entitled to a defense and indemnity from the manufacturer of the defective product.[66] Even if no liability is found, the innocent supplier may nonetheless be entitled to recover from the manufacturer its reasonable actual attorney's fees and costs in defending the action.[67] However, a supplier who is independently negligent is completely barred from recovery under the theory of implied indemnity.[68]

G. SUBSEQUENT REMEDIAL MEASURES/POST-ACCIDENT DESIGN CHANGES

Subsequent design changes relevant to plaintiff's allegation of defect are admissible in a product liability action to prove the existence of a defective condition.[69]

H. COLLATERAL ESTOPPEL

Collateral estoppel has barred a defendant in a subsequent action from relitigating a finding that its concealment of a manufacturing defect constituted outrageous conduct and a reckless disregard of the rights of others.[70]

I. STATUTES

Statutes relevant to product liability actions in Alaska include the statutes of limitations,[71] limitations on liability,[72] and in cases where breach of warranty is alleged, the Uniform Commercial Code.[73]

John B. Thorsness
Ronald H. Bussey
Sean P. Edwards
HUGHES THORSNESS POWELL HUDDLESTON
& BAUMAN LLC
550 West Seventh Avenue, Suite 1100
Anchorage, Alaska 99501-3563
(907) 274-7522

ENDNOTES - ALASKA

1. Alaska Stat. §09.10.070.

2. Alaska Stat. §09.55.580.

3. *Hanebuth v. Bell Helicopter Intl.*, 694 P.2d 143, 144, 146 (Alaska 1984); *Greater Area Inc. v. Bookman*, 657 P.2d 828, 829 (Alaska 1982).

4. *Yurioff v. American Honda Motor Co.*, 803 P.2d 386, 389 (Alaska 1990); *Mine Safety Appliances v. Stiles*, 756 P.2d 288, 291-292 (Alaska 1988).

5. *Wettanen v. Cowper*, 749 P.2d 362, 365 (Alaska 1988).

6. *Kodiak Elec. Assn. v. Delaval Turbine, Inc.*, 694 P.2d 150, (Alaska 1984); Alaska Stat. §09.10.070(a) and 1997 SLA ch. 26 sec. 6.

7. *Kodiak Elec. Assn.*, 694 P.2d at 156-157; *Anderson v. Fairchild Hiller Corp.*, 358 F. Supp. 1392 (D. Alaska 1973); Alaska Stat. §45.02.725.

8. *Armour v. Alaska Power Auth.*, 756 P.2d 1372, 1375 (Alaska 1988).

9. *Clary v. Fifth Ave. Chrysler Center, Inc.*, 454 P.2d 244, 247 (Alaska 1969), *quoting Greenman v. Yuba Power Prods., Inc.*, 59 Cal. 2d 57, 377 P.2d 897, 900, 27 Cal. Rptr. 697, 700, 13 A.L.R.3d 1049 (1962).

10. *Northern Power & Eng. Corp. v. Caterpillar Tractor Co.*, 623 P.2d 324, 329 (Alaska 1981).

11. *Caterpillar Tractor Co. v. Beck*, 593 P.2d 871, 883 (Alaska 1979) *aff'd in part, rev'd in part*, 624 P.2d 790 (1981).

12. Id. at 878 n.15.

13. Id. at 884-885.

14. *Keough v. W. R. Grasle, Inc.*, 816 P.2d 1343 (Alaska 1991).

15. *Dura Corp. v. Harned*, 703 P.2d 396, 406 (Alaska 1985).

16. *Prince v. Parachutes, Inc.*, 685 P.2d 83, 88 (Alaska 1984).

17. *Kaatz v. State*, 540 P.2d 1037, 1049 (Alaska 1975), *rev'd on other grounds*, 572 P.2d 775 (1977).

18. *Butaud v. Suburban Marine & Sporting Goods, Inc.*, 555 P.2d 42, 45-46 (Alaska 1976).

19. *Lamer v. McKee Indus., Inc.*, 721 P.2d 611, 615 (Alaska 1986); *Dura Corp. v. Harned*, 703 P.2d 396, 404-405 (Alaska 1985).

20. Alaska Stat. §09.17.080.

21. Alaska Stat. §09.17.900.

22. *Benner v. Wichman*, 874 P.2d 949, 958 (Alaska 1994).

23. Alaska Stat. §09.17.080(a) and 1997 SLA ch. 26, Sec. 11 and 55.

24. The Alaska Supreme Court has recently accepted a petition for review to decide this issue.

25. *Bachner v. Pearson*, 479 P.2d 319 (Alaska 1970).

26. *Kodiak Elec. Assn.*, 694 P.2d at 154; *Swenson Trucking & Excav., Inc. v. Truckweld Equip. Co.*, 604 P.2d 1113, 1116-1117, 1119 (Alaska 1980).

27. *Sturm, Ruger & Co., Inc. v. Day*, 594 P.2d 38 (Alaska 1979).

28. *State v. Tyonek Timber, Inc.*, 680 P.2d 1148, 1154 (Alaska 1984).

29. *Clary*, 454 P.2d at 248.

30. *Morrow v. New Moon Homes, Inc.*, 548 P.2d 279, 288-289 (Alaska 1976).

31. Id. at 288 n.25.

32. *Prince v. Parachutes, Inc.*, 685 P.2d 83, 87 (Alaska 1984).

33. Id. at 88-89; *Ross Labs. v. Thies*, 725 P.2d 1076, 1078-1079 (Alaska 1986).

34. *Shanks v. Upjohn*, 835 P.2d 1189 (Alaska 1992).

35. *Alvey v. Pioneer Oilfield Servs., Inc.*, 648 P.2d 599, 600 (Alaska 1982).

36. *State v. Abbott*, 498 P.2d 712 (Alaska 1972); *Sharp v. Fairbanks North Star Borough*, 569 P.2d 178 (Alaska 1977).

37. *Caterpillar Tractor*, 593 P.2d at 886 n.52; *Hiller v. Kawasaki Motors Corp.*, 671 P.2d 369, 372 (Alaska 1983).

38. *Caterpillar Tractor Co. v. Beck*, 624 P.2d 790, 793 (Alaska 1981); *Hiller*, 671 P.2d at 372.

39. Id.

40. *Caterpillar Tractor*, 593 P.2d at 887.

41. *Sturm, Ruger*, 594 P.2d at 45.

42. *Caterpillar Tractor*, 593 P.2d at 887.

43. *Heritage v. Pioneer Brokerage & Sales, Inc.*, 604 P.2d 1059, 1063-1064 (Alaska 1979).

44. *Sturm, Ruger*, 594 P.2d at 45.

45. *Caterpillar Tractor*, 593 P.2d at 887.

46. *Caterpillar Tractor*, 624 P.2d at 794; *Harned*, 665 P.2d 5, 8 n.8 (Alaska 1983); *Johnson v. State*, 636 P.2d 47, 57 (Alaska 1981).

47. Alaska Stat. §09.17.080.

48. Alaska Stat. §09.17.900.

49. *Benner*, 874 P.2d at 958.

50. *Clary*, 454 P.2d at 248-249.

51. *Tyonek Timber*, 680 P.2d at 1151-1154; *Morrow*, 548 P.2d at 285-286.

52. *Sturm, Ruger*, 594 P.2d at 46.

53. Alaska Stat. §09.17.020.

54. Alaska Stat. §09.17.020(f) and (g); and 1997 SLA ch. 26, Sec. 10 and 55.

55. Alaska Stat. §09.17.080.

56. *Benner*, 874 P.2d at 956-957.

57. Alaska Stat. §09.17.010(c).

58. *Northern Lights Motel, Inc. v. Sweeney*, 561 P.2d 1176, 1190 (Alaska 1977).

59. Id.

60. *Hibpshman v. Prudhoe Bay Supply, Inc.*, 734 P.2d 991 (Alaska 1987).

61. *Gillispie v. Beta Constr.*, 842 P.2d 1272 (Alaska 1992).

62. *Croft by Croft v. Wicker*, 737 P.2d 789 (Alaska 1987); *Tommy's Elbow Room, Inc. v. Kavorkian*, 727 P.2d 1038 (Alaska 1986).

63. Id.

64. *Hancock v. Northcutt*, 808 P.2d 251 (Alaska 1991).

65. *Mattingly v. Sheldon Jackson College*, 743 P.2d 356, 365-366 (Alaska 1987); *Chizmar v. Mackie*, 896 P.2d 196, 205, 214 (Alaska 1995).

66. *Ross Labs*, 725 P.2d at 1081.

67. *Heritage*, 604 P.2d 1059.

68. *Ross Labs*, 725 P.2d at 1081; *Koehring Mfg. Co. v. Earthmovers of Fairbanks, Inc.*, 763 P.2d 499, 504 (Alaska 1988).

69. See Alaska Rule of Evidence 407; *Caterpillar Tractor Co. v. Beck*, 624 P.2d 790 (Alaska 1981); *Bachner v. Pearson*, 479 P.2d 319, 329 (Alaska 1970).

70. *Borg-Warner Corp. v. Avco Corp. (Lycoming Div.)*, 850 P.2d 628, 637 (Alaska 1993).

71. See discussion at section B, *supra.*

72. Alaska Stat. §09.17.010 et seq.

73. Alaska Stat. §45.02.101 et seq.

ARIZONA

A. CAUSES OF ACTION

Product liability case may proceed on the theories of strict liability, negligence, or breach of express warranty.[1]

B. STATUTES OF LIMITATION

Negligence, strict liability, and breach of warranty[2] causes of action for personal injury, property damage, or wrongful death must be brought within two years after the cause of action accrues.[3] Arizona recognizes a "discovery" rule for tort actions.[4]

Arizona has ruled unconstitutional a statute of repose that formerly barred product liability actions that accrued more than twelve years after a product was first sold for use and consumption.[5]

C. STRICT LIABILITY

1. The Standard

Arizona has adopted section 402A of the Restatement (Second) of Torts.[6] In actions filed after December 31, 1987, each defendant is liable only for the amount of damages allocated to that defendant in direct proportion to that defendant's percentage of fault.[7]

2. "Defect"

There are three types of general defects that form the basis for most product liability actions in Arizona: manufacturing defects, design defects, and informational defects.[8]

A defective article is one that is not reasonably fit for the ordinary purposes for which such articles are sold and used.[9] A product in a defective condition unreasonably dangerous is one in a condition not contemplated by the ultimate consumer that will be unreasonably dangerous to him.[10]

3. Contributory Negligence

Contributory negligence is not a defense,[11] but assumption of risk is a defense.[12] In order to prove that a plaintiff "assumed the risk," there must be clear evidence that he not only had specific knowledge of the danger but that he also knew the specific foreseeable consequences of using the product in the manner that caused injury.[13] Assumption of risk is an affirmative defense.[14] Under Arizona's comparative fault system (discussed in Section D below), a plaintiff's misuse of a product is a type of fault to be apportioned by the jury whether or not that misuse was the sole proximate cause of the plaintiff's injuries. Arizona's courts have not yet ruled on whether assumption of risk is also subject to comparative fault apportionment.[15]

4. Sale or Lease

Strict liability is imposed on manufacturers and sellers as well as commercial lessors.[16] Sellers of used products are also liable.[17] In certain circumstances even a trademark licensor may be strictly liable.[18]

5. Inherently Dangerous Products

Arizona has utilized the approach of comment k to section 402A of the Restatement (Second) of Torts, which immunizes the producers of some unavoidably unsafe products.[19]

6. Successor Liability

A successor corporation will be held liable for "all the liabilities and obligations" of corporations merged or consolidated.[20]

7. Privity

No privity of contract is required to recover under a strict liability claim.[21]

8. Failure to Warn

A manufacturer has a duty to provide an adequate, effective warning to foreseeable users of its product.[22]

The duty to warn is imposed if without a warning the product would be in a defective condition and unreasonably dangerous to a user or consumer, that is, dangerous to the extent beyond that contemplated by the ordinary consumer with ordinary knowledge.[23]

Under certain circumstances, a manufacturer is not required to warn of clearly obvious hazards.[24]

The plaintiff must prove that the absence of the warning was a proximate cause of the alleged injuries.[25]

9. Post-Sale Duty to Warn

In Arizona, the duty to warn is a "continuing" duty that extends past the time of sale and includes an obligation to warn of dangers the manufacturer discovers after sale.[26]

10. Learned Intermediary Doctrine

The manufacturer of certain drugs has the duty to warn the prescribing physician of the risks of the drug.[27]

11. Substantial Change/Abnormal Use

A manufacturer is not responsible for injuries caused by a substantial change in the condition of the product occurring after the initial sale,[28] or due to abnormal use,[29] but the substantial change or abnormal use must be one that could not be reasonably foreseeable or expected.[30]

12. State of the Art

Compliance with state of the art is a defense to a claim of a product defect.[31]

13. Standards

Evidence of industry standards, customs, and practices is admissible, as is evidence of compliance with federal and other regulatory standards, to assist in determining the state of the art at a given time.[32] Such standards can also be considered in strict liability cases on the issue of whether a product is in a defective condition unreasonably dangerous to the user.[33]

14. Other Accidents

Evidence of other accidents is generally inadmissible unless plaintiff shows a substantial factual similarity between the products and circumstances of the accidents.[34]

15. Misrepresentation

Arizona has adopted section 402B of the Restatement dealing with misrepresentation.[35]

D. NEGLIGENCE

1. In negligence actions, standard negligence principles are applied.[36] The type of product that will trigger tort liability is one that is defective in a way that poses an unreasonable danger to those who use or consume it.[37]

2. Arizona's comparative fault statute diminishes the plaintiff's recovery in proportion to plaintiff's negligence.[38] Contributory negligence is a defense.[39] The conduct of nonparties can be considered by the jury if prior notice is given of an intention to present such evidence. Each party is liable only for the percentage of fault assigned to it by the jury.[40] Evidence of fault of nonparties is admissible, including in crashworthiness cases.[41]

E. BREACH OF WARRANTY

1. Breach of warranty occurs when goods are not fit for purposes for which such goods are used.[42]

2. An action for breach of warranty is based on strict liability and is virtually the same as a strict liability action.[43]

3. Breach of warranty claims require privity if based on contract.[44]

F. PUNITIVE DAMAGES

Punitive damages are recoverable in actions in strict liability and negligence.[45] Recovery in negligence actions requires more than mere negligence; some type of outrageous conduct is required.[46] Punitive damages are not allowed in actions based on breach of warranty purely in the context of contract.[47]

G. STATUTES

Relevant statutes for product liability actions are the statutes of affirmative defenses,[48] indemnification,[49] and limitation of actions.[50]

Warren E. Platt
Bruce P. White
SNELL & WILMER
One Arizona Center
Phoenix, Arizona 85004-0001
(602) 382-6000

ENDNOTES - ARIZONA

1. *Estabrook v. J. C. Penney Co.*, 10 Ariz. App. 114, 456 P.2d 960, *vacated on other grounds*, 105 Ariz. 302, 464 P.2d 325 (1969).

2. *Gates v. LaBelle's Distrib. of Ariz., Inc.*, 147 Ariz. 23, 708 P.2d 114 (App. 1985). See also *Drew v. United Producers and Consumers*, 778 P.2d 1227, 161 Ariz. 331 (1989).

3. Ariz. Rev. Stat. Ann. §12-542 (1991 Cum. Pocket Part).

4. *Lawhon v. L.B.J. Inst. Supply, Inc.*, 159 Ariz. 179, 765 P.2d 1003 (Ariz. App. 1988).

5. *Hazine v. Montgomery Elevator Co.*, 176 Ariz. 340, 861 P.2d 625 (1993).

6. *Sullivan v. Green Valley Mfg. Co.*, 118 Ariz. 181, 186, 575 P.2d 811, 816 (App. 1977).

7. Ariz. Rev. Stat. Ann. §§12-2506(A), 12-2509(A), (C).

8. *Gosewisch v. American Honda Motor Co., Inc.*, 153 Ariz. 400, 737 P.2d 376 (1987). See also Ariz. Rev. Stat. Ann. §12-681(3).

9. *Bailey v. Montgomery Ward and Co.*, 6 Ariz. App. 213, 431 P.2d 108 (App. 1967). See also *Dietz v. Waller*, 685 P.2d 744, 141 Ariz. 107 (Ariz. 1984).

10. *Dart v. Wiebe Mfg., Inc.*, 147 Ariz. 242, 244, 709 P.2d 876, 878 (1985).

11. *Gosewisch*, 153 Ariz. 400.

12. *Cota v. Harley Davidson*, 141 Ariz. 7, 684 P.2d 888 (App. 1984).

13. Id.

14. A.R.S. §12-682; *O.S. Stapley Co. v. Miller*, 103 Ariz. 556, 447 P.2d 248 (1968).

15. *Jimenez v. Sears, Roebuck & Co.*, 183 Ariz. 399, 904 P.2d 861 (1995).

16. *Sullivan*, 118 Ariz. at 186; Ariz. Rev. Stat. Ann. §12-681(1), (3), (5).

17. *Jordan v. Sunnyslope Appliance Propane & Plumbing Supplies Co.*, 135 Ariz. 309, 660 P.2d 1236 (App. 1983).

18. *Torres v. Goodyear Tire & Rubber Co.*, 163 Ariz. 88, 786 P.2d 935 (1990).

19. *Gaston v. Hunter*, 121 Ariz. 33, 46-47, 588 P.2d 326, 339-340 (App. 1978).

20. Ariz. Rev. Stat. Ann. §10-076(B)(5); *Schmidt v. Financial Resources Corp.*, 140 Ariz. 135, 680 P.2d 845 (App. 1984).

21. *Nastri v. Wood Bros. Homes, Inc.*, 142 Ariz. 439, 690 P.2d 158 (App. 1984).

22. *Brown v. Sears, Roebuck & Co.*, 136 Ariz. 556, 667 P.2d 750 (App. 1983); *Kavanaugh v. Kavanaugh*, 131 Ariz. 344, 641 P.2d 258 (App. 1981).

23. Id.

24. *Raschke v. Carrier Corp.*, 146 Ariz. 9, 703 P.2d 556 (App. 1985); *Brown*, 136 Ariz. 556.

25. Id.

26. *Readenour v. Marion Power Shovel*, 149 Ariz. 442, 719 P.2d 1058 (1986); *Rodriguez v. Besser Co.*, 115 Ariz. 454 , 565 P.2d 1315 (App. 1977).

27. *Gaston*, 121 Ariz. 33; *Dyer v. Best Pharmacal*, 118 Ariz. 465, 577 P.2d 1084 (App. 1978).

28. Ariz. Rev. Stat. Ann. §12-683(2); *Kuhnke v. Textron, Inc.*, 140 Ariz. 587, 684 P.2d 159 (App. 1984).

29. Ariz. Rev. Stat. Ann. §12-683(3); *Deyoe v. Clark Equip. Co., Inc.*, 134 Ariz. 281, 655 P.2d 1333 (App. 1982).

30. See *supra*, notes 27, 28.

31. Ariz. Rev. Stat. Ann. §12-683(1); *Deyoe,* 134 Ariz. 281.

32. Id.

33. Id.

34. *Readenour*, 149 Ariz. 442.

35. *Baroldy v. Ortho Pharmaceutical Corp.*, 157 Ariz. 574, 760 P.2d 574 (App. 1988).

36. *Dart,* 147 Ariz. 244; *Salt River Project Agr. v. Westinghouse Elec.,* 143 Ariz. 368, 376, 694 P.2d 198, 206 (1984); *Byrns v. Riddell, Inc.,* 113 Ariz. 264, 550 P.2d 1065 (1976).

37. *Salt River,* 143 Ariz. 368.

38. Ariz. Rev. Stat. Ann. §12-2505.

39. Id. §12-2509(B).

40. Id. §12-2501 et seq.

41. *Zwern v. Ford Motor Co.,* 188 Ariz. 486, 937 P.2d 676 (Ct. App. 1996) (intoxication of third party motorist).

42. Id. §47-2314(B)(1), (2); *Dietz v. Waller,* 141 Ariz. 107, 685 P.2d 744 (1984).

43. Id.

44. *Seekings v. Jimmy GMC of Tucson, Inc.,* 130 Ariz. 596, 638 P.2d 210 (1981).

45. *Salt River,* 143 Ariz. at 380, 694 P.2d at 210.

46. *Volz v. Coleman Co.,* 155 Ariz. 567, 748 P.2d 1191 (1987); *Smith v. Chapman,* 115 Ariz. 211, 564 P.2d 900 (1977).

47. *Richards v. Powercraft Homes, Inc.,* 139 Ariz. 264, 678 P.2d 427 (App. 1983), *vacated on other grounds,* 139 Ariz. 242, 678 P.2d 427 (1984).

48. Ariz. Rev. Stat. Ann. §12-683.

49. Id. §12-684.

50. Id. §12-551.

ARKANSAS

A. CAUSES OF ACTION

A "product liability action" includes all actions brought for or on account of personal injury, death, or property damage caused by, or resulting from, the manufacture, construction, design, formula, preparation, assembly, testing, service, warning, instruction, marketing, packaging, or labeling of any product.[1] Arkansas has endorsed the minority rule allowing recovery in instances where the only damages are to the product itself.[2]

B. STATUTES OF LIMITATION

Negligence and strict liability actions must be commenced within three years after the date the death, injury, or damage occurred.[3] Accrual is established by reference to a claimant's awareness of injury and the probable causal connection between the injury and the product's use — in essence, the time when an individual would have sufficient knowledge and understanding of an injury to initiate a lawsuit.[4] It is not necessary for the full extent of the injury to be manifested for the period to start running.[5] The general limitations period found in Arkansas' version of the UCC states that breach of warranty claims must be brought within four years from the date of sale and delivery unless a warranty explicitly extends to future performance of the goods, and discovery of the breach must await the time of such performance, in which case the cause accrues when the breach is or should have been discovered.[6] However the Eighth Circuit affirmed the holding of a district court sitting in Arkansas that breach-of-warranty actions seeking damages for personal injury are products liability actions under Arkansas law and that, consequently, the three-year statute of limitations found in the Products Liability Act governs a breach-of-warranty suit when damages for personal injury are sought.[7] An action timely filed and later nonsuited may be refiled within one year even though otherwise barred by the statute of limitations.[8]

C. STRICT LIABILITY

1. The Standard

(a) A supplier of a product is subject to liability in damages for harm to a person or to property if:

   (1) the supplier is engaged in the business of manufacturing, assembling, selling, leasing, or otherwise distributing the product;

   (2) the product was supplied by him in a defective condition which rendered it unreasonably dangerous; and

(3)   the defective condition was a proximate cause of the harm to person or to property.

(b)   The provisions of subsection (a) of this section apply although the claiming party has not obtained the product from or entered into any contractual relation with the supplier.[9]

2.   "Defect"

"Defective condition" is defined as a condition that renders a product unsafe for reasonably foreseeable use and consumption.[10] Proof of a specific defect is not required when common experience teaches that the accident or damage would not have occurred in the absence of a defect.[11]

3.   "Unreasonably Dangerous"

"Unreasonably dangerous" means that a product is dangerous to an extent beyond that which would be contemplated by the ordinary and reasonable buyer, consumer, or user who acquires or uses the product, assuming the ordinary knowledge of the community or of similar buyers, users, or consumers as to its characteristics, propensities, risks, dangers, and proper and improper uses, as well as any special knowledge, training, or experience possessed or required to be possessed by the particular buyer, user, or consumer. However, as to a minor, "unreasonably dangerous" means that a product is dangerous to an extent beyond that which would be contemplated by an ordinary and reasonably careful minor considering the minor's age and intelligence.[12] The fact that a product does not meet the expectations of the user does not mean that it is unreasonably dangerous.[13]

A manufacturer is not relieved of liability in a negligence or strict liability case based on defective design because the danger is open and obvious.[14]

4.   Proximate Cause

Proximate cause is defined as that which in a natural and continuous sequence, unbroken by any efficient intervening cause, produces the injury, and without which the result would not have occurred.[15] Proximate cause is usually a question for the jury, but it becomes a question of law if reasonable minds could not differ.[16] Proximate cause may be established by circumstantial or direct evidence.[17] The evidence must tend to eliminate other causes that may fairly arise from the evidence, and the jury must have more than speculation and conjecture in deciding between two equally probable possibilities.[18]

5.   Sale or Lease

"Supplier" means any individual or entity engaged in the business of selling a product, whether the sale is for resale, or for use or consumption. "Supplier" includes a retailer, wholesaler, or distributor and also includes a lessor or bailor engaged in the business of leasing or bailment of a product.[19] Strict liability applies to property damage in a house sold by a builder-vendor,[20] but a street designed and built by a residential developer is not a product within the meaning of the statute.[21] The provision of personal services does not constitute the sale of a product under the statute.[22] A commercial lease of an industrial building is not a product under the Arkansas strict liability statute.[23] A supplier of a defectively manufactured product has a cause of action for indemnity from the manufacturer.[24]

6. **Inherently Dangerous Products**

Comment k to section 402A of the Restatement (Second) of Torts (unavoidably unsafe products) has been adopted as an affirmative defense in certain prescription pharmaceutical cases when a design defect is alleged. There must be no feasible alternative design that accomplishes the product's purposes at lesser risk, and the product must be used under the direction of a prescribing physician with adequate warning of potential dangers inherent in its intended or foreseeable uses.[25]

7. **Privity**

Strict liability applies although the claiming party has not obtained the product from or entered into any contractual relation with the supplier.[26]

8. **Failure to Warn**

A failure to warn or the giving of an inadequate warning may be relevant to an action based on strict liability, negligence, or breach of warranty.[27] There is no duty, however, to warn a user of obvious dangers or those known to him or those that he should reasonably discover for himself.[28] Once a plaintiff proves the lack of an adequate warning or instruction, a presumption arises that the user would have read and heeded adequate warnings or instructions. This presumption may be rebutted by evidence that persuades the trier of fact that an adequate warning or instruction would have been futile under the circumstances.[29] The alleged defect, whether resulting from a failure to warn or otherwise, must constitute a proximate cause of the injury.[30]

9. **Post-Sale Duty to Warn**

Arkansas appellate courts have had no occasion to decide whether there are any circumstances when a manufacturer has a duty to warn of a danger in the use of a product learned subsequent to its sale.

10. **Substantial Change/Abnormal Use**

The fact that a product was made unreasonably dangerous by subsequent unforeseeable alteration, change, improper maintenance, or abnormal use may be considered as evidence of fault on the part of the user.[31] Supplying a product to a distributor after the anticipated expiration of life date placed on the product as required by law is a defense to a claim brought by the distributor against the manufacturer. Use of a product beyond its anticipated life by a consumer who knows or should have known the anticipated life of the product is evidence of fault on the part of the consumer.[32]

11. State of the Art

Compliance by a manufacturer or supplier with any federal or state statute or administrative regulation, existing at the time a product was manufactured and prescribing standards of design, inspection, testing, manufacturing, labeling, warning, or instructions for use of a product, is evidence that the product was not in an unreasonably dangerous condition in regard to the matters covered by the standards.[33] On the other hand, a reasonable jury can conclude that a machine was negligently designed despite evidence that the machine complied with applicable industry standards in place at the time of manufacture and that the machine was as safe as other similar machines manufactured at the same time.[34]

12. Malfunction

A defect may be inferred by the fact finder if the injury or damage would not have occurred in the absence of some defect.[35] Proof of existence of a defect may be by circumstantial evidence.[36] However, if direct proof is lacking, a plaintiff must negate other possible causes of the accident by a preponderance of the probabilities.[37]

13. Standards

See section 11, State of the Art.[38]

14. Other Accidents

Evidence of other accidents involving the same product may be admissible to demonstrate existence of a defect, notice to the defendant, or causation, but to be probative and admissible, the accidents must be sufficiently similar in time, place, or circumstances.[39]

15. Misrepresentation

Arkansas has not adopted Restatement (Second) of Torts section 402B, but it recognizes claims for damages based on deceit.[40]

D. NEGLIGENCE

A *prima facie* case of negligence requires the plaintiff to prove that he or she sustained damages, that the defendant was negligent, and that such negligence was a proximate cause of the damages.[41] To constitute negligence, an act must be one from which a reasonably careful person would foresee such an appreciable risk of harm to herself or others as to cause her not to do the act, or to do it in a more careful manner.[42] To constitute actionable negligence, it is not necessary that the actor foresee the particular injury that occurred, but only an appreciable risk of harm.[43]

E.   BREACH OF WARRANTY

A breach of warranty action does not arise unless there is an actual sale or a transaction analogous to a sale, such as a lease. Lack of privity is not a defense as long as the injured party was a person whom the manufacturer or seller might reasonably have expected to use, consume, or be affected by the goods.[44] Giving reasonable notice of the breach to the seller must be alleged and proved.[45] To some degree, the strict liability statute has rendered the personal injury action in warranty obsolete. The required proof of defectiveness and the defenses are identical.[46]

F.   SUCCESSOR LIABILITY

A corporation that purchases the assets of another corporation does not succeed to the liability of the selling corporation except (1) where the transferee assumes the debts of the transferor by express or implied agreement; (2) where there is a consolidation or merger of the two corporations; (3) where the transaction is fraudulent or lacking in good faith; and (4) where the purchasing corporation is a mere continuation of the selling corporation.[47] Arkansas courts have not yet had occasion to consider adoption of the more liberal "product line" exception.[48]

G.   COMPARATIVE FAULT/ASSUMPTION OF RISK

"Fault" is defined by statute to include any act, omission, conduct, risk assumed, breach of warranty, or breach of any legal duty that is a proximate cause of any damages sustained by a party.[49] Thus, a plaintiff's negligence that was a proximate cause of his own injury may be compared with a defendant's fault in supplying an unreasonably dangerous product.[50] The fault of a claiming party does not bar recovery unless it equals or exceeds in degree any fault on the part of a party or parties from whom a recovery is sought. On the other hand, if the fault of a claiming party is of less degree, his damages are reduced in proportion to the degree of his own fault.[51] In cases where there are multiple defendants, a plaintiff can recover if his relative fault is less than the combined fault of all defendants.[52] A plaintiff may recover from an individual defendant in a multiple defendant case even though the negligence of the individual defendant is less than that of the plaintiff.[53] However, the fault of the plaintiff is compared with the fault of only the party or parties from whom he seeks to recover, i.e., the fault of a third party defendant should not be combined with the fault of the defendant(s) in the absence of an amended complaint by the plaintiff seeking recovery from the third party defendant.[54] Whether comparative fault has completely subsumed the assumption of risk doctrine remains to be seen.[55] Failure to wear a seat belt is admissible in a civil action to show causation if the claim is timely asserted and is not based on an alleged failure of a seat belt.[56]

H. PUNITIVE DAMAGES

Punitive damages are recoverable in product liability actions.[57] Punitive damages are not recoverable unless compensatory damages are also awarded.[58] When punitive damages are claimed against more than one defendant, the right to introduce evidence of the financial condition of any of the defendants is waived.[59]

Kathryn Bennett Perkins
ROSE LAW FIRM
120 East Fourth Street
Little Rock, Arkansas 72201-2893
(501) 375-9131

ENDNOTES - ARKANSAS

1. Ark. Code Ann. §16-116-102.

2. *Farm Bureau Ins. Co. v. Case Corp.*, 317 Ark. 467, 878 S.W.2d 741 (1994); *Alaskan Oil, Inc. v. Central Flying Serv., Inc.*, 975 F.2d 553 (8th Cir. 1992).

3. Ark. Code Ann. §16-116-103.

4. *Adkison v. G. D. Searle & Co.*, 971 F.2d 132 (8th Cir. 1992).

5. *Spickes v. Medtronic, Inc.*, 275 Ark. 421, 631 S.W.2d 5 (1982).

6. Ark. Code Ann. §4-2-725.

7. *Follette v. Wal-Mart Stores, Inc.*, 41 F.3d 1234 (8th Cir. 1994), *supp. opinion on reh'g*, 47 F.3d 311 (8th Cir. 1995).

8. Id. §16-56-126; *Carton v. Missouri Pac. R.R.*, 295 Ark. 126, 747 S.W.2d 93 (1988).

9. Ark. Code Ann. §4-86-102.

10. Id. §16-116-102(4).

11. *Higgins v. General Motors Corp.*, 287 Ark. 390, 699 S.W.2d 741 (1985).

12. Ark. Code Ann. §16-116-102; *Berkeley Pump Co. v. Reed-Joseph Land Co.*, 279 Ark. 384, 653 S.W.2d 128 (1983).

13. *Berkeley Pump Co. v. Reed-Joseph Land Co.*, 279 Ark. 384, 653 S.W.2d 128 (1983).

14. *Lockley v. Deere & Co.*, 933 F.2d 1378 (8th Cir. 1991); *Forest City Mach. Works, Inc. v. Aderhold*, 273 Ark. 33, 616 S.W.2d 720 (1981).

15. *Anslemo v. Tuck*, 325 Ark. 211, 924 S.W.2d 798 (1996).

16. Id.

17. Id.; see also *Kaplon v. Howmedia, Inc.*, 83 F.3d 263 (8th Cir. 1996).

18. *St. Paul Fire & Marine Co. v. Brady*, 319 Ark. 301, 891 S.W.2d 351 (1995).

19. Ark. Code Ann. §§16-116-102(3), 4-86-102(a)(1); *Parker v. Seaboard Coastline R.R.*, 573 F.2d 1004 (8th Cir. 1978).

20. *Blagg v. Fred Hunt Co.*, 272 Ark. 185, 612 S.W.2d 321 (1981).

21. *Milam v. Midland Corp.*, 282 Ark. 15, 665 S.W.2d 284 (1984).

22. *Mason v. Jackson*, 323 Ark. 252, 914 S.W.2d 728 (1996).

23. *McMichael v. United States*, 856 F.2d 1026 (8th Cir. 1988).

24. Ark. Code Ann. §16-116-107.

25. *West v. Searle & Co.*, 305 Ark. 33, 806 S.W.2d 608 (1991). For further definition of "unavoidably unsafe," see Annot., 70 A.L.R.4th 16 (1989). See also *Hill v. Searle Labs.*, 884 F.2d 1064 (8th Cir. 1989); Note, 14 U. Ark. Little Rock L.J. 199 (1992).

26. Ark. Code Ann. §4-86-102.

27. *Hill*, 884 F.2d 1064.

28. *Hergeth, Inc. v. Green*, 293 Ark. 119, 733 S.W.2d 409 (1987); see Arkansas Model Jury Instructions 1002 and 1005.

29. *Bushong v. Garman Co.*, 311 Ark. 228, 843 S.W.2d 807 (1992).

30. *Flippo v. Mode O'Day Frock Shops of Hollywood*, 248 Ark. 1, 449 S.W.2d 692 (1970).

31. Ark. Code Ann. §16-116-106.

32. Id. §16-116-105(b), (c).

33. Id. §16-116-105(a).

34. *Buchanna v. Diehl Mach., Inc.*, 98 F.3d 366 (8th Cir. 1996).

35. *Harrell Motors, Inc. v. Flanery*, 272 Ark. 105, 612 S.W.2d 727 (1981); *Williams v. Smart Chevrolet Co.*, 292 Ark. 376, 730 S.W.2d 479 (1987).

36. *Petrus Chrysler-Plymouth v. Davis*, 283 Ark. 172, 671 S.W.2d 749 (1984).

37. *Farm Bureau Ins. Co. v. Case Corp.*, 317 Ark. 467, 878 S.W.2d 741 (1994); *Yielding v. Chrysler Motor Co.*, 301 Ark. 271, 783 S.W.2d 353 (1990).

38.   Ark. Code Ann. §16-116-105(a).

39.   *Thomas v. Chrysler Corp.*, 717 F.2d 1223 (8th Cir. 1983); *Firestone Tire & Rubber Co. v. Little*, 276 Ark. 511, 639 S.W.2d 726 (1982); *Lockley v. Deere & Co.*, 933 F.2d 1378 (8th Cir. 1991).

40.   *Lancaster v. Shilling Motors, Inc.*, 299 Ark. 365, 772 S.W.2d 349 (1989).

41.   *Mason v. Jackson*, 323 Ark. 252, 914 S.W.2d 728 (1996).

42.   Ark. Model Jury Instruction 301.

43.   *Jordan v. Adams*, 259 Ark. 407, 533 S.W.2d 210 (1976).

44.   *Sawyer v. Pioneer Leasing Corp.*, 244 Ark. 943, 428 S.W.2d 46 (1968); Ark. Code Ann. §4-86-101.

45.   Ark. Code Ann. §4-2-607(3)(a); *Gatlin v. Cooper Tire & Rubber Co.*, 252 Ark. 839, 481 S.W.2d 338 (1972); *L. A. Green Seed Co. v. Williams*, 246 Ark. 463, 438 S.W.2d 717 (1969).

46.   Woods, *The Personal Injury Action in Warranty — Has the Arkansas Strict Liability Statute Rendered It Obsolete?*, 28 Ark. L. Rev. 335 (1974).

47.   *Swayze v. A. O. Smith Corp.*, 694 F. Supp. 619 (E.D. Ark. 1988); *Ford Motor Co. v. Nuckolls*, 320 Ark. 15, 894 S.W.2d 897 (1995); Annot., 66 A.L.R.3d 824 (1975).

48.   *Swayze*, 694 F. Supp. at 624.

49.   Ark. Code Ann. §16-64-122(c).

50.   *Skinner v. R.J. Griffin & Co.*, 313 Ark. 430, 855 S.W.2d 913 (1993); *Elk Corp. of Ark. v. Jackson*, 291 Ark. 448, 725 S.W.2d 829 (1987).

51.   Ark. Code Ann. §16-64-122(a) and (b).

52.   Ark. Code Ann. §16-54-122(b).

53.   *Riddell v. Little*, 253 Ark. 686, 488 S.W.2d 34 (1972); see also *Bonds v. Snapper Power Equip. Co.*, 935 F.2d 985 (8th Cir. 1991).

54.   *Hiatt v. Mazda Motor Corp.*, 75 F.3d 1252 (8th Cir. 1996).

55. *Rini v. Oaklawn Jockey Club*, 861 F.2d 502 (8th Cir. 1988); *Dawson v. Fulton*, 294 Ark. 624, 745 S.W.2d 617 (1988); *Bryant v. Eifling*, 301 Ark. 172, 782 S.W.2d 580 (1990).

56. Ark. Code Ann. §27-37-703 (Supp. 1995).

57. *Forrest City Mach. Works, Inc. v. Aderhold*, 273 Ark. 33, 616 S.W.2d 720 (1981); *Airco, Inc. v. Simmons First Natl. Bank*, 276 Ark. 486, 638 S.W.2d 660 (1982).

58. *Takeya v. Didion*, 294 Ark. 611, 745 S.W.2d 614 (1988).

59. *Berkeley Pump Co. v. Reed-Joseph Land Co.*, 279 Ark. 384, 653 S.W.2d 128 (1983).

CALIFORNIA

A. CAUSES OF ACTION

Product liability lawsuits commonly include causes of action for strict liability, negligence, and breach of warranty.

B. STATUTES OF LIMITATION

1. Personal Injury and Wrongful Death

One year.[1] Under discovery rule applicable to statute of limitations for actions for personal injury, the statute begins to run when a plaintiff has knowledge of injury, and knowledge of facts creating, or which in any reasonable person would create, a suspicion of wrongdoing on part of someone, even if plaintiff is unable to identify the wrongdoer.[2] A wrongful death action must be commenced within one year of the decedent's death.[3]

2. Property Damage (Real or Personal)

Three years.[4]

3. Breach of Warranty

Four years.[5]

4. Asbestos Exposure

Either within one year after the date of plaintiff's initial disability (or the decedent's death) or within one year after plaintiff knew, or through the exercise of reasonable diligence should have known, that the disability (or death) was caused or contributed to by asbestos exposure, whichever is later.[6]

C. STRICT LIABILITY

1. The Standard

Under California law, "a manufacturer is strictly liable in tort when an article he placed on the market, knowing that it is to be used without inspection for defects, proves to have a defect that causes injury to a human being."[7]

While California's strict tort liability doctrine was incorporated in Restatement (Second) of Torts Section 402A,[8] California has not adopted the Restatement's "unreasonably dangerous" basis for imposition of strict liability.[9] Instead, California requires a less restrictive determination of whether the product was "defective."[10]

2. Establishing a "Defect"

California allows strict products liability claims based upon defect in manufacture, design, and failure to provide adequate warning.[11]

a. Defect in Manufacture

A manufacturing defect exists if the product deviates from the manufacturer's intended result or from other seemingly identical products from the manufacturer's same product line.[12] A manufacturer's failure to comply with its own design specifications can constitute a manufacturing defect.[13]

b. Defect in Design

California uses two alternative tests to establish the existence of a design defect. A product is defective in design if (1) it fails to perform as safely as an ordinary consumer would expect when used in an intended or reasonably foreseeable manner, or (2) the risk of danger inherent in the challenged design outweighs the benefits of such design.[14]

c. Defect Based Upon "Failure to Warn"

Inadequate warnings or a failure to warn can constitute a defect in a strict products liability action.[15] Manufacturers and distributors may be subject to strict liability if a reasonably foreseeable use of the product involves a substantial danger not readily recognizable to an ordinary consumer, and there is a failure to adequately warn of a substantial danger that was known or knowable given the accepted scientific knowledge at the time of manufacture and distribution.[16] There is no duty to warn of an obvious or known danger.[17]

The requisite warnings can either instruct the consumer how to use the product, or inform the consumer of potential risks that could be associated with foreseeable use of the product.[18]

3. Inherently Unsafe Products

A manufacturer or seller is not liable for an inherently unsafe product if (1) the product is one that is known to be inherently unsafe by the ordinary consumer; and (2) the product is a common consumer product intended for personal consumption, such as sugar, castor oil, alcohol, and butter.[19]

In 1997, the California legislature removed the statutory bar against tobacco-related tort claims against tobacco manufacturers and their successors-in-interest.[20] However, retailers and distributors of tobacco products are still exempt from such claims.[21]

Firearms and ammunition cannot be found to be defective in design on the basis that "the benefits of the product do not outweigh the risk of injury posed by its potential to cause serious injury, damage or death when discharged."[22]

4.   **Causation**

A manufacturer is liable if a defect in its product was a legal cause[23] or substantial factor[24] in producing the injury. In addition, proximate causation principles apply.[25]

5.   **Comparative Fault**

California applies comparative fault principles to strict liability and negligence actions, and requires a comparison of fault attributable to the plaintiff's conduct and that attributable to the defendant's product.[26] Plaintiff's recovery is reduced in direct proportion to her fault.[27]

6.   **Privity**

Privity is not required in California product liability actions, whether based on negligence, warranty, or strict liability.[28] Claims for strict products liability can be brought by heirs of a decedent killed by a defective product,[29] and by third parties or mere bystanders who did not purchase or use the defective product.[30] Sophisticated commercial purchasers are precluded from recovery in strict liability.[31]

7.   **Liability**

Strict products liability extends to those enterprises that place defective products in the stream of commerce, including manufacturers, suppliers, retailers, and distributors.[32] Persons who are in a class that is intended to be protected by the doctrine of strict liability, such as an ultimate consumer, are not liable.[33] Strict liability can also apply to commercial lessors and bailors,[34] as well as to licensors and franchisors.[35] Residential landlords are not strictly liable if they are not involved in the manufacturing or marketing of the defective product that causes injury. [36]

8.   **Successor Liability**

A successor corporation does not assume the predecessor's liabilities unless (1) there is an agreement of assumption; (2) there is a consolidation or merger of the two corporations; (3) the successor corporation is a continuation of the predecessor; or (4) the transfer of assets to the successor corporation is fraudulent.[37] However, a successor corporation can be liable even when it did not continue the predecessor's identical product line.[38] A parent corporation is not liable for damages caused by a product of a wholly owned subsidiary where the predecessor corporation only acquired stock of the subsidiary, and not assets.[39]

9. Substantial Change/Abnormal Use

The manufacturer of a product is not liable for damages arising from a reasonably unforeseeable misuse[40] of the product or a substantial change[41] to a product after it leaves the manufacturer's possession. California law essentially imposes a duty on the manufacturer to foresee careless behavior by the user of its product.[42] Alteration may constitute an affirmative defense.[43]

10. Government Contractor Defense

The government contractor defense is available to non-military manufacturers in a product liability action.[44] However, compliance with government specifications is not a defense to such a claim.[45]

11. State of the Art

Evidence of "the state of the art" may be admitted in a failure to warn case to show that the particular risk was neither known or knowable by the application of scientific knowledge available at the time of manufacture or distribution.[46] Evidence that a product's design was "state of the art" is relevant to the feasibility and cost of alternative designs.[47]

12. Subsequent Remedial Measures

California *Evidence Code*, §1151, which makes evidence of subsequent remedial or precautionary measures inadmissible to prove negligent or culpable conduct, does not apply to strict products liability claims.[48]

13. Standards

Evidence of industry custom and usage is not permitted to establish that a product is not defective.[49]

D. NEGLIGENCE

1. The Standard

A plaintiff establishes a prima facie case of negligence by showing duty, breach, proximate causation and injury.[50]

2. Breach of Duty

A products claim based on negligence focuses on the conduct of the defendant instead of the condition of the product.[51]

3. Duty to Inspect/Test

The scope of the duty to inspect and test a product depends on what the manufacturer knows or should know about the intended use of the product.[52] Negligent failure to test, when the defendant has a duty to test, can provide a basis for liability even where the product is not defective.[53]

E. BREACH OF WARRANTY

In California a product liability claim based upon breach of warranty is governed by three statutory schemes.[54] Recovery can be based on express warranty,[55] implied warranty of merchantability[56] or implied warranty of fitness for a particular purpose.[57]

While disclaimers of liability are not valid in strict liability and negligence claims,[58] it is possible under California law for a seller to negate implied warranties and preclude warranty liability for economic loss,[59] and possibly consequential damages.[60]

F. RECOVERABLE DAMAGES

1. Punitive Damages

California law permits recovery of punitive damages in product liability actions.[61] Plaintiff is required to prove, by clear and convincing evidence, that the defendant is guilty of malice, oppression or fraud.[62] "Malice" is defined as "despicable conduct . . . with a willful and conscious disregard of the rights and safety of others."[63] Conscious disregard can be established by consumer complaints, similar products, failure to test, and adequacy of testing.[64]

Punitive damages are not recoverable in a wrongful death action;[65] however, punitive damages that the decedent would have been entitled to recover had she lived, are recoverable in a survival action, which may be brought on behalf of a decedent's estate.[66]

Mere negligence, even gross negligence is not sufficient to justify an award of punitive damages.[67] Punitive damages are also not recoverable in claims based on breach of contract or breach of warranty.[68]

A corporate defendant is liable for punitive damages where an officer, director or managing agent of the corporation (1) knew of an employee's unfitness, yet employed her anyway in "conscious disregard of the rights and safety of others"; (2) authorized or ratified the wrongful conduct for which punitive damages are sought; or (3) is personally guilty of oppression, fraud or malice.[69]

2. Limit on Non-Economic Damages

Uninsured motorists and drunk drivers are precluded from recovering non-economic damages in any action arising out of the operation or use of a motor vehicle.[70]

3. Commercial or Economic Loss

Recovery of commercial or economic loss (the diminished value of a defective product that does not meet the consumer's needs as well as a non-defective product) is not allowed in California under a strict product liability claim.[71] Such damages might be recoverable in California under an express warranty or misrepresentation claim.[72]

4. Fear of Cancer Claims

In a negligence action damages for fear of developing cancer are recoverable if plaintiff alleges and proves such a fear is based on a toxic exposure and is corroborated by reliable medical and scientific evidence that the exposure would "more likely than not" lead to cancer in the future.[73] Where the defendant responsible for the toxic exposure acted with oppression, fraud, or malice plaintiff need only plead and prove a "serious, genuine and reasonable" fear of cancer, not the probability of its development.[74] The estimated future cost of medical monitoring is an appropriate element of damages.[75]

G. OTHER ASPECTS OF CALIFORNIA LAW

1. Joint and Several Liability

In California actions based on comparative fault, liability for economic damages is joint and several,[76] while liability for non-economic damages is limited to the proportion of such damages that is equal to the defendant's percentage of fault.[77] Damages are apportioned among the "universe of tortfeasors," including non-joined tortfeasors.[78]

Where a defendant's "joint and several liability" is not based on her own negligence, but on vicarious liability or strict liability, the defendant cannot invoke the doctrine of joint and several liability to reduce her responsibility for the plaintiff's non-economic damages.[79]

A joint tortfeasor who settles with the plaintiff may obtain an adjudication that the settlement is in "good faith," which bars any further claims against the settling tortfeasor for equitable contribution or indemnity.[80] A non-settling joint tortfeasor is only entitled to a set-off as to a money judgment against it in an amount equal to the economic portion of another tortfeasor's settlement with plaintiff.[81] The non-settling tortfeasor has the burden of showing which percentage of the jury award is attributable to economic damages.[82]

2. Market Share Doctrine

Under the market share doctrine, the burden of proof shifts to the defendant when various defendants produced an identical product and the plaintiff, through no fault of her own, is unable to establish the identity of the manufacturer of the defective product.[83]

3. Affirmative Defenses

Requisite affirmative defenses generally include comparative negligence;[84] assumption of the risk;[85] and statute of limitations.[86]

Arnold D. Larson, Esq.
Mary P. Lightfoot, Esq.
IVERSON, YOAKUM, PAPIANO & HATCH
One Wilshire Building
624 South Grand Avenue, 27th Floor
Los Angeles, California 90017-3328
(213) 624-7444
(213) 629-4563 (Fax)

ENDNOTES - CALIFORNIA

1. Cal. Civ. Proc. Code §340(3) (West 1998 Supp.).

2. *Jolly v. Eli Lilly & Co.*, 44 Cal. 3d 1103, 245 Cal. Rptr. 658 (1988); *Benson v. Browning-Ferris Industries*, 7 Cal. 4th 926, 931, 30 Cal. Rptr. 2d 440 (1994); *Bristol-Myers Squibb Company v. Superior Court*, 32 Cal. App. 4th 959, 38 Cal. Rptr. 2d 298 (1995).

3. Cal. Civ. Proc. Code §340(3) (West Supp. 1998).

4. Cal. Civ. Proc. Code §338(b) (West Supp. 1998) (real property); Cal. Civ. Proc. Code §338(c) (West Supp. 1998) (personal property).

5. Cal. Comm. Code §2725 (West Supp. 1998).

6. Cal. Civ. Proc. Code §340.2 (West 1982).

7. *Greenman v. Yuba Power Prods., Inc.*, 59 Cal. 2d 57, 27 Cal. Rptr. 697 (1963); *Vandermark v. Ford Motor Co.*, 61 Cal. 2d 256, 37 Cal. Rptr. 896 (1964).

8. 6 Witkin, *Summary of Cal. Law*, (9th ed. 1988) Torts, §1243; *Cronin v. J.B.E. Olson Corp.*, 8 Cal. 3d 121, 104 Cal. Rptr. 433 (1972).

9. *Cronin*, 8 Cal. 3d 121; *Barker v. Lull Engineering Co.*, 20 Cal. 3d 413, 143 Cal. Rptr. 225 (1978).

10. *Id.*

11. *Greenman*, 59 Cal. 2d 57; *Thomas v. General Motors Corp.*, 13 Cal. App. 3d 81, 91 Cal. Rptr. 301 (1970); *DeLeon v. Commercial Mfg. & Supply Co.*, 148 Cal. App. 3d 336, 195 Cal. Rptr. 867 (1983).

12. *Barker*, 20 Cal. 3d 413; *Lewis v. American Hoist & Derrick Co.*, 20 Cal. App. 3d 570, 97 Cal. Rptr. 798 (1971); *Campbell v. GMC*, 32 Cal. 3d 112, 123, 184 Cal. Rptr. 891 (1982).

13. *Lewis*, 20 Cal. App. 3d 570.

14. *Barker*, 20 Cal. 3d 413.

15. *Anderson v. Owens-Corning Fiberglas Corp.*, 53 Cal. 3d 987, 281 Cal. Rptr. 528 (1991).

16. Id.

17. *Rosburg v. Minnesota Mining & Mfg. Co.*, 181 Cal. App. 3d 726, 226 Cal. Rptr. 299 (1986).

18. *Finn v. Searle (G.D.) & Co.*, 35 Cal. 3d. 691, 200 Cal Rptr. 870 (1984).

19. Cal. Civ. Code §1714.45 (West Supp. 1998).

20. Cal. Civ. Code §1714.45(b) (West Supp. 1998).

21. Id.

22. Cal. Civ. Code §1714.4 (West 1985).

23. *Soule v. General Motors Corp.*, 8 Cal. 4th 548, 34 Cal. Rptr. 2d 607 (1994).

24. *Mitchell v. Gonzales*, 54 Cal. 3d 1041, 1 Cal. Rptr. 2d 913 (1991).

25. *Sindell v. Abbott Laboratories*, 26 Cal. 3d 588, 163 Cal. Rptr. 132 (1980), *cert. denied*, 449 U.S. 912 (Oct. 14, 1980).

26. *Daly v. General Motors Corp.*, 20 Cal. 3d 725, 144 Cal. Rptr. 380 (1978); *Fluor Corp. v. Jeppesen & Co.*, 170 Cal. App. 3d 468, 216 Cal. Rptr. 68 (1985).

27. Id.

28. *Greenman*, 59 Cal. 2d 57; *Vandermark*, 61 Cal. 2d 256; *Klein v. Duchess Sandwich Co., Ltd.*, 14 Cal. 2d 272, 93 P.2d 799 (1939).

29. *Barrett v. Superior Court*, 222 Cal. App. 3d 1176, 272 Cal. Rptr. 304 (1990).

30. *Elmore v. American Motors Corp.*, 70 Cal. 2d 578, 75 Cal. Rptr. 652 (1969).

31. *International Knights of Wine, Inc. v. Nave Pierson Winery, Inc.*, 110 Cal. App. 3d 1001, 168 Cal. Rptr. 301 (1980).

32. *Greenman*, 59 Cal. 2d 57; *Barth v. B.F. Goodrich Tire Co.*, 265 Cal. App. 2d 228, 71 Cal. Rptr. 306 (1968) (including component part manufacturers); *Jenkins v. T & N Plc.*, 45 Cal. App. 4th 1224, 53 Cal. Rptr. 2d 642 (1996); *Vandermark*, 61 Cal. 2d 256. However, retailers who sell to dealers will not be held liable. *Fruehauf Corp. v. Lakeside Chevrolet Co.*, 117 Cal. App. 3d 783, 173 Cal. Rptr. 55 (1981).

33. *Ramsey v. Marutamaya Ogatsu Fireworks Co.*, 72 Cal. App. 3d 516, 140 Cal. Rptr. 247 (1977).

34. *Price v. Shell Oil Co.*, 2 Cal. 3d 245, 85 Cal. Rptr. 178 (1970); *Fakhoury v. Magner*, 25 Cal. App. 3d 58, 101 Cal. Rptr. 473 (1972); *Golden v. Conway*, 55 Cal. App. 3d 948, 128 Cal. Rptr. 69 (1976).

35. *Garcia v. Halsett*, 3 Cal. App. 3d 319, 82 Cal. Rptr. 420 (1970); *Kasel v. Remington Arms Co.*, 24 Cal. App. 3d 711, 101 Cal. Rptr. 314 (1972).

36. *Peterson v. Superior Court*, 10 Cal. 4th 1185, 43 Cal. Rptr. 2d 836 (1995).

37. *Ray v. Alad Corp.*, 19 Cal. 3d 22, 136 Cal. Rptr. 574 (1977).

38. *Rawlings v. D.M. Oliver, Inc.*, 97 Cal. App. 3d 890, 159 Cal. Rptr. 119 (1979).

39. *Potlatch Corp. v. Superior Court*, 154 Cal. App. 3d 1144, 201 Cal. Rptr. 750 (1984).

40. *Horn v. General Motors Corp.*, 17 Cal. 3d 359, 131 Cal. Rptr. 78 (1976); *Campbell v. Southern Pacific Co.*, 22 Cal. 3d 51, 148 Cal. Rptr. 596 (1978).

41. *Moerrer v. Ford*, 57 Cal. App. 3d 114, 129 Cal. Rptr. 112 (1976).

42. *Bates v. John Deere Co.*, 148 Cal. App. 3d 40, 195 Cal. Rptr. 637 (1983).

43. *Williams v. Beechnut Nutrition Corp.*, 185 Cal. App. 3d 135, 229 Cal. Rptr. 605 (1986).

44. *McLaughlin v. Sikorsky Aircraft*, 148 Cal. App. 3d 203, 195 Cal. Rptr. 764 (1983); *Vermeulen v. Superior Court*, 204 Cal. App. 3d 1192, 251 Cal. Rptr. 805 (1988).

45. *McLaughlin*, 148 Cal. App. 3d at 203.

46. *Anderson*, 53 Cal. 3d 987; *Vermeulen v. Superior Court*, 204 Cal. App. 3d 1192, 251 Cal. Rptr. 805 (1988).

47. *McLaughlin v. Sikorsky Aircraft*, 148 Cal. App. 3d 203, 195 Cal. Rptr. 764 (1983).

48. *Ault v. International Harvester Co.*, 13 Cal. 3d 113, 117 Cal. Rptr. 812 (1974); *Schelbauer v. Butler Manufacturing Co.*, 35 Cal. 3d 442, 198 Cal. Rptr. 155 (1984); *Burke v. Almaden Vineyards, Inc.*, 86 Cal. App. 3d 768, 150 Cal. Rptr. 419 (1978); Cal. Ev. Code §1151 (West 1995).

49. *Grimshaw v. Ford Motor Company*, 119 Cal. App. 3d 757, 174 Cal. Rptr. 348 (1981).

50.   6 Witkin, *Summary of Cal. Law* (9th ed. 1988) Torts, §732.

51.   *Finn*, 35 Cal. 3d 691.

52.   *Warner v. Santa Catalina Island Co.*, 44 Cal. 2d 310, 282 P.2d 12 (1955).

53.   *Hasson v. Ford Motor Co.*, 19 Cal. 3d 530, 138 Cal. Rptr. 705 (1977).

54.   Cal. Comm. Code §§2101-2725 (West 1990 & Supp. 1997); The Song-Beverly Consumer Warranty Act, Cal. Civ. Code §§1790-1795.7 (West 1985 & Supp. 1998); Magnuson-Moss Warranty Act, 15 U.S.C.A. §§2301-2312 (1998).

55.   Cal. Comm. Code §2313(1) (West 1990); Cal. Civ. Code §1791.2(a) (West 1985).

56.   Cal. Comm. Code §2314(1) (West 1990); *Hauter v. Zogarts*, 14 Cal. 3d 104, 120 Cal. Rptr. 681 (1975); Cal. Civ. Code §1792 (West 1985).

57.   Cal. Comm. Code §2315 (West 1990); Cal. Civ. Code §§1791.1(b) (defining implied warranty of fitness in consumer goods context); 1792.1 (warranty by manufacturer); and 1792.2 (warranty by retailer or distributor) (West 1985).

58.   *Greenman*, 59 Cal. 2d 57; *Southern Cal. Edison Co. v. Harnischfeger Corp.*, 120 Cal. App. 3d 842, 175 Cal. Rptr. 67 (1981).

59.   Cal. Comm. Code §2316(2) and (3) (West 1990); *Seely v. White Motor Co.*, 63 Cal. 2d 9, 45 Cal. Rptr. 17 (1965).

60.   Cal. Comm. Code §2719(3) (West 1990).

61.   Cal. Civ. Code §3294 (West 1997).

62.   Id.

63.   Cal. Civ. Code §3294(c)(1) (West 1997).

64.   *West v. Johnson & Johnson Prods, Inc.*, 174 Cal. App. 3d 831, 220 Cal. Rptr. 437 (1986); *Hilliard v. A.H. Robins Co.*, 148 Cal. App. 3d 374, 196 Cal. Rptr. 117 (1983).

65.   Cal. Civ. Proc. Code §377.61 (West 1992); Cal. Civ. Proc. Code §377.34 (West 1992).

66. Cal. Civ. Code §377.34 (West 1992); *Grimshaw v. Ford Motor Company*, 119 Cal. App. 3d 757, 174 Cal. Rptr. 348 (1981).

67. Cal. Civ. Code §3294 (West Supp. 1997); Cal. Comm. Code §§2314-2315 (West 1990).

68. *Ebaugh v. Rabkin*, 22 Cal. App. 3d 891, 99 Cal. Rptr. 706 (1972).

69. Cal. Civ. Code §3294(b) (West Supp. 1997).

70. *Seely*, 63 Cal. 2d 9.

71. Id.

72. Cal. Civ. Code §3333.4. (West Supp. 1997) (§3333.4, which was created by the Personal Responsibility Act of 1996, a voter initiative designated as Proposition 213, has been declared constitutional in two lower Appellate Court reviews, although a California Supreme Court review is likely to follow); *Yoshioka v. Superior Court*, 58 Cal. App. 4th 972, 68 Cal. Rptr. 553 (1997); *Quakenbush v. Superior Court*, (1997) WL 789980 (Cal. App. 1 Dist.).

73. *Potter v. Firestone Tire and Rubber Co.*, 6 Cal. 4th 965, 25 Cal. Rptr. 2d 550 (1993).

74. Id.

75. *Miranda v. Shell Oil Co.*, 17 Cal. App. 4th 1651, 51 Cal. Rptr. 2d 569 (1993).

76. Cal. Civ. Code §1431.2(a) (West Supp. 1997).

77. Id.

78. *Roslan v. Permea, Inc.*, 17 Cal. App. 4th 110, 21 Cal. Rptr. 2d 66 (1993).

79. *Wimberly v. Derby Cycle Corp.*, 56 Cal. App. 4th 618, 65 Cal. Rptr. 2d 532 (1997).

80. Cal. Civ. Proc. Code §877.6.

81. *Conrad v. Ball*, 24 Cal. App. 4th 439, 29 Cal. Rptr. 2d 441 (1994).

82. Id.

83. *Sindell v. Abbott Labs.*, 26 Cal. 3d 588, 163 Cal. Rptr. 132 (1980), *cert. denied*, 449 U.S. 912 (Oct. 14, 1980).

84. *Li v. Yellow Cab Co.*, 13 Cal. 3d 804, 119 Cal. Rptr. 858 (1975).

85. *Knight v. Jewett*, 3 Cal. 4th 296, 11 Cal. Rptr. 2d 2 (1992); *Milwaukee Electric Tool Corp. v. Superior Court*, 15 Cal. App. 4th 547, 19 Cal. Rptr. 2d 24 (1993); *Romito v. Red Plastic Company, Inc.*, 38 Cal. App. 4th 59, 44 Cal. Rptr. 834 (1995).

86. *Minton v. Cavaney*, 56 Cal. 2d 576, 15 Cal. Rptr. 641 (1961).

COLORADO

A. CAUSES OF ACTION

Product liability actions may be based on strict liability, negligence, breach of warranty or misrepresentation. In Colorado, all product liability actions are covered by the Product Liability Act of 1977.[1] This statute limits the scope of product liability by mandating that strict liability actions may be brought only against manufacturers. The UCC is also relevant to actions involving breach of warranty.

B. STATUTES OF LIMITATION AND REPOSE

1. Statutes of Limitation

Because breach of warranty actions are governed by the UCC, they are subject to a three year statute of limitation.[2] All other product liability actions are subject to a two year statute of limitation.[3] A cause of action for an injury accrues on the date both the injury and its cause are known or should have been known by the exercise of reasonable diligence.[4]

2. Statute of Repose

There is a special statute of repose for manufacturers, sellers and lessors of new manufacturing equipment.[5] No product liability action may be brought against the manufacturer, seller or lessor of new manufacturing equipment on a claim arising more than seven years after the equipment was first used.[6] This statute of repose does not apply to injuries caused by hidden defect or prolonged exposure to hazardous material.[7]

C. STRICT LIABILITY

1. The Restatement Section 402A

Under Section 402A(2)(a), a plaintiff need not show that the defendant was negligent in manufacturing or selling the product. The plaintiff has the burden to prove that the product was "in a defective condition unreasonably dangerous."

2. Basic Elements

Colorado law applies the strict liability principles set forth in Restatement (Second) of Torts Section 402A.[8] Relying on Section 402A, the Colorado Supreme Court has enumerated the basic elements of strict liability as follows:

(1) the product is in a defective condition unreasonably dangerous to the user or consumer;

(2) the product is expected to and does reach the consumer without substantial change in the condition in which it was sold;

(3) the design defect caused the plaintiff's injury;

(4) the defendant sold the product and is engaged in the business of selling products; and

(5) the plaintiff sustained damages.[9]

3.   **The 1977 Product Liability Act**

Under Section 402A, strict liability applies to every manufacturer and every seller in the chain of distribution of the product. In 1977, the Colorado Legislature responded to this overly broad liability by enacting the Product Liability Act. The Act allows actions in strict liability only against manufacturers, unless jurisdiction cannot be obtained over the manufacturer.[10] It is important to note, however, that "manufacturer" is defined to include "a person or entity who designs, assembles, fabricates, produces, constructs, or otherwise prepares a product or a component part of a product prior to the sale of the product to a user or consumer." Colorado courts have interpreted this statutory definition very broadly to give plaintiffs strict liability claims in contexts that initially appear to involve only sellers.

4.   **Defective Condition Unreasonably Dangerous**

Various criteria go into the determination of whether a product was in a defective condition unreasonably dangerous. The tests that are applied are the expectations of the ordinary consumer, the risks and benefits associated with the product, and the adequacy of warnings communicated to the user.

D.   **NEGLIGENCE**

The basic elements of a product liability negligence claim are:

(1) The product was in a defective condition unreasonably dangerous;

(2) The defect resulted from the defendant's breach of a duty owed to the plaintiff;

(3) The defect caused injury to the plaintiff; and

(4) The plaintiff has suffered damages as a result of the injury.[11]

Manufacturers and sellers have a general duty to use reasonable care to avoid injuring those who could foreseeably be injured by their actions. An important factor in the determination of the duty to warn is the extent to which the danger was open and obvious. If a danger is open and obvious, there is no duty to warn unless there is a substantial likelihood that the proposed warning would have prevented injury to the ordinary user.

E.   BREACH OF WARRANTY

Breach of warranty actions are controlled by the UCC.[12] An action for breach of warranty may be brought on the basis of either express warranties or implied warranties. To state a cause of action for breach of warranty, a plaintiff must show:

(1) that timely notice was provided to the defendant;
(2) if the action is based on breach of an express warranty, that an express warranty was actually made and that he relied on the warranty in purchasing the product; and
(3) that a warranty was breached.

A seller's warranties, whether express or implied, extend to any person who may reasonably be expected to use, consume, or be affected by the goods and who is injured by the breach of the warranty. A seller may not exclude or limit the operation of this rule.[13]

F.   MISREPRESENTATION

The Colorado Supreme Court adopted the doctrine of strict liability for misrepresentation from Restatement section 402B.[14] The theory does not require proof that the product was defective or unreasonably dangerous. The basic elements required for strict liability based on misrepresentation are:

(1) there must be a misrepresentation of a material fact concerning the character or quality of a chattel;
(2) the misrepresentation must be made to the public; and
(3) physical harm must have resulted to a consumer from justifiable reliance upon the misrepresentation.

G.   DEFENSES

Certain affirmative defenses are available to the product liability defendant. Most defenses serve only to reduce the percentage of the damages for which the defendant is liable.

1.   Comparative Fault

In Colorado, the effect of comparative fault in product liability actions is governed by the Product Liability Act.[15] Under the statute, comparative fault is a partial defense that reduces the percentage of damages the defendant must pay.

2.   Assumption of Risk

The Supreme Court of Colorado has explicitly adopted this defense[16] in *Jackson v. Harsco Corp.* The Court defined assumption of risk as "voluntarily and unreasonably proceeding to encounter a known danger."[17] The defense focuses on the subjective knowledge of the injured party.[18] The burden of establishing the elements of this defense is on the party asserting it.[19] The defendant must demonstrate that the plaintiff had actual knowledge of the specific danger posed by the defect in design, and not just general knowledge that the product could be dangerous.[20] This defense reduces, but does not bar, recovery.

3. Misuse

Under Colorado law, misuse by an injured party which cannot reasonably be anticipated by the manufacturer can be utilized as a defense in a products liability case.[21] If the defendant can prove the defense, it will bar recovery regardless of the product's defective condition.[22] Misuse is a question of causation.[23] The defendant must show that:

(1) the plaintiff misused the product;
(2) the misuse, rather than the alleged defect in the product, caused the injury; and
(3) the misuse was unforeseeable.[24]

4. Unavoidably Unsafe Product

A manufacturer must prove four factors to be entitled to an "unavoidably dangerous" defense:

(1) the product's utility must greatly outweigh the risk created by its use;
(2) the risk must be a known one;
(3) the product's benefits must not be achievable in another manner; and
(4) the risk must be unavoidable under the present state of knowledge.[25]

As with all affirmative defenses, the defendant has the burden of going forward with evidence to prove each element of the unavoidably unsafe defense.[26]

5. Open and Obvious

In appropriate cases, if a danger is open and obvious, the manufacturer may be relieved of its duty to warn. If a product liability claim is based on an actual defect in the product, then the open and obvious nature of that defect is irrelevant.[27]

The open and obvious nature of a danger is not an affirmative defense. Rather, it opens up the question of whether a warning was even necessary. Since the necessity of a warning is part of the plaintiff's prima facie case, it is the plaintiff's burden to prove that there is a substantial likelihood that the proposed warning would have prevented injury to the ordinary user.

6. Firearms

A product liability action may not be brought on the basis of the inherent danger of a firearm. By statute in Colorado, "the inherent potential of a firearm or ammunition to cause injury, damage, or death when discharged shall not be a basis for a finding that the product is defective in design or manufacture."[28]

7. Learned Intermediary Doctrine

In a product liability case, a prescription drug manufacturer's duty to warn is owed to the physician.[29] It is the physician's responsibility as the learned intermediary to assess the risks and benefits of a particular course of treatment.[30] A warning is adequate when it explains to the physician the risks which the plaintiff is asserting to be associated with a drug and which caused injury.[31]

8. Successor Corporations

In general, successor corporations may not be sued in product liability for products their predecessor corporations manufactured or sold.[32] Colorado courts have expressly rejected the "product line doctrine" and the "continuity of enterprise" exceptions to the traditional rule of non-liability for successor corporations.[33]

H. PRESUMPTIONS

1. State of the Art Presumption of Non-Defectiveness

If the product conformed to the state of the art in existence at the time of the sale, it is rebuttably presumed that the product was not defective.[34]

2. Compliance with Government Codes Presumption of Non-Defectiveness

If at the time of the sale the product complied with any applicable government code, standard, or regulation, then it is rebuttably presumed that the product was not defective.[35] Compliance with federal and state codes will raise this presumption, but compliance with local codes will not.[36] Likewise, it at the time of sale the product violated a government code, standard or regulation, then it is rebuttably presumed that the product was defective.

3. Ten-Year Presumption of Non-Defectiveness

If there are no injuries for ten years after a product is first sold, it is rebuttably presumed that the product was not defective and that warnings were proper and adequate.[37]

I. EVIDENTIARY ISSUES

In any product liability action, evidence of scientific advancements that occurred after the product was sold are not admissible to show defectiveness.[38] Evidence of post-sale advancements in scientific knowledge may be admitted to show a duty to warn.[39]

Colorado Rule of Evidence 407 provides:

When, after an event, measures are taken which, if taken previously, would have made the event less likely to occur, evidence of the subsequent measures is not admissible to prove negligence or culpable conduct in connection with the event. This rule does not require the exclusion of evidence of subsequent measures when offered for another purpose, such as proving ownership, control, or feasibility of precautionary measures, if controverted, or impeachment.

In product liability cases based on failure to warn or on inadequate warnings, Rule 407 does apply to exclude evidence of subsequent changes to the warning. *Uptain v. Huntington Lab, Inc.*, 723 P.2d 1322 (Colo. 1986). This is because concepts from strict liability and negligence are so intricately intertwined in duty to warn cases. Id. It is still uncertain whether Rule 407 applies in strict liability cases, because strict liability is theoretically unrelated to the defendant's culpable conduct.

J. DAMAGES

The product liability plaintiff will be entitled to recover the same damages as the general personal injury plaintiff including lost earnings and profits, lost earning capacity, lost time, medical expenses, special damages, loss of consortium, pain and suffering, lost enjoyment of life, emotional distress, and interest.

Colorado does impose certain statutory limits on damages. The legislature has enacted a statutory cap on non-economic damages. In any given case, the total recovery for non-economic losses may not exceed $250,000 unless the court finds justification for increasing the amount by clear and convincing evidence.[40] If the court allows higher non-economic damages, the amount may not exceed $500,000.[41] No damages may be awarded for derivative non-economic losses, unless the court finds justification for an award by clear and convincing evidence.[42] If the court does allow derivative non-economic damages, the amount may not exceed $250,000. These limits do not apply to compensatory damages for physical impairment or disfigurement.[43] Caps apply to each defendant rather than to the plaintiff.[44] Thus, if a plaintiff proves the liability of multiple defendants, he will be allowed to max out the caps against each defendant.

In wrongful death actions, non-economic losses are absolutely capped at $250,000 unless the act causing death constituted a felonious killing.[45] However, subject to the cap, surviving plaintiffs are expressly allowed to recover for grief, loss of companionship, pain and suffering, and emotional stress.[46]

K. PUNITIVE OR EXEMPLARY DAMAGES

Exemplary damages are available in Colorado pursuant to statute.[47] The amount of exemplary damages shall not exceed an amount which is equal to the amount of the actual damages awarded to the injured party.[48] The statute provides that the court may increase the award of exemplary damages to a sum not to exceed three times the amount of actual damages. The appropriateness of exemplary damages must be proved beyond a reasonable doubt rather than by the usual civil standard of preponderance of the evidence. Exemplary damages are not recoverable in wrongful death cases.

R. Eric Peterson, Esq.
A. W. Victoria Jacobs, Esq.
WHITE AND STEELE, P.C.
1225 Seventeenth Street
Suite 2800
Denver, Colorado 80202
(303) 220-8979

ENDNOTES - COLORADO

1. Colo. Rev. Stat. §13-21-401, et seq.

2. Colo. Rev. Stat. §13-80-101(1)(a).

3. Colo. Rev. Stat. §13-80-107(1).

4. Colo. Rev. Stat. §13-80-108.

5. Colo. Rev. Stat. §13-80-107.

6. Colo. Rev. Stat. §13-80-107(1)(b).

7. Colo. Rev. Stat. §13-80-107(1)(b).

8. *Barton v. Adams Rental*, 1997 Colo. LEXIS 459 (Colo. 1997).

9. Id.

10. Colo. Rev. Stat. §13-21-402.

11. See *Mile Hi Concrete, Inc. v. Matz,* 842 P.2d 198 (Colo. 1992).

12. Uniform Commercial Code.

13. Colo. Rev. Stat. §4-2-318.

14. *American Safety Equipment Corp. v. Winkler*, 640 P.2d 218.

15. Colo. Rev. Stat. §13-21-406.

16. See comment n in *Jackson v. Harsco Corp.*, 673 P.2d 363 (Colo. 1983).

17. Id.

18. Id.

19. Id.

20. Id.

21. *Uptain v. Huntington Lab, Inc.*, 723 P.2d 1322 (Colo. 1986).

22. Id.

23. Id.

24. Id.

25. Id.

26. *Ortho Pharmaceutical Corp. v. Heath,* 722 P.2d 410 (Colo. 1986).

27. See *Armentrout v. FMC Corp.,* 842 P.2d 175 (Colo. 1992).

28. Colo. Rev. Stat. §13-21-503(3).

29. *Hamilton v. Hardy,* 549 P.2d 1099 (Colo. App. 1976).

30. *Caveny v. Ciba-Geigy Corp.,* 818 F. Supp. 1404 (D. Colo. 1992).

31. *Caveny v. Ciba-Geigy Corp.,* 818 F. Supp. 1404 (D. Colo. 1992).

32. *Johnston v. Amsted Industries, Inc.,* 830 P.2d 1141 (Colo. App. 1992).

33. *Johnston v. Amsted Industries, Inc.,* 830 P.2d 1141 (Colo. App. 1992).

34. Colo. Rev. Stat. §13-21-403(1)(a).

35. Colo. Rev. Stat. §13-21-403(1)(b).

36. Colo. Rev. Stat. §13-21-403(1)(b).

37. Colo. Rev. Stat. §13-21-403(3).

38. Colo. Rev. Stat. §13-21-404.

39. Colo. Rev. Stat. §13-21-404.

40. Colo. Rev. Stat. §13-21-102.5(3)(a).

41. Colo. Rev. Stat. §13-21-102.5(3)(a).

42. Colo. Rev. Stat. §13-21-102.5(3)(b).

43. Colo. Rev. Stat. §13-21-102.5(5).

44. *General Elec. Co. v. Neimer,* 866 P.2d 1361 (Colo. 1994).

45.   Colo. Rev. Stat. §13-21-203.

46.   Colo. Rev. Stat. §13-21-203.

47.   Colo. Rev. Stat. §13-21-102.

48.   Colo. Rev. Stat. §13-21-102(1).

CONNECTICUT

A. THE PRODUCTS LIABILITY ACT

In Connecticut the Products Liability Act[1] (the Act) creates an exclusive remedy for all claims of injury and property damage alleged to have been caused by defective products.[2] Although the Act generally does not affect the substantive theories of traditional product liability law, that is, strict liability, negligence, and warranty, it does create uniform procedural rules governing those claims.

B. PRODUCT SELLERS

A product liability claim may be brought against any person or entity engaged in the business of selling a product alleged to be defective, including lessors.[3]

C. THEORIES AND ELEMENTS OF LIABILITY

1. Strict Liability

a. The Standard

Connecticut has adopted Restatement (Second) of Torts section 402A (1965). To recover under the doctrine of strict liability, the plaintiff must prove that: (1) the defendant was engaged in the business of selling the product; (2) the product was in a defective condition unreasonably dangerous to the consumer or user; (3) the defect caused the injury or damage; (4) the defect existed at the time of the sale; and (5) the product was expected to and did reach the consumer without substantial change in condition.[4]

b. Definition of "Defect"

Connecticut courts define "unreasonably dangerous" as "dangerous to an extent beyond that which is contemplated by the ordinary consumer who purchases it, with the ordinary knowledge common to the community as to its characteristics."[5] Connecticut employs a modified consumer expectation test with respect to determining whether products are unreasonably dangerous.[6] The ordinary consumer expectation test is appropriate when the everyday experience of a particular product user permits the inference that a product does not meet minimum safety standards.[7] In situations involving complex product design, however, the consumer expectation test is modified, and involves the balancing of different risk utility factors including relative cost of the product, gravity of potential harm from the claimed defect, cost and feasibility of eliminating or minimizing the risk, usefulness of the product, the likelihood and severity of the danger imposed by the design, feasibility of an alternative design, financial costs of an improved design, the ability to reduce the product's danger without impairing usefulness or making it too expensive, and feasibility of spreading the loss by increasing a product's price.[8] The trial court must determine whether an instruction based on the ordinary consumer expectation test or the modified consumer expectation test, or both, is appropriate in light of evidence presented at trial.[9]

c. Evidence Admissible to Prove Defect

In addition to the factors identified above, the existence of a defect may also be shown through direct evidence or reference to: (1) prior or contemporaneous design features;[10] (2) subsequent design modifications;[11] (3) learned treatises establishing the feasibility of alternative design;[12] (4) other "similar" accidents;[13] (5) OSHA regulations;[14] (6) state of the art;[15] (7) "unspecified dangerous condition" and (8) *res ipsa loquitur*.

In certain cases, a plaintiff need not establish the presence of a specific defect, and may proceed on a theory of an "unspecified dangerous condition" where "other identifiable causes are absent,"[16] or under the doctrine of *res ipsa loquitur*. An instruction on *res ipsa loquitur* may be given, even when there is evidence of negligence on the part of the injured party if "a court can reasonably find that the event is one that ordinarily would not have occurred in the absence of someone [else's] negligence."[17]

d. No Substantial Change in Condition

One of the elements of section 402A of the Restatement (Second) of Torts is that the product is expected to and did reach the consumer without substantial change in condition.[18] The Act provides that product sellers will not be held liable for harm occurring because of a modification or alteration of the product by a third party, unless such modification was specified by the seller, made with the seller's consent or could have been reasonably anticipated by the seller.[19]

The Connecticut Supreme Court has held that the Act is consistent with the common-law requirement that the plaintiff must prove the product arrived without a substantial change in condition.[20] While not an affirmative defense, the defendant may claim that modification or alteration was the sole proximate cause of a plaintiff's injury, after the plaintiff has established, as part of its prima facie case, that the product reached the ultimate consumer without substantial change.[21] The plaintiff then bears the burden of disproving the alleged substantial change, by showing the harm would have occurred notwithstanding alteration or modification,[22] or by establishing that the alteration or modification was made at the seller's instruction, with its consent, or reasonably should have been anticipated.[23]

e. Crashworthiness

Connecticut superior courts have followed the majority rule imposing upon automobile manufacturers a duty to use reasonable care in designing a motor vehicle to avoid subjecting the user to an unreasonable risk of enhanced injury in the event of a collision.[24] Although the Connecticut Supreme and Appellate courts have not ruled on the issue, a number of trial courts in unreported decisions have followed the holding of the Court of Appeals for the Second Circuit that the plaintiff has the burden of proving both the existence of a defect and the extent to which that defect enhanced the injuries sustained.[25]

2. Negligence

Plaintiffs often will plead negligence as an alternative theory of liability. In addition to the strict liability requirements that the product seller sold the product in question, that it was defective, and that it caused the injuries, plaintiffs pursuing a negligence cause of action must also establish the existence of a duty and subsequent breach of duty by the defendant, resulting in the defective design, manufacture or warning.[26]

3. Breach of Warranty

Plaintiffs may bring claims for breach of warranty under the Act, but they may not recover "commercial losses" — consequential losses such as lost profits — unless they prevail on a claim under the Uniform Commercial Code.[27] Plaintiffs do not need to establish privity to prevail on a breach of warranty claim under the Act.[28] There is a split of authority among the trial courts on the issue of whether privity is required in a breach of warranty claim under the Uniform Commercial Code.[29]

4. Failure to Warn

a. The Standard

A plaintiff must prove that the product was defective in that adequate warning or instructions were not provided and that, if adequate warnings had been provided, the plaintiff would not have suffered harm.[30] A product seller has a duty to warn of dangers either he knows or should know about, but is not obligated to warn of obvious dangers.[31]

The Act, like recent case law adopting a modified consumer expectation standard, employs a "risk-utility" standard for determining the adequacy of warnings and instructions.[32] Under this standard, the trier of fact considers (1) the likelihood that the product would cause the harm suffered by the claimant; (2) the ability of the product seller to anticipate at the time of manufacture that the expected product user would be aware of the risk and the nature of potential harm; and (3) technological feasibility and cost of warnings.[33]

A product may be defective only because a manufacturer or seller fails to warn of the product's unreasonably dangerous propensities.[34] Warnings are presumptively inadequate if the trier of fact determines that they were not devised to communicate to the person best able to take precaution against the harm.[35] Even though the statute indicates that liability may be imposed for a failure to warn "whether negligent or innocent,"[36] in practical terms, there is no difference between the statutory strict liability of section 52-572q and negligence with respect to the law of warnings.[37]

b. State of the Art

State-of-the-art evidence is a factor for the jury to consider whether under the modified consumer expectation test, and is admissible on the issue of failure to warn.[38]

c. Continuing Duty

Connecticut law also imposes on product sellers a continuing duty to warn.[39] The plaintiff's awareness of the problem, however, ends the continuing duty to warn.[40] There is some question today, however, as to the necessity of the continuing duty to warn doctrine. The doctrine was developed in response to the general tort statute of limitations which ran two years from the seller's act or omission, potentially barring a cause of action before the accident giving rise to the claim occurred.[41] Unlike the general tort statute of limitations, however, the current statute of limitations governing product liability cases begins to run from the date the injury is sustained or discovered, obviating the need for a continuing duty to warn.

d. Learned Intermediary Doctrine

Connecticut recognizes the learned intermediary doctrine with respect to prescription drugs. Under this doctrine, a prescription drug seller satisfies its duty to warn of the risks inherent in the use of a drug by warning the prescribing physician. The courts have reasoned that prescribing physicians are in the best position to weigh the potential medical risks associated with the use of the drug against the needs and susceptibilities of their patients.[42]

e. Sophisticated User

While not an affirmative defense, the Act does allow the trier of fact to consider the impact of a purchaser's sophistication and knowledgeability.[43] Depending on the purchaser's degree of knowledge and sophistication, and the seller's knowledge thereof, warnings may not be mandated.[44]

5. Causation

a. Actual and Proximate Cause

Plaintiffs must prove not only that the product was defective but also that the defect was the actual and proximate cause of their injuries.[45] To establish a causal connection between the defect and the plaintiff's damages, a plaintiff must prove that the defect was a "substantial factor" in producing its damages.[46]

b. Superseding Cause

The doctrine of superseding cause, or cause which breaks the connection between a negligent defendant's conduct and the result, is recognized in Connecticut.[47] The function of the doctrine of superseding cause allows an admittedly negligent party to shift liability by identifying another's superseding conduct.[48]

c. Causation in Warning Cases

In product liability cases based on lack of adequate warnings, the claimant must prove only that the issuance of adequate warnings would have prevented the harm to the claimant.[49] Therefore, a product seller may not be held liable for failure to warn the user of dangers of which he was already aware.[50] The issue of causation in failure to warn cases is generally reserved for the trier of fact.[51]

6. Third-Party and Cross Claims

Product sellers may bring third-party actions for both indemnity and contribution against other product sellers and nonproduct sellers, including individuals, who may be liable for all or part of the plaintiffs' damages.[52] Where all potential defendants are parties to the suit, however, courts do not permit cross claims.[53]

A question remains, however, as to whether product sellers may bring common law indemnity actions against employers of individuals who have brought product liability actions for injuries sustained in the course of employment.[54]

D. DEFENSES

1. Assumption of Risk

Assumption of risk is a proper special defense under the Act.[55]

---

2. Comparative Responsibility

Even if the plaintiff establishes that the defendant is legally responsible, the jury may reduce the amount of any award if the defendant establishes that plaintiff contributed to the injuries or damage through misuse, negligence, or knowingly using the product in a defective condition.[56] The Act establishes a system of pure comparative responsibility, so that plaintiff may recover as long as it demonstrates that any defendant is partly responsible for the accident.[57]

3. Statutes of Limitation and Repose

Claims made under the Act must be brought within three years from the date when the injury is first sustained or discovered or in the exercise of reasonable care should have been discovered,[58] except for claims alleged to be caused by exposure to asbestos. For those claims, the Act bars claims brought more than thirty years from the date of the claimant's last exposure.[59] The Act also establishes a statute of repose barring all claims arising out of workplace accidents brought more than ten years after the date the seller parted with possession of the product.[60] Indemnity actions must be brought within three years of the date on which the underlying action is settled or adjudicated.[61]

4. Government Contractor Defense

A supplier of military equipment to the United States government may not be held liable for design defects pursuant to state law, when the United States approved reasonably precise specifications, the equipment conformed to those specifications, and the supplier warned the United States about the dangers in the use of the equipment that were known to the supplier but not to the United States.[62] Additionally, the government contractor defense may function as an affirmative defense to a failure to warn claim, but a failure to warn claim is not automatically precluded by the government contractor defense.[63]

5. Knowing Use of Defective Product

Knowing use of a defective product is a defense available to a product liability defendant.[64]

6. Preemption

Several Connecticut Superior Court decisions have addressed whether product liability claims based on failure-to-warn principles are preempted by other statutes.[65]

7. Spoliation

A trier of fact may draw an inference from the intentional spoliation of evidence that the destroyed evidence would have been unfavorable to the party that destroyed it.[66] An adverse inference may be drawn against a party who has destroyed evidence only if three conditions are established: (1) the spoliation must have been intentional; (2) the destroyed evidence must be relevant to the issue or matter for which the party seeks the inference; and (3) the spoliator must have been put on notice that the evidence should be preserved.[67]

E. DAMAGES

1. Workers' Compensation Offset

The provisions of the Act concerning workers' compensation issues such as offset were repealed on July 1, 1993.[68] Connecticut now allows the employer or its workers' compensation insurance carrier to place a lien against any judgment or settlement received by an injured employee from a product defendant.[69]

2. Joint and Several Liability

Product sellers are jointly and severally liable to a consumer or user for damages caused by a defective product.[70]

3. Punitive Damages and Sanctions

The Act allows for punitive damages when the seller acts with reckless disregard for the safety of product users. Plaintiff must introduce evidence permitting a jury to find that the seller's conduct was "outrageous."[71] The trier of fact determines whether punitive damages should be awarded and the trial court determines the amount, but the award may not exceed twice the amount of compensatory damages.[72] The Act also allows for attorney's fees for bringing a frivolous claim or asserting a frivolous defense.[73] The Act does not, however, allow for punitive damages for either property damage claims[74] or subrogation cases.[75]

Francis H. Morrison III
James H. Rotondo
Jessica J. Mitchell
DAY, BERRY & HOWARD
Cityplace
Hartford, Connecticut 06103-3499
(860) 275-0100

ENDNOTES - CONNECTICUT

1. Conn. Gen. Stat. §§52-240a, 52-240b, 52-572m to 52-572r, and 52-577a (1995).

2. *Gajewski v. Pavelo*, 36 Conn. App. 601, 611, 652 A.2d 509 (1994), *aff'd*, 236 Conn. 27, 670 A.2d 318 (1996) (the Act was intended to merge the various common law theories of products liability in one cause of action); *Winslow v. Lewis-Shepard, Inc.*, 212 Conn. 462, 471, 562 A.2d 517, 521 (1989) ("products liability act [is] an exclusive remedy for claims falling within its scope"); *Daily v. New Britain Mach. Co.*, 200 Conn. 562, 571, 512 A.2d 893, 899 (1986) (the Act provides exclusive remedy and by asserting claims under the Act, the plaintiff is precluded from also bringing common law claims). See *Lynn v. Haybuster Inc.*, 226 Conn. 282, 292, 627 A.2d 1288 (1993).

3. Conn. Gen. Stat. §52-572m(a).

4. *Giglio v. Connecticut Light & Power Co.*, 180 Conn. 230, 234, 429 A.2d 486, 488 (1980); *Rossignol v. Danbury School of Aeronautics, Inc.*, 154 Conn. 549, 559, 227 A.2d 418, 423 (1967); *Garthwait v. Burgio*, 153 Conn. 284, 289-290, 216 A.2d 189, 192 (1965).

5. *Giglio*, 180 Conn. at 234, 429 A.2d at 488; *Slepski v. Williams Ford, Inc.*, 170 Conn. 18, 23, 364 A.2d 175, 178 (1975) (both quoting Restatement (Second) of Torts §402A, comment *i* (1965)).

6. *Potter v. Chicago Pneumatic Tool Co.*, 241 Conn. 199, 219-221, 694 A.2d 1319, 1321 (1997).

7. *Potter*, 241 Conn. at 211-213; *Giglio*, 180 Conn. at 234; *Slepski*, 170 Conn. at 23.

8. *Potter*, 241 Conn. at 219-221.

9. Id. at 223.

10. *Ames v. Sears, Roebuck & Co.*, 8 Conn. App. 642, 643-644, 514 A.2d 352, 354, *cert. denied*, 210 Conn. 809, 515 A.2d 378 (1986); *Hartmann v. Black & Decker Mfg. Co.*, 16 Conn. App. 1, 14, 547 A.2d 38, 45 (1988).

11. *Sanderson v. Steve Snyder Enters.*, 196 Conn. 134, 147-148, 491 A.2d 389, 396 (1985); *Wagner v. Clark Equip. Co.*, 243 Conn. 168, 186-191, 700 A.2d 38, 45 (1997); but see *Cann v. Ford Motor Co.*, 656 F.2d 54, 59-60 (2d Cir.), *cert.*

denied, 456 U.S. 960 (1982); *Fish v. Georgia-Pac. Corp.,* 779 F.2d 836, 839-840 (2d Cir. 1985).

12. *Ames,* 8 Conn. App. at 650-651, 514 A.2d at 357; *Wagner,* 243 Conn. at 186-191.

13. *Hall v. Burns,* 213 Conn. 446, 452-453, 569 A.2d 10, 16 (1990); *Facey v. Merkle,* 146 Conn. 129, 136, 148 A.2d 261, 265 (1959).

14. *Wagner,* 243 Conn. at 186-191 (OSHA regulations are admissible in action against a product seller if the regulation addresses the safety of a product, evidence of industry standards and compliance with federal regulations with respect to product safety may also be admissible on the issue of defect.)

15. State of the art, defined as "relevant, scientific, technological and safety knowledge existing and reasonably feasible at the time of the design and rather than merely industry custom" is admissible and probative with respect to expectations of a reasonable consumer and with respect to the risk utility factors of alternative design features relating to safety. It does not, however, constitute an affirmative defense to a design defect claim. *Potter,* 241 Conn. at 248-253.

16. *Living and Learning Ctr., Inc. v. Griese Custom Signs, Inc.,* 3 Conn. App. 661, 664, 491 A.2d 433, 435 (1985); *Standard Structural Steel Co. v. Bethlehem Steel Corp.,* 597 F. Supp. 164, 183 (D. Conn. 1984); *Liberty Mut. Ins. Co. v. Sears, Roebuck & Co.,* 35 Conn. Supp. 687, 691, 406 A.2d 1254, 1256-1257 (1979).

17. *Barretta v. Otis Elevator Co.,* 41 Conn. App. 856, 860, 677 A.2d 979 (1996); *Giles v. City of New Haven,* 228 Conn. 441, 455, 626 A.2d 1335, 1348 (1994).

18. *Prokolkin v. General Motors Corp.,* 170 Conn. 289, 299, 365 A.2d 1180, 1191 (1976); *Rossignol,* 154 Conn. at 559.

19. Conn. Gen. Stat. §52-572p (1997) defines alteration or modification to include changes in the design, formula, function or use of the product from that originally designed, tested or intended by the product seller. See also *Elliot v. Sears, Roebuck & Co.,* 229 Conn. 500, 642 A.2d 709 (1994).

20. *Potter,* 241 Conn. at 236.

21. Id.

22. Id. at 237.

23. *Potter,* 221 Conn. at 236; *Elliott,* 229 Conn. at 508.

24. *Balboni v. America Honda Motor Co.*, 6 Conn. L. Trib. No. 13, 17 (Super. Ct. Hartford-New Britain Feb. 14, 1980); *LaPlante v. Honda Motor Co., Ltd.*, 6 Conn. L. Trib. No. 7 at 15 (Super. Ct. Hartford-New Britain Jan. 22, 1980), as corrected in 6 Conn. L. Trib. No. 9 at 2 (Mar. 3, 1980).

25. *Caiazzo v. Volkswagenwerk A.G.*, 647 F.2d 241, 250-251 (2d Cir. 1981) (interpreting New York law) (to establish a prima facie of crashworthiness, the plaintiff has an affirmative burden to prove: (1) that there existed at the time of the accident alternative, safe or practicable design, (2) that the plaintiff would have sustained less severe injuries had such alternative design been used, by offering proof of what injuries if any would have been sustained with an alternative design and (3) establish the extent of enhanced injuries attributable to the design defect).

26. *Coburn v. Lenox Homes, Inc.*, 186 Conn. 370, 372, 441 A.2d 620, 622 (1982); *Schenck v. Pelkey*, 176 Conn. 265, 251, 405 A.2d 665, 669 (1978); *LaMontagne v. E.I. DuPont de Nemours & Co., Inc.*, 41 F.3d 846, 856-858 (2d Cir. 1994).

27. Conn. Gen. Stat. §§52-572m(e), 52-572n(c).

28. Id. §52-572n(b); see also *Rossignol*, 154 Conn. at 561, 227 A.2d at 424.

29. Compare *Resnick v. Sikorsky*, 660 F. Supp. 415, 418 (D. Conn. 1987) and *Ferguson v. Sturm, Ruger & Co.*, 524 F. Supp. 1042, 1048 (D. Conn. 1981) (imposing privity requirement) with *Quadrini v. Sikorsky Aircraft Div.*, 505 F. Supp. 1049, 1051 (D. Conn. 1981) (dispensing with privity requirement where other remedy not available).

30. Conn. Gen. Stat. §52-572q(a), (c); see also *Haesche v. Kissner*, 229 Conn. 213, 640 A.2d 89 (1994) (upholding trial court's entry of summary judgment on the ground that the defendant's alleged failure to warn could not have proximately caused plaintiff's injuries); *Sharp v. Wyatt*, 31 Conn. App. 824, 627 A.2d 1347 (1993), *aff'd*, 230 Conn. 12, 644 A.2d 871 (1994) (the issues of the existence and adequacy of warnings are typically factual issues for the trier of fact); *but see Battistoni v. Weatherking Prods., Inc.*, 41 Conn. App. 555, 676 A.2d 890 (1996) (summary judgment in favor of the defendant reversed where the appellate court found a material issue of fact based upon the plaintiff's testimony that she did not understand the *consequences* of her action).

31. *Giglio*, 180 Conn. at 235-236; *Tomer v. American Home Prods. Corp.*, 170 Conn. 681, 687-688, 368 A.2d 35, 38-39 (1976); *Basko v. Sterling Drug Inc.*, 416 F.2d 417, 426 (2d Cir. 1969); *LaMontagne*, 41 F.2d at 859-860; *Gajewski*, 31 Conn. App. at 617; *Haesche*, 229 Conn. at 217.

32. *Potter*, 241 Conn. at 219-221.

33. Conn. Gen. Stat. §52-572q(b).

34. *Gajewski,* 36 Conn. App. at 604; *Sharp,* 31 Conn. App. at 833.

35. Id. §52-572q(d).

36. Conn. Gen. Stat. §52-572m(b).

37. *Gajewski,* 36 Conn. App. at 612; *Sharp,* 31 Conn. App. at 833.

38. *Potter,* 241 Conn. at 253; id. §52-572q(b); *Tomer,* 170 Conn. at 687-688; *Greenwood v. Eastman-Kodak Co.,* No. 92 0452919 S, 1994 Conn. Super. LEXIS 3453 (Aug. 30, 1993); *Sylvain v. Madison,* No. 92-0449656 S, 1992 Conn. Super. LEXIS 3230 (Nov. 10, 1992)).

39. *Giglio,* 180 Conn. at 241 (quoting *Handler v. Remington Arms Co.,* 144 Conn. 316, 321, 130 A.2d 793, 795 (1957)).

40. *Beckenstein v. Potter and Carrier, Inc.,* 191 Conn. 156, 162, 464 A.2d 18, 23 (1983).

41. Conn. Gen. Stat. §52-577; see also *Prokolkin v. General Motors Corp.,* 170 Conn. 289, 365 A.2d 1180 (1976).

42. *Basko v. Sterling Drug, Inc.,* 416 F.2d 417, 426 (2d Cir. 1969) (applying Connecticut law and addressing the learned intermediary doctrine); *Goodson v. Searle Labs.,* 471 F. Supp. 456, 548 (D. Conn. 1978) (applying the learned intermediary doctrine to enter summary judgment for drug manufacturer).

43. Conn. Gen. Stat. §52-572q; *Sharp,* 31 Conn. App. at 847-848.

44. Id.

45. *Slepski,* 170 Conn. at 22-23, 364 A.2d at 178; *Marko v. Stop & Shop, Inc.,* 169 Conn. 550, 553, 364 A.2d 217, 219 (1975).

46. See *Mahoney v. Beatman,* 110 Conn. 184, 195-198, 147 A. 762, 767-768 (1929) (establishing the "substantial factor" standard); *Wierzbicki v. W. W. Grainger Inc.,* 20 Conn. App. 332, 334, 566 A.2d 1369, 1370 (1989) (plaintiff satisfied burden of proving proximate cause by providing expert testimony that "it was highly probable that the defects caused the plaintiff's fall"). Although language in *Champagne v. Raybestos-Manhattan, Inc.,* and *Sharp v. Wyatt, Inc.,* seems to suggest that Connecticut courts would not strictly adhere to the "substantial factor" standard in cases in which product identification is at issue, close analysis of these opinions reveals

that neither court specifically decided this issue. *Champagne v. Raybestos-Manhattan, Inc.*, 212 Conn. 509, 530, 562 A.2d 1100, 1112 (1989) (finding sufficient evidence for the jury to conclude that plaintiff's decedent was exposed to the defendant's product); *Sharp*, 31 Conn. App. at 842 (holding there was sufficient evidence to establish that the defendant's products significantly contributed to the dangerous condition and therefore summary judgment was inappropriate).

47. *Wagner*, 243 Conn. at 182-183 (Connecticut courts use the terms "superseding" and "intervening" cause interchangeably).

48. Id.

49. Conn. Gen. Stat. §52-572q(c); *Sharp*, 31 Conn. App. at 835-837.

50. *Beckenstein*, 191 Conn. at 161-162; see also *Haesche*, 229 Conn. at 219-220.

51. *Battistoni*, 41 Conn. App. at 563; *Sharp*, 31 Conn. App. at 85.

52. Conn. Gen. Stat. §52-577a(b); *Burkert v. Petrol Plus of Naugatuck*, 216 Conn. 65, 73, 579 A.2d 26, 31 (1990); *Malerba v. Cessna Aircraft Co.*, 210 Conn. 189, 194, 554 A.2d 287, 289 (1989).

53. *Kyrtatas v. Stop & Shop, Inc.*, 205 Conn. 694, 701, 535 A.2d 357, 360 (1988).

54. On July 1, 1993, the legislature repealed Conn. Gen. Stat. section 52-572r, which prohibited product sellers from bringing such third-party claims. Conn. Pub. Act 93-228, §34. According to two unreported trial court decisions, however, section 52-572r still governs product actions involving injuries sustained before July 1, 1993. The repeal, moreover, did not disturb a recent Connecticut Supreme Court decision holding that, in negligence actions, a special defense of the employer's contributory negligence cannot be asserted. *Durniak v. August Winter & Sons, Inc.*, 222 Conn. 775, 781-782, 610 A.2d 1277, 1280 (1992). *Durniak* has yet to be applied in a product liability action.

55. *Martens v. Wild Bill Surplus Inc.*, No. CV 94-539091S, 1995 Conn. Super. LEXIS 1870, at *2-4 (Conn. Super. Ct., Hartford, June 20, 1995).

56. *Champagne v. Raybestos-Manhattan, Inc.*, 212 Conn. 509, 541, 562 A.2d 1100, 1117 (1989) (reducing compensatory and punitive awards in asbestosis case based on plaintiff's own conduct); *Norrie v. Heil Co.*, 203 Conn. 594, 600, 525 A.2d 1332, 1335 (1987) (jury entitled to consider defense that plaintiff knowingly used product in defective condition).

57.   Conn. Gen. Stat. §52-572o; *Elliot v. Sears, Roebuck & Co.*, 229 Conn. 500, 642
        A.2d 709 (1994) (holding that the bar created by section 52-572p applies
        only where a third party, and not the plaintiff, has made the alteration);
        but note *Sterling v. Vesper Corp. d/b/a/ Penco Products*, 10 Conn. L. Rep. 58
        (Conn. Super. Ct., Litchfield, Aug. 30, 1993); *Petrol Plus, Inc. v. D'Onofio*,
        CV 93-0351700S, 1995 WL 569612 (Conn. Super. Ct. Sept. 19, 1995,
        Hartmere, J.); *Greenwood v. Eastman-Kodak Co.*, No. 92-0452919S, 1994
        Conn. Super. LEXIS 851 (Conn. Super. Ct., Hartford-New Britain, Mar. 25,
        1994) (reasoning that comparative responsibility under the Act only
        diminishes plaintiff's recovery and is not an appropriate special defense).

58.   Id. §52-577a(a); *Champagne*, 212 Conn. at 521, 526 A.2d at 1107-1108; see
        also *Catz v. Rubenstein*, 201 Conn. 39, 43, 513 A.2d 98, 100 (1986).

59.   Conn. Gen. Stat. §52-577a(e).

60.   Id. §52-577a(c); see *Baxter v. Sturm, Ruger & Co.*, 230 Conn. 335, 644 A.2d
        1297 (1994) (reviewing criteria for determining whether statute of repose
        is procedural or substantive for choice of law purposes), *rev'd*, 32 F.3d 48
        (2d Cir. 1994).

61.   Conn. Pub. Act 93-370, §1.

62.   *Miller v. United Technologies Corp.*, 233 Conn. 732, 660 A.2d 810 (1995); see
        also *Boyle v. United Technologies Corp.*, 487 U.S. 500 (1988).

63.   Id. at 782, 660 A.2d at 835-836.

64.   *Norrie*, 203 Conn. at 600.

65.   *See, e.g., Graves v. Metrex Research Corp.*, 14 Conn. L. Rep. 574 (Conn.
        Super. Ct., Hartford, July 7, 1995) (granting summary judgment for
        product seller on the ground that the plaintiffs' product liability claim as
        preempted by FIFRA); *Buddington v. Sterling Winthrop, Inc.*, 10 Conn. L.
        Rep. 358 (Conn. Super. Ct., New Haven, Nov. 12, 1993) (allowing special
        defense which asserted that the plaintiff's product liability claim based on
        failure-to-warn principles was preempted by FIFRA); but see *Pacific Ins.
        Co. v. Dymon, Inc.*, 17 Conn. L. Rep. 502 (Conn. Super. Ct., Bridgeport,
        Aug. 26, 1996); *Duplin v. Whink Prods. Co.*, 11 Conn. L. Rep. 468 (Conn.
        Super. Ct., Hartford, May 5, 1994) (the Federal Hazardous Substances Act
        did not preempt a state product liability claim); *LaMontagne*, 834 F. Supp.
        576, 583-584 (D. Conn. 1993), *aff'd on other grounds*, 41 F.3d 846 (2d Cir.
        1994) (preemption of state tort claims with respect to medical prosthesis
        under the Medical Device Amendments of 1976 to the Federal Food, Drug
        and Cosmetic Act was inappropriate).

66.   *Beers v. Bayliner Marine Corp.*, 236 Conn. 769, 675 A.2d 829 (1996).

67.   Id.; see also *MacLauchlin v. General Motors Corp.*, No. CV 94-533959S, 1996 Conn. Super. LEXIS 1725 (Conn. Super. Ct., Hartford, July 3, 1996) (following *Beers*, the court declined to impose sanctions for spoliation and enter default against the defendant, which was never put on notice by the plaintiff that evidence was to be preserved, and had not acted in bad faith in destroying damaged warranty items in accordance with company policy); *Ampak Seafoods Corp. v. Crown, Cork & Seal Co.*, No-3-92-CV00112 (JAC), slip op. (D. Conn. February 22, 1996).

68.   Conn. Pub. Act 93-228, §34.

69.   Conn. Gen. Stat. §31-293(a) (as amended by Conn. Pub. Act 93-228, §7).

70.   Conn. Gen. Stat. §52-572o; *Marko,* 169 Conn. at 556, 364 A.2d at 220.

71.   *Ames,* 8 Conn. App. at 654-655, 514 A.2d at 359.

72.   Conn. Gen. Stat. §52-240a.

73.   Id. §52-240b.

74.   *Sacred Heart Church v. F. F. Hitchcock Co.*, 14 Conn. L. Rep. 297 (Conn. Super. Ct. Waterbury May 11, 1995).

75.   *Utica Mut. Ins. Co. v. Denwat Corp.*, 778 F. Supp. 592, 594 (D. Conn. 1991). *Accord Colorado Farm Bureau Mut. Ins. Co. v. CAT Continental, Inc.*, 649 F. Supp. 49, 52 (D. Colo. 1986); *Colonial Penn Ins. Co. v. Ford*, 172 N.J. Super. 242, 411 A.2d 736, 737 (1979); *Maryland Casualty Co. v. Brown*, 321 F. Supp. 309, 312 (N.D. Ga. 1971); *Bituminous Fire & Marine Ins. Co. v. Culligan Fyrprotexion, Inc.*, 437 N.E.2d 1360, 1371 (Ind. Ct. App. 1982). See also *Continental Ins. Co. v. Connecticut Natural Gas Corp.*, 5 Conn. App. 53, 60, 497 A.2d 54, 59 (1985) (a subrogee's rights can arise no higher than those of a subrogor).

DELAWARE

A. CAUSES OF ACTION

Product liability lawsuits commonly include causes of action for negligence and breach of warranty under the Uniform Commercial Code as adopted in Delaware. The doctrine of strict liability in tort has been rejected by the Delaware Supreme Court as inconsistent with the Delaware version of the UCC.[1]

B. STATUTES OF LIMITATION

An action for personal injury due to negligence is subject to a two-year statute of limitations.[2] The statute of limitations may be tolled for an "inherently unknowable injury"[3] or when "fraudulent concealment" of the cause of action is present.[4] An action for wrongful death or for injury to personal property is also subject to a two-year statute of limitations.[5] The statute of limitations may be tolled in a wrongful death action when an "inherently unknowable injury" was involved, but the statute of limitations begins to run when a qualifying survivor is chargeable with knowledge of a potential cause of action.[6] Most other actions are subject to a three-year statute of limitations.[7] An action for breach of contract for sale arising under the Uniform Commercial Code must be commenced within four years after the cause of action has accrued.[8] Under a product liability action arising from breach of the implied warranties of merchantability and fitness for a particular purpose, a four-year statute of limitations applies.[9] A party's lack of knowledge of a breach of warranty does not toll the applicable statute of limitations,[10] although the statute may be tolled due to the presence of other factors including fraudulent concealment of the cause of action.[11]

C. STRICT LIABILITY

Strict liability is not a recognized cause of action in Delaware for product liability claims.[12] The only exception is for a lease-bailment transaction.[13]

D. NEGLIGENCE

A plaintiff seeking to recover under a negligence theory must establish that the manufacturer failed to exercise the care of a reasonably prudent manufacturer under all the circumstances.[14]

E. COMPARATIVE NEGLIGENCE/ASSUMPTION OF RISK

Delaware has adopted a comparative negligence statute that precludes recovery if a plaintiff is more than 50 percent negligent under the facts of the case and diminishes plaintiff's recovery in proportion to any negligence less than or equal to 50 percent of defendant's negligence.[15] If there are two alternate paths, one known to be safe, the other known to be risky, the unnecessary choice of the risky path constitutes contributory negligence.[16] In order for the negligence of a third party to absolve a negligent defendant, such negligence must be the sole proximate cause of the accident.[17] Assumption of the risk is also a defense in a product liability action.[18]

F.   BREACH OF WARRANTY

Warranty actions may involve an implied warranty of merchantability[19] and an implied warranty of fitness for a particular purpose.[20] The elements of the merchantability cause of action are (1) that a merchant sold goods that (2) were not merchantable at the time of sale, and (3) injury and damages resulted to the claimant or his property (4) that were proximately and in fact caused by the defective nature of the goods, and (5) notice was given to the seller of the injury.[21] When a purchaser knows of the dangers of a product, or where that danger is obvious, there is no duty to warn and no implied warranty of merchantability arises.[22] The crucial element in an implied warranty of fitness for a particular purpose is that the buyer relies on the seller's skill or judgment to select or furnish suitable goods.[23] A seller's warranty extends to any natural person who may reasonably be expected to use, consume, or be affected by the goods and who is injured by breach of the warranty.[24]

G.   WRONGFUL DEATH

An action for wrongful death may be brought by the wife, husband, parent, and child of the deceased or, if these persons do not exist, by "any person related to the deceased person by blood or marriage."[25]

H.   RES IPSA LOQUITUR

Res ipsa loquitur may be invoked in a product liability suit and gives rise to an inference of negligence.[26]

I.   PUNITIVE DAMAGES

Punitive damages may be awarded in a product liability case, but only when outrageous conduct is present.[27] The imposition of punitive damages may be sought for persistent distribution of an inherently dangerous product with knowledge of its injury-causing effect among the consuming public.[28] Mere negligence is not enough to warrant punitive damages.[29]

J.   DEFECT

A product is defective in design if it is not reasonably fit for its intended purpose.[30] Some evidence of the existence of a defect at the time of delivery is an essential element of a cause of action for the breach of the implied warranty of merchantability.[31]

K.   SALE OR LEASE

A sale of a product is governed by provisions of the UCC as adopted in Delaware.[32] However, the doctrine of strict liability may apply to a lease-bailment transaction.[33]

L. INHERENTLY DANGEROUS PRODUCTS

A product is inherently dangerous when it poses a threat of serious physical harm if it proves to be defective.[34]

M. SUCCESSOR LIABILITY

The general rule is that, when one company sells or transfers all of its assets to another, the purchaser does not become liable for the debts and liabilities, including torts, of the transferor.[35] There are four exceptions to this rule: (1) the purchaser expressly or impliedly assumes such obligations; (2) the transaction amounts to a consolidation or merger of the seller into the purchaser; (3) the purchaser is merely a continuation of the seller; or (4) the transaction has been entered into fraudulently.[36]

N. PRIVITY

There is no privity requirement in post-UCC warranty cases. A manufacturer may be liable to those it should expect to be endangered by the probable use of the product.[37]

O. FAILURE TO WARN

A product, although virtually faultless in design, material, and workmanship, may nevertheless be deemed defective where the manufacturer fails to discharge a duty to warn.[38] However, a supplier should normally be able to rely on a knowledgeable purchaser/employer to warn its employees of the hazards of a product.[39]

P. CHOICE OF LAW

Local law of the state with the most significant relationship to the occurrence and the parties, rather than law of the state of occurrence (lex loci delicti), governs tort suits.[40]

Q. POST-SALE DUTY TO WARN

A rule of law imposing successor liability based on a continuing duty to warn has not been expressly adopted in Delaware.[41]

R. SUBSTANTIAL CHANGE/ABNORMAL USE

Post-manufacturing alterations may relieve the manufacturer of liability if the alterations rendered the product defective and were the actual and proximate cause of the injury.[42]

S. STATE OF THE ART

Evidence of a nationally accepted standard is admissible in a design failure case.[43]

T. STANDARDS

Evidence of industry-wide standards may be admissible, but such evidence is neither controlling nor always necessary.[44]

U. OTHER ACCIDENTS

Evidence of other accidents may be used to show knowledge on the part of the manufacturer.[45]

V. MISREPRESENTATION

Misrepresentation consists of (1) a false representation, usually one of fact, made by the defendant; (2) the defendant's knowledge or belief that the representation was false, or was made with reckless indifference to the truth; (3) an intent to induce the plaintiff to act or to refrain from acting; (4) the plaintiff's action or inaction taken in justifiable reliance on the representation; and (5) damage to the plaintiff as a result of such reliance.[46] Misrepresentation may be raised in a product liability case.[47]

W. STATUTES

Relevant statutes for product liability actions are the statutes of limitation and the UCC provisions when a breach of warranty is alleged.[48]

X. ECONOMIC LOSS DOCTRINE

Under Delaware law, the economic loss doctrine is a complete bar to the recovery of economic loss caused by qualitatively defective products, notwithstanding the presence of privity of contract.[49] An exception to the economic loss rule is a claim for negligent misrepresentation that may allow recovery in tort for economic loss.[50]

Allen M. Terrell, Jr.
Frederick L. Cottrell, III
RICHARDS, LAYTON & FINGER
One Rodney Square
P.O. Box 551
Wilmington, Delaware 19899
(302) 658-6541

ENDNOTES - DELAWARE

1. *Cline v. Prowler Indus. of Md., Inc.*, 418 A.2d 968 (Del. 1980); *Amoroso v. Joy Mfg. Co.*, 531 A.2d 619 (Del. Super. 1987).

2. Del. Code Ann. tit. 10, §8119.

3. *Bendix Corp. v. Stagg*, 486 A.2d 1150 (Del. 1984).

4. *Walls v. Abdel-Malik*, 440 A.2d 992 (Del. 1982).

5. Del. Code Ann. tit. 10, §8107.

6. *In re Asbestos Litigation West Trial Group*, 622 A.2d 1090, 1092 (Del. Super 1992).

7. Del. Code Ann. tit. 10, §8106.

8. Id. tit. 6, §2-725.

9. *Amoroso*, 531 A.2d 619.

10. Del. Code Ann. tit. 6, §2-725(2).

11. Id. tit. 6, §2-725(4); *Sellon v. General Motors Corp.*, 571 F. Supp. 1094 (D. Del. 1983).

12. *Cline*, 418 A.2d 968.

13. *Martin v. Ryder Truck Rental, Inc.*, 353 A.2d 581 (Del. 1976).

14. *Massey-Ferguson, Inc. v. Wells*, 383 A.2d 640 (Del. 1978).

15. Del. Code Ann. tit. 10, §8132; *Culver v. Bennett*, 588 A.2d 1094, 1098 (Del. 1991).

16. *Johnson v. Hockessin Tractor, Inc.*, 420 A.2d 154 (Del. 1980).

17. *Lynch v. Athey Prods. Corp.*, 505 A.2d 42 (Del. Super. 1985).

18. *Massey-Ferguson*, 383 A.2d 640.

19. Del. Code Ann. tit. 6, §2-314.

20. Id. tit. 6, §2-315.

21. *F. E. Myers Co. v. Pipe Maintenance Servs., Inc.*, 599 F. Supp. 697 (D. Del. 1984).

22. *In re Asbestos Litig. Mergenthaler*, 542 A.2d 1205 (Del. Super. 1986).

23. Id.

24. Del. Code Ann. tit. 6, §2-318.

25. Del. Code Ann. tit. 10, §§3721-3725.

26. *General Motors Corp. v. Dillon*, 367 A.2d 1020 (Del. 1976).

27. *Sheppard v. A. C. and S. Co.*, 484 A.2d 521 (Del. Super. 1984).

28. *Jardel Co. v. Hughes*, 523 A.2d 518 (Del. 1987).

29. Id.

30. *Dillon v. General Motors Corp.*, 315 A.2d 732 (Del. Super. 1974).

31. *Towe v. Justis Bros., Inc.*, 290 A.2d 657 (Del. Super. 1972).

32. *Martin*, 353 A.2d 581.

33. Id.

34. *Franchetti v. Intercole Automation, Inc.*, 529 F. Supp. 533 (D. Del. 1982).

35. *Elmer v. Tenneco Resins, Inc.*, 698 F. Supp. 535 (D. Del. 1988).

36. Id.

37. *Nacci v. Volkswagen of America, Inc.*, 325 A.2d 617 (Del. Super. 1974).

38. *Wilhelm v. Globe Solvent Co.*, 373 A.2d 218 (Del. Super. 1977), *aff'd in part and rev'd in part*, 411 A.2d 611 (Del. 1979).

39. *In re Asbestos Litig.*, 542 A.2d 1205.

40. *Travelers Indem. Co. v. Lake*, 594 A.2d 38 (Del. 1991).

41. *Elmer*, 698 F. Supp. 535.

42. *Lynch v. Athey Prods. Corp.*, 505 A.2d 42 (Del. Super. 1985).

43. *Slover v. Fabtek, Inc.*, 517 A.2d 293 (Del. Super. 1986).

44. *Massey-Ferguson, Inc. v. Wells*, 383 A.2d 640 (Del. 1978).

45. *Firestone Tire and Rubber Co. v. Adams*, 541 A.2d 567 (Del. 1988).

46. *Stephenson v. Capano Dev., Inc.*, 462 A.2d 1069 (Del. 1983).

47. *Nicolet, Inc. v. Nutt*, 525 A.2d 146 (Del. 1987).

48. Del. Code Ann. tit. 10, §§8106, 8107, 8119, and tit. 6, §§2-314, 2-315, 2-318, 2-725.

49. *Danforth v. Acorn Structures, Inc.*, 608 A.2d 1194, 1198 (Del. 1992).

50. *Guardian Const. Co. v. Tetra Tech Richardson, Inc.*, 583 A.2d 1378 (Del. Super. 1990).

DISTRICT OF COLUMBIA

A. CAUSES OF ACTION

Causes of action in product liability lawsuits include strict liability, negligence, and warranty.

B. STATUTES OF LIMITATION

Causes of action for the recovery of damages for personal injury or an injury to real or personal property, whether based on strict liability, negligence, or breach of warranty, must be brought within three years.[1] Negligence and strict liability causes of action generally accrue from the time of injury;[2] liability for breach of implied and express warranty accrues from the time a product is sold.[3] A "discovery" rule is recognized, however, in certain cases.[4] The "discovery" rule is most frequently applied in professional malpractice cases.[5]

C. STRICT LIABILITY

1. The Standard

In the District of Columbia, a merchant who sells a defective and unreasonably dangerous product to a consumer is liable for resultant injuries, regardless of fault or privity of contract.[6]

2. "Defect"

Strict liability will be imposed in those situations where a product leaves a seller's hands in a condition which is not contemplated by or would be unreasonably dangerous to the consumer.[7]

3. Contributory Negligence/Assumption of Risk

Contributory negligence is not a defense to a strict liability claim, but assumption of the risk is a defense.[8]

4. Sale or Lease

A consumer has a cause of action against all who participated in placing the product into the stream of commerce.[9] This includes manufacturers as well as intermediate sellers.[10] No District of Columbia cases have discussed the issue of strict liability in a lease relationship; under Maryland law, however, strict liability is not applicable to lessors of products.[11]

5. Inherently Dangerous Products

A product that can never be made completely safe for all users is not unreasonably dangerous if it is accompanied by an adequate warning.[12]

6. Successor Liability

A successor corporation generally is not responsible for the unliquidated tort liabilities of its predecessor corporation. Liability for dangerous or defective products will be imposed on a successor corporation, however, where there has been an express or implied assumption of liability.[13] An implied assumption of liability may be found to exist where a predecessor corporation has dissolved, gone out of business, or is no longer available to be sued.[14]

7. Privity

Strict liability for defective products does not depend on any contractual relationship between the manufacturer and the ultimate user or consumer.[15]

8. Design Defects

To prove the existence of a design defect, a plaintiff must show that a safer alternative design was commercially feasible at the time the product at issue was manufactured.[16] A plaintiff need not show that the alternative was commercially available.[17]

9. Failure to Warn

Manufacturers and sellers have a duty to warn consumers of attendant risks associated with normal use of their products and to provide specific instructions for safe use. A plaintiff may seek damages for negligent failure to warn or based on strict liability arising from the same failure.[18]

10. Post-Sale Duty to Warn

A manufacturer may have a post-sale duty to warn consumers about the dangerous propensities of its products where the manufacturer acquires knowledge or has a reasonable opportunity to learn about a defect.[19] No District of Columbia or Maryland courts have ordered product recall[20] or replacement on the basis of strict liability.

11. Learned Intermediary Doctrine

Manufacturers of prescription drugs and medical prostheses need only warn prescribing physicians of risks associated with their product. The manufacturer is not under a duty to warn individual patients.[21]

12. Substantial Change/Abnormal Use

Manufacturers are not liable for injuries caused by a substantial alteration of the product or due to misuse; however, a manufacturer will be liable for injuries resulting from alteration or unintended use of its product if such alteration or use was foreseeable.[22]

13. State of the Art

"State of the art" is a defense in strict liability tort cases.[23]

14. Malfunction

Unexplained malfunctioning of a product and absence of fault on the part of an accident victim is evidence of a product defect. A specific defect need not be shown.[24]

15. Standards and Government Regulations

Industry-wide custom influences, but does not conclusively determine, applicable standards of care for the manufacturer. Evidence of conformity to industry and legal standards will be conclusive if the person injured offers no contrary evidence that the product, as designed, created an unreasonable danger.[25]

16. Other Accidents

Evidence of substantially similar accidents is admissible, but the trial judge has broad discretion to exclude the evidence if overly prejudicial or likely to cause confusion.[26] The degree of "substantial similarity" required will vary based upon the proponent's theory of proof. Where dangerousness is at issue, a high degree of similarity is essential. If, however, an accident is offered to prove notice, a lack of similarity between conditions will not cause exclusion, provided that the accident was of a kind that should have served to warn the defendant.[27]

17. Misrepresentation

No District of Columbia cases have discussed Restatement (Second) of Torts section 402B or the issue of strict liability for misrepresentation.

D. NEGLIGENCE

Comparative negligence is not recognized.[28] Though contributory negligence is not a defense to a strict liability claim,[29] contributory negligence and assumption of the risk are complete bars to recovery in a negligence action.[30]

E. BREACH OF WARRANTY

District of Columbia courts have held that strict liability and implied warranty of merchantability represent one tort.[31] However, there are some substantive differences, including the statute of limitations and the categories of damages available, among others.[32] With respect to the statute of limitations, the "discovery rule" does not apply to breach of warranty.[33]

F. JOINT AND SEVERAL LIABILITY

The District of Columbia follows the principle of joint liability, which holds that when two or more tortfeasors contribute to harm to a plaintiff, each is potentially liable to the injured party for the entire harm.[34]

G. PUNITIVE DAMAGES

Punitive damages are not recoverable in actions in strict liability, negligence[35] (even gross negligence), or breach of warranty[36] without "clear and convincing evidence" that the defendant acted with actual malice or evil motive.[37] Punitive damages cannot be awarded in the absence of a verdict assessing compensatory damages.[38] It is within the trial court's discretion whether to bifurcate compensatory and punitive damages claims.[39]

H. STATUTES, INCLUDING APPLICABLE "TORT REFORM" STATUTES

Relevant statutes for product liability actions are the statutes of limitation[40] and the commercial code sections when a breach of warranty is alleged.[41]

Patrick W. Lee
Mark A. Behrens
Michael R. Greco
CROWELL & MORING LLP
1001 Pennsylvania Avenue, N.W.
Washington, D.C. 20004-2505
(202) 624-2500

ENDNOTES - DISTRICT OF COLUMBIA

1. D.C. Code Ann. §12-301 (1995 Repl. Vol. & Supp. 1996). See *Dawson v. Eli Lilly and Co.*, 543 F. Supp. 1330, 1332 (D.D.C. 1982); *Alley v. Dodge Hotel*, 501 F.2d 880 (D.C. Cir. 1974), *aff'd*, 551 F.2d 442 (D.C. Cir. 1976), *cert. denied*, 431 U.S. 958 (1977).

2. *Shehyn v. District of Columbia*, 392 A.2d 1008, 1013 (D.C. 1978); *Prouty v. National R.R. Passenger Corp.*, 572 F. Supp. 200, 205 (D.D.C. 1982). Cf. *Rochon v. Federal Bureau of Investigation*, 691 F. Supp. 1548, 1563 (D.D.C. 1988) ("continuing tort"); *Perkins v. Nash*, 697 F. Supp. 527, 533 (D.D.C. 1988).

3. *Hull v. Eaton Corp.*, 825 F.2d 448, 456-457 (D.C. Cir. 1987); *Long v. Sears Roebuck & Co.*, 877 F. Supp. 8, 14 (D.D.C. 1995).

4. See, e.g., *Bussineau v. President and Directors of Georgetown College*, 518 A.2d 423, 425 (D.C.), *reh'g denied*, 525 A.2d 595 (D.C. 1986), *reconsideration denied sub nom. Bussineau v. Georgetown Univ.*, 532 A.2d 89 (D.C. 1987); *Grigsby v. Sterling Drugs, Inc.*, 428 F. Supp. 242, 243 (D.D.C. 1975), *aff'd without opinion*, 543 F.2d 417 (D.C. Cir. 1976), *cert. denied*, 431 U.S. 967 (1977).

5. See, e.g., *Burns v. Bell*, 409 A.2d 614, 617 (D.C. 1979) (medical malpractice); *Stager v. Schneider*, 494 A.2d 1307, 1316 (D.C. 1985); *Knight v. Furlow*, 553 A.2d 1232, 1234 (D.C. 1989) (legal malpractice); *Duggan v. Keto*, 554 A.2d 1126, 1143 (D.C. 1989). But see *Shamloo v. Lifespring, Inc.*, 713 F. Supp. 14, 17 (D.D.C. 1989) ("discovery" rule not necessarily limited to licensed professionals); *Fearson v. Johns-Manville Sales Corp.*, 525 F. Supp. 671, 674 (D.D.C. 1981) (asbestos-related latent occupational disease).

6. See, e.g., *Young v. Up-Right Scaffolds, Inc.*, 637 F.2d 810, 812-813 (D.C. Cir. 1980); *Payne v. Soft Sheen Prods., Inc.*, 486 A.2d 712, 719 (D.C. 1985).

7. *Phipps v. General Motors Corp.*, 363 A.2d 955, 959 (Md. 1976). District of Columbia courts generally look to Maryland case law in the absence of any District of Columbia law on point. *Hull v. Eaton Corp.*, 825 F.2d 448, 453-454 (D.C. Cir. 1987); *Conesco Indus., Inc. v. Conforti and Eisele, Inc., D.C.*, 627 F.2d 312, 315 (D.C. Cir. 1980).

8. *East Penn Mfg. Co. v. Pineda*, 578 A.2d 1113, 1118-1119 (D.C. 1990).

9. *Berman v. Watergate West, Inc.*, 391 A.2d 1351, 1352 (D.C. 1978).

10. *Stewart v. Ford Motor Co.*, 553 F.2d 130, 137 (D.C. Cir. 1977).

11. *Bona v. Graefe*, 285 A.2d 607 (Md. 1972).

12. *Payne v. Soft Sheen Prods., Inc.*, 486 A.2d 712, 722 (D.C. 1985).

13. *Nissen Corp. v. Miller*, 594 A.2d 564, 565-566 (Md. 1991) (rejecting the continuity of enterprise theory of successor corporate liability and adhering to the general rule of nonliability of corporate successors).

14. *Smith v. Navstar Intl. Transp. Corp.*, 687 F. Supp. 201, 206, *republished as corrected*, 737 F. Supp. 1446, 1451 (D. Md. 1988).

15. *Bowler v. Stewart-Warner Corp.*, 563 A.2d 344, 346 (D.C. 1989); *Payne*, 486 A.2d at 719-720; *Picker X-Ray Corp. v. General Motors Corp.*, 185 A.2d 919, 921 (D.C. 1962).

16. *Artis v. Corona Corp. of Japan*, 703 A.2d 1214, 1217 (D.C. App. 1997).

17. Id.

18. *East Penn Mfg. Co.*, 578 A.2d at 1118; *Russell v. G.A.F. Corp.*, 422 A.2d 989, 991 (D.C. 1980); *Burch v. Amsterdam Corp.*, 366 A.2d 1079, 1086 (D.C. 1976).

19. *Owens-Illinois, Inc. v. Zenobia*, 601 A.2d 633, 646 (Md.), *reconsideration denied*, 602 A.2d 1182 (Md. 1992).

20. *Cf. Frericks v. General Motors Corp.*, 336 A.2d 118, 121 (Md. 1975).

21. *Brooks v. Medtronic, Inc.*, 750 F.2d 1227, 1231 (4th Cir. 1984); *Lee v. Baxter Healthcare Corp.*, 721 F. Supp. 89, 94-95 (D. Md. 1989), *aff'd without opinion*, 898 F.2d 146 (4th Cir. 1990).

22. *Young*, 637 F.2d at 815; *Payne*, 486 A.2d at 720 n.6.

23. *Lohrmann v. Pittsburgh Corning Corp.*, 782 F.2d 1156, 1164 (4th Cir. 1986).

24. *Hall v. General Motors Corp.*, 647 F.2d 175, 178 (D.C. Cir. 1980); *Stewart*, 553 F.2d at 136, 141.

25. *Westinghouse Elec. Corp. v. Nutt*, 407 A.2d 606, 610 (D.C. 1979).

26. *Brooks v. Chrysler Corp.*, 786 F.2d 1191, 1195 (D.C. Cir.), *cert. denied*, 479 U.S. 953 (1986).

27. *Exum v. General Elec. Co.*, 819 F.2d 1158, 1162 (D.C. Cir. 1987).

28. *District of Columbia v. C.F. & B., Inc.,* 442 F. Supp. 251, 257 (D.D.C. 1977); *National Health Labs., Inc. v. Ahmadi,* 596 A.2d 555, 561 (D.C. 1991).

29. *Young,* 637 F.2d at 814.

30. *Grogan v. General Maintenance Serv. Co.,* 763 F.2d 444, 448 (D.C. Cir. 1985); *Elam v. Ethical Prescription Pharmacy Inc.,* 422 A.2d 1288, 1289 n.2 (D.C. 1980); *Scoggins v. Jude,* 419 A.2d 999, 1005 (D.C. 1980).

31. *Bowler v. Stewart-Warner Corp.,* 563 A.2d 344, 347 (D.C. 1989). Under warranty liability, a product is defective if it is not reasonably fit for its intended purpose or not of merchantable quality. *Payne,* 486 A.2d at 720.

32. *Bowler,* 563 A.2d at 359 (Ferren, J., concurring).

33. *Hull v. Eaton Corp.,* 825 F.2d 448, 456 (D.C. Cir. 1987); *Dawson v. Eli Lilly and Co.,* 543 F. Supp. 1330, 1338 (D.D.C. 1982).

34. *National Health Labs.,* 596 A.2d at 557.

35. *Raynor v. Richardson-Merrell, Inc.,* 643 F. Supp. 238, 245 (D.D.C. 1986).

36. *Wesley Theological Seminary of the United Methodist Church v. United States Gypsum Co.,* 876 F.2d 119, 124 (D.C. Cir. 1989), *cert. denied,* 494 U.S. 1003 (1990).

37. *Jonathan Woodner, Co. v. Breeden,* 665 A.2d 929 (D.C. 1995).

38. *Franklin Inv. Co., Inc. v. Smith,* 383 A.2d 355, 358 (D.C. 1978).

39. *Merrell Dow Pharmaceuticals, Inc. v. Oxendine,* 593 A.2d 1023 (D.C. 1991).

40. D.C. Code Ann. §12-301 (1995 Repl. Vol. & Supp. 1996).

41. Id. §§28:2-313 to 2-318 (1996 Repl. Vol.).

FLORIDA

A. CAUSES OF ACTION

Product liability lawsuits commonly include causes of action for strict liability, negligence, and breach of warranty.

B. STATUTES OF LIMITATION

A product liability action based on strict liability, negligence, or breach of implied warranty must be brought within four years or it is barred.[1] An action based on breach of express warranty, however, has a five-year statute of limitations.[2] The limitation period generally runs from the time the defect is discovered or should have been discovered with the exercise of due diligence.[3] In certain limited circumstances, Florida's former statute of repose may bar a claim brought more than twelve years after delivery of the product to the original purchaser.[4]

C. STRICT LIABILITY

1. Section 402A

Florida has expressly adopted section 402A of the Restatement (Second) of Torts.[5]

2. Elements of Cause of Action

Florida requires that the plaintiff establish three elements:

a. the defendant's relationship to the product;

b. the defective and unreasonably dangerous condition of the product; and

c. the causal connection between the product's condition and the user's injuries.[6]

Several courts have also required that the defect exist at the time of the accident and when the product was in the possession of the defendant.[7]

3. "Product"

A "product" is property entered into the stream of commerce that can be sold for a profit to consumers.[8]

4. "Defect"

A product is "defective" when risks exceed a reasonable buyer's expectations.[9]

5. Defenses

The comparative fault of either the plaintiff[10] or a non-party,[11] misuse,[12] change of the product's condition,[13] and the "military contractor's defense"[14] are defenses to a strict liability action.[15]

6. Privity

Any consumer, user, or bystander injured by a defective product has standing to bring a product liability action.[16] Privity is not required.[17]

7. Sale or Lease

The plaintiff must allege a sale or other commercial transaction of the product by the defendant.[18]

Strict liability applies to any seller in the chain of a product's distribution.[19] Lessors may also be held strictly liable.[20] A single sale of a product, however, by a person not ordinarily in the business of distributing such products does not support a strict liability action.[21]

8. Used Products

A seller of used products will ordinarily not be strictly liable for a defective product if the defects are latent and not discoverable with reasonable care.[22]

9. Inherently Dangerous Products

A supplier of products will not be held strictly liable simply because the product is inherently dangerous. The court must evaluate the product based on the factors enumerated in section 402A of the Restatement (Second) of Torts.[23]

10. Unavoidably Dangerous Products

An unavoidably dangerous product cannot be made safe for its intended and ordinary use; if accompanied by sufficient directions and warnings it will not be considered unreasonably dangerous.[24] Some courts have applied a risk-benefit analysis to this determination.[25]

11. Harmless Products

A plaintiff may not recover damages incurred solely because a harmless product does not work.[26] Similarly, a manufacturer is not strictly liable for damages incurred through a product's normal wear and tear.[27]

D. NEGLIGENCE

A negligence action to recover for injuries caused by a defective product requires:

    a. the defendant's duty of reasonable care in manufacturing or distributing the product;

b. a breach of the duty; and

c. a causal connection between the breach and the injury.[28]

Unlike strict liability, the plaintiff must prove the defendant had actual or constructive knowledge of the defect.

The "patent danger" doctrine is rejected in Florida, but may otherwise reduce recovery through comparative negligence.[29]

An adjunct to a negligence claim may be based on the manufacturer or distributor's "failure to warn" of the product defect or the foreseeable manner in which the product could be used.[30]

E. BREACH OF WARRANTY

Unlike strict liability and negligence, a breach of warranty action requires "privity" of the parties.[31]

An action for breach of warranty is subject to both the Florida Uniform Commercial Code and Florida common law.[32]

F. DAMAGES

Strict liability and negligence actions permit recovery of damages for personal injury and injury to property. Breach of contract damages are recoverable only in warranty actions.[33] A contractual breach unaccompanied by personal injuries or property damages will not justify a tort claim solely for economic losses.[34]

Florida law requires that a judgment against a party found liable must be entered in proportion to that party's percentage of fault.[35] Thus, comparative fault operates to apportion damages.[36] However, where a party's percentage of fault equals or exceeds that of a particular plaintiff, judgment against that party as to economic damages must be entered on the basis of the doctrine of joint and several liability.[37] Non-economic damages must always be apportioned.[38]

Punitive damages are recoverable in strict liability, negligence, and warranty actions,[39] but various limitations exist.[40]

Lawrence P. Bemis, P.A.
Lance A. Harke
Sarah B. Clasby
STEEL HECTOR & DAVIS L.L.P.
200 South Biscayne Blvd.
Miami, Florida 33131-2398
(305) 577-7000

1.   Fla. Stat. §95.11(3)(a), (e), (k) (1997).

2.   Fla. Stat. §95.11(2)(b) (1997).

3.   Fla. Stat. §95.031(2) (1997); *Florida Power & Light Co. v. Allis Chalmers Corp.*, 85 F.3d 1514, 1519 (11th Cir. 1996) (granting summary judgment in favor of manufacturer where purchaser should have known of product defect nine years before filing suit).

4.   See *Melendez v. Dreis & Krump Mfg. Co.*, 515 So. 2d 735, 736 (Fla. 1987); see also *Mosher v. Speedstar Div. of AMCA Intl., Inc.*, 675 So. 2d 918, 920-921 (Fla. 1996) (recognizing "reliance exception" to former statute of repose); *Mosher v. Speedstar Div. of AMCA Int'l, Inc.*, 93 F.3d 746, 749 (11th Cir. 1996) (same); *Owens-Corning Fiberglass Corp. v. Corcoran*, 679 So. 2d 291, 294 (Fla. 3d DCA 1996) (former statute of repose may bar claims where injury has not occurred for more than 12 years after product was delivered, but will not bar claims where injury has not manifested itself for more than 12 years after delivery). The 12-year statute of repose, Fla. Stat. §95.031(2) (1985), was enacted in 1975 and repealed in 1986.

5.   See *Samuel Friedland Family Enter. v. Amoroso*, 630 So. 2d 1067, 1068 (Fla. 1994); *West v. Caterpillar Tractor Co.*, 336 So. 2d 80, 87 (Fla. 1976).

6.   *West*, 336 So. 2d at 84, 87; *Cintron v. Osmose Wood Preserving, Inc.*, 681 So. 2d 859, 861 (Fla. 5th DCA 1996).

7.   See, e.g., *Diversified Prods. Corp. v. Faxon*, 514 So. 2d 1161, 1162 (Fla. 1st DCA 1987); *Cassisi v. Maytag Co.*, 396 So. 2d 1140 (Fla. 1st DCA 1981).

8.   *Easterday v. Masiello*, 518 So. 2d 260, 261 (Fla. 1988); *Edward M. Chadbourne, Inc. v. Vaughn*, 491 So. 2d 551, 553 (Fla. 1986). See also *Pamperin v. Interlake Companies, Inc.*, 634 So. 2d 1137, 1140 (Fla. 1st DCA 1994) (storage rack system installed on a building, which was capable of being dismantled and resold, is a product and not a permanent improvement to real property).

9.   *Perez v. National Presto Indus., Inc.*, 431 So. 2d 667, 669 (Fla. 3d DCA), *review denied*, 440 So. 2d 352 (Fla. 1983); see also *Zyferman v. Taylor*, 444 So. 2d 1088, 1091 (Fla. 4th DCA), *petition denied*, 453 So. 2d 44 (Fla. 1984).

10.   See *West*, 336 So. 2d at 90; *Alderman v. Wysong & Miles Co.*, 486 So. 2d 673, 678 (Fla. 1st DCA 1986); *Goulah v. Ford Motor Co.*, 118 F.3d 1478, 1485 (11th

Cir. 1997) (defendant may argue that plaintiffs' action was the "sole legal cause" of the accident, even after withdrawal of comparative negligence defense).

11.   *Nash v. Wells Fargo Guard Servs., Inc.*, 678 So. 2d 1262, 1264 (Fla. 1996) (in order to apportion fault to non-party, defendant must plead it as an affirmative defense and "specifically identify the non-party").

12.   *High v. Westinghouse Elec. Corp.*, 610 So. 2d 1259, 1262 (Fla. 1992); *Tri-County Truss Co. v. Leonard*, 467 So. 2d 370, 371 (Fla. 4th DCA), *petition denied*, 476 So. 2d 676 (Fla. 1985). In other words, strict liability only applies if the product is used for the purpose for which it was intended when produced. *High*, 610 So. 2d at 1262.

13.   *Cintron v. Osmose Wood Preserving, Inc.*, 681 So. 2d 859, 861 (Fla. 5th DCA 1996).

14.   *Hercules, Inc. v. United States*, 116 S. Ct. 981 (1996); *Dorse v. Armstrong World Indus., Inc.*, 513 So. 2d 1265, 1269 (Fla. 1987).

15.   Res judicata may also apply against others in the chain of distribution. See *West v. Kawasaki Motors Mfg. Corp.*, 595 So. 2d 92, 97 (Fla. 3d DCA) (previous unsuccessful products liability claim against one party in the chain of distribution bars a subsequent claim, based on the same allegations, against another party in the same distribution chain), *review denied*, 604 So. 2d 489 (Fla. 1992).

16.   See, e.g., *West*, 336 So. 2d at 89; *Cedars of Lebanon Hosp. Corp. v. European X-Ray Distribs.*, 444 So. 2d 1068, 1070 (Fla. 3d DCA 1984).

17.   See *Easterday*, 518 So. 2d at 261.

18.   *Adorno Marketing, Inc. v. Da Silva*, 623 So. 2d 542, 543 (Fla. 3d DCA 1993); *Johnson v. Supro Corp.*, 498 So. 2d 528, 529 (Fla. 3d DCA 1986).

19.   *Johnson*, 498 So. 2d at 529.

20.   See *Samuel Friedland Family Enter.*, 630 So. 2d at 1071 (the doctrine of strict liability applies to commercial lease transactions just as it does to sales).

21.   Id.

22.   *Keith v. Russell T. Bundy & Assocs.*, 495 So. 2d 1223, 1228 (Fla. 5th DCA 1986).

23.   *Radiation Technology, Inc. v. Ware Constr. Co.*, 445 So. 2d 329, 331 (Fla. 1983).

24.   See *Buckner v. Allergan Pharmaceuticals, Inc.*, 400 So. 2d 820, 822-823 (Fla. 5th DCA), *review denied*, 407 So. 2d 1102 (Fla. 1981).

25.   See *Adams v. G. D. Searle & Co.*, 576 So. 2d 728, 733 (Fla. 2d DCA), *review denied*, 589 So. 2d 290 (Fla. 1991).

26.   *Monsanto Agric. Prod. Co. v. Edenfield*, 426 So. 2d 574, 575-576 (Fla. 1st DCA 1982).

27.   *Perez*, 431 So. 2d at 669.

28.   See *Cintron v. Osmose Wood Preserving, Inc.*, 681 So. 2d 859, 861 (Fla. 5th DCA 1996); *Westchester Exxon v. Valdez*, 524 So. 2d 452, 454 (Fla. 3d DCA 1988); *Stahl v. Metropolitan Dade County*, 438 So. 2d 14, 17 (Fla. 3d DCA 1983).

29.   *Auburn Mach. Works Co. v. Jones*, 366 So. 2d 1167, 1172 (Fla. 1979). Thus, a patent danger only bars liability where the negligence is solely in the lack of a warning. See *Mosher v. Speedstar Div. of AMCA Intl.*, 979 F.2d 823, 826 (11th Cir. 1992).

30.   See *E. R. Squibb & Sons, Inc. v. Farnes*, 697 So. 2d 825, 826 (Fla. 1997).

31.   See *Kramer v. Piper Aircraft Corp.*, 520 So. 2d 37, 39 n.4 (Fla. 1988); *T.W.M. v. American Med. Sys., Inc.*, 886 F. Supp 842, 844 (N.D. Fla. 1995); Fla. Stat. §672.318 (1996).

32.   See Fla. Stat. §672.313 (1997) (express warranty); §672.314 (implied warranty of merchantability); §672.315 (implied warranty of fitness for particular purpose).

33.   *Casa Clara v. Charley Toppino & Sons*, 620 So. 2d 1244, 1247 (Fla. 1993); *GAF Corp. v. Zack Co.*, 445 So. 2d 350, 351-352 (Fla. 3d DCA), *review denied*, 453 So. 2d 45 (Fla. 1984).

34.   See *Casa Clara*, 620 So. 2d at 1246; *AFM Corp. v. Southern Bell Tel. & Tel. Co.*, 515 So. 2d 180, 181-182 (Fla. 1987); see also *All American Semi Conductor, Inc. v. Mil-Pro Servs., Inc.*, 686 So. 2d 760, 761 (Fla. 5th DCA 1997).

35.   Fla. Stat. §768.81 (1997); see also *Fabre v. Marin*, 623 So. 2d 1182, 1185 (Fla. 1993) (the only means of determining a party's percentage of fault is to compare that party's percentage of fault to all other entities who contributed to the accident, regardless of whether they have been or could

have been joined as defendants); *Y.H. Investments, Inc. v. Godales*, 690 So. 2d 1273, 1278 (Fla. 1997) (party may add negligent tortfeasor on jury verdict form regardless of immunity, provided there is sufficient evidence of fault).

36.　*Nash v. Wells Fargo Guard Servs., Inc.*, 678 So. 2d 1262, 1263 (Fla. 1996); see also *Merrill Crossings Assocs. v. McDonald*, 705 So. 2d 560, 562 (Fla. 1997).

37.　Fla. Stat. §768.81(3) (1997); see also *Snoozy v. U.S. Gypsum Co.*, 695 So. 2d 767, 769 (Fla. 3d DCA 1997) (party must lay adequate foundation for allocation of fault pursuant to §768.81).

38.　*Nash*, 678 So. 2d at 1263-1264.

39.　See Fla. Stat. §768.73(1)(a) (1997).

40.　See, e.g., id. (generally limiting punitive damages to three times the amount of compensatory damages awarded).

GEORGIA

A. CAUSES OF ACTION

Product liability lawsuits may proceed on theories of strict liability, negligence, or breach of warranty.[1]

B. STATUTES OF LIMITATION

Negligence and strict liability actions must be brought within two years of the date of accrual for bodily injury[2] and within four years for property damage.[3] The discovery rule applies only to bodily injuries[4] and acts to toll the running of the statute of limitations until the injured knew or should have discovered, through the exercise of reasonable diligence, both (1) the nature of his injury and (2) the causal connection between the injury and the alleged conduct of the defendant.[5] Georgia has enacted a statute of repose that bars filing tort actions more than ten years after the date of the first sale for use or consumption of the product causing the injury.[6]

Warranty causes of action must be brought within four years of the tender of delivery of the good.[7] This period may be reduced by agreement to not less than a year but may not be extended.[8] If a written express warranty does not come within the Uniform Commercial Code, the statute of limitations for breach of warranty is six years.[9]

C. STRICT LIABILITY

1. The Standard

Rather than relying on common law or section 402A of the Restatement (Second) of Torts, Georgia has adopted a statutory standard for strict liability. A manufacturer will be liable in strict liability if its product when sold "was not merchantable and reasonably suited to the use intended, and its condition when sold is the proximate cause of the injury sustained."[10] This means that the product must be defective when sold.[11] The existence of a defect is critical because a manufacturer "is not an insurer against all risks of injury associated with its product."[12] In Georgia, a product need not be unreasonably dangerous before imposition of strict liability.[13]

Only manufacturers may be strictly liable in tort. "Product sellers" have been excluded from strict liability actions.[14] A "product seller" is defined as "a person who, in the course of a business conducted for the purpose leases or sells and distributes; installs; prepares; blends; packages; labels; markets; or assembles pursuant to a manufacturer's plan, intention, design, specifications, or formulation; or repairs; maintains; or otherwise is involved in placing a product in the stream of commerce."[15]

2.   "Defect"

In Georgia, a plaintiff may establish a "defect" by showing (1) an inadequate warning or marketing defect;[16] (2) a design or engineering defect;[17] (3) a manufacturing or construction defect;[18] or (4) a "semiwarranty" defect — that the product was not merchantable and not fit for use.[19] A product must be in a defective condition at the time it leaves the seller's hands.[20]

Georgia now applies a risk-utility standard in design defect cases,[21] rather than a reasonable foreseeability standard.[22] Under the new standard, a design defect is present where "the risks inherent in a product design [outweigh] the utility of the product so designed."[23] This is essentially a negligence standard.

Whether a product has a "defect" is decided on a case-by-case basis, and is usually a jury question.[24]

3.   Contributory Negligence/Assumption of Risk

Contributory negligence is not a defense to strict liability claims.[25]

Assumption of risk is a defense.[26] Two types of assumption of risk may be present: (1) assumption of risk of the product defect; or (2) assumption of risk of the physical injuries incurred.[27]

4.   Sale or Lease

Under the Georgia strict liability provision, a strict liability action may be brought for "any personal property sold as new property directly or through a dealer or any other person."[28]

This wording could permit an action for leased property if the lease is the substantial equivalent of a sale.[29] No case has specifically extended strict liability principles to leases. Although expressly declining to decide the issue, one case has noted that most courts extend strict liability to bailments and leases in a commercial setting.[30]

5.   Inherently Dangerous Products

There is no strict liability cause of action simply because an item is inherently dangerous.[31] However, if a product is so inherently dangerous that it requires a particular warning as to that characteristic, there may be a strict liability action for failure to warn.[32]

6.   Successor Liability

A purchasing corporation does not assume the liabilities of a seller unless (1) there is an agreement to assume liabilities; (2) the transaction is a merger; (3) the transaction is a fraudulent attempt to avoid liabilities; or (4) the purchaser is a mere continuation of the predecessor corporation.[33] To be a continuation, there must be some identity of ownership.[34]

7. Privity

No privity is required for an individual plaintiff to sue a manufacturer.[35] However, corporate plaintiffs must still establish privity.[36]

8. Failure to Warn

A manufacturer has a duty to give adequate warning where it has reason to believe that a use of the product may cause harm. If the product does not contain such a warning, the product is defective.[37]

A manufacturer has no duty to warn of an obvious or generally known danger.[38] Whether a peril is obvious is determined under the objective "open and obvious" rule.[39] Likewise, a duty to warn extends only to the manufacturer's reasonably contemplated and anticipated use of the product,[40] and does not extend to unexpected modifications or alterations.[41]

Whether a warning is adequate is a question for the jury.[42] Questions used in determining whether a warning was adequate are (1) Was there a danger that required a warning or instruction? (2) Was any warning or instruction given? (3) Was the warning or instruction read? (4) Was the warning label effective for those who would foreseeably be affected by the product? and (5) Did the label give adequate instructions on how to safely use the product?[43]

The lack or inadequacy of warning must be the proximate cause of the injury. If the plaintiff did not read the allegedly inadequate warning, there is no proximate causation.[44]

9. Post-Sale Duty to Warn

Georgia has not yet imposed a post-sale duty to warn in strict liability actions.

10. Learned Intermediary Doctrine

A manufacturer of prescription drugs has a duty to warn only the prescribing physician of the potential dangers related to the drug. The physician then acts as the "learned intermediary" between the manufacturer and the consumer.[45]

11. Substantial Change/Abnormal Use

A manufacturer may not be held strictly liable for injuries resulting from a substantial change in or an abnormal use of a product.[46]

12. State of the Art

The Georgia Supreme Court recently held that the state of the art is not a defense, but a factor to be considered in assessing whether a design defect exists.[47] Prior to the adoption of the new design defect standard an intermediate Georgia appellate court, applying a negligence standard, looked to the state of technology when a car was built and ruled that because the design met applicable federal standards it was not defectively designed.[48] However, the Georgia Supreme Court recently expressly declined to follow this analysis and held compliance with industry-wide practices, state of the art, or federal regulations does not eliminate conclusively a manufacturer's liability for its design of allegedly defective products.[49]

13. **Crashworthiness**

A manufacturer must use reasonable care in its design to avoid subjecting product users to enhanced injuries.[50] Once the plaintiff proves that a design defect was a substantial factor in producing damages over and above those that were probably caused as a result of the original impact or collision, the burden of proof shifts to the manufacturer to demonstrate a rational basis for apportioning liability for the injuries.[51]

14. **Standards**

In negligence actions, evidence as to industry standards is admissible and relevant as to whether an ordinary, prudent manufacturer would act in accordance with the standard.[52]

15. **Other Accidents**

Evidence of other similar accidents or lack thereof is admissible to demonstrate the manufacturer's knowledge of the alleged defect.[53] Such evidence is not admissible to prove that a product was defective.[54]

D. NEGLIGENCE

1. In negligence actions, "the duty imposed is the traditional one of reasonable care and the manufacturer need not provide . . . a product incapable of producing injury."[55]

2. Contributory and comparative negligence are defenses to a product liability suit under a negligence theory.[56] The Georgia comparative negligence standard permits a plaintiff to recover only if her negligence is less than that of the defendant.[57]

3. Intervening acts may prevent a negligent manufacturer from being liable.[58]

4. If a dealer, distributor, or other intermediary voluntarily agrees to notify consumers of a defect, he may be found negligent for failure to perform.[59]

E. BREACH OF WARRANTY

A breach of warranty occurs when a product is not fit for the ordinary purposes for which such goods are used.[60]

Breach of warranty claims require privity.[61] However, there is an exception for a natural person in the family or household of the buyer or a guest in the home where the warranty extends to the identifiable third person.[62] A person may not effectively assign a warranty to a subsequent purchaser of a product.[63]

If a purchaser fails to follow directions provided by a manufacturer, there can be no liability for breach of warranty.[64]

For breach of warranty claims, Georgia continues to distinguish between a "sale" and a "lease." However, the characteristics of an agreement, not its name, determine its treatment. Only if a "lease" is essentially a sale may the lessee be treated as an owner.[65]

If an express warranty provides the manufacturer with a right to repair defects, a breach of warranty would not occur unless and until the manufacturer has been given an opportunity to repair.[66]

F. DAMAGES

1. Joint and Several Liability

If the separate and independent acts of negligence of two or more persons combine to produce a single indivisible injury, then the actors are jointly and severally liable for the full amount of plaintiff's damages.[67] A manufacturer found liable in strict liability and another party found to be negligent may be joint tortfeasors where their combined acts result in a single indivisible injury.[68] When the plaintiff is partially responsible for the injury, this rule may be disregarded and separate judgments rendered among the persons who are liable and whose degree of fault is greater than that of the injured party.[69]

2. Collateral Source Rule

An injured party may recover damages from a manufacturer regardless of any compensation he may have received from other parties.[70] A litigant's insurance policy is therefore inadmissible because of its prejudicial nature.[71]

3. Punitive Damages

In 1988, the Georgia legislature enacted the Georgia Tort Reform Act to limit awards of punitive damages.[72] Punitive damages may be recovered only where "it is proven by clear and convincing evidence that the defendant's actions showed willful misconduct, malice, fraud, wantonness, oppression, or that entire want of care which would raise the presumption of conscious indifference to consequences."[73] The statute also provides that only one award of punitive damages may be awarded against a defendant for any act or omission[74] and required 75 percent of the award to go to the state.[75] These two provisions have been declared constitutional by the Georgia Supreme Court and have been found not to create an arbitrary and unreasonable classification between product liability plaintiffs and other tort plaintiffs.[76]

James R. Johnson
Erika B. Johnson
JONES, DAY, REAVIS & POGUE
3500 One Peachtree Center
303 Peachtree Street, NE
Atlanta, Georgia 30308-3242
(404) 521-3939

1. *Corbin v. Farmex, Inc.*, 227 Ga. App. 620, 490 S.E.2d 395 (1997); *Ogletree v. Navistar Intl. Transp. Corp.*, 194 Ga. App. 41, 390 S.E.2d 61 (1989), *cert. denied*, 194 Ga. App. 912 (1990), *overruled on other grounds by Weatherby v. Honda Motor Co.*, 195 Ga. App. 169, 393 S.E.2d 64 (1990).

2. O.C.G.A. §9-3-33.

3. Id. §§9-3-30, 9-3-31.

4. *Corporation of Mercer Univ. v. National Gypsum Co.*, 258 Ga. 365, 368 S.E.2d 732 (1988), *cert. denied*, 493 U.S. 965 (1989). But see *Smith v. Branch*, 226 Ga. App. 626, 487 S.E.2d 35 (1997).

5. *Welch v. Celotex Corp.*, 951 F.2d 1235 (11th Cir. 1992) (applying Georgia law); *Anderson v. Sybron Corp.*, 165 Ga. App. 566, 353 S.E.2d 816, *aff'd*, 251 Ga. 593, 310 S.E.2d 232 (1983); *King v. Seitzingers, Inc.*, 160 Ga. App. 318, 287 S.E.2d 252 (1981).

6. O.C.G.A. §51-1-11(b)(2). Ga. Code Ann. §51-1-11(c) (Supp. 1997) excepts from the operation of the statute of repose

   (1) actions in negligence against a manufacturer for products which cause a disease or birth defect, and
   (2) actions against manufacturers arising out of conduct which manifests a willful, reckless, or wanton disregard for life and property.

7. O.C.G.A. §11-2-725(1).

8. Id.

9. O.C.G.A. §9-3-24.

10. Id. §51-1-11(b)(1); *Center Chem. Co. v. Parzini*, 234 Ga. 868, 218 S.E.2d 580 (1975).

11. *Giordano v. Ford Motor Corp.*, 165 Ga. App. 644, 299 S.E.2d 897 (1983).

12. Id.

13. *Firestone Tire Co. v. King*, 145 Ga. App. 840, 244 S.E.2d 905 (1978); *Parzini*, 234 Ga. 868.

14. O.C.G.A. §51-1-11.1(b) (Supp. 1997); *Ream Tool Co. v. Newton*, 209 Ga. App. 226, 433 S.E.2d 67 (1993).

15. O.C.G.A. §51-1-11.1(a) (Supp. 1997); *Freeman v. United Cities Propane Gas Inc.*, 807 F. Supp. 1533 (M.D. Ga. 1992) (applying Georgia Law). But see *English v. Crenshaw Supply Co.*, 193 Ga. App. 354, 387 S.E.2d 628 (1989).

16. *Chrysler Corp. v. Batten*, 264 Ga. 723, 450 S.E.2d 208 (1994); *Wells v. Ortho Pharmaceutical Corp.*, 615 F. Supp. 262 (N.D. Ga. 1985) (applying Georgia law), *aff'd in part, modified on other grounds in part*, 788 F.2d 741 (11th Cir.), *cert. denied*, 479 U.S. 950 (1986).

17. *Barnes v. Harley-Davidson Co., Inc.*, 182 Ga. App. 778, 357 S.E.2d 127 (1987).

18. *Whirlpool Corp. v. Hurlbut*, 166 Ga. App. 95, 303 S.E.2d 284 (1983); *Firestone Tire & Rubber Co. v. Pinyan*, 155 Ga. App. 343, 270 S.E.2d 883 (1980).

19. *Parzini*, 234 Ga. 868.

20. *Coast Catamaran Corp. v. Mann*, 171 Ga. App. 844, 321 S.E.2d 353 (1984), *aff'd*, 254 Ga. 201, 326 S.E.2d 436 (1985), *overruled by Banks v. ICI Americas*, 264 Ga. 732, 450 S.E.2d 671 (1994).

21. *Hunt v. Harley-Davidson Motor Co., Inc.*, 147 Ga. App. 44, 248 S.E.2d 15 (1978).

22. *Banks v. ICI Americas*, 264 Ga. 732, 450 S.E.2d 671 (1994).

23. Id.

24. *SK Hand Tool Corp. v. Lowman*, 223 Ga. App. 712, 479 S.E.2d 103 (1996); *Parzini*, 234 Ga. 868.

25. *Continental Research Corp. v. Reeves*, 204 Ga. App. 120, 419 S.E.2d 48 (1992); *Deere & Co. v. Brooks*, 250 Ga. 517, 299 S.E.2d 704 (1983).

26. *Deere & Co. v. Brooks*, 250 Ga. 517; *Hunt*, 147 Ga. App. 44.

27. *Deere & Co.*, 250 Ga. 517.

28. O.C.G.A. §51-1-11(b)(1).

29. See, e.g., *Advanced Computer Sales, Inc. v. Sizemore*, 186 Ga. App. 10, 366 S.E.2d 303 (1988).

30. *Robert F. Bullock, Inc. v. Thorpe*, 256 Ga. 744, 353 S.E.2d 340 (1987).

31. *Blood Balm Co. v. Cooper*, 83 Ga. 457, 10 S.E. 118 (1889). See also McIntosh, §6A-5, at 45.

32. *Pepper v. Selig Chem. Indus., Inc.*, 161 Ga. App. 548, 288 S.E.2d 693 (1982).

33. *Bullington v. Union Tool Corp.*, 254 Ga. 283, 328 S.E.2d 726 (1985); *Corbin*, 227 Ga. App. 620.

34. *Bullington*, 254 Ga. 283.

35. O.C.G.A. §51-1-11(a).

36. *Best Canvas Prods. & Supplies, Inc. v. Ploof Truck Lines, Inc.*, 713 F.2d 618 (11th Cir. 1983) (applying Georgia law); *Chem Tech Finishers, Inc. v. Paul Mueller Co.*, 189 Ga. App. 433, 375 S.E.2d 881 (1988).

37. *Hunt*, 147 Ga. App. 44.

38. *Vax v. Albany Lawn & Garden Ctr.*, 209 Ga. App. 371, 433 S.E.2d 364 (1993). But see *Raymond v. Amada Co.*, 925 F. Supp. 1572 (N.D. Ga. 1996) (applying Georgia law).

39. *Weatherby v. Honda Motor Co.*, 195 Ga. App. 169, 393 S.E.2d 64 (1990).

40. *Talley v. City Tank Corp.*, 158 Ga. App. 130, 279 S.E.2d 264 (1981).

41. *Giordano*, 165 Ga. App. 644.

42. *Dorsey Trailers Southeast, Inc. v. Brackett*, 185 Ga. App. 172, 363 S.E.2d 779 (1987); *Omark Indus., Inc. v. Alewine*, 171 Ga. App. 207, 319 S.E.2d 24 (1984).

43. *Dorsey Trailers*, 185 Ga. App. 172; *Cobb Heating & Air Conditioning Co. v. Hertron Chem. Co.*, 139 Ga. App. 803, 229 S.E.2d 681 (1976).

44. *Cobb Heating*, 139 Ga. App. 803. But see *Wilson Foods Corp. v. Turner*, 218 Ga. App. 74, 460 S.E.2d 532 (1995).

45. *Presto v. Sandoz Pharmaceuticals Corp.*, 226 Ga. App. 547, 487 S.E.2d 70 (1997); *Hawkins v. Richardson-Merrell, Inc.*, 147 Ga. App. 481, 249 S.E.2d 286 (1978).

46. *Giordano*, 165 Ga. App. 644; *Greenway v. Peabody Intl. Corp.*, 163 Ga. App. 698, 294 S.E.2d 541 (1982); *Talley*, 158 Ga. App. 130.

47. *Doyle v. Volkswagenwerk Aktiengesellschaft*, 267 Ga. 574, 481 S.E.2d 518 (1997); *Banks v. ICI Americas, Inc.*, 264 Ga. 732, 450 S.E.2d 671 (1994).

48. *Honda Motor Co. v. Kimbrel*, 189 Ga. App. 414, 376 S.E.2d 379 (1988).

49. *Doyle v. Volkswagenwerk Aktiengesellschaft*, 267 Ga. 574.

50. *Friend v. General Motors Corp.*, 118 Ga. App. 763, 165 S.E.2d 734 (1968).

51. *Polston v. Boomershine Pontiac-GMC Truck, Inc.*, 262 Ga. 616, 423 S.E.2d 659 (1992).

52. *Ogletree*, 194 Ga. App. 41. See also *Honda Motor Co.*, 189 Ga. App. 414.

53. *Jackson v. International Harvester Co.*, 190 Ga. App. 765, 380 S.E.2d 306 (1989); *Skil Corp. v. Lugsdin*, 168 Ga. App. 754, 309 S.E.2d 921 (1983).

54. *Skil Corp.*, 168 Ga. App. 754.

55. *Weatherby*, 195 Ga. App. at 170 (citation omitted).

56. *Mann v. Hart County Elec. Membership Corp.*, 180 Ga. App. 340, 349 S.E.2d 215 (1986); *Union Carbide Corp. v. Holton*, 136 Ga. App. 726, 222 S.E.2d 105 (1975).

57. O.C.G.A. §51-11-7; *Union Camp Corp. v. Helmy*, 258 Ga. 263, 367 S.E.2d 796 (1988).

58. *Pepper*, 161 Ga. App. 548; *Union Carbide Corp.*, 136 Ga. App. 726.

59. *McGinty v. Goldens' Foundry & Mach. Co.*, 208 Ga. App. 248, 430 S.E.2d 185 (1993); *Blossman Gas Co. v. Williams*, 189 Ga. App. 195, 375 S.E.2d 117 (1988).

60. O.C.G.A. §11-2-314(2)(c).

61. *Best Canvas Prods. & Supplies, Inc.*, 713 F.2d 618; *Evershine Prods., Inc. v. Schmitt*, 130 Ga. App. 34, 202 S.E.2d 228 (1973).

62. O.C.G.A. §11-2-318; *Ellis v. Rich's, Inc.*, 233 Ga. 573, 212 S.E.2d 373 (1975).

63. *Decatur North Assocs., Ltd. v. Builders Glass, Inc.*, 180 Ga. App. 862, 350 S.E.2d 795 (1986).

64. *Evershine Prods., Inc.*, 130 Ga. App. 34.

65. *Advanced Computer Sales, Inc.*, 186 Ga. App. 10; *Citicorp Indus. Credit, Inc. v. Rountree*, 185 Ga. App. 417, 364 S.E.2d 65 (1987).

66. *DeLoach v. General Motors*, 187 Ga. App. 159, 369 S.E.2d 484 (1988).

67. *Colt Indus. Operating Corp. v. Coleman*, 246 Ga. 559, 272 S.E.2d 251 (1980); O.C.G.A. §51-12-30; O.C.G.A. §51-12-31 (Supp. 1997).

68. *Coleman*, 246 Ga. 559.

69. O.C.G.A. §51-12-33 (Supp. 1997).

70. *Bennett v. Haley*, 132 Ga. App. 512, 208 S.E.2d 302 (1974). But see *McGlohon v. Ogden*, 251 Ga. 625, 308 S.E.2d 541 (1983).

71. *Denton v. Con-Way Southern Express, Inc.*, 261 Ga. 41, 402 S.E.2d 269 (1991), *overruled on other grounds by Grissom v. Gleason*, 262 Ga. 374, 418 S.E.2d 27 (1992); *Amalgamated Transit Union Local 1324 v. Roberts*, 263 Ga. 405, 434 S.E.2d 450 (1993).

72. O.C.G.A. §51-12-5.1 (Supp. 1997).

73. Id. §51-12-5.1(b) (Supp. 1997).

74. Id. §51-12-5.1(e)(1) (Supp. 1997).

75. Id. §51-12-5.1(e)(2) (Supp. 1997).

76. *Mack Trucks, Inc. v. Conkle*, 263 Ga. 539, 436 S.E.2d 635 (1993); *State v. Moseley*, 263 Ga. 680, 436 S.E.2d 632 (1992), *cert. denied*, 114 S. Ct. 2101 (1994); but see *McBride v. General Motors Corp.*, 737 F. Supp. 1563 (M.D. Ga. 1990).

HAWAII

A. CAUSES OF ACTION

Hawaii recognizes actions for strict liability, negligence, and breach of warranty.

B. STRICT LIABILITY

1. The Standard

Hawaii courts have long followed the definition given in Restatement (Second) of Torts section 402A (1965) with one exception: Section 402A specifies a defective product that is unreasonably dangerous, while Hawaii omits the term "unreasonably."[1] However, a recent case acknowledged "defect" as an "unreasonably dangerous" condition.[2]

2. "Defect"

A product is dangerously defective if it does not meet the reasonable expectations of the ordinary consumer or user as to its safety, when the product is used in its intended or reasonably foreseeable manner.[3] The manufacturer's failure to equip its product with a safety device may constitute a design defect[4] although a manufacturer is not subject to an independent continuing duty to "retrofit" its product with after-market manufacturer safety equipment.[5] Design defect may be found alternatively if the plaintiff demonstrates that the product's design was a legal cause of the injuries[6] and the defendant fails to prove that the benefits of the design outweigh the risk of danger inherent in the design.[7] Evidence of a specific defect through expert testimony is not required.[8] Circumstantial evidence is sufficient,[9] and plaintiff need not produce the specific instrumentality involved.[10] In implied warranty cases, malfunction is not a prerequisite to establishing defect.[11]

3. Contributory Negligence/Assumption of Risk

Strict liability[12] and warranty[13] claims are subject to a pure comparative negligence analysis. Express assumption of risk is available as a complete bar to liability in tort and warranty strict product liability actions.[14] Primary implied assumption of risk is abolished; however, secondary implied assumption of risk, which is a form of contributory negligence, is preserved in and subsumed by comparative fault analysis.[15]

4. Sale or Lease

Occasional sellers who are engaged in isolated sales of products are not liable for strict liability, unlike manufacturers who are in the business of producing such products.[16]

5. Inherently Dangerous Products

The Hawaii Supreme Court appears to recognize asbestos[17] and chlorine[18] as inherently dangerous. It is obvious to all that swimming pools are dangerous to young children.[19]

6. Privity

All persons in the chain of distribution for component parts or final products are strictly liable for harm caused by products defectively designed or manufactured.[20] No privity is required; any consumer or ultimate user of the product may bring an action for product liability.[21]

7. Failure to Warn

A manufacturer must give appropriate warning of any known dangers which the users of its product would not ordinarily discover.[22] The duty to warn consists of two duties: a duty to give adequate instruction for safe use and a duty to give warning as to the dangers inherent in improper use.[23]

8. Substantial Change/Abnormal Use

In a product liability action, the product must have reached the consumer or ultimate user without substantial change or modification with respect to the alleged defect.[24]

9. State of the Art

State of the art is not a defense to a strict liability action.[25] Such evidence may be admissible in a negligence action, however, to show that the seller knew or reasonably should have known of the dangerousness of his or her product.[26]

10. Standards

Evidence of industry practices is relevant to but not determinative of the negligence issue of due care in the design of a product.[27] Nor is compliance with government regulations an absolute defense in strict liability cases involving inherently dangerous products.[28] A trial court must view a videotape before ruling on its admissibility.[29]

11. Other Accidents

Evidence of prior accidents may be admissible to show notice if there is sufficient similarity of circumstances to the subject accident.[30] Evidence of prior accidents may be admissible to show negligence, that the condition was dangerous, or that there was a defect only if there is substantial similarity between the accidents.[31]

12. Subsequent Remedial Measures

Hawaii Rules of Evidence Rule 407 specifically allows evidence of subsequent remedial measures for the purpose of proving dangerous defect in product liability cases.[32]

C. NEGLIGENCE

A person who manufactures or designs a product that injures someone is liable for negligence if he fails to take reasonable measures to protect against foreseeable dangers that pose an unreasonable risk of harm.[33] Among the factors to be considered in determining whether the manufacturer acted reasonably are: (1) balancing the likelihood and gravity of the potential harm against the burden of precautions that would effectively avoid the harm; (2) the style, type, and particular purpose of the product; (3) the cost of an alternative design, since the product's marketability may be adversely affected by a cost factor that greatly outweighs the added safety of the product; and (4) the price of the product itself.[34] The product must include adequate safety devices and warnings.[35]

A plaintiff whose negligence exceeds 50 percent is precluded from recovering under a negligence theory.[36]

A plaintiff may assert a market share theory of liability against a defendant even where the identity of the specific defendant is unknown.[37]

Although physical injury, overt symptoms of emotional distress and actually witnessing the tortious event are not prerequisites to a claim for negligent infliction of emotional distress, the presence or absence of these factors may be relevant to establishing such a claim. The question is not whether serious emotional distress might have resulted, but whether it actually resulted.[38]

D. BREACH OF WARRANTY

Merchant sellers are liable to all consumers and users who are injured if a product fails to meet its express warranties, the implied warranty of merchantability, or the implied warranty of fitness for a particular purpose.[39] Implied warranty claims based on strict liability can be maintained against the merchant seller even though the defect was not detectable by the seller.[40] On the other hand, nonmerchant (ordinary) sellers are not subject to the implied warranty of merchantability.[41]

Reliance is not an essential element of a breach of express warranty claim.[42] A plaintiff may recover for emotional distress in tort and implied warranty strict liability actions.[43]

E. DAMAGES

The "economic loss rule" applies to bar claims for relief based on either a negligence or strict products liability theory for economic loss stemming from injury only from the product itself.[44]

F. PUNITIVE DAMAGES

Punitive damages are allowed in product liability cases.[45] Hawaii requires clear and convincing proof of such damages.[46] The Hawaii Tort Reform Act provides that punitive damages are not covered by liability insurance policies unless specifically provided.[47]

G. STATUTES

Relevant statutes for product liability actions are the statutes of limitation[48] and the comparative negligence statute.[49] Hawaii's worker's compensation laws permit an action for indemnity based on an express agreement or on the existence of an independent duty.[50]

David J. Dezzani
Mark B. Desmarais
Roy J. Tjioe
Gregory F. Geary
GOODSILL ANDERSON QUINN & STIFEL
1800 Alii Place
1099 Alakea Street
Honolulu, Hawaii 96813
(808) 547-5600

ENDNOTES - HAWAII

1. *Brown v. Clark Equip. Co.*, 62 Haw. 530, 541-542, 618 P.2d 267, 274-275 (1980).

2. *Wagatsuma v. Patch*, 10 Haw. App. 547, 564, 879 P.2d 572, 583 (1994), *cert. denied*, 77 Haw. 373, 884 P.2d 1149 (1994).

3. *Ontai v. Straub Clinic and Hosp. Inc.*, 66 Haw. 237, 241, 659 P.2d 734, 739 (1983). This is also known as the "consumer expectation" test. *Wagatsuma*, 10 Haw. App. at 566, 879 P.2d at 584.

4. *Wagatsuma*, 10 Haw. App. at 564, 879 P.2d at 583, citing *Ontai*.

5. *Tabieros v. Clark Equip. Co.*, 85 Haw. 336, 358, 944 P.2d 1004, 1301 (1997).

6. Hawaii adopts the "substantial factor" test in determining legal cause. *Knodle v. Waikiki Gateway Hotel, Inc.*, 69 Haw. 376, 390, 742 P.2d 377, 386 (1987).

7. *Masaki v. General Motors Corp.*, 71 Haw. 1, 24, 780 P.2d 566, 579 (1989). This is also known as the "risk utility test," which shifts the burden to the defendant to prove the product was not defective, once the plaintiff makes a prima facie showing that the injury was legally caused by the product's design. *Wagatsuma*, 10 Haw. App. at 566-568, 879 P.2d at 584.

8. *Stewart v. Budget Rent-A-Car*, 52 Haw. 71, 76, 470 P.2d 240, 243 (1970).

9. Id.

10. *Beerman v. Toro Mfg. Corp.*, 1 Haw. App. 111, 115, 615 P.2d 749, 753 (1980).

11. *Larsen v. Pacesetter Systems, Inc.*, 74 Haw. 1, 25-26, 837 P.2d 1273, 1286 (1992).

12. *Hao v. Owens-Illinois, Inc.*, 69 Haw. 231, 236, 738 P.2d 416 (1987).

13. *Larsen*, 74 Haw. at 33, 837 P.2d at 1289-1290; *Armstrong v. Cione*, 69 Haw. 176, 180-183, 783 P.2d 79, 82-83 (1987).

14. *Larsen*, 74 Haw. at 36, 837 P.2d at 1291.

15. *Larsen*, 74 Haw. at 37-39, 837 P.2d at 1291-1292.

16. *Kaneko v. Hilo Coast Processing*, 65 Haw. 447, 459, 654 P.2d 343, 351 (1982).

17. *Nobriga v. Raybestos-Manhattan, Inc.*, 67 Haw. 157, 161, 683 P.2d 389, 392 (1984), *recon. den.*, 57 Haw. 683, 744 P.2d 779 (1984).

18. *Kajiya v. Department of Water Supply*, 2 Haw. App. 221, 225, 629 P.2d 635, 639 (1981).

19. *Wagatsuma*, 10 Haw. App. at 570, 879 P.2d at 585.

20. *Stewart*, 52 Haw. at 75, 470 P.2d at 243.

21. *Chapman v. Brown*, 198 F. Supp. 78, 118 (D. Haw. 1961).

22. *Ontai*, 66 Haw. at 248, 659 P.2d at 743.

23. Id.

24. *Stewart*, 52 Haw. at 75, 470 P.2d at 243.

25. *In re Haw. Fed. Asbestos Cases*, 665 F. Supp. 1454, 1460 (D. Haw. 1986).

26. *Johnson v. Raybestos-Manhattan, Inc.*, 69 Haw. 287, 288 n.2, 740 P.2d 548, 549 n.2 (1987).

27. *Brown*, 62 Haw. at 537, 618 P.2d at 272 (1980).

28. *Nobriga*, 67 Haw. at 161-162, 683 P.2d at 392.

29. *Tabieros*, 85 Haw. 336, 358, 944 P.2d 1004, 1301 (1997).

30. *Warshaw v. Rockresorts, Inc.*, 57 Haw. 645, 652, 562 P.2d 428, 434 (1977).

31. *American Broadcasting v. Kenai Air of Haw.*, 67 Haw. 219, 226-227, 686 P.2d 1, 6 (1984).

32. Haw. R. Evid., Rule 407.

33. *Ontai*, 66 Haw. at 247, 659 P.2d at 742; *Wagatsuma*, 10 Haw. App. at 565, 879 P.2d at 583.

34. *Wagatsuma*, 10 Haw. App. at 565, 879 P.2d at 583.

35. *Brown*, 62 Haw. at 539-540, 618 P.2d at 273.

36. Haw. Rev. Stat. §663-31 (1984).

37.   *Smith v. Cutter Biological, Inc.*, 72 Haw. 416, 823 P.2d 717 (1991).

38.   *Tabieros*, 85 Haw. at 361-362, 944 P.2d at 1304-1305.

39.   See *Ontai*, 66 Haw. at 249-252, 659 P.2d at 744.

40.   Id.

41.   Id.

42.   *Torres v. Northwest Engineering Co.*, 86 Haw. 383, 392, 949 P.2d 1004, 1013 (1997).

43.   *Larsen*, 74 Haw. at 43, 837 P.2d at 1294.

44.   *State by Bronster v. U.S. Steel Corp.*, 82 Haw. 32, 919 P.2d 294 (1996).

45.   *Beerman*, 1 Haw. App. at 118-119, 615 P.2d at 755.

46.   *Masaki*, 71 Haw. at 16, 780 P.2d at 575.

47.   Haw. Rev. Stat., §431:10-240 (1987).

48.   See, e.g., Haw. Rev. Stat. §657-7 (1972) (two years for personal injury actions); §490:2-725 (1965) (four years for breach of implied warranty of merchantability).

49.   Id. §663-31 (1984).

50.   *Kamali v. Hawaiian Elec. Co.*, 54 Haw. 153, 159, 504 P.2d 861, 865 (1972).

IDAHO

A. CAUSES OF ACTION

Litigation arising from the use of a product may include causes of action for strict liability under Restatement (Second) of Torts section 402A (1964); common law negligence; breach of warranty, including Uniform Commercial Code implied and express warranties;[1] the Idaho Consumer Protection Act;[2] and Idaho's Motor Vehicle Express Warranties Act (Lemon Law).[3] Product liability actions are governed by the Idaho Products Liability Reform Act (IPLRA).[4] IPLRA modified previously existing product liability law to the extent that it was inconsistent with the Act.[5]

B. STATUTES OF LIMITATION

An action for personal injuries based on negligence, strict liability, or breach of warranty must be brought within two years after the cause of action accrues.[6] A cause of action accrues when some damage relating to a wrongful act or omission becomes objectively certain.[7] Actions brought under IPLRA must be commenced within the two-year limitation period established for negligence actions.[8]

Product liability causes of action alleging property damage not arising from a breach of express or implied warranty must be commenced within two years after the cause of action accrues.[9] A cause of action for property damage arising from the breach of an express or implied warranty must be commenced within four years after the breach occurs.[10] Parties may reduce the period of limitations for express warranties to not less than one year.[11]

IPLRA bars product liability actions after the expiration of the product's "useful safe life."[12] A manufacturer may prove the expiration of the product's useful safe life by a preponderance of the evidence.[13] Alternatively, a manufacturer may rely on a rebuttable presumption that, ten years after the initial sale of a product, the useful safe life of the product has expired.[14] The presumption may only be rebutted by clear and convincing evidence.[15] This rebuttable presumption is statutorily characterized as a "statute of repose" and has survived constitutional challenge.[16] Exceptions to the useful safe life defense include express warranties exceeding the ten-year period, hidden defect, and fraudulent concealment.[17]

A six-year statute of repose applies to tort actions arising out of the design or construction of improvements to real property.[18] A cause of action accrues when damages are suffered or six years after the completion of the construction, whichever occurs first.[19] Idaho courts have applied this statute of repose to bar a product liability action stemming from an alleged defect in a control switch on equipment installed in a factory.[20] The court ruled that the equipment was a fixture and therefore an improvement to real property.[21] The limitation of action on improvements to real property has survived constitutional challenge.[22]

C. STRICT LIABILITY

1. The Standard

Idaho has adopted Restatement (Second) of Torts section 402A,[23] which gives rise to a cause of action for strict liability if a product is defective *and* is unreasonably dangerous to person or property. A product is unreasonably dangerous if it is more dangerous than would be expected by an ordinary person who may reasonably be expected to use it.[24] For example, whether irrigation equipment was defective and unreasonably dangerous should be viewed from the perspective of a farmer or qualified maintenance person.[25]

2. The Defect

A product may be defective due to a defect in design, a defect in the manufacturing process, or inadequate warnings accompanying the product at the time of sale.[26] A product is not necessarily defective and unreasonably dangerous merely because it poses some danger from its contemplated use; the danger posed by the product must be unreasonable.[27] A defect may be proved either by direct evidence or from circumstantial evidence and inferences arising therefrom.[28] The occurrence of a malfunction is circumstantial evidence of a defect.[29] This evidence may also be used to prove that the product defect is unreasonably dangerous.[30] If a plaintiff relies on circumstantial evidence, the plaintiff must exclude the possibility of other reasonably likely causes of the accident.[31] Plaintiff must prove that the product was defective when it left the control of the manufacturer.[32]

3. Contributory Negligence/Assumption of Risk

Comparative negligence is a defense to a product liability action sounding in negligence.[33] Comparative responsibility is a defense to a product liability action under IPLRA.[34] In either case, Idaho applies a modified comparative fault standard that precludes recovery by a plaintiff from a defendant if that plaintiff is *as* comparatively responsible as, or *more* comparatively responsible than, the defendant; for example, if a plaintiff is 50 percent at fault and a defendant is 50 percent at fault, the plaintiff does not recover. A plaintiff's comparative responsibility must be less than a particular defendant's comparative responsibility in order to recover from that defendant. For example, plaintiff is 20 percent at fault, defendant No. 1 is 70 percent at fault, and defendant No. 2 is 10 percent at fault; plaintiff recovers 70 percent of assessed damages from defendant No. 1, but plaintiff does not recover from defendant No. 2.[35] Comparative responsibility that does not bar a plaintiff's recovery results in a pro rata reduction in damages.[36]

Under IPLRA, comparative responsibility includes use of a product with an obviously defective condition, use of a product with knowledge of a defective condition, misuse of a product, and alteration of a product.[37]

A plaintiff's or third party's failure to inspect a product to discover a defect will not serve to reduce a plaintiff's award of damages.[38] Similarly, a third party's failure to observe an obviously defective condition will not serve to reduce a plaintiff's award of damages.[39]

4. Sale or Lease

IPLRA defines "product sellers" as persons or entities engaged in the business of selling products, whether for resale use or consumption, including manufacturers, wholesalers, distributors, and lessors.[40] IPLRA excludes from the definition of product sellers providers of professional services, some providers of nonprofessional services, commercial sellers of used products, and financial lessors.[41]

Product sellers, other than manufacturers, who neither warrant a product nor have a reasonable opportunity or expertise to perform an inspection of a product that would or should reveal a defect are not liable for injuries caused by the product.[42] This statutory limitation of liability does not apply if (1) the seller knew about the defect; (2) an alteration, modification, or installation of the product by the seller caused plaintiff's injuries; (3) the product design was provided by the seller and was a cause of plaintiff's injuries; (4) the seller is a wholly owned subsidiary of the manufacturer or vice versa; or (5) the product was sold after an expiration date placed on the product by the manufacturer.[43]

These defenses are not available to a nonmanufacturer product seller if the plaintiff is unable to pursue a claim against the manufacturer because of insolvency, inability to obtain service of process on the manufacturer, or a judicial determination that a judgment could not be collected against the manufacturer.[44] A product seller may be considered a manufacturer if it holds itself out as the manufacturer.[45]

A product seller entitled to the liability limitation of IPLRA is entitled to indemnification from the manufacturer for the costs of defense of the action incurred after the manufacturer rejects a tender of defense.[46]

5. Inherently Dangerous Products

Idaho has adopted comment k to the Restatement (Second) of Torts section 402A (1964), exempting from strict product liability providers of "unavoidably unsafe" products.[47]

6. Successor Liability

Idaho has not expressly addressed the potential liability of a successor corporation for products manufactured by its predecessor. Idaho courts have ruled that where a corporation sells most of its assets to another corporation, but the selling corporation continues to exist, the acquiring corporation will not be liable for the payment of royalties arising from a license agreement, absent an express assumption of the liability by the acquiring corporation.[48]

7. Privity

Privity of contract is not required to maintain a cause of action for personal injuries arising from the use of a product.[49] Privity is, in all probability, not necessary to maintain an action for economic damages stemming from a breach of warranty. However, due to plurality opinions, the Idaho decision that purportedly overruled the privity requirement never commanded a clear majority.[50]

8. Failure to Warn

A cause of action may be maintained in Idaho for failure to warn of dangers that are not open and obvious.[51] The duty to warn extends to dangers that arise during known or reasonably foreseeable uses of the product.[52]

Whether a danger is open and obvious is a question of fact to be decided by a jury.[53] The causal relationship between the alleged failure to warn and plaintiff's injury should not be decided as a matter of law notwithstanding plaintiff's admission that he was aware of the hazard that caused his injury.[54]

9. Post-Sale Duty to Warn

IPLRA recognizes the existence of a duty to warn of known defects discovered after a product is designed and manufactured.[55] However, evidence of changes in warnings or instructions is not admissible to prove that a product is defective.[56]

10. Substantial Change/Abnormal Use

Under IPLRA, "misuse" and "alteration" are defined as conduct affecting comparative responsibility.[57] Misuse occurs when a product is used in a manner that would not be expected of an ordinary reasonably prudent person using the product under similar circumstances.[58] A finding of misuse results in a reduction in the plaintiff's damage award to the extent that the misuse was the proximate cause of the harm.[59]

Alteration or modification occurs when the design, construction, or formula of a product is changed after sale by a party other than the seller.[60] Alteration or modification is not a defense if the alteration was made in accordance with the manufacturer's instructions, was made with the express or implied consent of the manufacturer, or could reasonably be anticipated.[61] Product alteration or modification results in a reduction of the claimant's damages to the extent that the alteration or modification was the proximate cause of the harm.[62]

11. State of the Art

Evidence of changes in a product's design, warning, technological feasibility or in the state of the art is not admissible to prove a product defect.[63] Such evidence may be admitted for purposes of impeachment or to prove ownership or control.[64] Before such evidence can be admitted, the court must determine, outside the presence of the jury, that the probative value of the evidence outweighs its prejudicial effect.[65] Of course, the state of the art of product design or manufacture is admissible to show what was technologically feasible *at the time* a product was manufactured, such evidence being relevant to the question of a defect.[66]

12. Malfunction

Malfunction of a product is circumstantial evidence of a defective condition.[67] When relying on the occurrence of a malfunction as circumstantial evidence of a defect, the plaintiff must exclude other reasonably likely causes of the accident.[68]

13. Other Accidents

Evidence of other accidents is admissible to show the existence of a particular physical condition or defect and, in the case of prior accidents, notice to the manufacturer of a dangerous condition.[69] The trial court in its discretion may exclude evidence of other accidents if they are not substantially similar to the subject case if the admission of evidence regarding other accidents will raise collateral issues, or if the evidence of the other accidents will tend to confuse the jurors.[70]

14. Misrepresentations

Idaho has not expressly recognized a cause of action for misrepresentation under Restatement (Second) of Torts section 402B (1964). Idaho does recognize a common law cause of action for fraud and fraudulent misrepresentation.[71] Negligent misrepresentation claims are narrowly confined to the accountant-client relationship.[72]

D. NEGLIGENCE

Strict product liability and negligence are not mutually exclusive theories; an injury may give rise to claims that can be asserted under either principle.[73] To prevail under a cause of action for negligence arising from the use of a product, a plaintiff must show the existence of a duty and breach of the duty that proximately caused damages.[74] Idaho courts have ruled that one who provides a product owes a duty to provide the product in a nondefective condition.[75]

E. BREACH OF WARRANTY

The Idaho Supreme Court has held that implied warranty and strict liability are coextensive causes of action except for the defenses of privity and disclaimer of warranty.[76] In a product liability-personal injury setting, the breach of implied warranty standard is most frequently stated as a failure of the goods to be fit for the ordinary purposes for which such goods are used (i.e., the goods are not merchantable).[77]

An implied warranty of fitness for a particular purpose arises at the time of purchase if the seller knows or has reason to know of a particular purpose for which the products will be used and that the buyer is relying on the seller's skill or judgment to select and furnish goods.[78] Implied warranties may be disclaimed if the disclaimer is a basis of the bargain.[79]

Even though an express affirmation of fact is not conveyed in the transaction, an express warranty may arise from a description of the goods conveyed in prior dealings.[80]

Absent personal injuries or property damage, breach of warranty is the sole remedy for recovery of purely economic damages.[81] Economic loss may be recoverable in tort under one of the three exceptions to the "economic loss rule"; (1) as a loss parasitic to an injury to person or property, (2) where unique circumstances require a different allocation of the risk, and (3) where a "special relationship" exists between the parties.[82]

A nonprivity breach of warranty action brought against a manufacturer or seller to recover for personal injuries from a defective product is not governed by the UCC but is governed by tort law.[83] Such an action finds support in comment m of section 402A of the Restatement (Second) of Torts (1965). The cause of action is for strict liability in tort and is subject to the common law and the IPLRA.[84]

F. IDAHO CONSUMER PROTECTION ACT

A private right of action exists under the Idaho Consumer Protection Act.[85] The Act declares unfair methods of competition and unfair or deceptive acts or practices in the conduct of any trade or commerce with respect to goods or services to be unlawful.[86] Violation of the Act arises when a person knows, or in the exercise of due care should know, that he has in the past, or is presently engaging in one of the enumerated proscribed acts or "in any act or practice which is otherwise misleading, false, or deceptive to the consumer."[87] The "due care" language has been suggested to imply a negligence standard.[88] Ascertainable loss of money or property is a prerequisite to private recovery under the Act.[89]

G. PUNITIVE DAMAGES

Punitive damages may be recovered in actions for strict liability, negligence, and breach of an implied warranty.[90] Punitive damages are defined by statute as noncompensatory damages that serve the public policy of punishing and deterring outrageous conduct.[91] In order to support an award for punitive damages, the evidence must show that the defendant acted in a manner that was an extreme deviation from reasonable standards of conduct, such as fraud, malice, oppression, or gross negligence, and that the defendant had an understanding of or disregard for the consequences of his act.[92] Punitive damages may not initially be pled as an element of damages in a complaint. A claim for punitive damages may be added by amendment after the plaintiff presents evidence to the court that there is a "reasonable likelihood" of proving facts at trial sufficient to support an award of punitive damages.[93] The Idaho Supreme Court has upheld the constitutionality of punitive damages awards.[94]

Punitive damages may be awarded, in the discretion of the court, in cases of repeated or flagrant violations of the Idaho Consumer Protection Act.[95] The statutory "repeated or flagrant" standard is independent of the common law standards.[96]

H. ATTORNEY'S FEES

Generally, attorney's fees are not recoverable in actions based upon the traditional strict liability, negligence, and warranty theories.[97] Attorney's fees may be awarded, however, if the gravamen of the lawsuit is the commercial transaction of the parties and constitutes the basis upon which the party is attempting to recover.[98] Attorney's fees may be recoverable in cases involving less than $25,000.[99] Attorney's fees are recoverable under the Idaho Consumer Protection Act.[100]

I. PREEMPTION OF STATE LAW CLAIMS

State damage awards are a form of state regulation.[101] State product liability and misrepresentation causes of action may be preempted by federal law.[102] Warranties, as a voluntary undertaking, may not be preempted.[103]

Rex Blackburn
Bruce C. Jones
David W. Gratton
EVANS, KEANE LLP
1101 West River Street, Suite 200
P.O. Box 959
Boise, Idaho 83701-0959
(208) 384-1800
Fax (208) 345-3514
EKIDALAW@MICRON.NET

1.   Idaho Code §§28-2-313 to 28-2-318.

2.   Id. §§48-601 to 48-619.

3.   Id. §§48-901 to 48-909.

4.   Id. §§6-1401 to 6-1410.

5.   Id. §6-1401.

6.   Id. §5-219(4).

7.   *Fairway Dev. Co. v. Peterson,* 124 Idaho 866, 865 P.2d 957 (1993); *Chicoine v. Dignall,* 122 Idaho 482, 835 P.2d 1293 (1992); *Griggs v. Nash,* 116 Idaho 228, 775 P.2d 120 (1989).

8.   Idaho Code §6-1403(5).

9.   *Wing v. Martin,* 107 Idaho 267, 688 P.2d 1172 (1984).

10.   Idaho Code §28-2-725(1).

11.   Id.

12.   Idaho Code §6-1403(1).

13.   Id.

14.   Idaho Code §6-1403(2)(a).

15.   Id.; *Oats v. Nissan Motor Corp.,* 126 Idaho 162, 879 P.2d 1095 (1994).

16.   *Olson v. J. A. Freeman Co.,* 117 Idaho 706, 791 P.2d 1285 (1990).

17.   Idaho Code §6-1403(2)(b).

18.   Id. §5-241.

19.   Id. §5-241(a).

20.   *West v. El Paso Prods.,* 122 Idaho 133, 832 P.2d 306 (1992).

21. *West*, 122 Idaho at 136, 832 P.2d at 309.

22. *West*, 122 Idaho at 137, 832 P.2d at 310.

23. *Shields v. Morton Chem. Co.*, 95 Idaho 674, 518 P.2d 857 (1973).

24. *Rojas v. Lindsay Mfg. Co.*, 108 Idaho 590, 701 P.2d 210 (1985).

25. *Rojas*, 108 Idaho at 591, 701 P.2d at 211.

26. *Rindlisbacker v. Wilson*, 95 Idaho 752, 519 P.2d 421 (1974); *Bryant v. Technical Research Co.*, 654 F.2d 1337 (9th Cir. 1981).

27. *Complaint of Diehl*, 610 F. Supp. 223 (D.C. Idaho 1985).

28. *Doty v. Bashara*, 123 Idaho 329, 848 P.2d 387 (1992); *Farmer v. International Harvester Co.*, 97 Idaho 742, 553 P.2d 1306 (1976).

29. Id.

30. *Westfall v. Caterpillar*, 120 Idaho 918, 821 P.2d 973 (1991).

31. *Mortensen v. Chevron Chem. Co.*, 107 Idaho 836, 693 P.2d 1038 (1984).

32. *Westfall*, 120 Idaho at 920, 821 P.2d at 975.

33. Idaho Code §6-801 (Negligence).

34. Id. §6-1404 (Product Liability).

35. *Ross v. Coleman Co.*, 114 Idaho 817, 761 P.2d 1169 (1988).

36. Idaho Code §§6-801 and 6-1404.

37. Id. §6-1405.

38. Id. §§6-1405(a), (c).

39. Id. §6-1405(c).

40. Id. §6-1402(1).

41. Id. §6-1402(1)(a)-(c).

42. Id. §6-1407(1); *Hoopes v. John Deere Co.*, 117 Idaho 386, 788 P.2d 201 (1990).

43.   Idaho Code §6-1407(1)(a)-(e).

44.   Id. §6-1407(4).

45.   *Hawks v. EPI Products USA, Inc.*, 129 Idaho 281, 923 P.2d 988 (1996).

46.   Id. §6-1407(2).

47.   *Toner v. Lederle Labs., a Div. of Am. Cyanamid Co.*, 112 Idaho 328, 732 P.2d 297 (1987), *answer to certification question conformed*, 828 F.2d 510 (9th Cir. 1987), *cert. denied*, 485 U.S. 942 (1988).

48.   *H.M. Chase Corp. v. Idaho Potato Processors, Inc.*, 96 Idaho 398, 529 P.2d 1270 (1974).

49.   *Green v. A. B. Haaglund & Soner*, 634 F. Supp. 790 (D.C. Idaho 1986).

50.   *State v. Mitchell Constr. Co.*, 108 Idaho 335, 699 P.2d 1349 (1985).

51.   *Complaint of Diehl*, 610 F. Supp. 223 (D.C. Idaho 1985).

52.   *Robinson v. Williamsen Idaho Equip. Co.*, 94 Idaho 819, 498 P.2d 1292 (1972).

53.   *Watson v. Navistar Intl. Transp.*, 121 Idaho 643, 827 P.2d 656 (1992).

54.   *Watson*, 121 Idaho at 662, 827 P.2d at 675.

55.   Idaho Code §6-1406(1).

56.   Id. §6-1406(1)(b).

57.   Id. §6-1405(3), (4).

58.   Id. §6-1405(3)(a).

59.   Id. §6-1405(3)(b).

60.   Id. §6-1405(4)(a).

61.   Id. §6-1405(4)(b)(1)-(3).

62.   Id. §6-1405(4)(b).

63.   Id. §6-1406(1)(a), (c), (d); Idaho Rule of Evidence 407.

64.   Idaho Code §6-1406(2).

65.   Id.

66.   *Fouche v. Chrysler Motor Corp.*, 107 Idaho 701, 692 P.2d 345 (1984).

67.   *Farmer v. International Harvester Co.*, 97 Idaho 742, 553 P.2d 1306 (1976).

68.   Id.

69.   *Sliman v. Aluminum Co. of Am.*, 112 Idaho 277, 731 P.2d 1267 (1986), *cert. denied*, 486 U.S. 1031 (1988).

70.   *Hawks v. EPI Products USA, Inc.*, 129 Idaho 281, 923 P.2d 988 (1996).

71.   *Faw v. Greenwood*, 101 Idaho 387, 613 P.2d 1338 (1980).

72.   *Duffin v. Idaho Crop Improvement Association*, 126 Idaho 1002, 895 P.2d 1195 (1995).

73.   *Chancler v. American Hardware Mut. Ins. Co.*, 109 Idaho 841, 712 P.2d 542 (1985).

74.   *Alegria v. Payonk*, 101 Idaho 617, 619 P.2d 135 (1980).

75.   *Metz v. Haskell*, 91 Idaho 160, 417 P.2d 898 (1966).

76.   *Robinson v. Williamsen Idaho Equip. Co.*, 94 Idaho 819, 498 P.2d 1292 (1972).

77.   Idaho Code §28-2-314(2)(c).

78.   Id. §28-2-315.

79.   *Duffin*, 126 Idaho 1002, 895 P.2d 1195 (1995).

80.   *Duffin*, 126 Idaho 1002, 895 P.2d 1195 (1995).

81.   *Clark v. International Harvester Co.*, 99 Idaho 326, 581 P.2d 784 (1978).

82.   *Duffin*, 126 Idaho 1002, 895 P.2d 1195 (1995).

83.   *Oats v. Nissan Motor Corp.*, 126 Idaho 162, 879 P.2d 1095 (1994).

84.   Id.

85.   Idaho Code §48-608(1).

86.   Id. §48-603.

87. Id.

88. William J. Batt, *Litigation Under the Idaho Consumer Protection Act*, 20 Idaho L. Rev. 63 (1984).

89. Idaho Code §48-608(1).

90. *Hatfield v. Max Rouse & Sons, Northwest*, 100 Idaho 840, 606 P.2d 944 (1980).

91. Idaho Code §6-1601(9).

92. *Cheney v. Palos Verdes Inv. Corp.*, 104 Idaho 897, 665 P.2d 661 (1983).

93. Idaho Code §6-1604.

94. *Garnett v. Transamerica Ins. Servs.*, 118 Idaho 769, 800 P.2d 656 (1990); see also *Walston v. Monumental Life Insurance Co.*, 129 Idaho 211, 923 P.2d 456 (1996).

95. Idaho Code §48-608(1).

96. *Mac Tools, Inc. v. Griffin*, 126 Idaho 193, 879 P.2d 1126 (1994) (punitive damage award in excess of 26 times the compensatory award upheld).

97. *Property Management West, Inc. v. Hunt*, 126 Idaho 897, 894 P.2d 130 (1995); *Chenery v. Agri-Lines Corp.*, 106 Idaho 687, 682 P.2d 640 (Ct. App. 1984).

98. *Brower v. E.I. DuPont De NeMours and Co.*, 117 Idaho 780, 792 P.2d 345 (1990); *Walker v. American Cyanamid Co.*, — Idaho —, 948 P.2d 1123 (Dec. 2, 1997) (Breach of Warranty).

99. Idaho Code §12-120(4).

100. Idaho Code §48-608(4).

101. *Zimmerman v. Volkswagen of America, Inc.*, 128 Idaho 851, 920 P.2d 67 (1996).

102. *Trinity Mountain Seed Co. v. MSD Aguet*, 844 F. Supp. 597 (D. Idaho 1994).

103. *Walker v. American Cyanamid Co.*, — Idaho —, 948 P.2d 1123 (Dec. 2, 1997).

ILLINOIS

Preliminary Note: Illinois product liability law has recently undergone a substantial change. On December 18, 1997, the 1995 Tort Reform Act was struck down in its entirety by the Illinois Supreme Court. After finding certain "core provisions" of the Act unconstitutional, the court held the entire remainder of the Act to be void on the grounds of severability. The court then invited the Illinois legislature to reenact any provisions struck down solely on the grounds of severability which it may deem "desirable or appropriate."[1]

A. CAUSES OF ACTION

Product liability lawsuits commonly include causes of action for strict liability, negligence, and breach of warranty.

B. STATUTES OF LIMITATION

Causes of action for personal injuries must be brought within two years, whether brought in negligence or strict liability.[2] Actions for property damage must be brought within five years.[3] The limitations period starts to run when the plaintiff knows or reasonably should know of his injury, and also knows or reasonably should know that it was wrongfully caused.[4] A cause of action for damages resulting from a breach of warranty must be brought within four years after tender of delivery,[5] except where there is an express warranty covering future performance beyond the four-year limitations period.[6]

There is a ten/twelve year statute of repose for strict product liability actions.[7] The action must be commenced within the shorter of ten years from the date of sale or delivery to an initial user or consumer or twelve years from the date of any first sale or delivery by the seller.[8]

There is a ten-year statute of repose relating to improvements to real property.[9]

C. STRICT LIABILITY

1. The Standard

Illinois has adopted section 402A of the Restatement (Second) of Torts.[10]

2. "Defect"

The jury is normally instructed that liability arises if the product left the control of the defendant having a condition that made it unreasonably dangerous.[11] A product is unreasonably dangerous if it is un-

---

safe when put to a use that is reasonably foreseeable considering the nature and function of the product.[12]

3. Contributory Negligence/Assumption of Risk

Contributory negligence is not a defense in strict liability cases. Comparative fault of the plaintiff is a damage-reducing factor[13] and a complete defense if the plaintiff is more than 50 percent at fault.[14] To constitute "comparative fault," the plaintiff's conduct must amount to an assumption of risk or an unforeseeable misuse of the product[15]. In this context, the plaintiff assumes the risk if he was subjectively aware of the unreasonably dangerous condition, but proceeded in the face of it.[16] A mere negligent failure to discover or guard against the condition will not constitute comparative fault in a strict liability case.[17]

4. Sale or Lease

Strict liability applies to any entity in the chain of a product's distribution[18] if it is in the business of supplying such products.[19] A nonmanufacturer defendant, however, can be dismissed from a strict liability action if the manufacturer is amenable to suit.[20]

Generally, strict liability applies to lessors who are in the business of supplying products.[21]

5. Inherently Dangerous Products

Strict liability applies to an inherently dangerous product if the manufacturer or seller fails to adequately warn of its potential risks or hazards.[22]

6. Successor Liability

A successor company that purchased the assets of a predecessor is generally not responsible for liabilities arising from the predecessor's products unless the successor agrees to assume those liabilities. Exceptions apply if the transfer amounts to a consolidation or merger, if the purchaser is a mere continuation of the seller, or if the transaction is for the fraudulent purpose of escaping liability.[23]

7. Privity

No privity is required; a plaintiff may sue even though he did not buy the product directly from the manufacturer.[24]

8. Failure to Warn

A product may be defective solely because it fails to warn of dangers attending its use.[25] A manufacturer or seller has a duty to warn if it knew or should have known of the danger presented by the product[26] at the time of production, unless that danger was or should have been known by the plaintiff.[27]

---

9. Post-Sale Duty to Warn

The duty to warn does not extend beyond the time the product leaves the manufacturer's control, despite the manufacturer's increased knowledge or expertise thereafter.[28]

10. Substantial Change/Misuse

A manufacturer is not responsible for injuries caused by a substantial change in the product occurring after the initial sale, or for injuries caused by misuse of the product, if the substantial change or misuse could not reasonably be foreseen.[29]

11. State of the Art

"State-of-the-art" evidence is admissible but is not conclusive.[30]

12. Malfunction

A malfunction of a product in the absence of evidence of abnormal use and reasonable secondary causes may be evidence of a defect,[31] but only where the product is of a type that would not otherwise be expected to malfunction in normal use.[32]

13. Standards

Evidence that the product complied with customary standards, industry standards, or government standards, is admissible but not conclusive.[33]

14. Other Accidents

Evidence of other accidents is admissible if the plaintiff proves that the accidents occurred under substantially similar conditions and are of a common cause.[34]

15. Misrepresentation

The Illinois Supreme Court has adopted section 311 of the Restatement (Second) of Torts governing claims for negligent misrepresentation.[35] Some Illinois appellate courts have recognized a cause of action for innocent misrepresentation under section 402B of the Restatement (Second) of Torts.[36]

16. Subsequent Remedial Measures

Illinois cases regarding the admissibility of subsequent remedial measures to prove defect lack consensus. Appellate courts remain divided on this issue.[37]

D. NEGLIGENCE

Negligence product liability case law in Illinois generally follows the common law.

Comparative negligence applies to reduce damages unless the plaintiff is more than 50 percent at fault, in which event recovery is barred.[38]

E.   BREACH OF WARRANTY

Generally, a plaintiff must establish privity with the defendant to state a cause of action for breach of implied warranty. The privity requirement is relaxed, however, in personal injury actions.[39]

With respect to the statute of limitations, the "discovery rule" does not apply. Instead, the cause of action accrues upon tender of delivery.[40]

To maintain a warranty action, the plaintiff must plead and prove that notice of the alleged breach was given.[41]

F.   PUNITIVE DAMAGES

Punitive damages are recoverable in product liability actions if the defendant acted willfully or with such gross negligence as to indicate a wanton disregard of others' rights.[42] However, a plaintiff may not request punitive damages in his original complaint. Such a request may be added by amendment only after the plaintiff establishes at a hearing a reasonable likelihood of proving facts sufficient to support an award.[43] Evidence of other accidents involving the product does not by itself establish a sufficient basis for punitive damages.[44] Punitive damages are not allowed in warranty actions unless the breach amounts to an independent, willful tort.[45]

G.   STATUTES

Relevant statutes for product liability actions are the Illinois Tort Reform Act of 1986,[46] the statutes of limitations[47] and, when a breach of warranty is alleged, applicable commercial code sections.[48]

Frances E. Prell
Colin Smith
BURKE, WEAVER & PRELL
55 West Monroe Street, Suite 800
Chicago, Illinois 60603
(312) 263-3600

ENDNOTES - ILLINOIS

1. *Best v. Taylor Mach. Works,* Docket Nos. 81891, 81892, 81893 cons., 1997 Ill. LEXIS 478 (Dec. 18, 1997).

2. 735 ILCS 5/13-202 (1992).

3. 735 ILCS 5/13-205 (1992).

4. *Witherell v. Weimer,* 85 Ill. 2d 146, 421 N.E.2d 869 (1981); *Hochbaum v. Casiano,* 292 Ill. App. 3d 589, 695 N.E.2d 626 (1997).

5. 810 ILCS 5/2-725 (1992).

6. Id.

7. 735 ILCS 5/13-213 (1992).

8. Id.

9. 735 ILCS 5/13-214 (Supp. 1996).

10. *Korando v. The Uniroyal Goodrich Tire Co.,* 159 Ill. 2d 335, 637 N.E.2d 1020 (1994); *Suvada v. White Motor Co.,* 32 Ill. 2d 612, 210 N.E.2d 182 (1965); see also *Perez v. Fidelity Container Corp.,* — Ill. App. 3d — , 682 N.E.2d 1150 (1997).

11. Ill. Pattern Jury Instr.-Civil 400.02 (1995 ed.).

12. Ill. Pattern Jury Instr.-Civil 400.06 (1995 ed.); *cf. Lamkin v. Towner,* 138 Ill. 2d 510, 563 N.E.2d 449 (1990) (court applied both consumer contemplation and risk-utility tests in addressing issue of design defect); *but cf. Todd v. Societe BIC, S.A.,* 21 F.3d 1402 (7th Cir. 1994) ("Illinois Supreme Court would not apply the risk-utility test to simple but obviously dangerous products."), *cert. denied,* 115 S. Ct. 359 (1994).

13. *Coney v. J.L.G. Indus.,* 97 Ill. 2d 104, 454 N.E.2d 197 (1983); 735 ILCS5/2-1116 (1992).

14. Id.

15. *Perez,* 682 N.E.2d 1156.

16. *Betts v. Manville Personal Injury Settlement Trust*, 225 Ill. App. 3d 882, 588 N.E.2d 1193 (1992).

17. *Coney*, 97 Ill. 2d 104.

18. *Crowe v. Public Building Commn. of Chicago*, 74 Ill. 2d 10, 383 N.E.2d 951 (1978).

19. *Timm v. Indian Springs Recreation Assn.*, 187 Ill. App. 3d 508, 543 N.E.2d 538 (1989); *Keen v. Dominick's Finer Foods, Inc.*, 49 Ill. App. 3d 480, 364 N.E.2d 502 (1977).

20. 735 ILCS 5/2-621 (1992).

21. *Crowe*, 74 Ill. 2d 10.

22. *Hammond v. North Am. Asbestos Corp.*, 97 Ill. 2d 195, 454 N.E.2d 210 (1983); *Skonberg v. Owens-Corning Fiberglass Corp.*, 215 Ill. App. 3d 735, 576 N.E.2d 28 (1991).

23. *Green v. Firestone Tire & Rubber Co.*, 122 Ill. App. 3d 204, 460 N.E.2d 895 (1984).

24. *Suvada*, 32 Ill. 2d 612.

25. *Hammond*, 97 Ill. 2d 195; *Illinois State Trust Co. v. Walker Mfg. Co.*, 73 Ill. App. 3d 585, 392 N.E.2d 70 (1979).

26. *Smith v. Eli Lilly & Co.*, 137 Ill. 2d 222, 560 N.E.2d 324 (1990).

27. *Proctor v. Davis,* — Ill. App. 3d —, 682 N.E.2d 1203 (1997); *McColgan v. Environmental Control Sys., Inc.*, 212 Ill. App. 3d 696, 571 N.E.2d 815 (1991).

28. *Collins v. Hyster Co.*, 174 Ill. App. 3d 972, 529 N.E.2d 303 (1988); *Carrizales v. Rheem Mfg. Co.*, 226 Ill. App. 3d 20, 587 N.E.2d 569 (1991).

29. *J. I. Case Co. v. McCartin-McAuliffe Plumbing & Heating, Inc.*, 118 Ill. 2d 447, 516 N.E.2d 260 (1987); *Woods v. Graham Engg.*, 183 Ill. App. 3d 337, 539 N.E.2d 316 (1989).

30. *Kerns v. Engelke*, 76 Ill. 2d 154, 390 N.E.2d 859 (1979).

31. *Tweedy v. Wright Ford Sales, Inc.*, 64 Ill. 2d 570, 357 N.E.2d 449 (1976).

32. *Shramek v. General Motors Corp.*, 69 Ill. App. 2d 72, 216 N.E.2d 244 (1966) (court held that given the nature and intended function of a vehicle tire, failure during normal use does not infer defect).

33. *Moehle v. Chrysler Motors Corp.*, 93 Ill. 2d 299, 443 N.E.2d 575 (1982); *Rucker v. Norfolk & Western Ry.*, 77 Ill. 2d 434, 396 N.E.2d 534 (1979).

34. *Rucker*, 77 Ill. 2d 434; *Gowler v. Ferrell-Ross Co.*, 206 Ill. App. 3d 194, 563 N.E. 2d 773 (1990).

35. *Board of Educ. v. A, C and S, Inc.*, 131 Ill. 2d 428, 546 N.E.2d 580 (1989).

36. See *Hollenbeck v. Selectone Corp.*, 131 Ill. App. 3d 969, 476 N.E.2d 746 (1985); *Pitler v. Michael Reese Hosp.*, 92 Ill. App. 3d 739, 415 N.E.2d 1255 (1980).

37. *Compare Burke v. Illinois Power Co.*, 57 Ill. App. 3d 498, 373 N.E.2d 1354 (1st Dist. 1978) (subsequent remedial measures admissible to prove defect), *with Davis v. International Harvester Co.*, 167 Ill. App. 3d 814, 521 N.E.2d 1282 (2d Dist. 1988) (post-occurrence change admissible only to establish feasible alternative design).

38. Ill. Pattern Jury Instr.-Civil B10.03 (1995 ed.); 735 ILCS 5/2-1107.1 (1992).

39. *Board of Educ.*, 131 Ill. 2d 428.

40. 810 ILCS 5/2-725 (1992).

41. 810 ILCS 5/2-607 (1992); *Board of Educ.*, 131 Ill. 2d 428.

42. *J. I. Case Co.*, 118 Ill. 2d 447; see also *Proctor*, 682 N.E.2d 1203.

43. 735 ILCS 5/2-604.1 (Supp. 1996).

44. *Loitz v. Remington Arms Co.*, 138 Ill. 2d 404, 563 N.E.2d 397 (1990).

45. *McGrady v. Chrysler Motors Corp.*, 46 Ill. App. 3d 136, 360 N.E.2d 818 (1977).

46. See, e.g., 735 ILCS 5/2-604.1, 2-1116, 2-1118 (1992).

47. 735 ILCS 5/13-202, 13-203, 13-204, 13-205, 13-211, 13-213, 13-214 (1992 and Supp. 1996).

48. 810 ILCS 5/2-101 to 2-725 (1992 and Supp. 1996).

INDIANA

A. CAUSES OF ACTION

Product liability lawsuits have commonly been based upon theories of negligence and strict liability. Causes of action for breach of implied warranty sounding in tort are identical to strict liability imposed by the Indiana Product Liability Act (IPLA).[1] Generally, negligence and breach of warranty actions were governed not by the IPLA but by Indiana's common law, the Comparative Fault Act (CFA) and Indiana's commercial code.[2] Effective July 1, 1995, the Indiana legislature passed new legislation amending the IPLA, the CFA, and statutes on punitive damages.[3]

As amended, the application of the IPLA is no longer limited to strict liability claims. It now governs all actions against a manufacturer or seller for physical harm caused by a product regardless of the theories upon which the action is brought.[4] Some of the amendments and new statutes effective July 1, 1995, are expressly applicable only to causes of action that accrue after June 30, 1995.[5] It is doubtful whether other provisions in that legislation would be construed to be applicable retroactively to causes of action that accrued prior to July 1, 1995.[6]

B. STATUTES OF LIMITATION

1. Two-Year Statute of Limitation

In an action based on negligence or strict liability a two-year statute of limitation begins to run when the plaintiff knew or in the exercise of ordinary diligence could have discovered that an injury has been sustained as a result of the tortious act of another.[7]

2. Statute of Repose

The IPLA contains a statute of repose.[8] Under this statute a cause of action based on negligence or strict liability must be commenced within two years of accrual or within ten years after the delivery of the product to the initial user or consumer.[9] If the cause of action accrues at least eight years but less than ten years after initial delivery, the action may be commenced at any time within two years after accrual.[10] The statute of repose is implicated only if the complained-of defect was present at or before the time the product was delivered to the initial user or consumer.[11] The statute of repose applies regardless of minority or legal disability of the plaintiff.[12]

Delivery under the statute of repose occurs when the product is delivered to the first "consuming entity."[13] The ten-year period may recommence when a product has been reconditioned, altered, or modified to the extent that a "new" product has been introduced into the stream of commerce.[14] A cause of action accrues when all of the elements necessary for recovery are met.[15] Accrual does not necessarily occur merely because the plaintiff is aware that he has suffered physical harm, but it does accrue when the plaintiff knew or should have known that the alleged product defect caused his physical harm.[16]

The statute of repose under the IPLA may not apply when the injury is caused by a disease contracted because of protracted exposure to an inherently dangerous foreign substance, such as asbestos.[17]

3. Asbestos-Related Injuries

The IPLA has a separate statute of limitation for certain asbestos-related injuries. Any cause of action resulting from an initial exposure to asbestos must be commenced within two years after the cause of action accrues. The cause of action accrues when the injured person knows that she has an asbestos-related injury. However, this statute of limitation applies only to product liability actions against persons who mined and sold commercial asbestos and to actions which seek to recover from certain bankruptcy funds that have been created for payment of asbestos-related claims.[18]

4. Breach of Contract or Warranty

An action for breach of any contract for sale must be commenced within four years after the cause of action has accrued. A cause of action accrues when a breach occurs, regardless of the aggrieved party's lack of knowledge of the breach. Generally, a breach of warranty occurs when tender of delivery is made.[19]

C. STRICT LIABILITY

1. The Standard

Prior to passage of the IPLA, Indiana recognized strict liability in tort as embodied in section 402A of the Restatement (Second) of Torts.[20] Strict liability actions are now governed by the IPLA, which was enacted in 1978.[21] The central burden for a plaintiff is to prove the product was in a "defective condition unreasonably dangerous."[22] Generally, this is a question of fact.[23]

2. "Defect"

A product is defective if, at the time it is conveyed by the seller to another party, it is in a condition (a) not contemplated by reasonable persons among those considered expected users or consumers of the product; and (b) that will be unreasonably dangerous to the expected user or consumer when used in reasonably expectable ways of handling or consumption. A product may also be defective if the seller fails to (a) properly package or label the product to give reasonable warnings of danger about the product; or (b) give reasonably complete instructions on proper use of the product when the seller, by exercising reasonable diligence, could have made such warnings or instructions available to the user or consumer.

A product is not defective if it is safe for reasonably expectable handling and consumption. If an injury results from handling, preparation for use, or consumption that is not reasonably expectable, the seller is not liable.

A product is not defective if it is incapable of being made safe for its reasonably expectable use when manufactured, sold, handled, and packaged properly.[24]

Under the amendments to the IPLA that became effective July 1, 1995, a party claiming that a product is defective by design or because of inadequate warnings must establish that the manufacturer failed to exercise reasonable care in designing the product or providing warnings.[25]

3. "Physical Harm"/"Property Damage"

The IPLA subjects a seller of a defective product to liability for physical harm caused by that product to the user or consumer or to his property. Recovery for damages to property can be had under the IPLA only if the injury results in sudden, major damage to property; gradually evolving damage to property and economic losses incurred on account of such gradual damage are not recoverable under the Act. Moreover, if only economic losses are sought, strict liability is not a basis for recovery.[26]

4. Contributory Negligence/Assumption of Risk

Prior to July 1, 1995, contributory negligence or comparative fault was not a defense in product liability actions based on strict liability.[27]

In an action based on fault (negligence), any contributory fault chargeable to the claimant diminishes proportionately the amount awarded as compensatory damages for an injury attributable to the claimant's contributory fault. Generally, the claimant may be barred from recovery if his contributory fault is greater than the fault of all persons whose fault proximately contributed to the claimant's damages.[28]

Effective July 1, 1995, comparative fault applies to all product liability actions that accrued subsequent to June 30, 1995. The fault of the person suffering the physical harm and the fault of all others who caused the harm are to be compared in accordance with the allocation provisions of the CFA.[29]

5. Sale or Lease

While a technical and complete sales transaction is the most easily recognizable commercial type of transaction, it is not the only transaction within the purview of the IPLA.[30] The plaintiff need only show that defendant placed the product into the stream of commerce.[31]

Strict liability is not imposed on the occasional seller of food or other such products who is not engaged in that activity as part of her business.[32]

6. Inherently Dangerous Products

A product is not defective if it is incapable of being made safe for its reasonably expectable use when manufactured, sold, handled, and packaged properly.[33] The open and obvious danger rule is not a defense to strict liability claims brought under the IPLA, but is a defense to product liability claims based on negligence.[34] Whether the dangerous condition of the product was open and obvious is a factor to be considered in strict liability cases in determining whether or not a product is defective and unreasonably dangerous.[35]

7. Successor Liability

Whether a successor corporation assumed a duty to a person injured by a product may be a jury question. An agreement between the successor and the predecessor absolving the successor of liability is not dispositive of whether the successor owed such a duty.[36]

8. Privity

Lack of privity between plaintiff and defendant does not bar plaintiff's personal injury claim sounding in strict liability or negligence.[37] The user or consumer need not have bought the product from or entered into any contractual relation with the seller.[38] Where only property damages are sustained, however, liability may be barred for lack of privity.[39] Lack of privity may bar a contract action for breach of warranty against a manufacturer.[40] For breach of implied warranty under the Uniform Commercial Code as adopted in Indiana, the buyer seeking recovery must be in privity of contract with the manufacturer.[41]

9. Failure to Warn

Under the IPLA, a product is defective if the seller fails to properly package or label the product to give reasonable warnings of danger about the product or give reasonably complete instructions on proper use of the product. The rule applies when the seller, by exercising reasonable diligence, could have made such warnings or instructions available to the user or consumer.[42] This statutory requirement is generally governed not by strict liability concepts but by those of negligence.[43] A manufacturer need only warn of reasonably foreseeable dangers.[44] The threshold question before the manufacturer is held liable for failure to warn is whether there was a duty to warn.[45]

As noted above, the July 1, 1995, amendments to the IPLA expressly require proof that the manufacturer failed to act with reasonable care in a product liability case predicated on lack of warnings.[46]

10. Post-Sale Duty to Warn

The post-sale duty to warn in a negligence case arises when the manufacturer knew or should have known of the risk.[47] In a case involving a drug product, the duty to warn is limited to what the manufacturer knew during the period the plaintiff took the drug in question.[48]

11. Substantial Change/Abnormal Use

A manufacturer is not liable when a substantial change has occurred to the product between the time it left the manufacturer's hands and the time of the accident.[49] Misuse of the product is also a defense if the misuse was not reasonably foreseeable.[50] If the injured person is reckless with regard to his own safety, recovery against even a reckless manufacturer will be barred.[51]

12. State of the Art

Prior to July 1, 1995, the IPLA provided a defense if the design, manufacture, inspection, packaging, warnings, or labeling of the product conformed with the generally recognized state of the art at the time the product was designed, manufactured, packaged, and labeled.[52]

The amendments to the IPLA effective July 1, 1995, deleted the former state of the art defense and created a rebuttable presumption that the product was not defective and the manufacturer or seller was not negligent if, before the sale, the product:

1. was in conformity with the generally recognized state of the art applicable to the safety of the product; or
2. complied with codes, standards, regulations, or specifications of the United States, Indiana, or their agencies.[53]

13. Malfunction

Evidence of a malfunction is insufficient to make a prima facie case that the alleged defective condition was attributable to the defendant manufacturer.[54] Any alteration by the user or consumer that increases the likelihood of a malfunction is a substantial change that may bar recovery under the IPLA.[55]

14. Standards

Standards set by the industry do not define the standard of reasonable care against which the conduct of a manufacturer in such industry is measured in a negligence case.[56]

15. Other Accidents

In a product liability action evidence of prior accidents may be admissible. However, the proponent of such evidence must lay a proper foundation by demonstrating sufficient similarity of circumstances and conditions of the other accidents to the one in issue.[57] Evidence of prior accidents may also be admissible as proof on the issue of punitive damages.[58]

16. Enhanced Injury/Crashworthiness

Indiana recognizes the enhancement of injury theory of liability under the IPLA.[59] A question exists as to whether or not the theory would apply outside of the motor vehicle context to other products.[60]

17. Bystander

A bystander injured by the product who would reasonably be expected to be in the vicinity of the product during its reasonably expected use may recover.[61] The bystander is not required to sustain bodily injury to be able to maintain an action under the IPLA for damage to his property.[62]

D. NEGLIGENCE

Strict liability in Indiana is governed by statute; negligence is based on common law authorities and the Comparative Fault Act.[63] However, as noted above, the IPLA was amended effective July 1, 1995, to make its provisions applicable to all product liability actions regardless of the legal theory utilized for recovery.[64]

E. BREACH OF WARRANTY

Product liability actions based upon breach of implied warranty have been held to be identical to strict liability actions.[65]

F. PUNITIVE DAMAGES

Punitive damages may be recovered in a product liability suit based on negligence or strict liability.[66] To support a claim for punitive damages, there must be clear and convincing evidence that the tortious conduct was committed oppressively, fraudulently, or with malice or gross negligence.[67] In order to recover punitive damages in a lawsuit founded on a breach of contract, the plaintiff must plead and prove the existence of an independent tort that would permit recovery of such damages.[68]

Effective July 1, 1995, the Indiana legislature enacted certain punitive damages statutes that relate to causes of action that accrue subsequent to June 30, 1995. Pursuant to those statutes punitive damages awards may not be more than the greater of: (1) three times the amount of compensatory damages; or (2) fifty thousand dollars. In most cases the person who received the punitive damage award will be paid 25 percent and the state treasurer will be paid 75 percent of the award.[69]

G. STATUTES

As noted in the preceding sections, statutes other than the IPLA that may be relevant to product liability actions include the Uniform Commercial Code sections applicable to breach of warranty claims and the Comparative Fault Act, which applies to negligence actions.[70]

Richard D. Wagner
Mark J.R. Merkle
KRIEG DeVAULT ALEXANDER & CAPEHART
One Indiana Square, Suite 2800
Indianapolis, Indiana 46204-2017
(317) 636-4341

ENDNOTES - INDIANA

1. *Masterman v. Veldman's Equip., Inc.*, 530 N.E.2d 312 (Ind. App. 1988).

2. *Miller v. Todd*, 551 N.E.2d 1139, 1143 (Ind. 1990); Ind. Code §§34-4-33-1 et seq.; Ind. Code §33-1-1.5-1; Ind. Code §§26-1-2-101 et. seq.; see also *Insul-Mark Midwest, Inc. v. Modern Materials, Inc.*, 612 N.E.2d 550, 554 (Ind. 1993).

3. Ind. Code §§33-1-1.5-1 et seq. (1995); §§34-4-33-2 et seq. (1995); and §§34-4-34-3 through 34-4-34-6 (1995).

4. Ind. Code §33-1-1.5-1 (1995).

5. House Bill No. 1741, §16 (1995).

6. See, e.g., *Brane v. Roth*, 590 N.E.2d 587 (Ind. App. 1992); and *Turner v. Town of Speedway*, 528 N.E.2d 858 (Ind. App. 1988).

7. Ind. Code §34-1-2-2(1) and Ind. Code §33-1-1.5-5; *Wehling v. Citizens Natl. Bank*, 586 N.E.2d 840 (Ind. 1992); *Rogers v. R. J. Reynolds Tobacco Co.*, 557 N.E.2d 1045 (Ind. App. 1990).

8. Ind. Code §33-1-1.5-5.

9. Id. §33-1-1.5-5(b).

10. Id.

11. *Stump v. Indiana Equip. Co., Inc.*, 601 N.E.2d 398 (Ind. App. 1992).

12. Ind. Code §§33-1-1.5-5(a).

13. *Whittaker v. Federal Cartridge Corp.*, 466 N.E.2d 480 (Ind. App. 1984).

14. *Wenger v. Weldy*, 605 N.E.2d 796, 798 (Ind. App. 1993).

15. *Wojcik v. Almase*, 451 N.E.2d 336 (Ind. App. 1983).

16. Id.; *Barnes v. A. H. Robins Co. Inc.*, 476 N.E.2d 84 (Ind. 1985).

17. *Covalt v. Carey Canada, Inc.*, 543 N.E.2d 382 (Ind. 1989).

18. Ind. Code §33-1-1.5-5.5(a), (b), (d).

19.   Ind. Code §26-1-2-725.

20.   *Reed v. Central Soya Co. Inc.*, 621 N.E.2d 1069, 1072 (Ind. 1993), *modified on rehearing*; 644 N.E. 2d 84 (Ind. 1994); *Koske v. Townsend Engineering Co.*, 551 N.E.2d 437, 442 (Ind. 1990).

21.   *Reed*, 621 N.E.2d at 1073.

22.   *Miller*, 551 N.E.2d 1139; Ind. Code §33-1-1.5-3(a).

23.   *Corbin v. Coleco Indus., Inc.*, 748 F.2d 411 (7th Cir. 1984).

24.   Ind. Code §33-1-1.5-2.5; *Peters v. Judd Drugs, Inc.*, 602 N.E.2d 162 (Ind. App. 1992).

25.   Ind. Code §33-1-1.5-3(b) (1995).

26.   *Reed*, 621 N.E.2d at 1074.

27.   *Jarrell v. Monsanto Co.*, 528 N.E.2d 1158, 1167 (Ind. App. 1988).

28.   Ind. Code §§34-4-33-3, 34-4-33-4; Note, *Partial Settlement of Multiple Tortfeasor Cases Under the Indiana Comparative Fault Act*, 22 Ind. L. Rev. 939 (1989).

29.   Ind. Code §33-1-1.5-10 (1995).

30.   Ind. Code §33-1-1.5-3; *Link v. Sun Oil Co.*, 160 Ind. App. 310, 312 N.E.2d 126 (1974).

31.   Id.

32.   *Perfection Paint & Color Co. v. Konduris*, 147 Ind. App. 106, 258 N.E.2d 681 (1970).

33.   Ind. Code §33-1-1.5-2.5; Wade, *A Conspectus of Manufacturers' Liability for Products*, 10 Ind. L. Rev. 755, 767 (1977).

34.   *Koske v. Townsend*, 551 N.E.2d 437 (Ind. 1990).

35.   *Johnson v. Kempler Industries, Inc.*, 677 N.E.2d 531 (Ind. App. 1997).

36.   *Lucas v. Dorsey Corp.*, 609 N.E.2d 1191, 1201 (Ind. App. 1993).

37.   *General Elec. Co. v. Drake*, 535 N.E.2d 156 (Ind. App. 1989); *Citizens Gas & Coke Util. v. American Econ. Ins.*, 486 N.E.2d 998 (Ind. 1985).

38.   Ind. Code §33-1-1.5-3(b)(2).

39.   *Citizens Gas & Coke*, 486 N.E.2d 998 at 1001.

40.   *Lane v. Barringer*, 407 N.E.2d 1173 (Ind. App. 1980).

41.   Ind. Code §§26-1-2-314(1), (2)(c), 26-1-2-315.

42.   Id. §33-1-1.5-2.5(b).

43.   *Moss v. Crossman Corp.*, 945 F. Supp. 1167 (N.D. Ind. 1996); *Jarrell*, 528 N.E.2d at 1166; cf. *Ortho Pharmaceutical Corp. v. Chapman*, 180 Ind. App. 33, 388 N.E.2d 541, 550 (1979).

44.   *Wingett v. Teledyne Indus., Inc.*, 479 N.E.2d 51 (Ind. 1985).

45.   *American Optical Co. v. Weidenhamer*, 457 N.E.2d 181 (Ind. 1983); *York v. Union Carbide Corp.*, 586 N.E.2d 861 (Ind. App. 1992).

46.   Ind. Code §33-1-1.5-3(b) (1995).

47.   *Smith v. Ford Motor Co.*, 908 F. Supp. 590 (N.D. Ind. 1995).

48.   *Ortho Pharmaceutical,* 388 N.E.2d at 548, 558.

49.   *Bishop v. Firestone Tire & Rubber Co.*, 814 F.2d 437 (7th Cir. 1987).

50.   Ind. Code §33-1-1.5-4.

51.   *Koske*, 551 N.E.2d at 443-444, *aff'd* 526 N.E.2d 985 (Ind. App. 1988).

52.   Ind. Code §33-1-1.5-4(4); *FMC Corp. v. Brown*, 526 N.E.2d 719 (Ind. App. 1988), *aff'd*, 551 N.E.2d 444 (Ind. 1990).

53.   Ind. Code §33-1-1.5-4.5 (1995).

54.   *Cornette v. Searjeant Metal Prods., Inc.*, 147 Ind. App. 46, 258 N.E.2d 652 (1970).

55.   *Cornette*, 258 N.E.2d at 657.

56.   *Thiele v. Faygo Beverage, Inc.*, 489 N.E.2d 562 (Ind. App. 1986).

57.   *Indiana State Highway Commn. v. Fair*, 423 N.E.2d 738 (Ind. App. 1981).

58. *Sipes v. Osmose Wood Preserving Co. of America, Inc.*, 546 N.E.2d 1223, 1225-1226 (Ind. 1989).

59. *Miller v. Todd*, 551 N.E.2d 1139 (Ind. 1990); *Rogers v. Ford Motor Co.*, 952 F. Supp. 606 (N.D. Ind. 1997).

60. *Moss v. Crossman Corp.*, 945 F. Supp. 1167 (N.D. Ind. 1996).

61. Ind. Code §33-1-1.5-2.

62. *General Elec. Co. v. Drake*, 535 N.E.2d 156 (Ind. App. 1989).

63. *Koske*, 551 N.E.2d at 443 (Ind. 1990); Ind. Code §34-4-33-1 et seq.

64. See n.4, *supra*.

65. *Thiele*, 489 N.E.2d 562.

66. *Sipes*, 546 N.E.2d 1223.

67. *Ragsdale v. K-Mart Corp.*, 468 N.E.2d 524 (Ind. App. 1984).

68. *Miller Brewing Co. v. Best Beers of Bloomington*, 608 N.E.2d 975 (Ind. 1993); *Austin v. Disney Tire Co., Inc.*, 815 F. Supp. 285 (S.D. Ind. 1993).

69. Ind. Code §§34-4-34-3 through 34-4-34-6 (1995).

70. Ind. Code §§26-1-2-101 et seq.; and §34-4-33-1 et seq.

IOWA

A. CAUSES OF ACTION

A product liability lawsuit is an action in strict liability. It commonly includes actions in negligence and breach of warranty. Less commonly, a product liability lawsuit includes actions alleging misrepresentation and violation of federal or state statutes.

B. STATUTES OF LIMITATION

Causes of action for personal injuries must be brought within two years, whether based in contract or tort.[1] Causes of action founded on unwritten contracts (breach of implied warranty)[2] must be brought within five years.[3] Causes of action founded on written contracts (breach of warranty) must be brought within ten years.[4] A rather liberal "discovery" rule applies.[5] There is a fifteen-year statute of repose limited to improvements to real property.[6]

The repose statute is interpreted broadly; it does not require that the product become a "fixture" to real estate, only that the product improve realty.[7]

C. STRICT LIABILITY

1. The Standard

Iowa has adopted section 402A of the Restatement (Second) of Torts.[8] If technical issues are involved, the plaintiff may be required to offer an expert witness to explain to the jury how the product is unreasonably dangerous.[9]

2. "Defect"

In Iowa a product is defective if it is unreasonably dangerous. A defective product is unreasonably dangerous if:

a. the danger is greater than an ordinary consumer with knowledge of the product's characteristics would expect it to be;

b. the danger outweighs the utility of the product; or

c. the benefits of the design do not outweigh the risk. Factors to consider include:

1. the seriousness of the harm posed by the design;

2. the likelihood that such danger would occur;

3. the mechanical feasibility of a safer alternate design;

4. the cost of an improved alternate design; and

5. the adverse consequences to the product and the user that would result from an alternate design.[10]

3. Contributory Negligence/Assumption of the Risk

Contributory negligence is not a complete defense under the Iowa Comparative Fault Act.[11] Assumption of the risk bars plaintiff's recovery if the plaintiff knew that the defect or dangerous condition was present, understood the nature of the danger to himself or herself, and yet fully and voluntarily used the product and such use was the proximate cause of plaintiff's injury.[12] However, unreasonable assumption of risk caused by misuse of a product will not otherwise bar the injured party's recovery, but will rather subject the claim to that party's comparative fault.[13] In a product liability case, the plaintiff must show he or she used the product in its intended manner or in a manner reasonably foreseeable by defendant.[14] A strict liability claim is offset by other partys' fault, including the injured party's, as defined in the Iowa Comparative Fault Act.[15]

4. Sale or Lease

Strict liability applies to the seller when the following conditions are met: "1) manufacture of a product by defendant; 2) the product was in a defective condition; 3) the defective condition was unreasonably dangerous to the user or consumer when used in a reasonably foreseeable manner; 4) the manufacturer was engaged in the business of manufacturing such a product; 5) said product was expected to and did reach the user without substantial change in condition, i.e., the defect existed at the time of the sale; 6) said product was the proximate cause of personal injuries or property damage suffered by the user or consumer; 7) damages suffered by the user or consumer."[16]

In general, strict liability applies to the retailer as well as the manufacturer of a defective product.[17] (See discussion on privity.) Iowa no longer recognizes the common carrier exception to strict liability.[18]

Nonmanufacturers are immune from strict liability when the cause of action arises solely from the original design or manufacture of the product and no causal link exists between the nonmanufacturer and the assembled product.[19]

5. Inherently Dangerous Products

A supplier of products will not be held strictly liable simply because the product is inherently dangerous unless it fails to give adequate warning of the danger.[20] "Some products, in the present state of human knowledge, cannot be made safe for their intended and ordinary use. Such a product properly prepared and accompanied by proper directions and warnings, is not defective, nor is it unreasonably dan-

---

gerous, even though its use may result in damage. These are unavoidably unsafe products."[21]

6. **Successor Liability**

A successor corporation may be liable for the debts and liabilities of the predecessor corporation if any of four circumstances exist: (1) there is an agreement to assume such debts or liabilities; (2) there is a consolidation of the two corporations; (3) the purchasing corporation is a mere continuation of the selling corporation; or (4) the transaction is fraudulent in fact.[22]

7. **Privity**

A product manufacturer, seller, or distributor will not be held to strict liability in the absence of privity of contract with the product purchaser where the damage caused by a defective product results in economic loss.[23] A remote manufacturer or seller of a product will be held to strict liability to a product user when the damage from a defective product results in personal injury, or the significant threat of personal injury, to the user of the product, or bystanders, or otherwise results in sudden, major damage to the user's property.[24] This rule is an adoption of the doctrine first set forth in the *Seely* case[25] that has also been adopted by Restatement (Second) of Torts section 402A.[26]

8. **Failure to Warn**

A manufacturer has no duty to warn when it did not know and should not have known of the danger of its product.[27] A manufacturer has a duty to warn of dangers known to it that would not be known to users of its product.[28] Factors to consider regarding the necessity of a warning are: (a) the likelihood that harm will occur if the warning is not passed on to the final user; (b) the seriousness of the probable harm; (c) the probability that the warning will be passed on; and (d) the ease or burden of the giving of a warning by the manufacturer to the final user.[29] Whether the factors exist is usually a jury question.[30] The plaintiff must prove that the seller of the allegedly defective product was negligent in its failure to warn; a strict liability claim based on failure to warn is not recognized in Iowa.[31]

9. **Post-Sale Duty to Warn**

After the sale of a product, a manufacturer may have a duty to warn concerning subsequently acquired knowledge of a defect or dangerous condition that would render the product unreasonably dangerous for its foreseeable use, depending on the circumstances.[32] A post-sale duty to warn may affect a product seller's ability to raise the state-of-the-art defense.

10. Substantial Change/Abnormal Use

A manufacturer has a duty to deliver its product using the precautions necessary to ensure that the product is free from defects for a normal length of time when handled in a normal manner.[33] A plaintiff whose misuse of a product results in injury is not barred from recovery for strict liability; the plaintiff's misuse of a product is a matter of comparative fault to be determined by the trier of fact.[34] (See Negligence, section D.)

11. State of the Art

A manufacturer may assert a state-of-the-art defense if it pleads and proves that the product conformed to the state of the art in existence at the time the product was designed, tested, manufactured, formulated, packaged, provided with a warning, or labeled.[35] The state of the art is a complete defense, but the manufacturer still has a duty to warn regarding defects subsequently discovered that are unreasonably dangerous.[36] (See Post-Sale Duty to Warn, *supra.*)

12. Malfunction

No Iowa case has addressed this issue.

13. Standards

Evidence of subsequent remedial or precautionary measures is admissible in strict liability and breach of warranty to prove that the product was defective.[37] Evidence of subsequent remedial measures is not admissible to prove negligence or culpable conduct, but it may be used for the purpose of proving ownership, control, feasibility of precautionary measures, if controverted, or impeachment.[38]

14. Other Accidents

Evidence of similar accidents is admissible.[39] A requirement of substantial similarity between the accident at issue and other accidents is a matter of relevance to be decided in the discretion of the trial judge.[40]

15. Misrepresentation

Iowa tort law is strongly influenced by the Restatement (Second) of Torts. No Iowa case has addressed section 402B and its application to misrepresentation. However, it is common to join claims of negligent misrepresentation under Restatement (Second) of Torts section 552 in product liability cases.[41]

16. Crashworthiness

To prevail on a claim of crashworthiness, the plaintiff must first make a showing of design defect, then establish (1) proof of practicable alternative safer design; (2) the types of injuries that would have resulted with a safer design; and (3) the extent of enhanced injuries attributable to defective design.[42]

D. NEGLIGENCE

Under the Iowa Comparative Fault Act, contributory negligence is not a defense.[43] Iowa has adopted a comparative fault statute, identified as Iowa Code ch. 668. The statute applies to strict liability actions. A plaintiff found to be more than 50 percent at fault is barred from recovery.[44]

E. BREACH OF WARRANTY

In the product setting, a cause of action for breach of warranty and a cause of action for strict liability are not mutually exclusive.[45] Each cause of action may be brought if supportable under the facts.[46]

The "discovery rule" does not apply to warranty claims.[47]

F. PUNITIVE DAMAGES

Punitive damages are recoverable in actions in strict liability[48] and negligence[49] when defendant's conduct amounts to willful and wanton disregard for the rights or safety of another (actual or legal malice).[50] Punitive damages are not recoverable in actions for breach of warranty unless the breach amounts to an independent, willful tort where actual or legal malice is shown.[51]

G. STATUTES

Relevant statutes for product liability actions are the statutes of limitation, the Iowa Comparative Fault Act, and the commercial code sections when a breach of warranty is alleged.[52]

S. P. DeVolder
LEWIS, WEBSTER, JOHNSON, VAN WINKLE & DEVOLDER
620 Liberty Building
418 6th Avenue
Des Moines, Iowa 50309-2407
(515) 243-1000
Fax: (515) 288-7000

IOWA - ENDNOTES

1.   Iowa Code §614.1(2).

2.   Id. §§554.2725, 614.1(5); *Fell v. Kewanee Farm Equip. Co.*, 457 N.W.2d 911 (Iowa 1990).

3.   Iowa Code §614.1(4).

4.   Id. §§614.1, 554.2725, 614.1(5).

5.   *LeBeau v. Dimig*, 446 N.W.2d 800 (Iowa 1989); *Sparks v. Metalcraft, Inc.*, 408 N.W.2d 347 (Iowa 1987).

6.   Iowa Code §614.1(11).

7.   *Krull v. Thermegas Co. of Northwood*, 522 N.W.2d 607 (Iowa 1994); *Bob McKiness Excavating & Grading, Inc.*, 507 N.W.2d 405 (Iowa 1993).

8.   *Hawkeye-Security Ins. Co. v. Ford Motor Co.*, 174 N.W.2d 672 (Iowa 1970); *Duggan v. Hallmark Pool Mfg. Co.*, 398 N.W.2d 175 (Iowa 1986).

9.   *James v. Swiss Valley Agric. Serv.*, 449 N.W.2d 886 (Iowa 1989); *Wernimont v. International Harvester Corp.*, 309 N.W.2d 137 (Iowa 1981).

10.   *Chown v. USM Corp.*, 297 N.W.2d 218 (Iowa 1980); *Kleve v. General Motors Corp.*, 210 N.W.2d 568 (Iowa 1973); Iowa Civil Jury Instructions, No. 1000.4 (Nov. 1988).

11.   *Speck v. Unit Handling Div., Litton Sys.*, 366 N.W.2d 543 (Iowa 1985); Iowa Code §668.1 et seq.; Iowa Civil Jury Instructions, No. 1000.9 (June 1987).

12.   *Speck, supra* note 10; Iowa Civil Jury Instructions, No. 1000.9 (June 1987).

13.   Iowa Code §668.1(1) (1995).

14.   *Hughes v. Massey-Ferguson, Inc.*, 490 N.W.2d 75 (Iowa App. 1992).

15.   *Bredberg v. PepsiCo, Inc.*, 551 N.W.2d 321 (Iowa 1996); Iowa Code 668.1.

16.   *Osborn v. Massey-Ferguson, Inc.*, 290 N.W.2d 893, 901 (Iowa 1980).

17.   *Kleve*, 210 N.W.2d 568.

18. *National Steel Serv. Center, Inc. v. Gibbons*, 319 N.W.2d 269 (Iowa 1982).

19. Iowa Code §613.18.

20. *Beeck v. Aquaslide 'N' Dive Corp.*, 350 N.W.2d 149 (Iowa 1984).

21. Iowa Civil Jury Instructions, No. 1000.7 (June 1987).

22. *DeLapp v. Xtraman*, 417 N.W.2d 219 (Iowa 1987); *C. Mac Chambers Co. v. Iowa Tae Kwon Do Academy*, 412 N.W.2d 593 (Iowa 1987).

23. *Nelson v. Todd's, Ltd.*, 426 N.W.2d 120 (Iowa 1988).

24. Id.

25. *Seely v. White Motor Co.*, 63 Cal. 2d 9, 45 Cal. Rptr. 17, 403 P.2d 145 (1965).

26. Restatement (Second) of Torts §402A.

27. *Moore v. Vanderloo*, 386 N.W.2d 108 (Iowa 1986).

28. *Nichols v. Westfield Indus., Ltd.*, 380 N.W.2d 392 (Iowa 1985); *Beeman v. Manville Corp. Asbestos Fund*, 496 N.W.2d 247 (Iowa 1993).

29. *Henkel v. R and S Bottling Co.*, 323 N.W.2d 185 (Iowa 1982); Iowa Civil Jury Instructions, No. 1000.6 (June 1987).

30. *Beeman*, 496 N.W.2d 247.

31. *Olson v. Prosoco, Inc.*, 522 N.W.2d 284 (Iowa 1994).

32. Iowa Code §668.12.

33. *Henkel*, 323 N.W.2d 185; *Cooley v. Quick Supply Co.*, 221 N.W.2d 763 (Iowa 1974); Iowa Civil Jury Instructions, No. 1000.5 (June 1987).

34. *Fell*, 457 N.W.2d 911; *Slager v. H.W.A. Corp.*, 435 N.W.2d 349 (Iowa 1989); Iowa Code §668.1.

35. Iowa Code §668.12.

36. *Fell*, 457 N.W.2d 911.

37. *Bandstra v. International Harvester Co.*, 367 N.W.2d 282 (1985); Iowa R. Evid. 407.

38.   Id.

39.   *Rattenborg v. Montgomery Elevator Co.*, 438 N.W.2d 602 (Iowa 1989).

40.   Id.

41.   *Beeck v. Kapalis*, 302 N.W.2d 90 (Iowa 1981); *Larsen v. United Fed. Sav. &
       Loan Assn.*, 300 N.W.2d 281 (Iowa 1981); Restatement (Second) of Torts
       §552.

42.   *Reed v. Chrysler Corp.*, 494 N.W.2d 224 (Iowa 1992).

43.   Iowa Code §668.1 et seq.

44.   Id.

45.   *Hawkeye-Security Ins. Co. v. Ford Motor Corp.*, 199 N.W.2d 373 (Iowa 1972).

46.   Id.

47.   *City of Carlisle v. Fetzer*, 381 N.W.2d 627 (Iowa 1986); Iowa Code §554.2725.

48.   *Beeck,* 350 N.W.2d 149.

49.   *Cedar Falls Bldg. Center, Inc. v. Vietor*, 365 N.W.2d 635 (Iowa 1985).

50.   Iowa Code §668A.1.

51.   *Parks v. City of Marshalltown*, 440 N.W.2d 377 (Iowa 1989).

52.   Iowa Code §§554.2725; 613.18; 614.1(2), (4), (5), (11); 668.1 et seq.; 668A.1.

KANSAS

A. **CAUSES OF ACTION**

Negligence, breach of warranty, and strict liability are alternative theories of liability.[1]

B. **STATUTES OF LIMITATION AND REPOSE**

A product liability action for personal injuries, death, or property damage must be brought within two years of the date of substantial injury or the date such injury becomes reasonably ascertainable, whether in negligence, strict liability, or breach of warranty.[2]

The Kansas Product Liability Act includes a "useful safe life" statute of repose. A product seller is not liable if it proves by a preponderance of the evidence that the harm was caused after the product's useful safe life had expired.[3] Where the harm was caused more than ten years after delivery of the product, it is presumed that the harm was caused after the expiration of the product's useful safe life. This presumption may only be rebutted by clear and convincing evidence.[4] The Kansas general statute of repose, which purports to state a ten-year statute of repose for all tort cases,[5] has been held not to apply to cases brought under the Kansas Product Liability Act.[6]

C. **STRICT LIABILITY**

1. **The Standard**

    Kansas's strict liability standard is modeled after section 402A of the Restatement (Second) of Torts.[7] The plaintiff must prove that the injury resulted from an unreasonably dangerous condition of the product that existed at the time the product left the defendant's control.[8] A product is considered unreasonably dangerous when, used in the way it is ordinarily used, it is more dangerous than the ordinary consumer who purchased it would expect.[9]

2. **"Defect"**

    The plaintiff must prove a specific defect to recover in strict liability.[10] The product is considered defective if it leaves the manufacturer's or seller's hands in a condition unreasonably dangerous to the ordinary user. The defect may be in the product's manufacturing or design, in its container or packaging, or in the instructions or warnings necessary for the product's safe use.[11] The Kansas Product Liability Act limits a *seller's* liability arising from an alleged defect when certain enumerated conditions are met.[12]

3. Contributory Negligence/Assumption of Risk/Comparative Fault

Contributory negligence is not a complete defense to a claimant's recovery.[13] Assumption of the risk remains an absolute bar to recovery, but applies only in limited circumstances involving employer-employee relationships.[14]

The comparative fault doctrine governs product liability cases in negligence, strict liability, and breach of implied warranty.[15] Under Kansas comparative fault principles, recovery is barred only if the claimant's fault is greater than the combined causal negligence of all the defendants.[16]

If the plaintiff's fault is less than that of the defendants, the jury may attribute fault to plaintiff, the defendants, and any other entity whose causal negligence is claimed to have contributed to the plaintiff's damages.[17] Each party is liable only for that percentage of the total damages attributed to it.[18] The negligence of any entity, whether joined as a party or not, may be compared if supported by the evidence, even if recovery against that entity is barred.[19]

4. Sale or Lease

The plaintiff must show that a defendant had some relationship to the allegedly defective product, for example, as a manufacturer, retailer, or distributor.[20] A lessor may contractually limit its liability to the lessee for negligence in the manufacture of a product.[21]

The seller of a used product who has not repaired or remanufactured the product is not subject to strict liability if that product is defective.[22] However, remanufacturers and sellers in the chain of distribution after remanufacture are subject to strict liability.[23]

5. Inherently Dangerous Products

Kansas recognizes the unavoidably unsafe product exception to strict liability for products that have been properly prepared and accompanied by proper directions and warnings.[24]

6. Successor Liability

To establish the liability of a successor entity for failure to warn, there must be some basis in the successor's relationship with the predecessor entity's customers of benefit to the successor, and the successor must be aware of the defective condition of the product.[25] This is a very narrow exception to the traditional rule of successor nonliability.

7. Privity

Privity is not required. Liability for a defective product extends to those individuals to whom injury from that product may reasonably be foreseen and then only where the product is being used for the purpose for which it was intended or for which it is reasonably fore-seeable that it may be used.[26]

8.   **Failure to Warn**

A manufacturer or seller that knows or should know that a product is potentially dangerous to users has a duty to give adequate warnings of such danger where injury to a user can be reasonably anticipated if an adequate warning is not given.[27] Manufacturers have a duty to re-search and test their products to establish a basis for warning con-sumers.[28] Kansas recognizes a rebuttable presumption that an adequate warning will be heeded and that an inadequate warning caused the injury.[29] As a practical matter, the adequacy of a warning is determined by application of a negligence standard. An adequate warning is one that is reasonable under the circumstances.[30] The Kansas Product Liability Act addresses situations in which there is some legislative or administrative regulatory safety standard relating to warnings or instructions.[31]

There is no duty to warn when the user already knows of the dan-ger.[32] Further, a product is *not* unreasonably dangerous when its de-gree of danger is obvious and generally known or recognized or the manufacturer has given adequate warnings that sufficiently alert the user to the risk of danger in using the product.[33] The duty to warn is commensurate with the seriousness of the danger.[34]

9.   **Post-Sale Duty to Warn**

A manufacturer has a post-sale duty to warn ultimate consumers who purchased the product who can be readily identified or traced when a defect that originated at the time the product was manufactured and was unforeseeable at the point of sale is discovered to present a life-threatening hazard. Determining the nature of the duty to warn and the persons to whom the warning should be given involves a case-by-case analysis.[35] Where a successor corporation has a relationship with its predecessor's customers and knows of a defective condition in the predecessor's product, it too may incur a post-sale duty to warn.[36]

10.   **Substantial Change/Abnormal Use**

Kansas courts instruct jurors that a consumer must exercise ordinary care with reference to those obvious defects and dangerous conditions about which he does or should know and understand. The consumer also has a duty to use a product in accordance with adequate instruc-tions and warnings and to use the product in a normal manner.[37] A manufacturer may be relieved of liability for a defective design if the product has been modified in a manner that the manufacturer could not reasonably have foreseen.[38] Failure to fulfill any of these duties constitutes negligence on the part of the consumer, which the jury may consider in determining the comparative fault of the parties.[39]

11. **State of the Art**

Evidence relating to technological advancements or changes made, learned, or placed into common use *subsequent* to the time the product in use was designed, formulated, tested, manufactured, or sold by the manufacturer is inadmissible unless such evidence is offered to impeach a witness who has expressly denied the feasibility of such advancements or changes.[40]

12. **Standards**

The Kansas Product Liability Act allocates evidentiary burdens according to whether the product was in compliance with legislative or administrative regulatory standards at the time of manufacture.[41]

When the injury-causing aspect of the product complied with legislative or administrative safety standards at the time of manufacture, the product is deemed not defective unless the plaintiff proves that a reasonably prudent seller could and would have taken added precautions.[42] When the injury-causing aspect of the product did not comply with existing standards, the product is deemed defective unless the seller proves its failure to comply was reasonably prudent under the circumstances.[43] Compliance with voluntary industry standards does not give rise to the presumption.[44]

13. **Other Accidents**

Evidence of the occurrence of other accidents is admissible, pursuant to a strict liability theory, to establish notice (relevant in punitive cases only) or the existence of a defect or to refute testimony by a defense witness that a given product was safely designed.[45] Admission of testimony regarding other accidents is usually predicated on a showing that the circumstances are substantially similar to those involved in the present case.[46]

14. **Misrepresentation**

A seller's misrepresentation may give rise to a cause of action for breach of implied or express warranty.[47]

15. **Disclaimers**

The defense of disclaimer of a warranty is not available in a suit based on strict liability.[48]

D. **NEGLIGENCE**

To recover for negligence, plaintiffs must prove the existence of a duty, breach of that duty, injury and a causal connection between the duty breached and the injury suffered.[49] Proof of a defect in the product is also required to recover in negligence in product liability, as it is for strict liability.[50]

A manufacturer has a duty to use reasonable care in designing its products so that they will be reasonably safe for their intended use.[51] Jurors are instructed that negligence is the lack of ordinary care under the existing circumstances.[52]

E. DAMAGES

In actions accruing on or after July 1, 1988, noneconomic damages are capped at $250,000 by statute.[53]

Federal courts in Kansas have held that Kansas law precludes the recovery in tort of purely economic losses.[54] Economic loss includes loss of bargain damages, repair and replacement costs, loss of profits, loss of goodwill, and loss of business reputation.[55] Some courts have focused on the type of risk involved, allowing tort recovery only where the product is unreasonably dangerous.[56]

F. PUNITIVE DAMAGES

Punitive damages may be awarded when the plaintiff proves by clear and convincing evidence that the defendant acted with fraud, malice, gross negligence or oppression. An award of punitive damages is to be viewed in light of the actual damages sustained, the actual damage award, the circumstances of the case, the evidence presented, the relative positions of the plaintiff and the defendant and the defendant's financial worth.[57]

Under Kansas law, the jury determines whether punitive damages are to be awarded and the court determines the amount of such damages.[58] Kansas statutes cap the amounts that can be awarded for punitive damages.[59]

G. STATUTES

Relevant statutes for product liability actions are the statutes of limitation,[60] the comparative negligence statute,[61] the commercial code sections (when a breach of warranty is alleged),[62] the Kansas Product Liability Act[63] and statutes placing caps on amounts to be awarded for punitive damages and noneconomic losses.[64]

Heather S. Woodson
STINSON, MAG & FIZZELL, P.C.
7500 West 110th Street
Overland Park, Kansas 66210-2329
(913) 451-8600

Thomas P. Schult
STINSON, MAG & FIZZELL, P.C.
1201 Walnut Street
P.O. Box 419251
Kansas City, Missouri 64141-6251
(816) 842-8600

ENDNOTES - KANSAS

1. Kan. Stat. Ann. §60-3302(c) (1994).

2. Kan. Stat. Ann. §60-513 (1997 Supp.); *Grey v. Bradford-White Corp.*, 581 F. Supp. 725, 728 (D. Kan. 1984).

3. Kan. Stat. Ann. §60-3303(a)(1) (1994).

4. Id. §60-3303(b)(1) (1994); *Grider v. Positive Safety Mfg. Co.*, 887 F. Supp. 251, 252 (D. Kan. 1995).

5. Kan. Stat. Ann. §60-513(b) (1997 Supp.).

6. *Speer v. Wheelabrator Corp.*, 826 F. Supp. 1264, 1272 (D. Kan. 1993); *Kerns v. G.A.C., Inc.*, 255 Kan. 264, 272, 875 P.2d 949, 956 (1994); *Baumann v. Excel Indus., Inc.*, 17 Kan. App. 2d 807, 814, 845 P.2d 65, 71 (1993).

7. *Wessinger v. Vetter Corp.*, 716 F. Supp. 537, 539 (D. Kan. 1989); *Brooks v. Dietz*, 218 Kan. 698, 702, 545 P.2d 1104, 1108 (1976).

8. *Jenkins v. Amchem Products, Inc.*, 256 Kan. 602, 630, 886 P.2d 869, 886 (1994), *cert. denied*, 516 U.S. 820 (1995).

9. Pattern Instructions Kansas (Civil) (Third) §128.17 (1997) (modifying the consumers expectation test adopted by *Lester v. Magic Chef, Inc.*, 230 Kan. 643, 653, 641 P.2d 353, 361 (1982), to conform with *Jenkins*, 256 Kan. at 635, 886 P.2d at 889).

10. *Jenkins*, 256 Kan. at 637, 886 P.2d at 890.

11. Pattern Instructions Kansas (Civil) (Third) §128.17 (1997); *Brooks,* 218 Kan. at 704, 545 P.2d at 1109-1110.

12. Kan. Stat. Ann. §60-3306 (1994).

13. Kan. Stat. Ann. §60-258a (1994).

14. *Smith v. Massey-Ferguson, Inc.*, 256 Kan. 90, 94-95, 883 P.2d 1120, 1125 (1994); *Tuley v. Kansas City Power & Light Co.*, 252 Kan. 205, 210-211, 843 P.2d 248, 252 (1992).

15. *Deines v. Vermeer Mfg. Co.*, 755 F. Supp. 350, 354 (D. Kan. 1990); *Kennedy v. City of Sawyer*, 228 Kan. 439, 449-451, 618 P.2d 788, 796-797 (1980); *cf.*

Haysville U.S.D. No. 261 v. GAF Corp., 233 Kan. 635, Syl. 4, 666 P.2d 192, Syl. 4 (1983) (comparative negligence not applicable to breach of warranty cases where result of breach is simple economic loss).

16.   Kan. Stat. Ann. §60-258a (1994); *Deines*, 755 F. Supp. at 354.

17.   Kan. Stat. Ann. §60-258a(b), (c) (1994).

18.   Id. §60-258a(d) (1994).

19.   *Hefley v. Textron, Inc.*, 713 F.2d 1487, 1496 (10th Cir. 1983); *Hardin v. Manitowoc-Forsythe Corp.*, 691 F.2d 449, 454 (10th Cir. 1982); *Cerretti v. Flint Hills Rural Electric Co-op Assn.*, 251 Kan. 347, 371, 837 P.2d 330, 347 (1992); *Brown v. Keill*, 224 Kan. 195, 206-207, 580 P.2d 867, 875-876 (1978).

20.   *Lenherr v. NRM Corp.*, 504 F. Supp. 165, 168 (D. Kan. 1980).

21.   *Mid-America Sprayers, Inc. v. United States Fire Ins. Co.*, 8 Kan. App. 2d 451, 459, 660 P.2d 1380, 1387 (1983).

22.   *Sell v. Bertsch and Co., Inc.*, 577 F. Supp. 1393, 1399 (D. Kan. 1984).

23.   *Stillie v. AM Intern. Inc.*, 850 F. Supp. 960, 962 (D. Kan. 1994).

24.   *Savina v. Sterling Drug, Inc.*, 247 Kan. 105, 115, 121-122, 795 P.2d 915, 923-924, 927-928 (1990).

25.   *Stratton v. Garvey Intern., Inc.*, 9 Kan. App. 2d 254, 258, 676 P.2d 1290, 1294 (1984).

26.   *Kennedy*, 228 Kan. at 445-446, 618 P.2d at 794.

27.   Pattern Instructions Kansas (Civil) (Third) §128.05 (1997); *Meyerhoff v. Michelin Tire Corp.*, 70 F.3d 1175, 1179 (10th Cir. 1995).

28.   *Richter v. Limax Intern., Inc.*, 45 F.3d 1464, 1470 (10th Cir. 1995).

29.   *Arnold v. Riddell, Inc.*, 882 F. Supp. 979, 996 (D. Kan. 1995) (citing *Wooderson v. Ortho Pharmaceutical Corp.*, 235 Kan. 387, 410, 681 P.2d 1038, 1057, *cert. denied*, 469 U.S. 965 (1984)).

30.   *Brand v. Mazda Motor Corp.*, 978 F. Supp. 1382, 1388 (D. Kan. 1997); *Wooderson*, 235 Kan. 387, Syl. 9, 681 P.2d 1038, Syl 9. See also *Deines*, 755 F. Supp. at 353 (inadequate warning is one that is unreasonable under the circumstances).

31. Kan. Stat. Ann. §60-3304 (1994); See *Alvarado v. J.C. Penney Co., Inc.*, 735 F. Supp. 371 (D. Kan. 1990) (plaintiff may attempt to demonstrate that standard does not meet necessary safety level).

32. *Brand*, 978 F. Supp. at 1389; *Mays v. Ciba-Geigy Corp.*, 233 Kan. 38, 60, 661 P.2d 348, 364 (1983).

33. *Delaney v. Deere & Co.*, 985 F. Supp. 1009, 1016 (D. Kan. 1997); *Wheeler v. John Deere Co.*, 862 F.2d 1404, 1413 (10th Cir. 1988). See also Kan. Stat. Ann. §60-3305 (1994) (limitation on duty to warn); *Wessinger*, 716 F. Supp. at 540 (same).

34. *Wooderson*, 235 Kan. 387, Syl. 4, 681 P.2d 1038, Syl. 4; *Neff v. Coleco Indus., Inc.*, 760 F. Supp. 864, 866-867 (D. Kan. 1991), *aff'd*, 961 F.2d 220 (10th Cir. 1992).

35. *Patton v. Hutchinson Wil-Rich Mfg. Co.*, 253 Kan. 741, Syl. 2, 761, 861 P.2d 1299, Syl. 2, 1314-1315 (1993).

36. *Patton v. TIC United Corp.*, 77 F.3d 1235, 1240-1241 (10th Cir.), *cert. denied*, 518 U.S. 1005 (1996).

37. Pattern Instructions Kansas (Civil) (Third) §128.06 (1997).

38. *Mason v. E. L. Murphy Trucking Co., Inc.*, 769 F. Supp. 341, 345 (D. Kan. 1991).

39. Pattern Instructions Kansas (Civil) (Third) §128-06 (1997).

40. Kan. Stat. Ann. §60-3307 (1994); *Blackburn, Inc. v. Harnischfeger Corp.*, 773 F. Supp. 296, 302 (D. Kan. 1991).

41. Kan. Stat. Ann. §60-3304 (1994).

42. Kan. Stat. Ann. §60-3304(a) (1994). See also *O'Gilvie v. International Playtex, Inc.*, 821 F.2d 1438, 1442-1443 (10th Cir. 1987), *cert. denied*, 486 U.S. 1032 (1988); *Alvarado*, 735 F. Supp. at 374.

43. Kan. Stat. Ann. §60-3304(b) (1994).

44. *Pfeiffer v. Eagle Mfg. Co.*, 771 F. Supp. 1141, 1143 (D. Kan. 1991); *cf. Rexrode v. American Laundry Press Co.*, 674 F.2d 826 (10th Cir.), *cert. denied*, 459 U.S. 862 (1982).

45. *Wheeler*, 862 F.2d at 1407; *King v. Emerson Elec. Co.*, 837 F. Supp. 1096, 1099 (D. Kan. 1993), *aff'd*, 69 F.3d 548 (10th Cir. 1995). See *Schaeffer v. Kansas Dept. of Transp.*, 227 Kan. 509, 517, 608 P.2d 1309, 1317 (1980).

46. *Wheeler*, 862 F.2d at 1407; *King*, 837 F. Supp. at 1099; *Schaeffer*, 227 Kan. at 517.

47. Kan. Stat. Ann. §60-3302(c) (1994).

48. *Elite Professionals Inc. v. Carrier Corp.*, 16 Kan. App. 2d 625, Syl. 1, 827 P.2d 1195, Syl. 1 (1992).

49. *Miller v. Lee Apparel Co. Inc.*, 19 Kan. App. 2d 1015, 1023, 881 P.2d 576, 583 (1994).

50. Id., 19 Kan. App. 2d at 1032, 881 P.2d at 589.

51. *Garst v. General Motors Corp.*, 207 Kan. 2, 19, 484 P.2d 47, 60 (1971).

52. Pattern Instructions Kansas (Civil) (Third) §128.01 (1997); *Timsah v. General Motors Corp.*, 225 Kan. 305, 313-314, 591 P.2d 154, 162 (1979).

53. Kan. Stat. Ann. §60-19a02 (1994). See also §60-19a01 (1994) (for actions accruing between July 1, 1987, and July 1, 1988).

54. E.g., *Winchester*, 983 F.2d at 996; *Sithon Maritime Co. v. Holiday Mansion*, 983 F. Supp. 977, (D. Kan. 1997). See *Elite Professionals*, 16 Kan. App. 2d at 633, 827 P.2d at 1202.

55. *Professional Lens Plan, Inc. v. Polaris Leasing Corp.*, 234 Kan. 742, 752-53, 675 P.2d 887, 897 (1984); *Nature's Share, Inc. v. Kutter Products, Inc.*, 752 F. Supp. 371, 380 (D. Kan. 1990).

56. E.g., *Daitom*, 741 F.2d at 1582.

57. *Tetuan v. A. H. Robins Co.*, 241 Kan. 441, 481-482, 738 P.2d 1210, 1238-1239 (1987); *Wooderson*, 235 Kan. at 415, 681 P.2d at 1061. See Pattern Instructions Kansas (Civil) (Third) §171.44 (1997).

58. Kan. Stat. Ann. §60-3701(a) (1994).

59. Kan. Stat. Ann. §60-3701 (1994).

60. Id. §60-513 (1997 Supp.).

61. Id. §60-258a (1994).

62.   Id. §84-2-101 et seq. (1996).

63.   Id. §60-3301 et seq. (1994).

64.   Id. §§60-3701, 60-19a01, 60-19a02 (1994).

KENTUCKY

A.   CAUSES OF ACTION

Kentucky product liability law allows three causes of action: strict liability in tort, negligence, and breach of warranty.[1] Kentucky's Product Liability Act applies to all damage claims arising from the use of a product, regardless of the legal theory advanced.[2] Kentucky also recognizes concert of action principles, but it has rejected enterprise liability, alternate liability, and market share liability.[3]

B.   STATUTES OF LIMITATION

The statute of limitations for personal injury claims not based on warranty is one year after the cause of action accrues.[4] Generally, a cause of action accrues at the time of injury.[5] In actions involving a delayed appearance of the injury, the cause of action will not accrue until the plaintiff discovers or reasonably should have discovered the injury and its cause.[6] The Sixth Circuit, predicting Kentucky law, has held that the limitations period is not tolled while the plaintiff seeks the identity of the person or entity causing the injury.[7] For a cause of action to accrue, the plaintiff must suffer a present injury. The fear of future harm or fear of increased risk of harm does not constitute a present injury for which a cause of action accrues.[8] Wrongful death and survival actions must be filed within one year from the date of appointment of the personal representative. The personal representative must be appointed within one year of the date of death or the date of death is considered the date of appointment.[9]

The statute of limitations for warranty actions is four years from the date of delivery.[10] That period may not be extended, but it may be reduced by the original agreement of the parties to not less than one year.[11] The cause of action for an express warranty extending to the future performance of a product accrues when the breach is or should have been discovered.[12]

An exception to these rules occurs when an injury arises out of a motor vehicle accident. For those actions, the limitations period is two years from the date of the injury.[13] The statute of limitations for personal property damage is two years.[14]

There is a statutory presumption, rebuttable by a preponderance of the evidence, that a product is not defective if the injury, death, or property damage occurred either more than five years after the date of the sale to the first consumer or more than eight years after date of manufacture.[15]

C. STRICT LIABILITY

1. The Standard

Kentucky recognizes the theory of strict product liability as expressed in section 402A of the Restatement (Second) of Torts.[16] Kentucky law provides for recovery when injury results from the use of a product that was "in a defective condition unreasonably dangerous," even though all due care was used in its manufacture and there was no privity of contract.[17]

2. "Defect"

A product is defective if an ordinarily prudent seller, being fully aware of the risks, would not place the product on the market.[18] The plaintiff must prove a causal link between the defect and the injury.[19]

3. Contributory Negligence/Assumption of Risk

Although Kentucky's Product Liability Act provides that contributory negligence is a complete defense in all product liability actions,[20] Kentucky's highest court recently ruled that Kentucky's comparative fault statute, enacted ten years after the Product Liability Act, supersedes the contributory negligence provisions in the Product Liability Act.[21] Pure comparative fault principles apply to products liability cases in Kentucky.[22] Comparative fault principles also apply to all other personal injury and property damage causes of action in Kentucky.[23]

The voluntary assumption of a known, unreasonable risk is a factor to be considered in assessing comparative fault; it is not a separate defense.[24]

4. Sale or Lease

A plaintiff must prove that the defendant is a "seller engaged in the business of selling such a product."[25] Strict liability applies to each member of the product's chain of distribution, including manufacturers or others whose primary business may not be selling.[26] If a manufacturer is identified and subject to the court's jurisdiction, a wholesaler, distributor, or retailer who sells the product without modification is not liable absent special circumstances.[27] Kentucky courts have not decided whether strict product liability applies to lessors or bailors of products that prove defective.

A federal trial court has held electricity to be a product subject to strict liability.[28]

5. Inherently Dangerous Products

Kentucky follows the principle in comment k of section 402A that an unavoidably unsafe product that is properly prepared and accompanied by proper directions and warnings is not defective or unreasonably dangerous. An unavoidably unsafe product is one that, in the present state of human knowledge, is incapable of being made completely safe for its intended use. Because its benefit outweighs the risk of injury, marketing such a product is justified.[29]

6. Successor Liability

A defendant that is a successor company to the seller will not be responsible for the seller's liability unless (1) the successor agreed to assume liabilities; (2) the companies merged; (3) the purchasing company is a continuation of the selling company; or (4) the transaction was entered into fraudulently to escape liability.[30]

7. Privity

No privity is required in strict liability actions; a plaintiff may sue even though she did not buy the product from the manufacturer.[31]

8. Failure to Warn

Kentucky law imposes a duty on manufacturers and suppliers of products to warn of known dangers or reasonably foreseeable misuse.[32] However, a manufacturer or supplier is not responsible to warn of open and obvious dangers. A plaintiff is adequately warned if given "fair and adequate notice of the danger and possible consequences of using or even misusing" the product.[33] There is presumption that a proper warning will be read and heeded.[34]

A manufacturer has a nondelegable duty to warn the ultimate user of latent product dangers.[35] The duty is not abrogated by a warning to the immediate buyer unless the buyer takes responsibility for correcting the defect.[36] However, the learned intermediary doctrine has been implicitly adopted by a Kentucky federal court.[37]

Product liability plaintiffs are entitled to a separate jury instruction on each theory of liability on which there is evidence to sustain it, including a theory of recovery based upon failure to warn.[38]

9. Post-Sale Duty to Warn

Kentucky has not decided whether to impose a continuing duty to warn after sale. A manufacturer who undertakes the duty to make a post-sale warning, however, must make the warning available to the end user.[39] A Kentucky federal court has held that a continuing duty to warn may arise if the manufacturer learns of significant product failures, unexpected or dangerous uses, or if a high accident rate demonstrates that a danger thought to be obvious was not recognized by users.[40]

10. Substantial Change/Abnormal Use

To establish liability, a product must reach the ultimate consumer without substantial change in the condition in which it was sold.

"Substantial change" is any change that increases the likelihood of malfunction.[41] Kentucky's Product Liability Act provides that a manufacturer is liable only if the injury would have occurred if the product was used in its original, unaltered, and unmodified condition. Product modification includes failure to observe routine maintenance and care, but not ordinary wear and tear, and applies to alterations made by any person or entity except those made in accordance with the manufacturer's specifications or instructions.[42]

Product alteration or modification includes the failure to follow a warning.[43] Comparative fault principles apply to product alteration defenses.[44] An unknowledgeable user, unaware of the danger, using the product for its intended purpose, is not necessarily negligent when using the product in a different manner from its intended use if such use is reasonably foreseeable.[45]

11. **State of the Art**

There is a presumption, rebuttable by a preponderance of the evidence, that a product is not defective if the design, methods of manufacture, and testing conform to the generally recognized and prevailing standards or the state of the art in existence at the time the design was prepared and the product was manufactured.[46] According to the Fourth Circuit, interpreting Kentucky law, proof that technology existed that, if implemented, could have feasibly avoided the dangerous condition does not alone establish a product's defectiveness.[47]

12. **Malfunction**

When an accident occurs that in common experience would not ordinarily occur without a defect in a product, the inference of a defect is permitted.[48]

13. **Standards**

Compliance and noncompliance with government or industry standards is admissible, but not determinative, on the issue of liability.[49]

14. **Similar Product Failure**

Evidence of similar product failures under similar conditions is relevant and admissible.[50] Evidence of lack of prior claims against a manufacturer is admissible to show lack of defective design and notice of defect.[51] Plaintiffs do not have to establish substantial similarity before discovery of other product failures.[52]

15. **Post-Accident Repairs**

When, after an event, measures are taken that if taken previously would have made an injury or harm allegedly caused by the event less likely to occur, evidence of the subsequent measures is not admissible to prove negligence in connection with the event. This rule does not require the exclusion of evidence of subsequent measures in product liability cases or when offered for another purpose.[53]

16. Misrepresentation

Kentucky has not expressly adopted Section 402B of the Restatement (Second) of Torts regarding innocent or strict liability misrepresentation.

A seller is liable for representing a product as safe or concealing known defects when injury occurs from the product's use.[54] An actionable misrepresentation is a representation of false, material fact that, at the time of its making, the seller knew was false or made recklessly, without knowledge of its truth. The seller must have intended to induce the buyer to act, and the buyer must have, in fact, relied on its misrepresentation.[55] Kentucky has adopted Section 552 of the Restatement (Second) of Torts, but Kentucky courts have not applied it to a product liability action.[56]

D. NEGLIGENCE

The negligence standard in Kentucky product liability law is whether a prudent seller by the exercise of ordinary care should have discovered and foreseen the condition and potential problems with the product when the seller put the product on the market.[57] Product liability plaintiffs are entitled to a separate jury instruction on a theory of negligence if there is evidence to sustain it.[58] However, the Sixth Circuit, interpreting Kentucky product liability law, decided that a negligence claim based on the failure to use ordinary care in design and manufacture required proof of a defect, and therefore a jury verdict for the defendant on the strict liability instruction and against the defendant on a negligence instruction was logically inconsistent.[59]

E. BREACH OF WARRANTY

A warranty that goods are merchantable is implied in a contract for their sale.[60] Liability for breach of implied warranty of merchantability depends on the condition of the goods, not on misconduct or fault of the seller.[61]

Any affirmation of fact or promise made by the seller to the buyer that relates to the goods and becomes part of the basis of the bargain creates an express warranty that the goods shall conform to affirmation or promise.[62] Although Kentucky courts have not defined "basis of the bargain," a federal court found in a pharmaceutical case involving package inserts that when the plaintiff did not see the package inserts any warranty included in them was not part of the basis of the bargain and no express warranty arose.[63]

Traditional horizontal privity is not required; however, actions on an express or implied warranty extend only to buyer's family, household, or guests reasonably expected to use the goods.[64] Vertical privity is required in warranty actions; the plaintiff must be in privity with the seller-defendant.[65]

Kentucky also recognizes an implied warranty of fitness for a particular purpose. Liability attaches if the seller had reason to know of the purpose to which the goods were to be put and the buyer relied on the seller's skill or judgment in selecting the appropriate goods.[66]

There is no implied warranty of habitability imposed on a builder/seller of a home beyond the initial buyer.[67]

F. DAMAGES

Past and future medical expenses, lost wages, permanent impairment of the power to labor and earn money, and past and future physical and mental pain and suffering are recoverable damages in personal injury cases in Kentucky.[68] The increased likelihood of future complications, including mental distress created by the increased risk of future complications, may also be compensable.[69] However, a harmful change of some nature (present injury) must exist before a plaintiff can recover for enhanced risk of future complications and accompanying mental distress.[70] Under Kentucky law, mere increased risk or fear of future harm does not alone constitute a present physical injury for which a plaintiff may recover.[71] The spouse of an injured plaintiff may recover for loss of consortium.[72] Minor children have an independent claim for parental loss of consortium.[73]

Kentucky's version of the Uniform Commercial Code governs damages for breach of warranty and includes the difference between the value of the goods as warranted and the value of the goods accepted, and incidental or consequential damages if appropriate.[74]

Damage to the product itself is recoverable under a warranty theory, but in an action based on tort, the plaintiff may need to prove that the damage to the product occurred as a result of "damaging event."[75] In cases involving a commercial transaction in which the only damages to the product occurred, a federal court has predicted that Kentucky would apply the "economic loss rule" and deny recovery in tort.[76]

Punitive damages are recoverable upon clear and convincing evidence of oppression, fraud or malice.[77] Punitive damages may not be recoverable in breach of warranty actions, if the action is considered a breach of contract.[78]

G. GOVERNMENT CONTRACTOR DEFENSE

Manufacturers are not liable for product failures if the government approves reasonably precise specifications, the product conforms to the specifications, and the supplier warns the government of the danger in using the product.[79]

H. STATUTES

Relevant statutes for product liability actions are the Kentucky Product Liability Act,[80] statutes of limitation, and the commercial code sections when a breach of warranty is alleged.

John L. Tate
W. Kennedy Simpson
Catharine Crawford Young
STITES & HARBISON
400 West Market Street
Suite 1800
Louisville, Kentucky 40202
(502) 587-3400

1.   *Clark v. Hauck Mfg. Co.*, 910 S.W.2d 247, 249 (Ky. 1995); *Williams v. Fulmer*, 695 S.W.2d 411, 413 (Ky. 1985).

2.   Ky. Rev. Stat. Ann. §§411.300 (1978) et seq.; *Monsanto Co. v. Reed*, 950 S.W.2d 811 (Ky. 1997).

3.   *Dawson v. Bristol Labs.*, 658 F. Supp. 1036 (W.D. Ky. 1987); *Farmer v. City of Newport*, 748 S.W.2d 162 (Ky. App. 1988).

4.   Ky. Rev. Stat. Ann. §413.140(1)(a) (Michie 1974).

5.   *Caudill v. Arnett*, 481 S.W.2d 668 (Ky. 1972), *overruled in part by Louisville Trust Co. v. Johns-Mansville Products Corp.*, 580 S.W.2d 497 (Ky. 1979).

6.   *Perkins v. Northeastern Log Homes*, 808 S.W.2d 809, 818-819 (Ky. 1991); *Drake v. B. F. Goodrich Co.*, 782 F.2d 638, 641 (6th Cir. 1986); *Louisville Trust Co. v. Johns-Manville Prods. Corp.*, 580 S.W.2d 497, 501 (Ky. 1979).

7.   *Simmons v. South Central Skyworkers, Inc.*, 936 F.2d 268, 269 (6th Cir. 1991).

8.   *Capital Holding Corp. v. Bailey*, 873 S.W.2d 187, 192 (Ky. 1994).

9.   Ky. Rev. Stat. Ann. §413.180 (Michie 1988); *Conner v. George W. Whitesides Co.*, 834 S.W.2d 652 (Ky. 1992).

10. Ky. Rev. Stat. Ann. §355.2-725(1) (Michie 1987).

11. Id. §355.2-725(1) (Michie 1987).

12. Ky. Rev. Stat. Ann. §355.2-725(2) (Michie 1987).

13. Id. §304.39-230(6) (Michie 1988); *Troxell v. Trammel*, 730 S.W.2d 525, 528 (Ky. 1987).

14. Ky. Rev. Stat. Ann. §413.125 (Michie 1988).

15. Ky. Rev. Stat. Ann. §411.310(1) (Michie 1978). (The presumption has not been interpreted by a Kentucky court.)

16. *Dealers Transp. Co. Inc. v. Battery Distrib. Co., Inc.*, 402 S.W.2d 441, 446-447 (Ky. 1965).

17. Id.

18. *Tobin v. Astra Pharmaceutical Prod., Inc.*, 993 F.2d 528, 536 (6th Cir. 1993), *cert. denied*, 510 U.S. 914 (1993); *Nichols v. Union Underwear Co., Inc.*, 602 S.W.2d 429, 433 (Ky. 1980).

19. *Morales v. American Honda Motor Co.* 71 F.3d 531, 537 (6th Cir. 1995); *Calhoun v. Honda Motor Co.*, 738 F.2d 126, 130 (6th Cir. 1984); *Holbrook v. Rose*, 458 S.W.2d 155, 157 (Ky. 1970).

20. Ky. Rev. Stat. Ann. §411.320(3) (Michie 1973).

21. *Caterpillar, Inc. v. Brock*, 915 S.W.2d 751 (Ky. 1996) (holding comparative fault statute supersedes KRS §411.320(1). *rev'd on other grounds, Brock v. Caterpillar, Inc.*, 94 F.3d 220 (6th Cir. 1996). *Smith v. Louis Berkman Co.*, 894 F. Supp. 1084, 1090 (W.D. Ky. 1995) (holding comparative fault statute supersedes KRS §411.320(2); *Ingersoll Rand Co. v. Rice*, 775 S.W.2d 924, 930 (Ky. App. 1988) (holding, *in dicta*, that comparative fault statute supersedes KRS §411.320(3), *overruled in part, Continental Marine v. Bayliner Marine Corp.*, 929 S.W.2d 206 (Ky. App. 1996).

22. Ky. Rev. Stat. Ann. §411.182; *Caterpillar*, 915 S.W.2d at 752.

23. *Hilen v. Hays*, 673 S.W.2d 713 (Ky. 1984) (superseded by statute).

24. *Parker v. Redden*, 421 S.W.2d 586, 590-593 (Ky. 1967).

25. *Dealers Transp. Co.*, 402 S.W.2d at 445.

26. *Embs v. Pepsi-Cola Bottling Co. of Lexington, Ky., Inc.*, 528 S.W.2d 703, 704 (Ky. 1975).

27. Ky. Rev. Stat. Ann. §411.340 (Michie 1978).

28. *Bryant v. Tri-County Elec. Membership Corp.*, 844 F. Supp. 347, 352 (W.D. Ky. 1994).

29. *Tobin*, 993 F.2d at 540; *McKee v. Cutter Labs., Inc.*, 866 F.2d 219 (6th Cir. 1989) (blood transfusion found to be a rendition of service, not a sale under the Kentucky Blood Shield Statute, strict product liability inapplicable); *McMichael v. American Red Cross*, 532 S.W.2d 7, 9 (Ky. 1975) (blood used in transfusion is an unavoidably unsafe product).

30. *Conn v. Fales Div. of Mathewson Corp.*, 835 F.2d 145, 146 (6th Cir. 1987) (applying Kentucky law); *American Ry. Express Co. v. Commonwealth*, 190 Ky. 636, 228 S.W. 433, 441 (1920), *error dismissed*, 263 U.S. 674 (1923).

31. *Dealers Transp. Co., Inc.*, 402 S.W.2d at 446 (Ky. 1965).

32. *Watters v. TSR, Inc.*, 904 F.2d 378, 381 (6th Cir. 1990); *Post v. American Cleaning Equip. Corp.*, 437 S.W.2d 516, 520 (Ky. 1968).

33. *Post*, 437 S.W.2d at 520.

34. *Bryant v. Hercules, Inc.*, 325 F. Supp. 241 (W.D. Ky. 1970).

35. *Montgomery Elevator Co. v. McCullough*, 676 S.W.2d 776, 782 (Ky. 1984).

36. *Bohnert Equip. Co., Inc. v. Kendall*, 569 S.W.2d 161, 166 (Ky. 1978), *overruled and limited to cases in which purchaser assumed responsibility for correcting defect, Montgomery Elevator Co. v. McCullough*, 676 S.W.2d 776 (Ky. 1984).

37. *Snawder v. Cohen*, 749 F. Supp. 1473, 1480 (W.D. Ky. 1990).

38. *Clark v. Hauck Mfg. Co.*, 910 S.W.2d 247, 249 (Ky. 1995).

39. *Montgomery Elevator Co.*, 676 S.W.2d at 779, 782.

40. *Louis Berkman Co.*, 894 F. Supp. at 1092.

41. *C&S Fuel, Inc. v. Clark Equip. Co.*, 552 F. Supp. 340, 345-346 (E.D. Ky. 1982).

42. Ky. Rev. Stat. Ann. §411.320(1) (Michie 1978).

43. *Sturm, Ruger & Co. v. Bloyd*, 586 S.W.2d 19 (Ky. 1979); *Ingersoll-Rand Co.*, 775 S.W.2d 924; see also *Hutt v. Gibson Fiber Glass Prods., Inc.*, 914 F.2d 790, 794 (6th Cir. 1990).

44. *Caterpillar*, 915 S.W.2d at 752.

45. *Burke Enters.*, 700 S.W.2d at 793.

46. Ky. Rev. Stat. Ann. §411.310(2) (Michie 1978).

47. *Sexton v. Bell Helmets, Inc.*, 926 F.2d 331, 333 (4th Cir. 1991), *cert. denied*, 502 U.S. 820, 112 S. Ct. 79, 116 L. Ed. 2d 52 (1991).

48. *Embs*, 528 S.W.2d at 706; *Perkins v. Trailco Mfg. and Sales Co.*, 613 S.W.2d 855, 858 (Ky. 1981).

49. *Jones v. Hutchinson Mfg. Co., Inc.*, 502 S.W.2d 66, 70 (Ky. 1973).

50. *Montgomery Elevator*, 676 S.W.2d at 783.

51. *Hines v. Joy Mfg. Co.*, 850 F.2d 1146 (6th Cir. 1988).

52. *Volvo Car Corp. v. Hopkins*, 860 S.W.2d 777, 779 (Ky. 1993).

53. Ky. Rules Evid. 407 (1992); *Ford Motor Co. v. Fulkerson*, 812 S.W.2d 119, 127 (Ky. 1991) (interpreting Ky. Rev. Stat. §411.330, repealed July 1992).

54. *Siler v. Morgan Motor Co.*, 15 F. Supp. 468 (E.D. Ky. 1936); *Coca-Cola Bottling Works v. Shelton*, 214 Ky. 118, 282 S.W. 778, 779 (1926).

55. *Keck v. Nacke*, 413 F. Supp. 1377, 1383 (E.D. Ky. 1976).

56. *Seigle v. Jasper*, 867 S.W.2d 476, 482 (Ky. App. 1993).

57. *Ulrich v. Kasco Abrasives Co.*, 532 S.W.2d 197, 200 (Ky. 1976).

58. *Hauck Mfg.*, 910 S.W.2d at 249.

59. *Tipton v. Michelin Tire Co.*, 101 F.3d 1145, 1150 (6th Cir. 1996).

60. Ky. Rev. Stat. Ann. §355.2-314 (Michie 1987).

61. *Belcher v. Hamilton*, 475 S.W.2d 483, 485 (Ky. 1971).

62. Ky. Rev. Stat. Ann. §355.2-313(1)(a) (Michie 1987).

63. *Snawder*, 749 F. Supp. at 1481.

64. Id. §355.2-318 (Michie 1987).

65. *Munn v. Pfizer Hosp. Prods. Group*, 750 F. Supp. 244, 248 (W.D. Ky. 1990); *Williams*, 695 S.W.2d at 414.

66. Ky. Rev. Stat. Ann. §355.2-315 (Michie 1987).

67. *Real Estate Marketing, Inc. v. Franz*, 885 S.W.2d 921, 926 (Ky. 1994).

68. 2 Palmore and Eades, *Kentucky Instructions to Juries*, §§39.02-39.05 (1989).

69. *Davis v. Graviss*, 672 S.W.2d 928 (Ky. 1984).

70. *Bailey*, 873 S.W.2d at 194.

71. *Bailey*, 873 S.W.2d at 192.

72. Ky. Rev. Stat. Ann. §411.145 (Michie 1988).

73.   *Giuliani v. Guiler*, 951 S.W.2d 318, 323 (Ky. 1997).

74.   Ky. Rev. Stat. §355.2-714(2), (3).

75.   *Real Estate Marketing*, 882 S.W.2d at 924.

76.   *Bow'ing Green Municipal Utils. v. Thomasson Lumber Co.*, 902 F. Supp. 134, 138 (W.D. Ky. 1995).

77.   Ky. Rev. Stat. Ann. §411.184(1), (2) (Michie 1988).

78.   Id. §411 184(4) (Michie 1988).

79.   *Lindgraf v. McDonnell Douglas Helicopter Co.*, 993 F.2d 558, 563 (6th Cir. 1993) (interpreting Kentucky law).

80.   Ky. Rev. Stat. Ann. §§411.300 et seq. (Michie 1978).

LOUISIANA

A. CAUSES OF ACTION

The Louisiana Products Liability Act (LPLA), La. Rev. Stat. Ann. §2800.51 et seq., has codified the law and established the exclusive theories of liability for manufacturers for damage caused by their products.

B. STATUTE OF LIMITATION (PRESCRIPTION)

Delictual actions are subject to a liberative prescription of one year. This prescription commences to run from the day injury or damage is sustained.[1]

C. BURDEN OF PROOF

In a product liability suit, plaintiff has the burden of proving the following:

1. the defendant was the manufacturer[2] of the product;[3]

2. the claimant's[4] damage[5] was proximately caused[6] by a characteristic of the product;

3. the characteristic made the product unreasonably dangerous in one or more of four ways (see discussion *infra*); and

4. the claimant's damage arose from a reasonably anticipated use[7] of the product by the claimant or someone else.[8]

D. UNREASONABLY DANGEROUS

1. Unreasonably Dangerous in Construction or Composition

A product is unreasonably dangerous in construction or composition if, at the time the product left its manufacturer's control, the product deviated in a material way from the manufacturer's specifications or performance standards for the product or from otherwise identical products manufactured by the same manufacturer.

Prior to 1996, the LPLA liability for a defect in construction or composition was *strict liability*. The claimant did not have to prove manufacturer negligence, that is, that the manufacturer knew or should have known of the product deviation and could have prevented it.[9] Effective April 1997, the legislature repealed La. Civ. Code art. 2317, Louisiana's strict liability article and changed it to a negligence standard. It is unclear if this will affect plaintiff's burden under LPLA.

2. Unreasonably Dangerous in Design

A product is unreasonably dangerous in design if, at the time the product left its manufacturer's control (a) there existed an alternative design for the product that was capable of preventing the claimant's damage; and (b) the likelihood that the product's design would cause the claimant's damage and the gravity of the damage outweighed the burden on the manufacturer of adopting such alternative design and the adverse effect, if any, of such alternative design on the utility of the product.[10]

An adequate warning about a product shall be considered in evaluating the likelihood of damage when the manufacturer has used reasonable care to provide the adequate warning to users and handlers of the product.[11]

The characteristic of the product that renders it unreasonably dangerous must exist at the time the product left the control of its manufacturer or result from a reasonably anticipated alteration or modification[12] of the product.[13] Plaintiff must also be using the product in a reasonably anticipated fashion.[14]

The standard of liability for defective design appears to be *negligence*, since the LPLA apparently requires proof of both manufacturer's knowledge of the purported design defect and the manufacturer's ability to prevent it as predicates to liability.[15]

A manufacturer of a product shall not be liable for damage proximately caused by a characteristic of the product's design if the manufacturer proves that, at the time the product left his control, (a) he did not know and, in light of then-existing reasonably available scientific and technological knowledge could not have known, of the design characteristic that caused the damage or the danger of such characteristic; (b) he did not know and, in light of then-existing reasonably available scientific and technological knowledge, could not have known of the alternative design identified by the claimant; or (c) the alternative design identified by the claimant was not feasible, in light of then-existing reasonably available scientific and technological knowledge or then-existing economic practicality.[16]

3. Unreasonably Dangerous Because of Inadequate Warning

A product is unreasonably dangerous because an adequate warning[17] about the product has not been provided if, at the time the product left its manufacturer's control, the product possessed a characteristic that might cause damage and the manufacturer failed to use reasonable care to provide an adequate warning of such characteristic and its danger to users and handlers of the product.

A manufacturer is not required to provide an adequate warning about his product when (a) the product is not dangerous to an extent beyond that which would be contemplated by the ordinary user or handler of the product, with the ordinary knowledge common to the community as to the product's characteristics; or (b) the user or handler of the product already knows or reasonably should be expected to know of the characteristic of the product that may cause damage and the danger of such characteristic.[18]

a. Post-Sale Duty to Warn

A manufacturer of a product who, after the product has left his control, acquires knowledge of a characteristic of the product that may cause damage and the danger of such characteristic, or who would have acquired such knowledge had he acted as a reasonably prudent manufacturer, is liable for damage caused by his subsequent failure to use reasonable care to provide an adequate warning of such characteristic and its danger to users and handlers of the product.[19]

b. Affirmative Defense

The manufacturer of a product should not be liable for damage proximately caused by a characteristic of the product if the manufacturer proves that, at the time the product left its control, the manufacturer did not know and, in light of then existing reasonably available scientific and technological knowledge, could not have known of the characteristic that caused the damage or the danger of such characteristic.[20]

This section appears to establish the requirement of scienter by providing that a manufacturer is only responsible for warning about known or knowable product characteristics and dangers. Thus, the standard of liability appears to be *negligence*.

4. Unreasonably Dangerous Because of Nonconformity to an Express Warranty

A product is unreasonably dangerous when it does not conform to an express warranty[21] made at any time by the manufacturer about the product if the express warranty has induced the claimant or another person or entity to use the product and the claimant's damage was proximately caused because the express warranty was untrue.[22]

Breach of express warranty is *strict liability*. Whether the manufacturer knew or should have known that the express warranty was untrue and whether the manufacturer could have prevented the claimant's damages are irrelevant.[23]

E. NON-MANUFACTURING SELLER

Non-manufacturing seller of defective product is not responsible for damages in tort absent showing that he knew or should have known that product was defective and failed to declare it.[24]

F. LEARNED INTERMEDIARY DOCTRINE

To recover for failure to warn under the Louisiana Learned Intermediary Doctrine, plaintiff must show that (1) defendant failed to warn physician of

---

risk associated with use of a product not otherwise known to the physician, and (2) failure to warn the physician was both the cause in fact and proximate cause of plaintiff's injury; as to the latter factor, plaintiff must show that a proper warning would have changed the decision of the treating physician, i.e., "but for" the inadequate warning, treating physician would not have used or prescribed product.[25]

G. MARKET SHARE LIABILITY

Market share liability cannot serve as a liability theory to support proof of proximate cause under the LPLA.[26]

H. DEFENSES

1. The defense of contributory negligence is not a complete bar to recovery in product liability cases, but the doctrine of comparative fault may be applied in certain categories of cases to reduce a plaintiff's recovery.[27]

2. Compliance and non-compliance of governmental or industry standards is admissible, but not determinative on the issue of liability.[28]

I. PUNITIVE DAMAGES

Punitive damages are not recoverable.[29]

William J. Hamlin
William C. Ellison
BORDELON, HAMLIN & THERIOT
701 South Peters Street, Suite 100
New Orleans, Louisiana 70130
(504) 524-5328

ENDNOTES - LOUISIANA

1. La. Code Civ. P. Art. 3492 (1990).

2. A "manufacturer" is the following:

    (a) A person or entity who is in the business of manufacturing a product for placement into trade or commerce;

    (b) A person or entity who labels a product as his own or who otherwise holds himself out to be a manufacturer of the product;

    (c) A seller of a product who exercises control over or influences a characteristic of the design, construction or quality of the product that causes damage;

    (d) The manufacturer of a product who incorporates into the product a component or part manufactured by another manufacturer; and

    (e) A seller of a product of an alien manufacturer, if the seller is in the business of importing or distributing the product for resale and the seller is the alter ego of the alien manufacturer. La. Rev. Stat. Ann. §9:2800.53(1)(a-d).

3. A "product" is a corporeal movable that is manufactured for placement into trade or commerce, including a product that forms a component part of or that is subsequently incorporated into another product or an immovable. La. Rev. Stat. Ann. §9:2800.53(3).

4. The "claimant" is a person or entity who asserts a claim against the manufacturer of a product or his insurer for damage caused by the product. La. Rev. Stat. Ann. §9:2800.53(4).

    There is no requirement that the claimant be in contractual *privity* with the manufacturer in order to recover or that the claimant be a product user. *Media Prod. Consultants, Inc. v. Mercedes Benz of N. Am., Inc.*, 262 So. 2d 388 (La. 1972).

5. "Damage" means all damage caused by a product, including survival and wrongful death damages, for which Civil Code Articles 2315, 2315.1, and 2315.2 allow recovery. It also includes damage to the product itself and economic loss arising from a deficiency in or loss of use of the product only to the extent that section 3 of chapter 6 of title VII of book III of the Civil Code, entitled "Of the Vices of the Things Sold," does not allow recovery for such damage or economic loss. Attorney's fees are not recoverable. La. Rev. Stat. Ann. §9:2800.53(5). Claim for redhibition against manufacturer to seek recovery for economic loss is not prevented by exclusivity provision of Products Liability Act; damage compensable in redhibition is not "damage" under the Act. *Draten v. Winn Dixie of*

Louisiana, Inc., 652 So. 2d 675 (La. App. 1st Cir. 1995); *Monk v. Scott Truck and Tractor*, 619 So. 2d 890 (La. App. 3d Cir. 1993).

6. "Causation" under the LPLA and under prior law are identical. The LPLA does not change the duty/risk analysis of proximate cause or the notion of cause-in-fact as articulated in Louisiana case law. See, e.g., *Hill v. Ludin and Assocs., Inc.*, 256 So. 2d 620, 622-623 (La. 1972); *Dixie Drive-It-Yourself Sys. v. American Beverage Co.*, 137 So. 2d 298, 302-308 (La. 1962).

7. "Reasonably anticipated use" means a use or handling of a product that the product's manufacturer should reasonably expect of an ordinary person under the same or similar circumstances. La. Rev. Stat. Ann. §9:2800.53(7).

8. La. Rev. Stat. Ann. §9:2800.54(A).

9. *Weber v. Fidelity & Cas. Ins. Co. of N.Y.*, 250 So. 2d 754 (La. 1974); *Scott v. White Trucks*, 622 F.2d 714 (5th Cir. 1983).

10. This specific element codifies prior law and has come to be known as the "risk-utility balancing test" under pre-LPLA products jurisprudence. See, e.g., *Halphen v. Johns-Manville Sales Corp.*, 484 So. 2d 110, 114 n.2, 115 (La. 1986); *Hunt v. City Stores, Inc.*, 387 So. 2d 585, 588 (La. 1980).

11. La. Rev. Stat. Ann. §9:2800.56.

12. "Reasonably anticipated alteration or modification" means a change in a product that the product's manufacturer should reasonably expect to be made by an ordinary person in the same or similar circumstances, and also means a change arising from ordinary wear and tear. "Reasonably anticipated alteration or modification" does not mean the following: (1) alteration, modification, or removal of an otherwise adequate warning provided about a product; (b) the failure of a person or entity, other than the manufacturer of a product, reasonably to provide to the product user or handler an adequate warning that the manufacturer provided about the product, when the manufacturer has fulfilled his obligation to use reasonable care to provide the adequate warning by providing it to such a person or entity rather than to the product user or handler; (c) changes to or in a product or its operation because the product does not receive reasonable care and maintenance.

13. La. Rev. Stat. Ann. §9:2800.54.C.

14. See, e.g., *Daigle v. Audi of Am. Inc.*, 598 So. 2d 1304 (La. App. 3d Cir. 1992), wherein the appellate court upheld a dismissal granted at the close of the plaintiff's case. Notably, the court recognized that the "reasonably antici-

pated use standard" of the LPLA is narrower in scope than its pre-LPLA counterpart, "normal use," which included "all reasonably foreseeable uses and misuses of the product."

15. See, e.g., *Charles v. Bill Watson Hyundai, Inc.*, 559 So. 2d 872 (La. App. 4th Cir. 1990), and *Armstrong v. Lorino*, 580 So. 2d 528 (La. App. 4th Cir. 1991), wherein the court dismissed the manufacturer on the grounds that plaintiff had failed to establish causation.

16. La. Rev. Stat. Ann. §9:2800.59.A.

17. An "adequate warning" is a warning or instruction that would lead an ordinary reasonable user or handler of a product to contemplate the danger in using or handling the product and either to decline to use or handle the product or, if possible, to use or handle the product in such a manner as to avoid the damage for which the claim is made. La. Rev. Stat. Ann. §9:2800.53(9).

18. La. Rev. Stat. Ann. §9:2800.57. See, e.g., *Davis v. Avondale Indus., Inc.*, 975 F.2d 169 (5th Cir. 1992), wherein the Fifth Circuit held that when a manufacturer or distributor sells an industrial product to a sophisticated purchaser, and that purchaser then supplies that product to its employees for use, the manufacturer and distributor have no legal duty to provide any warnings to the employee/user concerning possible hazards or dangers associated with the product's use.

     A sophisticated purchaser is one who by experience and expertise is aware of the possible hazards and/or dangers associated with the use of the product and who has an obligation to inform its employees of such potential hazards.

19. La. Rev. Stat. Ann. §9:2800.57.C.

20. La. Rev. Stat. Ann. §9:2800.59.B.

21. An "express warranty" is a representation, statement of alleged fact, or promise about a product or its nature, material, or workmanship that represents, affirms, or promises that the product or its nature, material, or workmanship possesses specified characteristics or qualities or will meet a specified level of performance. Express warranty does not mean a general opinion about a general praise of a product. A sample or model of a product is an express warranty. La. Rev. Stat. Ann. §9:2800.53(6).

22. La. Rev. Stat. Ann. §9:2800.58.

23. See, e.g., *Entrevia v. Hood*, 427 So. 2d 1146 (La. 1983).

24. *Wilson v. State Farm Fire & Casualty Ins. Co.*, 654 So. 2d 385 (La. App. 3d Cir. 1995); *writ den.*, 661 So. 2d 476 (La. 1995).

25. *Zachary v. Dow Corning Corp.*, 884 F. Supp. 1061 (M.D. La. 1995).

26. *Jefferson v. Lead Indus. Ass'n Inc.*, 930 F. Supp. 241 (E.D. La. 1996), *aff'd*, 106 F.3d 1245 (5th Cir. 1997).

27. See, e.g., *Bell v. Jet Wheel Blast, Div. of Ervin Indus.*, 462 So. 2d 166 (La. 1985).

28. See, e.g., *Dunne v. Wal-Mart Stores, Inc.*, 679 So. 2d 1034 (La. Ct. App. 1st Cir. 1996).

29. See, e.g., *International Harvester Credit v. Seale*, 518 So. 2d 1039 (La. 1988); *Ricard v. State*, 390 So. 2d 882 (La. 1980).

MAINE

A. CAUSES OF ACTION

Product liability lawsuits include claims based on strict liability, negligence, and breach of warranty.

B. STATUTES OF LIMITATION

Claims based on strict liability, negligence, and breach of warranty where the injury is to the person must be brought within six years.[1] Claims based on breach of warranty where the injury is to property must be brought within four years.[2] There is a two-year statute of limitations for wrongful death actions[3] and lawsuits against ski areas.[4]

With regard to strict liability and negligence claims, the applicable limitations statute does not specify when a cause of action accrues.[5] The Supreme Judicial Court of Maine has ruled that the limitations period "commenc[es] to run against a plaintiff at the time when he ha[s] received a judicially recognizable injury."[6] In a strict liability case in which the injury resulted from inhalation of asbestos dust, the court held that "a judicially recognizable claim does not arise until there has been a manifestation of physical injury to a person, sufficient to cause him actual loss, damage or suffering from a defective, unreasonably dangerous product."[7]

With regard to claims based on breach of warranty, where the injury is to the person, the period begins to run when the injury takes place; where the injury is to property, the period begins to run at the time delivery of goods was tendered.[8]

C. STRICT LIABILITY

1. The Standard

Maine's strict liability statute[9] is based on section 402A of the Restatement (Second) of Torts and has been interpreted as closely resembling a negligence action. In a defective manufacturing/design case, the defect must be *unreasonably* dangerous; in a failure to warn case, the product's danger must be foreseeable based on the *reasonable* foresight of an expert.[10] In both instances, plaintiff must prove that the defendant's conduct proximately caused her injuries.[11]

2. "Defect"

A product can be in a defective condition, unreasonably dangerous to the user or consumer, as a result of: (a) an error in the manufacturing or design process or (b) the failure to warn of a danger associated with a foreseeable use of the product.[12]

3. Contributory Negligence/Assumption of Risk

Assumption of risk is a defense pursuant to Maine's comparative negligence statute.[13] There must be a comparison of a manufacturer's or seller's fault, if any, with a plaintiff's negligence, if any, consisting in voluntary and unreasonably proceeding to encounter a danger known to her. [14]

4. Sale or Lease

Maine's strict liability statute imposes liability on sellers of defective products.[15] The question whether a claim may be brought against a *lessor* of a defective product has not been decided in Maine.

5. Inherently Dangerous Products

A supplier of products will not be held strictly liable simply because the product is inherently dangerous unless plaintiff proves the product was defectively manufactured or designed, or that the manufacturer failed to give adequate warning of the danger, thereby exposing the user to an unreasonable risk of harm.[16] Such proof will involve an examination of the utility of its design, the risks of the design, and the feasibility of safer alternatives.

6. Successor Liability

There are no Maine cases addressing this issue.

7. Privity

Lack of privity is no defense to a claim based on strict liability.[17]

8. Failure to Warn

A product liability action for failure to warn requires a three-part analysis: (1) whether the defendant has a duty to warn the plaintiff; (2) whether the actual warning on the product, if any, was inadequate; and (3) whether the inadequate warning proximately caused the plaintiff's injury.[18]

9. Post-Sale Duty to Warn

Under limited circumstances, a manufacturer may have a post-sale duty to warn; evidence of "recalls" may be admissible.[19] Further, under section 407 of the Maine Rules of Evidence, evidence of any such post-sale warning is admissible against the defendant.[20]

10. Substantial Change/Abnormal Use

A manufacturer is not relieved of strict liability for injuries caused by substantive alterations in its product if the changes were reasonably foreseeable, were a contributing cause of the injury, enhanced the injury, or increased the likelihood of its occurrence.[21]

11. State of the Art

"State of the art" evidence is admissible in the context of a strict liability claim based on a failure to warn.[22]

12. Malfunction

There are no Maine cases specifically addressing this issue.[23]

13. Standards

There are no Maine cases addressing this issue.

14. Other Accidents

Evidence of similar accidents or the absence thereof is admissible on issues of defective conditions, notice, or causation as long as the foundational requirement of substantial similarity of conditions or adequate number of situations is met.[24]

15. Misrepresentation

There are no Maine cases addressing this issue.

D. NEGLIGENCE

Claims based on negligence and strict liability substantially overlap.[25]

Comparative negligence is a defense to product liability claims and precludes recovery when the plaintiff is 50 percent or more at fault.[26]

E. BREACH OF WARRANTY

Maine recognizes the implied warranties of merchantability and fitness for a particular purpose.[27] In order to recover under either of these theories, a product liability plaintiff must establish some defect in the product at the time it was sold.[28] The Maine legislature has removed claims for injuries to the person based on breach of warranty from the UCC four-year limitations provision, placing them under the general six-year provision.[29]

F. PUNITIVE DAMAGES

Punitive damages are recoverable on proof of malice, actual or implied.[30]

G. STATUTES

Relevant statutes regarding product liability actions are the strict liability statute,[31] statutes of limitations,[32] and the UCC sections involving warranties accompanying the sale of goods.[33]

Bernard J. Kubetz
Thad B. Zmistowski
EATON, PEABODY, BRADFORD & VEAGUE
Fleet Center, Exchange Street
P.O. Box 1210
Bangor, Maine 04401
(207) 947-0111

ENDNOTES - MAINE

1. Me. Rev. Stat. Ann. tit. 14, §752; tit. 11, §2-725.

2. Id. tit. 11, §2-725.

3. Id. tit. 18-A, §2-804.

4. Id. tit. 14, §752-B.

5. Id. tit. 14, §752.

6. *Williams v. Ford Motor Co.*, 342 A.2d 712 (Me. 1975).

7. *Bernier v. Raymark Indus., Inc.*, 516 A.2d 534 (Me. 1986).

8. Me. Rev. Stat. Ann. tit. 11, §2-725.

9. Id. tit. 14, §221.

10. Id.; *Bernier,* 516 A.2d 534.

11. *Ames v. Dipietro-Ray Corp.*, 617 A.2d 559 (Me. 1992).

12. Id. See also *Pottle v. Up-Right, Inc.*, 628 A.2d 672 (Me. 1993).

13. Me. Rev. Stat. Ann. tit. 14,§156.

14. *Austin v. Raybestos-Manhattan, Inc.*, 471 A.2d 280 (Me. 1984).

15. Me. Rev. Stat. Ann. tit. 14, §221.

16. *Stanley v. Schiavi Mobile Homes, Inc.*, 462 A.2d 1144 (Me. 1983).

17. Id.

18. *Pottle,* 628 A.2d 672.

19. *Majetta v. International Harvester Co.*, 496 A.2d 286 (Me. 1985).

20. M.R. Evid. 407.

21. *Marois v. Paper Converting Mach. Co.*, 539 A.2d 621 (Me. 1988).

22. *Bernier*, 516 A.2d 534.

23. But see *Pratt v. Freese's Inc.*, 438 A.2d 901 (Me. 1981) (suggesting that evidence establishing product malfunction will be sufficient to survive a directed verdict motion *only* where all reasonable alternative explanations have been disproved). See also *Walker v. General Elec. Co.*, 968 F.2d 116 (1st Cir. 1992).

24. *Stanley*, 462 A.2d 1144; *Simon v. Town of Kennebunkport*, 417 A.2d 982 (Me. 1980).

25. *Marois*, 539 A.2d 621; *Stanley*, 462 A.2d 1144; *Ames*, 617 A.2d 559.

26. Me. Rev. Stat. Ann. tit. 14, §156; *Austin*, 471 A.2d 280.

27. Me. Rev. Stat. Ann. tit. 11, §§2-314, 2-315. See also *Lorfano v. DuraStone Steps, Inc.*, 569 A.2d 195 (Me. 1990); *Porter v. Pfizer Hospital Products Group, Inc.*, 783 F. Supp. 1466 (D. Me. 1992).

28. *Walker*, 968 F.2d 116 (1st Cir. 1992).

29. Me. Rev. Stat. Ann. tit. 11, §2-725.

30. *Tuttle v. Raymond*, 494 A.2d 1353 (Me. 1985).

31. Me. Rev. Stat. Ann. tit. 14, §221.

32. Id. tit. 14, §752; tit. 11, §2-725; tit. 18-A, §2-804; tit. 14, §752-B.

33. Id. tit. 11, §2-314 et seq.

MARYLAND

A. CAUSES OF ACTION

Maryland recognizes causes of action in negligence, breach of warranty, and strict liability.[1] In any of these causes of action, the plaintiff must (1) prove that the product was defective or in a defective condition; (2) attribute that product to a "seller"; and (3) prove that the defect proximately caused plaintiff's injury.[2]

B. STATUTES OF LIMITATION

Maryland has a three year statute of limitations for all negligence actions and tort based claims.[3] Actions founded in strict liability must also be brought within three years of the time the cause of action accrues.[4] Under the Maryland "discovery rule," a cause of action in negligence or strict liability accrues once a plaintiff knows or should know he or she has been wronged.[5] In a product liability action, therefore, the discovery rule mandates that the statute of limitations should not begin to run until the plaintiff knows or, through the exercise of due diligence, should know of the injury, its probable cause, and either manufacturer wrongdoing or product defect.[6] If a product liability case arose in another jurisdiction and is barred by the limitations statute of that state, it is also barred in Maryland, except as to a Maryland resident plaintiff.[7] This exception does not apply to cases arising prior to July 1, 1991, nor to cases involving wrongful death actions.[8]

All actions based on a breach of warranty, whether express or implied, must be commenced within four years from the date of sale of the product, unless reduced by the original agreement of sale.[9] The limitations period may not be reduced to less than one year.[10]

C. STRICT LIABILITY

1. Standard of Strict Liability

Maryland has adopted the standard laid out in section 402A of the Restatement (Second) of Torts.[11] In order to recover under a theory of strict liability, the plaintiff need not prove any specific act of negligence, but must demonstrate that: (1) the product was in a defective condition at the time that it left the possession or control of the seller; (2) it was unreasonably dangerous to the user or consumer; (3) the defect was a cause of the injuries; and (4) the product was expected to and did reach the consumer without substantial change in its condition.[12]

2. "Defect"

A defect may arise from the manufacture or design of any product "which may reasonably be expected to be capable of inflicting substantial harm."[13] In addition, the failure to give adequate warning can constitute a defect for which recovery can be had.[14]

a. Manufacturing Defect

A plaintiff may prove a product has a manufacturing defect simply by showing that the product fails to conform to the manufacturer's specifications.[15] As one court has explained, in a case alleging a manufacturing defect, "the focus is on the conduct of the manufacturer."[16] By contrast, in a design defect case, "the inquiry focuses on the product itself."[17]

b. Design Defect

Although Maryland courts can apply a risk/utility test to determine whether a design defect exists,[18] they have held that the trial court must make a *preliminary determination* as to whether a product involves an "inherently unreasonable risk"[19] — if that is the case, the requirement of demonstrating a defective condition and unreasonable dangerousness are met if the condition causing the injury is not one that would be contemplated by an ordinary consumer. When a product fails to meet the reasonable expectations of the user, "the inference is that there was some sort of a defect, a precise definition of which is unnecessary."[20]

If the court determines that the product does not involve an inherently unreasonable risk, it applies the risk/utility test. Courts have cited to the following factors: (1) the usefulness and desirability of the product; (2) the safety aspects of the product; (3) the availability of a substitute product; (4) the manufacturer's ability to eliminate the unsafe character of the product without impairing its usefulness or making it too expensive to maintain its utility; (5) the user's ability to avoid danger by the exercise of care; (6) the user's anticipated awareness of the dangers inherent in the product and their avoidability, whether based on general knowledge, the obvious condition of the product, or the existence of suitable warnings or instructions; and (7) the feasibility of the manufacturer's spreading the loss by setting the price of the product or carrying liability insurance.[21]

3. Proof of Defect

Proof of a defect "must arise above surmise, conjecture, or speculation," and a plaintiff may not base recovery solely on any presumption that might arise from the happening of an accident.[22] Rather, it is the plaintiff's burden to establish that it is more probable than not that the defect existed at the time of sale.[23]

It is not always necessary for the plaintiff to provide expert testimony to establish a defect. Expert testimony is only required when the subject of the inference is so particularly related to a science or profession that it is beyond the ken of the average layman.[24]

4. Proof of Causation

A cause of action in strict liability requires proof of proximate causation.[25] Maryland law requires that the plaintiff introduce evidence that allows the jury to reasonably conclude that it is more likely than not that the conduct of the defendant was a "substantial factor" in bringing about the result.[26]

5. Defenses

Contributory negligence is not a defense to a strict liability claim.[27] Defenses recognized in Maryland are as follows:

a. Assumption of Risk

Assumption of risk is an affirmative defense. The defendant must show "(1) that the plaintiff knew and appreciated the particular risk or danger created by the defect; (2) that the plaintiff voluntarily encountered the risk while realizing the danger; and (3) that the plaintiff's decision to encounter the known risk was unreasonable."[28]

A recent decision has addressed the problematic area of "voluntariness" as it relates to assumption of risk. Although not specifically addressing the doctrine's applicability to the product liability arena, the court expressly held that conduct is to be regarded as "voluntary" "even though [a plaintiff] is acting under the compulsion of circumstances, not created by the tortious conduct of the defendant, which have left him no reasonable alternative."[29]

b. Misuse

Although not characterized as an affirmative defense in Maryland, misuse of a product can bar recovery where it is either the sole proximate cause of damage, or it is the intervening or superseding cause.[30] In one instance, the court held that the plaintiffs' conduct constituted misuse as a matter of law, when they stored a gasoline can in the basement of their home and allowed unsupervised children access to the can in spite of instructions on the can not to do either.[31] That misuse, according to the court, "negated" the element of defect and required dismissal of the plaintiff's claims.

c. Sophisticated User/Bulk Supplier Defense

This defense has been recognized in Maryland, and focuses upon the conduct of the supplier in light of the circumstances. The circumstances a court should examine include: (1) the feasibility of giving direct warnings to all who are entitled to them and (2) where that is not feasible, examining whether the supplier acted in a manner reasonably calculated to assure either that the necessary information would be passed on to the ultimate handlers of the product or that their safety would otherwise be addressed.[32]

d. State of the Art

Although not strictly speaking a "defense," the defendant may, in a design case, negate plaintiff's proof of the availability of a safer alternative design by showing that the technology did not exist to develop the design at the time of manufacture.[33] It should be noted, however, that in a negligence or strict liability case, the manufacturer of the product is responsible for knowing what was generally known in the scientific or expert community about a product's hazards; state of the art includes all available knowledge at a given time including scientific, medical, engineering, and any other available knowledge.[34]

e. Product Alteration

Alteration of a product after it leaves the manufacturer constitutes a defense to a strict liability claim.[35]

6. Subsequent Remedial Measures

Evidence of subsequent remedial measures is not admissible to prove culpable conduct. It may, however, be admitted for other purposes (consistent with FRE 407) such as proving ownership; control; feasibility of precautionary measures, if controverted; or impeachment.[36]

D. NEGLIGENCE

In addition to pursuing a product liability claim based on strict liability, a product liability plaintiff in Maryland may also pursue a claim grounded upon negligence.[37]

1. Elements

A cause of action in negligence requires evidence of each of the following: (1) a duty owed by the defendant to the plaintiff; (2) a breach of that duty by the defendant; (3) an injury to the plaintiff; and (4) that the injury was proximately caused by the defendant's breach.[38]

2. Theories of Recovery

Actions under theories of negligence in product liability suits may include causes of action for negligent failure to warn of dangerous attributes of the product;[39] negligent failure to provide adequate instructions for safe use of the product;[40] and negligent design or manufacture[41] that results in an unreasonably dangerous product or which enhances injuries.[42]

---

3. **Purely Economic Losses**

There is no recovery under a negligence theory for purely economic losses resulting from a defective product, unless the defect causes a dangerous condition creating risk of death or personal injury.[43] Under Maryland's two-part approach for determining degree of risk required to circumvent the economic loss rule and allow recovery in tort for economic loss suffered when a product fails to meet the contractual expectations of the purchaser, both the nature of the damage threatened and the probability of the damage occurring are examined to determine whether the two, viewed together, exhibit clear, serious, and unreasonable risk of death or personal injury.[44] For example, where the possible injury is extraordinarily severe, such as multiple death, the probability of injury is not required to be as high as if injury threatened were less severe.[45] In the absence of such a dangerous condition, a purchaser is normally limited to contract causes of action, including breach of implied and express warranties.[46]

4. **Defenses**

a. **Contributory Negligence**

In a negligence action, contributory negligence will operate as a complete bar to plaintiff's claim.[47]

b. **Assumption of Risk**

Maryland recognizes assumption of risk as an affirmative defense to a negligence claim.[48]

c. **Product Misuse or Abuse**

Product misuse or abuse is also recognized as a defense to a negligence claim.[49]

d. **Product Alteration**

A material alteration of the product once it has left the hands of the manufacturer is a defense to a negligence claim.[50]

e. **Statutory Compliance**

Compliance with a statute does not necessarily preclude a finding of negligence or product defectiveness when a reasonable person would take precautions beyond the statutorily required measure, but where no special circumstances require extra caution, a court may find that conformity with a statutory standard amounts to due care as a matter of law.[51]

E. BREACH OF WARRANTY

Actions based on a breach of implied or express warranties are found in sections 2-313 through 2-318 of the Commercial Law Article, Annotated

Code of Maryland.[52] They are based primarily on the Uniform Commercial Code.

1. **Breach of Express Warranty**

   An action will arise where goods do not conform to an affirmation of fact or promise made by the seller to the buyer that relates to the goods and becomes a basis of the bargain.[53]

2. **Breach of Implied Warranty of Merchantability**

   An action will arise where it is shown that a product is not fit for the ordinary purposes for which such goods are used.[54]

3. **Breach of Implied Warranty of Fitness for a Particular Purpose**

   An action will arise where the seller at the time of contracting has reason to know of a particular purpose for which the goods are required, the buyer relies upon the seller's skill and judgment to select suitable goods, and the goods ultimately are not suitable for this purpose.[55]

4. **Sale or Lease**

   Actions for breach of implied warranty arise equally from a lease or bailment for hire, and from sale.[56]

5. **Exclusion or Modification of Warranties**

   The right to disclaim or limit warranties on consumer goods has been eliminated in Maryland.[57]

   a. **Express Warranties**

   A manufacturer of consumer goods cannot limit or modify a consumer's remedies for breach of the manufacturer's express warranties unless reasonable and expeditious means of performing the warranty obligations are provided by the manufacturer.[58]

   b. **Implied Warranties**

   The implied warranties of merchantability and fitness for a particular purpose generally cannot be modified by a seller of consumer goods and services.[59]

   i. **Motor Vehicle Exception**

   Implied warranties can be excluded or modified for motor vehicles that are over six years old, and have over 60,000 miles. The exclusion or modification must be conspicuous, in writing, mention "merchantability," and be acknowledged separately in writing by the buyer.[60]

6. Privity

a. Actions Involving Personal Injury

The requirement of privity has been virtually eliminated by statute in actions for damages for personal injury grounded on breach of an express or implied warranty.[61]

b. Actions Not Involving Personal Injury

Privity is required in an action for breach of express warranty or an implied warranty of fitness for a particular purpose in which only economic loss is claimed.[62] By statute, Maryland has abolished the common law requirement of privity for all claims of breach of implied warranty of merchantability.[63]

7. Elements

A plaintiff must show that a warranty existed, that the product did not conform to the warranty, and that the breach of warranty was the proximate cause of the occurrence.[64] In an action based on an implied warranty of fitness for particular purpose, if a special or unusual purpose is intended, it must also be shown that the buyer communicated that purpose to the seller.[65]

8. Defenses

A plaintiff's use or misuse of a product can operate as a defense to a breach of warranty claim.[66] Knowledge by the purchaser of the breach or defect, prior to the injury, will bar recovery.[67] In certain circumstances, the purchaser's use of the product can break the chain of proximate causation, and also bar recovery.[68] Though reluctant to engage in the "semantics" of labeling this conduct, Maryland courts have recognized that such acts can be characterized as either contributory negligence or assumption of risk.[69]

F. DUTY TO WARN

Maryland recognizes actions for failure to warn under negligence and strict liability theories.[70] A failure to warn action arises when a manufacturer or seller either does not supply a warning, or supplies a warning that is inadequate.[71] The manufacturer has a duty to warn of latent dangers inherent in its product for all uses that are reasonably foreseeable.[72]

1. Elements

An action brought in negligence or strict liability for a failure to warn is based primarily on the Restatement (Second) of Torts section 388.[73] The plaintiff must show that the defendant knew or should have known of a defect or defective condition inherent in the product, and that distribution of the product involved unreasonable risk of causing injury or harm.[74] In addition, the plaintiff has the burden of proving any state of the art evidence.[75]

2. Latent/Patent Rule

While the manufacturer has a duty to warn of the latent dangers inherent in the reasonably foreseeable uses of a product, there is no duty to warn of a danger that should be obvious to a user.[76]

3. Learned Intermediary Doctrine

A licensed health care professional stands between a manufacturer or supplier of prescription drugs or medical devices and a patient receiving treatment. Therefore, a manufacturer or supplier meets the duty to warn by adequately warning the health care professional rather than the patient.[77]

4. Post-Sale Duty to Warn

The duty to warn continues after the sale of a product when a latent defect becomes known by the manufacturer or seller shortly after the product is put on the market.[78]

5. Defenses

a. Contributory Negligence and Assumption of the Risk

Contributory negligence and assumption of the risk remain defenses to a failure to warn claim grounded in negligence.[79] However, contributory negligence is not a defense to a strict liability failure to warn claim.[80]

b. Misuse

Misuse of the product is a defense to a failure to warn claim under both negligence and strict liability theories.[81] The same evidence used to support a defense of contributory negligence may be admissible to show product misuse in strict liability cases.[82]

c. Sophisticated User

In Maryland, when a manufacturer sells its product to a "sophisticated user," there is no duty to warn.[83]

G. SEALED CONTAINER

By statute, nonmanufacturer sellers cannot be held liable under any theory for the defective design or manufacture of a product if: (1) the product was acquired and sold in a sealed container; (2) the seller had no knowledge of the defect; (3) in the exercise of reasonable care, the seller could not have discovered the defect; and (4) the seller did not design, manufacture, or alter the product in any way.[84] A seller or nonmanufacturer who is only a conduit ordinarily has no liability unless it had "reason to know" of the defect or danger inherent in the use of the product.[85]

H. DAMAGES

Under Maryland law, "compensatory damages are not to be awarded in negligence or strict liability actions absent evidence that the plaintiff suffered a loss or detriment."[86]

1. Damages Cap

Maryland has imposed a statutory cap on non-economic damages in tort claims involving personal injury, including survival and wrongful death actions.[87] When first enacted in 1986 (and applicable only to causes of action arising on or after July 1, 1986), the cap imposed a limit on recovery of non-economic damages of $350,000. The Maryland Court of Appeals held that the initial cap did not apply to wrongful death actions.[88] The legislature then modified the statute in 1994 to include wrongful death actions and to increase the cap to $500,000 for causes of action arising after October 1, 1994. By further legislation, the cap increases by an additional $15,000 for each year thereafter in which a cause of action arises.[89]

2. Joint and Several Liability

Maryland has adopted in its entirety the Uniform Contribution Among Tortfeasors Act.[90] Under Maryland law, defendants may be held jointly and severally liable, with no apportionment of damages based on degrees of negligence between or among those defendants.[91]

3. Punitive Damages

To be held liable for punitive damages, a defendant must act with "actual malice," which is defined as "evil motive, intent to injure, or fraud" in strict liability cases. The most recent case in this area has evolved a two-part test to determine whether punitive damages should be awarded; the plaintiff must show actual knowledge of the defect, and deliberate disregard of the consequences — both as of the time the product left the defendant's possession or control.[92]

I. EMERGING THEORIES OF LIABILITY

1. Market Share Liability

Maryland courts have not been presented with the theory of market share liability to determine its applicability. Several federal courts, however, have determined that Maryland courts would not recognize this theory, as it represents a "radical departure from the traditional concepts of product liability law."[93]

2. Contributory/Comparative Negligence

Maryland has always adhered to the doctrine of contributory negligence, and the Maryland Court of Appeals has specifically declined to adopt the doctrine of comparative negligence.[94] Although outcry from the plaintiff's bar has threatened this well-established doctrine, as of

---

this writing the Legislature has similarly declined to adopt any form of comparative negligence by statute.

3.   Developments in Asbestos Cases

The most significant development in this area of late is the application of the cap on non-economic damages imposed by the legislature for actions "arising after" July 1, 1986. In one instance, the court held that in a strict liability asbestos case, the cause of action would not arise until a plaintiff suffered "functional impairment."[95] More recently, the Maryland Court of Appeals has held that "functional impairment" in the context of asbestos-related illness did not occur until the plaintiff began experiencing shortness of breath that curtailed his normal activities; because in that instance the functional impairment began in 1990, the Court held that the cap on non-economic damages applied to limit the plaintiff's claim.[96]

In a recent case, the Court of Special Appeals has overturned one of two multimillion dollar awards against Ford Motor Co., which at trial was found responsible for asbestos exposure from brake linings for the first time. The court held that the "evidence simply was too thin" to prove that the plaintiff, a mechanic, regularly and often worked where Ford brake and clutch products were used.[97]

Daniel R. Lanier
MILES & STOCKBRIDGE
10 Light Street
Baltimore, MD 21202-1487
(410) 385-3651

ENDNOTES - MARYLAND

1. *Owens-Illinois v. Zenobia*, 325 Md. 420, 461, 601 A.2d 633, 653 (1992).

2. *Loh v. Safeway Stores, Inc.*, 47 Md. App. 110, 121, 422 A.2d 16, 23 (1980).

3. Md. Code Ann., Cts. and Jud. Proc. §5-101 (1995 Repl. Vol., 1997 Supp.).

4. Md. Code Ann., Cts. and Jud. Proc. §5-101 (1995 Repl. Vol., 1997 Supp.); *Phipps v. General Motors Corp.*, 278 Md. 337, 350, 363 A.2d 955, 962 (1976).

5. *Poffenberger v. Riser*, 290 Md. 631, 634-635, 431 A.2d 677, 679 (1981).

6. *Pennwalt Corp. v. Nasios*, 314 Md. 433, 455-456, 550 A.2d 1155, 1167 (1988); see also *Helinsky v. Appleton Papers*, 952 F. Supp. 266 (D. Md. 1997) (Plaintiff's product liability action against manufacturer of carbonless copy paper (CCP) accrued when physicians first suggested to plaintiff that CCP could be causing some of her symptoms; the mere fact that plaintiff had earlier attempted to determine the genesis of her health problems, and even suspected CCP might be a factor, was not enough to commence the limitations period).

7. Md. Code Ann., Cts. and Jud. Proc. §5-115(b).

8. Id. §5-115(c).

9. Md. Code Ann., Com. Law I §2-725 (1997 Repl. Vol.).

10. Id.

11. *Phipps*, 278 Md. at 353, 363 A.2d at 963.

12. Id. at 344, 363 A.2d at 958; see also *Klein v. Sears Roebuck & Co.*, 92 Md. App. 477, 485, 608 A.2d 1276, 1280 (1992).

13. *Lahocki v. Contee Sand & Gravel Co.*, 41 Md. App. 579, 583, 398 A.2d 490, 493 (1979), *rev'd on other grounds sub nom. General Motors Corp. v. Lahocki*, 286 Md. 714, 410 A.2d 1039 (1980).

14. *Zenobia*, 325 Md. at 437, 601 A.2d at 641; see *infra* Part F.

15. *Singleton v. International Harvester Co.*, 685 F.2d 112, 114-115 (4th Cir. 1981) (citing *Phipps*, 278 Md. at 344, 363 A.2d at 959).

16. *Klein*, 92 Md. App. at 485, 608 A.2d at 1280.

17. Id., 608 A.2d at 1280.

18. *Phipps*, 278 Md. at 344, 363 A.2d at 959; see also *Lundgren v. Ferno-Washington Co.*, 80 Md. App. 522, 527-528, 565 A.2d 335, 338 (1989); *Ziegler v. Kawasaki Heavy Indus., Ltd.*, 74 Md. App. 613, 620-621, 539 A.2d 701, 705 (1988); *Troja v. Black & Decker Mfg. Co.*, 62 Md. App. 101, 107-108, 488 A.2d 516, 519 (1985). At least one court has noted, however, that the risk/utility test has yet to be expressly relied upon by the Maryland Court of Appeals. *Simpson v. Standard Container Co.*, 72 Md. App. 199, 204, 527 A.2d 1337, 1340 (1987).

19. An example of an inherently unreasonable risk is, as explained by the *Phipps* court, that "the steering mechanism of a new automobile should not cause the car to swerve off the road; the drive shaft of a new automobile should not separate from the vehicle when it is driven in a normal manner; the brakes of a new automobile should not suddenly fail; and the accelerator of a new automobile should not stick without warning, causing the vehicle suddenly to accelerate. Conditions like these, even if resulting from the design of the products, are defective and unreasonably dangerous without the necessity of weighing and balancing the various factors involved." *Phipps*, 278 Md. at 345-346, 363 A.2d at 959 (citations omitted).

20. *Virgil v. Kash N' Karry Service Corp.*, 61 Md. App. 23, 31, 484 A.2d 652, 656 (1984).

21. *Phipps*, 278 Md. at 345 n.4, 363 A.2d at 959 n.4; *Troja*, 62 Md. App. at 108, 488 A.2d at 519 (both citing Wade, *On the Nature of Strict Tort Liability for Products*, 44 Miss. L.J. 825, 837-838 (1973)).

22. *Jensen v. American Motors Corp.*, 50 Md. App. 226, 232, 437 A.2d 242, 245 (1981).

23. Id., 437 A.2d at 245.

24. *Virgil*, 61 Md. App. at 31, 484 A.2d at 656 (holding that it is not necessary to provide expert testimony to establish that a thermos bottle that explodes or implodes when liquids are poured into it is defective).

25. *Phipps*, 278 Md. at 344, 363 A.2d at 958; see also *Virgil*, 61 Md. App. at 33, 484 A.2d at 657 (holding that "the effect of lapse of time [between purchase and use that caused injury] is a factor to be considered by the trier of fact in determining the existence of a defect").

26. *Lohrmann v. Pittsburgh Corning Corp.*, 782 F.2d 1156, 1162 (1985) (citing to *Robin Express Transfer, Inc. v. Canton R.R.*, 26 Md. App. 321, 338 A.2d 335 (1975)).

27. *Zenobia*, 325 Md. at 439 n.8, 601 A.2d at 642 n.8; *Ellsworth v. Sherne Lingerie, Inc.*, 303 Md. 581, 597-598, 495 A.2d 348, 356 (1985).

28. *Ellsworth*, 303 Md. at 597-598, 495 A.2d at 356 (quoting *Sheehan v. Anthony Pools*, 50 Md. App. 614, 626 n.11, 440 A.2d 1085, 1092 n.11 (1982), *aff'd*, 295 Md. 285, 455 A.2d 434 (1983)).

29. *ADM Partnership v. Martin*, 1997 Md. LEXIS 563 at *12-13 (1997).

30. Id. at 596-597, 495 A.2d at 355.

31. See *Simpson*, 72 Md. App. at 206, 527 A.2d at 1341.

32. *Kennedy v. Mobay*, 84 Md. App. 397, 413, 579 A.2d 1191, 1199 (1990).

33 *Troja*, 62 Md. App. at 109, 488 A.2d at 519; *Ziegler*, 74 Md. App. at 625, 539 A.2d at 707.

34. *AC and S v. Asner*, 344 Md. 155, 164, 686 A.2d 250, 254 (1996).

35. *Ellsworth*, 303 Md. at 591, 495 A.2d at 353; *Holman v. Mark Indus., Inc.*, 610 F. Supp. 1195, 1201-1202 (D. Md.), *aff'd*, 796 F.2d 473 (4th Cir. 1985).

36. *Troja*, 62 Md. App. at 114, 488 A.2d at 522.

37. See *Banks v. Iron Hustler Corp.*, 59 Md. App. 408, 422, 475 A.2d 1243, 1250 (1984).

38. *Pennwalt Corp.*, 314 Md. at 453, 550 A.2d at 1165.

39. See *Moran v. Faberge, Inc.*, 273 Md. 538, 554, 332 A.2d 11, 21 (1975) (manufacturer may be held liable for injuries sustained when cologne was intentionally applied to lit candle to make it "scented," since manufacturer knew product was highly flammable and placed no warnings whatsoever on the product); see also *U.S. Gypsum Co. v. Mayor and City Council of Baltimore*, 336 Md. 145, 647 A.2d 105 (1994); *Mazda v. Rogowski*, 105 Md. App. 318, 659 A.2d 391, *cert. denied*, 340 Md. 501, 667 A.2d 342 (1995); *American Laundry Mach. Indus. v. Horan*, 45 Md. App. 97, 412 A.2d 407 (1980).

40. See *Moran*, 273 Md. at 554, 332 A.2d at 21.

41. See, e.g., *Frericks v. General Motors Corp.*, 274 Md. 288, 336 A.2d 118 (1975); *Banks*, 59 Md. App. 408, 475 A.2d 1243; *Harley Davidson Motor Co. v. Wisniewski*, 50 Md. App. 339, 437 A.2d 700 (1981); *American Laundry Mach. Indus.*, 45 Md. App. 97, 412 A.2d 407.

42. See, e.g., *Volkswagen of America, Inc. v. Young*, 272 Md. 201, 321 A.2d 737 (1974).

43. *A.J. Decoster Co. v. Westinghouse Elec. Corp.*, 333 Md. 245, 250, 634 A.2d 1330, 1332 (1994).

44. *Morris v. Osmose Wood Preserving*, 340 Md. 519, 667 A.2d 624 (1995) (home-owners failed to establish that defects in plywood used in construction of roofs in their homes had created serious and unreasonable risk of death or personal injury, and were barred from recovery in tort for economic loss rule, where there was no allegation that any injury had ever occurred since roofs were installed or that any roofs had collapsed because of weather conditions or alleged degradation of wood, even though home-owners contended that degradation caused risk of injury to occupants and persons with cause to be on the roof).

45. Id.

46. *U.S Gypsum*, 336 Md. at 156, 647 A.2d at 405; *A.J. Decoster Co.*, 333 Md. at 250, 634 A.2d at 1332.

47. *Moran*, 273 Md. 538, 554, 332 A.2d 11, 21 (1975); *Figgie Intl., Inc., Snorkel Economy Div. v. Tognocchi*, 96 Md. App. 228, 239, 624 A.2d 1285, 1291, *cert. denied*, 332 Md. 381, 631 A.2d 451 (1993).

48. *Ellsworth v. Sherne Lingerie, Inc.*, 303 Md. 581, 597-598, 495 A.2d 348, 356 (1985); *Harris v. Otis Elevator Co.*, 92 Md. App. 49, 52, 606 A.2d 305, 307 (1992).

49. *Harris*, 92 Md. App. at 52, 606 A.2d at 307.

50. *Ellsworth*, 303 Md. at 591, 495 A.2d at 353; *Holman v. Mark Indus., Inc.*, 610 F. Supp. 1195, 1201-1202 (D. Md.), *aff'd*, 796 F.2d 473 (4th Cir. 1985).

51. *Beatty v. Trailmaster Prods., Inc.*, 330 Md. 726, 743-744, 625 A.2d 1005, 1014 (1993).

52. Md. Code Ann., Com. Law I §§2-313 to 2-318 (1997).

53. See §2-313; *Lowe v. Sporicidin Int'l*, 47 F.3d 124, 131 (4th Cir. 1995).

54. See §2-314; *Eaton Corp. v. Wright*, 281 Md. 80, 91, 375 A.2d 1122, 1128 (1977); *Frericks v. GMC*, 274 Md. 288, 299, 336 A.2d 118, 125 (1975).

55. See §2-315; *Lowe*, 47 F.3d at 132; *Bond v. NIBCO, Inc.*, 96 Md. App. 127, 137, 623 A.2d 731, 736 (1993).

56. See §2-314(4); §2-315(2); *Virgil v. "Kash N' Karry" Service Corp.*, 61 Md. App. 23, 29, 484 A.2d 652, 655 (1984); *Certain-Teed Prod. Corp. v. Goslee Roofing & Sheet Metal, Inc.*, 26 Md. App. 452, 460, 339 A.2d 302, 308 (1975). But see *Bona v. Graefe*, 264 Md. 69, 285 A.2d 607 (1972) (reading section 2-313, dealing with express warranties, as applicable to bailments for hire would go beyond the limits of judicial restraint and into the area of judicial legislation).

57. See §2-316.1; *Anthony Pools v. Sheehan*, 295 Md. 285, 289, 455 A.2d 434, 436-437 (1983); *Phipps v. General Motors*, 278 Md. 337, 349, 363 A.2d 955, 961 (1976); *Boatel Industries Inc. v. Hester*, 77 Md. App. 284, 300-301, 550 A.2d 389, 397 (1988).

58. See §2-316.1(3); *Boatel Industries*, 77 Md. App. at 300-301, 550 A.2d at 397 (1988).

59. See §2-316.1; *Anthony Pools*, 295 Md. at 289, 455 A.2d at 436-437 (1983); *Houck v. DeBonis*, 38 Md. App. 85, 97, 379 A.2d 765, 772 (1977).

60. See §2-316.1(2).

61. See §2-318; *Copiers, Typewriters, Calculators, Inc. v. Toshiba Corp.*, 576 F. Supp. 312, 323 (D. Md. 1983).

62. See *Wood Products, Inc. v. CMI Corp.*, 651 F. Supp. 641, 649 (D. Md. 1986); *Copiers, Typewriters, Calculators, Inc.*, 576 F. Supp. at 322.

63. See §2-314(1)(b); *Copiers, Typewriters, Calculators, Inc.*, 576 F. Supp. at 323.

64. See *Bond v. NIBCO, Inc.*, 96 Md. App. 127, 138, 623 A.2d 731, 737; *Mattos Inc. v. Hash*, 279 Md. 371, 379, 368 A.2d 993, 997 (1977); *Fischbach & Moore Int'l v. Crane-Barge R-14*, 632 F.2d 1123, 1125 (4th Cir. 1980).

65. See *Weinberger v. Bristol-Myers Co.*, 652 F. Supp. 187, 190 (D. Md. 1986); *Myers v. Montgomery Ward & Co.*, 253 Md. 282, 295-296, 252 A.2d 855, 863-864 (1969).

66. See *Erdman v. Johnson Brothers Radio and Television Co.*, 260 Md. 190, 197, 271 A.2d 744, 748 (1970).

67. See *Fischbach & Moore Int'l v. Crane-Barge R-14*, 632 F.2d 1123, 1125 (4th Cir. 1980); *Erdman*, 260 Md. at 198, 271 A.2d at 744.

68. See *Higgins v. E.I. Dupont de Nemours & Co.*, 671 F. Supp. 1063, 1066 (D. Md. 1987).

69. See *Mattos*, 279 Md. at 382-383, 368 A.2d at 999 (1977); *Erdman*, 260 Md. at 197, 271 A.2d at 748.

70. See, e.g., *Moran v. Faberge , Inc.*, 273 Md. 538, 332 A.2d 11 (1975); *Liesener v. Weslo, Inc.*, 775 F. Supp. 857 (D. Md. 1991).

71. See, e.g., id.; *Liesener*, 775 F. Supp. 857; *Ellsworth*, 303 Md. 581, 495 A.2d 348; *American Laundry Mach. Indus.*, 45 Md. App. 97, 412 A.2d 407.

72. *Moran*, 273 Md. at 545, 332 A.2d at 15-16; *Ellsworth*, 303 Md. at 598 n.12, 495 A.2d at 356 n.12; *Anchor Packing Co. v. Grimshaw*, 115 Md. App. 134, 191-192, 692 A.2d 5, 34 (1997).

73. *Dechello v. Johnson Enters.*, 74 Md. App. 228, 236, 536 A.2d 1203, 1207 (1988); *Kennedy v. Mobay Corp.*, 84 Md. App. 397, 411, 579 A.2d 1191, 1198 (1990).

74. Id.

75. *Owens-Illinois, Inc. v. Zenobia*, 325 Md. 420, 438 n.8, 601 A.2d 633, 641 n.8 (1992).

76. *Moran*, 273 Md. at 545, 332 A.2d at 15-16; *Volkswagen of America v. Young*, 272 Md. 201, 216, 321 A.2d 737, 745 (1974); *Simpson v. Standard Container Co.*, 72 Md. App. 199, 207, 527 A.2d 1337, 1341 (1987); *Banks v. Iron Hustler Corp.*, 59 Md. App. 408, 423, 475 A.2d 1243, 1250 (1984); *Mazda Motor of America, Inc. v. Rogowski*, 105 Md. App. 318, 325, 659 A.2d 391, 394 (1995).

77. *Lee v. Baxter Healthcare Corp.*, 721 F. Supp. 89, 95 (D. Md. 1989); *Doe v. American Nat'l Red Cross*, 866 F. Supp. 242, 248 (D. Md. 1994).

78. *Zenobia*, 325 Md. at 446, 601 A.2d at 645; *U.S. Gypsum Co. v. Mayor and City Council of Baltimore*, 336 Md. 145, 160, 647 A.2d 405, 412 (1994).

79. See *Ellsworth*, 303 Md. at 597-598, 495 A.2d at 356; see *Simpson*, 72 Md. App. at 205-207, 527 A.2d at 1340-1341.

80. *Zenobia*, 325 Md. at 435 n.7, 601 A.2d at 640 n.7; *Mazda*, 105 Md. App. at 326, 659 A.2d at 395.

81. *Ellsworth*, 303 Md. at 596-598, 495 A.2d at 355-356; *Simpson*, 72 Md. App. at 204-205, 527 A.2d at 1340.

82. *Ellsworth*, 303 Md. at 596-598, 495 A.2d at 355-356.

83. *Higgins v. E.I. DuPont de Nemours & Co.*, Inc., 671 F. Supp. 1055, 1060 (D. Md. 1987); *Eagle-Picher Indus., Inc. v. Balbos*, 326 Md. 179, 218, 604 A.2d 445, 464 (1992); *Kennedy*, 84 Md. App. at 411, 579 A.2d at 1198.

84. Md. Code Ann., Cts. and Jud. Proc. §5-405 (1995 Repl. Vol., 1997 Supp.).

85. *Eagle-Picher Indus.*, 326 Md. at 202-203, 604 A.2d at 456.

86. *Owens-Illinois v. Armstrong*, 87 Md. App. 699, 735, 591 A.2d 544, 561 (1991).

87. See Md. Code Ann., Cts. & Jud. Proc. §11-108 (1986); see also *Edmonds v. Murphy*, 83 Md. App. 133, 573 A.2d 853 (1990), *aff'd*, 325 Md. 342, 601 A.2d 102 (1992) (holding cap on non-economic damages constitutional); *Oaks v. Connors*, 339 Md. 24, 37-38, 660 A.2d 423, 430 (1995) (holding that a single cap applies to both the action of the injured spouse and the joint award for loss of consortium).

88. *United States v. Streidel*, 329 Md. 533, 620 A.2d 905 (1993).

89. Md. Code Ann., Cts. & Jud. Proc. §11-108 (1996).

90. See Md. Code Ann. Art. 50, §§16-24 (1994); *Rivera v. Prince George's County Health Dep't*, 102 Md. App. 456, 649 A.2d 1212 (1994).

91. See *Orient Overseas Line v. Globemaster Baltimore, Inc.*, 33 Md. App. 372, 374, 365 A.2d 325, 330 (1976).

92. *Asner*, 344 Md. at 185, 686 A.2d at 265.

93. *Tidler v. Eli Lilly & Co.*, 95 F.R.D. 332, 334 (D.D.C. 1982); see also *McClelland v. Goodyear Tire & Rubber Co.*, 735 F. Supp. 172, 173 (D. Md. 1990).

94. *Harrison v. Montgomery County Bd. of Educ.*, 295 Md. 442, 463, 456 A.2d 894, 905 (1983).

95. *Owens-Illinois, Inc. v. Armstrong*, 326 Md. 107, 121-122, 604 A.2d 47, 54, *cert. denied*, 113 S. Ct. 204 (1992).

96. *AC and S v. Abate*, January 7, 1998 (Ct. App. No. 1857).

97. *Wood v. Ford Motor Co.*, January 8, 1998 (Ct. Spec. App. No. 280).

MASSACHUSETTS

A. CAUSES OF ACTION

Product liability lawsuits commonly include causes of action for negligence and breach of warranty (express or implied) and claims under the Massachusetts Consumer Protection Act.[1]

Massachusetts does not recognize the common law tort basis of strict liability set forth in Section 402A of the Restatement (Second) of Torts.[2] Instead, the Massachusetts version of the Uniform Commercial Code has been construed to provide a warranty remedy "fully as comprehensive" as the strict liability remedy of Section 402A.[3] This expanded remedy applies only to "tort-based" warranty claims (claims for personal injury or damage to property other than the product itself), and not to "contract-based" warranty claims (claims solely for "economic loss," such as lost profits or the cost of repairs).[4]

B. STATUTES OF LIMITATION AND REPOSE

Negligence actions must be brought within three years "after the cause of action accrues";[5] accrual does not occur, however, until the prospective plaintiff has received "[r]easonable notice" that "a particular product or a particular act of another person may have been a cause of harm to him."[6] Tort-based warranty actions must be brought within three years from the date "the injury and damage occurs,"[7] but a discovery rule similar to that used for negligence applies.[8] Contract-based warranty actions must be brought within four years after the breach occurs, which is generally when tender of delivery is made.[9] Actions under the Consumer Protection Act must be brought within four years.[10]

Massachusetts has no statute of repose for product liability actions. However, some product liability claims may be subject to Massachusetts' six-year statute of repose applicable to tort actions arising out of improvements to real proprty.[11] Also, statutes of repose in other states may, under certain circumstances, be applicable in product liability actions in Massachusetts courts.[12]

C. STRICT LIABILITY: TORT-BASED WARRANTY

1. The Standard

The standard for liability on a "tort-based" warranty claim is the same as the strict liability standard imposed by Section 402A of the Restatement (Second) of Torts. See section A, *supra*. The focus is on "whether the product was defective and unreasonably dangerous," without regard to the seller's exercise of due care.[13]

2. Privity

In tort-based warranty actions a plaintiff may sue in warranty even though he or she did not buy or lease the product from the defendant. No privity is required for liability for breach of warranty, express or implied, if the plaintiff is a person whom the defendant "might reasonably have expected to use, consume or be affected by" the product.[14]

3. Sale or Lease

Because Massachusetts' "strict liability" claims are based on the UCC's provisions with respect to express and implied warranties, the plaintiff's case must be grounded on a sale or lease of new or used goods.[15] Once a transaction of this type has occurred, the nature of the liability and the parties benefited are very similar to those recognized in section 402A of the Restatement.[16]

4. Economic Loss

When economic loss (such as lost profits or the cost of repairs to the product itself) is the only damage claimed, recovery in tort-based strict liability, based on an implied warranty, is not allowed.[17]

5. Definition of "Defect"

A seller or lessor impliedly warrants that its product is "fit for the ordinary purposes for which such goods are used."[18] These purposes include "the uses intended by the manufacturer and those which are reasonably foreseeable."[19] A product that is "unreasonably dangerous" is deemed to be unfit for its ordinary purposes. A product is not unreasonably dangerous "merely because some risk is associated with its use," but only if it is dangerous beyond the expectations of an "ordinary consumer . . . with the ordinary knowledge common to the community."[20] A breach of the implied warranty of merchantability may be established by proof of: (1) manufacturing defect, (2) design defect, or (3) inadequate warning.[21]

In a manufacturing defect case the jury must "compare the propensities of the product as sold with those which the product's designer intended it to have and thereby reach a judgment as to whether the deviation from the design rendered the product unreasonably dangerous and therefore unfit for its ordinary purposes."[22] The defect must be shown to have existed at the time of sale.[23]

In a design defect case, in order to determine whether the design choices of the manufacturer rendered the product unreasonably dangerous and unfit for its ordinary purposes, the jury should weigh the gravity and likelihood of the danger against the feasibility, cost, and adverse consequences of a safer alternative design.[24] In a design defect case premised either on breach of warranty or on negligence, there must be proof of the existence of a safer alternative design that reasonably should have been adopted.[25] The manufacturer need not design against "bizarre, unforeseeable accidents," but "must anticipate the environment in which its product will be used, and . . . design against the reasonably foreseeable risks attending the product's use in that setting."[26]

Failure of a product manufacturer to provide adequate warnings or instructions constitutes a breach of the implied warranty of merchantability.[27] There is, however, no duty to warn of product-connected dangers that are obvious.[28] The Supreme Judicial Court has said, in dictum, that the adequacy of a warning is measured by the warning that would have been given at the time of sale by a hypothetical prudent vendor who was fully aware of all the risks presented by the product. The vendor's actual knowledge of risks, as well as the knowledge it "reasonably should have had," are immaterial; it is "presumed to have been fully informed at the time of sale of all risks."[29] Subsequent decisions have cast doubt on whether this dictum correctly stated Massachusetts law.[30] However, in a more recent dictum the Supreme Judicial Court, seeking to "dissipate any confusion on this matter," stated that "the quoted language does indeed state Massachusetts law accurately, and, we think, clearly."[31]

Similar strict liability actions may be based on breach of the UCC's implied warranty of fitness for a particular purpose or breach of express warranties.[32]

6. **Manufacture to Specifications**

Implied warranties of merchantability and fitness for a particular purpose may be negated where a product has been manufactured in accordance with "detailed, precise and complete" specifications supplied by the buyer. However, the mere specification of a brand or trade name will not negate an implied warranty of merchantability.[33]

7. **Reasonably Foreseeable Use**

In a tort-based warranty action, a plaintiff "must prove that at the time of his injury he was using the product in a manner that the defendant seller, manufacturer, or distributor reasonably could have foreseen."[34]

8. **Alteration of Product**

The Massachusetts implied warranty remedy is "congruent in nearly all respects" with section 402A of the Restatement, which applies only when the product is defective "at the time it leaves the seller's hands."[35] However, a defendant who negligently fails to design against a reasonably foreseeable alteration of the product will also be held strictly liable in warranty for a design defect.[36]

9. Unreasonably Dangerous

In a tort-based warranty action the plaintiff must prove that the product is both defective and unreasonably dangerous.[37] Although useful everyday items such as toothpicks, pins, needles, knives, nails, razor blades, and many types of tools present obvious dangers to users, they are not unreasonably dangerous, in part because of the obviousness of the danger, and do not subject the manufacturer or distributor to strict liability.[38]

10. Causation

The plaintiff is not obligated to prove "but for" causation, nor does he have the burden of identifying the "particular effect" of the defendant's product in a way that distinguishes it from the effects of other products to which the plaintiff was exposed.[39] The defendant's product, although it need not be the only cause, must at least be a "substantial factor," tending along with other factors to produce the injury, as distinguished from a mere "negligible factor."[40]

11. Knowing and Unreasonable Use

"[A] plaintiff's knowing and unreasonable use of a defective product is an affirmative defense to a defendant's breach of warranty, even if the misuse was foreseeable."[41] The conduct of the plaintiff "implies consent to the risk and thus is viewed as the sole proximate cause of the injury." It is an "absolute bar" to recovery that is intended to "balance[] the strict liability placed on the seller."[42] The defendant must show that the plaintiff knew the product was defective, knew that the defect created a danger to the user, and also knew the magnitude of that danger.[43]

12. Sole Proximate Cause

A defendant's demonstration that the "sole proximate cause" of the plaintiff's injury "lies elsewhere" — not with the defendant, but with the plaintiff, other parties, or nonparties — is a complete defense against both tort-based warranty and negligence claims.[44]

13. Superseding Cause

A manufacturer is not liable for a defect in design where the buyer's subsequent modification of the product is found by the jury to be a superseding cause that broke the chain of causation between the design defect and the plaintiff's injury.[45] See section C.7, *supra*. The superseding cause defense also applies where the manufacturer of a prescriptive drug "fulfills its duty to warn the physician but the physician fails to communicate the warning to the patient."[46] In addition, Massachusetts recognizes as an available basis for superseding cause the failure of a third person to prevent the plaintiff's injury where, "because of lapse of time or otherwise," the duty to prevent the injury "is found to have shifted" from the defendant to a third person.[47]

14. Contributory Negligence/Comparative Negligence/Assumption of Risk

The defenses of contributory and comparative negligence are not available in a warranty action.[48] However, a plaintiff's "knowing and unreasonable use of a defective product," which is essentially equivalent to assumption of the risk, is a complete defense to a tort-based warranty claim.[49] See section C.10, *supra*.

15. Delay in Notice of Breach

In tort-based warranty actions, failure of the plaintiff to give the defendant adequate notice of the claimed breach of warranty bars recovery only if the defendant proves that he was "prejudiced thereby,"[50] as by loss of evidence.[51]

16. Warnings to Intermediaries

A manufacturer's warning to an immediate purchaser will not, as a general matter, discharge its duty to give warning of the product's dangers to all persons who foreseeably will come in contact with it. However, a manufacturer may in limited instances be absolved from blame, in warranty as well as in negligence, because of reasonable reliance on an intermediary with "superior knowledge" of the product's dangers, to whom adequate warning has been given.[52]

17. State-of-the-Art Evidence

In a design defect warranty case, "compliance with 'state of the art' safety standards at the time the product was designed or manufactured is usually immaterial."[53] Notwithstanding dictum to the contrary in one Supreme Judicial Court decision,[54] the First Circuit and the Massachusetts Appeals Court have held that under Massachusetts law a state-of-the-art defense is available in failure to warn warranty cases, and therefore state-of-the-art evidence is admissible in support of such a defense.[55]

18. Other Accidents

Evidence of prior accidents is admissible to prove the existence of a defect or causation only if such accidents occurred under "substantially similar" circumstances. Even then, admissibility is subject to the discretion of the trial judge, who must assess the dangers of unfairness, confusion, and undue devotion of time to collateral matters.[56]

19. Successor/Market Share/Enterprise/Concerted Action Liability

Massachusetts does not recognize the "product line" theory of successor liability in a purchase of assets.[57] In a merger context, the surviving corporation is liable where the predecessor would have been liable.[58] A market share claim that fails to ensure "that wrongdoers be held liable only for the harm they have caused" or that "create[s] a substantial possibility that tortfeasors and innocent actors would be impermissibly intermingled" cannot stand.[59] Enterprise liability, under which an entire industry may be held liable for its collective wrongdoing, is "not a viable cause of action" in Massachusetts.[60] In "isolated circumstances" concert of action theories tracking section 876 of the Restatement (Second) of Torts have been recognized, but recovery is not allowed where the plaintiff cannot prove, without speculation, that the defendant's concerted activity was a cause in fact of the result.[61]

20. Disclaimer or Limitation of Warranty

In a breach of warranty action seeking to impose strict liability for personal injury, a disclaimer or limitation of an implied warranty (e.g., by use of "as is") is unenforceable against the injured person. However, an agreement for indemnification or other allocation of risk with respect to claims for personal injury may be enforced as between the manufacturer, seller, or lessor of a product and an "organizational" buyer or lessee (such as an injured person's employer).[62]

D. NEGLIGENCE

Manufacturers, nonmanufacturing sellers, and testers and handlers of products, among others, are subject to a duty of reasonable care. The inquiry focuses not on the product's characteristics, but on the defendant's conduct.[63]

1. The Standard

Liability for negligence may be imposed "when a product's manufacturer or seller has failed to use reasonable care to eliminate foreseeable dangers which might subject a user to an unreasonable risk of injury."[64] The standard is that of "the ordinary, reasonably prudent manufacturer [or seller] in like circumstances,"[65] and therefore evidence of prevailing industry standards at the time of sale is material.[66]

2. Obvious Danger

Where the danger from a product is obvious, no duty to warn is required, because a warning will not reduce the likelihood of injury.[67]

3. Post-Sale Duty to Warn

A manufacturer that learns or should have learned, after the sale, of a risk created by its negligence before the sale has a duty to take reasonable post-sale steps to warn the immediate purchaser. However, Massachusetts courts have not imposed a duty to warn "remote" purchasers of risks discovered, or that have become discoverable, after the product's sale.[68]

4. Relationship to Breach of Warranty

If a defendant in a product liability case is found to have been negligent, it must also be found to have breached its implied warranty of merchantability. A jury's answers to special questions indicating otherwise will be held to be inconsistent as a matter of law. The reverse, however, is not true.[69]

5. Economic Loss

When economic loss (such as lost profits or the cost of repairs) is the only damage claimed, recovery in negligence is not allowed.[70]

6. Enhanced Injury

Where an accident was foreseeable, a defendant manufacturer will be liable for a negligent design that, although not the cause of the accident, foreseeably enhanced the plaintiff's injuries.[71]

7. Contributory Negligence/Comparative Negligence/Assumption of Risk

A plaintiff's negligence will bar recovery if it was greater than the total amount of negligence attributable to the parties against whom recovery is sought. If it was not, the claim is not barred, but each plaintiff's negligence will be compared to the total negligence of the parties against whom recovery is sought, and the plaintiff's damages will be reduced proportionately.[72] The defense of assumption of risk has been abolished in negligence actions by statute.[73]

8. Knowing and Unreasonable Use

In a negligence case, a plaintiff's knowing and unreasonable misuse of a product will not, as in a breach of warranty case, *ipso facto* bar recovery. The comparative negligence statute governs, and the plaintiff's recovery is not barred unless the plaintiff's negligence was greater than the total amount of negligence attributable to the parties against whom recovery is sought.[74] However, in a negligent failure to warn case, a plaintiff's admitted knowledge of the danger that the absent warning would have described does bar recovery, since "the failure to warn was not the proximate cause of the knowledgeable user's injury."[75]

9. Sole Proximate Cause

The rule in a negligence action is the same as in a tort-based warranty action. See section C.11, *supra*.[76]

E. JOINT AND SEVERAL LIABILITY

In both "tort-based" warranty actions and negligence actions, liability is joint and several, subject to a statutory right of contribution.[77] Each tortfeasor is liable for contribution to the extent of its own pro rata share of the entire common liability without regard to its relative degree of fault.[78] Thus, in a two-defendant case, a defendant found 1 percent negligent can be compelled to contribute 50 percent of the judgment amount.

F. PUNITIVE DAMAGES

Punitive damages are not available in Massachusetts unless provided for by statute,[79] as in wrongful death actions where death has been caused by the defendant's wanton or reckless conduct or gross negligence.[80]

G. CONTRACT-BASED WARRANTY

1. Economic Loss

When economic loss (such as lost profits or the cost of repairs) is the only damage claimed, the action is deemed a "contract-based" warranty action, and neither negligence nor strict liability principles apply.[81]

2. Privity/Disclaimer/Notice of Breach

Because section 2-318 of the Massachusetts version of the Uniform Commercial Code is "designed to cover breach of warranty actions that are in essence products liability actions, and is not designed as an alternative for contractually based warranty claims," it would seem that section 2-318's provisions (1) eliminating the requirement of privity, (2) prohibiting disclaimers or limitations of liability, and (3) restricting the defense of lack of notice of breach do not apply in contract-based warranty actions.[82] However, these provisions do apply in the case of *consumer* transactions, even though the only damages claimed are for economic loss.[83]

H. CONSUMER PROTECTION ACT (CHAPTER 93A)

Chapter 93A prohibits "[u]nfair methods of competition and unfair or deceptive acts or practices in the conduct of any trade or commerce."[84] The plaintiff need not be a consumer, nor need plaintiff be in privity with the defendant.[85] In any personal injury product liability action, findings of simple negligence and breach of implied warranty also can constitute, at least in some instances, a violation by the defendant of Chapter 93A, thus necessitating payment of the plaintiff's reasonable attorneys' fees and costs.[86] In contract-based implied warranty actions seeking compensation for economic loss, any breach of an implied warranty automatically constitutes an "unfair act" under Chapter 93A.[87] This rule however, does not apply to commercial claims, as distinguished from claims by consumers.[88] Double and triple damages are available against a party who commits a "willful or knowing" violation of Chapter 93A or refuses to make a good-faith settlement offer in response to a demand by the plaintiff.[89] Although there is no right to a jury trial of Chapter 93A claims,[90] the trial judge may, in his or her discretion, submit such claims to a jury.[91]

John C. Bartenstein
ROPES & GRAY
One International Place
Boston, Massachusetts 02110-2624
(617) 951-7000

ENDNOTES - MASSACHUSETTS

1. Mass. Gen. Laws Ann. ch. 93A (West 1984).

2. *Swartz v. General Motors Corp.*, 375 Mass. 628, 631, 378 N.E.2d 61, 64 (1978). Massachusetts courts have not yet considered the effect of the Restatement (Third) of Torts: Product Liability (Proposed Final Draft, Apr. 1, 1997), which was finally approved by the American Law Institute on May 20, 1997). See *Commonwealth v. Johnson Insulation*, 425 Mass. 650, 654 n.6, 682 N.E.2d 1323, 1327 (1997).

3. *Back v. Wickes Corp.*, 375 Mass. 633, 639, 378 N.E.2d 964, 968 (1978).

4. *Bay State-Spray & Provincetown S.S., Inc. v. Caterpillar Tractor Co.*, 404 Mass. 103, 107, 533 N.E.2d 1350, 1353 (1989).

5. Mass. Gen. Laws Ann. ch. 260, §2A (West 1992).

6. *Bowen v. Eli Lilly & Co.*, 408 Mass. 204, 208, 557 N.E.2d 739, 741 (1990).

7. Mass. Gen. Laws Ann. ch. 106, §2-318 (West 1990); id., ch. 260, §2A (West 1992); *Bay State-Spray*, 404 Mass. at 107, 533 N.E.2d 1350 at 1353 (1989).

8. *Fidler v. E. M. Parker Co., Inc.*, 394 Mass. 534, 545, 476 N.E.2d 595, 602 (1985).

9. Mass. Gen. Laws Ann. ch. 106, §2-725 (West 1990); *Bay State-Spray*, 404 Mass. at 110, 533 N.E.2d at 1355.

10. Mass. Gen. Laws Ann. ch. 260, §5A (West 1992).

11. Mass. Gen. Law Ann. ch. 260, §2B (West 1992); *McDonough v. Marr Scaffolding Co.*, 412 Mass. 636, 591 N.E.2d 1079 (1992) (ice rink bleachers); *Snow v. Harnischfeger Corp.*, 12 F.3d 1154 (1st Cir. 1993) (overhead cranes).

12. Applicability of the out-of-state statute of repose turns on whether Massachusetts or the other state has the "more significant relationship . . . to the parties and the occurrence." *Cosme v. Whitin Machine Works, Inc.*, 417 Mass. 643, 650, 632 N.E.2d 832, 836 (1994).

13. *Commonwealth v. Johnson Insulation*, 425 Mass. 650, 660, 682 N.E.2d 1323, 1330 (1997); *Colter v. Barber-Greene Co.*, 403 Mass. 50, 61-62, 525 N.E.2d 1305, 1313 (1988); *Correia v. Firestone Tire & Rubber Co.*, 388 Mass. 342, 355, 446 N.E.2d 1033, 1040 (1983).

14. Mass. Gen. Laws Ann. ch. 106, §2-318 (West 1990); Mass. Gen. Laws Ann. ch. 106, § 2A-216, 1996 Mass. Legis. Serv. 8 (West); *Cohen v. McDonnell Douglass Corp.*, 389 Mass. 327, 337, 450 N.E.2d 581, 587 (1983) (plaintiff not a person "reasonably . . . expected to use, consume or be affected by" the product); *Roth v. Ray-Stel's Hair Stylists, Inc.*, 18 Mass. App. 975, 470 N.E.2d 137 (1984) (express warranty; personal injuries).

15. As to sales, see Mass. Gen. Laws Ann. ch. 106, §§2-102, 2-106, 2-313, 2-314, 2-318 (West 1990); as to leases, see Mass. Gen. Laws Ann. ch. 106, §§2A-102, 2A-210, 2A-212, 2A-216, 1996 Mass. Legis. Serv. 8 (West); *Mason v. General Motors Corp.*, 397 Mass. 183, 188, 490 N.E.2d 437, 441 (1986); *Fernandes v. Union Bookbinding Co., Inc.*, 400 Mass. 27, 34, 507 N.E.2d 728, 732 (1987).

16. *Mason*, 397 Mass. at 189-190, 490 N.E.2d at 442.

17. *Bay State-Spray*, 404 Mass. at 107, 533 N.E.2d at 1353.

18. Mass. Gen. Laws Ann. ch. 106, §2-314 (West 1990); Mass. Gen. Laws Ann. ch. 106, §2A-212, 1996 Mass. Legis. Serv. 8 (West).

19. *Hayes v. Ariens Co.*, 391 Mass. 407, 412, 462 N.E.2d 273, 277 (1984).

20. *Commonwealth v. Johnson Insulation*, 425 Mass. 650, 660, 682 N.E.2d 1323, 1330 (1997).

21. *Cheshire Medical Center v. W.R. Grace & Co.*, 49 F.3d 26, 32 (1st Cir. 1995).

22. *Back*, 375 Mass. at 641, 378 N.E.2d at 970.

23. *Fernandes*, 400 Mass. at 37, 507 N.E.2d at 734; *Collins v. Sears, Roebuck and Co.*, 31 Mass. App. 961, 583 N.E.2d 873, *rev. denied*, 411 Mass. 1106, 587 N.E.2d 790 (1992).

24. *Back*, 375 Mass. at 642, 378 N.E.2d at 970 (quoting *Barker v. Lull Eng. Co.*, 20 Cal. 3d 413, 431 (1978)).

25. *Kotler v. American Tobacco Co.*, 926 F.2d 1217, 1225 (1st Cir. 1990), *vacated*, 112 S. Ct. 3019, *reaffirmed*, 981 F.2d 7 (1st Cir. 1992).

26. *Back*, 375 Mass. at 640-641, 378 N.E.2d at 970; *Allen v. Chance Mfg. Co., Inc.*, 398 Mass. 32, 34, 494 N.E.2d 1324, 1326 (1986).

27. *Yates v. Norton Co.*, 403 Mass. 70, 74, 525 N.E.2d 1317, 1320 (1988); *Kalivas v. A. J. Felz Co.*, 15 Mass. App. 482, 487, 446 N.E.2d 726, 728-729 (1983).

28. *Colter*, 403 Mass. at 59, 525 N.E.2d at 1312 (1988); *Fiorentino v. A. E. Staley Mfg. Co.*, 11 Mass. App. 428, 434-435, 416 N.E.2d 998, 1004 (1981).

29. *Hayes*, 391 Mass. at 413, 462 N.E.2d at 276.

30. *Bavuso v. Caterpillar Indus., Inc.*, 408 Mass. 694, 699 n.8, 563 N.E.2d 198, 201 (1990) (in failure to warn warranty cases, it is permissible to use "principles concerning the need for warnings that have been articulated in the context of negligence claims"); *Anderson v. Owens-Illinois, Inc.*, 799 F.2d 1, 4 (1st Cir. 1986) (*Hayes* dictum "not the law"); *Welch v. Keene Corp.*, 31 Mass. App. 157, 163, 575 N.E.2d 766, 770 (1991), *rev. denied*, 411 Mass. 1103, 579 N.E.2d 1361 (1992); cf. *Allen*, 398 Mass. 32, 494 N.E.2d 1324 (design defect; necessity of a reasonably foreseeable risk).

31. *Simmons v. Monarch Mach. Tool Co., Inc.*, 413 Mass. 205, 208 n.3, 596 N.E.2d 318, 320 (1992). Cf. *City of Boston v. U.S. Gypsum Co.*, 37 Mass. App. 253, 263, 738 N.E.2d 1387, 1393 (1994) (dictum that "it may well be" that adequacy of a warning depends upon "whether the damages were scientifically discoverable").

32. Mass. Gen. Laws Ann. ch. 106, §2-315 (West 1990); *Fernandes*, 400 Mass. at 34, 507 N.E.2d at 732-733 (1987); *Roth*, 18 Mass. App. at 976, 470 N.E.2d at 138.

33. *Commonwealth v. Johnson Insulation*, 425 Mass. 650, 655-656, 682 N.E.2d 1323, 1327-1328 (1997).

34. *Allen*, 398 Mass. 32, 494 N.E.2d 1324.

35. Restatement (Second) of Torts §402A, comment g; *Back*, 375 Mass. at 640, 378 N.E.2d at 970.

36. *Fahey v. Rockwell Graphic Sys., Inc.*, 20 Mass. App. 642, 652, 482 N.E.2d 519, 525-526 (1985); *Colter*, 403 Mass. at 57, 525 N.E.2d at 1311.

37. *Lubanski v. Coleco Indus., Inc.*, 929 F.2d 42, 48 (1st Cir. 1991).

38. *Killeen v. Harmon Grain Prods., Inc.*, 11 Mass. App. 20, 23, 413 N.E.2d 767, 770 (1980); *Kearney v. Philip Morris, Inc.*, 916 F. Supp. 61, 72-73 (D. Mass. 1996).

39. *O'Connor v. Raymark Indus.*, 401 Mass. 586, 591, 518 N.E.2d 510, 513 (1988).

40. *O'Connor*, 401 Mass. at 592, 518 N.E.2d at 513; *Kearney*, 916 F. Supp. at 64-69 (plaintiff failed to establish that alleged design defect was cause-in-fact of injury).

41. *Colter,* 403 Mass. at 60, 525 N.E.2d at 1312; *Allen v. Chance Mfg. Co.,* 398 Mass. 32, 35, 494 N.E.2d 1324, 1326 (1986); *Correia,* 388 Mass. at 355, 446 N.E.2d at 1040.

42. *Colter,* 403 Mass. at 60, 525 N.E.2d at 1314.

43. *Goulet v. Whitin Mach. Works, Inc.,* 30 Mass. App. 310, 314, 568 N.E.2d 1158, 1161 (1991).

44. *Allen v. Chance Mfg. Co.,* 873 F.2d 465, 467 (1st Cir. 1989); *Correia,* 388 Mass. at 346-352, 446 N.E.2d at 1035-1038. One example: In a failure to warn case (warranty and negligence), where the manufacturer failed to furnish an appropriate warning but the plaintiff was a knowledgeable user who already appreciated the danger the warning would have described, "[t]he failure to warn was not the proximate cause of the knowledgeable user's injury" and recovery was denied. *Lussier v. Louisville Ladder Co.,* 938 F.2d 299, 301-302 (1st Cir. 1991).

45. *Cocco v. Deluxe Sys., Inc.,* 25 Mass. App. 151, 155, 516 N.E.2d 1171, 1173 (1987), *rev. denied,* 401 Mass. 1103, 519 N.E.2d 595 (1988).

46. *Garside v. Osco Drug, Inc.,* 976 F.2d 77, 80 n.3 (1992).

47. Restatement (Second) of Torts §452(2) (1965); *Solimene v. Grauel & Co.,* 399 Mass. 790, 794-795, 507 N.E.2d 662, 665-666 (1987).

48. *Correia,* 388 Mass. at 354-355, 446 N.E.2d at 1039-1040; *Fernandes v. Unicorn Bookbinding Co.,* 400 Mass. 27, 37, 507 N.E.2d 728, 734 (1987).

49. *Colter,* 403 Mass. at 64 n.14; 525 N.E.2d at 1315 n.14.

50. Mass. Gen. Laws Ann. ch. 106, §2-318 (West 1990); id., ch. 106, §2A-216, 1996 Mass. Legis. Serv. 8 (West).

51. *Sacramona v. Bridgestone/Firestone, Inc.,* 106 F.3d 444, 449 (1st Cir. 1997) (claim barred where delayed notice may have "deprived the defense of useful evidence"; "[n]o showing is required that lost evidence would inevitably have altered the outcome"); *Castro v. Stanley Works,* 864 F.2d 961, 964 (1st Cir. 1989).

52. *MacDonald v. Ortho Pharmaceutical Corp.,* 394 Mass. 131, 136-139, 475 N.E.2d 65, 68-70 (1985), *cert. denied,* 474 U.S. 920 (1985); *Barbosa v. Hopper Feeds, Inc.,* 404 Mass. 610, 616, 537 N.E.2d 99, 102-103 (1989); *Slate v. Bethlehem Steel Corp.,* 22 Mass. App. 641, 646, 496 N.E.2d 449, 453 (1986), *rev'd on other grounds,* 400 Mass. 378, 510 N.E.2d 249 (1987); *Garside,* 976 F.2d at 80.

53. *Touch v. Master Unit Die Products, Inc.*, 43 F.3d 754, 757 (1st Cir. 1995).

54. *Hayes*, 391 Mass. at 411, 462 N.E.2d at 276.

55. *Anderson v. Owens-Illinois*, 799 F.2d 1, 4 (1st Cir. 1986); *Welch v. Keene Corp.*, 31 Mass. App. 157, 163-164, 575 N.E.2d 766, 770-771, *rev. denied*, 411 Mass. 1106, 579 N.E.2d 1361 (1991); but see *Simmons v. Monarch Mach. Tool Co. Inc.*, 413 Mass. 205, 208 n.3 596 N.E.2d 318, 320 (1992) (earlier dictum that "the state of the art is irrelevant" in strict liability cases is affirmed as stating Massachusetts law "accurately.") Cf. *City of Boston v. U.S. Gypsum Co.*, 37 Mass. App. 253, 263, 638 N.E.2d 1387, 1393 (1994).

56. *McKinnon v. Skil Corp.*, 638 F.2d 270, 277 (1st Cir. 1981) (applying Massachusetts law).

57. *Dayton v. Peck, Stow & Wilcox*, 739 F.2d 690, 694 (1st Cir. 1984); *Guzman v. MRM/Elgin*, 409 Mass. 563, 567 N.E.2d 929 (1991); *McCarthy v. Litton Indus., Inc.*, 410 Mass. 15, 21, 570 N.E.2d 1008, 1012 (1991) (rule that asset purchaser is not liable for seller's debts and liabilities is subject to four exceptions, not including the product line theory).

58. Mass. Gen. Laws Ann. ch. 156B, §80(b) (West Supp. 1990); *Gurry v. Cumberland Farms, Inc.*, 406 Mass. 615, 620, 550 N.E.2d 127, 130-131 (1990).

59. *Santiago v. Sherwin-Williams Co.*, 3 F.3d 546, 550-551 (1st Cir. 1993); *Payton v. Abbott Labs*, 386 Mass. 540, 571-574, 437 N.E.2d 171, 188-190 (1982).

60. *Santiago v. Sherwin-Williams Co.*, 794 F. Supp. 29, 33 (D. Mass. 1992), *aff'd on other grounds*, 3 F.3d 546 (1st Cir. 1993).

61. *Santiago*, 3 F.3d at 552.

62. Mass. Gen. Laws Ann. ch. 106, §§2-316A, 2A-214A, 1996 Mass. Legis. Serv. 8 (West); *Ferragamo v. Mass. Bay Transp. Auth.*, 395 Mass. 581, 590, 481 N.E.2d 477, 482-483 (1985).

63. *Correia*, 388 Mass. at 355, 446 N.E.2d at 1040; *Colter*, 403 Mass. at 61, 525 N.E.2d at 1313.

64. *Colter*, 403 Mass. at 61, 525 N.E.2d at 1313.

65. *Back*, 375 Mass. at 643, 378 N.E.2d at 971.

66. *Touch*, 43 F.3d at 757.

67. *Colter*, 403 Mass. at 59, 525 N.E.2d at 1312.

68. *Hayes*, 391 Mass. at 411, 462 N.E.2d at 276; *doCanto v. Ametek, Inc.*, 367 Mass. 776, 781, 328 N.E.2d 873, 876 (1975).

69. *Hayes*, 391 Mass. at 410, 462 N.E.2d at 275; *Caccavale v. Raymark Indus., Inc.*, 404 Mass. 93, 97, 533 N.E.2d 1345, 1348 (1989).

70. *Bay State-Spray*, 404 Mass. at 107, 533 N.E.2d at 1353.

71. *Smith v. Ariens Co.*, 375 Mass. 620, 623, 377 N.E.2d 954, 957 (1978).

72. *Colter*, 403 Mass. at 62, 525 N.E.2d at 1313-1314; Mass. Gen. Laws Ann. ch. 231, §85 (West 1985).

73. Id.

74. *Colter*, 403 Mass. at 63, 525 N.E.2d at 1314; *Yates v. Norton Co.*, 403 Mass. 70, 77, 525 N.E.2d 1317, 1321 (1988); Mass. Gen. Laws Ann. ch. 231, §85 (West 1985).

75. *Lussier v. Louisville Ladder Co.*, 938 F.2d 299, 301 (1st Cir. 1991); *Colter*, 403 Mass. at 59, 525 N.E.2d at 1312.

76. *Allen*, 873 F.2d at 471; *Colter*, 403 Mass. at 59, 525 N.E.2d at 1312 (negligent failure to warn; no proximate cause); *Lussier*, 938 F.2d at 301 (negligent failure to warn; no proximate cause).

77. *Wolfe v. Ford Motor Co.*, 386 Mass. 95, 98, 434 N.E.2d 1008, 1011 (1982); Mass. Gen. Laws Ann. ch. 231B, §§1-4 (West 1984).

78. Mass. Gen. Laws Ann. ch. 231B, §§1-2 (West 1984).

79. *Santana v. Registrars of Voters of Worcester*, 398 Mass. 862, 867, 502 N.E.2d 132, 135 (1966).

80. Mass. Gen. Laws Ann. ch. 229, §2 (West 1985).

81. *Bay State-Spray*, 404 Mass. 103, 533 N.E.2d 1350 (1989).

82. *Bay State-Spray*, 404 Mass. at 110, 533 N.E.2d at 1355 (quoting and expressly affirming language from *Wilson v. Hammer Holdings, Inc.*, 850 F.2d 3, 7-8 (1st Cir. 1988)); J. C. Bartenstein, *Recent Developments in Commercial Warranty Law: Bay State and Canal Electric*, 35 Boston Bar J. (No. 3) 4 (May/June 1991). However, the decisions to date reflect the confusion created by flaws in the drafting of §2-318. Compare *Delano Growers' Coop. Winery v. Supreme Wine Co.*, 393 Mass. 666, 674-675, 473 N.E.2d 1066, 1072 (1985) (commercial warranty claim for economic loss: court uses notice

provisions of §2-607 without mentioning the relaxed notice requirements of §2-318) with *Cameo Curtains, Inc. v. Philip Carey Corp.*, 11 Mass. App. 423, 416 N.E.2d 995 (1981) (commercial warranty claim for economic loss: court uses relaxed notice provisions of §2-318, not those of §2-607, and also holds that the privity requirement is eliminated by §2-318).

83. *Jacobs v. Yamaha Motor Corp., U.S.A.*, 420 Mass. 323, 330, 649 N.E.2d 758, 763, (1995); Mass. Gen. Laws Ann. ch. 106, §§2-316A, 2A-214A, 1996 Mass. Legis. Serv. 8 (West).

84. Mass. Gen. Laws Ann. ch. 93A, §2 (West Supp. 1990).

85. *Maillet v. ATF-Davidson Co., Inc.*, 407 Mass. 185, 191, 552 N.E.2d 95, 98 (1990).

86. *Maillet*, 407 Mass. at 194, 552 N.E.2d at 98-99.

87. *Burnham v. Mark IV Homes, Inc.*, 387 Mass. 575, 581, 441 N.E.2d 1027, 1031 (1982) (consumer case; Attorney General's regulation provides that failure to fulfill "any promises or obligations arising under a warranty" shall be "an unfair and deceptive act or practice"); *Linthicum v. Archambault*, 379 Mass. 381, 387-388, 398 N.E.2d 482, 487 (1979) (commercial case); *Lynn v. Nashawaty*, 12 Mass. App. Ct. 310, 312, 423 N.E.2d 1052, 1053 (1981) (commercial case); *Hannon v. Original Gunite Aquatech Pools, Inc.*, 385 Mass. 813, 821, 434 N.E.2d 611, 616 (1982) (consumer case).

88. *Knapp Shoes, Inc. v. Sylvania Shoe Mfg. Corp.*, 418 Mass. 737, 745, 640 N.E.2d 1101, 1105 (1994).

89. Mass. Gen. Laws Ann. ch. 93A, §9(3) (West Supp. 1990).

90. *Nei v. Burley*, 388 Mass. 307, 318, 446 N.E.2d 674, 680 (1983).

91. *Service Pubs., Inc. v. Goverman*, 396 Mass. 567, 577-578, 487 N.E.2d 520, 527 (1986).

MICHIGAN

A. CAUSES OF ACTION

Product liability lawsuits commonly include causes of action for negligence[1] and breach of implied warranty.[2] There is no separate cause of action for strict liability;[3] however, the requisite elements for a cause of action based on strict liability in tort are essentially the same as those for breach of implied warranty.[4]

B. STATUTES OF LIMITATION

The period of limitations is three years for a product liability action.[5] In a wrongful death action, the statute of limitations may be extended by up to an additional three years.[6] Under appropriate circumstances Michigan applies a discovery rule to determine when a claim accrues and the statute of limitations begins to run.[7]

C. NEGLIGENCE

1. The Standard

The plaintiff in an action based on a negligence theory must make out a prima facie case establishing that the manufacturer breached its duty to use reasonable or ordinary care under the circumstances in planning or designing the product so that it is reasonably safe for the purposes for which it is intended.[8] The "unreasonably dangerous" standard is generally applied in product liability actions premised on negligence principles.[9] Thus, a product is deemed defective if the risk of injury or harm is unreasonable in the light of foreseeable risk of injury.[10]

2. Comparative Negligence and Assumption of Risk

In a product liability action brought to recover damages, the damages sustained by the plaintiff must be diminished in proportion to the amount of negligence attributed to him or her. Assumption of the risk is not a defense to a product liability action.[11] Several cases have examined the issue of children's usage of adult products, as well.[12]

D. BREACH OF IMPLIED WARRANTY

1. The Standard

A cause of action for breach of implied warranty in a product liability case is established on proof of injury caused by a defect in the product, attributable to the manufacturer, that made it not reasonably fit for its intended, anticipated, or reasonably foreseeable use, including reasonably foreseeable misuse.[13] It is not necessary to show negligence on the part of a manufacturer.[14]

2. "Defect"

In actions grounded on a breach of implied warranty, a product is deemed defective if it is "not reasonably fit" for its intended, anticipated, or reasonably foreseeable use, including reasonably foreseeable misuse.[15]

3. Comparative Negligence

Comparative negligence applies where plaintiff is injured as a result of a breach of implied warranty. Plaintiff's recovery is reduced to the extent of plaintiff's own negligence, and plaintiff is not entitled to recover the full amount of damages if he or she was also negligent.[16]

E. ACTIONS AGAINST EMPLOYERS

Michigan's Worker's Disability Compensation Act[17] protects employers from negligence claims by an injured employee[18] and from contribution claims grounded in negligence.[19] However, fault can now be "allocated" to employers by product liability defendants under recent tort reform legislation (discussed below). Employee actions for intentional torts against employers, however, are not barred. Michigan has statutorily adopted a certainty test[20] for these actions.[21]

F. SUCCESSOR LIABILITY

As a general rule, a purchaser of all or substantially all of the assets of another corporation is not liable for injuries caused by products manufactured by the predecessor corporation before the sale so long as the successor corporation did not participate in the manufacture, sale, or installation of the product or assume liability either by contract or by law.[22] However, a successor corporation may be liable for a predecessor's injury-causing product where the totality of the acquisition demonstrates a basic continuity of enterprise between the seller and buyer.[23]

G. PRIVITY

No privity is required; a plaintiff may sue even though he or she did not buy the product from the manufacturer.[24]

H. FAILURE TO WARN

If a manufacturer or distributor of a product knows or ought to know of a danger inherent in the product or in the use for which the product is intended, it has a duty to give adequate warnings.[25] Whether a duty to warn exists depends on whether the consumer's use of the product and the injury sustained was foreseeable, not whether the use was intended.[26] The duty to warn has been relaxed for simple products where the danger is open and obvious to all.[27] The manufacturer of such a simple product (one whose essential characteristics are fully apparent) has no duty to warn of the product's potentially dangerous conditions or characteristics that are readily apparent or visible on casual inspection and reasonably expected to be recognized by the average user of ordinary intelligence.[28] The duty may also be relaxed where the product has been sold to a sophisticated user[29] or where the providing of an additional warning would have been futile.[30]

I. DEFECTIVE DESIGN

The focus of a design defect case is usually on the quality of the manufacturer's decisions: did the manufacturer properly weigh alternatives and evaluate trade-offs and thereby develop a reasonably safe product?[31] Michigan has specifically rejected the apparent manufacturer theory of liability, which would have held retailers liable for design defects where the retailer's only conduct was the relabeling of the product with its identity.[32] In Michigan, there is no continuing duty for a manufacturer to repair or recall a product to bring it up to the current state of the art for safety features.[33]

J. SUBSTANTIAL CHANGE/ABNORMAL USE

A plaintiff may not recover if the proximate cause of his or her injury is found to have stemmed from his or her own conduct, such as misuse of a product, and not from a product's lack of fitness.[34] However, the substantial change or misuse must be one that could not have been reasonably foreseen or anticipated.[35]

K. REMEDIAL CHANGES IN PRODUCT

Evidence of any subsequent change with regard to the product is not admissible in a product liability action to prove liability, but it is admissible when offered for another purpose, such as proving ownership, control or feasibility of precautionary measures, if controverted, or impeachment.[36]

L. MALFUNCTION

A demonstrable malfunction of a product may create an inference that the defect is attributable to the manufacturer where failure is caused by a defect in a relatively inaccessible part integral to the structure of the product and not generally required to be repaired, replaced, or maintained.[37]

M. STANDARDS

Evidence that a product complied with governmental and industrial standards is admissible, but compliance is not conclusive as to whether the defendant was negligent or the product was defective.[38]

N. OTHER ACCIDENTS

Evidence of other accidents is inadmissible unless plaintiff proves that the product is the same and there is substantial factual similarity in time, place, and circumstances.[39] Under these circumstances, such evidence is admissible on the issue of the manufacturer's knowledge and/or notice regarding same.[40] The absence of prior accidents is admissible to show lack of knowledge or notice where these issues have been presented in the plaintiff's case.[41]

O. PUNITIVE DAMAGES

Punitive damages are not recoverable in a product liability action. Exemplary damages may be awarded for mental suffering consisting of a sense of insult, indignity, humiliation, or injury to feelings.[42]

P. ECONOMIC LOSS DOCTRINE

Michigan has adopted the economic loss doctrine where the dispute is between commercial parties where the only damages alleged are economic, that is, lost profits or anticipated commercial benefits. The doctrine, as set forth by the Michigan Supreme Court, bars tort claims and provides that the UCC is the exclusive remedy in cases involving economic loss arising from the purchase of goods.[43]

Q. INTEREST

Michigan allows pre-judgment interest beginning from the date of filing of the complaint and post-judgment interest until the date of satisfaction, at varying rates.[44]

R. STATUTES

Relevant statutes for product liability actions are the statutes of limitation for product liability actions,[45] the UCC section for breach of warranty,[46] and the statute governing product liability actions in general.[47]

S. TORT REFORM

Michigan's tort reform provisions have been in effect for slightly over two years. No reported appellate decisions have yet substantially addressed any portion of the act.[48] Nonetheless, the following are among the more significant changes tort reform brought about:

- Venue that previously had been established "where all or part of the cause of action arose," recast as arising where "the original injury occurred."[49]
- Joint and several liability, which allowed an unfair shifting of responsibility for uncollectible defendants, was replaced by "several only and not joint" liability.[50] An exception does still exist for injuries that include medical malpractice or criminal conduct involving gross negligence or the use of drugs or alcohol.[51]
- Fault can be allocated to nonparties (including an employer protected by the Worker's Disability Compensation Act).[52]
- Pure comparative negligence was replaced by modified comparative negligence where a plaintiff more than 50 percent liable will have economic damages reduced by that percentage and noneconomic damages shall not be awarded.[53]

- An absolute defense exists where the Plaintiff was impaired due to alcohol or controlled substances and, as a result of that impairment, the Plaintiff was 50 percent or more at fault.[54]
- Non-economic damages are capped at $280,000 for less severe injuries and $500,000 for injuries where death or permanent loss of a vital bodily function occurred.[55]
- Manufacturers are not liable for alteration or misuse unless it was reasonably foreseeable.[56]
- The duty to warn is relaxed for sophisticated users or where such risks should be apparent to a reasonably prudent user.[57]
- Sellers are relieved of liability unless they have failed to exercise reasonable care or breach an express warranty.[58]
- There is rebuttable presumption of nonliability for compliance with governmental standards, with no inverse presumption for failure to comply.[59]
- Michigan codified Daubert v. Merrill Dow, 509 U.S. 579, 113 S. Ct. 2786 (1993), 125 L. Ed. 2d and the court's "gatekeeper" responsibility for expert witness testimony.[60]

Xhafer Orhan
Edward M. Kronk
Daniel P. Malone
Lynn A. Sheehy
Phillip C. Korovesis
BUTZEL LONG
150 West Jefferson, Suite 900
Detroit, Michigan 48226-4430
(313) 225-7000

1. *Moning v. Alfono*, 400 Mich. 425, 254 N.W.2d 759 (1977); *Prentis v. Yale Mfg. Co.*, 421 Mich. 670, 365 N.W.2d 176 (1984); *Shipman v. Fontaine Truck Equip. Co.*, 184 Mich. App. 706, 459 N.W.2d 30 (1990).

2. *Lemire v. Garrard Drugs*, 95 Mich. App. 520, 291 N.W.2d 103 (1980); *Holdsworth v. Nash Mfg., Inc.*, 161 Mich. App. 139, 409 N.W.2d 764 (1987), *lv. denied*, 429 Mich. 872 (1988).

3. *Pelc v. Bendix Mach. Tool Corp.*, 111 Mich. App. 343, 314 N.W.2d 614 (1981); *Dooms v. Stewart Bolling & Co.*, 68 Mich. App. 5, 241 N.W.2d 738 (1976); see also *Parr v. Central Soya Co. Inc.*, 732 F. Supp. 738 (E.D. Mich. 1990).

4. *Trotter v. Hamill Mfg. Co.*, 143 Mich. App. 593, 372 N.W.2d 622 (1985) *lv. denied*, 424 Mich. 882 (1986); *Owens v. Allis-Chalmers Corp.*, 83 Mich. App. 74, 268 N.W.2d 291 (1978), *aff'd*, 414 Mich. 413, 326 N.W.2d 372 (1982).

5. Mich. Comp. Laws §600.5805(9); Mich. Stat. Ann. §27A.5805(9).

6. Mich. Comp. Laws §600.5852; Mich. Stat. Ann. §27A.5852; *Hardy v. Maxheimer*, 429 Mich. 422, 416 N.W.2d 299 (1987).

7. *Larson v. Johns-Manville Sales Corp.*, 427 Mich. 301, 399 N.W.2d 1 (1986) (asbestos); *Moll v. Abbott*, 192 Mich. App. 724, 482 N.W.2d 197 (1992) (DES), *rev'd*, 444 Mich. 1, 506 N.W.2d 816 (1993).

8. *Bullock v. Gulf & Western Mfg.*, 128 Mich. App. 316, 340 N.W.2d 294 (1983); *Shipman*, 184 Mich. App. 706.

9. *Huff v. Ford Motor Co.*, 127 Mich. App. 287, 338 N.W.2d 387 (1983).

10. *Owens v. Allis-Chalmers Corp.*, 414 Mich. 413, 326 N.W.2d 372 (1982).

11. Mich. Comp. Laws §600.2949; Mich. Stat. Ann. §27A.2949; *Ferdig v. Melitta, Inc.*, 115 Mich. App. 340, 320 N.W.2d 369 (1982).

12. *Kirk v. Hanes Corp.*, 16 F.2d 705 (1994); *Moning*, 400 Mich. 425.

13. *Vincent v. Allen Bradley Co.*, 95 Mich. App. 426, 291 N.W.2d 66 (1980); *Glavin v. Baker Material Handling Corp.*, 132 Mich. App. 318, 347 N.W.2d 222 (1984), *on remand*, 144 Mich. App. 147, 373 N.W.2d 272 (1985).

14. *Manzoni v. Detroit Coca-Cola Bottling Co.*, 363 Mich. 235, 109 N.W.2d 918 (1961); *Smith v. E. R. Squibb & Sons, Inc.*, 69 Mich. App. 375, 381, 245 N.W.2d 52,55 (1976), aff'd, 405 Mich. 79, 273 N.W.2d 476 (1979).

15. *Hartford Fire Ins. Co. v. Walter Kidde & Co., Inc.*, 120 Mich. App. 283, 328 N.W.2d 29 (1982); *Villar v. E. W. Bliss Co.*, 134 Mich. App. 116, 350 N.W.2d 920 (1984), *lv. denied*, 422 Mich. 871, 365 N.W.2d 758 (1985).

16. Mich. Comp. Laws §600.2949; Mich. Stat. Ann. §27A.2949; *Young v. E. W. Bliss Co.*, 130 Mich. App. 363, 343 N.W.2d 553 (1983).

17. Mich. Comp. Laws §418.101 et seq.; Mich. Stat. Ann. §17.237(101) et seq.

18. Mich. Comp. Laws §418.131; Mich. Stat. Ann. §17.237(131).

19. *Husted v. Consumer Power*, 376 Mich. 41, 135 N.W.2d 370 (1965).

20. Mich. Comp. Laws §18.131(1) (as amended 5/14/87); Mich. Stat. Ann. §17.237(131)(1).

21. *Schefsky v. Evening News Assn.*, 169 Mich. App. 223, 425 N.W.2d 768 (1988); *McNees v. Cedar Springs Stamping Co.*, 184 Mich. App. 101, 457 N.W.2d 68 (1990), *lv. denied*, 437 Mich. 922, 469 N.W.2d 283 (1991); *Smith v. General Motors Corp.*, 192 Mich. App. 652, 481 N.W.2d 819 (1992); *Adams v. Shepherd Prods., U.S., Inc.*, 187 Mich. App. 695, 468 N.W.2d 332 (1991) *lv. denied*, 439 Mich. 914, 479 N.W.2d 634 (1993).

22. *Denolf v. Frank L. Jursik Co.*, 54 Mich. App. 584, 221 N.W.2d 458 (1974), *modified*, 395 Mich. 661, 238 N.W.2d 1 (1976).

23. *Langley v. Harris Corp.*, 413 Mich. 592, 321 N.W.2d 662 (1982); *Fenton Area Pub. Schools v. Sorenson-Gross Constr. Co.*, 124 Mich. App. 631, 335 N.W.2d 221 (1983).

24. *Gimino v. Sears, Roebuck & Co.*, 308 Mich. 666, 14 N.W.2d 536 (1944); *Gauthier v. Mayo*, 77 Mich. App. 513, 258 N.W.2d 748 (1977).

25. *Durkee v. Cooper of Canada, Ltd.*, 99 Mich. App. 693, 298 N.W.2d 620 (1980).

26. *Gutowski v. M&R Plastics & Coating, Inc.*, 60 Mich. App. 499, 231 N.W.2d 456 (1975); *Ferlito v. Johnson & Johnson Prods., Inc.*, 771 F. Supp. 196 (E.D. Mich. 1991), *aff'd*, 983 F.2d 1066 (6th Cir. 1992).

27. *Wiegernik v. Mitts and Merrill*, 182 Mich. App. 546, 452 N.W.2d 872 (1990), *lv. denied*, 437 Mich. 884 (1990) (woodchipper); *Raines v. Colt Indus.*, 757 F.

Supp. 819 (E.D. Mich. 1991) (guns and simple tools); *Kirk*, 16 F.3d 705 (cigarette lighter).

28. *Glittenburg v. Doughboy*, (on reh'g) 441 Mich. 379, 491 N.W.2d 208 (1992) (pool).

29. *Antcliff v. State Employees Credit Union*, 414 Mich. 624, 638, 327 N.W.2d 814 (1982), *reh'g denied*, 417 Mich. 1103 (1983); *Tasca v. GTE Prods. Corp.*, 175 Mich. App. 617, 438 N.W.2d 625 (1988); *Kudiza v. Carboloy Div. of Gen. Elec. Co.*, 190 Mich. App. 285, 475 N.W.2d 371 (1991), *lv. app. denied*, 439 Mich. 918, 479 N.W.2d 679 (1992) (cobalt to large scale manufacturer); *Nichols v. Clare Community Hosp.*, 190 Mich. App. 679, 476 N.W.2d 493 (1991) (pharmaceuticals to hospital); *Jodway v. Kennametal*, 1994 Mich. App. LEXIS 480, 1994 WL 687220 (Mich. App. Dec. 2, 1994).

30. *Spencer v. Ford Motor Co.*, 141 Mich. App. 356, 367 N.W.2d 393 (1985).

31. *Prentis*, 421 Mich. 670; *Hindelang v. R.D. Werner Co., Inc.*, 188 Mich. App. 122, 469 N.W.2d 2 (1991).

32. *Seasword v. Hilti*, 444 Mich. 938, 514 N.W.2d 762 (1994), *on remand*, 1994 Mich. App. LEXIS 453, 1994 WL 687238 (Mich. App. Nov. 22, 1994).

33. *Gregory v. Cincinnati, Inc.*, 450 Mich. 1, 538 N.W.2d 325 (1995).

34. *Wells v. Coulter Sales, Inc.*, 105 Mich. App. 107, 306 N.W.2d 411 (1981); *Trotter*, 143 Mich. App. 593; *Wiegernik*, 182 Mich. App. 546.

35. *Snider v. Bob Thibodeau Ford, Inc.*, 42 Mich. App. 708, 202 N.W.2d 727 (1972), *lv. denied*, 388 Mich. 812 (1972); *Shipman*, 184 Mich. App. 706.

36. Mich. Comp. Laws §600.2946(3); Mich. Stat. Ann. §27A.2946(3); *Smith v. E.R. Squibb & Sons, Inc.*, 405 Mich. 79, 273 N.W.2d 476 (1979); *Downie v. Kent Prods.*, 420 Mich. 197, 362 N.W.2d 605, *modified*, 421 Mich. 1202, 367 N.W.2d 831 (1984); Mich. Rule Evid. 407.

37. *Holloway v. General Motors Corp.*, 403 Mich. 614, 271 N.W.2d 777 (1978); *Chambers v. General Motors Corp.*, 123 Mich. App. 619, 333 N.W.2d 9 (1982).

38. Mich. Comp. Laws §600.2946(1); Mich. Stat. Ann. §27A.2946(1); *Granger v. Freuhauf Corp.*, 147 Mich. App. 190, 383 N.W.2d 162 (1985), *rev'd on other grounds*, 429 Mich. 1, 412 N.W.2d 199 (1987).

39. *Holbrook v. Koehring Co.*, 75 Mich. App. 592, 255 N.W.2d 698 (1977); see also *Anderson v. Whittaker Corp.*, 894 F.2d 804 (6th Cir. 1990); *Lohr v. Stanley-Bostitch, Inc.*, 812 F. Supp. 752, 135 F.R.D. 162 (W.D. Mich. 1991).

40. *Muilenberg v. Upjohn Co.*, 115 Mich. App. 316, 320 N.W.2d 358 (1982); *Dowood Co. v. Michigan Tool Co.*, 14 Mich. App. 158, 165 N.W.2d 450 (1968).

41. *Belfry v. Anthony Pools*, 80 Mich. App. 118, 262 N.W.2d 909 (1977).

42. *Wise v. Daniel*, 221 Mich. 229, 190 N.W. 746 (1922); *Smith v. Jones*, 382 Mich. 176, 169 N.W.2d 308 (1969); see also *Law Offices of Lawrence J. Stockler, P.C. v. Rose*, 174 Mich. App. 14, 436 N.W.2d 70 (1989), *lv. denied*, 434 Mich. 862 (1990).

43. *Neibarger v. Universal Coops., Inc.*, 439 Mich. 512, 486 N.W.2d 612 (1992).

44. Mich. Comp. Laws §600.6013(6); Mich. Stat. Ann. §27A.6013(6); *Ballog v. Knight Newspapers, Inc.*, 381 Mich. 527, 164 N.W.2d 19 (1968); *Department of the Treasury v. Central Wayne County Sanitation Auth.*, 186 Mich. App. 58, 463 N.W.2d 120 (1990).

45. Mich. Comp. Laws §600.5805(9); Mich. Stat. Ann. §27A.5805(9).

46. Mich. Comp. Laws §440.2314; Mich. Stat. Ann. §19.2314.

47. Mich. Comp. Laws §600.2945 et seq.; Mich. Stat. Ann. §27A.2945 et seq.

48. Michigan Senate Bill 344, Public Act 249 of 1995 and Public Act 161.

49. Mich. Comp. Laws §600.1629; Mich. Stat. Ann. §27A.1629; See also *Gross v. General Motors Corp.*, 448 Mich. 147, 528 N.W.2d 707 (1995).

50. Mich. Comp. Laws §600.6304(4); Mich. Stat. Ann. §27A.6304.

51. Mich. Comp. Laws §600.6312; Mich. Stat. Ann. §27A.6312.

52. Mich. Comp. Laws §§600.2957, 600.6304; Mich. Stat. Ann. §§27A.2957, 27A.6304.

53. Mich. Comp. Laws §600.2959; Mich. Stat. Ann. §27A.2959.

54. Mich. Comp. Laws §600.2955(a); Mich. Stat. Ann. §27A.2955(a).

55. Mich. Comp. Laws §§600.2946a; 600.2949a; Mich. Stat. Ann. §§27A.2946a, 27A.2949a (exceptions exist for gross negligence or actual knowledge of defect substantially likely to injure).

56. Mich. Comp. Laws §600.2947; Mich. Stat. Ann. §27A.2947 (the issue of foreseeability is legal question for court).

57. Mich. Comp. Laws §§600.2947(4); 600.2948(2); Mich. Stat. Ann. §§27A.2947(4), 27A.2948(2).

58. Mich. Comp. Laws §600.2947(6); Mich. Stat. Ann. §27A.2947(6).

59. Mich. Comp. Laws §600.2946(4); Mich. Stat. Ann. §27A.2946(4).

60. Mich. Comp. Laws §600.2955; Mich. Stat. Ann. §27A.2955.

MINNESOTA

A. CAUSES OF ACTION

Minnesota recognizes strict liability, negligence, and breach of warranty as theories of recovery in a product liability action.[1] In cases in which a design defect is alleged, the plaintiff must elect either a strict liability or a negligence theory, but not both.[2] Breach of implied warranty includes merchantability and fitness for a particular purpose.[3]

B. STATUTES OF LIMITATION

A cause of action for wrongful death must be brought within three years after the cause of action accrues.[4] A cause of action based on strict liability must be brought within four years after the cause of action accrues.[5] A cause of action for negligence resulting in personal injury or damage to property must be brought within six years after the cause of action accrues.[6] A cause of action for breach of warranty must be brought within four years after the cause of action accrues.[7] Except where the contract provides otherwise, breach of warranty occurs when tender of delivery is made.[8] Otherwise, a cause of action generally accrues when the breach occurs, regardless of whether the plaintiff is aware of the breach.[9] Claims "arising out of the defective and unsafe condition of an improvement to real property" may not be brought "more than two years after discovery of the injury" or "more than ten years after substantial completion of construction."[10]

C. STRICT LIABILITY

1. The Standard

Although Minnesota originally adopted the definition of strict liability set forth in section 402A of the Restatement (Second) of Torts,[11] the Minnesota Supreme Court has since stated that the Restatement definition will not be used in all product defect cases.[12] To recover under strict liability, the claimant must show (1) the product was in a defective condition and unreasonably dangerous for its intended use; (2) such defect existed when the product left defendant's control; and (3) the defect was the proximate cause of the injury sustained.[13]

2. "Defect"

A product is defective in manufacture if the product is unreasonably dangerous. Minnesota follows the "consumer expectation" standard in determining whether a product is unreasonably dangerous in manufacture.[14] In design defect cases, the Minnesota Supreme Court has rejected the Restatement's consumer expectation standard in favor of a "reasonable care" balancing test.[15] What constitutes reasonable care will vary with the surrounding circumstances and will involve a balancing of the likelihood of harm, and the gravity of the harm if it happens, against the burden on the manufacturer of preventing the harm.[16]

3. Contributory Negligence/Assumption of Risk

Minnesota has established a modified form of comparative fault as set forth in Minn. Stat. §604.01. This statute reduces the recovery of an at-fault plaintiff, in both strict liability and negligence, according to plaintiff's percentage of fault and bars the claim completely if plaintiff's percentage of fault is more than that of a defendant.[17] The fault of defendants is not aggregated for comparison purposes.[18]

A person in the chain of manufacture or distribution must contribute toward any amount uncollectible from another person in the chain, but liability is limited to the person's fault if less than the fault of persons not in the chain of manufacture or distribution.[19] However, a person whose fault is 15 percent or less is liable for a percentage of the whole award no greater than four times the percentage of fault.[20]

Minnesota may recognize primary assumption of the risk in a product liability case. Secondary assumption of the risk is treated as fault and compared under Minnesota's comparative fault statute.[21]

4. Sale or Lease

Strict liability can be imposed on manufacturers and all those within the chain of distribution.[22] Under certain circumstances, sellers may obtain indemnification from manufacturers.[23]

5. Inherently Dangerous Products

While Minnesota has not specifically adopted comment k to section 402A of the Restatement (Second) of Torts, the reasonable care balancing test applied in strict liability cases permits the jury to consider, in assessing a manufacturer's conduct, the usefulness and desirability of the product and the possibility of eliminating the danger without impairing the usefulness of the product.[24]

6. Successor Liability

A corporation purchasing the assets of another corporation will not succeed to liabilities of the selling corporation for products manufactured by the seller unless: (1) the successor corporation expressly or impliedly agrees to assume such debts or liabilities; (2) the transaction amounts to a consolidation or merger of the predecessor; (3) the successor is merely a continuation of the predecessor corporation; (4) the transfer of assets was entered fraudulently to escape liability for debts; or (5) there is inadequate consideration for the sale or transfer of assets.[25] Minnesota courts have rejected the "product line" exception to the nonliability rule.[26]

7. Privity

Lack of privity is not a defense in strict product liability actions.[27] A manufacturer's duty to warn extends to all reasonably foreseeable users.[28] A manufacturer may not delegate its duty to produce a reasonably safe product.[29]

8. Failure to Warn

A manufacturer has a duty to provide instructions for safe use of a product and a duty to warn of foreseeable dangers inherent in the proper use or foreseeable improper use of a product.[30] A manufacturer has no duty to warn of dangers of unforeseeable improper use[31] or dangers that are obvious.[32]

9. Post-Sale Duty to Warn

A post-sale duty to warn arises only in special cases, such as where the product has a long life span and is sold used to other consumers, where the manufacturer continues to advertise and sell components for the product, where the manufacturer is aware of the defect, where the product defect is hidden, where the manufacturer has previously warned of dangers, and where potential injuries are severe.[33]

10. Learned Intermediary Doctrine

Minnesota recognizes the "learned intermediary" doctrine, under which a manufacturer of a prescription drug may satisfy its duty to warn by supplying the prescribing physician with adequate warnings or instructions.[34] This doctrine applies to contraceptives.[35]

11. Substantial Change/Abnormal Use

A manufacturer is not liable for defects that develop after the product leaves the manufacturer's control.[36] A manufacturer has a duty to warn against dangers inherent in improper uses of a product.[37]

12. State of the Art

Industry custom and practice and state-of-the-art evidence are admissible.[38]

13. Standards and Government Regulations

Evidence of industry standards and governmental regulations is admissible, although not conclusive, on the issue of whether the defendant exercised reasonable care.[39]

14. Other Accidents

Evidence of accidents suffered by others under similar circumstances at times not too remote from the accident involved in the litigation is admissible to show notice or design defect.[40]

15. Misrepresentation

There are eleven elements in a misrepresentation action: (1) there must be a representation; (2) the representation must be false; (3) the representation must deal with past or present fact; (4) the fact must be material; (5) the fact must be susceptible of knowledge; (6) the representer must know the fact is false or assert it as of his or her own knowledge without knowing whether it is true or false; (7) the representer must intend to have the other person be induced to act or be justified in acting on it; (8) the other person must be induced to act or be justified in acting; (9) that person's actions must be in reliance on the representation; (10) that person must suffer damages; and (11) the misrepresentation must be the proximate cause of injury.[41]

16. Spoliation of Evidence

Trial courts have inherent power to impose sanctions for spoliation of evidence. When one party intentionally or negligently spoliates the alleged defective product, the trial court must determine whether the opposing party is prejudiced and what sanction, if any, is appropriate.[42]

17. Seat Belt Evidence

Minnesota's seat belt evidence "gag rule" provides that proof of use or nonuse of seat belts or child restraint systems, or proof of installation or failure to install seat belts or child restraints is not admissible "in any litigation involving personal injuries or property damage resulting from the use or operation of any motor vehicle.[43] The Minnesota courts have applied the "gag rule" to preclude crashworthiness actions premised on an allegedly defective seat belt system.[44]

D. NEGLIGENCE

Minnesota's comparative fault statute diminishes the plaintiff's recovery in proportion to the plaintiff's negligence. The plaintiff may not recover against the defendant if the plaintiff's negligence is greater than that of the particular defendant.[45]

In design defect cases, strict liability and negligence theories of recovery are merged.[46] A failure-to-warn case is submitted to the jury under a negligence standard.[47] In manufacturing flaw cases, the court may instruct the jury on both strict liability and negligence.[48]

E. BREACH OF WARRANTY

Minnesota has adopted the provisions of the Uniform Commercial Code dealing with express warranty,[49] implied warranty of merchantability,[50] and implied warranty of fitness for a particular purpose.[51]

If supported by the evidence, the plaintiff may assert both breach of express warranty and strict liability.[52] The Minnesota Court of Appeals has concluded that a strict liability claim preempts a claim of implied warranty of merchantability.[53]

F. PUNITIVE DAMAGES

Punitive damages are available in a product liability action only where a plaintiff suffers personal injury.[54] However, a plaintiff may not seek punitive damages in the complaint. After filing suit, a party may move to amend the pleadings to assert punitive damages.[55] Punitive damages are thereafter recoverable if the plaintiff proves by clear and convincing evidence that the defendant's conduct showed deliberate disregard for the rights or safety of others.[56] The trier of fact shall, if requested by any of the parties, first determine whether compensatory damages should be awarded. After a determination has been made, the trier of fact shall, in a separate proceeding, determine whether and in what amount punitive damages will be awarded.[57]

G. STATUTES, INCLUDING APPLICABLE "TORT REFORM" STATUTES

Under the 1986 Tort Reform Act, the plaintiff may not seek punitive damages in the complaint. After filing the suit, a party may move to amend the pleadings to assert punitive damages.[58]

Under Minn. Stat. §604.02, a person in the chain of manufacture or distribution must contribute toward any amount uncollectible from another person in the chain, but liability is limited to the person's fault if less than the fault of persons not in the chain of manufacture or distribution.[59] However, a person whose fault is 15 percent or less is liable for a percentage of the whole award no greater than four times the percentage of fault.[60]

George W. Soule
BOWMAN AND BROOKE LLP
150 South Fifth Street, Suite 2600
Minneapolis, Minnesota 55402
(612) 339-8682

ENDNOTES - MINNESOTA

1. *Hapka v. Paquin Farms*, 458 N.W.2d 683 (Minn. 1990); *Bilotta v. Kelley Co.*, 346 N.W.2d 616 (Minn. 1984).

2. *Hauenstein v. Loctite Corp.*, 347 N.W.2d 272, 275 (Minn. 1984); *Bilotta*, 346 N.W.2d at 623; see also *Piotrowski v. Southworth Products Corp.*, 15 F.3d 748, 751 (8th Cir. 1994).

3. Minn. Stat. Ann. §336.2-314, -315 (West 1975).

4. Minn. Stat. Ann. §573.02, subd. 1 (West 1988).

5. Minn. Stat. Ann. §541.05 (West 1988).

6. Id.

7. Minn. Stat. Ann. §336.2-725(1) (West Supp. 1994-95).

8. Minn. Stat. Ann. §336.2-725(2) (West Supp. 1994-95).

9. *Leisure Dynamics, Inc. v. Falstaff Brewing Corp.*, 298 N.W.2d 33 (Minn. 1980).

10. Minn. Stat. Ann. §541.051, subd. 1 (West Supp. 1994-95).

11. *Olson v. Babbitt*, 291 Minn. 105, 189 N.W.2d 701 (1971).

12. *Bilotta v. Kelley Co.*, 346 N.W.2d 616 (Minn. 1984).

13. *Lee v. Crookston Coca-Cola Bottling Co.*, 188 N.W.2d 426 (Minn. 1971); see also *Kallio v. Ford Motor Co.*, 407 N.W.2d 92 (Minn. 1987).

14. *Bilotta*, 346 N.W.2d at 621-622.

15. Id.

16. Id.

17. Minn. Stat. Ann. §604.01 (West 1988 & Supp. 1994-1995); see also *Omnetics, Inc. v. Radiant Tech. Corp.*, 440 N.W.2d 177 (Minn. Ct. App. 1989).

18. *Cambern v. Sioux Tools, Inc.*, 323 N.W.2d 795 (Minn. 1982).

19. Minn. Stat. Ann. §604.02, subd. 3 (West 1988).

20. Minn. Stat. Ann. §604.02, subd. 1 (West Supp. 1994-95).

21. *Andren v. White-Rogers Co.*, 465 N.W.2d 102 (Minn. Ct. App.), *rev. denied* (Minn. 1991).

22. *Tolbert v. Gerber Indus., Inc.*, 255 N.W.2d 362 (Minn. 1977).

23. *Jacobs v. Rosemount Dodge-Winnebago South*, 310 N.W.2d 71 (Minn. 1981).

24. *Kociemba v. G.D. Searle & Co.*, 695 F. Supp. 432, 434 (D. Minn. 1988); *Krein v. Raudabough*, 406 N.W.2d 315, 318 (Minn. Ct. App. 1987); *Bilotta v. Kelley Co.*, 346 N.W.2d 616 (Minn. 1984).

25. *Carstedt v. Grindeland*, 406 N.W.2d 39 (Minn. Ct. App. 1987).

26. *Niccum v. Hydra Tool Corp.*, 438 N.W.2d 96, 100 (Minn. 1989).

27. *Milbank Mut. Ins. Co. v. Proksch*, 244 N.W.2d 105 (Minn. 1976); *Farr v. Armstrong Rubber Co.*, 179 N.W.2d 64 (Minn. 1970).

28. *Smits v. E-Z Por Corp.*, 365 N.W.2d 352 (Minn. Ct. App. 1985).

29. *Bilotta v. Kelley Co.*, 346 N.W.2d 616 (Minn. 1984).

30. *Kallio v. Ford Motor Co.*, 391 N.W.2d 860 (Minn. Ct. App. 1986), *aff'd*, 407 N.W.2d 92 (Minn. 1987); *Germann v. F.L. Smithe Mach. Co.*, 381 N.W.2d 503 (Minn. Ct. App. 1986), *aff'd*, 395 N.W.2d 922 (Minn. 1986).

31. *Huber v. Niagara Mach. and Tool Works*, 430 N.W.2d 465 (Minn. 1988).

32. *Westerberg v. School Dist. No. 792*, 148 N.W.2d 312 (Minn. 1967); *Hart v. FMC Corp.*, 446 N.W.2d 194 (Minn. Ct. App. 1989); *Mix v. MTD Prods., Inc.*, 393 N.W.2d 18 (Minn. Ct. App. 1986).

33. *Hodder v. Goodyear Tire & Rubber Co.*, 426 N.W.2d 826, 833 (Minn. 1988), *cert. denied*, 492 U.S. 926 (1989); see also *Ramstad v. Lear Siegler Divers. Holdings Corp.*, 836 F. Supp. 1511, 1517 (D. Minn. 1993).

34. *Mulder v. Parke Davis & Co.*, 181 N.W.2d 882 (Minn. 1970); *Todalen v. United States Chem. Co.*, 424 N.W.2d 73, 79 (Minn. Ct. App. 1988), *overruled on other grounds, Tyroll v. Private Label Chems., Inc.*, 505 N.W.2d 54 (Minn. 1993).

35. *Kociemba v. G. D. Searle & Co.*, 680 F. Supp. 1293 (D. Minn. 1988).

36. *Western Surety and Cas. Co. v. General Elec. Co.*, 433 N.W.2d 444 (Minn. Ct. App. 1988).

37. *Huber v. Niagara Mach. and Tool Works*, 430 N.W.2d 465 (Minn. 1988).

38. See Minnesota Dist. Judges Assn., Minnesota Jury Instruction Guides, JIG 117, 4 Minnesota Practice 81 (3d ed. 1986) ("the manufacturer is obligated to keep informed of scientific knowledge and discoveries in its field"); see also *Kallio v. Ford Motor Co.*, 407 N.W.2d 92 (Minn. 1987) (upholding, without objection, instruction based on JIG 117 and adding that the jury may consider state-of-the-art-evidence); *Schmidt v. Beninga*, 173 N.W.2d 401 (Minn. 1970) (admitting evidence of industry custom on the issue of standard of care in negligence cases).

39. *Gryc v. Dayton-Hudson Corp.*, 297 N.W.2d 727 (Minn.), *cert. denied*, 449 U.S. 921 (1980).

40. *Hodder v. Goodyear Tire & Rubber Co.*, 426 N.W.2d 826, 834 (Minn. 1988), *cert. denied*, 492 U.S. 926 (1989); *Colby v. Gibbons*, 276 N.W.2d 170, 176 (Minn. 1979); *Buzzell v. Bliss*, 358 N.W.2d 695, 700 (Minn. Ct. App. 1984).

41. *Davis v. Re-Trac Mfg. Corp.*, 149 N.W.2d 37 (Minn. 1967).

42. *Patton v. Newmar Corp.*, 538 N.W.2d 116, 118-119 (Minn. 1995).

43. Minn. Stat. §169.685, subd. 4.

44. *Olson v. Ford Motor Co.*, 558 N.W.2d 491 (Minn. 1997); *Anker v. Little*, 541 N.W.2d 333, 339 (Minn. Ct. App. 1995), *rev. denied* (Minn. 1996); *Schlotz v. Hyundai Motor Co.*, No. C5-96-1207, 557 N.W.2d 613 (Minn. Ct. App.), *rev. denied* (Minn.), *cert. denied*, 118 S. Ct. 80 (U.S. 1997).

45. Minn. Stat. Ann. §604.01 (West Supp. 1994-95).

46. *Bilotta v. Kelley Co.*, 346 N.W.2d 616 (Minn. 1984).

47. *Hauenstein v. Loctite Corp.*, 347 N.W.2d 272, 275 (Minn. 1984).

48. *Bilotta*, 346 N.W.2d at 622.

49. Minn. Stat. Ann. §336.2-313 (West 1975).

50. Minn. Stat. Ann. §336.2-314 (West 1975).

51. Minn. Stat. Ann. §336.2-315 (West 1975).

52.   *Bilotta*, 346 N.W.2d at 625.

53.   *Continental Ins. Co. v. Loctite Corp.*, 352 N.W.2d 460, 463 (Minn. Ct. App. 1984).

54.   *Independent Sch. Dist. No. 622 v. Keene Corp.*, 511 N.W.2d 728, 732 (Minn. 1994); *Eisert v. Greenberg Roofing & Sheet Metal Co.*, 314 N.W.2d 226, 228 (Minn. 1982).

55.   Minn. Stat. Ann. §549.191 (West 1994-95).

56.   Minn. Stat. Ann. §549.20, subd. 1(a) (West Supp. 1994-95).

57.   Minn. Stat. Ann. §549.20, subd. 4 (West Supp. 1994-95).

58.   Minn. Stat. Ann. §549.191 (West 1988).

59.   Minn. Stat. Ann. §604.02, subd. 3 (West 1988).

60.   Minn. Stat. Ann. §604.02, subd. 1 (West Supp. 1994-95).

MISSISSIPPI

A. CAUSES OF ACTION

Product liability lawsuits commonly include causes of action for strict liability, negligence, and breach of warranty.

B. STATUTES OF LIMITATION

1. Personal Injury and Property Damage

Causes of action for negligence and strict liability accruing before July 1, 1989 must be brought within six years.[1] Causes of action for negligence and strict liability accruing on or after July 1, 1989 must be brought within three years.[2]

2. Breach of Warranty

Causes of action for personal injury and property damage resulting from breach of warranty must be brought within six years from tender of delivery of goods.[3]

3. Real Property

Causes of action for personal injury and injury to real and personal property from latent and patent deficiencies in design and construction of improvements to real property must be brought within ten years from the date of occupancy for causes of action accruing prior to January 1, 1986, and within six years from the date of occupancy for causes of action accruing on or after January 1, 1986.[4] Privity of contract is not required.[5]

4. Discovery Rule

In product liability actions involving latent injury or disease, the cause of action does not accrue until the plaintiff has discovered, or by reasonable diligence should have discovered, the injury.[6]

C. STRICT LIABILITY

1. The Standard

Mississippi has adopted Restatement (Second) of Torts section 402A (1964).[7]

2. "Defect"

The Mississippi Supreme Court recently adopted the risk-utility analysis. Under this analysis, a product is unreasonably dangerous if a reasonable person would conclude that the danger-in-fact, whether foreseeable or not, outweighs the utility of the product.[8]

3. Contributory Negligence/Assumption of Risk

Contributory negligence and assumption of risk are defenses to causes of action for negligence and strict liability.[9] Mississippi is a pure comparative negligence state, and all questions of contributory negligence are for the jury to determine.[10] Assumption of risk operates as a bar to recovery.[11] The elements of assumption of risk are knowledge of the condition, appreciation of the danger of the condition, and a deliberate and voluntary choice to expose oneself to the danger.[12]

4. Sales and Leases

Traditionally, Mississippi courts have not imposed liability on a retailer or wholesaler who has no control over the manufacture, design, or labeling of the product.[13] Recently enacted product liability reform legislation provides indemnification for the product seller under certain circumstances.[14]

There are no Mississippi cases to date addressing whether strict liability principles apply to lessors of products.[15]

5. Open and Obvious Dangers

In failure-to-warn cases, no duty is imposed on a manufacturer or seller to warn of dangers that are open and obvious to a reasonable consumer.[16]

6. Successor Liability

As a general rule, when one corporation purchases or acquires manufacturing assets from another corporation, the successor does not become responsible for the debts and liabilities of the predecessor.[17]

7. Privity

Privity is not required to maintain any action for negligence, strict liability, or breach of warranty.[18]

8. Failure to Warn

Mississippi follows Restatement (Second) of Torts section 388 (1964).[19]

9. Post-Sale Duty to Warn

Mississippi courts have not to date imposed a post-sale duty to warn on manufacturers.[20]

10. Substantial Change/Abnormal Use

The plaintiff must prove that the product reached the consumer without substantial change in its condition. A manufacturer is not liable for injuries resulting from abnormal or unintended use of the product if such use was not reasonably foreseeable.[21]

11. **State of the Art**

   "State-of-the-art" evidence is admissible.[22]

12. **Standards**

   Evidence that the product complied with customary or industry standards is admissible.[23]

13. **Other Accidents**

   Evidence of other accidents is inadmissible unless plaintiff proves similarity of product and circumstances.[24]

14. **Misrepresentation**

   Mississippi has not adopted Restatement (Second) of Torts section 402B (1964).

15. **Second Impact Doctrine**

   The second impact doctrine is a recognized theory of liability against motor vehicle manufacturers.[25]

D. NEGLIGENCE

Negligence is commonly used as a cause of action in product liability lawsuits. Contributory negligence is a defense to negligence and strict liability causes of action. Mississippi is a pure comparative negligence state. All questions of negligence and contributory negligence are for the jury to determine.[26]

E. BREACH OF WARRANTY

Breach of express warranty is available in product liability lawsuits for personal injury.[27] The cause of action and proof required for breach of warranty are generally similar to the cause of action and proof required for strict liability.[28]

F. PUNITIVE DAMAGES

Punitive damages are recoverable in causes of action for negligence, strict liability, and breach of warranty. Mississippi law requires bifurcated trial in product cases for assessing punitive damages.[29] Punitive damages may not be awarded unless the claimant proves by clear and convincing evidence that the defendant acted with actual malice or gross negligence that evinces a wilful, wanton, or reckless disregard for the safety of others or committed actual fraud.[30] Relevant factors for the jury to consider in assessing the amount of punitive damages to be awarded are (1) the amount necessary to punish and deter the defendant, (2) the amount necessary to make an example of the defendant to deter others, and (3) the pecuniary ability or financial net worth of the defendant.[31]

G. STATUTES

Relevant statutes for product liability actions are product liability reform legislation,[32] punitive damages reform legislation,[33] statutes of limitation,[34] abolition of the privity requirement,[35] and contributory negligence.[36]

Judgments rendered against two or more tortfeasors are joint and several, but a right of contribution exists if one tortfeasor pays more than its pro rata share of the judgment.[37] Legislation applicable to causes of action accruing on or after July 1, 1989 imposes limitations on joint and several liability and right of contribution and requires the jury to determine the percentage of fault of each tortfeasor.[38]

William H. Cox, Jr.
Lewis W. Bell
WATKINS & EAGER PLLC
The Emporium Building, Suite 300
400 East Capitol Street
Jackson, Mississippi 39201
Post Office Box 650
Jackson, Mississippi 39201
(601) 948-6470

ENDNOTES - MISSISSIPPI

1. Miss. Code Ann. §15-1-49 (1972).

2. Id. §15-1-49 (Supp. 1993).

3. Id. §75-2-725 (1972).

4. Id. §15-1-41 (1972 & Supp. 1993). See generally *Collins v. Trinity Indus., Inc.*, 861 F.2d 1364 (5th Cir. 1988); *Reich v. Jesco, Inc.*, 526 So. 2d 550 (Miss. 1988); *Smith v. Fluor Corp.*, 514 So. 2d 1227 (Miss. 1987).

5. Miss. Code Ann. §11-7-20 (Supp. 1993); *Keyes v. Guy Bailey Homes, Inc.*, 439 So. 2d 670 (Miss. 1983).

6. Miss. Code Ann. §15-1-49(2) (Supp. 1993); *Owens-Illinois, Inc. v. Edwards*, 573 So. 2d 704 (Miss. 1990). While there is a specific statute of limitations rule for medical malpractice, the Mississippi Supreme Court in *Williams v. Kilgore*, 618 So. 2d 51 (Miss. 1992), discusses latent injury. The discussion may have relevance to a products case. In a cigarette case, *Schiro v. American Tobacco Co.*, 611 So. 2d 962 (Miss. 1992), the court discusses the discovery rule as announced in *Edwards, supra,* and appears to add a doctor's diagnosis as a new requirement on the issue of plaintiff's reasonableness.

7. *State Stove Mfg. Co. v. Hodges*, 189 So. 2d 113 (Miss. 1966).

8. *Sperry-New Holland v. Prestage*, 617 So. 2d 248, 256 (Miss. 1993). Prior to this decision, Mississippi applied the consumer expectations analysis. See *Melton v. Deere & Co.*, 887 F.2d 1241 (5th Cir. 1989); *Ford Motor Co. v. Matthews*, 291 So. 2d 169 (Miss. 1974). Several provisions in recently enacted product liability reform legislation appear to adopt the consumer expectations analysis, creating confusion in this area. See, e.g., Miss. Code Ann. §11-1-63(b) & (f) (Supp. 1993).

9. Id. §§11-1-63(d) & (h) (Supp. 1993); *Nichols v. Western Auto Supply Co., Inc.*, 477 So. 2d 261 (Miss. 1985).

10. Miss. Code Ann. §§11-7-15, 11-7-17 (1972).

11. Id. §11-1-63(d) (Supp. 1993); *Nichols, supra* note 9; *Elias v. New Laurel Radio Station, Inc.*, 146 So. 2d 558 (Miss. 1962).

12. Miss. Code Ann. §11-1-63(d) (Supp. 1993); *Alley v. Praschak Mach. Co.*, 366 So. 2d 661 (Miss. 1979).

13. *Sam Shainberg Co. of Jackson v. Barlow*, 258 So. 2d 242 (Miss. 1972). But see *Coca Cola Bottling Co., Inc. of Vicksburg v. Reeves*, 486 So. 2d 374 (Miss. 1986) (distinguishing *Shainberg*).

14. Miss. Code Ann. §11-1-63(g) (Supp. 1993).

15. See generally *J. L. Teel Co., Inc. v. Houston United Sales, Inc.*, 491 So. 2d 851 (Miss. 1986); *Hertz Corp. v. Goza*, 306 So. 2d 657 (Miss. 1974).

16. Miss. Code Ann. §11-1-63(e) (Sup. 1993).

17. *Mozingo v. Correct Mfg. Corp.*, 752 F.2d 168 (5th Cir. 1985); *Johnston v. Pneumo Corp.*, 652 F. Supp. 1402 (S.D. Miss. 1987). The Mississippi Supreme Court has not, to date, addressed this issue.

18. Miss. Code Ann. §11-7-20 (Supp. 1993).

19. Id. §11-1-1-63(c) (Supp. 1993); *Gordon v. Niagara Mach. & Tool Works*, 574 F.2d 1182 (5th Cir. 1978); cf. *Ward v. Hobart Mfg. Co.*, 450 F.2d 1176, 1188 (5th Cir. 1971) (no duty to warn where user is fully conscious of danger). There is no duty to warn someone of a danger of which the person is aware or which is open and obvious. Miss. Code. Ann. §11-1-63(e) (Supp. 1993). Additionally, Mississippi follows the learned intermediary doctrine, which applies to products used under the supervision of a licensed professional. See id. §11-1-63(c)(ii) (Supp. 1993); *Davis v. Avondale Indus., Inc.*, 975 F.2d 169 (5th Cir. 1992); *Swan v. I.P., Inc.*, 613 So. 2d 846 (Miss. 1993); *City of Jackson v. Ball*, 562 So. 2d 1267 (Miss. 1990); Pridgett v. Jackson Iron & Metal Co., 253 So. 2d 837 (Miss. 1971).

20. Courts have consistently held that under Mississippi law a product manufacturer is liable only if the defect existed at the time the product left the control of the manufacturer. See Ward, 450 F.2d at 1184 n.23; *Coca-Cola Bottling Co., Inc. v. Reeves*, 486 So. 2d 374, 378 (Miss. 1986); *Early-Gary, Inc. v. Walters*, 294 So. 2d 181, 186 (Miss. 1974); *State Stove Mfg. Co. v. Hodges*, 189 So. 2d 113, 121 (Miss. 1966); but see *Ford Motor Co. v. Matthews*, 291 S.2d 169, 176 (Miss. 1974). Recently enacted product liability reform legislation codifies this principle and strengthens the argument that claims based on post-sale duties to warn, recall, or retrofit are not viable. See *Miss. Code Ann.* §11-1-63(a) & (f) (Supp. 1993).

21. Id. §11-1-63(a) (Supp. 1993).

22. Id. §11-1-63(f)(ii) (Supp. 1993); *Hall v. Mississippi Chem. Express, Inc.*, 528 So. 2d 796 (Miss. 1988); *Brown v. Williams*, 504 So. 2d 1188 (Miss. 1987); *Toliver v. General Motors Corp.*, 482 So. 2d 213 (Miss. 1985).

23. *Ward v. Hobart Mfg. Co.*, 450 F.2d 1176 (5th Cir. 1971); *Fincher v. Ford Motor Co.*, 399 F. Supp. 106 (S.D. Miss 1975); *aff'd*, 535 F.2d 657 (5th Cir. 1976); *Hall*, 528 So. 2d 796; *Brown*, 504 So.2d 1188; *Toliver*, 482 So. 2d 213.

24. *Johnson v. Ford Motor Co.*, 988 F.2d 573, 579 (5th Cir. 1993); *Hardy v. Chemetron Corp.*, 870 F.2d 1007 (5th Cir. 1989); *Shields v. Sturm, Ruger & Co.*, 864 F.2d 379 (5th Cir. 1989).

25. *Toliver*, 482 So. 2d 213.

26. Miss. Code Ann. §§11-7-15, 11-7-17 (1972).

27. Id. §11-1-63(a)(i)(4) (Supp. 1993).

28. Id. §11-1-63(a) (Supp. 1993).

29. Id. §11-1-65(1)(c) (Supp. 1993).

30. Id. §11-1-65(1)(a) (Supp. 1993).

31. Id. §11-1-65(1)(e) (Supp. 1993).

32. Id. §111-1-63 (Supp. 1993). This legislation is applicable to all actions filed on or after July 1, 1994.

33. Miss. Code Ann. §11-1-65 (Supp. 1993). This legislation is applicable to pending actions in which judgment has not been entered as of July 1, 1993, and to all actions filed on or after July 1, 1993.

34. Miss. Code Ann. §15-1-49 (1972 & Supp. 1990)) (negligence and strict liability); §75-2-725 (1972) (breach of warranty); §15-141 (1972 & Supp. 1990) (improvements to real property).

35. Id. §11-7-20 (Supp. 1993).

36. Id. §11-7-15 (1972).

37. Id. §85-5-7 (1972 Rev. 1991).

38. Id. §85-5-7 (1972 Rev. 1991).

MISSOURI

A. CAUSES OF ACTION

Product liability suits brought in Missouri commonly include causes of action for strict liability, negligence, and warranty.[1]

B. STATUTES OF LIMITATION

A cause of action for personal injury or property damage must be brought within five years, whether brought in negligence, strict liability, or breach of warranty.[2]

A cause of action accrues when the damage resulting therefrom is sustained and capable of ascertainment.[3] If death results from use of the product, a cause of action under the wrongful death statute must be brought within three years from the death.[4]

If at the time of the injury the plaintiff is under 21 years old, he has 5 years from the time he reaches 21 in which to bring the action.[5]

C. STRICT LIABILITY

1. The Standard

Missouri has adopted section 402A of the Restatement (Second) of Torts.[6] Unless the court can say as a matter of law that the product is not unreasonably dangerous, the question is one for the jury.[7]

2. "Defect"

The jury is instructed that the product is defective if the defendant sold the product in the course of defendant's business and the product was then in a defective condition unreasonably dangerous when put to a reasonably anticipated use. The jury must also find that the product was used in a manner reasonably anticipated and that plaintiff was damaged as a direct result of such defective condition as existed when the product was sold.[8] An unreasonably dangerous product may arise from a design defect, a manufacturing defect, or failure to warn of the danger.[9] A manufacturer is not obligated to market only one version of a product that is the very safest design possible.[10]

3. Contributory Negligence/Assumption of Risk/Comparative Fault

By legislation, contributory fault was abolished, and for causes of action arising after July 1, 1987, principles of pure comparative fault are applied in both negligence and strict liability cases.[11]

The statute allows the defendant to plead and prove the plaintiff's fault. "Fault" is defined as:

(a) failure to use the product as reasonably anticipated by the manufacturer;

(b) use of the product for a purpose not intended by the manufacturer;

(c) use of the product with knowledge of a danger involved in such use with reasonable appreciation of the consequences and the voluntary and unreasonable exposure to said danger;

(d) unreasonable failure to appreciate the danger involved in use of the product or the consequences thereof and the unreasonable exposure to said danger;

(e) failure to undertake the precautions a reasonably careful user of the product would take to protect himself against dangers that he would reasonably appreciate under the same or similar circumstances; or

(f) failure to mitigate damages.[12]

4. Sale or Lease

Strict liability applies to any seller in the chain of a product's distribution.[13] However, the seller must be in the business of selling such products.[14] The word "sold" does not have a technical meaning but rather indicates the time at which defendant relinquishes control or possession of the product.[15] A seller or retailer has no duty to test or inspect the product unless a reasonably prudent seller should have discovered the defect before selling.[16] In Missouri, strict liability applies to commercial lessors and bailors as well.[17]

For causes of action arising after July 1, 1987, a defendant in a product liability claim whose liability is based solely on her status as a seller may be dismissed if there is another defendant in the suit from which full recovery may be had.[18] The defendant seller should move for dismissal within the time for filing an answer or other responsive pleading or later for good cause shown. An affidavit should accompany the motion stating that the defendant seller knows of no reason why she should be liable other than her status as a seller in the stream of commerce.

5. Inherently Dangerous Products

A manufacturer has a duty to warn an ultimate user of an inherently dangerous product.[19] Liability is imposed where injury resulting from the use of the product is attributable to this breach of the duty to warn.[20]

6. **Successor Liability**

A successor corporation may be liable for injuries suffered by a plaintiff in a product liability action if certain conditions are met, among which are whether the purchaser expressly or impliedly agrees to assume such debts, the purchasing corporation is merely a continuation of the selling corporation, the transaction amounts to a consolidation or merger of the corporation, or the transaction is fraudulently entered into in order to escape liability for debts.[21]

7. **Privity**

No privity is required under Missouri product liability law.[22] Bystanders may recover under a theory of strict product liability[23] and in negligence.[24]

8. **Failure to Warn**

Plaintiff must prove a causal connection between lack of a warning and plaintiff's injuries.[25] However, the plaintiff does not have to prove with certainty that the warning would have been seen and heeded.[26] A manufacturer has no duty to warn of those dangers that are open and obvious. Additionally, a defendant does not have a duty to warn someone or instruct someone of things they already know or reasonably may be expected to know.[27] Even though a warning will not alter the inherently dangerous nature of a product, it may be required to warn it of the danger so it can take precautions to minimize the risk.[28]

9. **Substantial Change/Abnormal Use**

A manufacturer will not be liable in strict liability if substantial change[29] or abnormal use[30] of the product has occurred unless it was foreseeable.[31] Generally, substantial change and abnormal use will go to the issue of comparative fault. It has the burden of proving the product was not altered.[32]

10. **State of the Art**

Since July 1, 1987, Missouri has recognized the state-of-the-art defense only in strict liability failure to warn cases.[33] "State of the art" means that the dangerous nature of the product was not known and could not reasonably be discovered at the time the product was placed in the stream of commerce. It is a complete defense and shall be pleaded as an affirmative defense. The party asserting it shall have the burden of proof. This defense does not affect a cause of action in negligence.

11. **Industry Standards**

Evidence of industry standards can be used in Missouri as evidence that the product presents an unreasonable risk of danger.[34]

---

12. Other Accidents

Other accidents are admissible if the facts are substantially similar.[35] In determining if other accidents are admissible, how substantially similar other accidents must be is dependent on why they are being introduced. A greater showing of similarity is necessary to prove defect as opposed to notice.[36]

13. Second Collision Doctrine

Missouri recognizes the second collision doctrine. This doctrine extends liability for those situations in which the construction or design has caused separate or enhanced injuries in the course of an initial accident brought about by an independent cause.[37]

14. Subsequent Remedial Measures

In Missouri, evidence of post-sale remedial measures may be used in strict liability cases.[38]

D. NEGLIGENCE

A plaintiff needs to prove (1) the existence of a duty; (2) breach of that duty; and (3) injury resulting from that breach for an action in negligence to lie.[39] In negligence, the duty owed is based on the foreseeability of the harm that is a likely result of the manufacturer's acts or omissions.[40] Strict liability focuses on the product, while negligence focuses on the conduct of the manufacturer.[41] Principles of comparative fault apply to all actions in negligence. Joint and several liability applies, and the plaintiff is only precluded from recovering that percentage of fault attributable to the plaintiff. Thus, even if plaintiff was 99 percent at fault, she could still recover 1 percent of the total damages.

E. BREACH OF WARRANTY

In the context of personal injury, a breach of warranty claim is substantially similar to that of strict liability.[42]

F. PUNITIVE DAMAGES

In order to recover punitive damages in Missouri, the fact-finder must find defendant knew of the defect and danger in the product and that by selling the product with that knowledge, the defendant showed complete indifference or conscious disregard for the safety of others. Punitive damages may be awarded only if supported by clear and convincing evidence.[43]

Missouri does not permit submission of punitive damages on the theory of constructive knowledge. But a plaintiff may recover if there is evidence to show that defendant was put on notice that there was relevant information with regard to the dangerousness of the product available to show the product was actually known to constitute a health hazard to a given class of individuals and that the defendant chose to ignore this information.[44]

G. STATUTES/INSTRUCTIONS

The relevant statutes for a product liability action are the statutes of limitations, the Commercial Code, and Mo. Rev. Stat. §537.760-765. The relevant verdict directors are Missouri Approved Instructions 25.04, 25.05, 25.06, and 25.09.

H. PREEMPTION

Negligence and strict liability claims,[45] as wells as a failure to warn claim,[46] may be preempted by federal law.

Robert A. Horn
BLACKWELL SANDERS MATHENY WEARY & LOMBARDI
Two Pershing Square
2300 Main Street, Suite 1100
P.O. Box 419777
Kansas City, Missouri 64141-6777
(816) 274-6800

ENDNOTES - MISSOURI

1. *Ragland Mills v. General Motors*, 763 S.W.2d 357 (Mo. App. 1989).

2. Mo. Rev. Stat. §516.120 (1986).

3. Mo. Rev. Stat. §516.100 (1986); *King v. Nashua Corp.*, 763 F.2d 332 (8th Cir. 1985).

4. Mo. Rev. Stat. §537.100 (1986).

5. Mo. Rev. Stat. §516.170 (1990).

6. *Keener v. Dayton Elec. Mfg. Co.*, 445 S.W.2d 362, 364 (Mo. 1969); *Caulter v. Michelin Tire Corp.*, 622 S.W.2d 421 (Mo. App. 1981); *Missouri Approved Instructions* 25.05.

7. *Racer v. Utterman*, 629 S.W.2d 387, 394 (Mo. App. 1981); *Nesselrode v. Executive Beechcraft, Inc.*, 707 S.W.2d 371, 378 (Mo. banc 1987).

8. *Welkener v. Kirkwood Drug Store Co.*, 734 S.W.2d 253 (Mo. App. 1987); *Missouri Approved Instructions* 25.04.

9. *Racer*, 629 S.W.2d 387.

10. *Linegar v. Armour of Am., Inc.*, 909 F.2d 1150 (8th Cir. 1990).

11. Mo. Rev. Stat. §537.765 (1987).

12. Mo. Rev. Stat. §537.765(3) (1987).

13. *Zaft v. Eli Lilly & Co.*, 676 S.W.2d 241 (Mo. 1984).

14. *Winters v. Sears, Roebuck & Co.*, 554 S.W.2d 565, 569 (Mo. App. 1987).

15. *Welkener*, 734 S.W.2d 253.

16. Id.

17. *Wright v. Newman*, 735 F.2d 1073 (8th Cir. 1984).

18. Mo. Rev. Stat. §537.762(1), (2) (1987).

19. *Duke v. Gulf & Western Mfg. Co.*, 660 S.W.2d 404, 418 (Mo. App. 1983).

20.   *Griggs v. Firestone Tire & Rubber Co.*, 513 F.2d 851, 856 (8th Cir. 1975).

21.   *Young v. Fulton Ironworks Co.*, 709 S.W.2d 927 (Mo. App. 1986).

22.   *Williams v. Ford Motor Co.*, 545 S.W.2d 611, 617 (Mo. App. 1970).

23.   *Giberson v. Ford Motor Co.*, 509 S.W.2d 8 (Mo. 1974).

24.   *Stevens v. Durbin-DurCo*, 377 S.W.2d 343 (Mo. 1964).

25.   *Grady v. American Optical Corp.*, 702 S.W.2d 911 (Mo. App. 1985); *Church v. Martin-Baker AirCraft Co., Ltd.*, 643 F. Supp. 499 (E.D. Mo. 1986).

26.   *Hill v. Airshields, Inc.*, 721 S.W.2d 112 (Mo. App. 1986).

27.   *Grady*, 702 S.W.2d 911.

28.   *Heifner et al. v. Synergy Gas Corp.*, 883 S.W.2d 29 (Mo. App. 1994).

29.   *Williams v. Deere & Co.*, 598 S.W.2d 609 (Mo. App. 1980); *Glass v. Allis-Chalmers Corp.*, 789 F.2d 612 (8th Cir. 1986).

30.   *Nesselrode*, 707 S.W.2d 371.

31.   *Higgins v. Paul Hardeman, Inc.*, 457 S.W.2d 943 (Mo. App. 1970); *Threats v. General Motors Corp.*, 890 S.W.2d 327 (Mo. App. 1994).

32.   *Waggoner v. Mercedes Benz of North America, Inc.*, 879 S.W.2d 692 (Mo. App. 1994).

33.   Mo. Rev. Stat. §537.764 (1987).

34.   *Nesselrode*, 707 S.W.2d at 381 (Mo. banc 1987).

35.   *Pierce v. Platte-Clay Elec. Coop., Inc.*, 769 S.W.2d 769 (Mo. banc 1989).

36.   *Eagleburger v. Emerson Elec. Co.*, 794 S.W.2d 210 (Mo. App. 1990).

37.   *Polk v. Ford Motor Corp.*, 529 F.2d 259 (8th Cir. 1976).

38.   *Pollard v. Ashby*, 793 S.W.2d 394 (Mo. App. 1990); *SRM Stinson, et al. v. E.I. DuPont De Nemours & Company*, 904 S.W.2d 428 (Mo. App. 1995).

39.   *Chubb Group of Ins. v. C.F. Murphy & Assocs.*, 656 S.W.2d 766, 774 (Mo. App. 1983).

40. *Blevines v. Cushman Motors*, 551 S.W.2d 602, 607 (Mo. banc 1977).

41. *Racer v. Utterman*, 629 S.W.2d 387, 395 (Mo. App. 1981).

42. *Witherspoon v. General Motors Corp.*, 535 F.2d 432 (W.D. Mo. 1982); *Metulunas v. Baker*, 569 S.W.2d 791, 794 (Mo. App. 1978).

43. *Rodriguez v. Suzuki Motor Corp., et al.*, No. 78539 (Mo. en banc December 17, 1996).

44. *Angotti v. Celotex Corp.*, 812 S.W.2d 742, 746 (Mo. App. 1981).

45. *Connelly et al. v. Iolab Corporation*, slip op., 1995 W.L. 250794 (Mo. App. W.D., 1995).

46. *State ex rel. Jones Chemicals, Inc. v. Seier*, 871 S.W.2d 611 (Mo. App. 1994).

MONTANA

A. CAUSES OF ACTION

Product liability lawsuits commonly include causes of action for strict liability, negligence, and warranty.[1]

B. STATUTES OF LIMITATION

Causes of action for personal injuries or property damage must be brought within three years if the claim is in strict liability.[2] For strict liability actions involving damage to property, the Montana Supreme Court has held that the statute is three years.[3] A Montana federal district court has held that for strict liability actions involving damage to property the statute is two years.[4] For negligence actions, the statute is three years for personal injury and two years for property damage.[5] Breach of warranty covenants imposed by law have a three-year statute of limitations.[6] A discovery doctrine appears to apply to all causes of action under certain circumstances.[7]

There is a ten-year statute of repose with respect to improvements to real property.[8]

C. STRICT LIABILITY

1. The Standard

The Montana Suprerme Court has adopted section 402A of the Restatement (Second) of Torts.[9] However, in 1987, Montana passed a statute that incorporates the language of 402A and that provides for specific defenses.[10] Defects in firearm design and ammunition design are dealt with separately.[11] To the extent that the statute contains 402A's exact language, the prior judicial interpretation of 402A appears to apply.[12] Because both the caselaw and the statute provide for recovery for loss of property as well as personal injury, the unreasonably dangerous standard of 402A is modified.[13]

2. "Defect"

A product is in a defective condition if it is unreasonably unsuitable or unreasonably dangerous for its intended or foreseeable purposes.[14] Although the unreasonably dangerous language is used in the statute, because damage to the user's property may give rise to a cause of action, it is assumed that this standard has not changed from the case law. It would appear that an adequate warning may overcome some defects.[15]

3. Contributory Negligence/Assumption of Risk

Prior to the statute, subjective assumption of the risk and was the only defense.[16] The statute, however, provides for subjective assumption of the risk and apparently objective assumption of the risk as defenses when the defect is open and obvious and where the user or consumer unreasonably makes use of the product thereafter.[17] The statute also provides for a defense of unreasonable misuse.[18] The affirmative defenses are to be applied as comparative negligence is applied.[19]

4. Sale or Lease

The statute indicates that a "seller" is a manufacturer, wholesaler, or retailer.[20] Case law indicates that lessors can be held liable.[21] Although Montana law is somewhat confusing, it would appear that a wholesaler or retailer may obtain indemnity from a manufacturer of a defectively manufactured product.[22] However, indemnity may be barred if the manufacturer has settled.[23]

5. Inherently Dangerous Products

Montana recognizes that a product may be so dangerous that it is defective unless it contains an adequate warning of the danger.[24]

6. Successor Liability

The surviving corporation of a corporate merger acquires successor liability.[25]

7. Privity

No privity is required in a product action.[26]

8. Failure to Warn

If the product does not contain a warning, or if the warning is such that the unguided user exposes himself or his property to risk or danger in using the product, then the product is "in a defective condition unreasonably dangerous to the user or his property."[27] There may be a duty to warn even if the risk is known[28] or if the danger is open and obvious.[29] The plaintiff must prove that any warning would have caused him or her to avoid the injury.[30]

9. Post-Sale Duty to Warn

While there do not appear to be any cases directly on point, a post-sale duty to warn does not appear to be precluded, and certainly if the newly discovered risk were substantial, Montana law would appear to require such a warning.[31]

10. Substantial Change/Abnormal Use

If the defect is a manufacturing defect, then changes in the product appear to be a defense.[32] However, if the alteration was foreseeable[33] or if the claimed defect is a design defect,[34] then subsequent changes may not be a defense. Abnormal use, if not foreseeable, appears to be a defense.[35]

11. State of the Art

The Montana Supreme Court has rejected the state-of-the-art defense as set forth in comment j of §402A.[36] In design cases, the knowledge that was available at the time that the product was manufactured is relevant to the issue of misdesign.[37]

12. Malfunction

The Montana Supreme Court has recognized that malfunction may be evidence of defect.[38]

13. Standards

Industry standards appear to be admissible in Montana as evidence of defect.[39]

14. Other Accidents

In Montana, other accidents may be admitted as evidence of defect if the circumstances were substantially the same as or similar to those of the accident at issue.[40] Other accidents may also be used as the basis of an expert opinion under appropriate circumstances.[41]

15. Misrepresentation

Section 402B of the Restatement (Second) of Torts, dealing with misrepresentation, does not appear to have been adopted in Montana.

D. NEGLIGENCE

In Montana, a manufacturer must use reasonable care to avoid creating an undue risk of harm to those who might be reasonably expected to use its design or product.[42] Contributory negligence is a defense, but comparative negligence applies unless the negligence of the plaintiff is greater than the negligence of the defendant or defendants.[43]

E. BREACH OF WARRANTY

A cause of action for breach of warranty includes not only express warranty claims but also fitness for a particular use, merchantability, performance in a skillful manner, and the covenant of good faith and fair dealing.[44] If the express warranty includes warranty of the performance of the product, then the statute of limitations is extended at least for as long as would be necessary to discover a breach of this warranty.[45]

F. PUNITIVE DAMAGES

Punitive damages are recoverable in strict liability, negligence, and non-contract warranty actions.[46] For example, showing that a defendant knew that it had a defective product and attempted to prevent public knowledge of that defect might prove malice and be the basis for punitive damages.[47]

G. STATUTES

Relevant statutes for product liability actions are the various statutes of limitations and commercial code sections, as well as the express statutes relating to product liability and firearms in Montana.[48]

James A. Poore III
POORE & HOPKINS, PLLP
Suite 303 The Florence
111 North Higgins Avenue
Missoula, Montana 59802
(406) 543-3487

ENDNOTES - MONTANA

1. Montana cases indicate that items such as mechanical equipment that is affixed to a building (*Papp v. Rocky Mountain Oil and Minerals, Inc.*, 236 Mont. 330, 769 P.2d 1249 (1989)) and speedbumps (*Harrington v. Labelle's of Colo., Inc.*, 235 Mont. 80, 765 P.2d 732 (1988)) are not products.

2. *Thompson v. Nebraska Mobile Homes Corp.*, 198 Mont. 461, 647 P.2d 334 (1982); Mont. Code Ann. §27-2-202.

3. *Thompson*, 198 Mont. 461.

4. *Montana Pole & Treating Plant v. I. F. Laucks and Co.*, 775 F. Supp. 1339 (D. Mont. 1991); *Affd.* 993 F.2d 676 (9th Cir. 1993).

5. Mont. Code Ann. §§27-2-204, -207.

6. *Bennett v. Dow Chem. Co.*, 220 Mont. 117, 713 P.2d 992 (1986).

7. *Major v. North Valley Hosp.*, 233 Mont. 25, 759 P.2d 153 (1988); *Bennett*, 220 Mont. 117. In medical products cases the statute of limitations may be tolled during the time a related malpractice case is pending before the Montana Medical Legal Panel. *Eisenmenger by Eisenmenger v. Ethicon, Inc.*, 264 Mont. 393, 399, 871 P.2d 1313, 1317 (1994), *cert. denied, Ethicon, Inc. v. Eisenmenger by Eisenmenger*, 115 S. Ct. 298, 130 L. Ed. 2d 211 (1994). *Cf. Blackburn v. Blue Mountain Women's Clinic*, — Mont. —, 951 P.2d 1 (1997).

8. Mont. Code Ann. §27-2-208.

9. *Brandenburger v. Toyota Motor Sales, U.S.A., Inc.*, 162 Mont. 506, 513 P.2d 268 (1973).

10. Mont. Code Ann. §27-1-719.

11. Id. §27-1-720.

12. See, e.g., *Wise v. Ford Motor Co.*, — Mont. —, 943 P.2d 1310, 1310 (1997).

13. *McJunkin v. Kaufman and Broad Home Sys., Inc.*, 229 Mont. 432, 748 P.2d 910 (1987) (the lack of a dangerous aspect does not automatically preclude a finding that the product is defective); *Thompson*, 198 Mont. 461.

14. *McJunkin*, 229 Mont. 432.

15. *Gouthier v. AMF, Inc.*, 788 F.2d 634, 636 (9th Cir. 1986); *amended* 805 F.2d 337.

16. *Zahrte v. Sturm Ruger & Co., Inc.*, 203 Mont. 90, 661 P.2d 17 (1983).

17. Mont. Code Ann. §27-1-719(5)(a); *Sharp v. Altec Industries, Inc.*, 22 Montana Federal Reports 418 (D.C. Mont. 1997).

18. Id. §27-1-719(5)(b). *In Hart-Albin Co. v. McLees Inc.*, 264 Mont. 1, 870 P.2d 51, 53-54 (1994), the Montana Supreme Court held that "unreasonable misuse," as found in the statute, means that a manufacturer is not responsible for injuries resulting from abnormal or unintended use of a product, if such use was not reasonably foreseeable.

19. Id. §27-1-719(6). A "non party" defense that has been added in negligence actions may apply. See §27-1-703(6).

20. Id. §27-1-719(1).

21. *Canada v. Blain's Helicopters, Inc.*, 831 F.2d 920 (9th Cir. 1987).

22. *Jones v. Aero-Chem Corp.*, 680 F. Supp. 338 (D. Mont. 1987).

23. *State ex rel. Deere & Co. v. District Court*, 224 Mont. 384, 730 P.2d 396 (1986); *Modified by* Mont. Code Ann. §27-1-703.

24. *Knudson v. Edgewater Automotive Div.*, 157 Mont. 400, 486 P.2d 596 (1971).

25. *Travelers Ins. Co. v. Western Fire Ins. Co.*, 218 Mont. 452, 709 P.2d 639 (1985).

26. *Streich v. Hilton-Davis, a Div. of Sterling Drug, Inc.*, 214 Mont. 44, 692 P.2d 440 (1984); *Brandenburger,* 162 Mont. 506. As to negligence actions, see: *Singleton v. L. P. Anderson Supply Co., Inc.,* — Mont. — , 943 P.2d 968 (1997).

27. *Streich,* 214 Mont. 44.

28. *Tacke v. Vermeer Mfg. Co.*, 220 Mont. 1, 713 P.2d 527 (1986).

29. *Stenberg v. Beatrice Foods Co.*, 176 Mont. 123, 576 P.2d 725 (1978).

30. The Montana Supreme Court has refused to create a presumption that a consumer would have read an adequate warning and acted to prevent the accident. *Riley v. American Honda Motor Co., Inc.*, 259 Mont. 128, 856 P.2d 196, 200 (1993).

31.   See cases cited under failure to warn.

32.   *Duncan v. Rockwell Mfg. Co.*, 173 Mont. 382, 567 P.2d 936 (1977); *Brothers v. General Motors Corp.*, 202 Mont. 477, 658 P.2d 1108 (1983); *St. Paul Mercury Ins. Co. v. Jeep Corp.*, 175 Mont. 69, 572 P.2d 204 (1977).

33.   *Kuiper v. District Court*, 193 Mont. 452, 632 P.2d 694 (Mont. 1981).

34.   *Streich*, 214 Mont. 44.

35.   *Kuiper*, 632 P.2d 694; *Lutz v. National Crane Corp.*, 367 Mont. 268, 884 P.2d 455, 458-460 (1994). See §27-1-719(5)(b).

36.   *Sternhagen v. Dow Co.*, — Mont. — , 935 P.2d 1139 (1997).

37.   *Preston v. District Court*, — Mont. — , 936 P.2d 814 (1997).

38.   *Duncan v. Rockwell Mfg. Co.*, 173 Mont. 382, 567 P.2d 936 (1977).

39.   *Tacke*, 220 Mont. 1.

40.   *Kuiper*, 632 P.2d 694.

41.   *Krueger v. General Motors Corp.*, 240 Mont. 266, 783 P.2d 1340 (Mont. 1989).

42.   *Streich*, 214 Mont. 44.

43.   Mont. Code Ann. §27-1-702. A "non party" defense that has been added in negligence actions may apply. See §27-1-703(6).

44.   *Bennett v. Dow Chem. Co.*, 220 Mont. 117, 713 P.2d 992 (1986). U.C.C. warranties are contained in Mont. Code Ann. §§30-2-313-318; Warranties with respect to Automobiles contained in Mont. Code Ann. §61-4-501 et. seq.

45.   *Iowa Mfg. Co. v. Joy Mfg. Co.*, 206 Mont. 26, 669 P.2d 1057 (1983).

46.   Mont. Code Ann. §27-1-220; *Bennett*, 220 Mont. 117.

47.   *Kuiper*, 632 P.2d 694.

48.   See statutes cited in other notes.

NEBRASKA

A. CAUSES OF ACTION

Negligence, breach of warranty, and strict liability are alternative theories of product liability.[1]

B. STATUTES OF LIMITATION

All product liability actions must be brought within four years after the date of the damage and in no case longer than ten years after the date the product was first leased or sold for use or consumption.[2] The four-year limitation begins when the person bringing the cause of action discovers, or reasonably should have discovered, the existence of the injury or damage.[3] A defendant may be equitably estopped from asserting the statute because of wrongful concealment of a material fact necessary to accrual of a cause of action, but a plaintiff may not use estoppel to excuse failure to timely file suit if he or she had ample time to do so after the inducement for delay has ceased.[4] The statute is tolled by infancy (up to age 21), mental disorder, or imprisonment.[5] The ten-year period begins to run when the product is first released to a person for its ultimate consumption or use.[6] The product liability limits do not apply to indemnity or contributions actions brought by a manufacturer or seller.[7] There is a separate discovery rule for asbestos cases.[8] The product liability statute, rather than contract or UCC statutes, limits actions for personal injury or property damage caused by negligence in the performance of a contract.[9]

When the four-year limitations period for breach of warranty applies, the cause of action accrues upon tender of delivery, except that "where a warranty explicitly extends to future performance of the goods and discovery of the breach must await the time of such performance the cause of action accrues when the breach is or should have been discovered."[10] The future performance exception does not apply to implied warranties.[11]

C. STRICT LIABILITY

1. The Standard

Nebraska essentially follows section 402A of the Restatement (Second) of Torts,[12] which embodies the user-contemplation test.[13] A plaintiff is required to prove by a preponderance of evidence that (1) the defendant placed the product on the market for use and knew, or in the exercise of reasonable care should have known, that the product would be used without inspection for defects; (2) the product was in a defective condition when it was placed on the market and left the defendant's possession; (3) the defect was the proximate or a proximately contributing cause of plaintiff's injury sustained while the product was being used in the way and for the general purpose for which it was designed and intended; (4) the defect, if existent, rendered the product unreasonably dangerous and unsafe for its intended use; and (5) plaintiff's damages were a direct and proximate result of the alleged defect.[14] Whether a product is in a defective condition unreasonably dangerous to its user is, generally, a question of fact.[15] A product is unreasonably dangerous if it creates a risk of harm beyond that which would be contemplated by the ordinary foreseeable user.[16]

2. "Defect"

In Nebraska, a product is defectively manufactured if it differs from the manufacturer's intended result[17] or if it differs from apparently identical products from that same manufacturer.[18] A product is defectively designed if it fails to perform as safely as would be expected by an ordinary consumer when the product is used in a manner either intended or reasonably foreseeable by the manufacturer.[19] A product is defective if lack of sufficient warnings renders it unreasonably dangerous. To be sufficient, a warning must inform a product's user of any risk of harm that is not readily recognizable by an ordinary user while using the product in a manner reasonably foreseeable by the manufacturer.[20] But the duty to warn does not arise if the user knows or should know of the potential danger, especially when the user is a professional who should be aware of the characteristics of the product.[21] Neither the supplier nor the manufacturer is under a duty to anticipate improper use and warn against all possible dangers.[22] No Nebraska case has addressed whether there is a post-sale duty to warn.

3. Contributory Negligence/Assumption of Risk

Assumption of the risk is a complete defense by statute (before 1992, by common law); the elements are that (1) the person knew of and understood the specific danger, (2) the person voluntarily exposed himself or herself to the danger, and (3) the person's damages occurred as a result of his or her exposure to the danger.[23]

Contributory negligence, by statute, is a defense to strict liability in tort.[24] Until recently, contributory negligence barred recovery unless the plaintiff's negligence was slight and the defendant's negligence or act or omission giving right to strict liability was gross by comparison, with mitigation of damages for slight contributory negligence.[25] Effective for causes of action accruing on or after February 8, 1992, a modified comparative negligence scheme applies.[26] Under the new law, recovery is barred if the plaintiff's contributory negligence is equal to or greater than the total negligence of all persons against whom recovery is sought, including those released, and otherwise is diminished proportionately by the degree of negligence of the plaintiff and the released person(s).[27] In multiple-defendant cases, the defendants are separately liable for noneconomic damages and jointly and severally liable for economic damages, except that when defendants, as part of a common enterprise or plan, act in concert and cause harm, their liability for all damages is joint and several.[28]

4. Sale or Lease

A plaintiff may bring a product liability action in strict liability only against the manufacturer of the product. Therefore, unless the seller or lessor of the product is also the manufacturer, no such action may be brought.[29] This rule is specifically applicable in asbestos strict liability actions.[30] A seller may be liable for negligence.[31]

5. Inherently Dangerous Products

Nebraska recognizes the unavoidably unsafe product exception to strict liability.[32]

6. Successor Liability

A successor corporation may be liable for the debts and liabilities of the predecessor corporation if any one of the four circumstances exist:

(1) the buyer corporation expressly or impliedly agrees to assume the selling corporation's liability;

(2) there is a consolidation or merger of the buyer and seller corporations;

(3) the buying corporation is a continuation of the seller corporation; or

(4) the parties entered into the transaction fraudulently to escape liability for their obligations.[33]

7. Privity

No privity is required for strict liability in tort. A manufacturer will be held strictly liable when a defective product injures someone rightfully using the product,[34] unless the nature of the product or the conditions of the sale make it improbable that it will be resold or that the vendee will allow others to use it or to share its use, or unless the product is made to special order for the peculiar use of a particular person.[35]

8. Substantial Change/Abnormal Use

Misuse is a separate and complete defense.[36] Misuse is use of a product in a way not reasonably foreseeable by the supplier or manufacturer.[37] Misuse includes failure to follow instructions and using the product in a way that is not reasonably foreseeable to the manufacturer or supplier.[38] A manufacturer is likewise not responsible when the product is altered after leaving the manufacturer's hands.[39]

9. State of the Art

In Nebraska, the state-of-the-art defense is a complete defense to strict liability. The defendant must prove that the testing, design, or labeling of the product was in conformity with the generally recognized state of the art in the industry, which is defined as the best technology that was reasonably available at that time.[40] Accordingly, feasibility of a safer design is not an element of the plaintiff's case.[41]

10. Compliance with Administrative, Industry, Regulatory, or Statutory Standards

FDA-approved drugs that are properly prepared, packaged, compounded, and distributed and that display approved warnings and direction are, as a matter of law, not defective.[42]

11. Malfunction

Evidence that an accident occurred is insufficient to establish a defect when the evidence does not establish why the accident happened.[43]

12. Subsequent Remedial Measures

Evidence of subsequent measures is not admissible to prove negligence or culpable conduct. Such evidence is admissible to prove ownership, control, or feasibility of controverted precautionary measures or for purposes of impeachment, including impeachment of a defense witness who testifies that the product conformed to the state of the art.[44]

13. Other Accidents

Evidence of other accidents will be admissible if sufficiently similar to be considered relevant and if the evidence does not present a disproportionate risk of prejudice.[45]

14. Misrepresentation

Although Nebraska has not addressed this issue, the Nebraska Supreme Court is strongly influenced by the Restatement (Second) of Torts.[46] Thus, it is likely that the Court would adopt section 402B.

15. Injury to Property

Strict liability extends to physical harm to property.[47] Recovery includes the cost of repairing the defective property itself if caused by a sudden, violent event that aggravates the inherent defect or causes it to manifest itself, but not if caused by an inherent defect that reduces the property's value without physical harm to the product.[48]

D. NEGLIGENCE

A supplier or manufacturer is liable under a negligence theory if the supplier or manufacturer fails to use reasonable care to ensure that the goods supplied or manufactured are carefully made so as not to present an unreasonable risk of causing physical harm when used for a purpose which the manufacturer should expect, in view of the foreseeable risk of injury.[49] The basic elements are duty, breach of duty, proximate causation, and damages; the plaintiff need not prove a feasible alternative design.[50] Proof of product defectiveness is evidence of the manufacturer's negligence.[51]

A supplier or manufacturer can also be held liable for negligence liability based on the supplier's or manufacturer's failure to sufficiently warn foreseeable users of foreseeable dangers associated with the product's use if there is reason to believe they would not realize the danger.[52] But a warning is unnecessary if the supplier has reason to believe the users will have such special experience as will enable them to perceive the danger.[53]

Contributory negligence and assumption of risk are separate defenses by statute.[54] For actions that accrued before February 8, 1992, a slight-gross standard applies; for later actions, a modified comparative fault standard applies.[55] Assumption of risk is a complete defense, not subject to comparison.[56] Misuse is part of the contributory negligence defense in a negligence action, although it is a separate affirmative defense in strict liability.[57]

Instructions on specific acts of negligence and contributory negligence, if pled and supported by evidence, must be submitted to the jury, rather than general instruction.

E. BREACH OF WARRANTY

In the product liability area, a cause of action for breach of warranty exists for breach of express warranty,[58] breach of implied warranty of merchantability,[59] or breach of implied warranty of fitness for a particular purpose.[60] A product's failure in performing its customary function is not a breach of an implied warranty of fitness for a particular purpose.[61] Notice of breach within a reasonable time is a condition to any remedy.[62] Nebraska extends express and implied warranties to injured persons not in privity with the seller if the person is in the buyer's family or household or is a guest in his or her home if it is reasonable to expect that such person may use, consume, or be affected by the goods.[63] An express warranty in a product brochure may not be limited by fine print provisions in the brochure.[64] A seller adopts a manufacturer's warranty by using it to induce a sale, but not by merely giving notice of it.[65] Damages for breach of warranty are measured from the date damages were or could have been discovered.[66]

F. PUNITIVE DAMAGES

Punitive damages are not recoverable in Nebraska.[67]

G. STATUTES

Relevant statutes for product liability actions are the statute of limitations,[68] contributory negligence statutes,[69] the statute exempting the lessor or seller from strict liability in tort,[70] the state-of-the-art defense statute,[71] the statute defining "product liability action,"[72] evidence code provisions on subsequent remedial measures and relevancy,[73] and the commercial code warranty sections.[74]

William M. Lamson, Jr.
Raymond E. Walden
KENNEDY, HOLLAND, DeLACY & SVOBODA
Kennedy Holland Building
10306 Regency Parkway Drive
Omaha, Nebraska 68114-3743
(402) 397-0203

ENDNOTES - NEBRASKA

1. *Adams v. American Cyanamid Co.*, 498 N.W.2d 577 (Neb. App. 1992); *Hillcrest Country Club v. N. D. Judds Co.*, 236 Neb. 233, 461 N.W.2d 55 (1990); *Delgado v. Inryco, Inc.*, 230 Neb. 662, 433 N.W.2d 179 (1988); *Morris v. Chrysler Corp.*, 208 Neb. 341, 303 N.W.2d 500 (1981).

2. Neb. Rev. Stat. §25-224 (1995). See *Fritchie v. Alumax, Inc.*, 931 F. Supp. 662 (D. Neb. 1996) (repose period ran from date entire scaffold deck was sold by distributor to equipment leasing company, not when later sold to contractor and not when contractor installed replacement part, where the defect claim related to the design of the deck and the replacement part was the same as the original).

3. *Thomas v. Countryside of Hastings, Inc.*, 246 Neb. 907, 524 N.W.2d 311 (1994); *Lindsay Mfg. Co. v. Universal Sun Co.*, 246 Neb. 495, 519 N.W.2d 530 (1994); *Murphy v. Spelts-Schultz Lumber Co.*, 240 Neb. 275, 481 N.W.2d 422 (1992); *Condon v. A. H. Robins Co.*, 217 Neb. 60, 349 N.W.2d 622 (1984).

4. *Gillam v. Firestone Tire & Rubber Co.*, 241 Neb. 414, 489 N.W.2d 289 (1992); *MacMillen v. A. H. Roberts Co.*, 217 Neb. 338, 348 N.W.2d 869 (1984).

5. Neb. Rev. Stat. §25-213 (1995); *Lawson v. Ford Motor Co.*, 225 Neb. 725, 408 N.W.2d 256 (1987).

6. *Witherspoon v. Sides Const. Co.*, 219 Neb. 117, 362 N.W.2d 35 (1985); *Spilker v. City of Lincoln*, 238 Neb. 188, 469 N.W.2d 546 (1991) (upholding con- stitutionality of statute of repose). The repose provision is constitutional. *Gillam v. Firestone Tire & Rubber Co.*, 241 Neb. 414, 489 N.W.2d 289 (1992); *Radke v. H. C. Davis Sons' Mfg. Co.*, 241 Neb. 21, 486 N.W.2d 204 (1992). Even if an injury occurs after the ten-year period, no cause of action ever accrues and the claim is barred. *Gillam, supra.*

7. Neb. Rev. Stat. §25-224(3) (1995).

8. Id. §25-224(5) (1995); see *Givens v. Anchor Packing, Inc.*, 237 Neb. 565, 466 N.W.2d 771 (1991) (holding amendment of §25-224(5) could not resurrect a cause of action that the prior version of the statute had extinguished). The 1981 amendment adding the asbestos exception does not apply retro- actively to revive a cause of action already barred before the amendment. *Givens, supra.* See also *Norwest Bank v. W. R. Grace & Co.*, 960 F.2d 754 (8th Cir. 1992) (quoting *Givens, supra*).

9. *Thomas*, 246 Neb. 907 (fire caused by negligent installation of furnace sold with new mobile home); *Fritchie*, 931 F. Supp. 662.

10. Neb. UCC §2-275 (1992).

11. *Fritchie*, 931 F. Supp. 662.

12. *Rahmig v. Mosely Mach. Co.*, 226 Neb. 423, 412 N.W.2d 56 (1987); *Adams*, 498 N.W.2d 577 (quoting *Rahmig*).

13. *Rahmig*, 226 Neb. 423 (expressly leaving adoption of the risk/utility test as "a matter for the future").

14. Id.

15. Id.

16. Id.; Nebraska Jury Instructions §11.24 (2d ed. 1989). See also *Adams*, 498 N.W.2d 577.

17. *Kudlacek v. Fiat*, S.p.A., 244 Neb. 822, 509 N.W.2d 603 (1994); *Nerud v. Haybuster Mfg.*, 215 Neb. 604, 340 N.W.2d 369 (1983), *overruled on other grounds*, *Rahmig*, 226 Neb. 423.

18. Nebraska Jury Instructions §11.21 (2d ed. 1989).

19. *Peitzmeier v. Hennessy Indus., Inc.*, 97 F.3d 293 (8th Cir. 1996); *Meisner v. Patton Electric Co.*, 781 F. Supp. 1432 (1990); *Kudlacek v. Fiat S.p.A.*, 244 Neb. 822, 509 N.W.2d 603 (1994); *Erickson v. Monarch Indus., Inc.*, 216 Neb. 875, 347 N.W.2d 99 (1984); Nebraska Jury Instructions §11.22 (2d ed. 1989).

20. *Erickson*, 216 Neb. 875; *Waegli v. Caterpillar Tractor Co.*, 197 Neb. 824, 251 N.W.2d 370 (1977); Nebraska Jury Instructions §11.23 (2d ed. 1989); *Meisner v. Patton Elec. Co., Inc.*, 781 F. Supp. 1432 (D. Neb. 1990).

21. *Peitzmeier*, 97 F.3d 293; *Strong v. E.I. DuPont de Nemours Co.*, 667 F.2d 682 (8th Cir. 1981); *Waegli*, 197 Neb. 824.

22. *Erickson*, 216 Neb. 875.

23. Neb. Rev. Stat. §§25-21,185.12 (1995); *Rahmig*, 226 Neb. 423. Nebraska Jury Instructions §11.26 (2d ed. 1989) (labeling defense as "knowledge of the defect").

24. Neb. Rev. Stat. §25-21,185 (1995) (general contributory negligence statute, mentioning strict liability); *Tillwick v. Sears, Roebuck & Co.*, 963 F.2d 1097 (1992). The Nebraska Supreme Court has not addressed whether contributory or comparative negligence is a defense in strict liability. In *Rahmig*, 226 Neb. 423, the court, somewhat ambiguously, cited pre-amendment cases in stating that "contributory negligence, which consists merely of a plaintiff's failure to discover a defect or guard against the possibility of a defect's existence, is not a defense in an action based on strict liability for a defective and unreasonably dangerous product." The federal district court in Nebraska predicted that the Nebraska Supreme Court would hold that contributory negligence is no defense, writing in the context of a case involving a plaintiff's failure to see a warning on the product and use of a faulty extension cord. *Meisner*, 781 F. Supp. at 1442-1443. However, in *Tillwick*, the Eighth Circuit rejected an argument that contributory negligence is not a defense at all, but was not faced with the question of what the *Rahmig* quotation means.

25. Neb. Rev. Stat. §25-21,185 (1989) (before 1991 & 1992 amendments).

26. Id. §§25-21,185.07 to -21,185.12 (1995).

27. Id. §§25-21, 185.09, -21,185.11 (1995).

28. Id. §25-21,185.10 (1995).

29. Id. §25-21,181 (1995). The Nebraska Supreme Court has left open whether the apparent manufacturer doctrine of the Restatement (Second) of Torts §400 (1965) "is in conflict with the plain language of §25-21,181." *Stones v. Sears, Roebuck & Co.*, 251 Neb. 560, 558 N.W.2d 540 (1997).

30. Id. §25-224(5) (1995).

31. Nebraska Jury Instructions §11.11 (2d ed. 1989).

32. *McDaniel v. McNeil Labs., Inc.*, 196 Neb. 190, 241 N.W.2d 822 (1976).

33. *Earl v. Priority Key Servs.*, 232 Neb. 584, 441 N.W.2d 610 (1989).

34. *Kohler v. Ford Motor Co.*, 187 Neb. 428, 191 N.W.2d 601 (1971).

35. *Morris v. Chrysler Corp.*, 208 Neb. 341, 303 N.W.2d 500 (1981).

36. *Rahmig*, 226 Neb. 423; *Hawkins Constr. Co. v. Matthews Co., Inc.*, 190 Neb. 546, 209 N.W.2d 643 (1973), *overruled on other grounds, National Crane Corp. v. Ohio Steel Tube Co.*, 213 Neb. 782, 332 N.W.2d 39 (1983); *Hancock v. Paccar, Inc.*, 204 Neb. 468, 283 N.W.2d 25 (1979); *Meisner v. Patton Elec. Co.*,

Inc., 781 F. Supp. 1432 (D. Neb. 1990). Nebraska Jury Instructions §11.25 (2d ed. 1989).

37.   *Rahmig,* 226 Neb. 423.

38.   *Erickson v. Monarch Indus., Inc.,* 216 Neb. 875, 347 N.W.2d 99 (1984); *Rahmig v. Mosely Mach. Co.,* 226 Neb. 423, 412 N.W.2d 56 (1987); *Meisner,* 781 F. Supp. 1432.

39.   *Erickson,* 216 Neb. 875.

40.   Neb. Rev. Stat. §25-21,182 (1995); *Hancock,* 204 Neb. 468. Nebraska Jury Instructions §11.31 (2d ed. 1989).

41.   *Rahmig,* 226 Neb. 423.

42.   *McDaniel,* 196 Neb. 190.

43.   *Delgado v. Inryco, Inc.,* 230 Neb. 662, 433 N.W.2d 179 (1988).

44.   Neb. Rev. Stat. §27-407 (1995); *Rahmig,* 226 Neb. 423.

45.   Neb. Rev. Stat. §§27-401, 27-403 (1995); *Herman v. Midland Agric. Serv., Inc.,* 200 Neb. 356, 264 N.W.2d 161 (1978).

46.   See, e.g., *Rahmig,* 226 Neb. 423.

47.   *National Crane Corp. v. Ohio Steel Tube Co.,* 213 Neb. 782, 332 N.W.2d 39 (1983).

48.   *Hilt Truck Line, Inc. v. Pullman, Inc.,* 222 Neb. 65, 382 N.W.2d 310 (1986).

49.   *Morris,* 208 Neb. 341 (citing Restatement (Second) of Torts §395 (1965)); *Rahmig,* 226 Neb. 423; Nebraska Jury Instructions §11.10 (2d ed. 1989).

50.   *Rahmig,* 226 Neb. 423; Neb. Rev. Stat. §25-21,181 (1995), protecting sellers and lessors of products, does not apply to negligence actions.

51.   *Morris,* 208 Neb. 341.

52.   Nebraska Jury Instructions §11.11 (2d ed. 1989).

53.   *Erickson,* 216 Neb. 875 (citing Restatement (Second) of Torts §388, comment k (1965)).

54.   See discussion and notes in section C.3, *supra.*

55. See discussion and notes in section C.3, *supra*.

56. See discussion and notes in section C.3, *supra*. With respect to causes of action accruing before Feb. 8, 1992, see *Mandery v. Chronicle Broadcasting Co.*, 228 Neb. 391, 423 N.W.2d 115 (1988); *Makovicka v. Lukes*, 182 Neb. 168, 153 N.W.2d 733 (1967).

57. Nebraska Jury Instructions §11.12 comment (2d ed. 1989).

58. Neb. UCC §2-313 (1992); *Murphy v. Spelts-Schultz Lumber Co.*, 240 Neb. 275, 481 N.W.2d 422 (1992); *Hillcrest Country Club v. N.D. Judds Co.*, 236 Neb. 233, 461 N.W.2d 55 (1990); *Delgado v. Inryco, Inc.*, 230 Neb. 662, 433 N.W.2d 179 (1988).

59. Neb. UCC §2-314 (1992); *Murphy,* 240 Neb. 275; *Delgado,* 230 Neb. 662.

60. Neb. UCC §2-315 (1992); *Murphy,* 240 Neb. 275; *Delgado,* 230 Neb. 662.

61. *Stones v. Sears, Roebuck & Co.*, 251 Neb. 560, 558 N.W.2d 540 (1997).

62. Neb. UCC §2-607(3)(a) (1992).

63. Neb. UCC §2-318 (1992).

64. *Hillcrest Country Club,* 236 Neb. 233.

65. Id.

66. Id. (date when roof began to flake).

67. *Miller v. Kingsley*, 194 Neb. 123, 230 N.W.2d 472 (1975).

68. Neb. Rev. Stat. §25-224 (1995).

69. Neb. Rev. Stat. §§25-21,185, 25-21,185.07 to -21,185.12 (1995).

70. Neb. Rev. Stat. §§25-21,181, 25-224(5) (1995).

71. Neb. Rev. Stat. §25-21,182 (1995).

72. Neb. Rev. Stat. §25-21,180 (1995).

73. Neb. Rev. Stat. §§27-401, 27-403, 27-407 (1995).

74. Neb. UCC §§2-313, 2-314, 2-315, 2-318, 2-607 (1992).

NEVADA

A. CAUSES OF ACTION

Product liability suits commonly include causes of action for strict liability, negligence, and breach of warranty.[1] Since contributory negligence is not a defense to an action of strict liability, it is common for cases to be pled solely on the theory of strict liability when there is a possibility of contributory negligence.[2]

B. DAMAGES

Damages recoverable under a theory of strict product liability include injury to life or other property resulting from the use of a dangerously defective product. When a product "injures itself," redress must be sought through manufacturer's warranties and insurance.[3]

C. STATUTES OF LIMITATION

Causes of action for personal injuries must be brought within two years, irrespective of whether the theory is negligence or strict liability.[4] The statute of limitations for property damages, however, is three years, irrespective of the theory.[5]

A cause of action for personal injuries resulting from breach of warranty falls within the four or six year statute of limitations:[6] six years for an express promise in writing, four years for an implied warranty.

The statute of limitations applicable to causes of action for damage from construction is indeed another matter. The statute concerning injuries or wrongful death caused by deficiency of construction or improvements to real property has been the subject of much dispute and has resulted in a statute that, to say the least, is ambiguous. The statute runs for ten years after the substantial completion of such an improvement. The statute goes on to provide, however, that where an injury occurs in the tenth year after substantial completion, an action for damages for personal injury or death may be commenced within two years after the date of such injury, irrespective of the date of death. That statute provides that an action in no event shall be commenced more than twelve years after the substantial completion of the improvement.[7] The statute of limitations does not run for damages or injury that are caused by deficiencies that are fraudulently concealed.[8]

With respect to damages that are the result of known deficiencies, that is, deficiencies that are known, or should have been known, by the owner, occupier, or person who is in possession of the land, again, that action must be brought within ten years after substantial completion of the project.

However, in the event injury or death occurs in the tenth year, it must be brought within two years after the date of injury, irrespective of the date of death. In this specific case, the action cannot be commenced more than twelve years after substantial completion of the project.

The statute of limitations for latent and patent deficiencies is eight years after substantial completion; however, as in the case of known deficiencies, in the event there is an injury or death in the eighth year, that must be prosecuted within two years. However, no action can be commenced more than ten years after the substantial completion of the improvement.[9]

There is one further exception in the statute in that the limitations are not a defense to an action brought against the owner or keeper of a motel, inn, boarding house, and so on. Likewise, there does not appear to be any defense for a defect in the product.[10]

D. STRICT LIABILITY

1. The Standard

Nevada has specifically adopted section 402A of the Restatement (Second) of Torts. The trier of fact must find that the product is unreasonably dangerous. Plaintiff must prove that the defect in the product makes the product unreasonably dangerous and unsafe for its intended use.[11]

2. "Defect"

A product is defective if it fails to perform in a manner reasonably expected in light of its nature and intended function.[12]

Nevada has also adopted Restatement of Torts section 402A, paragraph (h). Where the defendant has reason to anticipate that danger may result from particular use of his product and fails to give adequate warning of such danger, a product sold without such a warning is in a defective condition.[13]

3. Contributory Negligence/Assumption of Risk

Contributory negligence is not a defense, but assumption of risk and misuse of the product remain.[14] The misuse that constitutes a defense is that use which the designer or manufacturer could not reasonably foresee.[15]

4. Privity

There is no privity requirement for a case predicated upon strict liability.[16]

5. Lease

While Nevada has not specifically ruled on whether a lessor may be held strictly liable in a product liability action, the *Burns*[17] decision suggests that a lessor may be a proper defendant to such an action.

6. Successor Liability

Strict liability applies only to one who sells a product in the regular course of her business. It is not applicable to the occasional seller of a product.[18]

7. Failure to Warn

Where defendant has reason to anticipate that danger may result from a particular use of his product, and he fails to warn adequately of such a danger, the product sold without a warning is in a defective condition.[19]

8. Post-Sale Duty to Warn

Evidence of post-accident warnings are admissible to prove the existence of a defect in the product, but not to prove negligence or culpable conduct. The court has discretion to exclude evidence of such warnings if the evidence would prove to be more prejudicial than probative.[20]

9. Substantial Change/Abnormal Use

A manufacturer can be held liable for a foreseeable misuse of a product in spite of adequate warning.[21]

10. Malfunction

It is not necessary to prove a specific defect in the product. Rather, it is sufficient to show an unexplained, dangerous malfunction. That is sufficient to establish a prima facie case for the existence of a product defect.[22]

11. Other Accidents

In strict tort liability cases, evidence of prior or subsequent mishaps similar to the one in issue, involving the same product, are admissible to show faulty design or manufacture or other elements of the strict liability cause of action.[23]

12. Misrepresentation

Nevada case law suggests that misrepresentation concerning a product may be a proper basis for a strict liability action against the manufacturer.[24]

13. Causation

Plaintiff has the burden to prove that the design defect in the product was a substantial factor in causing his injury. Where the injury is identical to that which would have been received absent the claimed defect, the manufacturer may be absolved of liability.[25]

An intentional intervening act by a third party that is both unforeseeable and the proximate cause of the injury may insulate the manufacturer of a defective product from liability. Id.

14. Unavoidably Unsafe Products

The Nevada Supreme Court has questioned Restatement (Second) of Torts, §402A, Comment k, as it applies to drugs that are incapable of being made safe for their intended and ordinary use. The court suggests that a manufacturer may avoid strict liability for injuries caused by unavoidably unsafe products only where ample warning that the product is unsafe has been given.[26]

15. Bulk Supplier Doctrine

The United States District Court of Nevada has opined that the Nevada Supreme Court would adopt some form of the so-called bulk supplier doctrine. Under this defense, a bulk supplier who supplies a dangerous product to a sophisticated purchaser cannot be held liable for not warning the ultimate users of the product of its dangers.[27]

E. NEGLIGENCE

If liability is to be placed on a retailer or manufacturer of goods, it must rest on negligence or a declared public policy, that is, strict liability.[28] While assumption of the risk is a defense to a strict liability claim, it is not a bar to a negligence claim.[29]

F. SAFETY DEVICES

A manufacturer may be liable for failure to provide a safety device if the inclusion of the device is commercially feasible, will not effect product efficiency, and is within the state of the art at the time the product was placed in the stream of commerce.[30]

G. BREACH OF WARRANTY

Nevada has adopted the Uniform Commercial Code with regard to breach of warranty.[31] Vertical privity is not required to bring a breach of warranty action.[32] The defendant must be engaged in the business of selling or supplying the goods that are the subject of the suit in her regular course of business.[33] A breach of warranty action may only be premised on the sale of "goods" as defined in the UCC.[34] Purely economic loss may be recovered under a breach of warranty theory, without need to show personal or property damages.[35]

H. PUNITIVE DAMAGES

Nevada's punitive damages statute, Nev. Rev. Stat §42.010, allows for an award of punitive damages where defendant has been guilty of oppression, fraud, or malice, express or implied. Malice refers to malice in fact. In the context of product liability, malice in fact may be established by a showing that the defendant consciously and deliberately disregarded known safety measures in reckless disregard of the possible results.[36] The amount of a punitive damages award is not statutorily limited in an action brought against the manufacturer, distributor, or seller of a defective product.[37]

I. STATUTES

A label conforming with FIFRA (Federal Insecticide, Fungicide, and Rodenticide Act, 7 U.S.C. §136 et seq.) requirements will not be held inadequate in a strict liability claim.[38]

The manufacturer or distributor of firearms or ammunition is not subject to suit merely because its product is capable of causing serious injury, damage, or death, nor is the product defective in design simply because such results may occur. This statute does not extinguish a cause of action against such a manufacturer or distributor based on defect in design or production.[39]

The lender of money that is used to finance the design, manufacture, construction, repair, modification, or improvement of real or personal property is not liable to the borrower or third persons injured by a defect therein, unless the loss or damage is the result of activity by the lender other than the loan transaction.[40]

On or before March 1 of each year, every insurer who issues policies covering the liability of manufacturers or sellers of defective products must submit a report to the insurance commissioner on an approved claim reporting form.[41]

Stacey A. Upson
VARGAS & BARTLETT
201 West Liberty Street
P.O. Box 281
Reno, Nevada 89504-0281
(702) 786-5000

1. *Shoshone Coca Cola v. Dolinsky*, 82 Nev. 439, 420 P.2d 855 (1966); *Ginnis v. Mapes*, 86 Nev. 408, 470 P.2d 135 (1970).

2. *Young's Mach. Co. v. Long*, 100 Nev. 692, 692 P.2d 24 (1984).

3. *National Union Fire Ins. v. Pratt & Whitney*, 107 Nev. Adv. Op. 88, 815 P.2d 601 (1991).

4. Nev. Rev. Stat. §11.190.

5. Id.

6. Id.

7. Nev. Rev. Stat. §11.203.

8. Nev. Rev. Stat. §11.202.

9. *Jasinski v. Showboat Operating Co.*, 644 F.2d 1277; *Oak Grove Inv. v. Bell & Gossett Co.*, 99 Nev. 616, 668 P.2d 1075 (1983).

10. Nev. Rev. Stat. §11.206.

11. *Ward v. Ford Motor Co.*, 99 Nev. 47, 657 P.2d 95 (1983).

12. *Ginnis*, 86 Nev. 408; *Allison v. Merck and Co. Inc.*, 110 Nev. 762, 878 P.2d 948 (1994).

13. *Outboard Marine v. Schupbach*, 93 Nev. 158, 561 P.2d 450 (1977).

14. *Young's Machine Co.*, 100 Nev. 692.

15. *Corella v. Crown Control*, 98 Nev. 35, 639 P.2d 555 (1982).

16. *Shoshone Coca Cola*, 82 Nev. 439; *Ginnis*, 86 Nev. 408.

17. *Burns v. District Court*, 97 Nev. 237, 627 P.2d 403 (1981).

18. *Elley v. Stephens*, 104 Nev. 413, 760 P.2d 768 (1988).

19. *General Elec. Co. v. Bush*, 88 Nev. 360, 498 P.2d 366 (1972); *Outboard Marine Corp.*, 93 Nev. 158; *Oak Grove Inv.*, 99 Nev. 616; *Fyssakis v. U.N.X. Chem. Inc.*, 108 Nev. 212, 826 P.2d 570 (1992).

20. *Jeep Corp. v. Murray*, 101 Nev. 640, 708 P.2d 297 (1985); see also Nev. Rev. Stat. §48.095.

21. *Robinson v. GGC, Inc.*, 107 Nev. 135, 808 P.2d 522 (1991).

22. *Stackiewicz v. Nissan*, 100 Nev. 443, 686 P.2d 925 (1984).

23. *Ginnis*, 86 Nev. 408; *Beattie v. Thomas*, 99 Nev. 579, 668 P.2d 268 (1983); *Robinson*, 107 Nev. 135.

24. *Jeep Corp.*, 101 Nev. 640.

25. *Price v. Blain Kern Artista, Inc.*, 111 Nev. 515, 893 P.2d 367 (1995).

26. *Allison v. Merck and Co., Inc.*, 110 Nev. 762, 878 P.2d 948 (1994).

27. *Forest v. E.I. DuPont, et al.*, 791 F. Supp. 1460 (1992).

28. *Long v. Flanigan Whse. Co.*, 79 Nev. 241, 382 P.2d 399 (1963).

29. *Central Tel. Co. v. Fixtures Mfg.*, 103 Nev. 298, 738 P.2d 510 (1987).

30. *Robinson*, 107 Nev. 135; *Fyssakis*, 108 Nev. 212.

31. *Long*, 79 Nev. 241; see Nev. Rev. Stat. §§104.2312-104.2318, inclusive.

32. *United Mortgage Co. v. Hildreth*, 93 Nev. 73, 560 P.2d 154 (1977).

33. Id.

34. *Worrell v. Barnes*, 87 Nev. 204, 484 P.2d 573 (1971).

35. *Central Bit Supply v. Waldrop Drilling*, 102 Nev. 139, 717 P.2d 35 (1986).

36. *Jeep Corp.*, 101 Nev. 640; *Leslie v. Jones Chem. Co.*, 92 Nev. 391, 551 P.2d 234 (1976).

37. Nev. Rev. Stat. §42.005(2)(a).

38. *Davidson v. Velsicol Chem. Corp.*, 108 Nev. 591, 834 P.2d 931 (1992).

39. Nev. Rev. Stat. §41.131.

40.   Nev. Rev. Stat. §41.590.

41.   Nev. Rev. Stat. §690B.120.

NEW HAMPSHIRE

A. CAUSES OF ACTION

Claims for injury arising out of a product liability setting may be pursued in negligence, strict liability in tort, and warranty.

B. STATUTES OF LIMITATION

Claims in negligence and strict liability tort are subject to a three-year statute of limitations.[1]

New Hampshire applies a "discovery" rule.[2]

Causes of action for breach of warranty, express or implied, must be brought within four years of date of sale.[3]

C. NEGLIGENCE

Standard common law negligence duties apply to claims of damage arising from product losses.

If a claim is made for economic or commercial losses, the plaintiff must rely on negligence or warranty principles.[4]

Comparative negligence principles apply to claims of negligence. A plaintiff's award will be reduced based on percentage of comparative negligence. A plaintiff's claim is barred if plaintiff is more than 50 percent at fault.[5]

D. STRICT LIABILITY

New Hampshire has adopted Restatement (Second) of Torts section 402A.[6]

The New Hampshire Supreme Court cites extensively from comments to section 402A in its decisions. However, the court has made it clear that it does not adopt the comments in their entirety and has specifically rejected "risk-spreading" analysis.[7]

Although strict liability in tort has been adopted in New Hampshire, the New Hampshire Supreme Court has made it clear that this does not establish absolute liability, and issues of product defect, causation, and foreseeability are important elements for a jury.[8]

The occurrence of an injury from a product is not sufficient evidence to prove either "defect" or "unreasonably dangerous." These are questions of fact for determination by a jury and normally will require expert testimony.[9]

Strict liability will not apply to providers of services, *Siciliano v. Capital City Shows, Inc.*, 124 N.H. 719 (1984), nor will it apply to nonmanufacturers and nonsellers.[10]

E. DEFENSES

Plaintiff misconduct acts as a defense in a fashion analogous to comparative negligence. Plaintiff's misconduct, including product misuse, abnormal use, assumption of the risk, and so on, will result in a proportionate reduction in award to a plaintiff. If plaintiff's misconduct is more than 50 percent of the cause of the accident, then plaintiff will be barred from recovery.[11]

A third party's misconduct acts as a defense only if it is the sole proximate cause of the plaintiff's injuries, and provided such misconduct was not foreseeable to a manufacturer such that the misconduct should be accounted for in the design.[12]

F. LEASING AGREEMENTS

Strict liability is likely to apply to a lessor of a product if that lessor is in the business of routinely leasing a product, but it will not apply to lessor-lessee arrangements that appear to be nothing more than financing arrangements.[13]

G. INHERENTLY DANGEROUS PRODUCTS

A supplier of products will not be held strictly liable simply because a product is inherently dangerous, unless the product is deemed otherwise defective for failure to give adequate warnings.[14]

H. WARNINGS

A failure to warn of dangers not otherwise obvious to a user can constitute a design defect giving rise to strict liability if the product was used in a fashion that would foreseeably incur an injury and the failure to properly warn was causal.[15]

The product manufacturer or seller has no duty to warn of obvious risks.[16]

The New Hampshire Supreme Court has not addressed the sophisticated user defense as it might apply to warnings.

The New Hampshire Supreme Court has suggested in dicta that imposing a duty to warn of risks unknowable at the time of sale is unreasonable and amounts to absolute liability.[17] However, the New Hampshire Supreme Court has not directly addressed the issue of a duty to warn after manufacture or sale under circumstances where a manufacturer or seller becomes aware of widespread buyer alterations, misuse, or increased hazards with a product.

I. PRIVITY

Privity is not required.[18]

J. SUBSTANTIAL CHANGE

A manufacturer or seller is not liable for injuries or damages caused by a product that has been substantially changed or that has been subject to abnormal use, provided the change or abnormal use is not that which could be reasonably foreseen or expected by the manufacturer and/or seller.[19]

K. STATE OF THE ART

While state of the art is available as a defense, post-manufacture evidence can be introduced to rebut defense claims of infeasibility.[20]

L. STANDARDS

Evidence that a product complies with state or federal standards does not require a finding that the product is not defective.[21]

M. LIABILITY AMONG MULTIPLE DEFENDANTS

New Hampshire has recognized the right of indemnification by non-negligent sellers against upstream sellers and/or manufacturers.[22] For claims arising after July 1, 1986, New Hampshire has adopted a statute providing for contribution among joint tortfeasors.[23] No appellate decision has addressed the applicability of contribution among tortfeasors in a strict liability claim. The contribution statute does not refer specifically to negligence claims, but rather applies to parties liable for the same indivisible claim or same injury. It is likely that this statute will apply to claims of strict liability and tort.

N. RELATED THEORIES OF LIABILITY

1. Successor Liability

Under limited circumstances, a successor corporation may be held liable for a product manufactured or sold by a predecessor.[24] However, this decision should be narrowly construed, as the New Hampshire Supreme Court has specifically disapproved of the *Sears* decision to the extent that it suggests that New Hampshire adopts a "risk-spreading" analysis for imposing strict liability.[25] The New Hampshire Supreme Court has specifically rejected the "product line" theory for successor liability.

2. Market Share Liability and Enterprise Liability

Neither of these concepts have been specifically addressed by the New Hampshire Supreme Court. It is likely that either theory would be rejected by the New Hampshire Supreme Court, because each is reliant upon a risk-spreading analysis.[26]

O. BREACH OF WARRANTY

While a breach of warranty claim is available in a product liability setting, this claim is virtually identical to the strict liability and tort theory. Some

---

trial judges will not allow counsel to proceed on both theories on the basis that it causes confusion to a jury.

P. PUNITIVE DAMAGES

Punitive damages are not recoverable in tort actions in New Hampshire.[27]

Q. NONECONOMIC DAMAGES

A statute limiting recovery for damages for noneconomic loss, such as pain and suffering, to $875,000 has been declared unconstitutional by the New Hampshire Supreme Court.

Fred J. Desmarais
Jeffrey B. Osburn
WIGGIN & NOURIE
The Parish House
20 Market Street
P.O. Box 808
Manchester, New Hampshire 03105
(603) 669-2211

ENDNOTES - NEW HAMPSHIRE

1. N.H. Rev. Stat. Ann. §508:4 I.

2. *Raymond v. Eli Lilly & Co.*, 117 N.H. 164 (1977); *Brown v. Mary Hitchcock Memorial Hosp.*, 117 N.H. 739 (1977).

3. N.H. Rev. Stat. Ann. §382-A:2-725.

4. *Ellis v. Robert C. Morris, Inc.*, 128 N.H. 358 (1986); *Public Serv. Co. of N.H. v. Westinghouse Elec. Corp.*, 685 F. Supp. 1281 (D.N.H. 1988).

5. N.H. Rev. Stat. Ann. §507:7-d.

6. *Buttrick v. Lessard*, 110 N.H. 36 (1969); *Thibeault v. Sears, Roebuck & Co.*, 118 N.H. 802 (1978).

7. *Simoneau v. South Bend Lathe, Inc.*, 130 N.H. 466 (1982).

8. *Thibeault*, 118 N.H. 802; *McLaughlin v. Sears, Roebuck & Co.*, 111 N.H. 265 (1971).

9. *Bellotte v. Zayre*, 116 N.H. 52 (1976).

10. *Moulton v. Groveton Paper Co.*, 112 N.H. 50 (1972).

11. *Thibeault*, 118 N.H. 802.

12. *Reid v. Spadone Machine Co.*, 119 N.H. 457 (1979); *Murray v. Bullard Co.*, 110 N.H. 220 (1970).

13. *Brescia v. Great Road Realty Trust*, 117 N.H. 154 (1977).

14. *Thibeault*, 118 N.H. 802.

15. Id.; *Reid v. Spadone Mach. Co.*, 119 N.H. 457 (1979).

16. *Thibeault*, 118 N.H. 802; *Plant v. Hobart Corp.*, 771 F.2d 617 (1st Cir. 1985).

17. *Heather v. Sears, Roebuck & Co.*, 123 N.H. 512 (1983).

18. N.H. Rev. Stat. Ann. §382-A:2-318.

19. *Reid*, 119 N.H. 457.

20.   *Estate of Spinosa,* 621 F.2d 1154 (1st Cir. 1980).

21.   *Raymond v. Riegel Textile Corp.,* 484 F.2d 1025 (1st Cir. 1973).

22.   *Consolidated Util. Equip. Servs., Inc. v. Emhart Mfg. Corp.,* 123 N.H. 258 (1983).

23.   N.H. Rev. Stat. Ann. §507:7-f.

24.   *Cyr v. B. Offen & Co., Inc.,* 501 F.2d 1145 (1st Cir. 1974).

25.   *Simoneau,* 130 N.H. 466.

26.   Id.

27.   N.H. Rev. Stat. Ann. §507:16.

NEW JERSEY

A. CAUSES OF ACTION

The Products Liability Act (the Act) applies to actions filed on or after July 22, 1987[1] and subsumes common law claims; basically, the Act is the sole basis of relief for harm caused by defective products.[2] The Act was not, however, intended to codify all issues of product liability law. For example, the Act does not address certain defenses such as product misuse.[3] Product liability lawsuits include claims based on strict liability, negligence, and breach of warranty. A state cause of action is commenced in a manner consistent with federal practice, except a response is required within thirty-five (35) days after service of the summons and complaint.[4]

B. STATUTES OF LIMITATION

A cause of action for personal injuries must be brought within two years after the cause of action accrues, regardless of whether the claim is based on strict liability, negligence, or warranty.[5]

Although strict liability and negligence claims generally accrue at the time of injury, New Jersey Courts apply a rather liberal "discovery rule." The discovery rule tolls the limitations period where a plaintiff was not, and reasonably could not have been, aware of the underlying factual basis for a cause of action.[6]

A cause of action for breach of warranty accrues from the time the product is delivered.[7] A cause of action for property damage must be brought within six years.[8] Claims for injuries arising from improvements to real property, however, have a ten-year statute of limitations.[9]

C. STRICT LIABILITY

1. The Standard

Under New Jersey law, manufacturers and sellers are strictly liable for damages resulting from the use of their products if they fail to produce and distribute products that are reasonably fit, suitable, and safe when used for their intended or reasonably foreseeable purposes.[10] Although the Act is intended to clarify certain issues related to product liability claims, it does not purport to be a comprehensive codification of all matters.[11] It applies to all actions for harm caused by products except actions based on breach of express warranties[12] and environmental tort actions.[13]

2. Definition of "Defect"

A plaintiff may show a "defect" by establishing: (1) a manufacturing defect; (2) a design defect; and/or (3) an inadequate warning. With respect to a manufacturing defect, the product is measured against the same product made in accordance with the manufacturers' standards.[14] In a design defect case, the trier of fact engages in a "risk-utility" analysis weighing the following factors: (1) usefulness and desirability of product aspects; (2) the safety aspects of the product; (3) availability of substitutes; (4) ability to eliminate its unsafe character without great expense or impairing usefulness; (5) user's ability to avoid danger; (6) user's anticipated awareness of inherent dangers and their avoidability; and (7) feasibility of spreading loss. The question in a strict liability design-defect case is whether, assuming that the manufacturer knew of the defect in the product, he acted in a reasonably prudent manner in marketing the product or in providing the warnings given.[15]

In an inadequate warnings case, the Act defines an adequate warning[16] and knowledge of the defect is imputed to the manufacturer.[17]

3. Contributory Negligence/Assumption of Risk

Plaintiff's negligence is a defense unless it consists of mere failure to discover a defect in the product or to guard against the possibility of its existence. Assumption of the risk is available as a defense when plaintiff's conduct amounts to voluntarily and unreasonably proceeding to encounter a known danger.[18]

4. Obvious Danger

An open and obvious danger is a complete defense to products liability claims under the Act. There are two circumstances in which this absolute defense is not available to the defendant: if the product is workplace equipment or if the danger can "feasibly be eliminated without impairing the usefulness of the product."[19]

5. Entities Liable

Under New Jersey law, liability extends not only to those who manufacture a defective product, but also to any party in the chain of distribution, including distributors, retailers,[20] and lessors.[21] However, strict liability does not extend to an occasional seller who is not in the business of supplying such products.[22] Strict liability may apply in hybrid transactions involving the provision of a product with services.[23] A component part manufacturer can be held strictly liable for injuries caused by a defect in that part, provided that the part did not undergo a substantial change after leaving its maker's control.[24] Manufacturers will not be held liable for defects created or caused by someone further down the distribution line.[25]

6. Inherently Dangerous/Unavoidably Unsafe Products

According to the Act, a manufacturer or seller will not be held liable under a design defect theory if the harm was caused by an unsafe aspect of the product that is an inherent characteristic of the product and if the harm would be recognized by the ordinary person.[26] A manufacturer will also not be held liable for an unavoidably unsafe aspect of a product that is accompanied by adequate warnings.[27]

7. Successor Liability

If the successor corporation acquires all or substantially all of the manufacturing assets of the predecessor corporation and undertakes essentially the same manufacturing operation, it may be subject to strict liability for injuries caused by defects in the product. This is so even if the product was manufactured and sold by the predecessor, especially if the predecessor is no longer financially viable.[28]

8. Privity

Privity is not required for recovery under strict products liability.[29]

9. Failure to Warn/Inadequate Warning

In a failure to warn case, the alleged product defect is the absence of a warning or an adequate warning to unsuspecting users that the product can potentially cause injury.[30] Plaintiff is required to prove that the absence of a warning was a proximate cause of his harm, and there is a rebuttable presumption that plaintiff would have heeded the warning.[31] An "adequate product warning or instruction" is defined by the Act and is evaluated in terms of what the manufacturer knew at the time it produced the product and what it should have known based on reasonably available information, taking into account the ordinary knowledge common to anticipated users of the product.[32]

10. Post-Sale Duty to Warn

When a manufacturer fails to include a warning on a product, but subsequently learns, or should have learned, of the dangers associated with the product, the manufacturer owes a duty to warn of the dangers as soon as reasonably feasible.[33]

11. Learned Intermediary Doctrine

Manufacturers of prescription drugs satisfy their duty to warn by providing the prescribing physicians with information regarding the risks associated with the products. Manufacturers are not required to warn individual patients.[34]

12. Substantial Alteration/Misuse

A manufacturer will not be held strictly liable if there were substantial alterations of the product that caused injury, and if those alterations were not reasonably foreseeable.[35] Plaintiff has the burden of proving there was no misuse of the product or that the misuse was objectively foreseeable.[36] Accordingly, misuse of a product is not an affirmative defense in a products liability case.

13. **State of the Art**

Under the Act, "state-of-the-art" is an absolute defense to claims based on design defects.[37] The burden on a defendant who claims a state-of-the-art defense is to prove only the technological state-of-the-art when the product was manufactured and not to prove its conformity with the state of the art. It remains plaintiff's burden to prove non-conformity.[38]

14. **Malfunction**

Malfunctioning of a product in the absence of abnormal use or reasonable secondary cause is evidence of a defect.[39]

15. **Standards and Governmental Regulations**

Although a defendant's compliance with legislative enactments, administrative regulations, or industry safety codes is admissible, it is not conclusive as to absence of defect or negligence.[40]

16. **Other Accidents**

Evidence of prior substantially similar accidents or occurrences is admissible in product liability actions to prove defect.[41]

17. **Misrepresentation**

Although New Jersey courts have not officially adopted Restatement (Second) of Torts section 402B, the courts have inferred that such a cause of action may be viable.[42]

D. NEGLIGENCE

Contributory negligence is a defense; however, the doctrine of comparative negligence is applied unless the plaintiff is more than 50 percent at fault. If plaintiff is found to be 51 percent or more at fault, recovery is barred.[43]

E. BREACH OF WARRANTY

The principles underlying strict liability and implied warranty are identical in New Jersey.[44] Strict liability theories impose warranty obligations without the need for contractual privity.[45]

F. PUNITIVE DAMAGES

Under the Act, punitive damages may be awarded only if the plaintiff proves that the manufacturer/seller acted with actual malice or with wanton and willful disregard for the safety of foreseeable users. The evidentiary standard for proving punitive damages is "preponderance of the evidence."[46]

The trial of the matter will be bifurcated and evidence relevant to punitive damages will not be admissible in the liability proceeding. The issue of whether punitive damages are recoverable and the amount, if any, is the subject of a separate proceeding after a determination of liability has been made.[47]

Punitive damages are not permissible for products that have been licensed or approved by the Food and Drug Administration, except where the manufacturer knowingly withheld or misrepresented material, relevant information required to be submitted under the agency's regulations.[48]

G. JOINT AND SEVERAL LIABILITY

1. The Rule

The New Jersey Comparative Negligence Act requires that defendants are jointly and severally liable. A party may seek recovery of the entire verdict from any party who is found to be 60 percent or more responsible for the total damages. A party may seek the full amount of economic damages, but only the percentage of noneconomic damages attributable to that party's negligence, from any party who is between 20 and 60 percent responsible for the total damages. A defendant will be required to pay only his proportionate share of the verdict if he is found to be 20 percent or less responsible.[49]

2. Contribution

A joint tortfeasor who is compelled to pay more than his percentage share may seek contribution from other tortfeasors who are liable for plaintiff's injuries.[50]

3. Effect of Settlement

Under New Jersey law, a nonsettling defendant does not have a viable crossclaim against a settling defendant and all crossclaims against a settling defendant should be dismissed as a matter of law.

Even though a nonsettling defendant's crossclaim for contribution against the settling tortfeasor will be dismissed, the nonsettling defendant is entitled to a credit reflecting the settlor's fair share of the amount of the verdict.[51]

H. STATUTES

Relevant statutes for product liability actions include the Products Liability Act,[52] statutes of limitations,[53] and the commercial code section when a breach of warranty is alleged.[54]

New Jersey state courts generally follow *Model Jury Charges: Civil* (4th ed.).[55]

Gerhard P. Dietrich
Tracy Canuso Nugent
DALLER GREENBERG & DIETRICH, LLP
2 White Horse Pike
Haddon Heights, NJ 08035
(609) 547-9068 / (609) 547-2391 (Fax)
gdietrich@dallergreenberg.com (Email)

ENDNOTES - NEW JERSEY

1. N.J. Stat. Ann. §2A:58C-1-58C-7 (West 1987); *Dewey v. R. J. Reynolds Tobacco Co.*, 121 N.J. 69, 577 A.2d 1239 (1990).

2. *Canty v. Ever-Last Supply Co.*, 296 N.J. Super. 68, 685 A.2d 1365 (1996); *Ramos v. Silent Hoist and Crane Co.*, 256 N.J. Super. 467, 607 A.2d 667 (1992); *Tirrell v. Navistar Intl., Inc.*, 248 N.J. Super. 390, 591 A.2d 643, *cert. denied*, 126 N.J. 390, 599 A.2d 166 (1991). Express warranty claims are preserved by the Act. N.J. Stat. Ann. §2A:58C-1b(3) (West 1987).

3. *Jurado v. Western Gear Works*, 131 N.J. 375, 619 A.2d 1312 (1993).

4. N.J. Court Rules 4:2-2, 4:6-1.

5. N.J. Stat. Ann. §2A:14-2 (West 1987).

6. See, e.g., *Graves v. Church & Dwight Co., Inc.*, 225 N.J. Super. 49, 541 A.2d 725 (1988), *aff'd*, 115 N.J. 256, 558 A.2d 463 (1989); *Vispisiano v. Ashland Chem. Co.*, 107 N.J. 416, 527 A.2d 66 (1987); *Cipollone v. Liggett Group, Inc.*, 893 F.2d 541 (3d Cir. 1990), *cert. granted*, 499 U.S. 935, 1115 S. Ct. 1386 (1991), *aff'd in part, rev'd in part*, 112 S. Ct. 2608, 120 L.Ed.2d 407 (1992); *Tevis v. Tevis*, 79 N.J. 422, 400 A.2d 1189 (1979).

7. N.J. Stat. Ann. §12A:2-725 (West 1987); *Yttro Corp. v. X-Ray Marketing*, 233 N.J. Super. 347, 559 A.2d 3 (1989); *Biocraft Labs., Inc. v. USM Corp.*, 163 N.J. Super. 570, 395 A.2d 521 (1978).

8. N.J. Stat. Ann. §2A:14-1,2 (West 1987).

9. N.J. Stat. Ann. §2A:14-1.1 (West 1987). This limitation applies to injuries to real or personal property, injuries to the person, and bodily injury or wrongful death. It preserves causes of action against those in possession or control.

10. N.J. Stat. Ann. §2A:58C-2 (West 1987); *Zaza v. Marguess and Nell, Inc.*, 144 N.J. 34, 675 A.2d 620 (1996); *Feldman v. Lederle Labs.*, 125 N.J. 117, 592 A.2d 1176 (1991), *cert. denied*, 505 U.S. 1214, 112 S. Ct. 3027, 120 L. Ed. 2d 898 (1992); *Soler v. Castmaster, Div. of H.P.M. Corp.*, 98 N.J. 137, 484 A.2d 1225 (1984); *Navarro v. George Koch & Sons, Inc.*, 211 N.J. Super. 558, 512 A.2d 507, *cert. denied*, 107 N.J. 48, 526 A.2d 138 (1986); *Molino v. B. F. Goodrich Co.*, 261 N.J. Super. 85, 617 A.2d 1235, *cert. denied*, 134 N.J. 482, 634 A.2d 528 (1993).

11. N.J. Stat. Ann. §2A:58C-1-58C-7 (West 1987); *Zaza*, 144 N.J. 34; *Fabian v. Minster Mach. Co., Inc.*, 258 N.J. Super. 261, 609 A.2d 487 (1992), *cert. denied*, 130 N.J. 598, 617 A.2d 1220 (1992).

12. N.J. Stat. Ann. §2A:58C-1b(3) (West 1987).

13. Id. §2A:58C-1(4) and 58C-6 (West 1987). The definition of "environmental tort actions" excludes matters involving drugs or products intended for personal consumption or use.

14. Id. §2A:58C-2 (West 1987); *O'Brien v. Muskin Corp.*, 94 N.J. 169, 463 A.2d 298 (1983).

15. *Zaza*, 144 N.J. 34; *McGarvey v. G.I. Joe Septic Service, Inc.*, 293 N.J. Super. 129, 679 A.2d 733 (1996); *Adelman v. Lupo*, 291 N.J. Super. 207, 677 A.2d 230 (1996); *Roberts v. Rich Foods, Inc.*, 139 N.J. 365, 654 A.2d 1365 (1995); *Johansen v. Makita U.S.A., Inc.*, 128 N.J. 86, 607 A.2d 637 (1992); *O'Brien*, 94 N.J. 169; *Fabian*, 258 N.J. Super. 261.

16. "An adequate product warning or instruction is one that a reasonably prudent person in the same or similar circumstances would have provided with respect to the danger and that communicates adequate information on the dangers and safe use of the product, taking into account the characteristics of, and the ordinary knowledge common to, the persons by whom the product is intended to be used. . . ." N.J. Stat. Ann. §2A:58C-4 (West 1987); *Zaza*, 144 N.J. 34; *Feldman v. Lederle Labs*, 97 N.J. 429, 479 A.2d 374 (1984).

17. *Zaza*, 144 N.J. 34; *Malin v. Union Carbide Corp.*, 219 N.J. Super. 428, 530 A.2d 794 (1987).

18. *Coffman v. Keene Corp.*, 257 N.J. Super. 279, 608 A.2d 416 (1992), *aff'd*, 133 N.J. 581, 628 A.2d 710 (1993); *Johansen*, 128 N.J. 86; *Cartel Capital Corp. v. Fireco*, 81 N.J. 548, 410 A.2d 674 (1980); *Suter v. San Angelo Foundry & Machine Co.*, 81 N.J. 150, 406 A.2d 140 (1979). In *Suter*, the court carved out an exception to the defense in factory settings involving employees engaged in assigned tasks. See also *Fabian*, 258 N.J. Super. 261; *Ramos v. Silent Hoist and Crane*, 256 N.J. Super. 467, 607 A.2d 667 (1992).

19. N.J. Stat. Ann. §2A:58C-3a(2) (West 1987); *Roberts*, 139 N.J. 365. In *Roberts*, the New Jersey Supreme Court held that the plaintiff bears the burden of proving the product is workplace equipment or that the danger of the product could feasibly be eliminated without impairing the usefulness of the product in order to preclude the defendant from using the 3a(2) absolute defense. See also *McWilliams v. Yamaha Motor Corp. U.S.A.*, 987 F.2d 200 (3d Cir. 1993); *Dewey*, 121 N.J. 69; *Fabian*, 258 N.J. Super. 261.

20. *Oscar Mayer Corp. v. Mining Trading Corp.*, 744 F. Supp. 79 (D.N.J. 1990); *Promaulayko v. Johns-Manville Sales Corp.*, 116 N.J. 505, 562 A.2d 202 (1989); *Michalko v. Cooke Color and Chem. Corp.*, 91 N.J. 386, 451 A.2d 179 (1982); *Ramos*, 256 N.J. Super. 467; *Johnson v. Cyklop Strapping Corp.*, 220 N.J. Super. 250, 531 A.2d 1078 (1987), *cert. denied*, 110 N.J. 196, 540 A.2d 189 (1988).

21. *Cintrone v. Hertz Truck Leasing & Rental Servs.*, 45 N.J. 434, 212 A.2d 769 (1965); *Santiago v. E. W. Bliss, Div. of Gulf & Western Mfg. Co.*, 201 N.J. Super. 205, 492 A.2d 1089 (1985).

22. *Ramos*, 256 N.J. Super. 467; *Santiago*, 201 N.J. Super. 205.

23. *Michalko*, 91 N.J. 386; *Newmark v. Gimbel's, Inc.*, 54 N.J. 585, 258 A.2d 697 (1969).

24. *Zaza*, 144 N.J. 34; *McGarvey*, 293 N.J. Super. 129; *Michalko*, 91 N.J. 386; *Seeley v. Cincinnati Shaper Co., Ltd.*, 256 N.J. Super. 1, 606 A.2d 378, *cert. denied*, 130 N.J. 598, 617 A.2d 1220 (1992); *Ramos*, 256 N.J. Super. 467.

25. *Miltz v. Borroughs-Shelving, A Div. of Lear Siegler, Inc.*, 203 N.J. Super. 451, 497 A.2d 516 (1985).

26. N.J. Stat. Ann. §2A:58C-3a(2) (West 1987); *Roberts*, 139 N.J. 365; *Dewey*, 121 N.J. 69; *Fabian*, 258 N.J. Super. 261.

27. N.J. Stat. Ann. §2A:58C-3a(3) (West 1987). This section is not intended to apply to machinery or other equipment encountered in the workplace for which dangers can feasibly be eliminated. See *Fabian*, 258 N.J. Super. 261; see also *Snyder v. Mekhjian*, 244 N.J. Super. 281, 582 A.2d 307 (1990), *aff'd*, 125 N.J. 328, 593 A.2d 318 (1991), and supra note 18.

28. *Saez v. S&S Corrugated Paper Machinery Co.*, 302 N.J. Super. 545, 695 A.2d 740 (1997); *Class v. American Roller Die Corp.*, 294 N.J. Super. 407, 683 A.2d 595 (1996); *Mettinger v. W.W. Lowensten, Inc.*; 292 N.J. Super. 293, 678 A.2d 1115 (1996); *Ramirez v. Amsted Indus., Inc.*, 86 N.J. 332, 431 A.2d 811 (1981); *Leo v. Kerr-McGee Chemical Corporation*, 37 F.3d 96 (3d Cir. 1994); *Ramos*, 256 N.J. Super. 467; *Brotherton v. Celotex Corp.*, 202 N.J. Super. 148, 493 A.2d 1337 (1985). *Contra Pacius v. Thermtroll Corp.*, 259 N.J. Super. 51, 611 A.2d 153 (1992), wherein the doctrine was extended in instances where the product line was not continued.

29. *Dewey*, 121 N.J. 69; *Spring Motor Distrib., Inc. v. Ford Motor Co.*, 98 N.J. 555, 489 A.2d 660 (1985); *H. Rosenblum, Inc. v. Adler*, 93 N.J. 324, 461 A.2d 138 (1983).

30.   N.J. Stat. Ann. §2A:58C-4 (West 1987); *Taylor by Wurgaft v. General Elec. Co.*, 208 N.J. Super. 207, 505 A.2d 190, *cert. denied*, 104 N.J. 379, 517 A.2d 388 (1986); *Coffman*, 257 N.J. Super. 279.

31.   *Reiff v. Convergent Technologies*, 957 F. Supp. 573 (D.N.J. 1997); *Campos v. Firestone Tire & Rubber Co.*, 98 N.J. 198, 485 A.2d 305 (1984); *Coffman*, 257 N.J. Super. 279; *Theer v. Philip Carey Co.*, 133 N.J. 610, 628 A.2d 724 (1993).

32.   N.J. State. Ann. §2A:58C-4 (West 1987); *Canty*, 296 N.J. Super. 68; *Butler v. PPG Indus., Inc.*, 201 N.J. Super. 558, 493 A.2d 619, *cert. denied*, 102 N.J. 298, 508 A.2d 186 (1985). See *supra* note 16 for definition of adequate warning. Section C-4 creates a rebuttable presumption of an adequate warning in the case of a drug, device, or food product approved or prescribed by the Food and Drug Administration.

33.   N.J. Stat. Ann. §2A:58C-4 (West 1987). *Molino*, 261 N.J. Super. 85; *Lally v. Printing Mach. Sales and Serv. Co., Inc.*, 240 N.J. Super. 181, 572 A.2d 1187 (1990).

34.   *London v. Lederle Labs Div. of American Cyanamid Co.*, 290 N.J. Super. 318, 675 A.2d 1133 (1996); *Niemiera v. Schneider*, 114 N.J. 550, 555 A.2d 1112 (1989); *Spychala v. G.D. Searle & Co.*, 705 F. Supp. 1024 (D.N.J. 1988); see also N.J. Stat. Ann. §2A:58C-4 (West 1987).

35.   *Rivera v. Westinghouse Elevator Co.*, 107 N.J. 256, 526 A.2d 705 (1987); *Brown v. United States Stove Co.*, 98 N.J. 155, 484 A.2d 1234 (1984).

36.   *London*, 290 N.J. Super. 318; *Jurado*, 131 N.J. 375.

37.   N.J. Stat. Ann. §2A:58c-3a(1) (West 1987). N.J. Stat. Ann. §2A:58c-3(b) recognizes an exception with certain egregiously unsafe or ultrahazardous products that have hidden risks or could seriously injure third persons and have little or no usefulness. See also *Roberts*, 139 N.J. 365; *Fabian*, 258 N.J. Super. 261.

38.   N.J. Stat. Ann. §2A:58C-3a(1), 3b (West 1987); *Lewis v. American Cyanamid Co.*, 294 N.J. Super. 53, 682 A.2d 724 (1996); *Seeley*, 256 N.J. Super. 1; *Fabian*, 258 N.J. Super. 261.

39.   *Scanlon v. General Motors Corp.*, 65 N.J. 582, 326 A.2d 673 (1974).

40.   *Sanna v. National Sponge Co.*, 209 N.J. Super. 60, 506 A.2d 1258 (1986); *Smith v. Kris-Bal Realty, Inc.*, 242 N.J. Super. 346, 576 A.2d 934 (1990).

41.   *Ryan v. KDI Sylvan Pools, Inc.*, 121 N.J. 276, 579 A.2d 1241 (1990); *Wolf by Wolf v. Procter & Gamble Co.*, 555 F. Supp. 613 (D.N.J. 1982).

42. *Herbstman v. Eastman Kodak Co.*, 68 N.J. 1, 342 A.2d 181 (1975); *Realmuto v. Straub Motors, Inc.*, 65 N.J. 336, 322 A.2d 440 (1974).

43. N.J. Stat. Ann. §2A:15-5.1-5.3 (West 1987); *Suter v. San Angelo Foundry & Mach. Co.*, 81 N.J. 150, 406 A.2d 140 (1979).

44. *Realmuto*, 65 N.J. 336; *Dawson v. Chrysler Corp.*, 630 F.2d 950 (3d Cir. 1980), *cert. denied*, 450 U.S. 959 (1981).

45. *Huddell v. Levin*, 537 F.2d 726 (3d Cir. 1976); called into question by *Crispin v. Volkswagen AG*, 248 N.J. Super. 540, 591 A.2d 966 (1991).

46. N.J. Stat. Ann. §2A:58C-5a (West 1987); *Ripa v. Owens-Corning Fiberglass Corp.*, 282 N.J. Super. 373, 660 A.2d 521 (1995); *Herman v. Sunshine Chem. Specialties, Inc.*, 133 N.J. 329, 627 A.2d 1081 (1993).

47. N.J. Stat. Ann. §2A:58C-5b and 5d (West 1987). The factors include (1) the likelihood that serious harm would arise; (2) the tortfeasor's awareness of reckless disregard of the likelihood that someone would be seriously harmed; (3) the tortfeasor's conduct on learning that its initial conduct would cause harm; (4) the duration and any concealment of the conduct; and, if punitives are to be awarded, (5) the profitability of the misconduct; (6) when the misconduct was terminated; and (7) the tortfeasor's financial condition. *Herman*, *supra* note 46.

48. N.J. Stat. Ann. §2A:58C-5c (West 1987).

49. N.J. Stat. Ann. §2A:15-5.3.

50. N.J. Stat. Ann. §2A:15-5.3(e); *Ripa*, 282 N.J. Super. 373; *Promaulayko*, 116 N.J. 505.

51. *Mort v. Bess*, 287 N.J. Super. 423, 671 A.2d 189 (1996); *Tefft v. Tefft*, 192 N.J. Super. 561, 471 A.2d 790 (1983); *Young v. Latta*, 123 N.J. 584, 589 A.2d 1020 (1991); *Ripa*, 282 N.J. Super. 373.

52. §2A:58C-1-58C-7 (West 1987).

53. §2A:14-1-14-2 (West 1987).

54. §12A:2-313-2-318 (West 1987).

55. New Jersey Institute for Continuing Legal Education, *Model Jury Charges: Civil* (4th ed. 1998 supplement).

NEW MEXICO

A. CAUSES OF ACTION

Generally, product liability lawsuits include causes of action for strict liability, negligence, and warranty. In a recent decision, the New Mexico Supreme Court held that strict liability (as well as negligence) is applicable in a crashworthiness case.[1] An action to recover for economic losses resulting from a product injuring itself can only be brought in contract, at least in commercial transactions where there is no great disparity in bargaining power of the parties.[2]

B. STATUTES OF LIMITATION

Causes of action must be filed within three years for personal injury,[3] and within four years for property damage,[4] whether brought in negligence or strict liability. Generally, causes of action based on breach of warranty must be brought within four years of the tender of delivery of the goods.[5] The four year Uniform Commercial Code statute of limitations applies in an action for personal injury that is predicated on breach of an implied warranty.[6]

C. STRICT LIABILITY

1. The Standard

New Mexico has adopted section 402A of the Restatement (Second) of Torts.[7] The Court of Appeals recently relied upon the Restatement (Third) of Torts: Product Liability (Tentative Draft Nov. 2, 1995) as stating the basic rule of strict product liability.[8]

2. "Defect"

A product is considered defective if an unreasonable risk of injury proximately results from a condition of the product or from the manner of its use.[9] An unreasonable risk of injury is one that a reasonably prudent person having full knowledge of the risk would find unacceptable.[10] A product does not present an unreasonable risk of harm simply because it is possible to be harmed by it.[11] In a design defect case, the product's design need not necessarily adopt features that represent the ultimate in safety; the jury should consider the ability to eliminate the risk without seriously impairing the usefulness of the product or making it unduly expensive.[12]

3. Contributory Negligence/Assumption of Risk

Comparative fault is a defense in a product liability case, whether brought in strict liability, negligence, or breach of warranty.[13] A plaintiff's negligence, whether consisting of what is conventionally known as contributory negligence or assumption of risk, reduces the amount of damages plaintiff may recover by the percentage of fault assessed against him.[14]

The jury apportions damages among the defendants based on each defendant's individual percentage of fault.[15] A percentage of fault may also be assessed against nonparties,[16] even if such nonparties are immune from suit.[17] Comparative fault is applicable to intentional conduct.[18]

There is generally no joint and several liability for the acts of concurrent tortfeasors.[19] However, joint and several liability exists for intentional acts, persons vicariously liable, persons strictly liable for the manufacture and sale of a defective product, and in other situations "having a sound basis in public policy."[20]

4.   **Sale or Lease**

The plaintiff must allege that the defendant sold, leased, or otherwise placed the product into the stream of commerce.[21] Strict liability extends to any "supplier" in the chain of distribution of the product, including manufacturers, retailers, distributors, and lessors.[22] The "supplier" must be in the business of putting this product on the market.[23] For public policy reasons, the New Mexico courts have declined to extend strict liability to hospitals and doctors for the distribution or supply of medical products designed and manufactured by others.[24] A supplier of a component part or raw material that is not inherently defective or dangerous at the time it leaves the manufacturer's control, and which part or material is used in the manufacture or making of another product, does not owe a duty to warn the ultimate consumer concerning the suitability or safety of the finished product; in such situation any duty to warn the ultimate consumer rests on the manufacturer of the device or finished product.[25] A bulk supplier is required to warn its immediate purchaser of any known dangers, with the intent such warning be passed on to the ultimate consumer.[26]

5.   **Inherently Dangerous Products**

A supplier of a product that is unavoidably unsafe, that is, one that cannot be made safe for its intended and ordinary use even when properly prepared and accompanied by proper directions and warnings, will not be held liable unless the product unreasonably exposes users to risk of injury.[27] Whether users are unreasonably exposed to risk of injury turns on a balancing of the dangers and benefits resulting from the product's use.[28]

6. Successor Liability

The general rule is that a corporation that purchases the assets of another corporation does not automatically acquire its liabilities except (1) where there is an agreement to assume those obligations; (2) where the transfer results in a consolidation or merger; (3) where there is a continuation of the transferor corporation; or (4) where the transfer is for the purpose of fraudulently avoiding liability.[29] However, New Mexico recently adopted the product line exception. A successor who continues to produce and market the same product, using the same designs, equipment, and name, is responsible for design defects in its predecessor's product. Such a successor may also have an independent duty to warn of defects in its predecessor's product, depending on whether there is a nexus between the successor, its predecessor's customers, and the product to warrant an inference the successor had actual or constructive notice of the alleged defect.[30]

7. Privity

A "supplier" is directly liable to an injured consumer, despite the presence of an intermediate seller.[31]

8. Failure to Warn

A product presents an unreasonable risk of injury if put on the market without warning of a risk that could be avoided by the giving of an adequate warning.[32] However, based on comparative negligence principles, the duty to avoid unreasonable risk of injury to others is not necessarily satisfied by an "adequate" warning.[33] The warning must be communicated by a means that can reasonably be expected to reach the user.[34] Also, the warning must (1) be in a form that can reasonably be expected to catch the attention of the reasonably foreseeable user; (2) be understandable to the reasonably foreseeable user; and (3) disclose the nature and extent of the danger. The warning must specify any harmful consequences that a reasonably foreseeable user would not understand from a general warning of the product's danger or from a simple directive to use or not to use the product for a certain purpose or in a certain way.[35] If an adequate warning would have been noticed and acted on to guard against the danger, a failure to give an adequate warning is a proximate cause of injury.[36]

9. Post-Sale Duty to Warn

A supplier's duty to use ordinary care continues after the product has left its possession. A supplier who later learns, or in the exercise of ordinary care should know, of a risk of injury caused by a condition of the product or a manner in which it could be used, must then use ordinary care to avoid the risk.[37]

10. Substantial Change/Abnormal Use

In order for a supplier to be liable, the injury must have been proximately caused by a condition of the product that was not substantially changed from the condition in which the supplier placed the product on the market or in which the supplier could have reasonably expected it to be used. For a substantial change in the product to relieve a supplier of liability, the change itself must be a proximate cause of the harm done.[38] Incorporation of a component into a final product may not necessarily be a "substantial change" of the component.[39]

The supplier's duty is limited to use of the product for a purpose or in a manner that could reasonably be foreseen. Where an injury is caused by a risk or misuse of the product that was not reasonably foreseeable to the supplier, he is not liable.[40]

11. State of the Art

The New Mexico Supreme Court has not expressly approved of the state-of-the-art defense. However, it has indicated that in appropriate cases, state-of-the-art evidence and the state-of-the-art defense may be utilized.[41]

12. Malfunction

A product that malfunctions by not performing as intended may be unreasonably dangerous.[42] However, no New Mexico authority expressly establishes malfunction as evidence of a defect.

13. Standards

Proof that a product complies with industry standards or custom is evidence of whether a risk of injury would be acceptable to a reasonably prudent person,[43] and in a negligence case, is evidence of ordinary care.[44] However, industry standards or custom and usage are not dispositive of whether a manufacturer was negligent or whether a product was defective.[45]

14. Other Accidents

There are no reported New Mexico cases deciding whether evidence of other accidents is admissible in a product liability action. This question would probably be governed by application of Rules 401-403 or 404(b) of the Federal Rules of Evidence, which have been adopted in New Mexico.[46]

Guidance can be found in several reported New Mexico cases addressing the admissibility of other accidents in negligence actions.[47] In general, other accidents are not admissible.[48] However, other accidents may be admissible, in limited circumstances, if they are probative of a relevant fact.[49] Even if other accidents are relevant, a court may choose to exclude them under New Mexico Rule of Evidence 403[50] if their admission would cause unfair prejudice, confusion of the issues, mislead the jury, cause undue delay, waste time, or if such admission constitutes the needless presentation of cumulative evidence.[51]

15. Misrepresentation

Section 402B of the Restatement (Second) of Torts, dealing with the product liability theory of misrepresentation, has neither been adopted nor rejected in New Mexico.[52]

D. NEGLIGENCE

Manufacturers and suppliers have a duty to use ordinary care to avoid foreseeable risks of injury caused by the condition of a product or the manner in which it is used.[53] This duty is owed to all persons who can reasonably be expected to use the product or be in the vicinity during use.[54] The duty continues after the product has left the supplier's hands. See section C9, *supra*.

New Mexico has adopted the doctrine of pure comparative negligence. See section C3, *supra*. In "crashworthiness" cases, the fault of those responsible for the "first collision" is to be compared with the fault of those responsible for the "second collision" (crashworthiness injuries).[55]

E. BREACH OF WARRANTY

The creation and exclusion of warranties, both express and implied, are governed by the Uniform Commercial Code.[56] Implied warranty theories do not differ significantly from strict liability claims.[57]

F. PUNITIVE DAMAGES

Punitive damages are not available for mere negligence, but they are available in both tort and contract actions[58] (including breach of warranty),[59] where the defendant's conduct is willful, wanton, malicious, oppressive, fraudulent, reckless, in bad faith or grossly negligent.[60]

G. STATUTES

Relevant statutes in product liability actions are the statutes of limitation,[61] the commercial code sections dealing with warranties,[62] and the statute dealing with joint and several liability.[63]

Kenneth L. Harrigan
MODRALL, SPERLING, ROEHL, HARRIS & SISK
Sunwest Building
500 Fourth Street, N.W., Suite 1000
P.O. Box 2168
Albuquerque, New Mexico 87103-2168
(505) 848-1800

1. *Brooks v. Beech Aircraft Corp.*, 120 N.M. 372, 383, 902 P.2d 54, 65 (1995), *overruling Duran v. General Motors Corp.*, 101 N.M. 742, 688 P.2d 779 (Ct. App. 1983), *writ quashed*, 101 N.M. 555, 685 P.2d 963 (1983).

2. *In re Consol. Vista Hills Litigation*, 119 N.M. 542, 551, 893 P.2d 438, 447 (1995); *Utah Intl. v. Caterpillar Tractor*, 108 N.M. 539, 542, 775 P.2d 741, 744 (Ct. App. 1989), *cert. denied*, 108 N.M. 354, 772 P.2d 884 (1989).

3. N.M. Stat. Ann. 1978, §37-1-8 (Repl. Pamp. 1990).

4. Id. §37-1-4 (Repl. Pamp. 1990).

5. Id. §55-2-725 (Repl. Pamp. 1993).

6. *Fernandez v. Char-Li-Jon, Inc.*, 119 N.M. 25, 128, 888 P.2d 471, 474 (Ct. App.), *cert. denied*, 119 N.M. 20, 888 P.2d 466 (1994).

7. *Stang v. Hertz Corp.*, 83 N.M. 730, 735, 497 P.2d 732, 737, 52 A.L.R.3d 112 (1972).

8. *Spectron Dev. v. American Hollow*, 123 N.M. 170, 174, 936 P.2d 852, 856 (Ct. App. 1997).

9. SCRA 1986 (1998 Repl.), 13-1406 (Supreme Court Rules Annotated, Uniform Civil Jury Instructions). A product is defective if, at the time of sale or distribution, it contains a manufacturing defect, if defective in design or is defective because of inadequate instruction or warnings. *Spectron Dev. v. American Hollow*, 123 N.M. 170, 174, 936 P.2d 852, 856 (Ct. App. 1997).

10. Id. 13-1407; *Fernandez v. Ford Motor Co.*, 118 N.M. 100, 879 P.2d 101 (Ct. App.), *cert. denied*, 118 N.M. 90, 879 P.2d 91 (1994).

11. Id.

12. Id.

13. See SCRA 1986 (1998 ed.), 13-1427 and Committee Comment.

14. See id.; *Williamson v. Smith*, 83 N.M. 336, 491 P.2d 1147 (1971); *Scott v. Rizzo*, 96 N.M. 682, 634 P.2d 1234 (1981); *Marchese v. Warner Communications, Inc.*, 100 N.M. 313, 670 P.2d 113 (Ct. App. 1983), *cert. denied*, 100

N.M. 259, 669 P.2d 735 (1983); *Jaramillo v. Fisher Controls Co.*, 102 N.M. 614, 698 P.2d 887 (Ct. App. 1985), *cert. denied*, 102 N.M. 613, 698 P.2d 886 (1985); *Diaz v. McMahon*, 112 N.M. 788, 814 P.2d 1346 (Ct. App. 1991).

15. SCRA 1986 (1998 ed.), 13-2219.

16. *Bartlett v. N.M. Welding Supply, Inc.*, 98 N.M. 152, 646 P.2d 579 (Ct. App.) *cert. denied*, 98 N.M. 336, 648 P.2d 794 (1982); *Lamkin v. Garcia*, 106 N.M. 60, 738 P.2d 932 (Ct. App. 1987).

17. *Taylor v. Delgarno Transp., Inc.*, 100 N.M. 138, 667 P.2d 445 (1983).

18. *Reichert v. Atler*, 117 N.M. 623, 875 P.2d 379 (1994); *Barth v. Coleman*, 118 N.M. 1, 878 P.2d 319 (1994).

19. *Bartlett v. New Mexico Welding Supply, Inc.*, 98 N.M. 152, 646 P.2d 579 (Ct. App. 1982), *cert. denied*, 98 N.M. 336, 648 P.2d 794 (1982); *Medina v. Graham Cowboys, Inc.*, 113 N.M. 471, 827 P.2d 859 (Ct. App. 1992); *Saiz v. Belen School Dist.*, 113 N.M. 387, 827 P.2d 102 (1992).

20. N.M. Stat. Ann. 1978, §41-3A-1 (Repl. Pamp. 1996); *Saiz*, 113 N.M. 387. When joint and several liability applies, see Uniform Contribution Among Tortfeasors Act, N.M. Stat. Ann. 1978, §41-3-1 et seq. (Repl. Pamp. 1996).

21. *Stang v. Hertz*, 83 N.M. 730, 497 P.2d 732 (1972).

22. *Livingston v. Begay*, 98 N.M. 712, 652 P.2d 734 (1982); *Stang*, 83 N.M. 730.

23. *Arenivas v. Continental Oil Co.*, 102 N.M. 106, 692 P.2d 31 (Ct. App. 1983), *cert. quashed*, 102 N.M. 88, 691 P.2d 881 (1984).

24. *Parker v. St. Vincent Hospital*, 122 N.M. 39, 919 P.2d 1104 (Ct. App. 1996); *Tanuz v. Carlberg*, 122 N.M. 113, 921 P.2d 309 (Ct. App. 1996).

25. *Parker v. DuPont*, 121 N.M. 120, 909 P.2d 1 (N.M. Ct. App. 1995).

26. Id.

27. SCRA 1986 (1998 ed.), 13-1419 and Committee Comment; *Davila v. Bodelson*, 103 N.M. 243, 704 P.2d 1119 (Ct. App. 1985), *cert. denied*, 103 N.M. 177, 704 P.2d 431 (1985); *Perfetti v. McGhan Medical*, 99 N.M. 645, 662 P.2d 646 (Ct. App. 1983), *cert. denied*, 99 N.M. 644, 622 P.2d 645 (1983).

28. SCRA 1986 (1998 ed.), 13-1419.

29. *Southwest Dist. Co. v. Olympia Brewing Co.*, 90 N.M. 502, 565 P.2d 1019 (1977); *Pankey v. Hot Springs Natl. Bank*, 46 N.M. 10, 119 P.2d 636 (1941).

30. *Garcia v. Coe Manufacturing Co.*, 123 N.M. 34, 933 P.2d 243 (1997).

31. See *Sanchez v. City of Espanola*, 94 N.M. 677, 678, 615 P.2d 993, 995 (Ct. App. 1980); *Stang*, 83 N.M. at 735, 497 P.2d at 737.

32. SCRA 1986 (1998 ed.), 13-1415.

33. *Klopp v. Wackenhut Corp.*, 113 N.M. 153, 157, 824 P.2d 293, 297 (1992) (*overruling Skyhook Corp. v. Jasper*, 90 N.M. 143, 560 P.2d 934 (1977) and *Garrett v. Nissen Corp.*, 84 N.M. 16, 498 P.2d 1359 (1972)). Although a premises liability and not a product liability case, *Klopp* includes sweeping language that indicates it also applies in the context of product liability.

34. SCRA 1986 (1998 Ed.), 13-1417.

35. Id. 13-1418.

36. Id. 13-1425.

37. Id. 13-1402.

38. Id. 13-1422. See *Standhardt v. Flintkote Co.*, 84 N.M. 796, 802, 508 P.2d 1283, 1289 (1973); and *Tenney v. Seven-Up Co.*, 92 N.M. 158, 159, 584 P.2d 205, 206 (Ct. App.), *cert. denied*, 92 N.M. 180, 585 P.2d 324 (1978).

39. *Fernandez v. Ford Motor Co.*, 118 N.M. 100, 108-109, 879 P.2d 101, 109-110 (Ct. App.), *cert. denied*, 118 N.M. 90, 879 P.2d 91 (1994).

40. SCRA 1986 (1998 ed.), 13-1403; *Van de Valde v. Volvo of America Corp.*, 106 N.M. 457, 460, 744 P.2d 930, 933 (Ct. App. 1987).

41. *Brooks v. Beech Aircraft Corp.*, 120 N.M. 372, 381, 902 P.2d 54, 63 (1995); see *Saiz v. Belen School Dist.*, 113 N.M. 387, 402, 827 P.2d 102 (1992).

42. See *Stang v. Hertz*, 83 N.M. 730, 732, 497 P.2d 732, 734 (1972); *Armijo v. Ed Black's Chevrolet Center, Inc.*, 105 N.M. 422, 424, 733 P.2d 870, 872 (Ct. App. 1987); *Fernandez v. Ford Motor Co.*, 118 N.M. 100, 108, 879 P.2d 101, 109 (Ct. App.), *cert. denied*, 118 N.M. 90, 879 P.2d 91 (1994).

43. SCRA 1986 (1998 ed.), 13-1408.

44. SCRA 1986 (1998 ed.) 13-1405.

45. *Brooks v. Beech Aircraft Corp.*, 120 N.M. 372, 381, 902 P.2d 54, 63 (1995).

46. SCRA 1986 (1998 Ed.) 11-401, 11-402, 11-403, 11-404(b).

47. *Kirk Co. v. Ashcraft*, 101 N.M. 462, 684 P.2d 1127 (1984); *Ohlson v. Kent Nowlin Const. Co.*, 99 N.M. 539, 542, 660 P.2d 1021, 1024 (Ct. App.), *cert. denied*, 99 N.M. 477, 660 P.2d 119 (1983); *Ruiz v. Southern Pacific Transp. Co.*, 97 N.M. 194, 638 P.2d 406, 414 (Ct. App.), *cert. quashed*, 97 N.M. 242, 638 P.2d 1087 (1981).

48. *Ruiz v. Southern Pacific Transp. Co.*, 97 N.M. 194, 202, 638 P.2d 406, 414 (Ct. App.), *cert. quashed*, 97 N.M. 242, 638 P.2d 1087 (1981).

49. Id.; *Ohlson v. Kent Nowlin Const. Co.*, 99 N.M. 539, 660 P.2d 1021, 1026 (Ct. App.), *cert. denied*, 99 N.M. 477, 660 P.2d (1983).

50. SCRA 1986 (1998 Ed.), 11-403.

51. Id.; *Ohlson v. Kent Nowlin Const. Co.*, 99 N.M. 539, 660 P.2d 1021, 1026 (Ct. App.), *cert. denied*, 99 N.M. 477, 660 P.2d 119 (1983).

52. See SCRA 1986 (1998 ed.) 13-1409, 13-1426, Committee Comments.

53. Id. 13-1402.

54. Id.

55. *Duran v. General Motors Corp.*, 101 N.M. 742, 744, 688 P.2d 779, 781 (Ct. App. 1983), *writ quashed*, 101 N.M. 555, 685 P.2d 963 (1984) *overruled on other grounds, Brooks*, 120 N.M. 372, 902 P.2d 54 (1995); *Cleveland v. Piper Aircraft Corp.*, 890 F.2d 1540, 1549 (10th Cir. 1989), *reh'g denied*, 898 F.2d 778 (10th Cir. 1990). But see *Lujan v. Healthsouth*, 120 N.M. 422, 902 P.2d 1025 (1995).

56. N.M. Stat. Ann. 1978, §§55-2-313 to 318 (Repl. Pamp. 1993); see also SCRA 1986 (1998 ed.), 13-1428 to 1433.

57. See SCRA 1986 (1998 ed.), 13-1430, Committee Comment; see also *Armijo v. Ed Black's Chevrolet Ctr., Inc.*, 105 N.M. 421, 424, 733 P.2d 870, 872 (Ct. App. 1987).

58. SCRA 1986 (1998 ed.), 13-861 and 13-1827, Committee Comment; *Robinson v. Katz*, 94 N.M. 314, 321, 610 P.2d 201, 208 (Ct. App. 1980), *cert. denied*, 94 N.M. 675, 615 P.2d 992 (1980).

59. *Grandi v. LeSage*, 74 N.M. 799, 810, 399 P.2d 285, 293 (1965).

60. SCRA 1986 (1998 ed.), 13-861 and 13-1827; *Green Tree Acceptance, Inc. v. Layton*, 108 N.M. 171, 174, 769 P.2d 84, 87 (1989).

61. N.M. Stat. Ann. 1978, §§37-1-4, 37-1-7, 37-1-8 (Repl. Pamp. 1990); id. 55-2-725 (Repl. Pamp. 1993).

62. Id., §§55-2-313 to 318.

63. Id., §41-3A-1 (Repl. Pamp. 1996).

NEW YORK

A. CAUSES OF ACTION

A plaintiff in New York may assert four separate causes of action for injuries resulting from allegedly defective products: strict product liability; negligence; breach of express warranty; and breach of implied warranty.[1]

B. STATUTES OF LIMITATION

1. Strict Product Liability and Negligence

A claim sounding in strict product liability or negligence for personal injury or property damage is governed by a three-year limitations period.[2] A cause of action accrues when injury occurs, unless provided otherwise by statute.[3]

2. Warranty Theories

A claim based on breach of warranty is governed by a four-year statute of limitations.[4] The limitations period is measured from the tender of delivery by the defendant to defendant's purchaser, regardless of when the plaintiff may have acquired or come into contact with the product.[5] Thus, the time of accrual may differ for each entity in the product's chain of distribution.[6]

3. Wrongful Death

A wrongful death action must be commenced within two years of the decedent's death.[7]

4. The Discovery Rule

In 1986, the New York Legislature modified the three-year statute of limitations period for actions to recover for personal injury or property damage "caused by the latent effects of exposure to any substance or combination of substances, in any form, upon or within the body or upon or within the property...."[8] The Court of Appeals recently made clear that the "discovery rule" only applies to latent injuries caused by exposure to a "toxic substance."[9] The three-year statute of limitations period for these latent injuries begins to run from the earlier of the date of discovery of the injury by the plaintiff or from the date when, through the exercise of "reasonable diligence," the plaintiff should have discovered the injury.[10] The date on which a plaintiff discovered or should have discovered an injury has been treated as a mixed question of law and fact.[11] The Court of Appeals recently clarified what constitutes discovery of an "injury" within the meaning of CPLR §214-c. The Court ruled that a plaintiff will be deemed to have discovered an "injury" when he becomes aware of the primary medical condition underlying his claim.[12] The Court rejected decisions by several federal and state courts that held that a plaintiff will not be deemed to have discovered an "injury" until he becomes aware of both the medical condition at issue and facts demonstrating that the condition is attributable to an injury inflicted upon the plaintiff by a third party.[13]

There is no continuing-wrong exception to the discovery rule;[14] nor may a plaintiff extend the statute of limitations by alleging breach of a continuing duty to warn.[15] In addition, the rule has been held inapplicable to a cause of action for personal injuries based on breach of implied warranty.[16] Although a claim for breach of express warranty of future performance accrues with discovery of the breach (rather than delivery of the offending product), the limitations period will not be extended based on continuing breaches of the same warranty of future performance.[17]

There also is authority holding that the "discovery rule" supplied by CPLR 214-c does not apply to wrongful death actions because its express language limits it to actions to recover for personal injuries or property damage.[18]

The discovery statute permits an action to be commenced more than three years after the discovery of the injury where the *cause* of the injury is unknown at the time of injury. Under this rule, if the cause is discovered within five years of the injury or when, with reasonable diligence, the injury should have been discovered, the plaintiff has an additional one-year period from that date to commence an action. The plaintiff has the burden of alleging and proving that "technical, scientific or medical knowledge and information sufficient to ascertain the cause of his injury had not been discovered, identified or determined within three years of discovery of the injury."[19]

One appellate case has held that a plaintiff can only have the benefit of the one-year extension provided by CPLR 214-c(4) if he or she has, in fact, discovered the cause of the injury.[20] In other words, a plaintiff otherwise time-barred, because he sued more than three years after discovery of the injury, cannot maintain that he sued within a year of discovery of the cause if he has not actually discovered it; otherwise, he could indefinitely extend the statute of limitations (up to five years from discovery of the injury) while he searches for the cause.[21]

Another issue under 214-c concerns the so-called "two-injury" rule. Some cases have held that, even if suit is barred as to one injury, because it is discovered more than three years before suit is filed, it may be timely as to "separate and distinct" injuries caused by the defective product if they are discovered within the three years before suit is commenced.[22] It has been held, moreover, that the two-injury rule applies even if the exposure and discovery of the first injury pre-date the effective date of CPLR 214-c.[23]

The discovery rule of CPLR §214-c is not applicable to actions which satisfy the following three criteria: (a) acts or omissions that occurred prior to July 1, 1986, (b) that caused or contributed to an injury that either was discovered or, through the exercise of reasonable diligence, should have been discovered prior to July 1, 1986, *and*, (c) such action was or would have been barred due to the expiration of the applicable limitations period prior to July 1, 1986.[24]

C. STRICT LIABILITY

1. The Standard

Strict product liability is imposed upon a manufacturer or nonmanufacturing entity in a product's chain of distribution for personal injury or property damage caused by a defect in the product.[25] In order to establish liability, the plaintiff must prove that the defect was a substantial factor in bringing about the injury and that: at the time of the occurrence, the product was being used by the injured person, or a third person, for the purpose and in the manner normally intended; if the injured person was the user of the product, that he could not, by the exercise of reasonable care, have discovered the defect and perceived its danger; and, by the exercise of reasonable care, the injured person could not have avoided the injury.[26]

2. Establishing a Defect

Strict product liability claims may take one of three forms: manufacturing mistake or defect; defective or improper design; or failure to provide adequate warning.[27]

In a manufacturing defect case, the plaintiff claims that the product as manufactured deviated from the defendant's design or internal quality standards.[28] A plaintiff alleging a design defect must show that the manufacturer "marketed a product designed so that it was not reasonably safe and that the defective design was a substantial factor in causing plaintiff's injury."[29] Whether a product is defectively designed turns on the following factors: (a) the utility of the product to the public as a whole and to the individual user; (b) the nature of the product and the likelihood of its causing injury; (c) the availability of a safer design; (d) the potential for designing and manufacturing the product so that it is safer but remains functional and reasonably priced; (e) the ability of the plaintiff to have avoided injury by careful use of the product; (f) the degree of awareness of the potential danger of the product reasonably attributable to the plaintiff; and (g) the manufacturer's ability to spread any cost related to improving the safety of the design.[30] It has been held that plaintiff need not adduce direct evidence of a defect, but may prove it circumstantially by showing that the product failed to perform as intended by the manu-facturer.[31]

A defendant is liable for the absence or inadequacy of a warning of "latent dangers resulting from foreseeable uses of its products of which it knew or should have known."[32] A manufacturer's duty to warn applies not only to intended uses of its product, but also to unintended but reasonably foreseeable uses.[33] To prove causation in a failure-to-warn case, plaintiff must show that adequate warnings would have prevented the use or misuse of the product that caused the injury.[34]

3. Ultrahazardous Activity Doctrine

Courts applying New York law have stated that this doctrine primarily applies to activities conducted on lands. Courts have refused to extend the doctrine to include manufacturers of allegedly defective products.[35]

4. Damages Recoverable

New York's highest court has held that tort recovery in strict product liability (and negligence) for economic loss flowing from damage to the product is not available to a downstream purchaser of the product.[36] The relevant factors in determining whether or not tort liability will attach are: the nature of the defect; the injury; the manner in which the injury occurred; and the damages sought.[37] The focus of this test is whether or not the plaintiff is merely seeking the benefit of the bargain, which sounds in contract, or for injury to person or property, which, in appropriate circumstances, may be recoverable in tort.[38] Thus, tort damages are not generally recoverable where the product fails to meet the expectations of a customer and where the claimed injury is solely to the product itself.[39]

5. Contributory Negligence/Assumption of Risk

Plaintiff's own negligence or assumption of risk will not bar his or her recovery; however, the amount of the plaintiff's recovery will be reduced in proportion to the culpable conduct attributable to plaintiff.[40] Both contributory negligence and assumption of risk are affirmative defenses which the defendant must assert in its answer and prove at trial.[41]

6. Entities Liable

In addition to manufacturers,[42] strict product liability may be imposed upon those who are regularly engaged in the sale of products, such as wholesalers, retailers, and distributors.[43] Strict product liability does not apply, however, to the casual or occasional seller of an allegedly defective product.[44] The occasional seller may be held liable for negligent failure to warn where he has actual knowledge of "known defects that are not obvious or readily discernible."[45] Recent cases have rejected plaintiffs' efforts to hold parent corporations liable for their subsidiaries' products, where the parent corporations had no meaningful role in the development, design, manufacture, or distribution of the products. In these cases, the courts rejected attempts to impose liability on the parent corporations under one or more of the following theories: alter ego[46]; agency[47]; apparent manufacturer[48]; and concerted action.[49] A state court has held that a parent corporation is not liable, on a theory of "negligent undertaking," for its testing of component materials, which its subsidiary relied upon to make an allegedly defective product. The court found that the parent owed no duty to unknown, future purchasers of the finished goods made by the subsidiary.[50] A federal court recently has refused to dismiss a cause of action for conspiracy to market defective products against a manufacturer.[51]

7. Successor Liability

Although a successor corporation is generally not liable for torts committed by its predecessor, including product liability,[52] there are four exceptions to the general rule. A successor corporation will be liable in a product liability action for a defective product manufactured by the predecessor corporation if: (a) the successor expressly or impliedly agreed to assume liability; (b) the transfer of assets was a consolidation or merger; (c) the successor was a continuation of the predecessor corporation; or (d) the transfer of assets was entered into fraudulently to escape liabilities.[53] In addition, a successor corporation also may be liable based on its own conduct subsequent to the corporate change. New York's highest court has not adopted either the "continuity of the enterprise" or the "product line" exception to the general rule that successor corporations are not liable for their predecessor's torts.[54]

8. Privity

Privity is not a requirement for recovery under strict product liability.[55]

9. Post-Sale Duty to Warn

The duty to issue warnings can extend past the delivery of the product. Even though a product may "be reasonably safe when manufactured and sold and involve no then-known risks of which warning need be given, risks thereafter revealed by user operation and brought to the attention of the manufacturer or vendor may impose upon one or both a duty to warn."[56] The question of what triggers the post-delivery duty to warn is a function of the degree of danger that the product presents and the number of instances reported.[57] A manufacturer also must keep abreast of the state of the art and may be liable for failing to warn of dangers that come to light after initial distribution of the product.[58]

10. Substantial Change/Abnormal Use

The manufacturer of a product that is reasonably safe for its intended use cannot be held liable for personal injury under strict liability (or negligence) based upon a design defect if, after the product leaves the possession and control of the manufacturer, there is a substantial modification that proximately causes the plaintiff's injuries.[59] An exception to the subsequent modification defense may be invoked under a design defect theory, even when the product's safety device is deliberately bypassed by a third party.[60] In such cases, it is usually for the jury to determine the scope of the product's intended purposes and whether the product was reasonably safe when sold.[61]

11. Commonly Known Dangers

A manufacturer or seller of a product will not be held liable for failure to warn against known or obvious risks or dangers.[62] The "obviousness" of the risk or danger is usually a question of fact for the jury.[63]

12. Admissibility of Subsequent Remedial Measures

Evidence of post-accident repairs or improvements is generally not admissible in negligence claims or in strict product liability claims based on design defect or failure to warn.[64] Evidence of subsequent remedial measures is admissible in a strict product liability claim based on a manufacturing defect[65] to establish feasibility of design, to prove defendant's control of the premises or instrumentality at the time of the accident, or for impeachment purposes.[66] However, if the defendant concedes feasibility, such evidence will not be admitted.[67]

13. Admissibility of Similar Accidents

Evidence of other, similar accidents may be introduced to establish a dangerous condition.[68] Evidence of prior accidents may not be offered, however, to establish the existence of a dangerous condition or to prove notice unless the requisite substantial similarity of circumstances is demonstrated.[69]

14. Learned Intermediary Doctrine/Bulk Supplier Doctrine

In certain failure to warn cases, manufacturers or sellers who supply products to sophisticated or knowledgeable purchasers or intermediaries are not liable for a failure to warn the ultimate users of product-related hazards. The learned intermediary or responsible intermediary doctrine typically is applied to cases involving prescription drugs and medical devices.[70] In order to invoke the doctrine, the warning supplied to the physician "must be correct, fully descriptive, and complete and it must convey updated information as to known side effects."[71] The bulk supplier doctrine is related in that it imposes practical limitations on a manufacturer's duty to warn the ultimate user of the product where the manufacturer sells the product in bulk with the contemplation that it will be repackaged and resold by the manufacturer's distributee. Under such circumstances, the manufacturer's duty to warn is satisfied by providing the distributee with an adequate warning.[72] Similarly, under certain circumstances, an employer's failure to provide warnings or instruction to its employees about the hazards associated with a manufacturer's product may constitute an intervening and superseding cause that relieves the manufacturer of liability.[73]

15. State of the Art

A defendant may seek to avoid liability based on a claim that it complied with the then-applicable state of the art. While this is often termed a defense to a product claim, in reality it is less a defense and more a measure of whether the defendant has met its obligation of due care.[74] In fulfilling its duty, a manufacturer may not rest content with industry practice because the industry may be lagging behind in its knowledge about a product, or in what is reasonably knowable about a product.[75]

D. NEGLIGENCE

1. The Standard

In order to establish a prima facie case of negligence, a plaintiff must prove: (a) that defendant owed a duty to the plaintiff; (b) that the duty was breached; and (c) that the breach of the duty caused the injury.[76]

2. Breach of Duty

A manufacturer may breach its duty by, for example, inadequate testing,[77] inadequate design,[78] or failure to reasonably inspect the product.[79]

3. Component Part Manufacturer/Final Assembler

A manufacturer who incorporates a component produced by another into its product has a duty to inspect the component in a reasonably prudent fashion to achieve a finished product that is reasonably safe for its intended use. The failure to do so is negligence.[80] The manufacturer of a component or the processor of materials that are part of a finished product created by another may be held liable for defects in the component caused by its negligence, even though the assembler tests the component, or fails to do so.[81]

4. Privity

A plaintiff need not establish privity to recover on a negligence claim.[82]

E. WARRANTY THEORIES

A breach of warranty action is based on contract (i.e., the express or implied contract of sale); therefore, it is independent of negligence and obviates some of the proof problems arising in negligence cases. In order to

---

prove a breach of warranty claim, the plaintiff must demonstrate that: (a) he has been injured by a product; (b) the injury occurred because the product was defective and unfit for its intended purpose; and (c) the defect existed when the product left the control of the manufacturer.[83] New York's highest court recently held that a "defect" for recovery under warranty theories is different from the "defect" necessary to establish strict liability and further concluded that warranty theories may be broader than strict liability.[84]

The Uniform Commercial Code creates both express warranties[85] and implied warranties.[86] Express warranties are created where a manufacturer, in advertising or labelling its product, represents its quality so that the public is induced to purchase the product. If the product does not conform to the express warranty created, that warranty is breached.[87] The implied warranty of merchantability is breached where the product was not "fit for the ordinary purposes for which such goods are used."[88]

A seller's express or implied warranty extends to any person who may reasonably be expected to use, consume, or be affected by the goods.[89]

A breach of warranty claim requires a sale. A defendant retained primarily for servicing a product is liable only for negligence unless a contract establishes a higher duty.[90]

With few exceptions, lack of privity generally bars recovery for breach of warranty under either express or implied warranty theories.[91] If privity of contract exists, a plaintiff may recover direct and consequential damages resulting from the product's failure under both an express or implied warranty theory.[92] Even without privity, a plaintiff may recover under breach of warranty theories where plaintiff sustains a physical injury.[93] Privity also is not required where the plaintiff purchased a defective product based on the manufacturer's express representations in trade publications, direct mailings, or on product labels.[94]

F. JOINT AND SEVERAL LIABILITY

1. The Rule

With some exceptions provided by statute, the general rule in New York is that defendants are jointly and severally liable.[95] However, in a product liability case involving multiple tortfeasors where the manufacturer of the product is joined or subject to jurisdiction, a tortfeasor found to be 50 percent or less liable will not be required to pay more than his equitable share for noneconomic loss sustained by the plaintiff.[96]

2. Contribution and Indemnification

A joint tortfeasor may seek contribution from other tortfeasors who are liable for plaintiff's injuries.[97] The joint tortfeasor may seek contribution for any excess that it paid over its equitable share (its percentage of fault).[98] A party from whom contribution is sought, however, cannot be forced to pay more than its equitable share.[99]

3. Effect of Settlement

New York has codified its rules pertaining to the release of tortfeasors.[100] Under the statute, a release reduces the claim of the releasor against the other tortfeasors by the *greatest* of: the amount stipulated in the release; the amount actually paid for the release; or the amount of the released tortfeasor's equitable share of the damages.[101]

New York's highest court recently ruled that in multidefendant situations, the "aggregate" approach to offsetting the settling defendants' share of liability is to be used.[102] Under this approach, the *total* amounts paid in settlement by all settling defendants is compared to the *total* amount of apportioned liability. The greater amount represents the set-off.

A release further acts to relieve the settling party from liability for any claims for contribution; it similarly precludes the settling party from bringing any claim for contribution against any other person.[103]

G. OTHER ASPECTS OF NEW YORK LAW

1. Surveillance

In New York, a defendant's ability to surprise plaintiff at trial with secret surveillance tapes was virtually eliminated by a recent amendment to New York's disclosure rules. The amendment provides that "there shall be full disclosure of any films, photographs, video tapes or audio tapes, including transcripts or memoranda thereof" involving a party, including out-takes and *regardless* of whether a defendant intends to use the materials at trial.[104]

2. Claims Against Third-Party Employer

On September 10, 1996, the "Omnibus Workers' Compensation Reform Act of 1996" ("the Act") took effect, radically changing the previous rule, which had allowed manufacturers and sellers freely to implead employers for contribution or indemnity.[105] The Act amended the Workers' Compensation law, to prohibit third-party actions against employers except in cases in which a plaintiff has suffered a "grave injury," which is statutorily defined to include a list of specific injuries such as death, amputation, paraplegia, and others.[106] Impleader remains available against the employer in the absence of grave injury, where the basis for indemnity or contribution is a written contract entered into prior to the accident that caused the plaintiff's injury.[107] The Act also amended CPLR 1401 and 1601, to prohibit juries from apportioning fault to non-party employers in cases where the plaintiff did not sustain grave injury.[108] Although New York's highest court has not addressed the issue, the intermediate appellate courts have held that the Act applies prospectively only.[109]

3. Punitive Damages

Punitive damages may be recovered in tort actions, including product liability suits, where a plaintiff proves exceptional misconduct that surpasses negligence — such as where the evidence shows the defendant acted "maliciously, wantonly, or with a recklessness suggesting an improper motive or vindictiveness."[110] The evidentiary standard for proving punitive damages in New York appears to be "preponderance of the evidence."[111] Punitive damages are recoverable in a wrongful death action.[112]

A corporate defendant cannot be held liable for punitive damages unless it can be shown that a "superior officer" of the corporation in the course of employment ordered, participated in, or ratified the conduct.[113] Similarly, officers and directors are liable for punitive damages only if plaintiff proves complicity in the oppressive conduct — i.e., the officer of director authorized, participated in, or ratified the conduct giving rise to the punitive damages.[114]

Thomas E. Reidy[115]
Andrew M. Burns
NIXON, HARGRAVE, DEVANS & DOYLE LLP
Clinton Square
Post Office Box 1051
Rochester, New York 14603
(716) 263-1000

1. *Heller v. U.S. Suzuki Motor Corp.*, 64 N.Y.2d 407, 412, 477 N.E.2d 434 (1985); *Victorson v. Bock Laundry Machine Co.*, 37 N.Y.2d 395, 400, 355 N.E.2d 275 (1975).

2. N.Y. Civ. Prac. L. & R. §214 (McKinney 1990). See generally *Snyder v. Town Insulation, Inc.*, 81 N.Y.2d 429, 432, 615 N.E.2d 999 (1993).

3. *Snyder*, 81 N.Y.2d at 436 (holding accrual of cause of action against insulation manufacturer occurred at time of installation, i.e., when all elements of tort could be truthfully alleged in complaint); but see *Blanco v. AT&T*, 1997 N.Y. LEXIS 3693 at *22 (action for repetitive stress injury sustained from keyboard use accrues on date of injury or date of last use of keyboard, whichever is earlier); see also *Consorti v. Owens-Corning Fiberglas Corp.*, 86 N.Y.2d 449, 657 N.E.2d 1301 (1995) (rejecting wife's loss of consortium claim where husband's exposure to harmful substance and his injury occurred prior to date of marriage).

4. N.Y. U.C.C. §2-725 (McKinney 1993).

5. *Heller*, 64 N.Y.2d at 411.

6. Id.

7. N.Y. Est. Powers & Trusts Law §5-4.1 (McKinney Supp. 1996).

8. N.Y. Civ. Prac. L. & R. §214-c(2) (McKinney 1990).

9. *Blanco v. AT&T*, 1997 N.Y. LEXIS 3693 (N.Y. November 25, 1997) (CPLR 214-c does not apply to a claim alleging latent musculoskeletal injuries allegedly caused by use of keyboard, because "a keyboard is not a toxic substance . . . ". See McLaughlin, Practice Commentaries (McKinney's Cons Laws of NY, Book 7B, CPLR C214-c:1, p.631 (1990)). See also *Parajecki v. International Business Machines Corp.*, 899 F. Supp. 1050, 1053-1054 (S.D.N.Y. 1995) (holding New York's discovery rule under CPLR §214-c inapplicable to plaintiffs claiming latent "repetitive stress injuries" from keyboard use); "Latent Injuries and Statute of Limitations," New York Law Journal, December 1, 1994 (discussing two recent trail level decisions refusing application of the discovery rule to plaintiffs claiming latent "repetitive stress injuries" from typing on a keyboard).

10. N.Y. Civ. Prac. L. & R. §214-c(2) (McKinney 1990).

11. *Cochrane v. Owens-Corning Fiberglass Corp.*, 631 N.Y.S.2d 358, 360 (1st Dept. 1995). See also *Braune v. Abbott Laboratories*, 895 F. Supp. 530, 556 (S.D.N.Y. 1995) (applying New York law).

12. *Wetherill v. Eli Lilly & Co.*, 89 N.Y.2d 506, 678 N.E.2d 474 (1997).

13. Id. at 511-513.

14. *Jensen v. General Electric Co.*, 82 N.Y.2d 77, 88, 623 N.E.2d 547 (1993).

15. *Blanco v. AT&T*, 1997 N.Y. LEXIS 3693 (N.Y. November 25, 1997) ("the mere continuation of [the duty to warn] into the limitations period is not enough to resurrect a cause of action premised upon an injury occurring earlier.").

16. *Rothstein v. Tennessee Gas Pipeline Co.*, 204 A.D.2d 39, 45 (2d Dept. 1994), *aff'd on other grounds*, 1995 WL 708267 (Nov. 30, 1995). See also Alexander, Supplementary Practice Commentaries (McKinney's Cons Laws of NY, Book 7B, CPLR C213-c:2, p.136 (1996)).

17. See *Sackman v. Liggett Group, Inc.*, 167 F.R.D. 6, 15-16 (E.D.N.Y. 1996) (claim that cigarette maker breached express warranty that cigarettes would be safe was untimely when brought more than four years after plaintiff discovered injury was caused by cigarettes).

18. *Annunziato v. City of New York*, 224 A.D.2d 31 (2d Dept. 1996).

19. N.Y. Civ. Prac. L. & R. §214-c(4) (McKinney 1990). See also *Whitney v. Agway, Inc.*, 656 N.Y.S.2d 455 (3d Dept. 1997).

20. *Annunziato, supra.*

21. *Annunziato* actually involved a suit against the City of New York, which was governed by a one-year, 90-day limitations period supplied by General Municipal Law §§50-e and 50-i. The "discovery rule" created by CPLR 214-c, however, applied the same way it would have applied had the limitations period been supplied by CPLR 214(3).

22. See, e.g., *Sackman*, 167 F.R.D. at 13.

23. See *Sackman*, 167 F.R.D. at 14.

24. N.Y. Civ. Prac. L. & R. §214-c(6) (McKinney 1990). See also *Rothstein v. Tennessee Gas Pipeline Co.*, 1995 WL 708267 (Nov. 30, 1995).

25. *Amatulli v. Delhi Construction Corp.*, 77 N.Y.2d 525, 532, 571 N.E.2d 645 (1991); *Codling v. Paglia*, 32 N.Y.2d 330, 342, 298 N.E.2d 622 (1973).

26. *Codling*, 32 N.Y.2d at 342.

27. *Momen v. United States*, No. 94-CV-654, 1996 U.S. Dist. LEXIS 18067 (N.D.N.Y. Dec. 3, 1996); *Sage v. Fairchild-Swearingen Corp.*, 70 N.Y.2d 579, 585, 517 N.E.2d 1304 (1987); *Sukljian v. Charles Ross & Son Co.*, 69 N.Y.2d 89, 94, 503 N.E.2d 1358 (1986).

28. *Caprara v. Chrysler Corp.*, 52 N.Y.2d 114, 417 N.E.2d 545, *rearg. denied*, 52 N.Y.2d 1073 (1981); *Rainbow v. Elia Building Co.*, 79 A.D.2d 287, 294 (1982), *aff'd*, 56 N.Y.2d 550, 434 N.E.2d 1345 (1982).

29. *Voss v. Black & Decker Mfg. Co.*, 59 N.Y.2d 102, 107, 450 N.E.2d 204 (1983).

30. Id. at 109; *cf. McCarthy v. Sturm, Ruger & Co.*, 119 F.3d 148, 155 (2d Cir. 1997) (risk/utility analysis not relevant to case involving inherently dangerous product, such as gun or knife because "the risks arise from the function of the product, not any defect in the product.").

31. See *Taft v. Sports Page Shop Inc.*, 226 A.D.2d 974 (3d Dept. 1996).

32. *Rastelli v. Goodyear Tire Co.*, 79 N.Y.2d 289, 297, 591 N.E.2d 222 (1992); *Robinson v. Reed-Prentice*, 49 N.Y.2d 471, 478-479, 403 N.E.2d 440 (1980).

33. *Lugo v. LJN Toys Ltd.*, 75 N.Y.2d 850, 852, 552 N.E.2d 162 (1990).

34. *Banks v. Makita, USA, Inc.*, 226 A.D.2d 659 (2d Dept. 1996).

35. *Hamilton v. Accu-tek*, 935 F. Supp. 1307 (E.D.N.Y. 1996) (court distinguishes between injuries caused by abnormally dangerous activities, for which strict liability applies, and injuries caused by the use of a dangerous instrumentality, such as refrigerant, poison, pesticide, or firearm).

36. See *Bocre Leasing Corporation v. General Motors Corporation*, 84 N.Y.2d 685, 645 N.E.2d 1195 (1995); *Bellevue Associates v. HRH*, 78 N.Y.2d 282, 293-295, 579 N.E.2d 195 (1991); *Schiavone v. Timberland Equipment, Ltd.*, 56 N.Y.2d 667, 668, 436 N.E.2d 1322 (1982), *rev'g on dissent*, 81 A.D.2d 221, 227-234.

37. *Bocre Leasing Corp., supra; Bellevue*, 78 N.Y.2d at 293.

38. See *Village of Groton v. Tokheim Corp.*, 202 A.D.2d 728 (3d Dept. 1994).

39. *Bocre Leasing Corp., supra; Bellevue,* 78 N.Y.2d at 290-293. See *Ofsowitz v. Georgie Boy Mfg., Inc.,* 231 A.D.2d 858 (4th Dept. 1996) (extending rule to product seller and refusing to exclude consumer purchases).

40. N.Y. Civ. Prac. L. & R. §1411 (McKinney 1976).

41. N.Y. Civ. Prac. L. & R. §1412 (McKinney 1976).

42. The plaintiff bears the burden to prove the manufacturer's identity, but may do so with circumstantial proof if the product is no longer available. See *Healey v. Firestone Tire Co.,* 87 N.Y.2d 596, 601 (1996).

43. *Sukljian,* 69 N.Y.2d at 95; see also *In re New York State Silicone Breast Implant Litig.,* 227 A.D.2d 308 (1st Dept. 1996) (a party who gives advice to a manufacturer of consumer goods does not owe a duty to then-unknown individual purchasers of the finished goods).

44. *Stiles v. Batavia Atomic Horseshoes, Inc.,* 81 N.Y.2d 950, 951, 613 N.E.2d 572, *rearg. denied,* 81 N.Y.2d 1068, 619 N.E.2d 664 (1993); *Sukljian,* 69 N.Y.2d at 95-96; *Colopy v. Pitman Mfg. Co.,* 206 A.D.2d 864 (4th Dept. 1994).

45. *Sukljian,* 69 N.Y.2d at 97.

46. *Fletcher v. Atex, Inc.,* 68 F.3d 1451, 1458 (2d Cir. 1995) (applying law of Delaware, as state of subsidiary's incorporation, to issue of alter ego liability). See also *King v. Eastman Kodak Co.,* 631 N.Y.S.2d 832, 833 (1st Dept. 1995) (applying Delaware law to issue of alter ego liability).

47. *Fletcher,* 68 F.3d at 1461 (applying New York law and holding that parent corporation did not authorize subsidiary to act on its behalf). See also *King,* 631 N.Y.S.2d at 834 (holding that parent corporation never authorized actions of subsidiary); *Porter v. LSB Indus., Inc.,* 192 A.D.2d 205, 215 (4th Dept. 1993) (finding no evidence to support imposition of liability on parent corporation as principal of its subsidiary).

48. *Fletcher,* 68 F.3d at 1462 (applying New York law and holding apparent manufacturer theory inapplicable where parent corporation not involved in the chain of distribution, where parent corporation never held itself out as manufacturer of product, and where parent corporation's name never appeared on product). See also *King,* 631 N.Y.S.2d at 833 (apparent manufacturer liability inapplicable where parent corporation not involved in distribution of product and where parent corporation's name never appeared on product); *Pangallo v. Mitsubishi Intl. Corp.,* 632 N.Y.S.2d 647, 648 (2d Dept. 1995) (parent corporation not liable where product itself identified product's manufacturer as subsidiary of parent).

49. *Fletcher*, 68 F.3d at 1464 (applying New York law and holding that parent corporation did not engage in concerted action with subsidiary because parent not involved in decisions regarding manufacture, marketing, or warnings). See also *King*, 631 N.Y.S.2d at 833 (parent corporation not liable under concerted action theory where parent never agreed to pursue a tortious plan with subsidiary).

50. *In re New York State Silicone Breast Implant Litig.*, 227 A.D.2d 308 (1st Dept. 1996).

51. *Sackman v. Liggett Group, Inc.*, 965 F. Supp. 391 (E.D.N.Y. 1997) (court also held that concert of action claim may be maintained based on allegations that manufacturer conspired with other manufacturers to conceal health risks associated with product use).

52. *Schumacher v. Richards Shear Co.*, 59 N.Y.2d 239, 244, 451 N.E.2d 195 (1983).

53. Id. at 245; *Hartford Accident & Indemnity Co. v. Canron, Inc.*, 43 N.Y.2d 823, 825, 373 N.E.2d 364 (1977).

54. *Schumacher*, 59 N.Y.2d at 245 (not adopting either exception but noting that cases establishing those exceptions were factually distinguishable). But see *Rothstein v. Tennessee Gas Pipeline Co.*, 664 N.Y.S.2d 213 (Sup. Ct. Kings Co. 1997) (trial court adopts product line exception).

55. *Heller*, 64 N.Y.2d at 411; *Giuffrida v. Panasonic Indus. Co.*, 200 A.D.2d 713, (2d Dept. 1994).

56. *Cover v. Cohen*, 61 N.Y.2d 261, 275, 461 N.E.2d 864 (1984).

57. Id.

58. Id. at 274-275. See also *Lindsay v. Ortho Pharmaceutical Corp.*, 637 F.2d 87, 91 (2d Cir. 1980).

59. *Amatulli*, 77 N.Y.2d at 532; *Robinson*, 49 N.Y.2d at 479; *Wyda v. Makita Electric Works, Ltd.*, 648 N.Y.S.2d 154 (2d Dept. 1996); *Paul v. Ford Motor Co.*, 200 A.D.2d 724, 725-726 (2d Dept. 1994). See *Liriano v. Hobart Corp.*, 1998 U.S. App. LEXIS 1 (2d Cir. January 2, 1998) (court certifies question to New York's highest court as to whether a substantial modification would bar plaintiff's failure to warn claim).

60. *Lopez v. Precision Papers, Inc.*, 107 A.D.2d 667, 669 (2d Dept. 1985), *aff'd*, 67 N.Y.2d 871, 492 N.E.2d 1214 (1986) (forklift manufactured and marketed with an attached but removable overhead safety guard).

61. Id. See *LaPaglia v. Sears Roebuck & Co.*, 143 A.D.2d 173, 177 (2d Dept. 1988) (jury was warranted in refusing to absolve manufacturer from liability for design defect where lawn mower was manufactured with purpose of permitting, if not requiring, the facile removal of a chute deflector for purposes of installing a grass catcher).

62. See *Smith v. Stark*, 67 N.Y.2d 693, 694, 490 N.E.2d 841 (1986). See also *Banks v. Makita USA, Inc.*, 641 N.Y.S.2d at 877; *Wood v. Peabody*, 187 A.D.2d 824, 826 (3d Dept. 1992); *Belling v. Haugh's Pools Ltd.*, 126 A.D.2d 958, 959 (4th Dept. 1987), *appeal denied*, 70 N.Y.2d 602, *reconsideration dismissed*, 70 N.Y.2d 748 (1988).

63. *Frederick v. Niagara Machine & Tool Works*, 107 A.D.2d 1063, 1064 (4th Dept. 1985). But see *Bazerman v. Gardall Safe Corp.*, 203 A.D.2d 56 (1st Dept. 1994) (holding that danger from turning over a heavy safe was obvious as a matter of law).

64. *Cover*, 61 N.Y.2d at 270; *Caprara*, 52 N.Y.2d at 126.

65. *Cover*, 61 N.Y.2d at 270.

66. *Ramundo v. Town of Guilderland*, 142 A.D.2d 50, 54 (3d Dept. 1988), *appeal after remand*, 163 A.D.2d 712 (3d Dept. 1990); *Bolm v. Triumph Corp.*, 71 A.D.2d 429, 436 (4th Dept. 1979), *appeal dismissed*, 50 N.Y.2d 801 (1980).

67. *Cover*, 61 N.Y.2d at 270; *Demirovski v. Skil Corp.*, 203 A.D.2d 319 (2d Dept. 1994).

68. *Sawyer v. Dreis & Krump Mfg. Co.*, 67 N.Y.2d 328, 336, 493 N.E.2d 920 (1986); *Bolm*, 71 A.D.2d at 438.

69. *Sawyer*, 67 N.Y.2d at 336; *Hyde v. County of Rensselaer*, 51 N.Y.2d 927, 929, 415 N.E.2d 972 (1980); *White v. Timberjack, Inc.*, 209 A.D.2d 968 (4th Dept. 1994).

70. *Martin v. Hacker*, 83 N.Y.2d 1, 9, 628 N.E.2d 1308 (1993); *Wolfgruber v. Upjohn*, 72 A.D.2d 59, 61 (4th Dept. 1979), *aff'd*, 52 N.Y.2d 768, 417 N.E.2d 1002 (1980); *Polimeni v. Minolta Corp.*, 227 A.D.2d 64, 67 (3d. Dept. 1997).

71. *Martin*, 83 N.Y.2d at 11. See, e.g., *Fane v. Zimmer*, 927 F.2d 124, 130 (2d Cir. 1991) (where manufacturer of internal fixation device warned physician but not patient of risks, no liability imposed on manufacturer). See also *Rivers v. AT&T Technologies, Inc.*, 147 Misc. 2d 366, 372 (Sup. Ct. N.Y. Co. 1990) (same result in case involving purchase and use of bulk chemicals).

72. *Polimeni v. Minolta Corp.*, 227 A.D. 2d 64, 67 (3d Dept. 1997).

73. *Billsborrow v. Dow Chemical*, 177 A.D.2d 7, 16-19 (2d Dept. 1992); *In re Brooklyn Navy Yard Asbestos Litigation*, 971 F.2d 831, 838-839 (2d Cir. 1992).

74. *George v. Celotex Corp.*, 914 F.2d 26, 28 (2d Cir. 1990) (applying New York and federal law in holding that a manufacturer is held to the knowledge of an expert in its field and has a duty "to keep abreast of scientific knowledge, discoveries, and advances and is presumed to know what is "imparted thereby").

75. Id.

76. *Solomon v. City of New York*, 66 N.Y.2d 1026, 1027, 489 N.E.2d 1294 (1985).

77. *Bichler v. Eli Lilly & Co.*, 55 N.Y.2d 571, 436 N.E.2d 182 (1982).

78. *Micallef v. Miehle Co.*, 39 N.Y.2d 376, 348 N.E.2d 571 (1976); *Kriz v. Schum*, 75 N.Y.2d 25, 549 N.E.2d 1155 (1989).

79. *Markel v. Spencer*, 5 A.D.2d 400 (4th Dept. 1958), *aff'd without opinion*, 5 N.Y.2d 958 (1959).

80. *Mueller v. Teichner*, 6 N.Y.2d 903, 161 N.E.2d 14 (1959).

81. *Smith v. Peerless Glass Co.*, 259 N.Y. 292, 181 N.E. 576 (1932), *reh'g denied*, 259 N.Y. 664, 182 N.E. 225; *Mueller*, 6 N.Y.2d 903. See also *Feuerverger v. Hobart Corp.*, 738 F. Supp. 76 (E.D.N.Y. 1990) (applying New York law).

82. *Heller*, 64 N.Y.2d at 411; *Guiffrida*, 607 N.Y.S.2d at 74.

83. *Codling v. Paglia*, 38 A.D.2d 154 (3d Dept. 1972), *aff'd in part and rev'd in part on other grounds*, 32 N.Y.2d 330 (1973).

84. *Denny v. Ford Motor Co.*, 87 N.Y.2d 248, 662 N.E.2d 730 (1995) (refusing to overturn verdict that found manufacturer liable for a defect under breach of implied warranty, but not liable for any defect under strict product liability).

85. N.Y. U.C.C. §§2-313(1)(a)-(c) and §2-313(2) (McKinney 1993); *Cornier v. Spagna*, 101 A.D.2d 141 (1st Dept. 1984).

86. N.Y. U.C.C. §2-314 (implied warranty of merchantability); *Di Prospero v. R. Brown & Sons*, 100 A.D.2d 250 (3d Dept. 1985).

87. N.Y. U.C.C. §2-313(1)(a). See also *Randy Knitwear v. American Cyanamid Co.*, 11 N.Y.2d 5, 181 N.E.2d 399 (1962).

88.   N.Y. U.C.C. §2-314(2)(c) (McKinney 1993). See also *Denny*, 87 N.Y.2d at 248.

89.   N.Y. U.C.C. §2-318 (McKinney 1993).

90.   *Milau Associates v. North Ave. Dev. Corp.*, 42 N.Y.2d 482, 368 N.E.2d 1247 (1977).

91.   *Martin v. Julius Dierck Equip. Co.*, 43 N.Y.2d 583, 589-590, 374 N.E.2d 97 (1978); *Manufacturers & Traders Trust Co. v. Stone Conveyor, Inc.*, 91 A.D.2d 849, 850 (2d Dept. 1982); *Fargo Equipment Co., Inc. v. Carborundum Co.*, 103 A.D.2d 1002, 1003 (4th Dept. 1984).

92.   *All-O-Matic Industries, Inc. v. Southern Specialty Paper Co., Inc.*, 49 A.D.2d 935 (2d Dept. 1975).

93.   *Hole v. General Motors Corp.*, 83 A.D.2d 715, 716 (3d Dept. 1981); N.Y. U.C.C. §2-318.

94.   *Randy Knitwear*, 11 N.Y.2d at 14-15 (allowing express warranty claim).

95.   N.Y. Civ. Prac. L. & R. §§1601-1603 (McKinney Supp. 1996). See *Ravo v. Rogatnick*, 70 N.Y.2d 305, 309-310, 514 N.E.2d 1104 (1987).

96.   N.Y. Civ. Prac. L. & R. §1602 sub. 10.

97.   N.Y. Civ. Prac. L. & R. §1401 (McKinney 1976).

98.   N.Y. Civ. Prac. L. & R. §1402 (McKinney 1976).

99.   Id.

100. N.Y. Gen. Oblig. Law §15-108 (McKinney 1989).

101. N.Y. Gen. Oblig. Law §15-108(a) (McKinney 1989).

102. *Didner v. Keene Corp.*, 82 N.Y.2d 342, 353, 624 N.E.2d 979 (1993).

103. N.Y. Gen. Oblig. Law §§15-108(b), 15-108(c) (McKinney 1989).

104. N.Y. Civ. Prac. L. & R. §3101(i) (McKinney Supp. 1996).

105. *Dole v. Dow Chemical Co.*, 30 N.Y.2d 143, 152-153, 282 N.E.2d 288 (1972).

106. N.Y. Workers' Compensation Law §11 (McKinney Supp. 1996).

107. Id.

108. CPLR 1401; CPLR 1601(1) (McKinney Supp. 1996).

109. *Morales v. Walter J. Gross*, 230 A.D.2d 7 (2d Dept. 1997); *Majewski v. Broadalbin-Perth Central School Dist.*, 231 A.D.2d 102 (3d Dept. 1997); *Matie v. Sealed Air Corp.*, 1997 N.Y. App. Div. LEXIS 10394 (4th Dept. September 30, 1997); *Doria v. Cooke Poperties, Inc.*, 1997 N.Y. App. Div. LEXIS 12846 (1st Dept. December 9, 1997).

110. *Home Ins. Co. v. American Home Products*, 75 N.Y.2d 196, 203-204, 550 N.E.2d 930 (1991); *Camillo v. Geer*, 185 A.D.2d 192, 194 (1st Dept. 1992). See also *O'Neill v. Yield House, Inc.*, 892 F. Supp. 76 (S.D.N.Y. 1995) (applying New York law and upholding award of punitive damages against manufacturer of stepstool that made no meaningful efforts to ensure the safety of its product).

111. *Re Seventh Judicial District Asbestos Litig.*, 190 A.D.2d 1068, 1069 (4th Dept. 1993) (citing *Corrigan v. Bobbs-Merrill Co.*, 228 N.Y. 58 (1920)). See also *Simpson v. Pittsburgh Corning Corp.*, 901 F.2d 277, 282-283 (2d Cir. 1990) (applying New York preponderance standard while noting possibility that due process may require higher standard). But see *Camillo*, 185 A.D.2d at 194 (applying clear and convincing standard).

112. N.Y. Est. Powers and Trust Law §5-4.3(b) (McKinney Supp. 1995).

113. *Camillo*, 185 A.D.2d at 195-196 (citing *Loughry v. Lincoln First Bank*, 67 N.Y.2d 369, 494 N.E.2d 70 (1986)).

114. Roginsky v. Richarson-Merrell, Inc., 378 F.2d 832, 842 (2d Cir. 1967) (applying New York law).

115. The authors gratefully acknowledge the contributions of their colleagues, who prepared the comprehensive review of New York product liability law from which portions of this chapter was adapted.

NORTH CAROLINA

PREFACE

Topics of ongoing interest include:

- North Carolina continues to reject strict liability, and to recognize defense of contributory negligence as complete bar to recovery.

- Sealed container defense may be available to retailers and distributors.

- Manufacturer of prescription drug or device may only have duty to warn informed intermediary doctor, not patient directly.

- Punitive damages capped at greater of three times compensatory damages, or $250,000.

A. CAUSES OF ACTION

Product liability lawsuits are governed by a general products liability statute.[1] Causes of action commonly include negligence and warranty.

B. STATUTES OF LIMITATION AND REPOSE

Negligence causes of action for personal injuries or property damage[2] and contract actions for breach of warranty that involve *personal injury*[3] must be brought within three years. Contract or breach of warranty actions based on the sale of goods in which damages are limited to the product itself are subject to the four-year UCC statute of limitations.[4] Wrongful death suits are further limited to two years from the date of death.[5]

Statutes of repose have a substantial practical effect on litigation. A product liability cause of action on any theory is barred more than six years after the date of "initial purchase for use or consumption."[6] Sale to an intermediary or distributor is not a sale for initial use or consumption for purposes of beginning the repose period.[7] Suits involving improvements to real property are limited by a six-year statute of repose, with the triggering event being the later of the "specific last act or omission of the defendant" or "substantial completion of the improvement."[8] Any general negligence action accrues, as a matter of law, no "more than 10 years from the last act or omission of the defendant."[9] However, the period is tolled by statute for minors and others with disabilities whose claims accrue before expiration of the repose period.[10] Further, an action for willful and wanton misconduct may not be barred if the product is an improvement to realty.[11]

The statute of limitation for malpractice in the performance of professional services (e.g., medicine,[12] law,[13] accounting[14]), except for those professional services involving improvements to real property (e.g., architecture and engineering in some cases), is three years from the "last act of the defendant giving rise to the cause of action,"[15] with a one-year extension for losses "not readily apparent to the claimant" and a repose provision four years "from the last act of the defendant giving rise to the cause of action."[16] The statute of limitations for constructive fraud in breach of a fiduciary duty is ten years.[17]

C. STRICT LIABILITY

By statute, North Carolina does not recognize strict liability in product liability actions.[18] Evidence of negligence is required, except in cases of breach of warranty.

D. NEGLIGENCE

1. Discovery

The "discovery" rule was not codified until 1979[19] and is still interpreted reasonably strictly.[20] Additionally, its effect is severely limited by the statutes of repose discussed above.[21] It clearly applies to causes of action in negligence but arguably does not apply to causes of action for breach of warranty or contract since the cause of action is "complete" without physical harm to person or property.[22]

2. Degree and Standard of Care

The jury is instructed that the standard of care is that of a reasonably prudent person.[23] However, the degree of care varies according to the exigencies of the situation.[24]

3. Contributory Negligence/Assumption of Risk

Contributory negligence[25] and assumption of risk[26] are complete defenses to claims of negligence or breach of warranty.[27] However, contributory negligence does not bar damages based on an action for a breach of contract alone.[28] The "last clear chance" variation is also recognized as a complete defense where negligence of the defendant is established but injury could have been avoided by plaintiff.[29]

4. Sale or Lease

Negligence does not attach to a seller, lessor, or bailor in the chain of a product's distribution if that product was acquired and sold in a sealed container or if the product was acquired and sold under circumstances that afforded no reasonable opportunity to inspect the product for the defect alleged.[30] However, a breach of express warranty claim may survive.

5. Inherently Dangerous Products

North Carolina recognizes that control and possession of "dangerous instrumentalities" requires a high degree of care,[31] which, in very limited circumstances, may approach absolute liability.[32]

6. Successor Liability

Even when a successor corporation acquires all or substantially all of the manufacturing assets of another corporation, that alone is not sufficient to establish successor liability absent an express agreement to assume liabilities.[33] The successor may be liable for injuries caused by products made by the predecessor corporation if the manner of sale of the assets was fraudulent, or if the successor was a mere continuation of its predecessor.[34]

7. Privity

The privity requirement has been statutorily eliminated for many categories of plaintiffs.[35] However, significant privity restrictions remain. Where there is no privity, a plaintiff may not revoke acceptance of a product,[36] recover for economic injuries under an implied warranty theory,[37] or, under certain circumstances, recover for breach of express[38] or implied warranties.[39]

8. Failure to Warn

Failure to warn is based on the reasonable person standard.[40] Where plaintiff knew of the danger,[41] where the danger was obvious or a matter of common knowledge,[42] or where warnings were ignored,[43] no cause of action for failure to warn may be sustained. To prove claims for failure to warn or instruct, it must be shown that, at the time the product left defendant's control, it lacked adequate warning or instruction and created an unreasonably dangerous condition that the defendant knew or should have known to pose a substantial risk of harm to foreseeable plaintiffs.[44] Warnings directed by the responsible governmental agency may preempt a claim for negligent failure to warn.[45]

9. Post-Sale Duty to Warn

A statutory provision enacted in 1995 states that a failure to warn or instruct claim may be pursued by proof that, *after* the product left defendant's control, defendant became aware of or should have known that the product posed a substantial risk of harm to a foreseeable user, yet did not take reasonable steps to warn or instruct.[46] Cases alluding to a post-sale duty to warn dating from before this statute have concerned situations in which the knowledge of the alleged danger related to (a) an omitted safety feature known and available prior to the date of manufacture[47] and (b) a chemical whose alleged dangerous propensity was known at time of manufacture.[48]

10. Substantial Change/Abnormal Use

A manufacturer is not responsible for injuries caused by an alteration or modification to the product unless the alteration was made in accordance with instructions or specifications of or with the express consent of the manufacturer or seller.[49] Nor is a manufacturer responsible for misuse of the product.[50] Moreover, in negligence actions the chain of causation must not be broken by a third party.[51]

11. Standards

Generally, nonstatutory safety codes are inadmissible,[52] but this is not a hard and fast rule.[53] Particularly, when the nonstatutory standards are published by a source that is considered reliable by persons involved in the subject matter area[54] or adopted by the party, or have become a standard in the industry manufacturing the product,[55] they may be admissible.

12. Other Accidents

Evidence of similar events or conditions, when shown to be relevant[56] in terms of time and circumstances, may be admissible on the issue of causation, defect, or knowledge.[57]

13. *Res Ipsa Loquitur*

Neither negligence[58] nor proximate cause[59] may be presumed by the mere fact of accident or injury while using a product. However, *res ipsa loquitur* may apply in those cases in which the instrumentality is shown to be under the exclusive control of the defendant and the occurrence is one that does not occur in the ordinary course under proper care.[60]

14. Crashworthiness

Federal courts, predicting the views of the state courts, had generally anticipated rejection of crashworthiness in North Carolina.[61] However, the associated doctrine of "enhanced injury" was endorsed in a 1989 Court of Appeals decision.[62] A later Supreme Court case discussed the Court of Appeals decision without rejecting it.[63] Thus, crashworthiness may apply.

15. Seat Belt Use

By statute, evidence relating to the use or nonuse of seat belts is generally inadmissible in any action.[64]

16. Informed Intermediary

The manufacturer of a prescription drug or medical device is not required to warn or instruct individual patients if the manufacturer has adequately warned or instructed the physician or other legally authorized person who prescribes or dispenses the drug (unless the FDA requires such direct warning or instruction).[65]

17. No Liability for Inherent Characteristics

A manufacturer cannot be held liable for a design defect claim that is grounded on an inherent product characteristic, when such characteristic is recognized by an ordinary person with ordinary knowledge common to the community, and such characteristic cannot be eliminated without substantially compromising the product's usefulness or desirability.[66]

18. Market Share Liability

There are no North Carolina state court decisions on the issue of "market share" or "enterprise" liability. In 1986, a federal district court predicted that North Carolina would *not* adopt such theories of liability.[67]

E. BREACH OF WARRANTY

In the products setting, a cause of action for breach of warranty is generally quite similar to a negligence cause of action. However, with respect to the statute of limitations, the "discovery rule" does not apply. Breach of implied warranty does not require proof of negligence, although the courts have otherwise rejected theories of strict liability in tort. Damages tailored to the warranty context may be available.[68]

F. PSYCHOLOGICAL DAMAGES

North Carolina generally follows a conservative approach toward damages for alleged psychological harm. Recent cases have stated that claims in which plaintiffs did not personally witness the accident, and were not in close proximity, should ordinarily be rejected unless the plaintiff can produce evidence that the defendant had *actual knowledge* before the accident of plaintiff's particular susceptibility to emotional distress.[69] Further, where plaintiff alleges emotional distress, a strong showing of "severe" distress must be made.[70]

G. PUNITIVE DAMAGES

Punitive damages are recoverable in negligence actions only where plaintiff recovers compensatory damages and there is "clear and convincing evidence" of actual fraud, malice, or willful or wanton conduct related to the injury.[71] The conduct must be more than gross negligence.[72] Specificity is required in pleading.[73] Only nine categories of evidence may be considered by the jury.[74] Vicarious liability cannot be the basis for punitive damages.[75] Generally, the amount awarded is limited to the greater of three times compensatory damages or $250,000; and the jury is not so instructed.[76] Separate trial is required upon defendant's motion.[77] Attorney's fees shall be awarded for frivolous pleading regarding punitive damages.[78] Punitive damages are not recoverable in warranty.[79]

H. ECONOMIC LOSS

North Carolina has adopted the "economic loss rule," which states that purely economic loss is not recoverable in a product liability negligence action; rather, a contract/UCC claim must be brought.[80]

I. JOINT AND SEVERAL LIABILITY

Common law provides joint and several liability among tortfeasors for resulting injury.[81] There is no apportionment of fault.[82] The Uniform Contribution Among Tort-Feasors Act applies.[83]

J. STATUTES

Relevant statutes for product liability actions are the product liability chapter (see section A, *supra*), various statutes of limitation and repose (see section B, *supra*), the commercial code sections when a breach of warranty is alleged,[84] and the punitive damages chapter (see section G, *supra*).

H. Grady Barnhill, Jr.
William F. Womble, Jr.
WOMBLE CARLYLE SANDRIDGE & RICE, PLLC
P.O. Drawer 84
Winston-Salem, NC 27102
(336) 721-3600

ENDNOTES – NORTH CAROLINA

1. N.C. Gen. Stat. §99B et seq. (1996). It should be noted that the statute includes provisions that became effective January 1, 1996, and apply to claims for relief "arising on or after" that date.

2. Id. §1-52(16) for an action "[u]nless otherwise provided by statute, for personal injury or physical damages to claimant's property. . . ."

3. Id. §1-52(1) controls actions arising "out of a contract, express or implied" if the damages sought include personal injury. *Bernick v. Jurden*, 306 N.C. 435, 293 S.E.2d 405 (1982); *Smith v. Cessna Aircraft Co.*, 571 F. Supp. 433 (M.D.N.C. 1983).

4. N.C. Gen. Stat. §25-2-725(1); *Bobbitt v. Tannewitz*, 538 F. Supp. 654 (M.D.N.C. 1982); *Cessna Aircraft, supra* note 3. See also *Hanover Ins. Co. v. Amana Refrigeration, Inc.*, 106 N.C. App. 79, 415 S.E.2d 99, *rev. denied*, 332 N.C. 344, 421 S.E.2d 147 (1992) (choosing three-year statute of limitations for contract action over four-year statute of limitations for breach of warranty where product damaged real property); and see *Reece v. Homette Corp.*, 110 N.C. App. 462, 429 S.E.2d 768 (1993) (product liability remedies not available for damage to product; UCC limitation period ran from date of sale).

5. N.C. Gen. Stat. §1-53(4); *Bernick, supra* note 3.

6. N.C. Gen. Stat. §1-50(a)(6); *Hyer v. Pittsburgh Corning Corp.*, 790 F.2d 30 (4th Cir. 1986).

7. *Chicopee, Inc. v. Sims Metal Works, Inc.*, 98 N.C. App. 423, 391 S.E.2d 211, *rev. denied*, 327 N.C. 426, 395 S.E.2d 674 (1990).

8. N.C. Gen. Stat. §1-50(a)(5)a; *Forsyth Memorial Hosp., Inc. v. Armstrong World Indus., Inc.*, 336 N.C. 438, 444 S.E.2d 423 (1994).

9. Id. §1-52(16); *Doe v. Doe*, 973 F.2d 237 (4th Cir. 1992).

10. N.C. Gen. Stat. §1-17; *Bryant v. Adams*, 116 N.C. App. 448, 448 S.E.2d 832 (1994), *rev. denied*, 339 N.C. 736, 454 S.E.2d 647 (1995).

11. *Forsyth Hospital, supra* note 8.

12. *Nelson v. Patrick*, 58 N.C. App. 546, 293 S.E.2d 829 (1982).

13. *Clodfelter v. Bates*, 44 N.C. App. 107, 260 S.E.2d 672 (1979), *rev. denied*, 299 N.C. 329, 265 S.E.2d 394 (1980).

14. *Barger v. McCoy Hilliard & Parks*, 120 N.C. App. 326, 462 S.E.2d 252 (1995); *aff'd in part, rev'd in part*, 346 N.C. 650, 488 S.E.2d 215 (1997).

15. N.C. Gen. Stat. §1-15(c).

16. Id.

17. N.C. Gen. Stat. §99B-6(c); *Barger, supra* note 14; *Sharp v. Teague*, 113 N.C. App. 589, 597, 439 S.E.2d 792 (1994) *rev. denied*, 339 N.C. 730, 456 S.E.2d 771 (1995).

18. N.C. Gen. Stat. §99B-1.1; *Smith v. Fiber Controls Corp.*, 300 N.C. 669, 268 S.E.2d 504 (1980); *Warren v. Colombo*, 93 N.C. App. 92, 377 S.E.2d 249 (1989).

19. N.C. Gen. Stat. §1-52(16).

20. See *Ferris v. Haymore*, 967 F.2d 946 (4th Cir. 1992).

21. See *Bonestell v. North Topsail Shores Condominiums, Inc.*, 103 N.C. App. 219, 405 S.E.2d 222 (1991).

22. *United States Leasing Corp. v. Everett, Creech, Hancock, & Herzig*, 88 N.C. App. 418, 363 S.E.2d 665, *rev. denied*, 322 N.C. 329, 369 S.E.2d 364 (1988); *Carl Rose & Sons Ready Mix Concrete, Inc. v. Thorp Sales Corp.*, 36 N.C. App. 778, 245 S.E.2d 234 (1978).

23. *Bolkhir v. North Carolina State Univ.*, 321 N.C. 706, 365 S.E.2d 898 (1988); *Thomasville v. Lease-Afex, Inc.*, 300 N.C. 651, 268 S.E.2d 190 (1980). See N.C. Pattern Jury Instructions — Civil 750.00 and 750.21.

24. *Greene v. Meredith*, 264 N.C. 178, 141 S.E.2d 287 (1965).

25. N.C. Gen. Stat. §99B-4(3); *Fiber Controls, supra* note 18; N.C. Pattern Jury Instructions — Civil 750.23 and 755.60. Contributory negligence may apply to claims of failure to warn, defective design, and defective manufacture. *Cessna Aircraft, supra* note 3.

26. N.C. Gen. Stat. §99B-4(2); *Alston v. Monk*, 92 N.C. App. 59, 373 S.E.2d 463 (1988), *rev. denied*, 324 N.C. 246, 378 S.E.2d 420 (1989).

27. Contributory negligence applies to product liability actions. *Champs Convenience Stores, Inc. v. United Chem. Co.*, 329 N.C. 446, 406 S.E.2d 856 (1991).

28. *Steelcase, Inc. v. Lilly Co.*, 93 N.C. App. 697, 379 S.E.2d 40 (1989), *rev. denied*, 325 N.C. 276, 384 S.E.2d 530 (1989).

29. *Watson v. White*, 309 N.C. 498, 308 S.E.2d 268 (1983); *McCullough v. Amoco Oil Co.*, 64 N.C. App. 312, 307 S.E.2d 208 (1983), *rev'd on other grounds*, 310 N.C. 452, 312 S.E.2d 417 (1984).

30. N.C. Gen. Stat. §99B-2(a); *Davis v. Siloo Inc.*, 47 N.C. App. 237, 267 S.E.2d 354, *rev. denied*, 301 N.C. 234, 283 S.E.2d 131 (1980), N.C. Pattern Jury Instructions — Civil 755.55 and 755.56. Section 99B-2(a) applies to implied warranty claims. *Morrison v. Sears, Roebuck & Co.*, 319 N.C. 298, 354 S.E.2d 495 (1987). Identified manufacturer of component part may be liable. *Haymore v. Thew Shovel Co.*, 116 N.C. App. 40, 446 S.E.2d 865 (1994).

31. *McCollum v. Grove Mfg. Co.*, 58 N.C. App. 283, 293 S.E.2d 632 (1982), *aff'd*, 307 N.C. 695, 300 S.E.2d 374 (1983); *Haymore, supra* note 30; see N.C. Pattern Jury Instructions — Civil 750.20.

32. *Maybank v. S. S. Kresge Co.*, 46 N.C. App. 687, 266 S.E.2d 409 (1980), *aff'd in part, rev'd in part on other grounds*, 302 N.C. 129, 273 S.E.2d 681 (1981); *Jones v. Williamette Industries, Inc.*, 120 N.C. App. 591, 463 S.E.2d 294 (1995), *rev. denied*, 342 N.C. 656, 467 S.E.2d 714 (1996).

33. *Budd Tire Corp. v. Pierce Tire Co.*, 90 N.C. App. 684, 370 S.E.2d 267 (1988).

34. Id.; *Pendergrass v. Card Care, Inc.*, 333 N.C. 233, 424 S.E.2d 391 (1993).

35. See N.C. Gen. Stat. §99B-2(b); *Bernick v. Jurden, supra* note 3.

36. *Alberti v. Manufactured Homes, Inc.*, 329 N.C. 727, 407 S.E.2d 819 (1991).

37. *Gregory v. Atrium Door and Window Co.*, 106 N.C. App. 142, 415 S.E.2d 574 (1992); see also *Crews v. W.A. Brown & Son*, 106 N.C. App. 324, 416 S.E.2d 924 (1992).

38. A seller's express or implied warranty extends to any "natural person who is in the family or household of his buyer or who is a guest in his home if it is reasonable to expect that such person may use, consume or be affected by the goods and who is injured in person by breach of the warranty." N.C. Gen. Stat. §25-2-318.

39. Plaintiff cannot sue for implied warranty if plaintiff is not "a buyer . . . or . . . a member or a guest of a member of the family of the buyer, a guest of the buyer, or an employee of the buyer." N.C. Gen. Stat. §99B-2(b). *Crews, supra* note 37.

40. *Buck v. Tweetsie R.R., Inc.*, 44 N.C. App. 588, 261 S.E.2d 517, *rev. denied*, 299 N.C. 735, 267 S.E.2d 660 (1980). A nonmanufacturing seller may have a reduced duty to warn. *Crews, supra* note 37.

41. *Strickland v. Dri-Spray Equip.*, 51 N.C. App. 57, 275 S.E.2d 503 (1981).

42. N.C. Gen. Stat. §99B-5(b); *Ashe v. Acme Builders, Inc.*, 267 N.C. 384, 148 S.E.2d 244 (1966); *Britt v. Mallard-Griffin, Inc.*, 1 N.C. App. 252, 161 S.E.2d 155 (1968); N.C. Pattern Jury Instructions — Civil 755.62.

43. N.C. Gen. Stat. §99B-4(1); *Jenkins v. Helgren*, 26 N.C. App. 653, 217 S.E.2d 120 (1975); *Edwards v. ATRO S.p.A.*, 891 F. Supp. 1074, *order supplemented*, 891 F. Supp. 1085 (E.D.N.C. 1995).

44. N.C. Gen. Stat. §99B-5(a)(1); N.C. Pattern Jury Instructions — Civil 755.61. The duty to warn for prescription drugs or devices is addressed at §99B-5(c).

45. *Helms v. Sporicidin Intl.*, 871 F. Supp. 837 (E.D.N.C. 1994).

46. N.C. Gen. Stat. §99B-5(a)(2).

47. *Smith v. Selco Prods., Inc.*, 96 N.C. App. 151, 385 S.E.2d 173 (1989), *rev. denied*, 326 N.C. 598, 393 S.E.2d 883 (1990).

48. *Davis*, 47 N.C. App. 237.

49. N.C. Gen. Stat. §99B-3(a); N.C. Pattern Jury Instructions — Civil 755.57.

50. N.C. Gen. Stat. §99B-4; N.C. Pattern Jury Instructions — Civil 755.58 and 755.59.

51. *Goodman v. Wenco Foods, Inc.*, 333 N.C. 1, 423 S.E.2d 444 (1992).

52. *Sloan v. Carolina Power & Light Co.*, 248 N.C. 125, 102 S.E.2d 822 (1958).

53. *Manganello v. Permastone, Inc.*, 291 N.C. 666, 231 S.E.2d 678 (1977).

54. *Bucham v. King*, 182 N.C. 171, 108 S.E. 635 (1921); *Horne v. Owens-Corning Fiberglas Corp.*, 4 F.3d 276 (4th Cir. 1993) (industry standards and state of the art evidence); *ATRO S.p.A., supra* note 43.

55. *Stone v. Proctor*, 259 N.C. 633, 131 S.E.2d 297 (1963).

56. N.C.R. Evid. 401 (N.C. Gen. Stat. §8C-1) is identical to the federal rule and thus the developed federal case law may be helpful.

57. *Murrow v. Daniels*, 321 N.C. 494, 364 S.E.2d 392 (1988); see also *State v. Frazier*, 344 N.C. 611, 476 S.E.2d 297 (1996) (holding evidence of similar acts admissible); *Purvis v. Bryson's Jewelers*, 115 N.C. App. 146, 443 S.E.2d 768, *cert. denied*, 338 N.C. 520, 452 S.E.2d 816 (1994); *Sass v. Thomas*, 90 N.C. App. 719, 370 S.E.2d 73 (1988) and *Etheridge v. Atlantic Coast Line R.R.*, 206 N.C. 657, 175 S.E. 124 (1934) (excluding evidence of injury to another bridge worker).

58. *Kekelis v. Whitin Mach. Works*, 273 N.C. 439, 160 S.E.2d 320 (1968).

59. *Pack v. Auman*, 220 N.C. 704, 18 S.E.2d 247 (1942).

60. *Madden v. Carolina Door Controls*, 117 N.C. App. 56, 449 S.E.2d 769 (1994); *Schaffner v. Cumberland County Hosp. System, Inc.*, 77 N.C. App. 689, 336 S.E.2d 116 (1985), *rev. denied*, 316 N.C. 195, 341 S.E.2d 578 (1986).

61. See, e.g., *Erwin v. Jeep Corp.*, 812 F.2d 172 (4th Cir. 1987); *Martin v. Volkswagen of Am., Inc.*, 707 F.2d 823 (4th Cir. 1983).

62. *Colombo, supra* note 18.

63. *Murphey v. Georgia Pacific Corp.*, 331 N.C. 702, 417 S.E.2d 460 (1992); see generally Kerry A. Shad, *Warren v. Colombo: North Carolina Recognizes Claim for Enhanced Injury*, 68 N.C. L. Rev. 1330 (1990).

64. N.C. Gen. Stat. §20-135.2A(d); *Chaney v. Young*, 122 N.C. App. 260, 468 S.E.2d 837 (1996); *Hagwood v. Odom*, 88 N.C. App. 513, 364 S.E.2d 190 (1988); *Miller v. Miller*, 273 N.C. 228, 160 S.E.2d 65 (1968).

65. N.C. Gen. Stat. §99B-5(c); N.C. Pattern Jury Instructions — Civil 755.63; see also *Foyle v. Lederle Labs.*, 674 F. Supp. 530 (E.D.N.C. 1987); *Padgett v. Synthes Ltd.*, 677 F. Supp. 1329 (W.D.N.C. 1988), *aff'd*, 872 F.2d 418 (4th Cir. 1989).

66. N.C. Gen. Stat. §99B-6(c); N.C. Pattern Jury Instructions — Civil 755.66.

67. *Griffin v. Tenneco Resins, Inc.*, 648 F. Supp. 964, 967 (W.D.N.C. 1986) (plaintiffs alleged exposure to chemical dyes manufactured by some or all of the named defendants, but could not identify which specific defendant or defendants manufactured the dye that injured plaintiffs) (citing *Elledge v. Pepsi-Cola Bottling Co.*, 252 N.C. 337, 113 S.E.2d 435 (1960); *Wilder v. Amatex Corp.*, 314 N.C. 550, 336 S.E.2d 66 (1985)).

68. If the purchaser, before acceptance, has examined the goods fully or has refused to examine them, there may be no liability with regard to defects that examination should have found. See N.C. Gen. Stat. §25-2-316(3)(b);

Southeastern Adhesives Co. v. Funder Am., Inc., 89 N.C. App. 438, 366 S.E.2d 505 (1988). Plaintiff must show that the product was not merchantable at the time of the sale. *Goodman, supra* note 51; *Morrison, supra* note 30; *Sutton v. Major Prods. Co.*, 91 N.C. App. 610, 372 S.E.2d 897 (1988). See N.C. Pattern Jury Instructions — Civil 750.40, *et. seq.*

69.   E.g., *Hickman v. McKoin*, 337 N.C. 460, 446 S.E.2d 80 (1994) (parent-child relation insufficient to show foreseeable distress); *Andersen v. Baccus*, 335 N.C. 526, 439 S.E.2d 136 (1994); *Sorrells v. M.Y.B. Hospitality Ventures of Asheville*, 334 N.C. 669, 435 S.E.2d 320 (1993); *Gardner v. Gardner*, 334 N.C. 662, 435 S.E.2d 324 (1993).

70.   E.g., *Waddle v. Sparks*, 331 N.C. 73, 414 S.E.2d 22 (1992); *Pardasani v. Rack Room Shoes, Inc.*, 912 F. Supp. 187 (M.D.N.C. 1996). Further, proper medical documentation and diagnosis of the alleged emotional or mental condition is required. *Kaplan v. Prolife Action League*, 111 N.C. App. 1, 431 S.E.2d 828, *rev. denied*, 335 N.C. 175, 436 S.E.2d 379 (1993), *cert. denied*, 512 U.S. 1253 (1994); *Bryant v. Thalhimer Brothers Inc.*, 113 N.C. App. 1, 437 S.E.2d 519 (1993), *rev. denied*, 336 N.C. 71, 445 S.E.2d 29 (1994); *Clark v. Perry*, 114 N.C. App. 297, 442 S.E.2d 57 (1994).

71.   N.C. Gen. Stat. §1D-15(a), (b); §1D-5(4) (defining fraud). Chapter 1D, effective January 1, 1996, as to claims for relief *arising* on or after that date.

72.   Id. §1D-15(a); §1D-5(7).

73.   N.C.R. Civ. P. 9(k).

74.   N.C. Gen. Stat. §1D-35(2).

75.   Id. §1D-15(c).

76.   Id. §1D-25(b), (c) (cap; jury instructions); §1D-26 (exception for driving while impaired cases). See N.C. Pattern Jury Instructions — Civil 810.05 and 810.06.

77.   Id. §1D-30.

78.   Id. §1D-45.

79.   *Stanback v. Stanback*, 297 N.C. 181, 254 S.E.2d 611 (1979); *Newton v. Standard Fire Ins. Co.*, 291 N.C. 105, 229 S.E.2d 297 (1976); *Miller v. Nationwide Mut. Ins. Co.*, 112 N.C. App. 295, 435 S.E.2d 537 (1993), *rev. denied*, 335 N.C. 770, 442 S.E.2d 519 (1994).

80.   *Chicopee, supra* note 7; *AT&T Corp. v. Medical Review of North Carolina, Inc.,* 876 F. Supp. 91 (E.D.N.C. 1995).

81.   *Young v. Baltimore & Ohio R. Co.,* 266 N.C. 458, 465, 146 S.E.2d 441 (1966).

82.   *Hall v. Carroll,* 253 N.C. 220, 222, 116 S.E.2d 459 (1960); N.C. Gen. Stat. §1B-2(1) (relative degree of fault is not considered).

83.   N.C. Gen. Stat. §1B-1 et seq.

84.   See, e.g., N.C. Gen. Stat. §25-2-313 to 318.

NORTH DAKOTA

A. CAUSES OF ACTION

Product liability lawsuits commonly include causes of action for strict liability, negligence, and breach of warranty.

B. STATUTES OF LIMITATION AND REPOSE

The statute of limitations for strict product liability and negligence claims is six years.[1] When a case involves a latent injury, a discovery rule may apply.[2] The statute of limitations for wrongful death claims is two years from the date of death.[3] The six-year statute of limitations governs survival claims,[4] but there is a one-year extension from the date of death if the death occurs in the sixth year.[5] The statute of limitations for breach of warranty claims is four years from the date of delivery of the goods, unless the warranty explicitly extends to future performance of the goods.[6]

There is a statute of repose that bars product liability actions for products initially purchased more than ten years before, or manufactured more than eleven years before, the injury.[7] This statute of repose does not apply if the defendant issued a recall or became aware of a defect and failed to take reasonable steps to warn.[8]

There is a ten-year statute of repose for improvements to real property, with a two-year extension if the injury occurs in the tenth year.[9] This statute of repose does not protect manufacturers who lack involvement with the design or construction of the project where the product is used.[10]

C. STRICT LIABILITY

1. The Standard

The North Dakota Supreme Court has adopted the elements of section 402A of the Restatement (Second) of Torts.[11]

2. "Defect"

A product is defective if "there was a defect or defective condition in the product which made the product unreasonably dangerous."[12] A product is unreasonably dangerous if it is dangerous to an extent beyond that which would be contemplated by the ordinary buyer, consumer, or user, "considering the product's characteristics, propensities, risks, dangers, and uses, together with any actual knowledge, training or experience possessed by that particular buyer, user, or consumer."[13]

3. Defenses

Comparative negligence, assumption of risk, and unforeseeable product misuse are defenses on a modified comparative fault basis.[14] The plaintiff cannot recover if the plaintiff's fault is as great as or exceeds the combined fault of all other persons who contributed to the injury.[15]

4. Several Liability

North Dakota has abolished joint and several liability. The fact-finder must apportion the "fault" of all persons, whether or not a party, and liability is several only.[16]

5. Sale or Lease

To be liable for strict product liability, the defendant must have sold the product and be in the business of selling that type of product.[17] If a nonmanufacturing seller identifies the manufacturer, the court must dismiss a strict product liability claim against the nonmanufacturing seller unless certain exceptions exist.[18]

A manufacturer must assume the cost of defense and any liability that may be imposed on a nonmanufacturing seller when the nonmanufacturing seller did not substantially alter the product and the alleged defect existed when the product left the control of the manufacturer.[19]

6. Inherently Dangerous Products

There are no statutes or case law on inherently dangerous products.

7. Successor Liability

The North Dakota Supreme Court has rejected the continuity of enterprise and product line theories of successor liability.[20] The North Dakota Supreme Court has held that "a successor corporation may acquire an independent duty to warn where defects in its predecessor's products come to its attention."[21]

8. Privity

Privity is not required.[22]

9. Failure to Warn

When no warning has been given, there is a presumption that if an adequate warning had been given, the plaintiff would have read and heeded it.[23] The obviousness of danger does not automatically preclude liability in a failure-to-warn case, but is only one factor to be considered in determining whether the product is unreasonably dangerous.[24] The North Dakota Supreme Court held in a negligence case that it is a question of fact whether communicating a warning to an employer satisfies the duty to warn an employee.[25]

10. Substantial Change

By statute, no manufacturer or seller is liable when an alteration or modification of the product was a substantial contributing cause of the accident.[26] The North Dakota Supreme Court has held that the statute does not absolve a defendant from liability unless the alteration or modification was unforeseeable.[27]

11. State of the Art

The North Dakota Supreme Court has held that a trial court did not err in excluding state-of-the-art evidence.[28]

12. Rebuttable Presumption Against Defects

There is a rebuttable presumption that a product is free from defect if it complied with applicable government or industry standards.[29]

13. Malfunction

Under some circumstances, a defect may be inferred from proof that the product did not perform as intended by the manufacturer.[30]

14. Other Accidents

Evidence of another accident is not admissible unless the proponent shows that the circumstances of the accident are substantially similar to the circumstances of the accident in the pending lawsuit.[31]

15. Misrepresentation

The North Dakota Supreme Court has held that the substance of the representations, directions, and warnings on a product container provided minimal support for an instruction on section 402B of the Restatement (Second) of Torts.[32]

D. NEGLIGENCE

1. Separate Theories

The court must instruct the jury on both strict product liability and negligence and require the jury to assess fault separately for each theory.[33] The plaintiff is entitled to judgment on the theory that allows the greater recovery.[34]

2. Post-Sale Duty to Warn

A manufacturer that learns about dangers associated with its products after they are sold has a post-sale duty under negligence principles to take reasonable steps to warn foreseeable users about those dangers.[35]

3. Defenses

Comparative negligence, assumption of risk, and unforeseeable product misuse are defenses on a modified comparative fault basis.[36]

E. BREACH OF WARRANTY

1. Disclaimers and Limitations of Remedy

To be effective, a disclaimer or limitation of remedy provision must be part of the "basis of the bargain."[37] The North Dakota Supreme Court has held a limitation of remedy provision unconscionable in a commercial transaction.[38]

2. Economic Loss

A manufacturer of a product sold in a commercial transaction is limited to a breach of warranty claim for economic loss caused by the failure of a component part that causes damage only to the product itself.[39]

3. Defenses

Comparative negligence, assumption of risk, and unforeseeable product misuse are defenses on a modified comparative fault basis.[40]

F. COLLATERAL SOURCE RULE

A party responsible for paying damages is entitled to a reduction for payments from certain collateral sources like workers' compensation benefits and social security.[41]

G. PUNITIVE DAMAGES

1. Availability

Punitive damages are available "[i]n any action for the breach of an obligation not arising from contract, when the defendant has been guilty by clear and convincing evidence of oppression, fraud, or actual malice."[42] Punitive damages are not available if the product complied with federal statutes or regulations, or if an agency of the federal government gave pre-market approval or certification of the product.[43] This exception does not apply if the defendant withheld or misrepresented material information to the federal agency, or bribed it.[44]

The amount of punitive damages awarded in a case may not exceed the greater of twice the amount of compensatory damages or $250,000.[45] Upon election of either party, the court must try the issue of punitive damages separately from the issues of liability and compensatory damages.[46] Evidence of a defendant's financial condition is not admissible in the proceeding on punitive damages.[47]

2. Procedure

A party must offer affidavits showing the factual basis for the claim and obtain a court order to assert a claim for punitive damages.[48]

Patrick W. Durick
Larry L. Boschee
PEARCE & DURICK
314 East Thayer Avenue
P.O. Box 400
Bismarck, North Dakota 58502
(701) 223-2890

ENDNOTES – NORTH DAKOTA

1. N.D. Cent. Code §28-01-16(5) (1991).

2. *BASF Corp. v. Symington*, 512 N.W.2d 692, 695 (N.D. 1994).

3. N.D. Cent. Code §28-01-18(4) (1991).

4. *Hulne v. Intl. Harvester Co.*, 322 N.W.2d 474, 477 (N.D. 1982).

5. N.D. Cent. Code §28-01-26 (1991).

6. Id. §41-02-104(1) (Supp. 1997).

7. Id. §28-01.3-08 (Supp. 1997).

8. Id.

9. Id. §28-01-44 (1991).

10. *Vantage, Inc. v. Carrier Corp.*, 467 N.W.2d 446, 450-451 (N.D. 1991).

11. *Johnson v. American Motors Corp.*, 225 N.W.2d 57, 66 (N.D. 1974).

12. N.D. Cent. Code §28-01.3-06 (Supp. 1997).

13. Id. §28-01.3-01(4) (Supp. 1997).

14. Id. §32-03.2-02 (1996).

15. Id.

16. Id.

17. *Johnson*, 225 N.W.2d at 66.

18. N.D. Cent. Code §28-01.3-04 (Supp. 1997).

19. Id. §28-01.3-05 (Supp. 1997).

20. *Downtowner, Inc. v. Acrometal Prod., Inc.*, 347 N.W.2d 118, 125 (N.D. 1984).

21. Id.

22. *Johnson*, 225 N.W.2d at 66.

23. *Butz v. Werner*, 438 N.W.2d 509, 517 (N.D. 1989).

24. *Olson v. A. W. Chesterton Co.*, 256 N.W.2d 530, 537 (N.D. 1977).

25. *Seibel v. Symons Corp.*, 221 N.W.2d 50, 57 (N.D. 1974).

26. N.D. Cent. Code §28-01.3-03 (Supp. 1997).

27. *Oanes v. Westgo, Inc.*, 476 N.W.2d 248, 252 (N.D. 1991).

28. *Olson*, 256 N.W.2d at 540.

29. N.D. Cent. Code §28-01.3-09 (Supp. 1997).

30. *Herman v. General Irr. Co.*, 247 N.W.2d 472, 478 (N.D. 1976).

31. *Crowston v. Goodyear Tire & Rubber Co.*, 521 N.W.2d 401, 411 (N.D. 1994).

32. *Olson*, 256 N.W.2d at 541.

33. *Butz*, 438 N.W.2d at 516.

34. Id.

35. *Crowston*, 521 N.W.2d at 409.

36. N.D. Cent. Code §32-03.2-02 (1996).

37. *Fleck v. Jacques Seed Co.*, 445 N.W.2d 649, 654 (N.D. 1989).

38. *Construction Assocs., Inc. v. Fargo Water Equip. Co.*, 446 N.W.2d 237, 242, 244 (N.D. 1989).

39. *Cooperative Power Assoc. v. Westinghouse Elec. Corp.*, 493 N.W.2d 661 (N.D. 1992).

40. N.D. Cent. Code §32-03.2-02 (1996).

41. Id. §32-03.2-06 (1996).

42. Id. §32-03.2-11 (Supp. 1997).

43. Id.

44. Id.

45. Id.

46. Id.

47. Id.

48. Id.

OHIO

A. CAUSES OF ACTION

The product liability law of Ohio has been codified in the Ohio Products Liability Act, which became effective on January 5, 1988.[1] The Act governs the recovery of compensatory damages, as well as punitive or exemplary damages,[2] for product liability claims that arise on or after January 5, 1988, and are brought in actions commenced on or after this date.[3] Subjects addressed in the Act are discussed below, along with other closely related topics.

The Act defines a "product liability claim" as an action seeking compensatory damages from the manufacturer or supplier of a product "for death, physical injury to person, emotional distress, or physical damage to property other than the product in question."[4] The damages must have arisen from (1) the product's defective manufacture or construction; (2) the product's defective design or formulation; (3) inadequate warning or instruction associated with the product; or (4) the product's failure to conform to a representation or warranty.[5] Claims of compensatory damages for economic loss that are not based on product liability claims are not subject to the Act, but may be brought under Ohio's common law or other applicable sections of the Ohio Revised Code.[6] A claim for mere economic loss does not state a cause of action under the Act.[7]

B. ACCRUAL, LIMITATIONS, AND REPOSE

Actions for bodily injury or injury to personal property generally accrue when the injury or loss to person or property occurs.[8] Versions of the discovery rule apply in circumstances involving exposure to (1) hazardous chemicals, toxic chemicals, ethical drugs, or ethical medical devices; (2) asbestos or chromium; (3) chemical defoliants, herbicides, or similar agents; and (4) DES or similar compounds.[9] An action involving exposure to hazardous chemicals, for example, "accrues upon the date on which the plaintiff is informed by competent medical authority that the plaintiff has an injury that is related to the exposure, or upon the date on which by the exercise of reasonable diligence the plaintiff should have known that the plaintiff has an injury that is related to the exposure, whichever date occurs first."[10] The discovery rule does not apply in wrongful death actions.[11]

Ohio's General Assembly recently enacted legislation confirming that "an action based on a product liability claim and an action for bodily injury or injuring personal property" shall be brought within two years of the time the cause of action accrues.[12] The Ohio Supreme Court had previously held that a product liability action based on product-related personal injuries is controlled by the two-year statute of limitations that governs analogous common-law product liability actions.[13] It appears that an action for a product-related death would be governed by the two-year statute of limitations for wrongful death[14] and that product-related actions for damage to real property would be governed by a four-year or ten-year statute of limitations.[15]

The Ohio Revised Code generally prohibits product liability actions against product manufacturers or suppliers, including wrongful death actions, that are brought more than 15 years after delivery of the product to an end user.[16] However, this repose provision contains limited exceptions for actions accruing near the end of the repose period and for actions involving fraud, written warranties exceeding 15 years, and persons under disability.[17]

C. STRICT LIABILITY

1. The Standard for Liability

A manufacturer is subject to liability for compensatory damages based on a product liability claim brought under the Act only if the claimant establishes that the product in question is "defective," the defective aspect of the product proximately caused the claimant harm, and the manufacturer designed, produced, etc., the product.[18] A claimant may prove that a product is defective by showing (a) defective manufacture or construction;[19] (b) defective design or formulation;[20] (c) inadequate warning or instruction;[21] or (d) failure to conform to a representation made about the product.[22] Strict liability is not available as a basis for imposing liability against a manufacturer where the claimant is heavily involved in the process by which an allegedly defective product is manufactured.[23]

A supplier, as distinguished from a manufacturer, is subject to liability for compensatory damages based on a product liability claim brought under the Act only if the claimant establishes that (a) the supplier was negligent and the negligence proximately caused the claimant harm; or (b) the product in question, when it left the supplier's control, did not conform to a representation made by the supplier and the representation and failure to conform proximately caused the claimant harm.[24] Although the statutory definition of "supplier" excludes manufacturers,[25] a supplier may be held liable as if it were a manufacturer under certain specified conditions.[26]

2. Definition of "Product"

The Act defines the term "product" as tangible personal property[27] that is (a) delivered by itself, as a component, or as an ingredient; (b) made for introduction into trade or commerce; and (c) intended for sale or lease in commercial or personal use.[28]

3. Defective Manufacture or Construction

Claimants may establish defective manufacture or construction under the Act by showing that, when a product left the manufacturer's control, it deviated in a material way from "design specifications, formula, or performance standards of the manufacturer, or from otherwise identical units manufactured to the same design specifications."[29] A manufacturer's exercise of "all possible care in [a product's] manufacture or construction" does not preclude a conclusion that the product is defective.[30]

4. Defective Design or Formulation

Claimants may establish defective design or formulation under the Act only by showing that the foreseeable risks associated with a product's design or formulation exceeded the benefits.[31] The consumer expectation test is no longer available as a standard for determining whether a product is defective in design or formulation.[32]

A prescription drug or medical device prescribed, dispensed, or implanted by a physician or other person legally authorized to do so is not considered defective in design or formulation simply because an aspect of the drug or device is unavoidably unsafe, if adequate warning and instruction are provided.[33] A warning is adequate if it reasonably discloses all of the risks that are inherent in the use of a drug, which the manufacturer knew or should have known to exist.[34] The FDA's review, analysis, and approval of a drug package warning does not necessarily insulate a drug manufacturer from a claim that the warning is inadequate.[35]

A product is not defective in design or formulation if the claimant's injury was caused by "an inherent characteristic of the product which is a generic aspect of the product that cannot be eliminated without substantially compromising the product's usefulness or desirability and which is recognized by the ordinary person with the ordinary knowledge common to the community."[36] Likewise, a product is not defective in design or formulation if, when the product left the manufacturer's control, "a practical and technically feasible alternative design or formulation was not available that would have prevented the harm for which the claimant seeks to recover compensatory damages without substantially impairing the usefulness or intended purpose of the product, unless the manufacturer acted unreasonably in introducing the product into trade or commerce."[37]

5. Inadequate Warning or Instruction

Claimants may establish that a product is defective due to inadequate warning or instruction under the Act by showing that the manufacturer unreasonably failed to provide warning or instruction, at the time of marketing the product or after the product left the manufacturer's control, where the warning or instruction was required "in light of the likelihood that the product would cause harm of the type for which the claimant seeks to recover . . . and in light of the likely seriousness of that harm."[38]

A product is not defective due to inadequate warning or instruction where the manufacturer fails "to warn or instruct about an open and obvious risk or a risk that is a matter of common knowledge."[39] A prescription drug prescribed or dispensed by a physician or other person legally authorized to do so is not defective due to inadequate warning or instruction "if its manufacturer provides otherwise adequate warning and instruction to the physician or other legally authorized person who prescribes [it] . . . and if the federal food and drug administration has not provided that warning or instruction relative to that drug is to be given directly to the ultimate user of it."[40]

6. Conformance to Representation

Under the Act, claimants may establish that a product is defective due to its failure to conform to a representation made by the manufacturer or supplier by showing that the product did not so conform, even where the manufacturer or supplier did not act "fraudulently, recklessly, or negligently in making the representation."[41]

7. Privity

Privity is not required to state a product liability claim under the Act.

8. Theories of Liability

The Ohio Revised Code rejects enterprise liability as a theory for imposing industry-wide liability.[42] Furthermore, it appears that the Ohio courts would reject a market-share theory of liability.[43] Alternative liability may not be used to establish liability except when all possible tortfeasors are named and subject to the court's jurisdiction[44] and the tortfeasors' products create a substantially similar risk of harm.[45] A successor corporation in the sale-of-assets context may be held liable for injuries resulting from products made by a predecessor corporation, but only where (a) liability is assumed; (b) the sale amounts to a *de facto* merger or consolidation; (c) the successor is merely a continuation of the predecessor; or (d) the asset sale was aimed primarily at avoiding liability.[46]

9. Comparative Fault/Joint and Several Liability

Contributory negligence, other contributory tortious conduct, and assumption of risk may be asserted as affirmative defenses in product liability actions.[47] Assumption of risk, whether express or implied, generally serves as a complete bar to recovery.[48] A claimant's contributory tortious conduct does not bar the recovery of damages where it is no greater than the combined tortious conduct of the other parties from whom recovery is sought and certain entities from whom recovery is not sought, including settling entities and dismissed entities.[49]

Even where a claimant's assumption of risk or contributory tortious conduct does not bar recovery, recovery against a defendant is normally limited according to the defendant's proportionate share of the tortious conduct[50] (i.e., the defendant's liability is normally reduced to reflect the tortious conduct of (a) the claimant; (b) other parties from whom recovery is sought; and (c) certain entities from whom recovery is not sought, including settling entities and dismissed entities).[51] Specifically, for claims of noneconomic loss, a defendant's liability is always limited according to its proportionate share of the tortious conduct at issue.[52] Joint and several liability is retained for claims involving economic loss, but only against defendants that are more than 50 percent responsible for such loss.[53] Other defendants must only pay their proportionate share of the economic loss.[54]

10. Compliance with Safety Standards

A manufacturer's compliance with state safety standards is not necessarily a complete defense to a strict liability claim.[55] Similarly, compliance or noncompliance with industrial or professional safety standards does not constitute either a complete defense to or proof of a strict liability claim.[56] On the other hand, a split in authority is developing on the question of whether compliance with certain federal safety standards shields a manufacturer from liability.[57]

11. Prior Accidents and Occurrences

The Ohio Supreme Court has held that evidence of prior accidents and occurrences may be admissible in product liability cases, where the accidents or occurrences transpire under circumstances that are substantially similar to those in the case at hand.[58] Evidence of prior accidents and occurrences therefore may be admitted to establish the "nature and magnitude of the risks of harm associated with [a] design" under the Act.[59] However, such evidence is not admissible to show that a manufacturer knew or should have known of an injury-causing defect since proof of fault is not necessary to prevail on a product liability claim.[60]

12. Subsequent Remedial Measures

Evidence of subsequent remedial measures may not be admitted in product liability actions to show that implementing such measures would have made an injury less likely to occur.[61] Evidence of subsequent remedial measures still may be introduced for other purposes, including impeachment and proof of ownership or control when in dispute.[62]

D. COMMON LAW ACTIONS

It appears that the Act does not supplant common law product liability causes of action which are not specifically covered by the Act.[63] The Ohio Supreme Court has held that a common law negligent design claim survives enactment of the Act on this ground.[64]

E. BREACH OF WARRANTY

Product liability claims for "breach of warranty" are governed by sections of the Act dealing with conformance to representations made by manufacturers and suppliers.[65]

F. COMPENSATORY DAMAGES

There are no caps on damages for economic loss. On the other hand, damages for noneconomic loss are generally limited to the greater of $250,000 or three times the economic damages awarded to a maximum of $500,000.[66] The maximum award in cases involving "substantial permanent injury" is increased to the greater of $1,000,000 or $35,000 times the number of years the claimant is expected to live.[67]

G. PUNITIVE OR EXEMPLARY DAMAGES

Punitive damages awards are limited to the lesser of three times the amount of the compensatory damages awarded or $100,000 ($250,000 in cases against "large employers"—entities employing more than 25 people).[68] The claimant has the burden of establishing an entitlement to punitive damages by clear and convincing evidence.[69] Punitive damages are not recoverable unless compensatory damages have already been assessed and the defendant's actions demonstrate malice, aggravated or egregious fraud, or insult.[70] The fact that a product is defective does not, by itself, establish that punitive damages are warranted.[71] The trier of fact is responsible for determining the amount of punitive damages.[72]

Punitive damages generally may not be assessed against a defendant where punitive damages in excess of $100,000 (or $250,000 for a large employer) have already been assessed against the defendant for a particular act or course of conduct.[73] Manufacturers, including drug manufacturers, are immunized from liability for punitive damages where they comply with certain governmental standards and regulations.[74]

H. COLLATERAL BENEFITS

When determining a compensatory damages award, the trier of fact must consider evidence of certain collateral benefits that are not paid for by the claimant and do not require reimbursement.[75] The trier of fact retains discretion to decide whether to make a corresponding reduction in the damages award.[76]

I.   PREEMPTION

A product liability action for inadequate warning is not preempted by federal labelling requirements where the action seeks to impose labelling requirements that are identical to those of the federal statute.[77] However, such an action is preempted to the extent that it seeks to impose "more elaborate or different" labelling requirements.[78] Additionally, a split in authority is developing on the question of whether product liability claims are preempted in situations where a defendant has complied with certain federal standards.[79]

Robert C. Weber
JONES, DAY, REAVIS & POGUE
North Point
901 Lakeside Avenue
Cleveland, Ohio 44114
(216) 586-3939

1. Ohio Rev. Code Ann. §§2307.71-2307.80 (Page 1996).

2. Id. §2307.72.

3. 1987 H 1., effective Jan. 5, 1988.

4. Ohio Rev. Code Ann. §2307.71(M).

5. Id.

6. Id. §2307.72(C).

7. Id. §§2307.71(G), 2307.79; *LaPuma v. Collinwood Concrete*, 75 Ohio St. 3d 64, 66, 661 N.E.2d 714, 716 (1996).

8. Ohio Rev. Code Ann. §2305.10(A).

9. Id. §2305.10(B).

10. Id. §2305.10(B)(1).

11. *Shover v. Cordis Corp.*, 61 Ohio St. 3d 213, 217-218, 574 N.E.2d 457, 461 (1991).

12. Ohio Rev. Code Ann. §2305.10(A).

13. *McAuliffe v. Western States Import Co.*, 72 Ohio St. 3d 534, 540, 651 N.E.2d 957, 961 (1995) (citing §2305.10).

14. Ohio Rev. Code Ann. §2125.02(D).

15. *Taylor v. Multi-Flo, Inc.*, 69 Ohio App. 2d 19, 22-23, 429 N.E.2d 1086, 1089 (1980) (the statute of limitations applying in a product-related action for injury to real property is found in either §2305.09(D) [four-year time limit] or §2305.14 [ten-year time limit]).

16. Ohio Rev. Code Ann. §§2125.02(D)(2), 2305.011(C).

17. Id. §§2125.02(D)(2); 2305.011(C).

18. Id. §2307.73(A).

19. Id. §§2307.73(A)(1), 2307.74.

20. Id. §§2307.73(A)(1), 2307.75.

21. Id. §§2307.73(A)(1), 2307.76.

22. Id. §§2307.73(A)(1), 2307.77, 2307.78(A)(2).

23. *Queen City Terminals, Inc. v. General Am. Transp. Corp.*, 73 Ohio St. 3d 609, 620-623, 653 N.E.2d 661, 671-673 (1995) (discussing claims that arose before the Act became effective).

24. Ohio Rev. Code Ann. §2307.78(A); *Brown v. McDonald's Corp.*, 101 Ohio App. 3d 294, 301-303, 655 N.E.2d 440, 444-446 (1995) (affirming summary judgment for a supplier where plaintiffs failed to show that the supplier acted negligently in selling a product and presented no evidence that the supplier made any express representations about the product).

25. Ohio Rev. Code Ann. §2307.71(O)(2); *State Farm Fire & Casualty Co. v. Kupanoff Imports, Inc.*, 83 Ohio App. 3d 278, 281 n.1, 614 N.E.2d 1072, 1073 n.1 (1992) (under §2307.71(O), "a supplier can be a seller or distributor but is not a manufacturer").

26. Ohio Rev. Code Ann. §2307.78(B); *Convention Ctr. Inn, Ltd. v. Dow Chem. Co.*, 70 Ohio App. 3d 243, 248, 590 N.E.2d 898, 900 (1990) (under §2307.78(B), even "a non-negligent supplier of a defective product can be liable to an injured consumer as if it were the manufacturer").

27. Ohio Rev. Code Ann. §2307.71(L); *Wireman v. Keneco Distribs., Inc.*, 75 Ohio St. 3d 103, 105-106, 661 N.E.2d 744, 747 (1996).

28. Ohio Rev. Code Ann. §2307.71(L).

29. Id. §2307.74; *In re Air Crash Disaster at Sioux City*, 781 F. Supp. 1307, 1311 (N.D. Ill. 1991) (denying summary judgment where fact issue existed concerning whether product deviated materially from design specifications).

30. Ohio Rev. Code. Ann. §2307.74.

31. Id. §2307.75(A).

32. Id.

33. Id. §2307.75(D) (citing §2307.76).

34. *Wagner v. Roche Lab.*, 77 Ohio St. 3d 116, 120, 671 N.E.2d 252, 256 (1996).

35. Id. at 123, 671 N.E.2d at 258.

36. Ohio Rev. Code Ann. §2307.75(E); *Paugh v. R.J. Reynolds Tobacco Co.*, 834 F. Supp. 228, 231 (N.D. Ohio 1993) (as a matter of law, cigarettes are not defective in design under the Act because "the risks posed by smoking are an inherent characteristic of cigarettes, and because knowledge of these risks has been common to the community").

37. Ohio Rev. Code Ann. §2307.75(F); *Jacobs v. E.I. DuPont de Nemours & Co.*, 67 F.3d 1219, 1242 (6th Cir. 1995) (exempting a manufacturer from liability where the claimant failed to identify a safe and efficacious alternative design).

38. Ohio Rev. Code Ann. §2307.76(A); *Brown v. McDonald's Corp.*, 101 Ohio App. 3d 294, 298-299, 655 N.E.2d 440, 442 (1995) (citing §2307.76(A)(2)(b)).

39. Ohio Rev. Code Ann. §2307.76(B); *Hanlon v. Lane*, 98 Ohio App. 3d 148, 154, 648 N.E.2d 26, 30 (1994) (natural gas manufacturer has no duty to warn of the danger of carbon monoxide poisoning where danger is open and obvious).

40. Ohio Rev. Code Ann. §2307.76(C). The learned intermediary doctrine also applies to bulk suppliers. See *Midwest Specialties, Inc. v. Crown Indus. Prods. Co.*, 940 F. Supp. 1160, 1167 (N.D. Ohio 1996).

41. Id. §§2307.77, 2307.78(A)(2); *Gawloski v. Miller Brewing Co.*, 96 Ohio App. 3d 160, 164-165, 644 N.E.2d 731, 734 (1994) (citing §2307.77).

42. Ohio Rev. Code Ann. §2307.791(A).

43. *Kurczi v. Eli Lilly & Co.*, 113 F.3d 1426, 1434 (6th Cir. 1997).

44. Ohio Rev. Code Ann. §2307.791(B).

45. *Horton v. Harwick Chem. Corp.*, 73 Ohio St. 3d 679, 688, 653 N.E.2d 1196, 1203 (1995).

46. Ohio Rev. Code Ann. §2307.73(C); *Flaugher v. Cone Automatic Mach. Co.*, 30 Ohio St. 3d 60, 62, 507 N.E.2d 331, 334 (1987).

47. Ohio Rev. Code Ann. §2315.20.

48. Id. §2315.20(B); *Syler v. Signode Corp.*, 76 Ohio App. 3d 250, 253, 601 N.E.2d 225, 227 (1992) ("Assumption of the risk may be asserted as a defense of a products liability claim brought pursuant to [the Act]"); but see *Carrel v. Allied Prods. Corp.*, 78 Ohio St. 3d 284, 290 (1997) (assumption

of risk is a viable defense to a product liability action brought by an employee where the employee voluntarily exposes himself to risks but not where the employee is required to encounter the risk in performing normal job duties).

49.   Ohio Rev. Code Ann. §2315.20(C). In actions involving claims of negligence against a supplier, a claimant's contributory negligence, other contributory tortious conduct, or implied assumption of risk does not completely bar recovery where it is no greater than the combined negligence of the parties from whom recovery is sought and certain other entities, including settling entities and dismissed entities. Id. §2315.19(A)(2).

50.   Id. §2307.31(B).

51.   Id. §2307.31(C).

52.   Id. §2307.31(B)(3).

53.   Id. §2307.31(B)(1)(a).

54.   Id. §§2307(B)(1)(b), 2307(B)(2).

55.   *Hardiman v. Zep Mfg. Co.*, 14 Ohio App. 3d 222, 226, 470 N.E.2d 941, 946 (1984) (compliance with Ohio "safe-place-to-work" statutes does not insulate a manufacturer from liability in strict liability cases); cf. *Knitz v. Minster Mach. Co.*, 69 Ohio St. 2d 460, 464, 432 N.E.2d 814, 817 (1982) (statutory regulations only act as "guides" in determining the reasonableness of a manufacturer's design choice).

56.   *Welch Sand & Gravel, Inc. v. O & K Trojan, Inc.*, 107 Ohio App. 3d 218, 225, 668 N.E.2d 529, 534 (1995) (compliance with professional engineering standard does not conclusively defeat a design defect claim); *Evanoff v. Grove Mfg. Co.*, 99 Ohio App. 3d 339, 346, 650 N.E.2d 914, 919 (1994) (noncompliance with industrial safety guidelines does not necessarily establish strict liability).

57.   *Nelson v. Ford Motor Co.*, 108 Ohio App. 3d 158, 160-162, 670 N.E.2d 307, 310-311 (1996) (compliance with federal motor vehicle safety standards does not necessarily shield a defendant from common law product liability); *Minton v. Honda of Am. Mfg., Inc.*, No. 14949, 1996 Ohio App. LEXIS 3092, at *11-18 (Ohio Ct. App. July 19, 1996) (claims of manufacturer liability are not permitted where a manufacturer complies with federal motor vehicle safety standards).

58.   *Renfro v. Black*, 52 Ohio St. 3d 27, 31-32, 556 N.E.2d 150, 154-155 (1990).

59. *Ogden v. Raymond Corp.*, No. 95CA0001, 1995 Ohio App. LEXIS 5796, at *7-8 (Ohio Ct. App. Dec. 27, 1995) (quoting §2307.75(B)(1)).

60. *Onderko v. Richmond Mfg. Co.*, 31 Ohio St. 3d 296, 301, 511 N.E.2d 388, 392 (1987); *Mulloy v. Longaberger, Inc.*, 47 Ohio App. 3d 77, 81, 547 N.E.2d 411, 415-416 (1989).

61. Ohio Rev. Code Ann. §2307.73(D).

62. Id.

63. *Carrel v. Allied Prods. Corp.*, 78 Ohio St. 3d 284, 289 (1997).

64. Id.

65. Id. §§2307.71(M), 2307.77, 2307.78(A)(2); *Paugh v. R.J. Reynolds Tobacco Co.*, 834 F. Supp. 228, 232 (N.D. Ohio 1993).

66. Ohio Rev. Code Ann. §2323.54(B)(1).

67. Id. §2323.54(B)(2).

68. Id. §2315.21(D)(1).

69. Id. §2315.21(D)(2).

70. Id. §2315.21(C)(1).

71. Id.

72. Id. §2307.801(B).

73. Id. §2315.21(D)(3).

74. Id. §§2307.801(C), 2307.801(D).

75. Id. §2317.45.

76. Id.

77. *Jenkins v. James B. Day & Co.*, 69 Ohio St. 3d 541, 547, 634 N.E.2d 998, 1003 (1994).

78. Id.; *Martin v. Teletronic Pacing Sys., Inc.*, 105 F.3d 1090, 1098 (6th Cir. 1997) (to be preempted, a state law requirement respecting a medical device

must be different from or in addition to a relevant federal requirement and must relate to the safety or effectiveness of the medical device).

79.   *Nelson v. Ford Motor Co.*, 108 Ohio App. 3d 158, 160-162, 670 N.E.2d 307, 310-311 (1996) (compliance with federal motor vehicle safety standards does not necessarily preempt common law product liability actions); *Minton v. Honda of Am. Mfg., Inc.*, No. 14949, 1996 Ohio App. LEXIS 3092, at *11-18 (Ohio Ct. App. July 19, 1996) (claims of manufacturer liability are preempted where a manufacturer complies with federal motor vehicle safety standards).

OKLAHOMA

A. CAUSES OF ACTION

Product liability lawsuits in Oklahoma commonly include causes of action for negligence, manufacturers' products liability,[1] and breach of express and implied warranty as provided by the Oklahoma Uniform Commercial Code.[2]

Recovery under a theory of manufacturers' products liability is allowed for bodily injury and for damage to property other than the product itself.[3] Recovery of purely economic damages to the product itself must be based on the parties' contractual relationship and specifically the Uniform Commercial Code warranty provisions.[4] However, recovery for damage to the property itself has recently been allowed, where personal injuries result from the damages to the property.[5]

B. STATUTES OF LIMITATION

The statute that generally describes the period of limitations in Oklahoma is codified at Oklahoma Statute title 12, section 95 (1981). The limitations period for a cause of action in tort alleging personal injury or damage to property is two years from the date of injury.[6] Similarly, the statutory period to be applied in product liability actions is two years from the date of injury.[7] However, Oklahoma applies the "discovery rule," so that the two-year period in a product liability case does not commence until plaintiff actually knows or should have known that he has been injured and defendant's product caused such injury.[8]

A cause of action seeking recovery for damages resulting from breach of warranty must be brought within five years from the date of the delivery of the product.[9] Oklahoma has not adopted a statute of repose or a useful-life defense, for products liability *per se.*

While Oklahoma has not adopted a specific statute of repose for products, the state does allow for repose in tort actions for injury to property arising from "the design, planning, supervision or observation of construction or construction of an improvement to real property."[10] The "discovery rule" is applicable to an action sounding in tort against engineers and architects; but the statute of response prohibits its use to extend the time period for bringing an action beyond the ten-year statute of response.[11] [The argument has been raised that certain products may therefore be considered an "improvement to real property" and as such are subject to repose after the passage of ten years.[12] The Oklahoma Supreme Court has announced that in deciding whether a particular product constitutes an "improvement to real property" the determinative factor will be the state scheme of taxation.[13]] The Oklahoma Supreme Court upheld as constitutional the barring of a manufacturers' products liability action to recover for wrongful death.[14] The statute of repose was not intended to cover "prefabricated" products produced in mass quantities to be used in construction.[15]

C. MANUFACTURERS' PRODUCTS LIABILITY

In the seminal case of *Kirkland v. General Motors Corp.*, 521 P.2d 1353 (Okla. 1973), Oklahoma embraced the doctrine of strict product liability in tort as described in Restatement (Second) of Torts section 402A. In *Kirkland*, in addition to adopting 402A, the Oklahoma Supreme Court also accepted the Restatement definition of "unreasonably dangerous" found in comment g of that provision.[16] Consequently, Oklahoma is considered a "pure Restatement jurisdiction."[17]

In order to prevail in an action for manufacturers' products liability, plaintiff must establish that:

(1) the product in question was the cause of the injury;

(2) the product was defective when it left the hands of the manufacturer; and

(3) the defect made the product unreasonably dangerous to an extent beyond that which would be contemplated by the ordinary consumer.[18]

1. Causation

Oklahoma applies the "significant probability test" in assessing whether the product in question is the cause of the plaintiff's injury. The mere possibility of causation is not enough.[19]

Additionally, Oklahoma has specifically rejected the "market share" theory of liability, at least with respect to asbestos litigation.[20]

2. Definition of "Defect"

Oklahoma defines "defect" under the "consumer expectation test" found in comment i of Restatement (Second) of Torts section 402A.[21] Generally, a product is considered defective if it is more dangerous than the ordinary user or consumer would expect. *Kirkland* at 1362-1363. Thus, Oklahoma applies an "objective" standard in determining defectiveness.

However, Oklahoma has also endorsed the "knowledgable user" test. A consumer may have specialized knowledge, and her expectations may be tempered by this greater knowledge of the product.[22]

Under the consumer expectation test, a product cannot be defective where it contains an open and obvious danger, since it is definitionally not more dangerous than expected. See also *Lamke v. Futorian Corp.*, 709 P.2d 684, 686 (Okla. 1985); and *Woods v. Freuhauf Corp.*, 765 P.2d 770, 774 (Okla. 1988). Additionally, where the danger of using a product is obvious to the general community, plaintiffs may be automatically barred from recovery.[23]

The plaintiff need not identify the exact defect; circumstantial evidence may be used to support the probability of a defect.[24]

3. Affirmative Defenses

In addition to the potential defenses arising from the absence of proof of the basic elements of the "prima facie" case; Oklahoma recognizes two affirmative defenses to the cause of action of manufacturers' products liability: (1) abnormal use, sometimes called "misuse," and (2) assumption of the risk. These two defenses totally bar recovery; Oklahoma employs no system of comparative responsibility in product liability cases.

Abnormal use, or "misuse," has been defined under a common sense definition: use of a product for a purpose not intended, or use of a product in an unforeseeable way. (Although a consumer's failure to follow instructions or heed warnings does not constitute misuse, such conduct still may preclude recovery if it constitutes the sole proximate cause of the injuries.)[25] Assumption of the risk requires showing that (1) the danger was known; (2) the risk was appreciated or understood; and (3) the taking of the risk was unreasonable.[26] The Oklahoma definition of assumption of the risk parallels comment n of Restatement section 402A.[27] A consumer can assume the risk of a known defect without specific technical knowledge of the cause of the product's dangerous, defective condition.[28]

Liability for bodily injury or damage to property other than the product itself arises from a duty to the public and is independent of the parties' contractual relationship and the UCC warranty provisions.[29] Therefore, the parties may not contractually limit a manufacturer's liability for personal injury caused by defective products.[30]

4. Other Limitations on Recovery

Since Oklahoma has adopted the exclusivity doctrine of workers' compensation, employees may not bring actions against their employers for work-related injuries, even where the employer is the manufacturer of the defective product that injured the employee.[31] Similarly, since Oklahoma has no system of comparative responsibility, a manufacturer will remain fully liable for all injuries suffered as a result of a defective product despite fault of the employer that contributed to the injury.[32]

For a finding of liability, Oklahoma requires that the defect must have been resident in the product when it left the manufacturer's possession and control.[33]

Similarly, Oklahoma recognizes "state of the art" doctrine, which provides that liability is only imposed if a product was defective when first distributed, not at the time plaintiff was injured.[34] "State-of-the-art" evidence is admissible to establish the feasibility of safer design alternatives;[35] the reasonable expectations of consumer;[36] and whether the defect existed when the product left the defendant-seller's control.[37]

Regarding "unavoidably unsafe product," Comment k of the Restatement (Second) of Torts §402A serves as an affirmative defense when the product is incapable of being made safe under present technology but the social need for the product warrants its production.

Comment k applies to medical devices, particularly those which are implanted. However, it does not provide blanket protection for all medical devices; rather, it applies as an affirmative defense only when the following criteria are met:

1) the product is properly manufactured and contains adequate warnings;
2) its benefits justify its risks; and,
3) the product was, at the time of manufacture and distribution, incapable of being made more safe.

The comment k defense does not apply when the product is defective due to faulty manufacturing or inadequate warnings.[38]

Evidence of compliance with relevant government regulations is admissible.[39] Evidence of other accidents may be admissible provided such information is relevant and its probative value is not outweighed by its tendency to prejudice the outcome.[40]

By statute,[41] joint tortfeasors are allowed a set-off for a settlement paid in good faith by a codefendant liable for the same injury.[42] A recent Oklahoma Supreme Court case has acknowledged the theory that a set-off may be obtained for spousal or other third party settlements if it can be demonstrated that settlement was made without good faith; however, the Oklahoma Supreme Court has not decided the issue. An evidentiary hearing on the issue will be required.[43]

5. **Proper Parties**

    a. **Plaintiffs**

    Section 402A of the Restatement (Second) of Torts provides that "users or consumers" of products may bring product liability actions. Oklahoma has expanded the class of those protected under product liability to include bystanders.[44] No privity of contract is required to sue in strict liability for a defective product.[45]

    b. **Defendants**

    Section 402A assigns liability on a product liability action to sellers of products; however, occasional sellers of products are not liable under the theory.[46] Although Oklahoma has named the cause of action "manufacturers' products liability," retailers and wholesalers are also liable.[47] Similarly, lessors of products are considered "suppliers" of defective products and are liable under Oklahoma law.[48] Oklahoma has not decided the question of whether a seller of a used product is liable under product liability theory.

Oklahoma has not specifically ruled on the question of whether successor corporations retain liability under a product liability theory. However, the general standard for successor liability was set forth in *Pulis v. United States Electrical Tool Co.*, 561 P.2d 68 (Okla. 1977), which has been applied in product liability cases.[49]

Oklahoma extends liability under a theory of manufacturers' products liability not only to manufacturers and sellers but to "suppliers" as well.[50] A "supplier" is defined under Oklahoma law according to the Restatement (Second) of Torts as "one who injects a product into the stream of commerce 'whether through a sale or other means' and regardless of whether title to the product is retained by the supplier."[51] Oklahoma has yet to address the question of whether liability under a theory of manufacturers' products liability is extended to a bailor.[52]

6. Duty to Warn

Plaintiff may rely on failure to warn as a theory of recovery in product liability. However, in order to prevail on this cause of action, plaintiff must show that the failure to warn actually caused his injury.[53] The duty to warn extends only to ordinary consumers and users of the product. An "ordinary consumer" is defined as one who is "foreseeably expected to purchase the product involved."[54] Similarly, there is no duty to warn of a product-connected danger that is obvious or generally known. There is no duty to warn a knowledgeable user of the product of the dangers associated with the product's use.[55] Evidence of remedial measures, such as post-sale warnings, may not be used to prove negligence or otherwise evidence culpable conduct.[56] In an unpublished decision, one division of the Oklahoma Court of Appeals held that the proscription against evidence of subsequent remedial measures is applicable to a products case brought solely on a strict liability theory.[57]

7. Misrepresentation

Restatement (Second) of Torts section 402B, concerning misrepresentation, has never been adopted in Oklahoma.

D. NEGLIGENCE

A plaintiff who brings an action for manufacturers' strict products liability is not precluded from bringing a cause of action for negligence.[58] Oklahoma has adopted a "modified comparative negligence" system.[59] Therefore, if a plaintiff is more than 50 percent at fault, recovery is barred.[60] Under the Oklahoma system, the "plaintiff's percentage of negligence is to be compared with the aggregate negligence of all defendants combined."[61]

E. BREACH OF WARRANTY UNDER THE OKLAHOMA UNIFORM COMMERCIAL CODE

Any recovery under a warranty theory is restricted to the terms of Article 2 of the Oklahoma Uniform Commercial Code.

The Oklahoma Uniform Commercial Code authorizes recovery under theories of breach of the implied warranty of merchantability,[62] breach of the implied warranty of fitness for a particular purpose,[63] and breach of express warranty.[64]

Recovery for purely economic damages to the product itself must be based on the parties' contractual relationship, specifically, the warranty provisions, express or implied.[65] No action may be premised on manufacturers' products liability when injury occurs solely to the product itself.[66]

The sovereign immunity of a political subdivision is waived only in accordance with the strictures of the Oklahoma Governmental Tort Claims Act.[67] Pursuant to the Act, the state or a political subdivision is not liable under a theory of manufacturer's products liability or breach of warranty, either express or implied.[68] However, a recent Oklahoma Court of Appeals decision would allow the state or a political subdivision to remain liable for breach of express or implied warranties in contract.[69] The Appeals Court reasoned that the provisions of the Governmental Tort Claims Act did not apply to contractual warranties.[70]

F. PUNITIVE DAMAGES

Punitive damages are available for actions sounding in negligence[71] and strict product liability in tort,[72] but not for breach of warranty.[73]

John C. Niemeyer
Linda G. Alexander
Anne E. Zachritz
NIEMEYER, ALEXANDER, AUSTIN & PHILLIPS, P.C.
Three Hundred North Walker
Oklahoma City, Oklahoma 73102-1822
(405) 232-2725

ENDNOTES - OKLAHOMA

1. Although Oklahoma has adopted strict liability in tort under Restatement (Second) of Torts section 402A, the Oklahoma Supreme Court has designated this cause of action as "Manufacturers' Products Liability." See *Kirkland v. General Motors Corp.*, 521 P.2d 1353, 1361 cited in V. Lawrence-MacDougall, *Products Liability Law in Oklahoma* 9-10 (1990).

2. Okla. Stat. tit. 12A (1981).

3. *Waggoner v. Town & Country Mobile Homes*, 808 P.2d 649, 652 (Okla. 1990), citing *Kirkland*, 521 P.2d 1353 (Okla. 1974); *Kimbrell v. Zenith Radio Corp.*, 555 P.2d 590 (Okla. 1976).

4. Id. at 653.

5. *Dutsch v. Sea Ray Boats, Inc.*, 845 P.2d 187, 193 (Okla. 1992).

6. Okla. Stat. tit. 12 §95 (1981).

7. *Kirkland*, 521 P.2d at 1361.

8. *Daugherty v. Farmers Coop. Assoc.*, 689 P.2d 947 (Okla. 1984).

9. Okla. Stat. tit. 12A §2-725 (1981).

10. Okla. Stat. tit. 12 §109 (1981), which in full provides:

    No action in tort to recover damages
    (i) for any deficiency in the design, planning, supervision or observation of construction or construction of an improvement to real property,
    (ii) for injury to property, real or personal, arising out of any such deficiency, or
    (iii) for injury to the person or for wrongful death arising out of any such deficiency,
    shall be brought against any person owning, leasing, or in possession of such an improvement or performing or furnishing the design, planning, supervision or observation of construction or construction of such an improvement more than ten (10) years after substantial completion of such an improvement.

11. *Samuel Roberts Noble Foundation, Inc. v. Vick*, 840 P.2d 619 (Okla. 1992).

12. *Smith v. Westinghouse Elec. Corp.*, 732 P.2d 466 (Okla. 1987) (where the issue considered was whether transformers were an "improvement to real property" and, as such, subject to Okla. Stat. tit. 12 §109's ten-year repose period). See also *O'Dell v. Lamb-Grays Harbor Co.*, 911 F. Supp. 490 (W.D. Okla. 1995) (distinguishing *Smith* on the basis that the "product" was a "fixture").

13. Id. at 470.

14. *Riley v. Brown and Root, Inc.*, 836 P.2d 1298 (Okla. 1992).

15. *Ball v. Hahnischfeger*, 877 P.2d at 45 (Okla. 1994).

16. *Kirkland*, 521 P.2d 1362-1363.

17. V. Lawrence-MacDougall, *Products Liability Law in Oklahoma* 12 (1990).

18. *Kirkland*, 521 P.2d at 1363.

19. *Case v. Fibreboard*, 743 P.2d 1062 (Okla. 1987); *Dillon v. Fibreboard*, 919 F.2d 1488 (10th Cir. 1990); *Blair v. Eagle-Picher Indus., Inc.*, 962 F.2d 1492 (10th Cir. 1992).

20. *Case*, 743 P.2d 1062.

21. *Woods v. Fruehauf Trailer Corp.*, 765 P.2d 770, 773 (Okla. 1988).

22. Id.

23. *Kirkland*, 521 P.2d at 1362-1363.

24. *Dutsch*, 845 P.2d 193.

25. *Thrasher v. B&B Chemical Co.*, 2 F.3d 995 (10th Cir. 1993).

26. *Kirkland*, 521 P.2d at 1366-1367.

27. Id.

28. *Holt v. Deere & Co.*, 24 F.3d 1289, 1293 (10th Cir. 1994).

29. *Waggoner*, 808 P.2d at 652, *citing* Restatement (Second) of Torts §402A, comment m (1965). *Dutsch*, 845 P.2d at 193 ("When purely economic damages occur and there is no damage to person or other property, U.C.C. remedies are sufficient to protect the plaintiff.").

30. *Moss v. Polyco, Inc.*, 522 P.2d 622, 627 (Okla. 1974); Okla. Stat. tit. 12A, §7-219(3) (1981).

31. Okla. Const. Art. XXIII, §7; Okla. Stat. tit. 85 §12 (Supp. 1986); *Rios v. Nicor Drilling Co.*, 665 P.2d 1183 (Okla. 1983).

32. See *Field v. Volkswagen*, 555 P.2d 48, 57 (Okla. 1976).

33. *Kirkland*, 521 P.2d at 1363.

34. See, e.g., *Smith v. Minster Mach. Co.*, 669 F.2d 628 (10th Cir. 1982).

35. *Karns v. Emerson Elec. Co.*, 817 F.2d 1452, 1457 (10th Cir. 1987).

36. *Robinson v. Audi Nsu Auto Union*, 739 F.2d 1481, 1486 (10th Cir. 1984).

37. *Kirkland*, 521 P.2d at 1363.

38. *Tansy v. Dacomed Corp.*, 890 P.2d 881 (Okla. 1994).

39. *Bruce v. Martin-Marietta Corp.*, 544 F.2d 442, 446 (10th Cir. 1976), *aff'g* 418 F. Supp. 829, 836 (W.D. Okla. 1975).

40. Okla. Stat. tit. 12 §§2402, 2403 (1981). See, e.g., *Barringer v. Wal-Mart Stores, Inc.*, 699 F. Supp. 1496, 1498 n.2 (W.D. Okla. 1988).

41. Okla. Stat. tit. 12 §832 (1981).

42. *Dutsch*, 845 P.2d at 192.

43. Id.

44. *Moss*, 522 P.2d at 626.

45. See generally *Kirkland*, 521 P.2d 1353 (Okla. 1974); Restatement (Second) of Torts §402A (1965).

46. *Bruce*, 544 F.2d at 442, *aff'g* 418 F. Supp. 837 (W.D. Okla. 1975).

47. *Moss*, 522 P.2d at 626-627.

48. *Dewberry v. LaFollette*, 598 P.2d 241, 243 (Okla. 1979).

49. *Goucher v. Parmac, Inc.*, 694 P.2d 953 (Okla. 1984).

50. *Gonser v. Decker*, 814 P.2d 1056, 1057 (Okla. App. 1991), *citing Dewberry*, 598 P.2d at 242.

51. Id.; Restatement (Second) of Torts §402A, comments c and f (1965).

52. Id.

53. *Smith v. United States Gypsum Co.*, 612 P.2d 251, 253 (Okla. 1980); *Duane v. Oklahoma Gas & Elec. Co.*, 833 P.2d 284, 286 (Okla. 1992).

54. *Rohrbaugh v. Owens-Corning Fiberglas Corp.*, 965 F.2d 844, 846 (10th Cir. 1992), *citing Woods v. Fruehauf Trailer Corp.*, 764 P.2d 770, 774 (Okla. 1988).

55. See *Duane*, 833 P.2d at 286 (manufacturer had no duty to warn plaintiff that a power surge could transform dielectric oil into a volatile substance); *Hutchins v. Silicone Specialties, Inc.*, 881 P.2d 64 (Okla. 1993) (manufacturer that markets its product solely to professional consumers with specialized training is entitled to expect its instructions to be followed and has no duty additional to warn of dangers associated with product's use).

56. Okla. Stat. tit. 12 §2407 (1981).

57. *Brown v. Firestone Tire & Rubber Co.*, No. 79,598, slip op. at 15-21 (Okla. Ct. App. July 5, 1994). This case is apparently the only authority in Oklahoma.

58. *Kirkland*, 521 P.2d at 1365.

59. Okla. Stat. tit. 23 §§13, 14; *Laubach v. Morgan*, 588 P.2d 1071 (Okla. 1978).

60. Id. at 1073.

61. Id.

62. Okla. Stat. tit. 12A §2-314 (1981).

63. Okla. Stat. tit. 12A §2-315 (1981).

64. Okla. Stat. tit. 12 §2-313 (1981).

65. *Waggoner*, 808 P.2d at 653.

66. Id.; *Oklahoma Gas & Elec. v. McGraw-Edison*, 834 P.2d 980 (Okla. 1992).

67. Okla. Stat. tit. 51 §151 et seq. (Supp. 1992).

68. Okla. Stat. tit. 51 §155(26) (Supp. 1992).

69. *Lucas v. Canadian Valley Vo-Tech School*, 824 P.2d 1140 (Okla. Ct. App. 1992).

70. Id. at 1141-1142.

71. Okla. Stat. tit. 23 §9 (Supp. 1987).

72. *Thiry v. Armstrong World Indus.*, 661 P.2d 515 (Okla. 1983).

73. *Jackson v. Glasgow*, 622 P.2d 1088 (Okla. 1980).

OREGON

A. CAUSES OF ACTION

Product liability lawsuits commonly include causes of action for strict liability, negligence, and warranty.

B. STATUTES OF LIMITATION

Causes of action for personal injuries or property damage must be brought within two years of the date of the death, injury, or damage,[1] and not later than eight years after the date on which the product was first purchased for use or consumption.[2] There is a question whether the two-year limitation is subject to a "discovery" rule. The statute specifically states that the two-year limitation runs from the "date on which the death, injury or damage complained of occurred."[3] An intermediate appellate court has, however, applied a discovery rule in spite of this language.[4] A later Oregon Supreme Court case, construing a similar wrongful death statute, refused to apply a discovery rule.[5] The Oregon Supreme Court has ruled that the statute of limitations for wrongful death claims, rather than the statute of limitations for product liability actions, applies to a wrongful death claim based on a theory of product liability.[6] A cause of action seeking damages for breach of warranty must be brought within the two years for any products related claim.[7]

C. STRICT LIABILITY

1. The Standard

By statute, Oregon has adopted the rule of section 402A of the Restatement (Second) of Torts and has dictated that the rule is to be construed by comments a to m of that section of the Restatement.[8] Thus, the product must be shown to be both in a "defective condition" and as being "unreasonably dangerous" to the user. The tests imposed by comments g and i are used to determine if the necessary showings have been made.[9]

2. The Defective Condition

An action may be based on a defective design, a manufacturing flaw, or a failure to adequately warn or instruct in the use of the product.[10] The Restatement (Second) of Torts, section 402A, comments g, i, and j, define the terms "defective condition" and "unreasonably dangerous" and the obligation to give directions or warnings. Finally, the action may allege an indeterminate defect. Inability to specify a defect is not fatal to a claim if a showing can be made that the product failed under circumstances that reasonably tend to indicate that the defect existed at the time of the sale and that a defect is the only reasonable explanation for the accident.[11]

3. **Contributory Negligence**

Contributory negligence, in the sense of unreasonably proceeding to encounter a known danger in the product, is a defense.[12] Failure to discover a defect is not a defense, but any other unreasonable conduct by the injured party that is a cause of the injury is also a defense.[13] The contributory negligence in this regard is compared with the fault of the defendant, to reduce the injured person's damages, except that if the injured party's fault is greater than the defendant's fault, the injured party cannot recover.[14] In a crashworthiness case, failure to use a seat belt can be considered as an element of contributory negligence.[15]

4. **Sale or Lease**

For a strict liability claim, the plaintiff must allege a sale or lease of a product by defendant.[16] Sellers of used goods are generally not subject to strict liability as long as they are not the manufacturer; however, if the nature of the sale implies a representation as to safety, the seller of the goods may be liable.[17] A defendant who, as part of his business, modifies a product may be strictly liable.[18]

5. **Inherently Dangerous Products**

A supplier of products will not be held strictly liable simply because the product is inherently dangerous unless it fails to give adequate warning of the danger.[19] However, comment k of Restatement (Second) of Torts section 402A will apply.

6. **Successor Liability**

The Oregon courts have never held that a successor corporation that acquires all or substantially all of the manufacturing assets of another corporation and continues in its predecessor's commercial activity is liable for its predecessor's defective products.

7. **Privity**

No privity is required; a plaintiff may sue even though she did not buy the product from the manufacturer.[20] A plaintiff may be a user, consumer, or other injured party; therefore, bystanders may have strict liability protection.[21]

8. **Failure to Warn**

If the plaintiff relies on a theory of failure to warn, he must prove that the absence of the warning was a cause of his loss.[22] It is sufficient to prove causation if there is evidence (or the jury can draw an inference) that a warning is generally effective in preventing such accidents.[23] The provisions of comment j of Restatement (Second) of Torts section 402A apply by statute.

9. **Post-Sale Duty to Warn**

    While the Oregon courts have not specifically ruled regarding this issue, a post-sale duty to warn may exist.[24]

10. **Substantial Change/Abnormal Use**

    A manufacturer is not responsible for injuries caused by a substantial change[25] to the product occurring after initial sale or due to misuse,[26] but the substantial change or misuse must be one that could not reasonably be foreseen.[27]

11. **State of the Art**

    The question of whether evidence of the state of the art is admissible has not been settled by the Oregon appellate courts. However, comment j of section 402A of the Restatement (Second) of Torts would seem to require that a state-of-the-art analysis would apply to a failure-to-warn claim.

12. **Other Accidents**

    Evidence of other accidents is inadmissible unless the prior accidents occurred under substantially similar circumstances and conditions.[28]

13. **Misrepresentations**

    Section 402B of the Restatement (Second) of Torts, dealing with misrepresentation, appears to have been adopted in Oregon.[29]

D. NEGLIGENCE

Ordinary contributory negligence is a defense,[30] and comparative negligence applies unless plaintiff is more than 50 percent at fault.[31]

The recovery of economic loss in strict liability cases is more limited,[32] as is the recovery of punitive damages in a strict liability case.[33]

E. BREACH OF WARRANTY

In the product liability setting, a cause of action for breach of warranty is similar to a strict liability cause of action. The following main differences exist:

1. There must be privity between plaintiff and defendant unless the product is a consumer good within the meaning of Or. Rev. Stat. §72.8010(1).[34] Also, a member of a buyer's family or a guest in her home may recover for personal injuries if it was reasonable to assume the family member or guest would consume or be affected by the product.[35]

2. If a plaintiff is a consumer, the plaintiff asserting a claim for a breach of warranty may be entitled to attorneys' fees under the federal Magnuson-Moss Act.

3. The warranty may be express,[36] an implied warranty of merchantability,[37] or an implied warranty of fitness for a particular purpose.[38]

F.   PUNITIVE DAMAGES

Punitive damages are recoverable in Oregon in a "product liability civil action," which includes negligence and strict liability, if certain statutory criteria are met.[39] Oregon has recently adopted standards for judicial review of punitive damages awards.[40]

G.   STATUTES

Relevant statutes for product liability actions are Or. Rev. Stat. §30.900 et seq. and Or. Rev. Stat. Chapter 72 when breach of warranty is alleged.

Elizabeth A. Schleuning
Roland F. Banks, Jr.
SCHWABE WILLIAMSON & WYATT
Pacwest Center
1211 S.W. Fifth Avenue
Suites 1600-1950
Portland, Oregon 97204-3795
(503) 222-9981

ENDNOTES - OREGON

1. Or. Rev. Stat. §30.905(2) (1987); *Burns v. General Motors Corp.*, 133 Or. App. 555, 841 P.2d 1354 (1995).

2. Id. §30.905(1) (1993). Some products, such as asbestos, and breast implants, have been statutorily exempted from the eight-year statute of ultimate repose.

3. Id. §30.905(2) (1993).

4. *Dortch v. A. H. Robins Co.*, 59 Or. App. 310, 650 P.2d 1046 (1982); overruled by *Border v. Indian Head Indus., Inc.*, 101 Or. App. 556, 792 P.2d 111 (1990).

5. *Eldridge v. Eastmoreland Gen. Hosp.*, 307 Or. 500, 769 P.2d 775 (1989).

6. *Western Helicopter Servs. v. Rogerson Aircraft*, 311 Or. 361, 811 P.2d 361 (1991). See also *Western Helicopters, Inc. v. Rogerson Aircraft*, 765 F. Supp. 1041 (D. Or. 1991).

7. *Bancorp Leasing and Financial Corp. v. Augusta Aviation Corp.*, 813 F.2d 272 (9th Cir. 1987).

8. Id. §30.920(3) (1979).

9. *Ewen v. McLean Trucking Co.*, 300 Or. 24, 32, 706 P.2d 929 (1985); *Becker v. Barbur Blvd. Equip. Rental Inc.*, 81 Or. App. 648, 726 P.2d 967 (1986).

10. Or. Rev. Stat. §30.900 (1977).

11. *Brownell v. White Motor Corp.*, 260 Or. 251, 254, 490 P.2d 184 (1971). But see *Helms v. Halton Tractor Co.*, 66 Or. App. 890, 676 P.2d 347 (1984).

12. *Bacelleri v. Hyster Co.*, 287 Or. 3, 597 P.2d 351 (1979).

13. *Sandford v. Chevrolet Div. of Gen. Motors*, 292 Or. 590, 610, 642 P.2d 624 (1982); Or. Rev. Stat. §18.470 (1995).

14. Id.

15. *Dahl v. Bayerische Motoren Werk*, 304 Or. 558, 748 P.2d 77 (1987). But see Or. Rev. Stat. §18.590 (1989).

16. Id. §30.920 (1979).

17. *Tillman v. Vance Equip.*, 286 Or. 747, 596 P.2d 1299 (1979).

18. *Meyers v. Cessna Aircraft Corp.*, 275 Or. 501, 553 P.2d 355 (1976).

19. *Burkett v. Freedom Arms, Inc.*, 299 Or. 551, 556, 704 P.2d 118 (1985). See also note 7, *supra*.

20. Or. Rev. Stat. §30.920(2)(b) (1979).

21. Id.

22. *Bacelleri*, 287 Or. 3.

23. Id.

24. See *Erickson Air-Crane v. United Technologies Corp.*, 79 Or. App. 659, 720 P.2d 389 (1986), *rev'd on other grounds*, 303 Or. 281, 735 P.2d 614 (1987).

25. Or. Rev. Stat. §30.915 (1977).

26. *Finday v. Copeland Lumber*, 265 Or. 300, 509 P.2d 28 (1973).

27. *Russell v. Ford Motor Co.*, 281 Or. 587, 575 P.2d 1383 (1978).

28. *Davis v. Homasote Co.*, 281 Or. 383, 574 P.2d 1116 (1978). But see *Oberg v. Honda Motor Co. Ltd.*, 316 Or. 263, 851 P.2d 1084 (1993), *rev'd, remanded (on other grounds)*, 512 U.S. 415, 114 S. Ct. 2331, 129 L. Ed. 2d 336 (1994); where the court permitted introduction of Consumer Product Safety Commission records despite the absence of similar circumstances and conditions.

29. See *McGrath v. White Motor Corp.*, 258 Or. 583, 594-95, 484 P.2d 838 (1971).

30. Or. Rev. Stat. §18.470 (1995).

31. *Bacelleri*, 287 Or. 3.

32. See *Brown v. Western Farmers Assn.*, 268 Or. 470, 521 P.2d 537 (1974); *Russell*, 281 Or. 587.

33. Or. Rev. Stat. §30.925 (1995) and Or. Rev. Stat. §18.537 (1995) requires "clear and convincing" evidence that the defendant acted with malice or has shown a reckless and outrageous indifference to a highly inconsumable risk of harm and has acted with a conscious indifference to the health, safety and welfare of others.

34. See id. §§72.8020, 72.8030 (1973).

35. Id. §72.3180 (1961).

36. Id. §72.3130 (1961).

37. *B. W. Feed Co. Inc. v. General Equip. Co.*, 44 Or. App. 285, 605 P.2d 1205 (1980); Or. Rev. Stat. §§72.1040 (1987), 72.3140 (1961).

38. *Swan Island Sheet Metal Works v. Troy's Custom Smoking Co.*, 49 Or. App. 469, 619 P.2d 1326 (1980); Or. Rev. Stat. §72.3150 (1961).

39. Or. Rev. Stat. §30.925 (1995).

40. Or. Rev. Stat. §18.537 (1995).

PENNSYLVANIA

A. CAUSES OF ACTION

Product liability lawsuits commonly include causes of action for strict liability, negligence and breach of warranty.

B. STATUTES OF LIMITATION

Causes of action for personal injuries[1] or property damage[2] must be brought within two years, whether brought in negligence or strict liability. A rather liberal "discovery" rule applies.[3] A cause of action seeking personal injuries resulting from a breach of warranty must be brought within four years of the date of sale.[4]

A twelve-year statute of repose is applicable to claims involving improvements to real property.[5]

C. STRICT LIABILITY

1. The Standard

Pennsylvania has adopted section 402A of the Restatement (Second) of Torts.[6] However, the determination of whether the product is "unreasonably dangerous" is removed from jury consideration. That element must be decided by the court prior to submitting the case to the jury.[7] Since most courts fail to act at all, in most cases the "unreasonably dangerous" requirement is effectively removed. Pennsylvania courts strive to an unusual degree to remove negligence concepts from the strict liability cause of action, which is not always possible.[8] In some circumstances the doctrine of *res ipsa loquitur* may allow a jury to infer the existence of a manufacturing defect or negligence where injury would not have otherwise ordinarily occurred.[9]

2. Definition of Defect

The jury is instructed that the product is defective if it left the supplier's control lacking any element necessary to make it safe for its intended use or possessing any feature that renders it unsafe for its intended use.[10]

3. Causation

It is the plaintiff's burden in any product liability case to demonstrate that the injuries sustained were substantially caused by the product's defect.[11]

---

4. Contributory Negligence/Assumption of Risk

Contributory negligence is not a defense,[12] but assumption of risk is.[13] Evidence of contributory negligence probably is not admissible in strict liability cases, even as it relates to causation, unless the plaintiff's act initiated the accident.[14] The form of assumption of risk adopted is that the plaintiff knew and understood the specific danger and potential for serious injury and yet voluntarily chose to encounter it.[15]

5. Sale or Lease/Persons Liable

The plaintiff must allege a sale or other commercial transaction of the product by the defendant.[16]

Strict liability applies to any seller in the chain of a product's distribution.[17] However, the supplier must be in the business of supplying such products.[18] Under some circumstances, a distributor may obtain indemnity from the manufacturer.[19]

Generally, strict liability applies to lessors who are in the business of supplying products.[20] The occasional seller of a product may avoid liability under section 402A of the Restatement (Second) of Torts.[21]

6. Inherently Dangerous Products

A supplier of products will not be held strictly liable simply because the product is inherently dangerous, unless it fails to give adequate warning of the danger.[22]

7. Successor Liability

A successor corporation acquiring all or substantially all of the manufacturing assets of another corporation and continuing the same product line may be liable for injuries caused by products made by the predecessor corporation.[23] Lack of a remedy against the predecessor corporation is a prerequisite to an action against the successor.[24]

8. Market Share Liability/Enterprise Liability

Market share liability and enterprise liability have been rejected in the Commonwealth of Pennsylvania.[25]

9. Privity

No privity is required; plaintiffs may sue even though they did not buy the product from the manufacturer.[26]

10. Failure to Warn

Whether a warning is adequate and whether a product is defective due to inadequate warnings are questions of law for the trial judge.[27] If the plaintiffs rely on a theory of failure to warn, they must prove that the absence of the warning was a cause of the loss.[28] Under certain situations, this can be a very difficult burden to satisfy.

Pennsylvania has not yet adopted the sophisticated user doctrine.[29]

11. Post-Sale Duty to Warn and Remedial Measures

Under limited circumstances, a manufacturer may have a post-sale duty to warn, at least where a component manufacturer advises of a defect and a manufacturer fails to pass such information along to the customer.[30] Normally, post-manufacture remedial measures are not admissible.[31]

12. Learned Intermediary Doctrine

A seller of prescription drug products and vaccines has a duty to exercise reasonable care to inform users of the facts that make a product dangerous.[32] A seller of such products may satisfy its duty to warn by furnishing adequate warnings and instructions to the prescribing physician, but is not required to give them directly to the patient.[33]

13. Substantial Alteration/Abnormal Use

A manufacturer is not responsible for injuries caused by a substantial change in the product that occurs after initial sale[34] or due to abnormal use,[35] but the substantial change or abnormal use must be one that could not reasonably be foreseen or expected.

14. State of the Art

"State-of-the-art" evidence is generally not available as a defense.[36]

15. Malfunction

A malfunction of a product in the absence of evidence of abnormal use or reasonable secondary causes is evidence of a defect.[37]

16. Standards and Governmental Regulations

Evidence that the product complied with customary standards or industry standards is usually inadmissible with respect to the issue of defect.[38]

17. Other Accidents

Evidence of other accidents is inadmissible unless plaintiff proves that the product is the same and there is substantial factual similarity in time, place, and circumstance. Evidence of lack of prior claims or accidents may be admissible to rebut causation.[39]

18. Misrepresentation

Section 402B of the Restatement (Second) of Torts dealing with misrepresentation has been adopted in Pennsylvania.[40]

19. Destruction or Loss of Product

Pennsylvania courts often impose sanctions against parties when the product at issue has been altered, lost or destroyed. Whether sanctions are appropriate and the level of sanctions warranted is determined by: (1) the degree of fault of the party who altered or destroyed the evidence; (2) the degree of prejudice suffered by the opposing party; and (3) the degree of sanction necessary to avoid substantial unfairness to the opposing party and, if the opposing party is seriously at fault, to deter such conduct by others in the future.[41] Courts have disposed of cases on summary judgment when the plaintiff is relying on a manufacturing defect[42] and have imposed less severe sanctions depending upon the facts and circumstances of each particular case.[43] Where plaintiff is relying on a design defect, however, the case will likely proceed if defendant is able to inspect a product identical to the one no longer available.[44]

20. Economic Loss

Recovery is permitted only for personal injury or property damage. Recovery solely for economic loss is prohibited in strict liability and negligence actions.[45]

D. NEGLIGENCE

Unlike strict liability, there are few unique aspects of Pennsylvania product liability cases based on negligence.[46] A cause of action based on negligence may well be broader in scope than one based on strict liability. Thus, a manufacturer may be responsible in negligence for a foreseeable injury to an unintended user.[47]

Contributory negligence is a defense, but comparative negligence applies unless the plaintiff is more than fifty percent at fault, in which event recovery is barred.[48]

E. BREACH OF WARRANTY

A cause of action for breach of warranty is generally quite similar to a strict liability cause of action.[49]

However, with respect to the statute of limitations, the "discovery rule" does not apply.[50]

F. PUNITIVE DAMAGES

Punitive damages are recoverable in actions in strict liability[51] and negligence,[52] but not in lawsuits sounding only in breach of warranty.[53]

G. STATUTES

Relevant statutes for product liability actions are the statutes of limitation and the commercial code sections when a breach of warranty is alleged.[54]

The Pennsylvania Workmen's Compensation Act's "exclusive remedy provision" exempts the plaintiff's employer from liability and from being joined as a party to an action for an employee's injuries.[55] An employer may, however, contractually obligate itself to defend and indemnify a product manufacturer, provided that the employer "expressly" agrees to be liable for indemnification and contribution in a written contract.[56]

Morton F. Daller
Eileen M. Johnson
Mark S. Kirby
DALLER GREENBERG & DIETRICH, LLP
Valley Green Corporate Center
7111 Valley Green Road
Fort Washington, Pennsylvania 19034
(215) 836-1100
(215) 836-2845 (facsimile)
Email: mdaller@dallergreenberg.com

ENDNOTES - PENNSYLVANIA

1. 42 Pa. Cons. Stat. Ann. §5524(2) (Purdon Supp. 1993).

2. Id. §5524(3) (Purdon Supp. 1993).

3. *Bohus v. Beloff*, 950 F.2d 919 (3d Cir. 1991); *Grabowski v. Turner & Newall*, 516 F. Supp. 114 (E.D. Pa. 1980), *aff'd sub nom. DeMato v. Turner & Newall, Ltd.*, 651 F.2d 908 (3d Cir. 1981) (per curiam); *Mitchell v. Hendricks*, 431 F. Supp. 1295 (E.D. Pa. 1977); *Huber v. McElwee-Courbis Constr. Co.*, 392 F. Supp. 1379 (E.D. Pa. 1974); *Hayward v. Medical Center of Beaver County*, 530 Pa. 320, 608 A.2d 1040 (1992).

4. 42 Pa. Cons. Stat. Ann. §5525 (Purdon Supp. 1993); 13 Pa. Cons. Stat. Ann. §2725 (Purdon 1984 and Purdon Supp. 1993); *Williams v. West Penn. Power Co.*, 502 Pa. 557, 467 A.2d 811 (1983); *Patton v. Mack Trucks, Inc.*, 360 Pa. Super. 1, 519 A.2d 959 (1986).

5. 42 Pa. Cons. Stat. Ann. §5536 (Purdon Supp. 1992); *Noll by Noll v. Harrisburg Area YMCA*, 537 Pa. 274, 643 A.2d 81 (1994); *McCormick v. Columbus Conveyor Co.*, 522 Pa. 520, 564 A.2d 907 (1989).

6. *Mazur v. Merck & Co., Inc.*, 964 F.2d 1348 (3d Cir. 1992), *Conti v. Ford Motor Co.*, 743 F.2d 195 (3d Cir. 1984; *Webb v. Zern*, 422 Pa. 424, 220 A.2d 853 (1966); *Schriner v. Pennsylvania Power & Light Co.*, 348 Pa. Super. 177, 501 A.2d 1128 (1985).

7. *Fraust v. Swift and Co.*, 610 F. Supp. 711 (W.D. Pa. 1985); *Davis v. R.H. Dwyer Indus., Inc.*, 548 F. Supp. 667 (E.D. Pa. 1982).

8. *Habecker v. Clark Equip. Co.*, 36 F.3d 278 (3d Cir. 1994); *Skipworth v. Lead Indus.*, 547 Pa. 224, 690 A.2d 169 (1997); *Lewis v. Coffing Hoist Div.*, 515 Pa. 334, 528 A.2d 590 (1987).

9. *Bearfield v. Hauch*, 407 Pa. Super. 624, 595 A.2d 1320 (1991).

10. *Azzarello v. Black Brothers Co., Inc.*, 480 Pa. 547, 391 A.2d 1020 (1978).

11. *Blancha v. Raymark Indus.*, 972 F.2d 507 (3d Cir. 1992); *Jacobini v. V&O Press Co.*, 527 Pa. 32, 588 A.2d 476 (1991); *Sherk v. Daisy-Heddon*, 498 Pa. 594, 450 A.2d 615 (1982).

12. *Dillinger v. Caterpillar, Inc.*, 959 F.2d 430 (3d Cir. 1992); *Davis*, 548 F. Supp. 667.

13. *Wagner v. Firestone Tire & Rubber Co.*, 890 F.2d 652 (3d Cir. 1989); *Lonon v. Pep Boys, Manny, Moe & Jack*, 371 Pa. Super. 291, 538 A.2d 22 (1988).

14. *Dillinger*, 959 F.2d 430; *Kern*, 801 F. Supp. 1438.

15. *Mackowick v. Westinghouse Elec. Corp.*, 525 Pa. 52, 575 A.2d 100 (1990); *Mucowski v. Clark*, 404 Pa. Super. 197, 590 A.2d 348 (1991); *Staymates v. ITT Holub Indus.*, 364 Pa. Super. 37, 527 A.2d 140 (1987); *Walasavage v. Marinelli*, 334 Pa. Super. 396, 483 A.2d 509 (1984).

16. *Klein v. Council of Chem. Assocs.*, 587 F. Supp. 213 (E.D. Pa. 1984); *Francioni v. Gibsonia Truck Corp.*, 472 Pa. 362, 372 A.2d 736 (1977).

17. *Neal v. Carey Canadian Mines, Ltd.*, 548 F. Supp. 357 (E.D. Pa. 1982), *aff'd sub nom. Van Buskirk v. Carey Canadian Mines, Ltd.*, 760 F.2d 481 (3d Cir. 1985).

18. *Webb*, 422 Pa. 424; *Pennsylvania Natl. Mut. Ins. Co. v. Kaminski Lumber*, 397 Pa. Super. 484, 580 A.2d 401 (1990); *McKenna v. Art Pearl Works, Inc.*, 225 Pa. Super. 362, 310 A.2d 677 (1973).

19. *Walasavage*, 334 Pa. Super. 396; *Burch v. Sears, Roebuck & Co.*, 320 Pa. Super. 444, 467 A.2d 615 (1983).

20. *Francioni*, 472 Pa. 362.

21. *Acevedo v. Start Plastics, Inc.*, 834 F. Supp. 808 (E.D. Pa. 1993); *Jones v. SEPTA*, 834 F. Supp. 766 (E.D. Pa. 1993).

22. *Mazur*, 964 F.2d 1348; *Greiner v. Volkswagenwerk Aktiengeselleschaft*, 540 F.2d 85 (3d Cir. 1976); *Incollingo v. Ewing*, 444 Pa. 263, 282 A.2d 206 (1971); Restatement (Second) of Torts §402A, comment k (1965).

23. *Dawejko v. Jorgensen Steel Co.*, 290 Pa. Super. 15, 434 A.2d 106 (1981).

24. *Leo v. Kerr-McGee Chemical Corp.*, 37 F.3d 96 (3d Cir. 1994); *Conway v. White Truck*, 885 F.2d 90 (3d Cir. 1989); *LaFountain v. Webb Indus. Corp.*, 759 F. Supp. 236 (E.D. Pa. 1991), *aff'd*, 951 F.2d 544 (3d Cir. 1991); *Amader v. Pittsburgh Corning Corp.*, 546 F. Supp. 1033 (E.D. Pa. 1982); *Keselyak v. Reach-All, Inc.*, 443 Pa. Super. 71, 660 A.2d 1350 (1995).

25. *Skipworth*, 547 Pa. 224; *Pennfield Corp. v. Meadow Valley Elec.*, 413 Pa. Super. 187, 604 A.2d 1082 (1992); *Burnside v. Abbott Labs.*, 351 Pa. Super. 264, 505 A.2d 973 (1985); *Cummins v. Firestone Tire & Rubber Co.*, 344 Pa. Super. 9, 495 A.2d 963 (1985).

26. *Mannsz v. MacWhyte*, 155 F.2d 445 (3d Cir. 1946); *Thompson v. Reedman*, 199 F. Supp. 120 (E.D. Pa. 1961); *Moscatiello v. Pittsburgh Contractors*, 407 Pa. Super. 378, 595 A.2d 1198 (1991).

27. *Mazur*, 964 F.2d 1348; *Mackowick*, 525 Pa. 52; *Dauphin Deposit Bank and Tr. Co. v. Toyota Motor Corp.*, 408 Pa. Super. 256, 596 A.2d 845 (1991).

28. *Paulik v. Lane Limited/Tobacco Exporters International*, Nos. 97-1121 and 97-1199, 1998 WL 40655 (3d Cir. Feb. 4, 1998); *Overpeck v. Chicago Pneumatic Tool Co.*, 634 F. Supp. 638 (E.D. Pa. 1986), *aff'd*, 823 F.2d 751 (3d Cir. 1987); *Phillips v. A-Best Products Co.*, 542 Pa. 124, 665 A.2d 1167 (1995); *Morris v. Pathmark Corp.*, 405 Pa. Super. 274, 592 A.2d 331 (1991), *appeal granted*, 530 Pa. 644, 607 A.2d 254 (1992), *appeal dismissed*, 563 Pa. 104, 607 A.2d 254 (1994); *Remy v. Michael D's Carpet Outlets*, 391 Pa. Super. 436, 571 A.2d 446 (1990), *aff'd sub nom. Kimco Dev. Corp. v. Michael D's Carpet Outlets*, 536 Pa. 1, 637 A.2d 603 (1993); *O'Neill v. Checker Motors Corp.*, 389 Pa. Super. 430, 567 A.2d 680 (1989); *Staymates*, 364 Pa. Super. 37.

29. *Phillips v. A-Best Products Co.*, 542 Pa. 124, 665 A.2d 1167 (1995); *Phillips v. A. P. Green Refractories Co.*, 428 Pa. Super. 167, 630 A.2d 874 (1993), *appeal denied in part by Harmotta v. Walter C. Best, Inc.*, 537 Pa. 632, 642 A.2d 486 (1994), *and appeal granted in part by Phillips v. A-Best Products Co.*, 538 Pa. 614, 645 A.2d 1317 (1994); Restatement (Second) of Torts §388 (1965).

30. *Walton v. Avco Corp.*, 530 Pa. 568, 610 A.2d 454 (1992).

31. *Kelly v. Crown Equip. Co.*, 970 F.2d 1273 (3d Cir. 1992); *Leaphart v. Whiting Corp.*, 387 Pa. Super. 253, 564 A.2d 165 (1989).

32. *Incollingo*, 444 Pa. 263.

33. *Mazur*, 964 F.2d 1348; *Taurino v. Ellen*, 397 Pa. Super. 50, 579 A.2d 925 (1990).

34. *Sweitzer v. Dempster Sys.*, 372 Pa. Super. 449, 539 A.2d 880 (1988); *D'Antona v. Hampton Grinding Wheel Co.*, 225 Pa. Super. 120, 310 A.2d 307 (1973).

35. *Brill v. Systems Resources, Inc.*, 405 Pa. Super. 603, 592 A.2d 1377 (1991); *Pegg v. General Motors Corp.*, 258 Pa. Super. 59, 391 A.2d 1074 (1978).

36. *Santiago v. Johnson Mach. & Press Corp.*, 834 F.2d 84 (3d Cir. 1987); *Hoffman v. Niagra Mach. and Tool Works Co.*, 683 F. Supp. 489 (E.D. Pa. 1988); *Lewis*, 515 Pa. 334.

37. *Gordner v. Dynetics Corp.*, 862 F. Supp. 1303 (M.D. Pa. 1994); *Rogers v. Johnson & Johnson Prods.*, 523 Pa. 176, 565 A.2d 751 (1989); *Roselli v. General Elec. Co.*, 410 Pa. Super. 223, 599 A.2d 685 (1991).

38. *Hoffman*, 683 F. Supp. 489; *Leaphart*, 387 Pa. Super. 253; *Lewis*, 515 Pa. 334.

39. *Tait v. Armor Elevator Co.*, 958 F.2d 563 (3d Cir. 1992); *Gidlewski v. Bettcher Indus., Inc.*, 619 F. Supp. 87 (E.D. Pa.), *aff'd*, 779 F.2d 42 (3d Cir. 1985); *Spino v. John S. Tilley Ladder Co.*, 548 Pa. 286, 696 A.2d 1169 (1997); *DiFrancesco v. Excam, Inc.*, 434 Pa. Super. 173, 642 A.2d 529 (1994); *Madjic v. Cincinnati Mach. Co.*, 370 Pa. Super. 611, 537 A.2d 334 (1988).

40. *Klages v. General Ordnance Equip. Corp.*, 240 Pa. Super. 356, 367 A.2d 304 (1976).

41. *Schmid v. Milwaukee Elec. Tool Co.*, 13 F.3d 76 (3d Cir. 1994); *Dansak v. Cameron Coca-Cola Bottling Co., Inc.*, 703 A.2d 489 (Pa. Super. 1997).

42. *Schwartz v. Subaru of America, Inc.*, 851 F. Supp. 191 (E.D. Pa. 1994); *Smith v. American Honda Motor Co., Inc.*, 846 F. Supp. 1217 (M.D. Pa. 1994); *Sipe v. Ford Motor Co.*, 837 F. Supp. 660 (M.D. Pa. 1993); *Martin & Greenspan v. Volkswagen of America*, No. CIV.A.88-8261, 1989 WL 81296 (E.D. Pa. July 13, 1989); *Roselli v. General Elec. Co.*, 410 Pa. Super. 223, 599 A.2d 685 (1991).

43. *Baliotis v. McNeill*, 870 F. Supp. 1285 (M.D. Pa. 1994); *Mensch v. Bic Corp.*, No. CIV.A.90-6002, 1992 WL 236965 (E.D. Pa. Sept. 17, 1992).

44. *Troup v. Tri-County Confinement Systems, Inc.*, No. 13, 1998 WL 81459 (Pa. Super. Feb. 27, 1998); *Sebelin v. Yamaha Motor Corp.*, No. 1903, 1998 WL 1256. (Pa. Super. Jan. 5, 1998); *O'Donnell v. Big Yank, Inc.*, 696 A.2d 846 (Pa. Super. 1997).

45. *Lucker Mfg. v. Milwaukee Steel Foundry*, 777 F. Supp. 413 (E.D. Pa. 1991); *Spivack v. Berks Ridge Corp., Inc.*, 402 Pa. Super. 73, 586 A.2d 402 (1990); *REM Coal Co., Inc. v. Clark Equip. Co.*, 386 Pa. Super. 401, 563 A.2d 128 (1989); *compare 2J Corp. v. Tice*, 126 F.3d 539 (3d Cir. 1997) (economic loss doctrine does not preclude recovery for contents of warehouse when warehouse collapses).

46. *Thompson v. Pennsylvania Power Co.*, 402 F.2d 88 (3d Cir. 1968); *Rosa v. United States*, 613 F. Supp. 469 (M.D. Pa. 1985). In negligence actions generally, contributory negligence is a defense except where the defendant is wanton or willfully negligent.

47. *Griggs v. BIC Corp.*, 981 F.2d 1429 (3d Cir. 1992).

48. 42 Pa. Cons. Stat. Ann. §7102 (Purdon Supp. 1992); *Williams v. United States*, 507 F. Supp. 121 (E.D. Pa. 1981); *Elder v. Orluck*, 511 Pa. 402, 515 A.2d 517 (1986).

49. 13 Pa. Cons. Stat. Ann. §2315 (Purdon 1984); *Bogacki v. American Mach. & Foundry Co.*, 417 F.2d 400 (3d Cir. 1969); *Berkebile v. Brantly Helicopter Corp.*, 462 Pa. 83, 337 A.2d 893 (1975).

50. See note 4, *supra*.

51. *Neal v. Carey Canadian Mines, Ltd.*, 548 F. Supp. 357 (E.D. Pa. 1982), *aff'd sub nom. Van Buskirk v. Carey Canadian Mines, Ltd.*, 760 F.2d 481 (3d Cir. 1985).

52. *Takes v. Metropolitan Medicine Co.*, 440 Pa. Super. 101, 65 A.2d 138 (1995), *rev'd on other grounds*, 548 Pa. 92, 695 A.2d 397 (1997).

53. 13 Pa. Cons. Stat. Ann. §2715 (Purdon 1981); *Rose v. A&L Motor Sales*, 699 F. Supp. 75 (W.D. Pa. 1988).

54. 42 Pa. Cons. Stat. Ann. §§5524, 5525, 5536 (Purdon 1981 and Purdon Supp. 1993); 13 Pa. Cons. Stat. Ann. §2315 (Purdon 1984 and Purdon Supp. 1993).

55. 77 P.S. §481(b) (Purdon Supp. 1991).

56. 77 P.S. §481(b) (Purdon Supp. 1991); *Bester v. Essex Crane Rental Corp.*, 422 Pa. Super. 178, 619 A.2d 304 (1993).

RHODE ISLAND

A. CAUSES OF ACTION

Rhode Island recognizes product liability suits premised on strict liability, negligence, and breach of UCC warranties of merchantability and fitness.[1]

B. STATUTES OF LIMITATION

Claims for personal injuries or wrongful death sounding in strict liability, negligence, or breach of warranty, must be brought within three years of the date of injury. The UCC four-year statute of limitations for breach of warranty applies only where there is a direct buyer-seller relationship between the parties.[2] A discovery rule applies only in drug product liability actions.[3]

Claims for property damage must be brought within ten years of the date of damage.[4]

A ten-year statute of repose is limited to improvements to real property and material suppliers who furnished materials for the construction of improvements.[5] A general ten-year statute of repose limiting product liability actions to ten years following purchase was held to violate the Rhode Island State Constitution.[6]

C. STRICT LIABILITY

1. The Standard

Rhode Island has adopted section 402A of the Restatement (Second) of Torts.[7] There must be proof of a defect in the design or manufacture of a product when it leaves the manufacturer's hands that makes it unreasonably dangerous for its intended use.[8] The scope of strict liability has been extended to cover a seller's or manufacturer's failure to warn of the product's dangerous propensity.[9]

Generally, all elements, including the "unreasonably dangerous" requirement, are reserved for jury determination. However, where a prescription drug is defended as "unavoidably unsafe" under Restatement (Second) of Torts section 402A, comment k, the court must be satisfied that reasonable minds could differ in deciding whether a drug's risks outweigh its benefits before submitting the issue to the jury.[10]

2. "Defect"

Rhode Island uses a consumer expectation test, in that "unreasonably dangerous" means that the defect establishes a "strong likelihood of injury" not contemplated by the user or consumer.[11] Plaintiff need not establish a specific defect as long as there is evidence of some unspecified dangerous condition. The jury may rely on circumstantial evidence to establish the dangerous condition, and where the allegedly defective product is destroyed in the mishap, evidence of malfunction may be sufficient evidence of defect.[12]

3. Contributory Negligence/Assumption of Risk

Assumption of the risk is a complete defense to a product liability action, whether in strict liability or breach of warranty.[13] The standard for assumption of the risk is entirely subjective—plaintiff must personally have assumed an encounter with a perceived danger.[14] Rhode Island's comparative negligence statute, which reduces damages by the percent plaintiff was contributorily negligent (even as much as 99 percent), applies in product liability cases in strict liability, negligence, and warranty.[15]

4. Sale or Lease

A seller or commercial lessor is liable to the same extent as the manufacturer, as long as the defect existed as of the time of sale or lease.[16]

5. Inherently Dangerous Products

Rhode Island accords no special treatment to inherently dangerous products, except that Restatement (Second) of Torts section 402A, comment k, respecting unavoidably unsafe products, is applicable to drug product claims, including breach of warranty.[17] See section C1 above respecting the risk-benefit test applicable to drug products.

6. Successor Liability

A successor corporation that absorbs the predecessor's business and property by purchase or merger, and continues the predecessor's management personnel and policies, may be liable for injuries caused by the predecessor's products.[18]

7. Privity

Privity is not required.

8. Failure to Warn

A manufacturer or seller has a duty to warn of dangers that are not open and obvious.[19] Moreover, incident to the duty to warn is the duty to acquire knowledge about products through reasonably adequate inspections and tests.[20]

9. Substantial Change/Abnormal Use

By statute, R.I. Gen. Laws section 9-1-32, a product manufacturer or seller is not liable for personal injuries, death, or property damage where a substantial cause of the injury or damage is a post-sale product alteration or modification. The failure to follow routine maintenance requirements can be found an alteration or modification covered by the statute.[21]

Product misuse is a defense, but the improper use must be neither intended nor foreseeable.[22]

10.   State-of-the-Art Evidence

State-of-the-art evidence is generally not admissible. Evidence in the nature of state of the art evidence is admissible in failure to warn cases, because the duty to warn extends only to dangers reasonably foreseeable and knowable at the time of marketing.[23]

11.   Other Accidents

Evidence of other accidents or consumer complaints may be admissible as tending to show that the injury to plaintiff was probably caused by a product defect, as opposed to plaintiff's particular susceptibility, or as tending to show the dangerous character of the product and defendant's knowledge and duty to warn of that character. Such evidence, by itself, however, is not sufficient to establish defect, or causation as to a particular plaintiff.[24]

12.   Post-Accident Repairs

Under the Rhode Island Rules of Evidence, evidence of subsequent remedial measures is admissible if the subsequent measures would have made the injury less likely.[25]

13.   Market-Share Liability

Rhode Island refused to adopt the market-share doctrine California accepted in *Sindell v. Abbott Labs., Inc.*, 163 Cal. Rptr. 132 (1980). Under Rhode Island law, the imposition of liability requires the identification of the specific defendant responsible for the injury.[26]

D.   NEGLIGENCE

Rhode Island negligence law contains no aspects unique to claims for defective products. Most negligence defenses — such as comparative negligence and assumption of the risk — can also be asserted in strict liability cases.

Rhode Island has a so-called pure comparative negligence statute. Plaintiff may recover even if plaintiff's comparative fault is more than 50 percent.

E.   BREACH OF WARRANTY

In the products setting, a breach of warranty claim is substantively similar to a strict liability claim.[27] Differences in the statute of limitations do exist, as noted in section B above.

Under the Rhode Island version of the UCC, merchantability and fitness warranties extend to any person who may reasonably be expected to use, consume, or be affected by the goods and who is injured by the breach of the warranty. This extension cannot be limited or excluded.[28]

F. PUNITIVE DAMAGES

Punitive damages are recoverable in negligence and strict liability, but not in breach of warranty. Punitive damages are awarded where the defendant acted maliciously, intending to harm plaintiff.[29]

G. OTHER ASPECTS

Rhode Island has adopted a version of the Uniform Contribution Among Joint Tortfeasors Act. However, under the statute, a plaintiff's employer cannot be held liable in contribution for workplace injuries, nor does an employer's fault reduce the plaintiff's recovery. Similarly, equitable indemnity against the employer is not permitted, but express or implied contractual indemnity may be enforced against the employer.[30]

George Vetter
Gordon P. Cleary
VETTER & WHITE
20 Washington Place
Providence, Rhode Island 02903
(401) 421-3060

ENDNOTES – RHODE ISLAND

1. But see *Fry v. Allergam Medical Optics*, 695 A.2d 511 (R.I. 1997) (holding federal law preempts claims involving Class III medical devices).

2. *Pirri v. Toledo Scale Corp.*, 619 A.2d 429 (1993); *Kelley v. Ford Motor Co.*, 290 A.2d 607 (R.I. 1972); *Plouffe v. Goodyear Tire & Rubber Co.*, 373 A.2d 492 (R.I. 1977).

3. *Anthony v. Abbott Labs.*, 490 A.2d 43 (R.I. 1985); *Renaud v. Sigma-Aldrich Corp.*, 662 A.2d 711 (R.I. 1995).

4. *Romano v. Westinghouse Elec. Co.*, 336 A.2d 555 (R.I. 1975).

5. R.I. Gen. Laws §9-1-29.

6. *Kennedy v. Cumberland Engg. Co.*, 471 A.2d 195 (R.I. 1984).

7. *Ritter v. Narragansett Elec. Co.*, 283 A.2d 255 (R.I. 1971).

8. *Simmons v. Lincoln Elec. Co.*, 696 A.2d 273 (R.I. 1997); *Peters v. Jim Walter Door Sales of Tampa, Inc.*, 525 A.2d 46 (R.I. 1987).

9. *Thomas v. Amway Corp.*, 488 A.2d 716 (R.I. 1985).

10. *Castrignano v. E. R. Squibb & Sons, Inc.*, 546 A.2d 775 (R.I. 1988).

11. *Castrignano*, 546 A.2d at 779.

12. *Scittarelli v. Providence Gas Co.*, 415 A.2d 1040 (R.I. 1980).

13. *Castrignano*, 546 A.2d at 783.

14. *Fiske v. MacGregor, Div. of Brunswick*, 464 A.2d 719 (R.I. 1983).

15. Id.

16. *Brimbau v. Ausdale Equip. Rental Corp.*, 440 A.2d 1292 (R.I. 1982).

17. *Castrignano*, 546 A.2d at 783.

18. *Casey v. San-Lee Realty, Inc.*, 623 A.2d 16 (R.I. 1993).

19. *Kuras v. International Harvester Co.*, 820 F.2d 15 (1st Cir. 1987).

20. *Scittarelli*, 415 A.2d at 1043.

21. *LaPlante v. American Honda Motor Co.*, 27 F.3d 731 (1st Cir. 1994); *Pietrafesa v. Board of Governors for Higher Education*, 846 F. Supp. 1066 (D.R.I. 1994).

22. *Roy v. Star Chopper Co., Inc.*, 442 F. Supp. 1010 (D.R.I. 1977), *aff'd*, 584 F.2d 1124 (1st Cir. 1978); *Austin v. Lincoln Equip. Assocs., Inc.*, 888 F.2d 934 (1st Cir. 1989).

23. *Thomas*, 488 A.2d at 722; *Castrignano*, 546 A.2d at 782 (prescription drugs).

24. *Thomas*, 488 A.2d at 720-721.

25. R.I.R.E. 407.

26. *Gorman v. Abbott Labs., Inc.*, 599 A.2d 1364 (1991).

27. *Castrignano*, 564 A.2d at 783.

28. R.I. Gen. Laws §6A-2-318.

29. *Greater Providence Deposit Corp. v. Jenison*, 485 A.2d 1242 (R.I. 1984).

30. *Roy*, 442 F. Supp. at 1021-1022.

SOUTH CAROLINA

A. SCOPE OF PRODUCT LIABILITY

Product liability actions may include causes of action for strict liability, negligence, and breach of an implied or express warranty.[1]

B. CAUSES OF ACTION

A cause of action results when injury is caused by a defective product, through negligence, strict liability in tort,[2] and/or breach of warranty.[3] None are exclusive remedies. The standard of safety is essentially the same regardless of which theory is employed.[4] In a products liability case the Plaintiff must establish three things, regardless of the theory on which he seeks recovery: 1) that he was injured by the product; 2) that the product, at the time of the accident, was in essentially the same condition as when it left the hands of the defendant; and 3) that the injury occurred because the product was in a defective condition unreasonably dangerous to the user.[5]

Under any products liability theory, a plaintiff must prove the product defect was the proximate cause of the injury sustained.[6] Proximate cause requires proof of both causation in fact and legal cause.[7] Causation in fact is proved by establishing the injury would not have occurred "but for" the defendant's negligence.[8] Legal cause is proved by establishing fore-seeability.[9]

C. STATUTES OF LIMITATION

Because no "product liability" statute of limitations exists, the applicable statute of limitations is the equivalent of any personal injury, wrongful death, or property damage statute. For such actions, the limitations period is six years for causes of action accruing prior to April 5, 1988, and three years for causes of action arising on or after April 5, 1988.[10] For breach of warranty actions, the statute of limitations is six years.[11] The date of discovery is significant in determining the date to commence the running of the statute.

South Carolina also imposes a thirteen-year statute of repose[12] on improvements to real property.

D. STRICT LIABILITY

1. Scope

Liability is imposed regardless of whether the defendant used due care. However, certain defenses prevent liability from being absolute.

---

2. Standard

South Carolina has adopted legislatively Restatement (Second) of Torts, section 402A (1965) and comments.[13]

3. "Defect"

Plaintiff must prove product was "defective" and that the defect was unreasonably dangerous.[14] Two tests have evolved to determine whether a product is in a defective condition unreasonably dangerous for its intended use. The first test is whether the product is unreasonably dangerous to the ordinary consumer or user given the conditions or circumstances that foreseeably attend the use of the product.[15] Under the second test, a product is unreasonably dangerous and defective if the danger associated with the use of the product outweighs the utility of the product. The state of the art and industry standards are relevant to show both the reasonableness of design and that the product is dangerous beyond the expectations of the ordinary consumer.[16]

4. Contributory Negligence/Assumption of Risk

Contributory negligence is not a defense,[17] but assumption of risk will bar recovery.[18] Again in this area, South Carolina adopts the Restatement, including the comments.[19]

The continued use of a product after discovering a defect is not a complete bar to recovery unless the plaintiff's continued use of the product after discovering the defect was unreasonable. The question of reasonableness is generally one for the jury.[20]

5. Sale or Lease

Strict liability may be applied even though no sale has occurred.[21]

6. Successor Liability

A successor corporation continuing the business of its predecessor may be liable for product liability claims arising out of sales made prior to the defendant's purchase of assets.[22]

7. Privity

No privity of contract is required.[23]

8. Failure to Warn

A sufficient warning must specify the danger or cause of danger and plaintiff must show that a warning would have changed his or her behavior.[24]

A manufacturer of a product is responsible for failing to warn if it knows or has reason to know the product is or is likely to be dangerous for its intended use, and the manufacturer has no reason to believe that the user will realize the potential danger, and the manufacturer fails to utilize reasonable care to inform of the product's dangerous condition or of the facts that make it likely to be dangerous.[25]

The seller of a product is not required to warn of dangers or potential dangers that are generally known and recognized, and thus a product cannot be deemed defective or unreasonably dangerous if the danger associated with the product is one that the product's users generally recognize.[26]

9. Post-Sale Duty to Warn

A post-sale duty to warn arises when, after the sale, the manufacturer or seller learns of latent defects affecting the product.[27]

However, a manufacturer has no duty to notify previous purchasers of its products about later developed safety devices or to retrofit those products if the products were nondefective under standards existing at the time of manufacture or sale.[28]

A manufacturer has no duty to warn of potential risks or dangers inherent in a product if the product is distributed through a learned intermediary or distributed to a sophisticated user who is in the position to understand and assess the risk involved, and to inform the ultimate user of the risks, thereby warning the ultimate user of any alleged inherent dangers involved in the product.[29]

10. Substantial Change/Abnormal Use

Defendant is liable for reasonably foreseeable misuses of the product.[30] However, the defendant is under no duty to prevent the product from deteriorating because of use (absent an original defect in the product).[31] Liability may be imposed upon a manufacturer or seller notwithstanding subsequent alteration of the product when the alteration could have been anticipated by the manufacturer or seller, or did not causally contribute to the damages or injuries complained of.[32]

When an alteration to a product is shown, the foreseeability of the alteration must be examined. This foreseeability is normally a question of fact for the jury.[33]

11. State of the Art

The state of the art and industry standards are relevant to show both the reasonableness of the design and that the product is dangerous beyond the expectations of the ordinary consumer.[34] The Fourth Circuit Court of Appeals has also held that evidence of design customs and trade practices at the time of manufacture is admissible on the issue of design defects.[35]

12. Malfunction

The mere fact that a product malfunctions does not demonstrate the manufacturer's negligence nor does it establish that the product was defective.[36]

13. Standards

A product must be measured against the standard existing at the time of sale or against reasonable customer expectations held at the time of sale. Hindsight opinions by experts suggesting that more should have been done are insufficient to discredit the conclusion that the manufacturer met the standard of care.[37]

A product is not per se "defective" merely because safer equipment could be installed.[38] Also, the defendant has the duty to keep abreast of current standards.[39]

14. Other Accidents

Evidence of substantially similar incidents is admissible.[40]

15. Misrepresentation

South Carolina has not specifically adopted Restatement (Second) of Torts section 402B. Currently, South Carolina imposes a stricter standard than most jurisdictions. It requires proof of nine specific elements to sustain an action for misrepresentation.[41] In the commercial setting, misrepresentation regarding a product will not create a tort cause of action where only "economic losses" are suffered.[42]

16. Economic Loss

For now, South Carolina still recognizes the general rule that there is no tort liability for a product defect if the damage suffered by a plaintiff is only to the product itself. However, the Supreme Court has suggested that it is uncomfortable with the rule as it exists and has partially rejected the rule in the residential home building context.[43]

E. NEGLIGENCE

South Carolina follows the general negligence doctrine[44] of due care with regard to product liability. Also, the traditional defenses of assumption of risk and statute of limitations apply. The defense of contributory negligence has been judicially repealed in South Carolina for all causes of action arising after July 1, 1991.[45] For all causes of action arising after that date, the courts will apply the "not greater than" version of comparative negligence. Specifically, the South Carolina Supreme Court has explained:

> a plaintiff in a negligence action may recover damages if his or her negligence is not greater than that of the defendant. The amount of

the plaintiff's recovery shall be reduced in proportion to the amount of his or her negligence. If there is more than one defendant, the plaintiff's negligence shall be compared to the combined negligence of all defendants.[46]

To establish negligence the plaintiff must prove the defendant failed to exercise due care in some respect. The focus is upon the action of the defendant. The mere fact a product malfunctions does not demonstrate the manufacturer's negligence nor tend to establish the product was defective.[47]

Under a negligence theory, the plaintiff bears the burden of demonstrating the defendant (seller or manufacturer) failed to exercise due care in some respect, and, unlike strict liability, the focus is on the conduct of the seller or manufacturer, and liability is determined according to fault.[48]

The Court of Appeals recently held that assumption of risk is no longer a complete defense to a negligence claim but is instead treated as a factor in assessing comparative negligence.[49]

F. BREACH OF WARRANTY

Warranty of liability[50] is governed by the South Carolina version of the UCC.[51] A cause of action in warranty is advantageous where the loss was purely economic.[52]

G. PUNITIVE DAMAGES

Punitive damages may be awarded against the tortfeasor who acted in "conscious disregard" of the rights of others.[53] Punitive damages may not be awarded in cases based solely on strict liability in tort or on a warranty theory.[54]

H. STATUTES

See endnotes for relevant statutes, particularly for strict liability and breach of warranty.

Edward W. Mullins, Jr.
William H. Latham
NELSON MULLINS RILEY & SCARBOROUGH, L.L.P.
Keenan Building, 3d Floor
1330 Lady Street
P.O. Box 11070
Columbia, South Carolina 29201
(803) 799-2000

ENDNOTES – SOUTH CAROLINA

1. *Bragg v. Hi-Ranger, Inc.*, 319 S.C. 531, 462 S.E.2d 321 (Ct. App. 1995).

2. South Carolina adopted Restatement (Second) of Torts §402A (1965) in S.C. Code Ann. §15-73-10 to -30 (Law. Co-op. 1976), thereby establishing strict liability in tort in South Carolina.

3. S.C. Code Ann. §§36-1-101 et seq., 36-2-313, -314, -315, -318 (Law. Co-op. 1976 & Supp. 1991) impose UCC warranties.

4. *Chestnut v. Ford Motor Co.*, 445 F.2d 967, 969 (4th Cir. 1971).

5. *Madden v. Cox*, 284 S.C. 574, 579, 328 S.E.2d 108, 112 (Ct. App. 1985), *citing* Prosser, Law of Torts 671-672 (4th ed. 1970). See also S.C. Code Ann. §15-73-10 (Law Co-op. 1976) (South Carolina's strict liability statute).

6. *Small v. Pioneer Machinery, Inc.*, —S.C—, —S.E—, 1997 WL 722995 at *6 (S.C. App. 1997).

7. Id.

8. Id.

9. Id.

10. S.C. Code. Ann. §15-3-530, -535, -545 (Law. Co-op. 1976 & Supp. 1991).

11. Id. §36-2-725 (Law. Co-op. 1976).

12. Id. §15-3-640 (Law. Co-op. 1976 & Supp. 1991).

13. See S.C. Code Ann. §15-73-10, 20.

14. See Hubbard and Felix, at 221-222.

15. *Vaughn v. Nissan Motor Corp.*, 77 F.3d 736, 737 (4th Cir. 1996) (additionally holding that if a product is unreasonably dangerous to the ordinary consumer, recovery is not restricted to "ordinary consumers" alone; rather, the manufacturer must take the injured person as it finds her).

16. *Bragg*, 462 S.E.2d at 326.

17. S.C. Code Ann. §§15-73-10, -20; 36-2-316(3)(b) (Law. Co-op. 1976), Official Comment 8; Restatement (Second) of Torts §402A.

18. "If the user or consumer discovers the defect and is aware of the danger, and nevertheless proceeds unreasonably to make use of the product and is injured by it, he is barred from recovery." S.C. Code Ann. §15-73-20 (Law. Co-op. 1976).

19. Id. §15-73-10, -20 (Law. Co-op. 1976).

20. *Fleming v. Borden, Inc.,* 316 S.C. 452, 450 S.E.2d 589, 594 (S.C. 1994).

21. *Henderson v. Gould, Inc.,* 288 S.C. 261, 341 S.E.2d 806 (1986).

22. *Holloway v. John E. Smith's Sons Co., Div. of Hobam, Inc.,* 432 F. Supp. 454 (D.S.C. 1977).

23. *Salladin v. Tellis,* 247 S.C. 267, 146 S.E.2d 875 (1966); see also S.C. Code Ann. §36-2-318 (Law. Co-op. 1976) (addressing breach of warranty).

24. *Gardner v. Q.H.S., Inc.,* 448 F.2d 238 (4th Cir. 1971).

25. *Bragg,* 462 S.E.2d at 331.

26. *Anderson v. Green Bull, Inc.,* 322 S.C. 268, 471 S.E.2d 708, 710 (S.C. App. 1996) (holding that dangers of electrical conductivity of aluminum ladders is generally known).

27. See Hubbard and Felix, 195-196; *Carolina Home Bldrs., Inc. v. Armstrong Furnace Co.,* 259 S.C. 346, 191 S.E.2d 774 (1972).

28. *Bragg,* 462 S.E.2d at 331.

29. Id. at 331-332.

30. *Gardner,* 448 F.2d 238.

31. *Mickle v. Blackmon,* 252 S.C. 202, 166 S.E.2d 173 (1969).

32. *Fleming,* 450 S.E.2d 589.

33. Id. at 593.

34. *Bragg,* 462 S.E.2d 321 at 328.

35. Id. at 249, n.46; cf. id. at 250, n.48; *Reed v. Tiffin Motorhomes, Inc.*, 697 F.2d 1192 (4th Cir. 1982).

36. *Sun Villa Homeowners Assn. v. Square D Company*, 301 S.C. 330, 333, 391 S.E.2d 868, 870 (Ct. App. 1990).

37. *Bragg*, 462 S.E.2d at 331.

38. *Marchant v. Mitchell Distrib. Co.*, 270 S.C. 29, 240 S.E.2d 511 (1977).

39. *Carolina Home Bldrs.*, 259 S.C. 346.

40. *J.K.T. Co., Inc. v. Hardwick*, 274 S.C. 413, 265 S.E.2d 510 (1980), *appeal after remand*, 284 S.C. 10, 325 S.E.2d 329 (1984) (appeal after remand did not affect substantive products liability law).

41. *First State Sav. and Loan v. Phelps*, 299 S.C. 441, 385 S.E.2d 821 (S.C. 1989).

42. *Bishop Logging v. John Deere Indus.*, 317 S.C. 520, 455 S.E.2d 183, 189 (Ct. App. 1995).

43. *Kershaw Couty Bd. of Education v. U.S. Gypsum Co.*, 302 S.C. 390, 396 S.E.2d 369 (1990).

44. See *Carolina Home Bldrs.*, 259 S.C. 346 (manufacturer's standard of care is relative to that of others having expertise in his field).

45. *Nelson v. Concrete Supply Co.*, 303 S.C. 243, 399 S.E.2d 783 (1991).

46. Id.

47. *Sunvillas Homeowners Assoc. v. Square D. Corp.*, 310 S.C. 330, 391 S.E.2d 868 (Ct. App. 1990).

48. *Bragg*, 462 S.E.2d at 326.

49. *Davenport v. Cotton Hope Plantation,* —S.C.— , 482 S.E.2d 569 (Ct. App. 1997).

50. Express warranty, implied warranty of merchantability, and implied warranty of fitness for a particular purpose are warranted by the UCC.

51. S.C. Code Ann. §36-1-101 (Law. Co-op. 1976).

52. See *supra*, section D16, Economic Loss.

53. *Willis v. Floyd Brace Co.*, 279 S.C. 458, 463, 309 S.E.2d 295, 298 (Ct. App. 1983).

54. *Barnwell v. Barber Colman Co.*, 301 S.C. 534, 393 S.E.2d 162 (1989); *Pinckney v. Orkin*, 268 S.C. 430, 234 S.E.2d 654 (1977).

SOUTH DAKOTA

A. CAUSES OF ACTION

Product liability lawsuits include causes of action for strict liability, negligence, and warranty.

B. STATUTES OF LIMITATION

An action against a manufacturer, lessor, or seller of a product, regardless of the substantive legal theory upon which the action is brought, must be commenced within three years of the date when the damage occurred, became known, or should have become known to the injured party.[1] An action for personal injury must be brought within three years of its accrual.[2] A breach of warranty action must be brought within four years after the cause of action has accrued, which occurs when tender of delivery is made.[3]

C. PRODUCTS LIABILITY

1. The Standard

For strict liability cases, South Dakota has adopted section 402A of the Restatement (Second) of Torts.[4] The product must be unreasonably dangerous and in substantially the same condition as when placed in the stream of commerce.

2. "Defect"

Ordinarily, an expert is required to testify that the product is unreasonably dangerous in order to present a jury question, and the jury must then find (1) that the product was in a defective condition, (2) that the condition made it unreasonably dangerous, (3) that the defect existed at the time it left the control of the defendant, (4) that the product was expected to and did reach the plaintiff without any substantial change in condition, and (5) that the plaintiff used the product in a manner reasonably anticipated.[5] Three types of defect are actionable under strict liability: manufacturing defects, design defects, and defects due to failure to warn.[6]

3. Contributory Negligence/Assumption of Risk

Contributory negligence is not a defense in strict liability unless it is the sole cause.[7] Assumption of the risk is a defense.[8] Misuse is a defense in strict liability cases,[9] and the Eighth Circuit Court of Appeals has held that misuse is also a defense in a breach of warranty case, relevant to proximate cause.[10] The Eighth Circuit Court of Appeals has also held that assumption of risk and misuse defenses require

---

proof that the consumer or user is aware of the defect and never-theless proceeds to use the product.[11] Alteration or modification is a defense in strict liability and negligence cases.[12] Evidence regarding the use or non-use of a seatbelt is not admissible.[13] Defendant's conformity with government regulations is allowed as evidence of reasonable care but is not controlling.[14] The South Dakota Legislature has codified a state of the art defense.[15]

4. Evidence and Related Matters

Post-accident design is admissible in strict liability actions.[16] Recalls are also admissible into evidence.[17]

5. Used Goods

A seller of used goods, if rebuilt or reconditioned, is subject to strict liability.[18]

6. Successor Liability

A successor corporation may be liable; case law specifically determines the elements.[19]

7. Who Is Protected

No privity of contract is required, and consumers, users, and foreseeable bystanders are protected.[20]

8. Failure to Warn

The manufacturer and seller of a product must give adequate warning if danger is reasonably anticipated. They do not need to warn for obvious danger known to the injured person.[21] The Eighth Circuit Court of Appeals has held that the duty to warn includes a post-sale duty to warn of defects existing at the time of sale, but discovered after sale.[22]

9. Duty to Inspect

The manufacturer must make a reasonable inspection.[23] A manufacturer is not relieved by a duty of a third party to inspect.[24]

10. Duty to Inspect Component Part

A manufacturer has the duty to inspect the component part it has incorporated into a product.[25]

11. Component Part Manufacturer

A component part manufacturer has the same duty of care as the manufacturer.[26]

12. Seller's Duty to Inspect

One who sells a product in the ordinary course of trade does not have a duty to inspect or test unless the seller has reason to know that the product is likely to be dangerously defective.[27] By statute, a distributor, wholesaler, dealer, or retail seller cannot be strictly liable for an unreasonably dangerous latent defect, unless the seller knew or should have known of the defective condition.[28]

13. **Contributory Negligence**

In a negligence action, plaintiff may still recover if contributory negligence is slight compared with the negligence of the defendant.[29]

14. **Breach of Warranty**

The Uniform Commercial Code has been adopted.[30]

15. **Punitive Damages**

Punitive damages are permissible in actions not arising out of contract for injury to person or property through oppression, fraud, malice, or reckless disregard of plaintiff's rights.[31]

Arlo Sommervold
WOODS, FULLER, SHULTZ & SMITH
300 South Phillips Avenue, Suite 300
Sioux Falls, South Dakota 57102
(605) 336-3890

ENDNOTES – SOUTH DAKOTA

1. SDCL §15-2-12.2.

2. SDCL §15-2-14.

3. SDCL §57A-2-725.

4. *Engberg v. Ford Motor Co.*, 205 N.W.2d 104, 109 (S.D. 1973).

5. South Dakota Jury Pattern Instruction 150-01. *Engberg*, 205 N.W.2d at 109; *Smith v. Smith*, 278 N.W.2d 155, 158-159 n.2 (S.D. 1979); *Jahnig v. Coisman*, 283 N.W.2d 557, 560 (S.D. 1979).

6. *Peterson v. Safway Steel Scaffolds Co.*, 400 N.W.2d 909, 912 (S.D. 1987); *Rynders v. E. I. DuPont, DeNemours & Co.*, 21 F.3d 835, 842 (8th Cir. 1994).

7. *Smith*, 278 N.W.2d at 161; *Berg v. Sukup Mfg. Co.*, 355 N.W.2d 833, 835 (S.D. 1984).

8. Id.

9. Id.

10. *Herrick v. Monsanto Co.*, 874 F.2d 594, 598-599 (8th Cir. 1989).

11. *Novak v. Navistar Int'l Transp. Corp.*, 46 F.3d 844, 849 (8th Cir. 1995).

12. SDCL §20-9-10; *Peterson*, 400 N.W.2d at 913-914.

13. SDCL §32-38-4.

14. *Zachar v. Budd Co.*, 396 N.W.2d 122, 133-134 (S.D. 1986); *Hofer v. Mack Trucks*, 981 F.2d 377, 383 (8th Cir. 1992).

15. SDCL §20-9-10.1.

16. *Farner v. Paccar, Inc.*, 562 F.2d 518, 525-526 (8th Cir. 1977); *Shaffer v. Honeywell, Inc.*, 249 N.W.2d 251, 257 n.7 (S.D. 1976).

17. *Farner*, 562 F.2d at 526-527.

18. *Crandell v. Larkin and Jones Appliance Co.*, 334 N.W.2d 31, 34 (S.D. 1983); *Wynia v. Richard-Ewing Equip. Co.*, 17 F.3d 1084, 1087-1089 (8th Cir. 1994).

19. *Hamaker v. Kenwell-Jackson Mach., Inc.*, 387 N.W.2d 515, 518-521 (S.D. 1986).

20. *Engberg*, 205 N.W.2d at 109.

21. *Jahnig*, 283 N.W.2d at 560.

22. *Novak*, 46 F.3d at 850.

23. *Weidner v. Lineback*, 140 N.W.2d 597, 601 (S.D. 1966).

24. South Dakota Pattern Jury Instruction 150-04; Restatement (Second) of Torts §§386, 393.

25. South Dakota Pattern Jury Instruction 150-05. *American Radiator & Standard Sanitary Corp. v. Fix*, 200 F.2d 529, 536 (8th Cir. 1952).

26. South Dakota Pattern Jury Instruction 150-06; Restatement (Second) of Torts §595 note m.

27. *Peterson*, 400 N.W.2d at 915.

28. SDCL §20-9-9; *Wynia*, 17 F.2d at 1088-1089.

29. SDCL §20-9-2.

30. SDCL Ch. 57A.

31. Id. §21-3-2; *Holmes v. Wegman Oil Co.*, 492 N.W.2d 107, 113 (S.D. 1992); *Hofer*, 981 F.2d at 382-383.

TENNESSEE

A. CAUSES OF ACTION

In the State of Tennessee, a "product liability action" is defined by statute to include, but not be limited to, all actions based on the following theories: strict liability in tort; negligence; breach of warranty, express or implied; breach of or failure to discharge a duty to warn or instruct, whether negligent or innocent; misrepresentation, concealment, or nondisclosure, whether negligent or innocent; or any other substantive legal theory in tort or contract whatsoever.[1] Any complaint filed in a product liability action is required to state the amount of damages sought to be recovered from any defendant.[2]

B. STATUTES OF LIMITATION

Any action against a manufacturer or seller of a product for injury to the personal property which is caused by its defective or unreasonably dangerous condition must be brought within the periods set forth as follows:

A cause of action for personal injury accrues from the date of the personal injury, not the date of the negligence or the sale of the product, and the person may maintain the cause of action until one year from the date of injury.[3]

For tort actions resulting in injuries to personal or real property, the action must be commenced within three years from the accrual of the cause of action.[4]

Actions to recover damages for any deficiency in the design, planning, supervision, observation of construction, or construction of an improvement to real property for injury to property, real or personal, that arises out of that deficiency, or for injury to the person or for wrongful death arising out of any deficiency, shall be brought within four years after substantial completion of such an improvement.[5]

Additionally, any action for breach of any contract for sale must be commenced within four years after the cause of action has accrued, unless the parties by original agreement reduce the period of limitation to not less than one year.[6] A cause of action accrues when the breach occurs, and a breach of warranty occurs when tender of delivery is made, except that where a warranty explicitly extends to future performance of the goods and discovery of the breach must await the time of such conformance, the cause of action accrues when the breach is or should have been discovered.[7]

Notwithstanding these limitations of actions provisions, the action must be brought within six years of the date of the injury, and in any event the action must be brought within ten years from the date on which the product was first purchased for use or consumption, or within one year after the expiration of the anticipated life of the product, whichever is shorter.[8] An exception to this provision involves injury to minors, in which case the action must be brought within the limitations period as stated above or a period of one year after attaining the age of majority.[9]

Furthermore, note that the language requiring that in any event the action must be brought within the shorter of ten years from the date when the product was first purchased or within one year after the expiration of the anticipated life of the product does not apply to actions resulting from exposure to asbestos.[10] However, the asbestos exception cannot be applied retroactively to revive a plaintiff's cause of action which was already barred as of the enactment of the 1979 asbestos exception by the Tennessee legislature.[11]

The limitation of actions for the human implantation of silicone gel breast implants that are not pending or decided on or before May 26, 1993, provides that any action against a manufacturer or seller for injury to a person caused by a silicone gel breast implant must be brought within a period not to exceed twenty-five years from the date such product was implanted; however, such action must be brought within four years from the date the plaintiff knew or should have known of the injury.[12] In defining the statute of limitations for silicone gel breast implants, "seller" does not include a hospital or other medical care facility where the procedure took place, nor shall it include the physician or other medical personnel involved in the procedure.[13]

Under Tennessee law, a cause of action accrues when the injury occurs or is discovered, or when in the exercise of reasonable care and diligence it should have been discovered.[14]

Tennessee has recognized specific time and filing requirements for the joinder of additional defendants in civil actions where comparative fault is or becomes an issue and a defendant alleges in an answer or amended answer that a person not a party to the suit caused or contributed to the injury or damage for which the plaintiff seeks to recover.[15]

C. STRICT LIABILITY

1. The Standard

A manufacturer or seller of a product shall not be liable for any injury to person or property caused by the product unless the product is determined to be in a defective condition or unreasonably dangerous at the time it left the control of the manufacturer or seller.[16] Regardless of the legal theory, plaintiff must prove the product was defective.[17]

"Unreasonably dangerous" means a product is dangerous to an extent beyond that which would be contemplated by the ordinary consumer who purchases it, with the ordinary knowledge common to the community as to its characteristics, or that the product because of its dangerous condition would not be put on the market by a reasonable product manufacturer or seller assuming that he knew of its dangerous condition.[18]

2. "Defective Condition"

"Defective condition" means a condition of a product that renders it unsafe for normal or anticipatable handling and consumption.[19]

3. Contributory Negligence/Assumption of Risk

Tennessee has rejected the doctrine of contributory negligence in favor of a modified comparative fault doctrine.[20] Tennessee courts have ruled that the modified comparative fault doctrine applies to strict liability cases.[21] Tennessee courts now differentiate between express and implied assumption of risk, having abolished the latter doctrine.[22]

4. Sale or Lease

Under Tennessee law, "manufacturer" is defined as a designer, fabricator, producer, compounder, processor, or assembler of any product or its component parts.[23]

"Seller" includes a retailer, wholesaler, or distributor and any individual or entity engaged in the business of selling a product, whether such sale is for resale or for use or consumption. "Seller" also includes a lessor or bailor engaged in the business of leasing or bailment of a product.[24] The seller's liability is set forth by statute and provides that a seller is not liable when the product is acquired and sold by the seller in a sealed container and/or when the product is acquired and sold by the seller under circumstances in which the seller is afforded no reasonable opportunity to inspect the product in such a manner that would or should, in the exercise of reasonable care, reveal the existence of the defective condition.[25] This provision does not apply to actions based on breach of warranty, express or implied, to actions where the manufacturer of the product or part in question should not be subject to service of process in the State of Tennessee or by long-arm statutes of Tennessee, or in actions where the manufacturer has been judicially declared insolvent.[26]

A product liability action that is based on the doctrine of strict liability in tort shall not be commenced or maintained against any seller of a product that is alleged to contain or possess a defective condition unreasonably dangerous to the buyer, user, or consumer unless said seller is also the manufacturer of said product or the manufacturer of the part thereof claimed to be defective, or unless the manufacturer of the product or part in question shall not be subject to service of process in the State of Tennessee or service cannot be secured by the long-arm statutes of Tennessee or unless such manufacturer has been judicially declared insolvent.[27]

If the action is not a product liability action for personal injury or property damage, then provisions of the Uniform Commercial Code would control, and an actual sale would be required.[28]

5. Inherently Dangerous Products

A person who deals with inherently dangerous instrumentalities is recognized as having a duty to exercise caution commensurate with the danger or peril involved.[29] The basis of liability is negligence and not absolute liability.[30]

6. Successor Liability

There are no reported cases on this issue in Tennessee. However, the U.S. District Court for the Eastern District of Tennessee anticipated how Tennessee would handle this issue by applying the traditional corporate test that a corporate acquisition structured as a purchase of assets for cash does not give rise to liability on the part of the successor corporation for injuries caused by a defective product manufactured and sold by the predecessor and for which the successor assumed no liability.[31]

7. Privity

Privity is not a requirement for maintaining an action for personal injury or property damage brought on account of negligence, strict liability, or breach of warranty, including actions brought under the provisions of the Uniform Commercial Code.[32]

8. Failure to Warn

A plaintiff who relies on the theory of failure to warn must prove that the product was in a defective condition or unreasonably dangerous at the time it left the control of the manufacturer or seller.[33] A product is not recognized as being unreasonably dangerous because of failure to adequately warn of a danger or hazard that is apparent to the ordinary user.[34]

9. Post-Sale Duty to Warn

There are no reported decisions by Tennessee courts regarding a post-sale duty to warn. The courts may, however, base a future decision concerning a post-sale duty to warn on the statute that provides that regardless of the theory of recovery, a manufacturer or seller is not liable in a product liability action unless the product is determined to be in a defective condition or unreasonably dangerous at the time it left the control of the manufacturer or seller.[35]

10. Substantial Change/Abnormal Use

If a product is not unreasonably dangerous at the time it leaves the control of the manufacturer or seller but was made unreasonably dangerous by subsequent unforeseeable alteration, change, improper maintenance, or abnormal use, the manufacturer or seller is not liable.[36]

11. State of the Art

In determining whether a product is in a defective condition or unreasonably dangerous at the time it left the control of the manufacturer or seller, the state of scientific and technological knowledge available to the manufacturer or seller at the time the product was placed on the market, rather than at the time of injury, is applicable.[37] Consideration is given also to the customary designs, methods, standards, and techniques of manufacturing, inspecting, and testing by other manufacturers or sellers of similar products.[38]

12. Malfunction

In a product liability action in which recovery is based on the theory of strict liability, the plaintiff must establish the existence of a defect in the product.[39]

13. Standards and Government Regulations

A manufacturer's or seller's compliance with any federal or state statute or administrative regulation existing at the time a product was manufactured and prescribing standards for design, inspection, testing, manufacture, labeling, warning, or instructions for use of a product raises a rebuttable presumption that the product is not in an unreasonably dangerous condition with regard to matters covered by these standards.[40]

14. Other Accidents

Tennessee law does not require proof of the exact identity of conditions in order to render evidence of prior accidents admissible, but does require conditions to be substantially the same.[41]

15. Misrepresentation

Tennessee recognizes a product liability action based on misrepresentation, concealment, or nondisclosure, whether negligent or innocent.[42] Section 402B of the Restatement (Second) of Torts has been adopted by Tennessee.[43] Tennessee no longer recognizes Restatement of Torts section 552(D) as giving rise to a product liability cause of action for pecuniary loss based on innocent misrepresentation.[44]

D. NEGLIGENCE

In product liability cases based on negligence, the plaintiff must establish the existence of a defect in the product and has the additional burden of proving that the defective condition of the product was a result of neg-ligence in the manufacturing process or that the manufacturer or seller knew or should have known of the defective condition.[45] The negligence standard is the failure to do what a reasonable and prudent person would ordinarily do under the circumstances.[46]

Tennessee has adopted a modified comparative fault system that entitles the plaintiff to recover so long as the plaintiff's negligence remains less than that of the defendant(s).[47] The comparative fault principles are to be applied to all cases tried or retried after May 4, 1992, and to all cases on appeal in which the application of comparative fault had been requested or asserted in the trial court and in which the request or assertion was pre-served as a ground for appeal.[48] The doctrines of remote contributory negligence, last clear chance, and joint and several liability are now obso-lete.[49] Furthermore, the allegation that a nonparty caused or contributed to the injury or damage for which recovery is sought is an affirmative defense.[50] However, under the modified comparative fault doctrine, the fault of a nonparty may be attributed only to those persons against whom a plaintiff has a cause of action in tort.[51]

E. BREACH OF WARRANTY

Tennessee recognizes a product liability action based on the theories of breach of warranty, express or implied.[52]

The statute requiring that a manufacturer or seller of a product is not liable for any injury to person or property caused by the product unless the product is in a defective condition or is unreasonably dangerous at the time it left the control of the manufacturer or seller does not apply to an action based on express warranty.[53]

As in the case of negligence and strict liability, causes of action for personal injury or property damage brought on account of breach of warranty, including actions brought under the provisions of the Uniform Commercial Code, do not require privity in order for the plaintiff to maintain an ac-tion.[54]

F. PUNITIVE DAMAGES

Punitive damages are recoverable in product liability actions,[55] however, punitive damages are not recoverable as a matter of right, but rest within the sound discretion of the trier of fact.[56] To recover punitive damages, actual damages must be shown.[57] Punitive damages are awarded only in cases in which the court finds that the defendant acted intentionally, fraudulently, maliciously, or recklessly.[58] The plaintiff must find defen-dant's conduct by clear and convincing evidence.[59] On motion of defen-dant, the court shall bifurcate the trial with the fact finder determining liability for and the amount of compensatory damages, as well as liability for punitive damages, in the first phase; the amount of punitive damages shall be determined in the second phase pursuant to the factors listed in the *Hodges* opinion.[60]

G. STATUTES

The Tennessee Products Liability Act of 1978 provides the framework of law governing product liability actions.[61] Additionally, limitation of action statutes,[62] as well as particular Uniform Commercial Code Sections governing breach of warranty actions, are applicable.[63]

Reported cases as of December 31, 1997.

W. Kyle Carpenter
J. Ford Little
WOOLF, MCCLANE, BRIGHT,
ALLEN & CARPENTER, PLLC
Suite 900, Riverview Tower
P.O. Box 900
Knoxville, Tennessee 37901
(Phone) (423) 215-1000
(Fax) (423) 215-1001

ENDNOTES - TENNESSEE

1. Tenn. Code Ann. §29-28-102(6) (1980).

2. Id. §29-28-107 (1980).

3. Id. §28-3-104(b) (Supp. 1997).

4. Id. §28-3-105 (Supp. 1997).

5. Id. §28-3-202 (1980).

6. Id. §47-2-725(1) (1996).

7. Id. §47-2-725(2) (1996).

8. Id. §29-28-103(a) (Supp. 1997).

9. Id.; e.g., *Holt v. Hypro, a Div. of Lear Siegler, Inc.*, 746 F.2d 353 (6th Cir. 1984).

10. Tenn. Code Ann. §29-28-103(b) (Supp. 1997).

11. *Wyatt v. A-Best Products Co., Inc.*, 924 S.W.2d 98 (Tenn. Ct. App. 1995).

12. Id. §29-28-103(c) (Supp. 1997).

13. Id.

14. *Buckner v. GAF Corp.*, 495 F. Supp. 351 (E.D. Tenn. 1979); see also *McCroskey v. Bryant Air Conditioning Co.*, 524 S.W.2d 487 (Tenn. 1975); *Wyatt v. A-Best Company, Inc.*, 910 S.W. 2d 851 (Tenn. Ct. App. 1995).

15. Tenn. Code Ann. §20-1-119 (1994).

16. Id. §29-28-105(a) (1980); e.g., *Smith v. Detroit Marine Eng. Corp.*, 712 S.W.2d 472 (Tenn. Ct. App. 1985).

17. *Fulton v. Pfizer Hospital Products Group, Inc.*, 872 S.W.2d 908 (Tenn. Ct. App. 1993).

18. Tenn. Code Ann. §29-28-102(8) (1980); e.g., *Holman v. BIC Corp.*, 925 S.W.2d 527 (Tenn. 1996).

19. Id. §29-28-102(2) (1980).

20. *McIntyre v. Balentine*, 833 S.W.2d 52 (Tenn. 1992).

21. *Whitehead v. Toyota Motor Corp.*, 897 S.W.2d 684 (Tenn. 1995); see also *McKinnie v. Lundell Mfg. Co., Inc.*, 825 F. Supp. 834 (W.D. Tenn. 1993).

22. *Perez v. McConkey*, 872 S.W.2d 897 (Tenn. 1994).

23. Tenn. Code Ann. §29-28-102(4) (1980).

24. Id. §29-28-102(7) (1980).

25. Id. §29-28-106 (Supp. 1997).

26. Id.

27. Id.

28. *Baker v. Promark Prods. West, Inc.*, 692 S.W.2d 844 (Tenn. 1985).

29. *International Harvester Co. v. Sartain*, 222 S.W.2d 854 (Tenn. Ct. App. 1948).

30. Id. See also *Pierce v. United States*, 142 F. Supp. 721 (E.D. Tenn. 1955), *aff'd*, *United States v. Pierce*, 235 F.2d 466 (6th Cir. 1956); see also *Wilson v. Electric Power Bd. of Chattanooga*, 544 S.W.2d 92 (Tenn. 1976).

31. *Poole v. Amsted Indus., Inc.*, No. CIV-1-76-75 (E.D. Tenn. Oct. 5, 1976), 575 F.2d 1338 (6th Cir. 1972) (TABLE No. 76-2652). See generally *Woody v. Combustion Engineering, Inc.*, 463 F. Supp. 817 (E.D. Tenn. 1978).

32. Tenn. Code Ann. §29-34-104 (1980); e.g., *Commercial Truck and Trailer Sales v. McCampbell*, 580 S.W.2d 765 (Tenn. 1979).

33. *Pemberton v. American Distilled Spirits Co.*, 664 S.W.2d 690 (Tenn. 1984); *Smith v. Detroit Marine Engineering Corp.*, 712 S.W.2d 472 (Tenn. Ct. App. 1985).

34. Tenn. Code Ann. §29-28-105(d) (1980).

35. Id. §29-28-105(a) (1980).

36. Id. §29-28-108 (1980).

37. Id. §29-28-105(b) (1980).

38.   Id.

39.   *Browder v. Pettigrew*, 541 S.W.2d 402 (Tenn. 1976); *Whaley v. Rheem Mfg. Co.*, 900 S.W.2d 296 (Tenn. Ct. App. 1995).

40.   Tenn. Code Ann. §29-28-104 (1980).

41.   *Powers v. J. B. Michael and Co.*, 329 F.2d 674 (6th Cir. 1964), *cert. denied*, 377 U.S. 980 (1964); *see also Sweeney v. State*, 768 S.W.2d 253 (Tenn. 1989); *Graham v. Cloar*, 205 S.W.2d 764 (Tenn. Ct. App. 1947); *Winfree v. Coca-Cola Bottling Works of Lebanon*, 83 S.W.2d 903 (Tenn. Ct. App. 1935).

42.   Tenn. Code Ann. §29-28-102(6) (1980).

43.   *Ford Motor Co. v. Lonon*, 398 S.W.2d 240 (Tenn. 1966).

44.   *First Natl. Bank of Louisville v. Brooks Farms*, 821 S.W.2d 925 (Tenn. 1991).

45.   *Browder*, 541 S.W.2d 402.

46.   *Groce Provision Co. v. Dortch*, 350 S.W.2d 409 (Tenn. Ct. App. 1961).

47.   *McIntyre v. Balentine*, 833 S.W.2d 52 (Tenn. 1992).

48.   *Cook v. Spinnaker's of Rivergate, Inc.*, 846 S.W.2d 810 (Tenn. 1993); *rev'd on other grounds*, 878 S.W.2d 934 (Tenn. 1994).

49.   *McIntyre*, 833 S.W.2d at 57-58.

50.   Id. at 58.

51.   *Ridings v. The Ralph M. Parsons Co.*, 914 S.W.2d 79 (Tenn. 1996).

52.   Tenn. Code Ann. §29-28-102(6) (1980).

53.   Id. §29-28-105(c) (1980).

54.   Id. §29-34-104 (1980).

55.   *Cathey v. Johns-Manville Sales Corp.*, 776 F.2d 1565 (6th Cir. 1985), *cert. denied*, 478 U.S. 1021 (1986).

56.   *Huckeby v. Spangler*, 563 S.W.2d 555 (Tenn. 1978); *B. F. Myers & Son of Goodlettsville, Inc. v. Evans*, 612 S.W.2d 912 (Tenn. App. 1980).

57. *Solomon v. First Am. Natl. Bank of Nashville*, 774 S.W.2d 935 (Tenn. App. 1989).

58. *Hodges v. S. C. Toof & Co.*, 833 S.W.2d 896 (Tenn. 1992).

59. Id. at 901.

60. Id. at 901-902.

61. Tenn. Code Ann. §29-28-101 et seq. (1980 & Supp. 1997).

62. See id. §§28-3-104, 28-3-105, 28-3-202 (1980 & Supp. 1997); id. §47-2-725 (1996).

63. See id. §47-1-101 et seq. (1996).

TEXAS

A. CAUSES OF ACTION

Product liability lawsuits commonly included causes of action for strict liability, negligence, breach of warranty, and violation of the Texas Deceptive Trade Practices Act (DTPA).[1] The DTPA, however, will no longer apply to suits for personal injuries, for causes of action accruing on or after September 1, 1995, or filed on or after September 1, 1996.[2]

B. STATUTES OF LIMITATIONS

Causes of action for wrongful death, personal injury, or property damage must be brought within two years, whether brought in strict liability or in negligence, after the cause of action accrues.[3] Causes of action for wrongful death accrue on the death of the injured person.[4] Most other causes of action accrue at the time of the injury.[5] A cause of action under the DTPA must be brought within two years.[6] A liberal "discovery" rule applies.[7] A cause of action for breach of warranty under the Texas Uniform Commercial Code must be brought within four years of the date of delivery of the product.[8]

A fifteen-year statute of repose protects manufacturers or sellers of manufacturing equipment (equipment and machinery used in the manufacturing, processing, or fabrication of tangible personal property — but not agricultural machinery) for causes of action accruing on or after September 1, 1993, unless the manufacturer expressly represents that the equipment has a useful, safe life of longer than fifteen years.[9]

C. STRICT LIABILITY

1. The Standard

Texas has adopted section 402A of the Restatement (Second) of Torts.[10]

(1) Sale or Lease

Strict liability applies to any person in the chain of a product's distribution.[11] The defendant must, as a part of its business, be involved in selling, leasing, or otherwise placing into the course of commerce products similar to the one involved in the suit, by transactions that are essentially commercial in character.[12] Strict liability does not apply to a product that never actually entered the course of commerce.[13]

A seller is entitled to indemnity from the manufacturer so long as the seller did not negligently alter or modify the product, or engage in some other act or omission for which the seller is independently liable.[14]

2. **Privity**

Privity of contract is not required in strict product liability cases.[15]

2. **Economic Loss**

There can be no recovery in strict liability for purely economic loss,[16] which includes damage to the product itself.[17]

3. **Definition of "Defect"**

In a manufacturing defect or failure to warn case, the "consumer expectations" test applies. A "defect" is defined as a condition of the product that renders it "unreasonably dangerous,"[18] or dangerous to an extent beyond that which would be contemplated by the ordinary user of the product, with the ordinary knowledge common to the community as to the product's characteristics.[19]

In a design defect case, for claims accruing prior to September 1, 1993, the "risk-utility balancing" test applies, in which a "defectively designed" product is defined as a product that is unreasonably dangerous as designed, taking into consideration the utility of the product and the risk involved in its use.[20] For claims which accrued after September 1, 1993, to recover for a strict products liability claim based on design defect, the plaintiff must prove that there was a "safe alternative design" that would have prevented or significantly reduced the risk of injury and was economically and technologically feasible at the time the product left the seller's or manufacturer's control.[21]

4. **Substantial Change or Alteration**

A manufacturer is not responsible for injuries caused by a substantial change to or alteration of the product, but the change or alteration must be one that could not be reasonably foreseen or expected.[22] Similarly, an original designer of a product cannot be held strictly liable when he licenses the design to another party who modifies the design and manufactures and markets a defective product based on the modified design.[23]

5. **Causation**

Producing cause is required in strict liability cases. A "producing cause" is an efficient, exciting, or contributing cause that, in a natural sequence, produced the occurrence or injury. Foreseeability is not required. There may be more than one producing cause.[24]

6. **Claimant's Negligence/Comparative Responsibility/Assumption of Risk**

Comparative responsibility is a defense. For actions that accrued prior to September 1, 1995, a claimant's recovery against a strictly liable defendant is completely barred if the claimant is 60 percent responsible for the injury.[25] Where the claimant's percentage of responsibility is less than 60 percent, the claimant's damages are reduced by the claimant's percentage of responsibility.[26]

For claims which accrue on or after September 1, 1995, or are filed on or after September 1, 1996, a claimant may not recover damages if his percentage of responsibility is greater than 50 percent.[27] If the claimants' percentage of responsibility is 50 percent or less, the court must reduce the amount of damages to be recovered by the claimant by a percentage equal to the claimant's percentage of responsibility.[28]

There are also provisions for allocating responsibility to settling parties[29] and third-party defendants[30] and for reducing the plaintiff's damages to account for settlements.[31]

Assumption of the risk and misuse are subsumed in the contributory negligence question.[32]

A user or consumer is not negligent for failing to discover or guard against a product defect, unless such failure rises to the level of assumption of the risk.[33] In such a case, a plaintiff assumes the risk of injury if he or she actually knew of the condition that caused the injury, fully appreciated the nature and extent of the danger involved, and voluntarily encountered the danger.[34]

7. **Causation by Third Parties, Including Employers**

The defense of "sole cause" applies to product liability cases. If the conduct of a nonparty was the sole cause of the injury, then no other person or product could be a producing cause.[35] The conduct of a plaintiff's employer can constitute the sole cause of injury.[36] The conduct of a plaintiff's employer is not submitted, however, as a part of any comparative responsibility question. A plaintiff's recovery is not reduced by the percentage of the employer's responsibility if the employer is less than the sole cause.[37]

8. **Failure to Warn**

A strict liability action for failure to warn requires that the lack of an adequate warning renders the product unreasonably dangerous. Such a product is said to have a "marketing defect." A seller is liable if it fails to give adequate *warnings* of the product's dangers that were known or that should have been known, or if a seller fails to give adequate *instructions* to avoid such dangers, thereby rendering the product unreasonably dangerous.[38] The "consumer expectation" test applies.[39] A manufacturer does not have a duty to warn or instruct about another manufacturer's products, even though those products might be used in connection with the manufacturer's own product.[40] There is a rebuttable presumption that, if given, an adequate warning would have been read and heeded.[41] The existence of a duty to warn of the dangers of an alleged defective product is a question of law.[42]

"Adequate" warnings and instructions are defined as warnings and instructions in a form that could reasonably be expected to catch the attention of a reasonably prudent person in the circumstances of a product's use. Their content must be comprehensible to the average user and must convey a fair indication of the nature and extent of the danger and how to avoid it.[43]

9. Warnings to Intermediaries

In the case of prescription drugs and certain medical devices, a seller can satisfy the duty to warn by furnishing adequate warnings and instructions to the prescribing physician, who is considered a "learned intermediary."[44]

A seller whose product is not sold directly to the ultimate user may satisfy its duty to warn by reasonably assuring itself that its customer is adequately trained and warned, familiar with the characteristics and safe uses of the product, and capable of passing on its knowledge to the ultimate consumer.[45]

10. Inherently Unsafe Products

For cases filed prior to September 1, 1993, an inherently dangerous product was considered defective if it was not accompanied by adequate warnings and instructions.[46] For cases commenced on or after September 1, 1993, a manufacturer or seller is not liable if a product is inherently unsafe and is known to be unsafe by the ordinary consumer and the product is a common consumer product intended for personal consumption, such as sugar, castor oil, alcohol, tobacco, and butter, as identified in comment (i) to Section 402A of the Restatement (Second) of Torts.[47]

11. No Post-Sale Duties

There is no post-sale duty to warn or to recall a product.[48] If a manufacturer regains control of a used product and resells it, however, the product may be judged by the technology available at the time of resale.[49]

12. Subsequent Remedial Measures

The Texas Rule of Evidence on subsequent remedial measures differs from the Federal Rule in that it does not "preclude admissibility [of subsequent remedial measures] in products liability cases based on strict liability."[50]

13. State of the Art

Whether a product is defectively designed is judged in the context of the state of technical knowledge existing at the time the product was manufactured.[51]

Evidence that the product complied with customary industrial or governmental standards is admissible, but generally is not conclusive evidence that the product is free of defect.[52] In federal courts, compliance with government safety standards is considered "strong and substantial evidence that a product is not defective."[53]

14. Industry Liability

The Texas Supreme Court has expressly stated that theories of industry liability based on concert of action, market share, or enterprise liability are neither approved nor disapproved in product liability cases.[54] Lower courts have utilized the theory of alternative liability to shift the burden of proving the identity of a product's manufacturer to the defendants when the plaintiff has no means of identifying the product.[55] Although lower courts have recognized conspiracy as a products liability cause of action,[56] the Texas Supreme Court has rejected this idea by holding that civil conspiracy is an intentional tort requiring a specific intent, thus it cannot be based on negligence.[57]

15. Circumstantial Evidence

A defect may be proved by circumstantial evidence.[58]

16. Other Accidents

Evidence of other accidents is admissible if there is proof that the other accidents involved the same product and occurred under reasonably similar circumstances.[59]

17. Misrepresentation

Section 402B of the Restatement (Second) of Torts has been adopted in Texas.[60]

D. NEGLIGENCE

Negligence is a well-established product liability cause of action in Texas. Unlike strict liability, which focuses on the product itself, negligence focuses on the conduct of the product manufacturer.[61]

1. Causation

Proximate cause, including foreseeability, is required in negligence cases.[62]

2. Claimant's Negligence/Comparative Responsibility

In negligence actions, a claimant's recovery against a negligent defendant is barred if the claimant is more than 50 percent responsible for the occurrence or injury.[63] If a claimant's responsibility is 50 percent or less, the claimant's damages are reduced by the percentage of the claimant's responsibility.[64]

3. Subsequent Remedial Measures

Subsequent remedial measures are inadmissible unless the action is based on strict liability or if the subsequent remedial measure is offered to prove ownership, control or feasibility of precautionary measures, if controverted, or impeachment.[65]

E. BREACH OF WARRANTY

1. Warranties Recognized

Texas has adopted the Uniform Commercial Code, including its definitions of express and implied warranties.[66]

2. Causation

Proximate cause, including foreseeability, is required in warranty cases.[67]

3. Used Products

No warranty is implied when the purchaser knows the goods are used.[68]

4. Claimant's Negligence/Comparative Responsibility

The same system of comparative responsibility applies in warranty cases as in strict liability and negligence cases.[69]

5. Community Knowledge

Community knowledge must be considered in determining whether an implied warranty exists, and an implied warranty cannot contradict the community's common knowledge.[70]

6. Reliance

Express warranty claims require a showing of reliance on the part of the plaintiff.[71]

7. Deceptive Trade Practices Act Remedies

Breach of express and implied warranty are included among the violations of the Texas Deceptive Trade Practices Act,[72] which allows recovery of statutory penalties and up to three times the amount of "actual" damages (for actions accruing before September 1, 1995) or "economic" damages (for actions accruing on or after September 1, 1995, or suits filed on or after September 1, 1996).[73]

F. TEXAS DECEPTIVE TRADE PRACTICES-CONSUMER PROTECTION ACT ("DTPA")

For actions accruing before September 1, 1995, and filed before September 1, 1996, a consumer may recover "actual" damages for certain acts defined as deceptive trade practices. Additional damages of up to three times the amount of actual damages may be awarded if the defendant's conduct was knowing.[74]

For actions accruing on or after September 1, 1995, or suits filed on or after September 1, 1996, a consumer may recover "economic" or "mental anguish" damages for certain acts defined as deceptive trade practices. Additional damages of up to three times the amount of economic or mental anguish damages may be awarded if the defendant's conduct was knowing or intentional.[75]

1. Who Can Sue

Plaintiff must be a statutorily defined "consumer." A business consumer with assets of $25 million or more (or controlled by an entity with assets of $25 million or more) has no standing to bring suit under the DTPA.[76] For claims accruing on or after September 1, 1995, or suits filed on or after September 1, 1996, the DTPA does not apply to a claim for damages based on the rendering of a professional service, the essence of which is the providing of advice, judgment, opinion, or a professional skill, unless the claim involves:

(1) an express misrepresentation of a material fact that cannot be characterized as advice, judgment or opinion;

(2) a failure to disclose information in order to fraudulently induce a consumer into a transaction;

(3) an unconscionable action that cannot be characterized as advice, judgment, or opinion; and

(4) a breach of an express warranty that cannot be characterized as advice, judgment, or opinion.[77]

The DTPA also does not apply to:

(1) a claim for bodily injury, death, or the infliction of mental anguish, except to the extent that mental anguish damages would otherwise be properly recoverable under the DTPA or to the extent another statute permits recovery of DTPA damages;

(2) a claim arising out of a written contract if the transaction at issue involves consideration by a consumer of more than $100,000, the consumer is represented by counsel of his own choice while negotiating the contract, and the contract does not involve the consumer's residence; and

(3) a claim arising out of a transaction that involves consideration by the consumer of more than $500,000 and that does not involve the consumer's residence.[78]

2. Deceptive Practices and Misrepresentations

The DTPA penalizes a "laundry list" of 25 specific activities. A breach of warranty is also a DTPA violation.[79] However, the DTPA does not create any new warranties or extend existing warranties.[80]

3. In Connection With a Sale or Lease

The DTPA protects consumers from "deceptive trade practices *made in connection with the purchase or lease* of any goods or services."[81] The Texas Supreme Court recently characterized this as a limitation on the liability of parties along the distribution or production chain of a product, and determined that the DTPA was not intended "to reach upstream manufacturers and suppliers when their misrepresentations are not communicated to the consumer."[82] Nevertheless, the downstream seller found directly liable to the consumer may seek contribution if "the seller's DTPA liability is caused or contributed to by the otherwise actionable misconduct of upstream manufacturers or suppliers."[83]

4. Causation

Producing cause is required in a DTPA action.[84]

5. Damages

For claims accruing before September 1, 1995, and filed before September 1, 1996, "actual" damages are recoverable under the DTPA to the extent allowed by common law. "Actual" damages are either "out of pocket" or "benefit of the bargain" damages, whichever is greater.[85]

For claims accruing on or after September 1, 1995, or suits filed on or after September 1, 1996, "economic" damages are recoverable. "Economic" damages are "compensatory damages for pecuniary loss." "Economic" damages do not include exemplary damages or damages for physical pain and mental anguish, loss of consortium, disfigurement, physical impairment, or loss of companionship or society.[86] Mental anguish damages are allowed only if the defendant acted intentionally or knowingly.[87] For claims accruing on or after September 1, 1995, or suits filed on or after September 1, 1996, prejudgment interest awards are limited.[88]

For all DTPA claims, additional damages of up to three times the amount of actual, economic, or mental anguish damages may be awarded by the finder of fact to punish a knowing or intentional deceptive practice, misrepresentation, or breach of warranty.[89] A plaintiff may not recover both punitive damages and additional DTPA damages.[90] Additional DTPA damages and attorneys' fees require an award of actual or economic damages.[91] In computing additional DTPA damages for claims accruing on or after September 1, 1995, or suits filed on or after September 1, 1996, attorneys' fees, costs, and prejudgment interest may not be considered.[92]

6. Attorneys' Fees

Attorneys' fees and court costs may be recovered by a successful DTPA plaintiff.[93] Attorneys' fees and court costs may also be awarded against a party whose DTPA claim is groundless, brought in bad faith, or brought for the purpose of harassment.[94] However, attorneys' fees under the DTPA must be awarded as a specific dollar amount and not as a percentage of the judgment.[95]

7. Comparative Responsibility

The comparative responsibility statute applies to DTPA suits for personal injury or property damage filed after September 1, 1989.[96] The DTPA provides for contribution and indemnity rights to the extent provided by common law or statute.[97]

G. JOINT AND SEVERAL LIABILITY

A defendant is always liable for the percentage of actual damages equal to its own percentage of responsibility.[98]

For causes of action accruing before September 1, 1995, and filed before September 1, 1996, a defendant is only jointly and severally liable if (1) the plaintiff is not found responsible and (2) the defendant's share of responsibility is greater than 10 percent. In a negligence case, the defendant will also be jointly and severally liable if its share of responsibility is both greater than 20 percent and greater than that of the plaintiff.[99] A defendant found liable in a toxic tort case is always jointly and severally liable for all of the plaintiff's damages.[100]

For causes of action accruing on or after September 1, 1995, or suits filed on or after September 1, 1996, a defendant is only jointly and severally liable if the defendant's share of responsibility is greater than 50 percent. However, in cases involving toxic tort claims, a defendant is jointly and severally liable if the defendant's share of responsibility is 15 percent or greater.[101]

H. PUNITIVE DAMAGES

1. The Standard

For causes of action accruing before September 1, 1995, punitive damages may be awarded for gross negligence. Gross negligence is more than momentary thoughtlessness, inadvertence, or error of judgment. It means such an entire want of care as to establish that the act or omission was the result of actual conscious indifference to the rights, safety, or welfare of the person affected.[102] An act or omission that is merely thoughtless, careless, or not inordinately risky cannot constitute gross negligence. Only if a defendant's act or omission is unjustifiable and likely to cause serious harm can it be grossly negligent. Furthermore, a grossly negligent defendant must be consciously indifferent and have actual subjective knowledge of an extreme risk of serious harm.[103]

For causes of action accruing on or after September 1, 1995, punitive damages may be awarded if the plaintiff proves by clear and convincing evidence that the defendant acted fraudulently, with malice, or, in a wrongful death action, with willfulness or gross neglect.[104] "Fraud" is defined as any fraud except constructive fraud.[105] "Malice" and "gross neglect" are defined in the same manner as "gross negligence" under the pre-September 1, 1995, standard.[106]

2. Actual Damages Required

Punitive damages may not be awarded in the absence of actual damages.[107]

3. Limits on Punitive Damages

For claims accruing before September 1, 1995, punitive damages are limited to the greater of $200,000 or four times the amount of actual damages, unless the claim involves an intentional tort or actual malice is proved.[108]

For claims accruing on or after September 1, 1995, punitive damages are limited to the greater of (a) two times "economic damages" plus non-economic damages up to $750,000 or (b) $200,000.[109] "Economic damages" means compensatory damages for pecuniary loss and excludes damages for physical pain, mental anguish, loss of consortium, companionship, and society, disfigurement, and physical impairment.[110] The only exception to these damages limits arises if the defendant's conduct on which the request for punitive damages is based arises from the knowing or intentional commission of certain felony conduct.[111] The applicability of this exception to product liability actions is currently unknown.

4. No Joint and Several Liability for Punitive Damages

A defendant is liable only for the punitive damages assessed against it. There is no joint or several liability for punitive damages.[112]

I. SUCCESSOR LIABILITY

A successor corporation acquiring all or substantially all of the manufacturing assets of another corporation is not liable for injuries caused by products made by the predecessor corporation in the absence of an agreement to assume such liabilities or proof of actual fraud.[113]

J. STATUTES AND REFERENCES

Relevant statutes for product liability actions include the statutes of limitations,[114] comparative responsibility,[115] damage limitations,[116] the Uniform Commercial Code (Sales),[117] the Deceptive Trade Practices Act,[118] and the Products Liability Act.[119]

Texas state courts generally follow the *Texas Pattern Jury Charge*. The *Malpractice, Premises & Products* volume addresses product liability cases. The

Business, Consumer & Employment volume addresses the Deceptive Trade Practices Act.[120]

James Edward Maloney
Maria Wyckoff Boyce
John Withers Clay
BAKER & BOTTS, L.L.P.
One Shell Plaza
910 Louisiana
Houston, TX 77002-4995
(713) 229-1234

ENDNOTES - TEXAS

1.   Tex. Bus. & Comm. Code Ann. §17.46-17.63 (Vernon 1987) (for causes of action accruing before September 1, 1995, and which were filed before September 1, 1996), *amended by* Acts 1995, 74th Leg., ch. 414, §1.

2.   Tex. Bus. & Comm. Code Ann. §17.49(e) (Vernon Supp. 1998).

3.   Tex. Civ. Prac. & Rem. Code Ann. §16.003 (Vernon 1986 & Supp. 1998).

4.   Tex. Civ. Prac. & Rem. Code Ann. §16.003(b) (Vernon 1986).

5.   *Moreno v. Sterling Drug, Inc.*, 787 S.W.2d 348, 351 (Tex. 1990).

6.   Tex. Bus. & Comm. Code Ann. §17.565 (Vernon 1987).

7.   Tex. Bus. & Comm. Code Ann. §17.565 (Vernon 1987); see also *Burns v. Thomas*, 786 S.W.2d 266, 267 (Tex. 1990).

8.   Tex. Bus. & Comm. Code Ann. §2.725 (Tex. UCC) (Vernon 1994); see also *Weeks v. J. I. Case Co.*, 694 S.W.2d 634, 636 (Tex. App. — Texarkana 1985, writ ref'd n.r.e.).

9.   Tex. Civ. Prac. & Rem. Code Ann. §16.012 (Vernon Supp. 1998). A ten-year statute of repose for causes of action against persons making improvements to real property had been held to protect product manufacturers whose products were installed as improvements to real property. Tex. Civ. Prac. & Rem. Code Ann. §16.009 (Vernon 1986); *Conkle v. Builders Concrete Prods. Mfg. Co.*, 749 S.W.2d 489, 490-491 (Tex. 1988). The Texas Supreme Court, however, has recently overruled *Conkle*, and held that this statute of repose cannot be used to protect manufacturers of products. *Sonnier v. Chisholm Ryder Co. Inc.*, 909 S.W.2d 475, 478-483 (Tex. 1995); see *Astec Indus. Inc. v. Suarez*, 921 S.W.2d 794, 797 (Tex. App.—Fort Worth 1996, no writ).

10.   *Firestone Steel Prods. Co. v. Barajas*, 927 S.W.2d 608, 613 (Tex. 1996); *Caterpillar Inc. v. Shears*, 911 S.W.2d 379, 381 (Tex. 1995); *McKisson v. Sales Affiliates, Inc.*, 416 S.W.2d 787, 789 (Tex. 1967).

11.   Restatement (Second) of Torts §402A, cmt. f (1965); Tex. Civ. Prac. & Rem. Code Ann. §82.001 (Vernon Supp. 1998).

12.   Restatement (Second) of Torts §402A, cmt. f (1965); Tex. Civ. Prac. & Rem. Code Ann. §82.001 (Vernon 1997); *Firestone Steel Prods. Co. v. Barajas*, 927

S.W.2d 608, 613 (Tex. 1996); *Armstrong Rubber Co. v. Urquidez*, 570 S.W.2d 374, 375 (Tex. 1978); *McKisson v. Sales Affiliates, Inc.*, 416 S.W.2d 787, 788 (Tex. 1967); see also *Hernandez v. Kasco Ventures, Inc.*, 832 S.W.2d 629, 634 (Tex. App.—El Paso 1992, no writ) (recovery denied because defendant not regularly engaged in business of selling the product).

13. *Armstrong Rubber Co.*, 570 S.W.2d at 376.

14. Tex. Civ. Prac. & Rem. Code Ann. §82.002 (Vernon 1997).

15. *Bernard Johnson, Inc. v. Continental Constr.*, 630 S.W.2d 365, 370 n.4 (Tex. App.—Austin 1982, writ ref'd n.r.e.); *Milt Ferguson Motor Co. v. Zeretzke*, 827 S.W.2d 349, 354 (Tex. App.—San Antonio 1991, no writ); *Texas Processed Plastics, Inc. v. Gray Enters.*, 592 S.W.2d 412, 415 (Tex. Civ. App. —Tyler 1979, no writ).

16. *Nobility Homes of Texas, Inc. v. Shivers*, 557 S.W.2d 77, 80 (Tex. 1977); *Purina Mills, Inc. v. Odell*, 948 S.W.2d 927, 940 n.12 (Tex. App.—Texarkana 1997); see *Brewer v. General Motors Corp.*, 926 S.W.2d 774, 780 (Tex. App.— Texarkana 1996, n.w.h.).

17. *Mid-Continent Aircraft Corp. v. Curry County Spraying Serv., Inc.*, 572 S.W.2d 308, 313 (Tex. 1978); see also *Signal Oil & Gas Co. v. Universal Oil Prods.*, 572 S.W.2d 320, 325 (Tex. 1978) (allowing recovery for damage to product itself if collateral property damage has also occurred).

18. *Caterpillar Inc. v. Shears*, 911 S.W.2d 379, 381-382 (Tex. 1995) (marketing defect); *Lucas v. Texas Indus.*, 696 S.W.2d 372, 377 (Tex. 1984) (manufacturing defect).

19. Restatement (Second) of Torts §402A, cmt. i (1965); State Bar of Texas, Texas Pattern Jury Charges—Malpractice, Premises & Products PJC 71.3, 71.5 (1997); *Caterpillar Inc.*, 911 S.W.2d at 383 (marketing defect).

20. *Turner v. General Motors Corp.*, 584 S.W.2d 844, 847 and n.1, 851 (Tex. 1979).

21. Tex. Civ. Prac. & Rem. Code Ann. §82.005(a) (Vernon 1997) (this statute does not apply to a drug or device as those terms are defined by the Federal Food, Drug, and Cosmetic Act (21 U.S.C. §321) or to a toxic or environmental tort as defined by Tex. Civ. Prac. & Rem. Code Ann. §33.013(c)(2) and (3)); see also *Caterpillar Inc.*, 911 S.W.2d at 384.

22. State Bar of Texas, Texas Pattern Jury Charges—Malpractice, Premises & Products PJC 70.5 (1997); *Woods v. Crane Carrier Co.*, 693 S.W.2d 377, 379-380 (Tex. 1985) (affirming the use of a definition regarding substantial

change or alteration); *Miller v. Bock Laundry Mach. Co.*, 568 S.W.2d 648, 650 (Tex. 1977) (product must be defective at time sold). See also *Feldman v. Kohler Co.*, 918 S.W.2d 615, 631 (Tex. App.—El Paso 1996, writ denied) (finding that the reasonably foreseeable use or alteration of a product imposed strict liability on the manufacturer).

23. *Firestone Steel Prods. Co. v. Barajas,* 927 S.W.2d 608, 616 (Tex. 1996).

24. State Bar of Texas, Texas Pattern Jury Charges—Malpractice, Premises & Products PJC 70.1 (1997); *Union Pump Co. v. Allbritton,* 898 S.W.2d 773, 775 (Tex. 1995); *Rourke v. Garza,* 530 S.W.2d 794, 801 (Tex. 1975); see also Tex. Civ. Prac. & Rem. Code Ann. §82.005(a)(2) (Vernon 1997) (producing cause must be shown in a product liability action based on design defect).

25. Tex. Civ. Prac. & Rem. Code Ann. §33.001(b) (Vernon Supp. 1995) (for causes of action which accrued prior to September 1, 1995, and were filed before September 1, 1996), *amended by* Acts 1995, 74th Leg., ch. 136, §1.

26. Tex. Civ. Prac. & Rem. Code Ann. §33.012(a) (Vernon Supp. 1995) (for causes of actions which accrued prior to September 1, 1995, and which were filed before September 1, 1996), *amended* 1995.

27. Tex. Civ. Prac. & Rem. Code Ann. §33.001 (Vernon 1997).

28. Id. at §33.012(a).

29. Id. at §33.014.

30. Id. at §33.016.

31. Id. at §33.012(b).

32. *Duncan v. Cessna Aircraft Co.,* 665 S.W.2d 414, 428 (Tex. 1984).

33. *Keen v. Ashot Ashkelon, Ltd.,* 748 S.W.2d 91, 92 (Tex. 1988); *Duncan,* 665 S.W.2d at 422-423; *Torres v. Caterpillar, Inc.,* 928 S.W.2d 233, 242 (Tex. App. —San Antonio 1996, no writ); *Mooney Aircraft Corp. v. Altman,* 772 S.W.2d 540, 543 (Tex. App. — Dallas 1989, writ denied).

34. *Henderson v. Ford Motor Co.,* 519 S.W.2d 87, 90-91 (Tex. 1974) (rejecting the definition of assumption of risk found in §402A cmt. n of the Restatement (Second) of Torts). But see *Caterpillar Inc. v. Shears,* 911 S.W.2d 379, 386 (Tex. 1995) (dissent).

35. State Bar of Texas, Texas Pattern Jury Charges—Malpractice, Premises & Products PJC 70.3 (1997); *Ahlschlager v. Remington Arms Co.*, 750 S.W.2d 832, 835 (Tex. App.—Houston [14th Dist.] 1988, writ denied).

36. *Dresser Indus., Inc. v. Lee*, 880 S.W.2d 750, 754 (Tex. 1993); *Rankin v. Atwood Vacuum Mach. Co.*, 831 S.W.2d 463, 465 (Tex. App.—Houston [14th Dist.] writ denied per curiam, 841 S.W.2d 856 (Tex. 1992)).

37. *Dresser Indus.*, 880 S.W.2d at 754-755.

38. Restatement (Second) of Torts §402A, cmt. j (1965); *Caterpillar Inc. v. Shears*, 911 S.W.2d 379, 381-382 (Tex. 1995).

39. Restatement (Second) of Torts §402A, cmt. i (1965); State Bar of Texas, Texas Pattern Jury Charges—Malpractice, Premises & Products PJC 71.5 (1997); see also *Caterpillar Inc.*, 911 S.W.2d at 381-382; *Joseph E. Seagram & Sons, Inc. v. McGuire*, 814 S.W.2d 385, 388 (Tex. 1991). *But cf. Turner v. General Motors Corp.*, 584 S.W.2d 844, 850-851 (Tex. 1979) (rejecting consumer expectation test in design defect cases).

40. *Firestone Steel Prods. Co. v. Barajas*, 927 S.W.2d 608, 614 (Tex. 1996).

41. *General Motors Corp. v. Saenz*, 873 S.W.2d 353, 359 (Tex. 1993); *Magro v. Ragsdale Bros., Inc.*, 721 S.W.2d 832, 834 (Tex. 1986).

42. *Barajas*, 927 S.W.2d at 613.

43. *Saenz*, 873 S.W.2d at 363; *Shop Rite Foods, Inc. v. Upjohn Co.*, 619 S.W.2d 574, 578 (Tex. Civ. App.—Amarillo 1981, writ ref'd n.r.e.); *Bituminous Cas. Corp. v. Black & Decker Mfg. Corp.*, 518 S.W.2d 868, 872-873 (Tex. Civ. App. —Dallas 1974, writ ref'd n.r.e.); see also *Blackwell Burner Co. Inc. v. Cerda*, 644 S.W.2d 512, 515-516 (Tex. App.—San Antonio 1982, writ ref'd n.r.e.).

44. *Alm v. Aluminum Co. of Am.*, 717 S.W.2d 588, 591 (Tex. 1986); *Reyes v. Wyeth Labs.*, 498 F.2d 1264, 1276 (5th Cir. 1974), *cert. denied*, 419 U.S. 1096 (1974); *Rolen v. Burroughs Wellcome Co.*, 856 S.W.2d 607, 609 (Tex. App. —Waco 1993, writ denied); *Gravis v. Parke-Davis & Co.*, 502 S.W.2d 863, 870 (Tex. Civ. App.—Corpus Christi 1973, writ ref'd n.r.e.).

45. *Alm*, 717 S.W.2d at 591-592. The class of intermediaries through whom warnings may be provided was further defined by the Texas Supreme Court after remand. *Aluminum Co. of Am. v. Alm*, 785 S.W.2d 137 (Tex.), *cert. denied*, 498 U.S. 847, 111 S. Ct. 135 (1990).

46. *Morris v. Adolph Coors Co.*, 735 S.W.2d 578, 582-583 (Tex. App.—Fort Worth 1987, writ ref'd n.r.e.).

47. Tex. Civ. Prac & Rem. Code Ann. §82.004 (Vernon 1997); Restatement (Second) of Torts §402(a), cmt. i (1965).

48. *Dion v. Ford Motor Co.*, 804 S.W.2d 302, 311 (Tex. App.—Eastland 1991, writ denied); *Arkwright-Boston Mfrs. Mut. Ins. Co. v. Westinghouse Elec. Corp.*, 844 F.2d 1174, 1185 (5th Cir. 1988); *Syrie v. Knoll Int'l*, 748 F.2d 304, 311-312 (5th Cir. 1984). *But cf. Bell Helicopter Co. v. Bradshaw*, 594 S.W.2d 519, 531-532 (Tex. Civ. App.—Corpus Christi 1979, writ ref'd n.r.e.). See *American Tobacco Co., Inc. v. Grinnell*, 951 S.W.2d 420, 438 (Tex. 1997) (observing that Texas courts do not impose a post-sale duty to take remedial measures).

49. *Bell Helicopter Co.*, 594 S.W.2d at 530-532; see also *Torres v. Caterpillar, Inc.*, 928 S.W.2d 233, 240-241 (Tex. App.—San Antonio 1996, no writ) (holding that manufacturer may become subject to post-sale strict liability if it regains control over the product and the product becomes defective during the period of control).

50. Tex. R. Civ. Ev. 407(a).

51. Tex. Civ. Prac. & Rem. Code Ann. §82.005(b)(2) (Vernon 1997) (applies to claims which accrued after September 1, 1993); *Boatland of Houston, Inc. v. Bailey*, 609 S.W.2d 743, 746 (Tex. 1980); see also *American Tobacco Co., Inc. v. Grinnell*, 951 S.W.2d 420, 438 (Tex. 1997) (observing that whether a product is dangerous is determined when it leaves the manufacturer's hands and enters the stream of commerce).

52. *Simien v. S.S. Kresge Co.*, 566 F.2d 551, 557-558 (5th Cir. 1978).

53. *Lorenz v. Celotex Corp.*, 896 F.2d 148, 150 (5th Cir. 1990).

54. *Gaulding v. Celotex Corp.*, 772 S.W.2d 66, 71 (Tex. 1989).

55. *Click v. Owens-Corning Fiberglas Corp.*, 899 S.W.2d 376, 377 (Tex. App.—Houston [14th Dist.] 1995, n.w.h.); *Celotex Corp. v. Tate*, 797 S.W.2d 197 (Tex. App.—Corpus Christi 1990, no writ).

56. See *Rogers v. R. J. Reynolds Tobacco Co.*, 761 S.W.2d 788, 796 (Tex. App.—Beaumont 1988, writ denied).

57. *Triplex Comm. Inc. v. Riley*, 900 S.W.2d 716, 720 and n.2 (Tex. 1995); see *Barajas*, 927 S.W.2d at 614.

58. *Feldman v. Kohler Co.*, 918 S.W.2d 615, 630 (Tex. App.—El Paso 1996, writ denied); *Fitzgerald Marine Sales v. LeUnes*, 659 S.W.2d 917, 918 (Tex. App.—Fort Worth 1983, writ dismissed); *Bell Aerospace Corp. v. Anderson*, 478

S.W.2d 191, 197 (Tex. Civ. App.—El Paso 1972, writ ref'd n.r.e.); *cf. Plas-Tex v. U.S. Steel Corp.*, 772 S.W.2d 442, 444 (Tex. 1989) (in a breach of implied warranty of merchantability case, *prima facie* showing of defect can be made by proof of malfunction along with evidence of proper use of goods by plaintiff).

59. *McInnes v. Yamaha Motor Corp.*, 659 S.W.2d 704, 710 (Tex. App.—Corpus Christi 1983), *aff'd*, 673 S.W.2d 185 (Tex. 1984), *cert. denied*, 469 U.S. 1107 (1985); *Rush v. Bucyrus-Erie Co.*, 646 S.W.2d 298, 301 (Tex. App.—Tyler 1983, writ ref'd n.r.e.).

60. *American Tobacco Co., Inc. v. Grinnell*, 951 S.W.2d 420, 426 (Tex. 1997); *Crocker v. Winthrop Labs.*, 514 S.W.2d 429, 431 (Tex. 1974).

61. *Gonzales v. Caterpillar Tractor Co.*, 571 S.W.2d 867, 871 (Tex. 1978); *Lozano v. H.D. Indus., Inc.*, 953 S.W.2d 304, 314 (Tex. App.—El Paso 1997); *Syrie v. Knoll Int'l*, 748 F.2d 304, 307 (5th Cir. 1984).

62. *Rudes v. Gottschalk*, 324 S.W.2d 201, 203-204 (Tex. 1959); *Dico Tire, Inc. v. Cisneros*, 953 S.W.2d 776, 782-783 (Tex. App.—Corpus Christi 1997).

63. Tex. Civ. Prac. & Rem. Code Ann. §33.001(a) (Vernon Supp. 1990) (actions that accrue before September 1, 1995), *amended* 1995; Tex. Civ. Prac. & Rem. Code Ann. §33.001 (Vernon 1997) (actions that accrue on or after September 1, 1995, or suits filed on or after September 1, 1996).

64. Tex. Civ. Prac. & Rem. Code Ann. §33.012(a) (Vernon Supp. 1998).

65. Tex. R. Evid. 407(a).

66. Tex. Bus. & Comm. Code Ann. (Tex. U.C.C.) §§2.313-2.315 (Vernon 1994).

67. *Signal Oil & Gas Co. v. Universal Oil Prods.*, 572 S.W.2d 320, 329 (Tex. 1978).

68. *Southerland v. Northeast Datsun, Inc.*, 659 S.W.2d 889, 891 (Tex. App.—El Paso 1983, no writ); *Cheney v. Parks*, 605 S.W.2d 640, 642 (Tex. Civ. App.—Houston [1st Dist.] 1980, writ ref'd n.r.e.).

69. *Signal Oil & Gas Co.*, 572 S.W.2d at 329 n.13.

70. *American Tobacco Co., Inc. v. Grinnell*, 951 S.W.2d 420, 435 (Tex. 1997).

71. Id. at 436.

72. Tex. Bus. & Comm. Code Ann. §17.50(a)(2) (Vernon 1987).

73. Tex. Bus. & Comm. Code Ann. §17.50(b)(1) (Vernon Supp. 1990) (for causes of action that accrue before September 1, 1995), *amended* 1995; Tex. Bus. & Comm. Code Ann. §17.50(b)(1) (Vernon Supp. 1998) (for causes of action that accrue on or after September 1, 1995, or suits filed on or after September 1, 1996).

74. Tex. Bus. & Comm. Code Ann. §17.50(b)(1) (Vernon Supp. 1990).

75. Tex. Bus. & Comm. Code Ann. §17.50(b)(1) (Vernon Supp. 1998).

76. Tex. Bus. & Comm. Code Ann. §17.45(4) (Vernon 1987).

77. Tex. Bus. & Comm. Code Ann. §17.49(c) (Vernon Supp. 1998).

78. Id. at §17.49(e)-(g).

79. Id. at §17.46(b).

80. *Parkway Co. v. Woodruff*, 901 S.W.2d 434, 438 (Tex. 1995); *La Sara Grain Co. v. First Nat'l Bank of Mercedes*, 673 S.W.2d 558, 565 (Tex. 1984).

81. *Cameron v. Terrell & Garrett, Inc.*, 618 S.W.2d 535, 541 (Tex. 1981) (emphasis added).

82. *Amstadt v. United States Brass Corp.*, 919 S.W.2d 644, 649 (Tex. 1996).

83. Id. at 652.

84. Tex. Bus. & Comm. Code Ann. §17.50(a) (Vernon Supp. 1998).

85. *W. O. Bankston Nissan, Inc. v. Walters*, 754 S.W.2d 127, 128 (Tex. 1988).

86. Tex. Bus. & Comm. Code Ann. §17.45(11) (Vernon Supp. 1998).

87. Id. at §17.50(b)(1).

88. Id. at §17.50(f).

89. Id. at §17.50(b)(1).

90. Tex. Civ. Prac. & Rem. Code Ann. §41.004(b) (Vernon Supp. 1998).

91. *Wheelways Ins. Co. v. Hodges*, 872 S.W.2d 776, 783 (Tex. App.—Texarkana 1994, no writ); Tex. Bus. & Comm. Code Ann. §17.50(b)(1) (Vernon Supp. 1998).

92. Tex. Bus. & Comm. Code Ann. §17.50(e) (Vernon Supp. 1998).

93. Id. at §17.50(d).

94. Id. at §17.50(c).

95. *Arthur Andersen & Co. v. Perry Equip. Corp.*, 945 S.W.2d 812, 818-819 (Tex. 1997).

96. Tex. Civ. Prac. & Rem. Code Ann. §33.002(b)(2) (Vernon Supp. 1990), Tex. Bus. & Comm. Code Ann. §17.50(b)(1)(A) (Vernon Supp. 1990) (for causes of action that accrue before September 1, 1995), *amended* 1995; Tex. Civ. Prac. & Rem. Code Ann. §33.001 (Vernon 1997) (for causes of action that accrue on or after September 1, 1995, or suits filed on or after September 1, 1996).

97. Tex. Bus. & Comm. Code Ann. §17.555 (Vernon 1987); *Plas-Tex, Inc. v. U.S. Steel Corp.*, 772 S.W.2d 442, 446 (Tex. 1989).

98. Tex. Civ. Prac. & Rem. Code Ann. §33.013(a) (Vernon 1997).

99. Tex. Civ. Prac. & Rem. Code Ann. §33.013(b), (c)(1) (Vernon Supp. 1990).

100. Id. at §33.013(c)(3).

101. Tex. Civ. Prac. & Rem. Code Ann. §33.013(b)-(c) (Vernon 1997).

102. Tex. Civ. Prac. & Rem. Code Ann. §41.001(5) (Vernon Supp. 1990).

103. *Transportation Ins. Co. v. Moriel*, 879 S.W.2d 10, 22-23 (Tex. 1994).

104. Tex. Civ. Prac. & Rem. Code Ann. §41.003(a) (Vernon 1997).

105. Id. at §41.001(6).

106. Id. at §§41.001(7); 41.003(a)(3).

107. Id. at §41.004(a).

108. Tex. Civ. Prac. & Rem. Code Ann. §41.007 (Vernon Supp. 1990).

109. Tex. Civ. Prac. & Rem. Code Ann. §41.008(b) (Vernon 1997).

110. Id. at §41.001(4).

111. Id. at §41.008(c).

112. For claims that accrue before September 1, 1995, Tex. Civ. Prac. & Rem. Code Ann. §41.005 (Vernon Supp. 1990); *but cf. Transfer Prods., Inc. v. Texpar Energy, Inc.*, 788 S.W.2d 713, 717 (Tex. App.—Corpus Christi 1990, no writ) (allowed joint and several liability where companies were closely related). For claims that accrue on or after September 1, 1995, Tex. Civ. Prac. & Rem. Code Ann. §41.006 (Vernon 1997).

113. Tex. Bus. Corp. Act Ann. art. 5.10B and art. 7.12 (Vernon Supp. 1995); *Celotex Corp. v. Tate*, 797 S.W.2d 197, 206 (Tex. App.—Corpus Christi 1990, no writ).

114. Tex. Civ. Prac. & Rem. Code Ann. ch. 16.

115. Tex. Civ. Prac. & Rem. Code Ann. ch. 33.

116. Tex. Civ. Prac. & Rem. Code Ann. ch. 41.

117. Tex. Bus. & Comm. Code. Ann. ch. 2.

118. Tex. Bus. & Comm. Code Ann. §§17.41-17.63 (Vernon 1987 and Supp. 1998).

119. Tex. Civ. Prac. & Rem. Code §§82.001-82.006 (Vernon 1997).

120. State Bar of Texas, Texas Pattern Jury Charges (1997).

UTAH

A. CAUSES OF ACTION

The Utah Products Liability Act[1] applies. Product liability lawsuits may include claims based on strict liability, negligence, and breach of express or implied warranties.

B. STATUTES OF LIMITATION

1. Negligence

Claims for negligence must be brought within four years,[2] with the exception of claims for injury to personal property or to real property, which must be brought within three years.[3] The cause of action has been held to occur on the date of injury, not the date the plaintiff discovered that the defendant could be at fault.[4]

2. Strict Liability

All claims under the Products Liability Act, whether for personal injury, death, or property damage, must be brought within two years of the time the claimant discovered or should have discovered both the harm and the cause.[5] The statute is tolled until the plaintiff discovers, or in the exercise of due diligence should have discovered, the identity of the manufacturer.[6]

3. Construction Claims

Injuries due to defective design or construction of improvements to real property must be brought within two years of discovery of the claim. Breach of warranty claims must generally be brought within six years of completion of the improvement. In the absence of fraud, express warranty, or intentional wrongdoing, no claims may be commenced more than twelve years after the improvement is completed. Claims discovered in the last year may be brought within two years of the date of discovery.[7]

4. Breach of Warranty

Utah has adopted the Uniform Commercial Code, and warranty claims must be brought within four years of the tender of delivery,[8] unless the warranty explicitly extends to future performance. Discovery of breach of warranty for future performance can only occur after the materials are used in construction.[9] However, claims for breach of warranty seeking damages for personal injury or tortious injury to personal property are treated as tort claims and are subject to the applicable tort limitations period.[10]

C. STRICT LIABILITY

1. The Standard

Utah has adopted section 402A of the Restatement (Second) of Torts.[11]

2. "Defect"

A product is in a defective condition if it is unreasonably dangerous to the user or consumer or to his property.[12] The defective condition must exist at the time of the sale, and must be a cause of the plaintiff's injuries.[13]

3. Defenses

a. Misuse

Misuse of the product by the user or consumer is a defense.[14] However, if the fact finder determines the misuse is foreseeable, defendant cannot use this defense.[15]

b. Unreasonable Use

Knowledge of the defect by the user or consumer, who is aware of the danger and unreasonably proceeds to make use of the product, is a defense.[16]

c. State of the Art

The Tenth Circuit has ruled that Utah law requires plaintiff to show that an alternative safer design, practicable under the circumstances, was available at the time of sale of the product.[17] An open and obvious danger does not operate as a complete bar to recovery.[18]

4. Comparative Fault

Utah applies a comparative negligence scheme to strict liability claims, and the plaintiff's recovery is limited to the portion of damages attributable to the product defect.[19] In determining proportion of fault, the fault of any person who contributed to the injury, regardless of whether the person is immune from the suit or a named defendant, may be considered.[20]

5. Sale or Lease

Plaintiff must allege a sale or other commercial transaction of the product by the defendant, but strict liability applies to anyone in the chain of distribution, as long as the seller is engaged in the business of selling the product.[21]

The District Court for the District of Utah has held that Utah courts will apply strict liability to lessors of products, in addition to sellers, at least in some circumstances.[22]

6. Inherently Dangerous Products

The "basic policy" of comment k of section 402A has been adopted in Utah. All FDA-approved prescription drugs are exempt from design defect claims.[23]

7. Successor Liability

No Utah authority addresses the question of successor liability.

8. Privity

No privity is required; the ultimate user may sue any seller.[24]

9. Failure to Warn

To recover for a claimed failure to warn, the plaintiff must establish causation. An inadequate warning may make a product unreasonably dangerous.[25]

An adequate warning must be designed to reasonably catch the attention of the consumer, be comprehensible and give a fair indication of the specific risks involved, and be of an intensity justified by the magnitude of the risk.[26] Whether a "sophisticated user" standard changes the duty to warn has been found to be a fact question for the jury to decide.[27] Utah has adopted a rebuttable "heeding presumption" that an adequate warning would have been followed.[28]

10. Post-Sale Duty to Warn

Drug manufacturers have a continuous duty to warn the medical profession regarding additional side effects.[29] However, there are no other reported Utah cases regarding a continuing duty to warn in other circumstances.

11. Learned Intermediary Doctrine

The manufacturer of a prescription drug has a duty to warn the prescribing physician, but not the patient.[30]

12. Substantial Change/Abnormal Use

The manufacturer is not responsible for injuries caused by a substantial and unforeseeable change in the product.[31]

13. Standard for Summary Judgment/Directed Verdict

Expert testimony that expresses conclusions as to dispositive factual issues and identifies the specific grounds and facts on which the conclusions are based is adequate to avoid motions for summary judgment or directed verdict.[32]

D. NEGLIGENCE

Utah has the traditional standards of reasonableness for negligence cases.[33] Negligence cases apply modified comparative negligence principles, which limit each defendant to liability related to that defendant's proportion of fault.[34] Additionally, a plaintiff's claim is barred if her percentage of fault exceeds that of the defendants.[35] The proportion of fault of immune nonparties, such as the plaintiff's employer or dismissed parties, should be determined by the finder of fact.[36]

E.   BREACH OF WARRANTY

In a product setting, a cause of action for breach of warranty is generally quite similar to a strict liability cause of action.[37]

F.   PUNITIVE DAMAGES

Punitive damages are recoverable in actions of strict liability and negligence, but not in actions sounding only in breach of warranty. Punitive damages may not be awarded for injuries caused by drugs that receive premarket approval or licensing by the FDA, and are generally recognized as safe and effective, unless the drug manufacturer is shown by clear and convincing evidence to have knowingly withheld or misrepresented information submitted to the FDA that is relevant to the claimant's harm.[38]

G.   STATUTES

Relevant statutes for product liability actions are the statutes of limitation, the Utah Products Liability Act, the Punitive Damages Act regarding drug claims mentioned, the comparative negligence statute, and commercial code sections regarding breaches of warranty.[39]

Stephen B. Nebeker
Rick L. Rose
Eric D. Barton
RAY, QUINNEY & NEBEKER
400 Deseret Building
79 South Main Street
P.O. Box 45385
Salt Lake City, Utah 84145-0385
(801) 532-1500

ENDNOTES - UTAH

1. Utah Code Ann. §78-15-1 to -6 (1996, as amended).

2. Id. §78-12-25(3) (1996).

3. Id. §78-12-26 (1996).

4. *Atwood v. Sturm, Ruger & Co., Inc.*, 823 P.2d 1064-1065 (Utah 1992).

5. Utah Code Ann. §78-15-3 (1996).

6. *Aragon v. Clover Club Foods*, 857 P.2d 250 (Utah App. 1993).

7. Utah Code Ann. §78-12-25.5 (1996).

8. Id. §70A-2-725 (1990).

9. *Salt Lake City Corp. v. Kasler Corp.*, 855 F. Supp. 1560, 1568 (D. Utah 1994).

10. *Davidson Lumber v. Bonneville, Inv., Inc.*, 794 P.2d 1 (Utah 1990).

11. *Ernest W. Hahn, Inc. v. Armco Steel Co.*, 601 P.2d 152, 158 (Utah 1979).

12. Restatement (Second) of Torts, §402A(1); *Ernest W. Hahn*, 601 P.2d at 156.

13. *Lamb v. B&B Amusements Corp.*, 869 P.2d 926 (Utah 1993).

14. *Ernest W. Hahn*, 601 P.2d at 158, *citing* comment g to Restatement (Second) of Torts §402A.

15. *Allen v. Minnstar, Inc.*, 97 F.3d 1365, 1368-69 (10th Cir. 1996) (applying Utah law).

16. *Ernest W. Hahn*, 601 P.2d at 158; *Jacobson Constr. Co. v. Structo-lite Engg., Inc.*, 619 P.2d 306 (Utah 1980); Restatement (Second) of Torts §402A.

17. *Allen v. Minnstar, Inc.*, 8 F.3d 1470 (10th Cir. 1993).

18. *House v. Armour of America, Inc.*, 886 P.2d 542, 548 (Utah Ct. App. 1994) *aff'd*, 929 P.2d 340 (Utah 1996).

19. *Mulherin v. Ingersoll-Rand Co.*, 628 P.2d 1301, 1304 (Utah 1981); see also Utah Code Ann. §78-27-38 (1996).

20. Utah Code Ann. §78-27-38(4) (1996).

21. *Ernest W. Hahn*, 601 P.2d at 156; Restatement (Second) of Torts §402A(1).

22. *Ghionis v. Deer Valley Resort Co.*, 839 F. Supp. 794 (D. Utah 1993).

23. *Grundberg v. The Upjohn Co.*, 813 P.2d 89, 95 (Utah 1991); see also *Unthank v. United States*, 732 F.2d 1517, 1523 (10th Cir. 1984) (applying Utah law).

24. *Ernest W. Hahn*, 601 P.2d at 156; Restatement (Second) of Torts §402A(1).

25. *Unthank*, 732 P.2d 1521.

26. *House v. Armour of America, Inc.*, 886 P.2d at 551.

27. Id. at 550.

28. Id. at 553.

29. *Barson v. E. R. Squibb & Sons, Inc.*, 682 P.2d 832, 835 (Utah 1984).

30. Id.

31. *Ernest W. Hahn*, 601 P.2d at 156.

32. *Butterfield v. Okubo*, 831 P.2d 104 (Utah 1992); *Nay v. General Motors Corp., GMC Trucking Div.*, 850 P.2d 1264 (Utah 1993).

33. *Koer v. Mayfair Markets*, 431 P.2d 566 (Utah 1967).

34. Utah Code Ann. §78-27-38 (1996).

35. Id.

36. *Sullivan v. Scoular Grain Co. of Utah*, 853 P.2d 878 (Utah 1993), and Utah Code Ann. §78-27-38(4)(a) (1996).

37. *Ernest W. Hahn*, 601 P.2d at 159.

38. Utah Code Ann. §78-18-2 (1992). Applies only to causes of action accruing after July 1, 1989.

39. Utah Code Ann. §§70A-2-725, 78-12-25(3), 78-12-25.5, 78-12-26, 78-15-1 to 78-15-6, 78-18-2, 78-27-38 (1996).

VERMONT

A. CAUSES OF ACTION

Product liability lawsuits in the State of Vermont have been brought under the theories of strict product liability, negligence, or breach of an implied warranty of merchantability or of suitability for a particular purpose.[1] In many instances, all three causes of action may be alleged in the complaint.

B. STATUTES OF LIMITATION

The statute of limitation applicable to a strict product liability or negligence action depends upon the nature of the harm suffered by the plaintiff.[2] Actions for "injury to the person suffered by the act or default of another" or for "[d]amage to personal property" must be brought within three years after the cause of action accrues.[3] "[T]he cause of action shall be deemed to accrue as of the date of the discovery of the injury."[4] A six-year statute of limitation applies in most other situations.[5]

While the "discovery rule" has not been explicitly added to a section of the Vermont code that creates a cause of action for damage occurring to personal property,[6] a recent opinion by the Vermont Supreme Court has held that the "discovery rule" applies even in instances where the statute of limitations is silent.[7]

With respect to injuries suffered as a result of "noxious agents medically recognized as having prolonged latent development," Vermont law imposes a twenty-year statute of repose running from the "date of the last occurrence to which the injury is attributed."[8]

The State of Vermont has adopted the provisions of the Uniform Commercial Code concerning the express and implied warranties that arise in contracts for the sale of goods.[9] In contrast to the personal injury actions, a four-year statute of limitations governs causes of action brought for any breach of a contract for the sale of goods.[10]

C. STRICT LIABILITY

1. The Standard

In 1975, the Supreme Court of Vermont explicitly adopted the provisions of section 402A of the Restatement (Second) of Torts (1965).[11]

2. Duty to Warn

Manufacturers have a duty to warn purchasers when the manufacturer has knowledge of a product defect that makes the product "dangerous to an extent beyond that which would be contemplated by the ordinary purchaser, i.e., a consumer possessing the ordinary and common knowledge of the community as to the product's characteristics."[12]

However, manufacturers do not have a duty to warn in instances when the product at issue is neither designed nor manufactured defectively. For instance, a properly made BB gun "is not dangerous beyond that [danger] which would be contemplated by the ordinary consumer with the ordinary knowledge common to the community."[13]

The plaintiff bears the responsibility of demonstrating that the lack of warning made the product unreasonably dangerous.[14] In addition, the plaintiff has the burden of showing that the lack of warning was a proximate cause of the injury.[15] Assuming the defendant manufacturer had a duty to warn and did not do so, a presumption of causation is created, one which suggests that had a warning been present, the plaintiff would have read it and heeded it.[16]

3. Post-Sale Duty to Warn

One case, in finding that a manufacturer had a duty to warn *employees* of a product purchaser about the dangers of the product, arguably acknowledged a post-sale duty to warn; in another case, however, evidence of a post-injury warning to other persons has been ruled inadmissible under rule of evidence 407.[17]

4. Application of Comparative Fault to Strict Liability

In a 1996 products liability case, The Vermont Supreme Court could not agree on the role of comparative fault in product liability cases.[18] The case produced four separate opinions. Three of the five Justices agreed that "principles of comparative causation apply in this products liability action," but the three did not agree to a general rule on when comparative principles apply in strict products liability actions, nor on how to implement these principles when they do apply.[19] The remaining two Justices dissented, arguing that comparative principles are not applicable in products liability actions. A Vermont federal court recently adopted the position of one of the Vermont Supreme Court Justices in that case and held that principles of pure comparative fault apply in strict products liability actions.[20]

5. State of the Art

No reported Vermont products-liability case has addressed a "state of the art" defense, so the availability of the defense presents an open issue. In one non-products-liability case, however, the "state of the art" concept was used to *erode* a traditional assumption-of-the-risk defense.[21]

D. NEGLIGENCE

1. General Principles

In the view of Vermont courts, it makes little difference whether a cause of action for product liability arises under a theory of negligence or implied warranty. The seller's responsibility to the consumer is the same under either theory.[22] Moreover, once causation is established, lack of privity will not relieve any legal obligation for injuries inflicted by the sale of a defective product.[23]

2. Vicarious Liability

Under the doctrine of vicarious liability recently recognized by the Vermont Supreme Court, an assembler-manufacturer may be held liable for the negligence of the makers of components used by the assembler-manufacturer in the final product.[24] While application of this doctrine does not require that the plaintiff demonstrate that the assembler-manufacturer itself was negligent, the plaintiff still bears the burden of showing that some negligence took place, at least on the part of the component maker.[25] To that extent, vicarious liability differs from strict liability in tort, under which an assembler-manufacturer may be held liable regardless of the negligent or non-negligent source of the defect.[26]

3. Comparative Negligence

Vermont has adopted a "modified" comparative negligence statute, in which a plaintiff's award for damages may be reduced by the percentage of his own negligence up to 50 percent of the total liability. If the plaintiff is more than 50 percent liable, however, all recovery is barred.[27]

In a multiple-defendant lawsuit, a finding by the jury that the plaintiff was more negligent than some of the defendants will not bar recovery as long as the plaintiff's negligence was not greater than that of all the defendants put together.[28] Where more than one defendant is found liable, each defendant is responsible for its proportionate share of the defendants' collective liability; thus, in a case in which the jury finds a plaintiff 40 percent negligent, defendant A 30 percent negligent, and defendant B 30 percent negligent, the plaintiff will be able to recover 60 percent of her total damages, with each defendant contributing one-half of the award.

4. Compliance with Regulations

Evidence of compliance with governmental regulations is admissible to show whether a defendant satisfied the applicable standard of care in negligence actions, and is apparently admissible in strict liability actions as well.[29]

E. BREACH OF WARRANTY

The implied warranties of merchantability and fitness for a particular purpose are closely linked under Vermont law. The difference appears to lie in the scope of the seller's promise: an implied warranty of merchantability reflects the promise that the product is good for the purpose inherent in its nature, while that of fitness for a particular purpose is a promise that the product is good for a particular purpose specified by the buyer.[30]

1. Elements

Regardless of which particular implied warranty is at issue, the injured party must be able to show (a) that the product allegedly causing the injury was harmful or deleterious in some way; and (b) that the defect existed as of the time that the product was in the possession of or under the control of the seller.[31]

2. Time at Which Cause of Action Accrues

In a case based on an alleged breach of warranty, Vermont courts will focus on the time of purchase by the plaintiff as the pivotal point in determining possession and control of the product.[32]

F. SUCCESSOR CORPORATIONS

The Vermont Supreme Court has adopted a general rule that "the liabilities of a predecessor corporation will pass to the successor only when the change is occasioned by statutory merger or consolidation."[33] Thus, a company that takes over ownership of another corporation by purchasing all of its stock will be liable for the torts committed by the purchased corporation.

However, if change is accomplished through sale of physical assets only, the purchasing corporation assumes no liability unless

1. the buyer expressly or impliedly agrees to assume the liabilities;

2. the transaction amounts to a de facto merger or consolidation;

3. the purchasing corporation is merely a continuation of the selling corporation;

4. the sale is a fraudulent transaction intended to avoid debts and liabilities;

5. inadequate consideration was given for the sale.[34]

G. DEFENSES

The defenses usually raised in a product liability action include contributory negligence, assumption of risk, and misuse of the product. However, there are no Vermont cases specifically discussing the application of those defenses to product liability litigation.

H.   PUNITIVE DAMAGES

Although there are no Vermont cases explicitly discussing the application of punitive damages to the product liability field, there is no reason to think that such damages would not be awarded in an appropriate case.

The general rule in Vermont is that punitive damages may only be awarded where the plaintiff has successfully shown that the defendant acted with actual malice.[35] However, other cases have broadened the scope of the "actual malice," and have awarded punitive damages in instances where the defendant acted recklessly or with wanton disregard of the plaintiff's rights.[36]

I.   STATUTES

The relevant statutes for product liability actions are the various statutes of limitation and the commercial code sections when a breach of warranty is alleged.[37]

Karen McAndrew
Cathy Nelligan Norman
DINSE, KNAPP & McANDREW, P.C.
209 Battery Street
P.O. Box 988
Burlington, Vermont 05402-0988
(802) 864-5751

1. See *Page v. Smith-Gates Corp.*, 143 Vt. 280, 465 A.2d 1102 (Vt. 1983) (plaintiff asserted all three theories as a basis of recovery).

2. *University of Vt. and State Agric. College v. W.R. Grace & Co.*, 152 Vt. 287, 289, 565 A.2d 1354, 1356 (1989); *Kinney v. Goodyear Tire & Rubber Co.*, 134 Vt. 571, 574, 367 A.2d 677, 679-680 (1976).

3. Vt. Stat. Ann. tit. 12, §512(4) (1973 & 1997 Supp.). See also *Kinney*, 134 Vt. 571, 367 A.2d 677.

4. Vt. Stat. Ann. Tit. 12, §512(4), (5) (1973 & 1997 Supp.); see also *University of Vt.*, 152 Vt. 287, 565 A.2d 1354 (extending discovery rule to product liability action alleging property damage).

5. Vt. Stat. Ann. tit. 12, §511 (1973); see *University of Vt.*, 152 Vt. at 289, 565 A.2d at 1356.

6. Vt. Stat. Ann. tit. 12, §512(5) (1973).

7. *University of Vt.*, 152 Vt. 287.

8. Vt. Stat. Ann. tit. 12, §518(a) (1973). See *Cavanaugh*, 145 Vt. 516 (interpreting statute).

9. Vt. Stat. Ann. tit. 9A, §§2-312 to 2-315 (1966).

10. Id. tit. 9A, §2-725(1) (1966).

11. *Zaleskie v. Joyce*, 133 Vt. 150, 333 A.2d 110 (1975); see *Farnham v. Bombardier, Inc.*, 161 Vt. 619, 640 A.2d 47 (Vt. 1994) (stating elements of strict-liability cause of action).

12. *Menard v. Newhall*, 135 Vt. 53, 373 A.2d 505 (1977). See also *Ostrowski v. Hydra-Tool Corp.*, 144 Vt. 305, 479 A.2d 126 (1984).

13. *Menard*, 135 Vt. 53.

14. Id.

15. Id.

16. Id.

17. *McCullock v. H.B. Fuller Co.*, 981 F.2d 656, 658 (2d Cir. 1992) (warning given to purchaser, but did not reach employee: implicit acknowledgement of post-sale duty to warn); *Fish v. Georgia Pacific Corp.*, 779 F.2d 836, 839 (2d Cir. 1985) (post-injury warnings not admissible).

18. *Webb v. Navistar Int'l Transportation Corp.*, 692 A.2d. 343 (Vt. 1996).

19. Id.

20. *Jugle v. Volswagen of America, Inc.*, 1997 WL 467029 (D. Vt. 1997).

21. See *Estate of Frant v. Haystack Group, Inc.*, 162 Vt. 11, 641 A.2d 765, 770 (1994) (endemic hazards of skiing, whose risk is assumed by skiers, are reduced as result of advances in "state of the art" slope grooming techniques).

22. *O'Brien v. Comstock Foods, Inc.*, 125 Vt. 158, 212 A.2d 69 (1965). See also *DiGregorio v. Champlain Valley Fruit Co.*, 127 Vt. 562, 255 A.2d 183 (1969) (duty of wholesaler to indemnify retailer for injuries caused by a banana with a thermometer in it is not affected by whether the consumer's action was brought under negligence or breach of implied warranty).

23. *O'Brien*, 125 Vt. 158 (adopting principles of *McPherson v. Buick Motor Co.*, 217 N.Y. 382, 111 N.E. 1050 (1916)).

24. *Morris v. American Motors Corp.*, 142 Vt. 566, 459 A.2d 968 (Vt. 1982).

25. Id.

26. Id.

27. Vt. Stat. Ann. tit. 12, §1036 (1973 and 1997 Supp.).

28. Id.

29. *McCullock*, 981 F.2d at 658 (compliance with OSHA labelling regulations was admissible, but did not *per se* insulate manufacturer from failure to warn purchaser's employee of dangers); *Ball v. Melsur Corp.*, 161 Vt. 35, 43, 633 A.2d 705, 712 (1993) (in negligence action, compliance with OSHA regulations admissible on standard-of-care issue once a duty had been shown to independently exist; court deliberately refrained from addressing whether OSHA regulations could create a duty in the first place).

30. *Rogers v. W. T. Grant Co.*, 132 Vt. 485, 321 A.2d 54 (1974), quoting *Wing v. Chapman*, 49 Vt. 33, 35 (1876); see also *Green Mountain Mushroom Co. v. Brown*, 117 Vt. 509, 95 A.2d 679 (1952).

31.   Id.

32.   Id.

33.   *Ostrowski,* 144 Vt. 305.

34.   Id.

35.   *Appropriate Tech. Corp. v. Palma,* 146 Vt. 643, 508 A.2d 724 (1986).

36.   *Shortle v. Central Vt. Pub. Serv. Corp.,* 137 Vt. 32, 399 A.2d 517 (1979).

37.   See Vt. Stat. Ann. tit. 12, §§512(4) and (5), 518(a) (1973 & 1997 Supp.); id. tit. 9A, §§2-312 to 2-315, 2-725(1).

VIRGINIA

A. CAUSES OF ACTION

Product liability lawsuits commonly include causes of action for negligence and breach of warranty.

B. STATUTES OF LIMITATION AND REPOSE

Causes of action for personal injuries must be brought within two years, whether founded in negligence or in breach of warranty.[1] An action for property damage must be brought within five years, except that if property subject to contract has been damaged, the statute of limitations is four years.[2]

A cause of action for personal injury accrues at the date the injury is sustained and not when the resulting damage is discovered, except where injury is due to asbestos exposure or breast implants.[3]

There is a five-year statute of repose limited to damages arising out of the defective or unsafe condition of improvements to real property.[4]

C. STRICT LIABILITY

Virginia has not adopted strict liability as a theory of product liability.[5] However, federal courts interpreting Virginia law have opined that Virginia's warranty theory is the "functional equivalent" of strict tort.[6]

D. NEGLIGENCE

1. The Standard

Under negligence theory, the plaintiff must show that he was injured (1) by goods that were unreasonably dangerous either for the use to which they would ordinarily be put or for some other reasonably foreseeable purpose and (2) that the unreasonably dangerous condition existed when the goods left the defendant's hands.[7]

This duty to provide a product that is reasonably safe includes a duty to warn. Virginia has adopted the test formulated by section 388 of the Restatement (Second) of Torts. A manufacturer will be liable for a failure to warn if he (a) knows or has reason to know that the chattel is or is likely to be dangerous for the use for which it is supplied; (b) has no reason to believe that those for whose use the chattel is supplied will realize its dangerous condition; and (c) fails to exercise reasonable care to inform them of its dangerous condition or of the facts that make it likely to be dangerous.[8]

2. "Reasonably Safe"

To prevail, the plaintiff must prove that the manufacturer's conduct was unreasonable, namely, that the manufacturer failed to use "ordinary care" to provide a product that was reasonably safe.[9] The product need not be completely accident-proof or incorporate only features representing the ultimate in safety.[10]

3. Contributory Negligence/Assumption of Risk

Contributory negligence is a complete bar to recovery on a negligence claim.[11] Virginia law does not compare the negligence of the parties.[12] The test is not whether the plaintiff actually knew of the danger confronting him, but whether in the exercise of reasonable care he should have known he was in a situation of peril.[13]

Assumption of risk is also a defense. However, it is often a difficult defense to prove, as the court requires that the nature and extent of the risk must have been fully appreciated and that the risk was voluntarily incurred.[14]

4. Sale

Negligence applies to any seller in the chain of a product's distribution if the seller sells the product as its own.[15]

5. Inherently Dangerous Products

A supplier of products will not be held liable simply because the product is inherently dangerous unless it fails to give adequate warning of the danger.[16]

6. Successor Liability

If a corporation acquires all or substantially all of the assets of another corporation and continues the same manufacturing process, the successor is not liable for injuries caused by products made by the predecessor corporation unless (a) the successor agrees to assume such liabilities; (b) the circumstances evidence a consolidation of the two corporations; (c) the successor corporation was a mere continuation of the predecessor corporation; or (d) the transaction was fraudulent in fact.[17]

7. Privity

No privity is required. A plaintiff may sue for negligence even though he did not buy the product from the manufacturer.[18]

8. Failure to Warn

The duty to warn is only to give a reasonable warning, not the best possible one. A warning is not insufficient because plaintiff was not told exactly how a danger might operate. There is no liability for failing to warn of an open and obvious danger.[19]

A plaintiff's failure to read posted warnings or warnings printed in manuals preclude recovery for failure to warn.[20]

9. **Post-Sale Duty to Warn**

The manufacturer's duty to warn is a continuous duty not interrupted by the manufacture or sale of the product under a theory of negligence, but not under a theory of breach of warranty.[21] However, where the manufacturer has sold the product to a knowledgeable purchaser who serves as distributor to the ultimate user or consumer, the manufacturer may not owe a duty to warn that ultimate user or consumer.[22]

10. **Substantial Change/Abnormal Use**

A manufacturer may be responsible for injuries caused by a substantial change in the product occurring after initial sale or due to abnormal use if such change or use is one that could have been reasonably foreseen or expected.[23]

11. **State of the Art**

"State-of-the-art" or "custom in the industry" evidence is admissible.[24]

12. **Malfunction**

The mere fact that a product malfunctioned is not sufficient to establish the existence of a defect.[25]

13. **Standards**

Evidence that the product complied with customary or industry standards is admissible, although such does not establish conclusively that due care was exercised.[26] An employer's failure to comply with mandatory safety regulations may be an independent, intervening, and superseding act shielding a manufacturer from liability for its original negligence.[27]

14. **Other Accidents**

Evidence of similar accidents, when relevant, is admissible to establish that defendant had notice and actual knowledge of a defective condition, provided the prior incident occurred under substantially the same circumstances and had been caused by the same or similar defects and dangers as those at issue.[28]

E. **BREACH OF WARRANTY**

1. **The Standard**

The standard of safety imposed on the seller or manufacturer is said to be essentially the same whether the theory of liability is labeled warranty or negligence.[29] However, the focus under warranty is on whether the product itself is "unreasonably dangerous" rather than on the conduct of the manufacturer, and the condition must have existed when the goods left the manufacturer's hands.[30]

2. Defenses

Various defenses not available in negligence apply, namely, the contract doctrines of privity (although much diluted over the years), disclaimer, requirements of notice of breach, and a limitation through inconsistencies with express warranties.[31]

Warranty disclaimers and limitations can be enforced against third-party beneficiaries despite lack of privity. However, warranties created through specific and express representations between parties outside the chain of distribution, such as representations by the manufacturer directly to the consumer, must be disclaimed between those parties themselves, and not through an intermediate distributor.[32]

Contributory negligence is not a defense to a warranty action. However, the action can be barred by the similar defense that a manufacturer is not liable for danger that is known, visible, or obvious to the plaintiff or where the product has been misused.[33] Assumption of risk is not a defense in an action for breach of implied warranty.[34]

F. PUNITIVE DAMAGES

Punitive damages are recoverable in actions of negligence as well as warranty if the plaintiff proves a conscious disregard of the rights of others or wanton, willful, or malicious conduct by defendant. But plaintiff must prove more than simple negligence.[35]

G. STATUTES

Relevant statutes for product liability actions are the statutes of limitation and the commercial code sections when a breach of warranty is alleged.[36]

Michael W. Smith
Mary Metil Grove
CHRISTIAN, BARTON, EPPS, BRENT & CHAPPELL
909 East Main Street, Suite 1200
Richmond, Virginia 23219-3095
(804) 697-4100

ENDNOTES - VIRGINIA

1. Va. Code §§8.01-243, 8.01-246 (1992); *Friedman v. Peoples Serv. Drug Stores, Inc.*, 208 Va. 700, 160 S.E.2d 563 (1968).

2. Va. Code §§8.01-243, 8.01-246 (1992); Va. Code §8.2-725 (1991).

3. Va. Code §§8.01-230, 8.01-249 (1992); *Hawks v. DeHart*, 206 Va. 810, 146 S.E.2d 187 (1966).

4. Va. Code §8.01-250 (1992).

5. *Quillen v. International Playtex, Inc.*, 789 F.2d 1041 (4th Cir. 1986).

6. *Bly v. Otis Elevator Co.*, 713 F.2d 1040 (4th Cir. 1983).

7. *Logan v. Montgomery Ward & Co.*, 216 Va. 425, 219 S.E.2d 685 (1975).

8. *Owens-Corning Fiberglas Corp. v. Watson*, 243 Va. 128, 413 S.E.2d 630 (1992); *Besser v. Hansen*, 243 Va. 267, 415 S.E.2d 138 (1992); *Featherall v. Firestone Tire & Rubber Co.*, 219 Va. 949, 252 S.E.2d 358 (1979); Restatement (Second) of Torts §388.

9. *Turner v. Manning, Maxwell & Moore, Inc.*, 216 Va. 245, 217 S.E.2d 863 (1975).

10. *Marshall v. H. K. Ferguson Co.*, 623 F.2d 882 (4th Cir. 1980).

11. *Smith v. Virginia Elec. & Power Co.*, 204 Va. 128, 129 S.E.2d 655 (1963).

12. *Litchford v. Hancock*, 232 Va. 496, 352 S.E.2d 335 (1987); *Ford Motor Co. v. Bartholomew*, 224 Va. 421, 297 S.E.2d 675 (1982).

13. *Reed v. Carlyle & Martin, Inc.*, 214 Va. 592, 202 S.E.2d 874, *cert. denied*, 419 U.S. 859 (1974); *Smith, supra* note 11.

14. *Lust v. Clark Equip. Co.*, 792 F.2d 436 (4th Cir. 1986).

15. *Carney v. Sears, Roebuck & Co.*, 309 F.2d 300 (4th Cir. 1962).

16. *Spruill v. Boyle-Midway, Inc.*, 308 F.2d 79 (4th Cir. 1962).

17. *Crawford Harbor Assoc. v. Blake Constr. Co., Inc.*, 661 F. Supp. 880 (E.D. Va. 1987).

18. Va. Code §8.2-318 (1991).

19. *Austin v. Clark Equipment Co.*, 48 F.3d 833 (4th Cir. 1995); *Pfizer, Inc. v. Jones*, 221 Va. 681, 272 S.E.2d 43 (1980); *Sadler v. Lynch*, 192 Va. 344, 64 S.E.2d 664 (1951).

20. *Begley v. Gehl Co.*, 1996 U.S. Dist. LEXIS 8198 (W.D.Va. 1996).

21. *Estate of Kimmel v. Clark Equip. Co.*, 773 F. Supp. 828 (W.D. Va. 1991); *Bly*, 713 F.2d 1040.

22. *Ann McAlpin, etc. v. Leeds & Northrop Co., et al.*, 912 F. Supp. 207 (W.D. Va. 1996); *Marshall, supra* note 10; *Morsberger v. Uniking Conveyer Corp.*, 647 F. Supp. 1297 (W.D. Va. 1986); *Goodbar v. Whitehead Bros.*, 591 F. Supp. 552 (W.D. Va. 1984), *aff'd sub nom. Beale v. Hardy*, 769 F.2d 213 (4th Cir. 1985).

23. *Featherall*, 219 Va. 949.

24. *Turner v. Manning, Maxwell & Moore, Inc.*, 216 Va. 245, 217 S.E.2d 863 (1975).

25. *Alevromagiros v. Hechinger Company*, 993 F.2d 417 (4th Cir. 1993); *White Consol. Indus., Inc. v. Swiney*, 237 Va. 23, 376 S.E.2d 283 (1989); *Logan v. Montgomery Ward & Co.*, 216 Va. 425, 219 S.E.2d 685 (1975).

26. *Turner*, 216 Va. 245; *Alevromagiros*, 993 F.2d 417.

27. *Cooper v. Ingersoll Rand Co.*, 628 F. Supp. 1488 (W.D. Va. 1986).

28. *Ford Motor Co. v. Phelps*, 239 Va. 272, 389 S.E.2d 454 (1990); *General Motors Corp. v. Lupica*, 237 Va. 516, 379 S.E.2d 311 (1989).

29. *Logan*, 216 Va. 425.

30. *Cooper*, 628 F. Supp. 1488; *Bly v. Otis Elevator Co.*, 713 F.2d 1040 (4th Cir. 1983).

31. *Chestnut v. Ford Motor Co.*, 445 F.2d 967 (4th Cir. 1971).

32. *Virginia Transformer Corp. v. P.D. George Co.*, 932 F. Supp. 156 (W.D. Va. 1996); *Begley, supra*, 1996 U.S. Dist. LEXIS 8198.

33. *Besser v. Hansen*, 243 Va. 267, 415 S.E.2d 138 (1992); *Lust v. Clark Equip. Co.*, 792 F.2d 436 (4th Cir. 1986); *Turner v. Manning, Maxwell & Moore, Inc.*, 216 Va. 245, 217 S.E. 2d 863 (1975).

34. *Darrel Wood v. Bass Pro Shops, Inc.*, 250 Va. 297, 462 S.E.2d 101 (1995).

35. *Wallen v. Allen*, 231 Va. 289, 343 S.E.2d 73 (1986); *Ford Motor Co. v. Bartholomew*, 224 Va. 421, 297 S.E.2d 675 (1982).

36. Va. Code §§8.01-243, 8.01-246, 8.01-249 (1992); Va. Code §8.2-725 (1991).

WASHINGTON

I. WASHINGTON PRODUCT LIABILITY ACT

The Washington legislature passed the Washington Product Liability Act (WPLA) in 1981.[1] The WPLA applies to all product liability claims arising on or after July 26, 1981.[2]

Based in large part on the Model Uniform Product Liability Act,[3] the WPLA, on its face, substantially changes Washington's product liability law. However, subsequent interpretations of the WPLA by the Washington Supreme Court make the substance of the WPLA more consistent with prior common law than at first it might appear.

A. CAUSES OF ACTION

1. "Product Liability Claim"

The WPLA creates a single product liability cause of action, called a "product liability claim," that consolidates most of the common law theories of liability, including "[s]trict liability in tort; negligence; breach of express or implied warranty; breach of, or failure to, discharge a duty to warn or instruct . . . ; misrepresentation, concealment, or nondisclosure . . . ; or other claim or action previously based on any other substantive legal theory."[4]

Although the WPLA does not contain an express preemption clause, and notwithstanding the WPLA's reservation clause,[5] the Washington Supreme Court has determined that the "product liability claim" preempts the enumerated common law remedies.[6]

2. Other Causes of Action

The WPLA specifically excepts from this preemptive definition "fraud, intentionally caused harm or a claim or action under the [Washington] consumer protection act."[7]

B. DAMAGES

The WPLA restricts recovery for direct or consequential economic loss to the law of sales.[8] In drawing this line between contract and tort remedies, Washington has adopted "risk of harm" analysis for defining "economic loss."[9] Punitive damages are generally disfavored in Washington[10] and are not available in a product liability action.[11] Neither the WPLA nor Washington common law provides for recovery of attorneys' fees in product liability cases.

C. STATUTE OF LIMITATION

A product liability claim must be brought within three years from the time the claimant discovers "the harm and its cause."[12] The Washington Supreme Court has held the discovery rule satisfied when the claimant "discovered, or . . . should have discovered, a factual causal relationship of the product to the harm."[13] Where a claimant has sustained "separate and distinct" injuries, as distinguished from a progressive injury or disease, the discovery rule applies separately as to each injury.[14]

Although Washington imposes an absolute six-year statute of limitations on causes of action based on real estate improvements,[15] a 1986 amendment to this statute specifically excludes manufacturers from its coverage.[16]

D. STATUTE OF REPOSE

The WPLA protects product sellers (including manufacturers) from liability for harm caused after "expir[ation]" of the product's "useful safe life."[17] The defendant must prove expiration by a preponderance of the evidence, but the WPLA provides a rebuttable presumption that a product's useful safe life expires 12 years from the date of delivery.[18]

E. "CLAIMANT"

The WPLA broadly defines "claimant" as including "any person or entity that suffers harm."[19] The statute specifically abolishes any privity requirement.[20]

F. "DEFECT"

The WPLA avoids the term "defect," and the Washington courts have held that the claimant need not establish that the product was "defective" in order to recover.[21]

G. LIABILITY OF PRODUCT SELLERS OTHER THAN MANUFACTURERS

The WPLA subjects manufacturers and "product sellers other than manufacturers"[22] to different levels of liability. Generally, if a solvent manufacturer is subject to the jurisdiction of the court, the WPLA limits the liability of product sellers other than manufacturers to harm proximately caused by (1) common law negligence,[23] (2) breach of express warranty,[24] or (3) intentional misrepresentation or concealment.[25] There are, however, five circumstances under which a product seller "shall have the liability of a manufacturer."[26]

H. LIABILITY OF MANUFACTURERS

The WPLA defines five categories of potential liability for product manufacturers:[27] construction defects, breach of warranty, design defects, failure to warn, and post-sale duty to warn.

1. Categories of Potential Liability

a. Construction Defects

The WPLA uses the term "strict liability" to describe a manufacturer's responsibility for products that materially deviate from the manufacturer's design specifications or performance standards or materially deviate from otherwise identical units of the same product line.[28] If the deviation proximately causes the claimant's harm, the product is "not reasonably safe in construction" and the manufacturer is strictly liable.[29]

b. Breach of Warranty

The manufacturer is also strictly liable for any breach of express warranty,[30] or breach of implied warranty,[31] as to any nonconformity rendering the product "not reasonably safe."[32]

c. Design Defects

Although the WPLA uses the term "negligence" to describe a manufacturer's liability for claims based on design defects,[33] the Washington Supreme Court equates this statutory negligence with the strict liability standard as defined in the pre-WPLA Washington cases.[34]

In defining when design defects render a product "not reasonably safe," the WPLA adopts a risk-utility balancing test:

> A product is not reasonably safe as designed, if, at the time of manufacture, the likelihood that the product would cause the claimant's harm or similar harms, and the seriousness of those harms, outweighed the burden on the manufacturer to design a product that would have prevented those harms and the adverse effect that an alternative design that was practical and feasible would have on the usefulness of the product. . . .[35]

A claimant can recover under Washington Revised Code section 7.72.030(1)(a) without proving the availability of an alternative, safer design.[36]

d. Failure to Warn

The WPLA also adopts a risk-utility balancing test for determining when inadequate warnings or instructions render a product "not reasonably safe":

> A product is not reasonably safe because adequate warnings or instructions were not provided with the product, if, at the time of manufacture, the likelihood that the product would cause the claimant's harm or similar harms, and the seriousness of those harms, rendered the

warnings or instructions of the manufacturer inadequate and the manufacturer could have provided the warnings or instructions which the claimant alleges would have been adequate.[37]

As with design defects, strict liability is the standard for inadequate warnings,[38] notwithstanding that the WPLA purports to impose liability only where "the claimant's harm was proximately caused by the negligence of the manufacturer."[39] Consequently, "foreseeability" is not an element of a strict liability claim based on failure to warn.[40]

e. Post-Sale Duty to Warn

The WPLA adopts a common law negligence standard for providing warnings or instructions where the manufacturer learned or should have learned about a danger after the product was manufactured. The manufacturer must act as a "reasonably prudent manufacturer" and "exercise[] reasonable care to inform product users."[41]

2. Consumer Expectation Test

In addition to the five specific categories of liability discussed above, the WPLA provides: "In determining whether a product was not reasonably safe . . . , the trier of fact shall consider whether the product was unsafe to an extent beyond that which would be contemplated by the ordinary consumer."[42] The Washington Supreme Court has determined that "consumer expectations" are not merely a factor to consider under risk-utility balancing; instead, consumer expectations provide an alternative test for manufacturer liability.[43]

I. EVIDENTIARY ISSUES

The trier of fact may consider evidence of industry custom, technological feasibility, (i.e., "state of the art"),[44] or compliance with private, legislative, or administrative standards.[45] Washington recognizes compliance with a "specific mandatory government contract specification" as an absolute defense to a design defect claim;[46] noncompliance with a "specific mandatory government specification" (the word "contract" is not included here) gives rise to an automatic finding that the product is "not reasonably safe."[47]

Extant evidentiary rules other than those discussed above are unchanged under the WPLA.[48] Thus, evidence of subsequent remedial changes is generally inadmissible,[49] and the admissibility of "prior accident" evidence is left to trial court discretion.[50]

II. PRODUCT LIABILITY ISSUES OUTSIDE OF THE WPLA

A. APPORTIONMENT OF FAULT

Under Washington's general tort contributory fault rules, modified in 1993, fault is apportioned as follows:

[T]he trier of fact shall determine the percentage of the total fault which is attributable to every entity which caused the claimant's damages except entities immune from liability to the claimant under Title 51 RCW. The sum of the percentages of the total fault attributed to at-fault entities shall equal one hundred percent. The entities whose fault shall be determined include the claimant or person suffering personal injury or incurring property damage, defendants, third-party defendants, entities released by the claimant, entities with any other individual defense against the claimant, and entities immune from liability to the claimant, but shall not include those entities immune from liability to the claimant under Title 51 RCW.[51]

B. EFFECT OF PLAINTIFF'S FAULT

Washington's 1981 "Tort Reform" Act created a statutory system of "pure" comparative fault under which plaintiff's compensatory damages are diminished in proportion to the contributory fault chargeable to plaintiff.[52] This system applies to product liability claims.[53]

C. JOINT AND SEVERAL LIABILITY

Additional tort reform in 1986 abolished joint and several liability of defendants in cases where the plaintiff carries a share of the fault.[54] Even if the plaintiff is blameless, the defendants against whom judgment is entered are only jointly and severally liable "for the sum of their proportionate shares of the claimant[']s total damages."[55] Since shares of fault are allocated to all responsible entities, the named defendants may be jointly responsible for only a portion of plaintiff's total damages, and cannot be held jointly and severally liable for damages allocated to nonparties.[56]

D. CONTRIBUTION

In general, "[a] right of contribution exists between or among two or more persons who are jointly and severally liable upon the same indivisible claim for the same injury, death or harm" and "may be enforced either in the original action or by a separate action brought for that purpose."[57] A 1993 Washington Supreme Court decision emphasizes that one tortfeasor may not seek contribution "from another tortfeasor who has prevailed on summary judgment with dismissal of the plaintiff's tort claim."[58]

E. DEFENSES

The WPLA does not preempt existing common law defenses,[59] including obvious danger,[60] assumption of the risk,[61] and product alteration or modification.[62] Under Washington's system of comparative fault, however, these factors do not bar recovery, but instead merely reduce the claimant's recoverable damages.[63]

F. SUCCESSOR LIABILITY

In addition to the traditional bases of successor liability (agreement to assume liability, de facto merger, mere continuation, fraud),[64] Washington recognizes product line liability where the successor acquires substantially all of the predecessor's assets, holds itself out as a continuation, and benefits from the predecessor's good will.[65]

G. MARKET-SHARE ALTERNATE LIABILITY

The Washington Supreme Court has adopted a somewhat unique rule of market-share alternate liability in DES cases.[66] To date, the court has refused to extend this theory into other contexts.[67]

H. CHOICE OF LAW

Washington has adopted the "most significant relationship" rule for choice of law problems, as developed in the Restatement (Second) of Conflict of Laws.[68]

John D. Dillow
PERKINS COIE LLP
1201 Third Avenue, 40th Floor
Seattle, Washington 98101-3099
(206) 583-8888

ENDNOTES - WASHINGTON

1. Laws of 1981, ch. 27.

2. Wash. Rev. Code §4.22.920(1); see also *Viereck v. Fibreboard Corp.*, 81 Wash. App. 579, 583, 915 P.2d 581, 584, *rev. denied*, 130 Wash.2d 1009, 928 P.2d 414 (1996).

3. 44 Fed. Reg. 62,714 (1979); see also *Washington State Physicians Ins. Exch. & Assn. v. Fisons Corp.*, 122 Wash. 2d 299, 319, 858 P.2d 1054, 1065 (1993).

4. Wash. Rev. Code §7.72.010(4); *Hue v. Farmboy Spray Co.*, 127 Wash. 2d 67, 74 n.10, 896 P.2d 682, 686 n.10 (1995) (WPLA "creates a single cause of action for product-related harm with specified statutory requirements for proof.").

5. "The previous existing applicable law of this state on product liability is modified only to the extent set forth in this chapter." Wash. Rev. Code §7.72.020(1).

6. *Washington Water Power Co. v. Graybar Elec. Co.*, 112 Wash. 2d 847, 851-856, 774 P.2d 1199, 1202-1205 (1989).

7. Wash. Rev. Code §7.72.010(4).

8. *Washington Water Power Co.*, 112 Wash. 2d at 856-859, 774 P.2d at 1205-1207 (discussing Wash. Rev. Code §7.72.010(6)); see also *Berschauer/Phillips Constr. Co. v. Seattle Sch. Dist. No. 1*, 124 Wash. 2d 816, 822, 881 P.2d 986, 990 (1994).

9. *Washington Water Power Co.*, 112 Wash. 2d at 860-867, 774 P.2d at 1207-1211 (discussing "sudden and dangerous" and "evaluative" risk of harm formulas, without choosing between them); see also *Touchet Valley Grain Growers, Inc. v. Opp & Seibold Gen. Constr. Inc.*, 119 Wash. 2d 334, 350-355, 831 P.2d 724, 732-735 (1992) (same). Note, however, that where a claim arises under admiralty jurisdiction, federal admiralty rules preclude application of the analysis in *Washington Water Power Co.* See *Stanton v. Bayliner Marine Corp.*, 123 Wash. 2d 64, 87-88, 866 P.2d 15, 28 (1993) ("[S]ubstantive admiralty law precludes recovery for economic loss"; only remedy, if any, is under the Uniform Commercial Code.), *cert. denied*, 513 U.S. 819 (1994).

10. *Barr v. Interbay Citizens Bank*, 96 Wash. 2d 692, 699-700, 635 P.2d 441, 444 (1981), *amended*, 649 P.2d 827 (Wash. 1982) (100-year history disfavoring

punitive damages); see also *Dailey v. North Coast Life Ins. Co.*, 129 Wash. 2d 572, 919 P.2d 589 (1996).

11. See *Sofie v. Fibreboard Corp.*, 112 Wash. 2d 636, 665-666, 771 P.2d 711, 726 (1989).

12. Wash. Rev. Code §7.72.060(3).

13. *North Coast Air Servs., Ltd. v. Grumman Corp.*, 111 Wash. 2d 315, 319, 759 P.2d 405, 406 (1988). Washington Revised Code section 7.72.060(3) modifies and narrows the liberal common law discovery rule stated in *Ohler v. Tacoma Gen. Hosp.*, 92 Wash. 2d 507, 510-511, 598 P.2d 1358, 1360 (1979).

14. *Green v. American Pharm. Co.*, 86 Wash. App. 63, 67, 935 P.2d 652, 655, *rev. granted*, 133 Wash. 2d 1016, 948 P.2d 388 (1997).

15. Wash. Rev. Code §4.16.310.

16. Id. §4.16.300.

17. Id. §7.72.060(1); see *Rice v. Dow Chem. Co.*, 124 Wash. 2d 205, 212, 875 P.2d 1213, 1217 (1994).

18. Id. §7.72.060(2); see *Rice*, 124 Wash. 2d at 212, 875 P.2d at 1217.

19. Id. §7.72.010(5). Even one acting as a rescuer "may recover [under the WPLA] for injuries against the party who created the peril." *McCoy v. American Suzuki Motor Corp.*, 86 Wash. App. 107, 114, 936 P.2d 31, 33, *rev. granted*, 133 Wash. 2d 1027, 950 P.2d 478 (1997).

20. Id. The WPLA's exclusion of recovery for economic loss, however, effectively imposes a privity requirement for such claims, reversing Washington's common law rule that allowed tort-based actions for economic loss. See *Washington Water Power Co.*, 112 Wash. 2d at 852, 857-858 and n.7, 774 P.2d at 1203, 1205-1206 and n.7.

21. *Couch v. Mine Safety Appliances Co.*, 107 Wash. 2d 232, 239, 728 P.2d 585, 589 (1986).

22. "Product seller" includes manufacturers, wholesalers, distributors and retailers, as well as parties engaged in leasing and bailing. Wash. Rev. Code §7.72.010(1).

23. Id. §7.72.040(1)(a); see *Martin v. Schoonover*, 13 Wash. App. 48, 54, 533 P.2d 438, 442 (1975).

24. Wash. Rev. Code §7.72.040(1)(b). Although Washington Revised Code section 7.72.030(2) makes a manufacturer potentially liable for breach of UCC implied warranties, section 7.72.040(1) extinguishes a seller's liability for UCC implied warranties except for economic loss that is pursued as a UCC claim. See Wash. Rev. Code §7.72.010(6).

25. Id. §7.72.040(1)(c).

26. Id. §7.72.040(2) (no solvent manufacturer subject to court's jurisdiction; judgment-proof manufacturer; parent-subsidiary relationship; seller provided plans or specifications; product marketed under seller's brand or trade name).

27. Id. §7.72.010(2) broadly defines "manufacturer."

28. Id. §7.72.030(2), (2)(a).

29. Id. §7.72.030(2).

30. Id. §7.72.030(2)(b). The warranty must be "part of the basis of the bargain."

31. Id. §7.72.030(2)(c), incorporating Title 62A (the UCC).

32. Id. §7.72.030(2).

33. Id. §7.72.030(1).

34. *Falk v. Keene Corp.*, 113 Wash. 2d 645, 651-653, 782 P.2d 974, 978-979 (1989) (WPLA sets forth same "strict liability" design defect standard adopted in *Seattle-First Natl. Bank v. Tabert*, 86 Wash. 2d 145, 542 P.2d 774 (1975)).

35. Wash. Rev. Code §7.72.030(1)(a).

36. *Couch*, 107 Wash. 2d at 234, 728 P.2d at 586.

37. Wash. Rev. Code §7.72.030(1)(b).

38. *Ayers v. Johnson & Johnson Baby Prods. Co.*, 117 Wash. 2d 747, 762-763, 818 P.2d 1337, 1345 (1991).

39. Wash. Rev. Code §7.72.030(1).

40. *Ayers*, 117 Wash. 2d at 763, 818 P.2d at 1345.

41. Wash. Rev. Code §7.72.030(1)(c); see *Couch*, 107 Wash. 2d at 239 n.5, 728 P.2d at 589 n.5.

42. Wash. Rev. Code §7.72.030(3).

43. *Falk*, 113 Wash. 2d at 654-655, 782 P.2d at 980 (design defect); *Ayers*, 117 Wash. 2d at 765, 818 P.2d at 1346 (failure to warn).

44. Wash. Rev. Code §7.72.050(1); cf. *Lenhardt v. Ford Motor Co.*, 102 Wash. 2d 208, 210-211, 683 P.2d 1097, 1099 (1984) (pre-WPLA case discussing and distinguishing "state of the art" and "industry custom"). Neither type of evidence was relevant under prior caselaw, and thus in this context at least the WPLA significantly changes Washington common law. See also *Crittenden v. Fibreboard Corp.*, 58 Wash. App. 649, 658, 794 P.2d 554, 559 (1990), *amended*, 803 P.2d 1329 (Wash. Ct. App. 1991); *Falk*, 113 Wash. 2d at 654, 782 P.2d at 979-980.

45. Wash. Rev. Code §7.72.050(1).

46. Id. §7.72.050(2); see *Koehler v. Fibreboard Corp. (In re Estate of Foster)*, 55 Wash. App. 545, 779 P.2d 272 (1989), *review denied*, 114 Wash. 2d 1004, 788 P.2d 1079 (1990). The Washington Supreme Court more recently held, however, that "compliance with specific mandatory government contract specifications *relating to design* does not give rise to the absolute defense in [§]7.72.050(2) to a postmanufacture *failure-to-warn* claim." *Timberline Air Serv., Inc. v. Bell Helicopter-Textron, Inc.*, 125 Wash. 2d 305, 318, 884 P.2d 920, 927 (1994) (emphasis added).

47. Wash. Rev. Code §7.72.050(2).

48. Id. §7.72.020(1).

49. "[E]vidence of subsequent remedial measures should not be admitted in a strict products liability action absent an exception under ER 407." *Hyjek v. Anthony Indus.*, 133 Wash. 2d 414, 428, 944 P.2d 1036, 1043 (1997).

50. See *Seay v. Chrysler Corp.*, 93 Wash. 2d 319, 324, 609 P.2d 1382, 1385 (1980).

51. Wash. Rev. Code §4.22.070(1); see also id. §4.22.060; *Schmidt v. Cornerstone Inv., Inc.*, 115 Wash. 2d 148, 157-159, 795 P.2d 1143, 1147 (1990) (recovery reduced by amount paid in settlement or reasonable amount). A decision offsetting an amount paid rather than the much higher reasonable settlement amount is of interest in the structured settlement context. See *Brewer v. Fibreboard Corp.*, 127 Wash. 2d 512, 532, 901 P.2d 297, 307-308 (1995).

52. Wash. Rev. Code §4.22.005.

53. Id. §4.22.015; see also *Lundberg v. All-Pure Chem. Co.*, 55 Wash. App. 181, 186-187, 777 P.2d 15, 19, *review denied*, 113 Wash. 2d 1030, 784 P.2d 530 (1989).

54. Wash. Rev. Code §4.22.070.

55. Id. §4.22.070(1)(b); see *Washburn v. Beatt Equip. Co.*, 120 Wash. 2d 246, 293-299, 840 P.2d 860, 886-889 (1992).

56. *Washburn*, 120 Wash. 2d at 296-297, 840 P.2d at 887-888; see also id. at 294, 840 P.2d at 886 ("*only* defendants against whom judgment is entered are jointly and severally liable and only for the sum of *their* proportionate shares of the total damages").

57. Wash. Rev. Code §4.22.040(1).

58. *Gerrard v. Craig*, 122 Wash. 2d 288, 298-299, 857 P.2d 1033, 1038-1039 (1993). *Gerrard* does not explicitly overrule a prior Washington Supreme Court decision, *Smith v. Jackson*, 106 Wash. 2d 298, 721 P.2d 508 (1986), but there is tension between the two cases. In *Smith*, the named defendant was allowed to bring a contribution action against certain third parties even though the statute of limitation would have precluded a direct action between the plaintiff and the third parties. 106 Wash. 2d at 304, 721 P.2d at 511. *Gerrard*, following *Washburn*, 120 Wash. 2d at 294, 840 P.2d at 886-887, holds that "only those defendants against whom a claimant has obtained a judgment can be jointly and severally liable" and thus susceptible to a contribution action. See also Wash. Rev. Code §4.22.070(1).

59. Wash. Rev. Code §7.72.020(1).

60. *Haysom*, 89 Wash. 2d at 479, 573 P.2d at 789.

61. *Campbell v. ITE Imperial Corp.*, 107 Wash. 2d 807, 819-820, 733 P.2d 969, 976 (1987).

62. *Bich v. General Elec. Co.*, 27 Wash. App. 25, 29, 614 P.2d 1323, 1326 (1980).

63. See Wash. Rev. Code §4.22.005.

64. *Martin v. Abbott Labs.*, 102 Wash. 2d 581, 609, 689 P.2d 368, 384-385 (1984).

65. *Martin*, 102 Wash. 2d at 615, 689 P.2d at 388 (adopting "product line" successor liability in product liability action as defined in *Ray v. Alad Corp.*, 19 Cal. 3d 22, 560 P.2d 3, 136 Cal. Rptr. 574 (1977)); see also *Hall v.*

Armstrong Cork, Inc., 103 Wash. 2d 258, 692 P.2d 787 (1984) (product line exception unavailable where plaintiff can pursue claim against predecessor corporation).

66. *Martin*, 102 Wash. 2d 581, 689 P.2d 368; see also *George v. Parke-Davis*, 107 Wash. 2d 584, 733 P.2d 507 (1987).

67. See, e.g., *Lockwood v. AC & S, Inc.*, 109 Wash. 2d 235, 245 n.6, 744 P.2d 605, 612 n.6 (1987) (court declined to apply market-share alternate liability in asbestos case).

68. See *Rice v. Dow Chem. Co.*, 124 Wash. 2d at 213, 875 P.2d at 1217; *Barr v. Interbay Citizens Bank*, 96 Wash. 2d 692, 697, 635 P.2d 441, 443 (1981); *Johnson v. Spider Staging Corp.*, 87 Wash. 2d 577, 580, 555 P.2d 997, 1000 (1976).

WEST VIRGINIA

A. CAUSES OF ACTION

Product liability lawsuits commonly include causes of action for strict liability, negligence, and breach of warranty.

B. STATUTES OF LIMITATION

A cause of action for personal injury damages or tortious injury to personal property must be brought within two years, whether brought in negligence, strict liability, or breach of warranty.[1] A "discovery" rule applies, and a cause of action in negligence, strict liability, or breach of warranty accrues when the plaintiff knows, or by the exercise of reasonable diligence should know, (1) that he has been injured, (2) the identity of the maker of the product, and (3) that the product had a causal relation to his injury, which is a question of fact.[2]

A cause of action for economic or contractual damages resulting from a breach of warranty must be brought within four years.[3] A cause of action for breach of warranty accrues when the breach occurs, regardless of the aggrieved party's lack of knowledge of the breach.[4] A breach of warranty occurs when tender of delivery is made; however, where a warranty explicitly extends to future performance of the goods and discovery of the breach must await the time of such performance, the cause of action accrues when the breach is or should have been discovered.[5]

C. STRICT LIABILITY

1. The Standard

West Virginia has not adopted section 402A of the Restatement (Second) of Torts. The West Virginia rule does not require that the defective condition be "unreasonably dangerous."[6] The general test for establishing strict liability in tort in West Virginia is whether the involved product is "defective" in the sense that it is not reasonably safe for its intended use as determined by what a reasonably prudent manufacturer's standards should have been at the time the product was made.[7]

The theory of strict liability in tort does not apply to an independent contractor who assembles a product unless it can be shown that the condition complained about was so obvious and egregious that no reasonably competent assembler would have left the product in that condition.[8]

Strict liability in tort may be used to recover for property damage when the defective product damages property only.[9] Property damage to defective products that results from a sudden calamitous event, such as a fire, is recoverable under a strict liability cause of action.[10] Damages that result merely because of a "bad bargain," such as deterioration, internal breakage, or depreciation, are outside the scope of strict liability.[11] In addition, the theory of strict liability cannot be used to recover loss of profits. This item of damages must be pursued under a warranty or contract theory.[12]

2. "Defect"

The product is to be tested by what a reasonably prudent manufacturer would accomplish with regard to the safety of the product, having in mind the general state of the art of the manufacturing process, including design, labels, and warnings, as it relates to economic costs, at the time the product was made.[13]

Direct evidence of the defect is not required. Circumstantial evidence may be sufficient to make a prima facie case in a strict liability action, provided the evidence shows that a malfunction in the product occurred that would not ordinarily happen in the absence of a defect. In addition, the plaintiff must show that there was neither abnormal use nor a reasonable secondary cause for the malfunction.[14]

3. Contributory Negligence/Assumption of Risk

The defense of comparative negligence is available against the plaintiff in a product liability action; however, the plaintiff's negligence must be something more than failing to discover a defect or to guard against it.[15]

The defense of comparative assumption of the risk is available against the plaintiff in a product liability action in which it is shown that with full appreciation of the defective condition (actual knowledge on the part of the plaintiff), the plaintiff continued to use the product.[16]

4. Sale

The seller of a product may be entitled to implied indemnity from the manufacturer; however, a party seeking implied indemnity must be without fault.[17] Settlement will bar an action for contribution by the non-settling party, but settlement is not a bar to implied indemnity when liability is not predicated on independent fault or negligence of the non-settling party.[18]

5. Inherently Dangerous Products

West Virginia has declined to adopt the doctrine of *Rylands v. Fletcher* into its tort product liability law.[19]

6. Privity

No privity is required; a plaintiff may sue even though she did not buy the product from the manufacturer.[20]

7. Failure to Warn

In failure-to-warn cases, "the focus is not so much on a flawed physical condition of the product, as on its unsafeness arising out of the failure to adequately label, instruct, or warn.[21] The duty to warn exists when the use made of the product is foreseeable to the manufacturer or seller.[22] The basic inquiry in this regard is whether it was "reasonably foreseeable to the manufacturer that the product would be unreasonably dangerous if distributed without a warning."[23]

8. Substantial Change/Abnormal Use

The defense of abnormal use is available against the plaintiff in a product liability action.[24] Plaintiff must show that there was neither "abnormal"[25] use nor a reasonable secondary cause for the malfunction."[26]

9. State of the Art

"State-of-the-art" evidence is admissible.[27]

10. Standards and Government Regulations

Failure to comply with a statute or regulation constitutes prima facie negligence if an injury proximately results from the noncompliance and is of the type the statute or regulation was intended to prevent. Conversely, compliance with the appropriate statute or regulation may serve competent evidence of due care, but it does not constitute due care per se, nor does it create a presumption of due care.[28]

11. Unavoidably Unsafe Products

Comment k to section 402A, which defines an exception to the doctrine of strict liability for "unavoidably unsafe" products, has not been explicitly adopted by the Supreme Court of Appeals of West Virginia. However, a federal district court sitting in West Virginia has predicted that "[i]t seems likely . . . the West Virginia courts would also apply the comment k exception where a product is proven to be unavoidably unsafe."[29]

12. Crashworthiness

West Virginia has adopted the "crashworthiness" theory.[30] To recover on a theory of crashworthiness against the manufacturer of a motor vehicle, the plaintiff only has to show that a defect in the vehicle's design was "a factor in causing some aspect of the plaintiff's harm.[31] The manufacturer may then limit its liability by showing that the plaintiff's "injuries are capable of apportionment between the first and second collisions."[32]

D. NEGLIGENCE

Unlike strict liability, there are few unique aspects of West Virginia product liability cases based on negligence.

West Virginia has adopted the doctrine of comparative negligence. Under the West Virginia approach, which is known as modified comparative negligence, if the negligence of the plaintiff equals or exceeds the combined negligence of *all* of the parties involved in the accident, and not just the alleged negligence or fault of the defendant, the plaintiff is barred from recovery.[33]

West Virginia has also adopted the doctrine of comparative assumption of the risk. Under that doctrine, a plaintiff is not barred from recovery by the doctrine of assumption of risk unless his degree of fault arising therefrom equals or exceeds the combined fault or negligence of the other parties to the accident.[34]

The duty of reasonable care owed by the assembler of a product is to recognize an unreasonable risk of harm to those who use the product as assembled unless the assembler "has a specialized skill or competence, or has represented that he has such a skill, to modify the product to enhance its safety."[35]

E. BREACH OF WARRANTY

There is no requirement of privity of contract to mention an action for breach of an express or implied warranty in West Virginia.[36]

Lack of notice of the breach is not a defense in a product liability action for personal injuries.[37]

F. PUNITIVE DAMAGES

Punitive damages are recoverable in product liability actions.[38] A jury may award punitive or exemplary damages against a defendant for punishment of willful, wanton, or malicious behavior toward the plaintiff.[39] Punitive damages should bear a reasonable relationship to the potential of harm caused by the defendant's actions, and that generally means that punitive damages should bear a reasonable relationship to compensatory damages.

G. SUCCESSOR LIABILITY

The West Virginia Supreme Court of Appeals has recognized that a successor corporation is liable for the obligations of a predecessor if there is an agreement to assume liability, fraud, lack of good faith, statutory consolidation, or merger and the successor is a mere continuation or reincarnation of its predecessor.[40]

H. STATUTES, INCLUDING APPLICABLE "TORT REFORM" STATUTES

Relevant statutes for product liability actions are the statutes of limitation, the lemon law, which establishes a manufacturer's duty to repair or replace a new motor vehicle,[41] and, when a breach of warranty is alleged, the commercial code sections.

R. Kemp Morton
Krista L. Duncan
HUDDLESTON, BOLEN, BEATTY, PORTER & COPEN
611 Third Avenue
P. O. Box 2185
Huntington, West Virginia 25722-2185
(304) 529-6181

1. W. Va. Code §55-2-12 (1994); *Taylor v. Ford Motor Co.*, 408 S.E.2d 270, 274 (W. Va. 1991).

2. *Cecil v. Airco, Inc.*, 416 S.E.2d 728, 730-31 (W. Va. 1992); *Taylor*, 408 S.E.2d at 274; *Hickman v. Grover*, 358 S.E.2d 810, 813 (W. Va. 1987).

3. W. Va. Code §46-2-725(1) (1993).

4. W. Va. Code §46-2-725(2) (1993); see *Roxalana Hills, Ltd. v. Masonite Corp.*, 627 F. Supp. 1194, 1199-1201 (S.D.W. Va. 1986), *aff'd*, 813 F.2d 1228 (4th Cir. 1987); *Basham v. General Shale*, 377 S.E.2d 830, 835 (W. Va. 1988).

5. *Id.*

6. *Morningstar v. Black & Decker Mfg. Co.*, 253 S.E.2d 666, 684 (W. Va. 1979).

7. *Id.* at 683.

8. *Yost v. Fuscaldo*, 408 S.E.2d 72, 77 (W. Va. 1991).

9. *Capitol Fuels, Inc. v. Clark Equip. Co.*, 382 S.E.2d 311, 313 (W. Va. 1989); *Basham*, 377 S.E.2d 830; *Star Furn. Co. v. Pulaski Furn. Co.*, 297 S.E.2d 854, 857 (W. Va. 1982).

10. *Id.*

11. *Roxalana Hills, Ltd. v. Masonite Corp.*, 627 F. Supp. 1194, 1195-99 (S.D.W. Va. 1986), *aff'd*, 813 F.2d 1228 (4th Cir. 1987); *Taylor v. Ford Motor Co.*, 408 S.E.2d 270 (W. Va. 1991); *Capitol Fuels, Inc.*, 382 S.E.2d at 313; *Basham*, 377 S.E.2d at 834; *Star Furn. Co.*, 297 S.E.2d at 859 & 859, n.4.

12. *Kaiser Aluminum & Chem. Corp. v. Westinghouse Elec. Corp.*, 981 F.2d 136, 145-147 (4th Cir. 1992); *Star Furn. Co.*, 297 S.E.2d at 859-860.

13. *Morningstar v. Black & Decker Mfg. Co.*, 253 S.E.2d 666, 682-683 (W. Va. 1979).

14. *Anderson v. Chrysler Corp.*, 403 S.E.2d 189, 193-194 (W. Va. 1991).

15. *Star Furn. Co.*, 297 S.E.2d at 862-863; see also *Morningstar*, 253 S.E.2d at 683.

16. *In re State Public Bldg. Asbestos Litigation*, 454 S.E.2d 413, 424 (W. Va. 1994) *cert. denied*, 115 S. Ct. 2614 (1995); *King v. Kayak Mfg. Corp.*, 387 S.E.2d 511, 518 (W. Va. 1989); *see also Star Furn. Co.*, 297 S.E.2d at 863 n.5; *Morningstar*, 253 S.E.2d at 683-684.

17. *Hill v. Joseph T. Ryerson & Son, Inc.*, 268 S.E.2d 296, 301 (W. Va. 1980).

18. *Dunn v. Kanawha County Board of Education*, 459 S.E.2d 151, 156-158 (W. Va. 1995).

19. *Morningstar*, 253 S.E.2d at 684.

20. *Morningstar*, 253 S.E.2d at 680.

21. *Ilosky v. Michelin Tire Corp.*, 307 S.E.2d 603, 609 (W. Va. 1983).

22. *Id.*

23. *Church v. Wesson*, 385 S.E.2d 393, 396 (W. Va. 1989).

24. *Star Furn. Co. v. Pulaski Furn. Co.*, 297 S.E.2d 854, 862-863 (W. Va. 1982); *Morningstar*, 253 S.E.2d at 683.

25. *Morningstar*, 253 S.E.2d at 683.

26. *Anderson v. Chrysler Corp.*, 403 S.E.2d 189, 193-194 (W. Va. 1991).

27. *Church*, 385 S.E.2d at 396; *Morningstar*, 253 S.E.2d at 666.

28. *Miller v. Warren*, 390 S.E.2d 207, 208-209 (W. Va. 1990).

29. Restatement (Second) of Torts §402A, cmt. k (1965). See *Rohrbough v. Wyeth Labs., Inc.*, 719 F. Supp. 470, n.1 (N.D.W. Va. 1989), *aff'd*, 916 F.2d 970 (4th Cir. 1990) citation omitted; *Johnson v. General Motors Corp.*, 438 S.E.2d 28 (W. Va. 1993).

30. *Blankenship v. General Motors Corp.*, 406 S.E.2d 781, 786 (W. Va. 1991).

31. *Id.*

32. *Id.* at 786.

33. *Bowman v. Barnes*, 282 S.E.2d 613, 618 (W. Va. 1981); *Bradley v. Appalachian Power Co.*, 256 S.E.2d 879, 885 (W. Va. 1979).

34. *King v. Kayak Mfg. Corp.*, 387 S.E.2d 511, 517-518 (W. Va. 1989).

35. *Yost v. Fuscaldo*, 408 S.E.2d 72, 76 (W. Va. 1991).

36. *Taylor v. Ford Motor Co.*, 408 S.E.2d 270, 272 (W. Va. 1991); *Sewell v. Gregory*, 371 S.E.2d 82, 86 (W. Va. 1988); see generally *Dawson v. Canteen Corp.*, 212 S.E.2d 82, 83-84 (W. Va. 1975).

37. W. Va. Code §46-2-607(3)(a) (1993); *Hill v. Joseph T. Ryerson & Son, Inc.*, 268 S.E.2d 296, 305 (W. Va. 1980).

38. *Rohrbough v. Wyeth Labs., Inc.*, 719 F. Supp. 470, 479 (N.D.W. Va. 1989) (dicta), *aff'd*, 916 F.2d 970 (4th Cir. 1990).

39. *Ilosky v. Michelin Tire Corp.*, 307 S.E.2d 603, 619 (W. Va. 1983).

40. *In re State Public Bldg. Asbestos Litigation*, 454 S.E.2d 413, 424-425 (W. Va. 1994) *cert. denied*, 115 S. Ct. 2614 (1995); *Davis v. Celetox Corp.*, 420 S.E.2d 557, 563 (W. Va. 1992).

41. See generally W. Va. Code §46A-6A-1 et seq. (1996), *Bostic v. Mallard Coach Co.*, 406 S.E.2d 725 (W. Va. 1991); *Adams v. Nissan Motor Corp.*, 387 S.E.2d 288 (W. Va. 1989).

WISCONSIN

A. CAUSES OF ACTION

Strict liability and negligence constitute alternative theories of recovery for product liability.[1] Wisconsin does not recognize a separate product liability cause of action for breach of warranty.[2]

B. STATUTES OF LIMITATION

Causes of action for personal injury or wrongful death must be brought within three years after the cause of action accrues.[3] Causes of action for property damage must be brought within six years after the cause of action accrues.[4] Wisconsin recognizes a "discovery" rule for tort actions.[5]

There is no statute of repose in Wisconsin.

C. STRICT LIABILITY

1. The Standard

Wisconsin has adopted section 402A of the Restatement (Second) of Torts.[6] A finding of strict liability is equivalent to a finding of negligence per se, for purposes of applying Wisconsin's comparative negligence law.[7] Strict liability may extend to include injury to bystanders as well as to users or consumers.[8]

2. "Defect"

A product is defective if it is unfit for its intended purpose at the time that it leaves the control of the manufacturer.[9] The defect may relate to design, manufacture, or failure to warn.[10]

To state a claim in strict liability, a plaintiff must also allege that the product was unreasonably dangerous. Wisconsin recognizes the "consumer contemplation" test for determining "unreasonable danger," that is, the product must be dangerous "beyond that which would be contemplated by the ordinary consumer who purchases it," with the ordinary knowledge common to the community as to its characteristics.[11]

3. Contributory Negligence/Assumption of Risk

Assumption of risk has been abolished as a separate defense in Wisconsin. Contributory negligence is a partial defense to product liability actions. Evidence of contributory negligence on the part of the plaintiff is admissible and may bar recovery, with respect to strict liability or negligence, if the plaintiff is found to be equally or more negligent, on a percentage basis, than the defendant.[12]

4. Sale or Lease

Strict liability is imposed on manufacturers and sellers[13] as well as on commercial lessors.[14]

The seller of a used product may be held liable for strict liability if the seller is engaged in the business of selling such product and the hidden defective condition of the used product arises out of the original manufacturing process.[15]

A reconditioner of a used product who does not manufacture, distribute, or sell the products it reconditions is not liable in strict products liability for defects in the products it reconditions.[16]

5. Inherently Dangerous Products

Wisconsin has not adopted comment k to section 402A of the Restatement (Second) of Torts. Sellers of inherently dangerous products may be found strictly liable for injuries resulting from the products.[17]

6. Successor Liability

A corporation purchasing the assets of another corporation will not succeed to the selling corporation's liability for products manufactured by the seller unless (1) the buyer expressly or impliedly agrees to assume the seller's liability; (2) the transaction is a consolidation or merger of the buyer and seller; (3) the buyer is a mere continuation of the seller; or (4) the corporations fraudulently enter into the transaction in order to escape liability.[18] Wisconsin does not recognize the "product line" exception to the nonliability rule. "Mere continuation" is proved through identity of ownership, management, and control rather than continuation of a particular product line.

7. Privity

Privity is not required to state a cause of action in strict product liability.[19]

8. Failure to Warn

The manufacturer, distributor, or retailer of an unreasonably dangerous product is required to warn the potential user of the danger. The duty arises if the seller has, or should have, knowledge of a dangerous use of the product.[20] The duty to warn is a duty to give a warning that is adequate and appropriate under the circumstances.[21] The plaintiff must prove that the absence of a warning was a proximate cause (substantial factor) of the alleged injuries. In some circumstances, a failure to warn constitutes negligence as a matter of law.[22]

It is a defense to a strict liability action that the plaintiff voluntarily confronted an open and obvious condition if a reasonable person in the position of the plaintiff would recognize the condition and the risk that it presents.[23] This defense applies even when the reasonable person in the plaintiff's position would not appreciate the gravity of the harm threatened.[24]

9.   **Post-Sale Duty to Warn**

Under limited circumstances, a manufacturer may be under a post-sale duty to warn. Wisconsin does not recognize an absolute, continuing duty to warn of new safety devices that eliminate potential hazards. The post-sale duty to warn is most likely to be found where there is a limited market and a limited number of products in existence. The post-sale duty to warn does not generally apply to mass-marketed manufactured goods that become increasingly safer with each new model.[25]

10. **Substantial Change/Abnormal Use**

A manufacturer is not responsible for injuries caused by a substantial change in the condition of the product occurring after initial sale, or due to abnormal use, but the substantial change or abnormal use must be one that could not reasonably be foreseen or expected.[26]

11. **State of the Art**

"State-of-the-art" evidence is admissible for the purpose of providing the jury with a basis to determine whether the design of the product was unreasonably dangerous.[27]

12. **Malfunction**

Where evidence rebuts the existence of other probable causes, evidence of malfunction may be considered evidence of defect.[28]

13. **Standards and Government Regulations**

Evidence of industry custom and safety standards is admissible, but not conclusive, on the question of reasonable safety or defect.[29]

14. **Other Accidents**

Evidence of other accidents may be admitted on the issues of notice, defect, or causation, but only where the other accidents are shown to have occurred under conditions and circumstances substantially similar to those of the accident in question.[30]

15. **Misrepresentation**

Misrepresentation is an independent tort in Wisconsin.[31] Wisconsin has not adopted section 402B of the Restatement (Second) of Torts. Where plaintiffs sue under both strict liability and misrepresentation, Wisconsin will evaluate misrepresentation as a contractual claim, not a tort claim.[32]

D. NEGLIGENCE

A plaintiff may recover for negligence in designing, constructing, inspecting, or warning about a product.[33] Wisconsin's comparative fault statute diminishes the plaintiff's recovery in proportion to the plaintiff's negligence. Plaintiff may not recover against the defendant if the plaintiff's negligence is greater than that of the particular defendant.[34] A plaintiff's negligence is measured separately against the negligence of each person found to be causally negligent.[35] Multiple defendants have a right to contribution from one another in proportion to their causal negligence, but a change in Wisconsin law has modified joint and several liability. Where previously there was unlimited joint and several liability,[36] there is now conditional joint and several liability for cases brought after May 15, 1995. If a defendant's negligence is less than 51 percent, its liability is limited to its percentage of causal negligence. Defendants whose causal negligence is 51 percent or more are jointly and severally liable.[37] The new statute does not apply to cases involving concerted action.[38]

E. BREACH OF WARRANTY

Wisconsin does not recognize a product liability cause of action for breach of warranty.[39]

F. PUNITIVE DAMAGES

Punitive damages are now regulated by statute in Wisconsin, for cases brought after May 15, 1995.[40] To receive punitive damages, a plaintiff must show that a defendant acted maliciously toward him or in intentional disregard of his rights.[41] Previously, punitive damages were recoverable if a plaintiff proved that a defendant's conduct was "outrageous" or in reckless disregard of plaintiff's rights.[42] Punitive damages are not recoverable in wrongful death cases[43] and not without a recovery of compensatory damages.[44]

G. STATUTES

Wisconsin has a statute of limitations for personal injury actions, which includes product liability claims. A "borrowing statute" applied to foreign statutes of limitation. Wis Stat. §893.07. Section 895.045 governs comparative negligence, and section 895.85 is the punitive damages statute.

Frank J. Daily
Michael J. Gonring
QUARLES & BRADY
411 East Wisconsin Avenue
Milwaukee, Wisconsin 53202-4497
(414) 277-5000

ENDNOTES - WISCONSIN

1. See *Vincer v. Esther Williams All Aluminum Swimming Pool Co.*, 69 Wis. 2d 326, 230 N.W.2d 797 (1975).

2. See *Austin v. Ford Motor Co.*, 86 Wis. 2d 628, 273 N.W.2d 233 (1979).

3. See Wis. Stat. §893.54 (1995).

4. See Wis. Stat. §893.52 (1995).

5. See *Hansen v. A. H. Robins, Inc.*, 113 Wis. 2d 550, 335 N.W.2d 578 (1983).

6. See *Dipple v. Sciano*, 37 Wis. 2d 443, 155 N.W.2d 55 (1967).

7. See *Dipple*, 37 Wis. 2d at 461.

8. See *Howes v. Hansen*, 56 Wis. 2d 247, 201 N.W.2d 825 (1972).

9. See Wisconsin Civil Jury Instruction 3260.

10. See *Arbet v. Gussarson*, 66 Wis. 2d 551, 225 N.W.2d 431 (1975).

11. See *Vincer*, 69 Wis. 2d at 331; *Arbet*, 66 Wis. 2d at 557.

12. See Wis. Stat. §895.045(1) (1995); see also *Powers v. Hunt-Wesson Foods, Inc.*, 64 Wis. 2d 532, 219 N.W.2d 393 (1974); *Jagmin v. Simonds Abrasive Co.*, 61 Wis. 2d 60, 211 N.W.2d 810 (1973).

13. See *Dipple*, 37 Wis. 2d at 459-460.

14. See *Kemp v. Miller*, 154 Wis. 2d 538, 453 N.W.2d 872 (1990).

15. *Nelson v. Nelson Hardware, Inc.*, 160 Wis. 2d 689, 467 N.W.2d 518 (1991).

16. *Rolph v. EBI Cos.*, 159 Wis. 2d 518, 464 N.W.2d 667 (1991).

17. See *Collins v. Eli Lilly Co.*, 116 Wis. 2d 166, 342 N.W.2d 37 (1984).

18. See *Fish v. Amsted Indus., Inc.*, 126 Wis. 2d 293, 376 N.W.2d 820 (1985).

19. See *Dipple*, 37 Wis. 2d at 459.

20. See *Flaminio v. Honda Motor Co. Ltd.*, 733 F.2d 463 (7th Cir. 1984).

21. See *Schuh v. Fox River Tractor Co.*, 63 Wis. 2d 728, 218 N.W.2d 279 (1974).

22. See, e.g., *Anderson v. Alfa-Laval Agri, Inc.*, 209 Wis. 2d 337, 564 N.W.2d 788 (Ct. App. 1997).

23. *Griebler v. Doughboy Recreational, Inc.*, 160 Wis. 2d 547, 466 N.W.2d 897 (1991).

24. Id.

25. See *Gracyalny v. Westinghouse Elec. Corp.*, 723 F.2d 1311 (7th Cir. 1983); *Kozlowski v. John E. Smith's Sons Co.*, 87 Wis. 2d 882, 275 N.W.2d 915 (1979).

26. See *Powers*, 64 Wis. 2d 532; *Dipple*, 37 Wis. 2d at 460.

27. See *D. L. v. Huebner*, 110 Wis. 2d 581, 329 N.W.2d 890 (1983); *Wisconsin Elec. Power Co. v. Zallea Bros., Inc.*, 606 F.2d 697 (7th Cir. 1979); *Schuh v. Fox River Tractor Co.*, 63 Wis. 2d 728, 218 N.W.2d 279 (1974).

28. See *City of Franklin v. Badger Ford Truck Sales Inc.*, 58 Wis. 2d 641, 207 N.W.2d 866 (1973).

29. See *Sumnicht v. Toyota Motor Sales U.S.A., Inc.*, 121 Wis. 2d 338, 360 N.W.2d 2 (1984); *D. L. v. Huebner*, 110 Wis. 2d at 595; *Raim v. Ventura*, 16 Wis. 2d 67, 113 N.W.2d 827 (1962).

30. See *Farrell v. John Deere Co.*, 151 Wis. 2d 45, 443 N.W.2d 50 (Ct. App. 1989).

31. See *Lundin v. Shimanski*, 124 Wis. 2d 175, 368 N.W.2d 676 (1985).

32. See *Wisconsin Power and Light Co. v. Westinghouse Elec. Corp.*, 645 F. Supp. 1129 (W.D. Wis. 1986), *aff'd*, 830 F.2d 1405 (7th Cir. 1987).

33. See *Smith v. Atco Co.*, 6 Wis. 2d 371, 94 N.W.2d 697 (1959); *Kutsugeras v. AVCO Corp.*, 973 F.2d 1341 (7th Cir. 1992).

34. See Wis. Stat. §895.045, *Delvaux v. Vanden Langenberg*, 130 Wis. 2d 464, 387 N.W.2d 751 (1986).

35. Wis. Stat. 895.045(1) (1995).

36. See *Fitzgerald v. Badger State Mut. Cas. Ins. Co.*, 67 Wis. 2d 321, 227 N.W.2d 444 (1975); *City of Franklin v. Badger Ford Truck Sales, Inc.*, 58 Wis. 2d 641, 207 N.W.2d 866 (1973).

37.   Wis. Stat. 895.045(1) (1995).

38.   Wis. Stat. 895.045(2) (1995).

39.   See *Austin v. Ford Motor Co.*, 86 Wis. 2d 628, 273 N.W.2d 233 (1979).

40.   Wis. Stat. 895.85 (1995).

41.   Wis. Stat. 895.85(3) (1995).

42.   See *Wangen v. Ford Motor Co.*, 97 Wis. 2d 260, 294 N.W.2d 437 (1980).

43.   See *Wangen*, 97 Wis. 2d 260, 294 N.W.2d 437 (1980).

44.   *Tucker v. Marcus*, 142 Wis. 2d 425, 418 N.W.2d 818 (1988).

WYOMING

A. CAUSES OF ACTION

Product liability claims may be premised on any or all of negligence,[1] breach of express and implied warranties,[2] or strict liability[3] theories.

B. STATUTES OF LIMITATION

1. Negligence

The statute of limitations is four years after cause of action accrues. The four-year statute of limitations "is triggered when the plaintiff knows or has reason to know the existence of the cause of action."[4] The plaintiff's lack of knowledge of the identity of the tortfeasor does not prevent the statute of limitations from running.[5]

2. Breach of Warranty

The Wyoming legislature has adopted the official version of Uniform Commercial Code section 2-725 (Wyo. Stat. §34.1-2-725), and the statute of limitations therein has not been modified by other statutes of limitation. The statute of limitations is not more than four years after the cause of action has accrued, and can be less if the agreement of the parties reduces that period, but it cannot be reduced to less than one year. A cause of action accrues when the breach occurs, and, subject to certain exceptions in Wyoming Statutes section 34.1-2-725, a breach of warranty occurs when tender of delivery is made.[6]

3. Strict Liability

The general four year tort statute applies. See section B1, *supra*. Actions based on strict product liability are tortious rather than contractual in nature.[7]

4. Exception for Improvements to Real Property

Wyoming has a statutory exception to the discovery provisions that delay triggering the statute of limitations for negligence and strict liability actions. For manufacturers, suppliers, and others, no action can be brought in tort, contract, indemnity, or otherwise more than 10 years after substantial completion of an improvement to real property.[8]

C. STRICT LIABILITY

1. The Standard

The standard of Restatement, (Second) of Torts section 402A (1965) was adopted in *Ogle v. Caterpillar Tractor Co.*[9] The Wyoming Supreme

Court had declined to adopt the same standard on several previous occasions,[10] although a number of earlier product liability cases were tried on strict liability theories.[11] In *Ogle*, the court stated that the Restatement definition formed "the best starting point from which the cause of action can evolve," pointing out that many of the "finer points" not explicitly covered in section 402A and the official comments had already been considered and decided elsewhere.[12]

2.   **"Defect"**

"A product is defective when it is in an unreasonably dangerous condition. The term 'unreasonably dangerous' means unsafe when put to a use that is reasonably foreseeable considering the nature and function of the product."[13]

The erroneous choice of a product, however, is not a defective product for purposes of strict liability.[14] In *McLaughlin v. Michelin Tire Corp.*, tires installed on a scraper created severe bouncing and vibration problems and made the scraper hard to control. An accident resulted. Summary judgment was upheld for the defendant on the cause of action based on strict liability because plaintiff failed to show an actual defect. Still available to the plaintiff was a cause of action based on implied warranty of fitness for a particular purpose.[15]

3.   **Contributory Negligence/Assumption of Risk**

The 1994 Legislature amended Wyo. Stat. §1-1-109 to make it a comparative fault statute. Modified comparative principles, formerly applicable only to negligence actions, apply to all actions accruing after July 1, 1994, whether based upon negligence, breach of warranty, or strict liability. (See section G, *infra*.) All fault attributed to a plaintiff, including contributory negligence, assumption of risk, and misuse or alteration, will reduce the plaintiff's recoverable damages and will bar recovery completely if the plaintiff's fault exceeds 50 percent of the total fault of all actors. Previously, in 1991, the Wyoming Supreme Court held that Wyoming's then comparative negligence statute did not apply to strict liability or warranty claims, but specifically left open the question as to whether comparative principles would be judicially applied.[16] Later decisions made it clear that the court was not disposed to do so.

In 1992, the court again refused to apply Wyoming's comparative negligence statute to an indemnity action by a negligent defendant, who had previously settled with the plaintiff, against a strictly liable product manufacturer.[17] In response to certified questions from the Tenth Circuit Court of Appeals, the Wyoming Supreme Court adopted section 886B of the Restatement of Torts (Second), holding that "all-or-nothing" implied indemnity rules would be applied in product liability actions based on strict liability or breach of warranty. (The court adopted "comparative partial indemnity" for equitable indemnity actions premised on negligence.) The lone dissent begins with the observation, "This case may produce more litigation, more business for lawyers, more costs and expenses to the legal system, and more confusion and uncertainty in the law than anything. . . ."[18]

Assumption of risk and misuse can be absolute affirmative defenses in strict liability actions accruing before July 1, 1994. Assumption of risk is use with knowledge of the danger. Misuse is using a product for an unintended or unforeseeable purpose, or using the product in an obviously dangerous manner.[19] The Wyoming Supreme Court found no error in the giving of the following instruction pertaining to misuse: "A manufacturer or seller is entitled to expect a use of his product which is reasonably foreseeable by the ordinary consumer who purchases or uses it with the ordinary knowledge common to the community as to its characteristics. Community means those who ordinarily use a product in question."[20]

4. Sale or Lease

There are no Wyoming Supreme Court cases addressing whether lessors may be strictly liable.[21] A "plain reading" of both section 402A and the comments to that section mention only sellers of products. An injured lessee can sue the manufacturer or another previous seller of the product prior to the lessor. (Comment l to section 402A). However, the Federal District Court for the District of Wyoming has held that strict liability applies to bailments for mutual benefit.[22]

5. Inherently Dangerous Products

No cases on point discuss inherently dangerous products since the adoption of the strict liability standard. Probably comment k to section 402A applies. Electricity is not a product within the definition of section 402A.[23]

6. Successor Liability

No Wyoming cases discuss this issue.

7. Privity

While no Wyoming case specifically discusses privity in relationship to strict liability, the Supreme Court's embrace of section 402A and its comments eliminate a privity requirement between buyer and seller. (See comment l to section 402A.)

8. Failure to Warn

The parameters of failure to warn as a theory of strict liability in tort have not been discussed in any Wyoming Supreme Court case. Plaintiff's theories of liability in a recent case appealed to the Wyoming Supreme Court included negligent failure to warn and failure to warn that made the product defective for purposes of strict liability in tort. Interestingly, by special verdict, the jury in the district court found that the manufacturer did negligently fail to warn of reasonable dangers associated with the product, but that the failure was not a proximate cause of the injury and that the product was not in an unreasonably dangerous defective condition.[24]

Failure to warn as a theory of strict liability in tort also appears in Wyoming Civil Pattern Jury Instruction 11.05: "A defective condition can include a defect . . . in the instructions or warnings reasonably necessary for the product's safe use."

9. Post-Sale Duty to Warn

No case explicitly adopts a post-sale duty to warn as a basis for strict liability. But see W.C.P.J.I. 12.06. There is no post-sale duty to warn of defects that cause damage only to the product itself. Damage to the product itself is a pure economic loss, which is better adjusted under contract than tort principles.[25]

10. Substantial Change/Abnormal Use[26]

Comment g to section 402A of the Restatement (Second) of Torts was given approval in a 1988 Wyoming Supreme Court decision. Plaintiffs, in a car that was on fire, suffered damages because a seatbelt buckle would not release. Adopting the "inference of defect" rule, the Wyoming Supreme Court upheld the directed verdict in favor of defendant, holding that the plaintiffs had failed to prove that there was no abnormal use and no reasonable secondary causes for the malfunction.[27] Whether a different result will be reached under the new comparative fault statute is unknown. Misuse or alteration of a product are specifically listed acts to which comparative fault principles apply. See section C3.

11. State of the Art

"State of the art" is an area in which there is guidance from decisions that were tried on strict liability theories but that predated Wyoming's formal adoption of section 402A. "There is no duty upon a manufacturer to adopt every possible new device which has been conceived or invented."[28] A "standard of conduct" by which to judge the defendant's product may be established by showing that other manufacturers have adopted a certain design.[29] Cases to date have not distinguished between "state of the art" and custom. See W.C.P.J.I. 3.08.

12. Malfunction

The Wyoming Supreme Court has quoted with approval the following:

> A prima facie case that a product was defective and that the defect existed when it left the manufacturer's control

is made by proof that *in the absence of abnormal use or reasonable secondary causes* the product failed "to perform in the manner reasonably to be expected in light of [its] nature and intended function."[30]

13. Standards and Government Regulations

No Wyoming cases discuss the relationship between evidence of, violations of, or compliance with, standards or government regulations and strict liability.[31]

14. Other Accidents

Evidence of other accidents or absence of other accidents is admissible, subject to the discretion of the judge as to reliability, authentication, probative value, and a host of other factors. The trial judge has broad discretion as to admissibility of such evidence.[32]

15. Misrepresentation

Wyoming has not specifically adopted Restatement (Second) of Torts section 402B. Note, however, that *Phillips v. Duro-Last Roofing*, (see note 17) was tried in Federal District Court on various theories, including section 402B. The case was certified to the Wyoming Supreme Court on the question of the applicability of Wyoming's comparative negligence statute. Whether section 402B liability is recognized in Wyoming was not an issue in that certification. See W.C.P.J.I. 11.02A.

D. NEGLIGENCE

Negligence means the failure to use ordinary care.[33] The essential elements of a negligence claim are (1) a duty, (2) a violation of the duty, (3) proximate causation, and (4) an injury.[34] For apportionment, see section G, *infra*.

The Wyoming Supreme Court has held that showing a defect is a required common element to every products liability case.[35] Based upon that holding, the Tenth Circuit Court of Appeals has ruled that a jury's finding that a product was not defective, but that the manufacturing defendant was negligent, was an inconsistent verdict. The jury verdict in favor of the plaintiff was remanded for a new trial.[36]

E. BREACH OF WARRANTY

Warranties covering goods are governed by Wyoming Statutes sections 34.1-2-313, 314, 315, corresponding to the Uniform Commercial Code. Breach of these warranties is often alleged in the same complaint with the theories of negligence and strict liability. However, as mentioned above, there is a difference as to when statutes of limitation will be deemed to be triggered. Also, certain damages may be recoverable only under contract or warranty theory, that is, when there is economic loss only.

F. PUNITIVE DAMAGES

Punitive damages may be awarded if, and only if, a preponderance of the evidence shows that the defendant was guilty of willful and wanton misconduct. "Willful and wanton misconduct is the intentional doing of an act, or an intentional failure to do an act, in reckless disregard of the consequences, and under such circumstances and conditions that a reasonable person would know, or have reason to know, that such conduct would, in a high degree of probability, result in harm to another."[37]

G. STATUTES

There is no title or chapter of the Wyoming Statutes specifically devoted to product liability. Relevant statutes have been cited above and in the end-notes, including breach of warranty, statutes of limitations, statute of repose, and perhaps most significantly, the comparative fault statute.

Wyoming Supreme Court decisions made determinations of ultimate liability in product liability actions accruing before July 1, 1994 very complex. See C.3, *supra*. In 1994, the Wyoming Legislature amended the comparative negligence statute to make it a comparative fault statute.[38]

The amendments now bring strict tort, strict products liability, breach of warranty, assumption of risk, and misuse or alteration of a product within the statutory definition of fault and within the comparative principles of the statute. The amendments apply to all causes of action accruing after July 1, 1994.

The comparative fault statute apportions fault among all actors in product liability cases, regardless of the legal basis of fault. A defendant will still not be entitled to credit for settlements made by other parties or actors.[39]

Greg Greenlee
MURANE & BOSTWICK, L.L.C.
2020 Carey Avenue
Suite 750
Cheyenne, Wyoming 82001
(307) 634-7500
fax (307) 638-7882
email: lawfirm@murane.com

Thomas R. Smith
MURANE & BOSTWICK, L.L.C.
201 North Wolcott
Casper, Wyoming 82601
(307) 234-9345
fax (307) 237-5110
email: lawfirm@murane.com

ENDNOTES - WYOMING

1. *Ford Motor Co. v. Arguello*, 382 P.2d 886 (1963).

2. For express warranty, see Wyo. Stat. §34.1-2-313 (1977); for implied warranty of merchantability, see Wyo. Stat. §34.1-2-314 (1977); for implied warranty of fitness for a particular purpose, see Wyo. Stat. §34.1-2-315 (1977).

3. *Ogle v. Caterpillar Tractor Co.*, 716 P.2d 334, 341 (Wyo. 1986).

4. Wyo. Stat. §1-3-105(a)(iv)(C); *Olson v. A. H. Robins Co., Inc.*, 696 P.2d 1294, 1297 (Wyo. 1985).

5. *Nowotny v. L & B Contract Industries*, 933 P.2d 452 (Wyo. 1997).

6. Discussed in *Ogle*, 716 P.2d 334.

7. Id.

8. Wyo. Stat. §1-3-111. The constitutionality of this statute was upheld in *Worden v. Village Homes*, 821 P.2d 1291 (Wyo. 1991). The statute was termed a "statute of repose" in contrast to a statute of limitation.

9. *Ogle*, 716 P.2d 334 (Wyo. 1986); see also *Estate of Coleman v. Casper Concrete*, 939 P.2d 233 (Wyo. 1997).

10. E.g., *Buckley v. Bell*, 703 P.2d 1089 (Wyo. 1985).

11. E.g., *Caldwell v. Yamaha Motor Co., Ltd.*, 648 P.2d 519 (Wyo. 1982).

12. *Ogle*, 716 P.2d 334 (Wyo. 1986).

13. Wyoming Civil Pattern Jury Instruction 11.04.

14. *Buckley*, 703 P.2d 1089; *McLaughlin v. Michelin Tire Corp.*, 778 P.2d 59 (Wyo. 1989).

15. Id.

16. *Phillips v. Duro-Last Roofing, Inc.*, 806 P.2d 834 (Wyo. 1991).

17. *Schneider Natl., Inc., v. Holland Hitch Co.*, 843 P.2d 561 (Wyo. 1992).

18. *Schneider Natl., Inc.*, 843 P.2d at 588 (Cardine, J., dissenting).

19. See section C1, *supra*, and *Anderson v. Louisiana Pacific*, 859 P.2d 85 (Wyo. 1993); *Schneider Natl., Inc.*, 843 P.2d 561; *Zierke v. Agri-Systems*, 992 F.2d 276 (10th Cir. 1993).

20. *Anderson*, 859 P.2d at 88.

21. In *Ortega v. Flaim*, 902 P.2d 199 (Wyo. 1995), the Wyoming Supreme Court refused to extend strict liability to a landlord for a leased residential dwelling, or to an integral component of the dwelling.

22. *Gray v. Snow King Resort*, 889 F. Supp. 1473 (D. Wyo. 1995).

23. *Wyrulec Co. v. Schutt*, 866 P.2d 756 (Wyo. 1993).

24. *Anderson*, 859 P.2d 85.

25. *Continental Ins. v. Page Engg. Co.*, 783 P.2d 641 (Wyo. 1989).

26. For misuse, see section C3, *supra*.

27. *Sims v. General Motors Corp.*, 751 P.2d 357 (Wyo. 1974).

28. *Maxted v. Pacific Car & Foundry Co.*, 527 P.2d 832 (Wyo. 1974).

29. *Wells v. Jeep Corp.*, 532 P.2d 595 (Wyo. 1975).

30. *Sims*, 751 P.2d at 361, citing a previous Wyoming case and *Tweedy v. Wright Ford Sales, Inc.*, 357 N.E.2d 449, 452 (Ill. 1976).

31. In *Distad v. Cubin*, 633 P.2d 167 (Wyo. 1981), the Wyoming Supreme Court adopted the standards of the Restatement (Second) of Torts sections 286, 287, 288, 288A, 288B, and 288C to govern the relevance of a violation of a statute, ordinance, or regulation as to questions of negligence. See also *Dubray v. Howshar*, 884 P.2d 23 (Wyo. 1994); *Pullman v. Outzen*, 924 P.2d 416 (Wyo. 1996).

32. Cf. *Caterpillar Tractor v. Donohue*, 674 P.2d 1276 (Wyo. 1983) (evidence admitted), with *Sims*, *supra* note 26; see also *Caldwell v. Yamaha Motor Co. Ltd.*, 648 P.2d 519 (Wyo. 1982).

33. Wyoming Civil Pattern Jury Instruction 3.02. "The concept of ordinary care accommodates all circumstances so that the degree of care varies with the circumstances." *Wyrulec*, 866 P.2d at 762.

34.   *McClellan v. Tottenhoff*, 666 P.2d 408 (Wyo. 1983).

35.   *McLaughlin v. Michelin*, 788 P.2d 59 (Wyo. 1989).

36.   *Bradley v. General Motors Corp.*, 1997 WL 354721 (10th Cir. 1997).

37.   Wyoming Pattern Jury Instruction 4.06; for a discussion of willful and wanton misconduct, see *Danculovich v. Brown*, 593 P.2d 187 (Wyo. 1979).

38.   1994 Wyo. Session Laws, ch. 98; Wyo. Stat. §1-1-109 (1994).

39.   *Haderlie v. Sondgeroth*, 866 P.2d 703 (Wyo. 1993).